Reading Freud

Reading Freud provides an accessible outline of the whole of Freud's work from *Studies in Hysteria* through to *An Outline of Psycho-Analysis*. It succeeds in expressing even the most complex of Freud's theories in clear and simple language while avoiding oversimplification.

Each chapter concentrates on one or more individual texts and includes valuable background information, relevant biographical and historical details, descriptions of Post-Freudian developments and Freud's new concepts. By putting each text into the context of Freud's life and work as a whole, Jean-Michel Quinodoz manages to produce an overview which is chronological, correlative and interactive. Texts discussed include:

• *The Interpretation of Dreams*
• "The 'Uncanny' "
• *Civilization and its Discontents*

The clear presentation, with regular summaries of the ideas raised, encourages the reader to fully engage with the texts presented and gain a thorough understanding of each text in the context of its background and impact on the development of psychoanalysis.

Drawing on his extensive experience as a clinician and a teacher of psychoanalysis, Jean-Michel Quinodoz has produced a uniquely comprehensive presentation of Freud's work which will be of great value to anyone studying Freud and Psychoanalysis.

Jean-Michel Quinodoz is a Psychoanalyst in private practice in Geneva. He is a member of the Swiss Psychoanalytical Society and Honorary Member of the British Psychoanalytical Society, both of which are component societies of the International Psychoanalytical Association founded by Freud in 1910. After ten years of activity as Editor for Europe of *The International Journal of Psychoanalysis*, he is now Editor-in-Chief of the *News Annual* published in various languages by the *Journal*. He is the author of *The Taming of Solitude* (1993) and *Dreams that Turn Over a Page* (2002).

THE NEW LIBRARY OF PSYCHOANALYSIS: TEACHING SERIES

General Editor   Dana Birksted-Breen

The New Library of Psychoanalysis was launched in 1987 in association with the Institute of Psycho-Analysis, London. It took over from the International Psychoanalytical Library which published many of the early translations of the works of Freud and the writings of most of the leading British and Continental psychoanalysts.

The purpose of the New Library of Psychoanalysis is to facilitate a greater and more widespread appreciation of psychoanalysis and to provide a forum for increasing mutual understanding between psychoanalysts and those working in other disciplines.

The **New Library of Psychoanalysis Teaching Series** extends the aims and achievements of the New Library of Psychoanalysis to those studying psychoanalysis and related fields such as the social sciences, philosophy, literature and the arts. Each text provides a comprehensive yet accessible introduction to central subjects in psychoanalysis, expressing even the most complex psychoanalytic concepts in clear and simple language whilst avoiding over simplification.

The Institute, together with the British Psycho-Analytical Society, runs a low-fee psychoanalytic clinic, organizes lectures and scientific events concerned with psychoanalysis and publishes the *International Journal of Psycho-Analysis*. It also runs the only UK training course in psychoanalysis which leads to membership of the International Psychoanalytical Association – the body which preserves internationally agreed standards of training, of professional entry, and of professional ethics and practice for psychoanalysis as initiated and developed by Sigmund Freud. Distinguished members of the Institute have included Michael Balint, Wilfred Bion, Ronald Fairbairn, Anna Freud, Ernest Jones, Melanie Klein, John Rickman and Donald Winnicott.

Previous General Editors include David Tuckett, Elizabeth Spillius and Susan Budd.
Previous and current Members of the Advisory Board include Christopher Bollas, Ronald Britton, Donald Campbell, Stephen Grosz, John Keene, Eglé Laufer, Juliet Mitchell, Michael Parsons, Rosine Jozef Perelberg, David Taylor, Mary Target Catalina Bronstein, Sara Flanders, Richard Rusbridger.

ALSO IN THE NEW LIBRARY OF PSYCHOANALYSIS

Impasse and Interpretation Herbert Rosenfeld
Psychoanalysis and Discourse Patrick Mahony
The Suppressed Madness of Sane Men Marion Milner
The Riddle of Freud Estelle Roith
Thinking, Feeling, and Being Ignacio Matte Blanco
The Theatre of the Dream Salomon Resnik
Melanie Klein Today: Volume 1, Mainly Theory Edited by Elizabeth Bott Spillius
Melanie Klein Today: Volume 2, Mainly Practice Edited by Elizabeth Bott Spillius
Psychic Equilibrium and Psychic Change: Selected Papers of Betty Joseph Edited by Michael Feldman and Elizabeth Bott Spillius
About Children and Children-No-Longer: Collected Papers 1942–80 Paula Heimann. Edited by Margret Tonnesmann
The Freud – Klein Controversies 1941–45 Edited by Pearl King and Riccardo Steiner
Dream, Phantasy and Art Hanna Segal
Psychic Experience and Problems of Technique Harold Stewart
Clinical Lectures on Klein & Bion Edited by Robin Anderson
From Fetus to Child Alessandra Piontelli
A Psychoanalytic Theory of Infantile Experience: Conceptual and Clinical Reflections E Gaddini. Edited by Adam Limentani
The Dream Discourse Today Edited and introduced by Sara Flanders
The Gender Conundrum: Contemporary Psychoanalytic Perspectives on Feminitity and Masculinity Edited and introduced by Dana Breen
Psychic Retreats John Steiner
The Taming of Solitude: Separation Anxiety in Psychoanalysis Jean-Michel Quinodoz
Unconscious Logic: An Introduction to Matte-Blanco's Bi-logic and its Uses Eric Rayner
Understanding Mental Objects Meir Perlow
Life, Sex and Death: Selected Writings of William Gillespie Edited and introduced by Michael Sinason
What Do Psychoanalysts Want?: The Problem of Aims in Psychoanalytic Therapy Joseph Sandler and Anna Ursula Dreher
Michael Balint: Object Relations, Pure and Applied Harold Stewart
Hope: A Shield in the Economy of Borderline States Anna Potamianou
Psychoanalysis, Literature & War: Papers 1972–1995 Hanna Segal
Emotional Vertigo: Between Anxiety and Pleasure Danielle Quinodoz
Early Freud and Late Freud Ilse Grubrich-Simitis
A History of Child Psychoanalysis Claudine and Pierre Geissmann
Belief and Imagination: Explorations in Psychoanalysis Ronald Britton
A Mind of One's Own: A Kleinian View of Self and Object Robert A Caper
Psychoanalytic Understanding of Violence and Suicide Edited by Rosine Jozef Perelberg
On Bearing Unbearable States of Mind Ruth Riesenberg-Malcolm
Psychoanalysis on the Move: The Work of Joseph Sandler Edited by Peter Fonagy, Arnold M. Cooper and Robert S. Wallerstein
The Dead Mother: The Work of André Green Edited by Gregorio Kohon
The Fabric of Affect in the Psychoanalytic Discourse André Green
The Bi-Personal Field: Experiences of Child Analysis Antonino Ferro
The Dove that Returns, the Dove that Vanishes: Paradox and Creativity in Psychoanalysis Michael Parsons
Ordinary People, Extra-ordinary Protections: A Post Kleinian Approach to the Treatment of Primitive Mental States Judith Mitrani
The Violence of Interpretation: From Pictogram to Statement Piera Aulagnier
The Importance of Fathers: A Psychoanalytic Re-Evaluation Judith Trowell and Alicia Etchegoyen
Dreams That Turn Over a Page: Paradoxical Dreams in Psychoanalysis Jean-Michel Quinodoz
The Couch and the Silver Screen: Psychoanalytic Reflections on European Cinema Andrea Sabbadini

ALSO IN THE NEW LIBRARY OF PSYCHOANALYSIS

In Pursuit of Psychic Change: The Betty Joseph Workshop Edited by Edith Hargreaves and Arturo Varchevker

The Quiet Revolution in American Psychoanalysis: Selected Papers of Arnold M. Cooper Arnold M. Cooper, Edited and Introduced by Elizabeth L. Auchincloss

Seeds of Illness and Seeds of Recovery: The genesis of suffering and the role of psychoanalysis Antonino Ferro

The Work of Psychic Figurability: Mental States Without Representation César Botella and Sára Botella

Key Ideas for a Contemporary Psychoanalysis: Misrecognition and Recognition of the Unconscious André Green

The Telescoping of Generations: Listening to the Narcissistic Links Between Generations Haydée Faimberg

Glacial Times: A Journey through the World of Madness Salomon Resnik

THE NEW LIBRARY OF PSYCHOANALYSIS:
TEACHING SERIES

General Editor: Dana Birksted-Breen

Reading Freud

A Chronological Exploration of Freud's Writings

Jean-Michel Quinodoz

Translated by David Alcorn

First published as *Lire Freud,*
Presses Universitaires de France, 2004

Routledge
Taylor & Francis Group
LONDON AND NEW YORK

First published as *Lire Freud* in 2004 by Presses Universitaires de France, Paris

This edition published 2005 by Routledge
27 Church Road, Hove, East Sussex, BN3 2FA

Simultaneously published in the USA and Canada
by Routledge
711 Third Avenue, New York 10017

Routledge is an imprint of the Taylor & Francis Group, an Informa business

© 2005 Jean-Michel Quinodoz
Translation © David Alcorn

Typeset in Times by RefineCatch Limited, Bungay, Suffolk

Paperback cover design by Sandra Heath

All rights reserved. No part of this book may be reprinted or reproduced or utilized in any form or by any electronic, mechanical, or other means, now known or hereafter invented, including photocopying and recording, or in any information storage or retrieval system, without permission in writing from the publishers.

This publication has been produced with paper manufactured to strict environmental standards and with pulp derived from sustainable forests.

British Library Cataloguing in Publication Data
A catalogue record for this book is available from the British Library

Library of Congress Cataloging in Publication Data

Quinodoz, Jean-Michel.
 [Lire Freud. English]
 Reading Freud : a chronological exploration of Freud's writings /
Jean-Michel Quinodoz ; translated by David Alcorn.
   p. cm.
 Includes bibliographical references and indexes.
 ISBN 1-58391-746-2 – ISBN 1-58391-747-0 (pbk) 1. Freud, Sigmund, 1856-1939. I. Title.

BF109.F74Q56 2005
150.19′52′092–dc22

2004027662

ISBN 978-1-58391-747-3

CONTENTS

Explanatory note   xi
Sigmund Freud (1856–1939) chronological table   xii
Reading Freud   1

I
THE DISCOVERY OF PSYCHOANALYSIS
(1895–1910)

Studies on Hysteria (Freud and Breuer 1895d)	9
Letters to Wilhelm Fliess (1887–1904)	21
"Project for a Scientific Psychology" (1950c [1895])	26
"The Neuro-Psychoses of Defence" (1894a); "On the Grounds for Detaching a Particular Syndrome from Neurasthenia under the Description 'Anxiety Neurosis' " (1895b); "Further Remarks on the Neuro-Psychoses of Defence" (1896b); "Sexuality in the Aetiology of the Neuroses" (1898a); "Screen Memories" (1899a)	31
The Interpretation of Dreams (1900a); *On Dreams* (1901a)	36
The Psychopathology of Everyday Life (1901b)	45
Jokes and their Relation to the Unconscious (1905c)	50
Three Essays on the Theory of Sexuality (1905d)	57
"Fragment of an Analysis of a Case of Hysteria" (Dora) (1905e)	65
Delusions and Dreams in Jensen's "Gradiva" (1907a)	73
"Analysis of a Phobia in a Five-Year-Old Boy ('Little Hans')" (1909b)	78
"Notes upon a Case of Obsessional Neurosis (The 'Rat Man')" (1909d)	88
Leonardo da Vinci and a Memory of his Childhood (1910c)	94

II
THE YEARS OF MATURITY
(1911–1920)

"Psycho-Analytic Notes on an Autobiographical Account of a Case of Paranoia (Dementia Paranoides)" (1911c)	101
Papers on Technique Written between 1904 and 1919; "Remembering, Repeating and Working-Through" (1914g); "Observations on Transference-Love" (1915a); "Lines of Advance in Psycho-Analytic Therapy" (1919a)	108
Totem and Taboo (1912–1913)	121

"On Narcissism: An Introduction" (1914c) 128
Papers on Metapsychology Written between 1915 and 1917; *Introductory Lectures on Psycho-Analysis* (1916–1917) 135
"From the History of an Infantile Neurosis" (The "Wolf-Man") (1918b [1914]) 156
"The 'Uncanny' "(1919h) 165
"A Child is Being Beaten (A Contribution to the Study of the Origin of Sexual Perversions)" (1919e); "The Psychogenesis of a Case of Female Homosexuality" (1920a) 171

III

FRESH PERSPECTIVES
(1920–1939)

Beyond the Pleasure Principle (1920g) 185
Group Psychology and the Analysis of the Ego (1921c) 194
The Ego and the Id (1923b) 203
"The Economic Problem of Masochism" (1924c) 212
Inhibitions, Symptoms and Anxiety (1926d) 217
The Future of an Illusion (1927c); *The Question of Lay Analysis* (1926e) 227
Civilization and its Discontents (1930a); *New Introductory Lectures on Psycho-Analysis* (1933a [1932]) 235
Papers on Denial of Reality and Splitting of the Ego Written between 1924 and 1938; *An Outline of Psycho-Analysis* (1940a [1938]) 243
"Analysis Terminable and Interminable" (1937c); "Constructions in Analysis" (1937d) 254
Moses and Monotheism (1939a [1934–1938]) 264

Reading Freud Today? 273
Appendix (names of those who participated in the Seminar between 1988 and 2003) 275
Bibliography 276
Name index 287
Subject index 290

EXPLANATORY NOTE

TITLES

Books: *italics* – for example:

The Psychopathology of Everyday Life or *THE PSYCHOPATHOLOGY OF EVERYDAY LIFE*

Articles: roman type, between inverted commas – for example:

"On Narcissism: An Introduction" or "ON NARCISSISM: AN INTRODUCTION"

BIBLIOGRAPHICAL REFERENCES

The title of each of Freud's books or articles is followed by the year in which the text was first published, with reference to the chronological listing of the *Freud–Bibliographie mit Werkkonkordanz* (Meyer-Palmedo and Fichter, 1989) and of the *Standard Edition of the Complete Psychological Works of Sigmund Freud*, e.g. *The Psychopathology of Everyday Life* (1901b).

Where the year of publication does not correspond to the date at which Freud wrote the text in question, I have indicated the year of publication followed by that of actual writing between square brackets, e.g. *An Outline of Psycho-Analysis* (1940a [1938]).

QUOTATIONS: PAGE REFERENCES TO FREUD'S PUBLISHED TEXTS

Page numbers for quotations refer to *The Standard Edition of the Complete Psychological Works of Sigmund Freud*.

HIGHLIGHTED FEATURES

Biographies and history

Elements from Freud's personal life which have to do with the text under discussion, together with biographical details concerning some of his earliest followers. These are placed in the historical context of the time.

Post-Freudians

Major post-Freudian developments relating to the text under discussion.

Development of Freud's concepts

A longitudinal study of some of Freud's major themes on which he continued to work over several years. Two examples of these are the Oedipus complex and transference.

New concepts

The principal concepts introduced by Freud are referred to as and when they appear in his writings, the aim being to highlight the history of his ideas.

SIGMUND FREUD (1856–1939) CHRONOLOGICAL TABLE

Biographical details	*Publications*
1856: 6 May. Birth of Freud at Freiberg (in modern Slovakia)	
1860: Jakob Freud's family settles in Vienna	
1873: Sigmund Freud enters Vienna University as a medical student	
1876–1882: Assistant at the Institute of Physiology in Vienna (Prof. E. Brücke)	Paper on the discovery of testicles in eels (1877)
1880: Meets Dr Josef Breuer	
1881: Graduates as Doctor of Medicine – Breuer treats Anna O.	
1882: Engagement to Martha Bernays	
1883–1884: Research into the clinical uses of cocaine	
1885: Appointed *Privatdozent* – Studies under Charcot at the Salpêtrière hospital in Paris	Papers on cocaine (1884)
1886: Sets up private practice in Vienna – Marriage to Martha Bernays	
1887: Birth of Mathilde – Meets Wilhelm Fliess, from Berlin	Letters to Wilhelm Fliess (1887–1902)
1888:	1877–1883: Papers on nerve cells in fish
1889: Birth of Martin – Visits Bernheim in Nancy (France)	1888–1893: Several articles on hypnosis
1890–1891: Moves house to no. 19, Berggasse, Vienna – Birth of Oliver	*On Aphasia* (1891b)
1892: Birth of Ernst	"Clinical Study of the Unilateral Cerebral Palsies of Children" (1891a)
1893: Birth of Sophie	"Preliminary Communication" (Freud and Breuer, 1893)
1894:	"The Neuro-Psychoses of Defence" (1894a)
1895: Birth of Anna – The paradigmatic dream ("Irma's injection")	*Studies on Hysteria* (1895d) – "Anxiety Neurosis" (1895b)
1896: Death of Freud's father, Jakob Freud – Breaks off relations with Breuer	"Project for a Scientific Psychology" (1950c [1895])
1897: Beginning of his self-analysis (1896–1902) – Abandons the seduction theory	"Further Remarks on the Neuro-Psychoses of Defence" (1896b)
1898: *Oedipus Rex*, *Hamlet*	"Sexuality in the Aetiology of the Neuroses" (1898a)
1899:	"Screen Memories" (1899a)
1900: Analysis of Dora (Ida Bauer)	*The Interpretation of Dreams* (1900a)
1901: First trip to Rome, with his brother Alexander	*On Dreams* (1901a)
	The Psychopathology of Everyday Life (1901b)
1902: Founds the Wednesday Society – Meets W. Stekel and A. Adler	
1903: Appointed Professor Extraordinarius in the Vienna University Medical School	
1904: Beginning of international recognition	*Jokes and their Relation to the Unconscious* (1905c)
1905: Meets O. Rank	*Three Essays on the Theory of Sexuality* (1905d)
1906:	"Fragment of the Analysis of a Case of Hysteria" (Dora) (1905e)
1907: Meets C. G. Jung, K. Abraham, M. Eitingon	*Delusions and Dreams in Jensen's "Gradiva"* (1907a)
1908: Meets S. Ferenczi, E. Jones, H. Sachs, P. Federn	
1909: Vienna Psycho-Analytical Society – Meets the Protestant clergyman, O. Pfister	"Analysis of a Phobia in a Five-Year-Old Boy ('Little Hans')" (1909b)
	"Notes upon a Case of Obsessional Neurosis (The 'Rat Man')" (1909d)

Year	Events	Works
1910	Foundation of the International Psychoanalytical Association (IPA)	*Leonardo da Vinci and a Memory of his Childhood* (1910c)
1911	Dissension within the Vienna Society – Secession of Adler	"Psycho-Analytic Notes on an Autobiographical Account of a Case of Paranoia" (Schreber) (1911c)
1912	Foundation of the "Secret Committee" – Secession of Stekel	Papers on Technique (1904–1919)
1913	Meets Lou Andreas-Salomé – Breaks off relationships with Jung	*Totem and Taboo* (1912–1913)
1914	Outbreak of the First World War – Martin and Ernst are called up	"On Narcissism: An Introduction" (1914c)
1915	Ferenczi's analysis with Freud (in three phases, 1914–1916)	Papers on Metapsychology (1915–1917)
1916	Oliver is called up	*Introductory Lectures on Psycho-Analysis* (1916–1917)
1917		
1918	End of First World War – Anna's first analysis with her father	"From the History of an Infantile Neurosis" (The "Wolf-Man") (1918b)
1919	Tausk commits suicide – death of the patron A. von Freund	"The 'Uncanny'" (1919h)
		"A Child is Being Beaten" (1919e)
		"The Psychogenesis of a Case of Female Homosexuality" (1920a)
1920	Death of Freud's daughter Sophie – Jones founds *The International Journal of Psycho-Analysis*	*Beyond the Pleasure Principle* (1920g)
1921		*Group Psychology and the Analysis of the Ego* (1921c)
1922		
1923	First operation for cancer	*The Ego and the Id* (1923b)
1924	Rank publishes *The Trauma of Birth*	"The Economic Problem of Masochism" (1924c)
1925	Death of Abraham – Death of Breuer	
1926	Freud is 70 years of age – Secession of Rank – M. Klein arrives in London	*Inhibitions, Symptoms and Anxiety* (1926d)
		The Question of Lay Analysis (1926e)
1927	Innsbruck Congress	*The Future of an Illusion* (1927c)
1928		
1929	Beginning of the world-wide economic Depression	
1930	Death of Freud's mother, aged 95 – Freud is awarded the Goethe Prize	*Civilization and its Discontents* (1930a)
1931	Rise of anti-Semitism in Austria and Germany	
1932	Wiesbaden Congress	
1933	Death of Ferenczi – Hitler seizes power	*New Introductory Lectures on Psycho-Analysis* (1933a)
1934		
1935		Papers on Denial of Reality and Splitting of the Ego (1924-1938)
1936	Freud is 80 years of age – Meets R. Rolland	"Analysis Terminable and Interminable" (1937c)
1937	Death of Lou Andreas-Salomé	"Constructions in Analysis" (1937d)
1938	With the assistance of Jones and Princess Marie Bonaparte, Freud leaves Vienna for London	*Moses and Monotheism* (1939a)
1939	23 September. Death of Freud in London, aged 83	*An Outline of Psycho-Analysis* (1940a [1938])

READING FREUD

The culmination of personal and group research

Reading Freud is the outcome of a long journey, on both personal and group levels. In the first place, this volume is based on my personal encounter with psychoanalysis and on my long experience as a psychoanalyst in private practice with patients who have classic psychoanalytic treatment: lying on the couch, with in most cases four sessions per week. Clinical experience has taught me that Freud's ideas are living theories which throw light on our everyday work with our patients and are a continual inspiration for contemporary psychoanalysts. *Reading Freud* is based also on my familiarity with the various post-Freudian currents of thought which exist at present. I was able to appreciate the diversity and creativity of these thanks to the contacts I have had with many colleagues in the course of my work as editor for Europe of the *International Journal of Psycho-Analysis*. My knowledge of German was another element that prompted me to write *Reading Freud*. Whenever I read the original version of one of Freud's texts, I am struck by the sheer simplicity of the way he wrote, using for the most part everyday expressions and avoiding neologisms. I have tried to write this book in the same spirit in order to make Freud's ideas accessible to as wide a readership as possible – it is perfectly feasible to respect the complexity of an author's thinking while expressing his ideas in clear and simple language. Lastly, *Reading Freud* is the result of the work done in a seminar devoted to a chronological reading of Freud's writings. The seminar began in 1988 as part of the training programme for prospective psychoanalysts at the Raymond de Saussure Psychoanalytic Institute in Geneva, and at the time of writing this work is still ongoing. Since the seminar provided the raw material on which both the form and the content of this book are based, I feel it important to mention that group experience.

There are many ways of reading Freud

Freud's published work is both impressive in scope and complex in nature. His psychoanalytic papers alone fill some twenty-four volumes, while his pre-psychoanalytic writings and his correspondence comprise over a hundred books in all. How can we possibly have a global view of such an imposing body of work?

There are many ways of reading Freud, and though each has its advantages and disadvantages, they all complement one another. We can read Freud selectively, choosing *à la carte* an article or a book, or we can choose a theme and the papers in which it is discussed. A selective approach has the advantage of closely examining each paper, spending as much time as need be to mull over it; this is a particularly apposite approach, because Freud's writings do lend themselves to a "Talmudic" form of exegesis, i.e. analysis of the meaning of each sentence (and even of each word) and of its relationship to other texts. However, with this kind of approach, it would take many years before the reader could complete such an undertaking.

Another way to read Freud's major psychoanalytic works would be to adopt a chronological approach, beginning with *Studies on Hysteria*, published in 1895, and going all the way through to *An Outline of Psycho-Analysis*, written in 1938, the year before he died. Reading Freud's texts in the order in which they were published, without spending too much time on each one individually, gives the reader a grasp of how Freud's thinking developed over the years. In order to maximize the advantages to be gained from a chronological reading, I think that, from the outset, a time-limit should be set, even though this kind of approach does not allow the reader to analyse each paper in as detailed a fashion as the text itself deserves. It is above all important that the reader keeps the overall picture in mind, for when we succeed in acquiring a panoramic view of Freud's writings, this helps us to realize that the various psychoanalytic schools of thought have often seized on certain particular aspects rather than on others. We can see too that this narrowing of focus tends to increase as it is handed down from generation to generation, with the concomitant risk of leaving aside more and more aspects of Freud's writings which are just as valuable.

These two approaches, selective and chronological, do not stand in opposition one to the other – in fact, they are complementary, for each in its own way illustrates how Freud himself kept revising his way of looking at things, turning uncertainty to his advantage and taking his clinical experience into account in order further to develop what he had discovered. It is of course possible for a single person to embark on such an undertaking, but it would demand a great deal of time and tenacity before the reader could complete the bulk of the work so as to have an overview of how Freud's thinking developed over the years. That is why I feel that such an experience is particularly stimulating for a *group* of readers, more able to sustain a long-term effort of this type.

Reading Freud: *directions for use*

A crazy undertaking?

For a long time, the idea of writing a book on the entire range of Freud's texts did not even cross my mind; the project seemed to me to be over-ambitious. In addition, I could not see how the approach that made for the originality of the seminar – working on Freud's writings in a way that was not only chronological but also correlative and interactive – could be carried over on to the pages of a book. Then, one day, I had the idea of using typography, page layout and colour all at the same time so as to offer a visual representation of this combined approach to Freud's writings. This layout enabled me to adopt for each chapter of *Reading Freud* the same pattern used in the seminar session devoted to studying one of Freud's texts.

Chapter heading

With very few exceptions, each chapter heading is the title of a single one of Freud's texts. To distinguish between books and papers, inverted commas are used for the latter. The title is followed by the date of first publication of the text, as referenced in the chronological table of *Freud–Bibliographie mit Werkkonkordanz* (Meyer-Palmedo and Fichter 1989) and in the *Standard Edition of the Complete Psychological Works of Sigmund Freud*. When the date of publication does not coincide with the year which a given text was actually completed, I follow the usual practice: the first date given is that of publication, the second, in square brackets, is when it was written, e.g. *An Outline of Psycho-Analysis* (1940a [1938]).

Introductory note

Each chapter carries an introductory heading which evokes the topic about to be examined, together with a short presentation of Freud's paper. The idea here is to give the reader an outline of the contents of the chapter and to situate the text briefly within the context of Freud's writings as a whole.

Biographies and history

In this highlighted feature, the reader will find information concerning Freud's personal life insofar as it relates to the text studied in the chapter, as well as some indication of the wider historical context. I have noted the principal elements which influenced to a certain extent the writing of Freud's text, and I have included a short biography of some of Freud's most important followers at the time, as well as information relating to those of his patients who played a significant role.

Discovering the text

References: for each of Freud's texts, I have indicated the volume and page number references to the *Standard Edition of the Complete Psychological Works of Sigmund Freud* (*S.E.*, London: Hogarth Press and The Institute of Psycho-Analysis). In addition, the reader will find in the Bibliography the references corresponding to the various volumes of *Sigmund Freud, Gesammelte Werke* (*G.W.*).

Bringing out the salient points of the text

How was I to present a text in such a way as to avoid both pitfalls: oversimplification in my attempt to summarize and being encyclopaedic by overwhelming the reader with references? Faced with this dilemma, I decided to present each text in a way that would arouse the reader's curiosity and perhaps lead him or her to read the full text either in its original version or in translation. Whenever possible, I have tried also to present the main points of the text in simple, everyday language – taking as my example Freud's own style of writing in German.

Following Freud's writings in this way enables us to discover the ongoing development of his thinking; he sometimes abandons an old idea to pick up a new one, then he comes back to the original one, even though they may be contradictory. Reading Freud's original text helps us to see how his writings stimulate our own thinking and opens up new avenues; as such, Freud's writings are truly "open" in Umberto Eco's sense, as Ferro (1996) has pointed out. Freud wrote like an explorer discovering a new territory, noting down his impressions as he went along, drawing a rough map in his notebook and, from time to time, staying a while to set up his easel and turn his sketch of the landscape into a *chef d'oeuvre*.

A preference for the clinical approach

In writing *Reading Freud*, I have preferred to adopt a clinical approach both as to my own reading of Freud and concerning other contributions which shed light on his texts. I think it is important to keep in mind the fact that psychoanalysis is not only a theory and a method of investigation into the human mind, but also and above all a clinical and technical approach which enables many of our patients to resolve the unconscious conflicts which they could not have eliminated by any other means, even the most modern.

New concepts

At the end of each chapter, I highlight the most important concepts which can be found in the text being studied, at the point in time when Freud attributed to them the status of a true psychoanalytic concept.

However, this way of presenting a concept – locating it at a precise moment in Freud's development – is not without its problems. Fixing the point at which a concept first appeared in Freud's writings can be quite arbitrary; when we read Freud retrospectively, we come to realize that he described phenomena corresponding to a given concept in various contexts and at different periods in time, yet it is only later that these phenomena are accorded the status of a psychoanalytic concept. For example, the term "transference" appears as early as 1895, in *Studies on Hysteria*, but it is only 10 years later, in 1905, that it will be described as a psychoanalytic concept (in the "Dora" clinical case).

Development of Freud's concepts

Some of Freud's major concepts evolved over several decades. That is why I have given a selection of these – transference, the Oedipus complex, etc. – a special feature of their own in which to describe their development over time.

Post-Freudians

Under this heading, I highlight the most significant contributions which helped develop Freud's ideas, whether by his immediate disciples or by other major figures in psychoanalysis who have succeeded him down to the present day. To avoid overwhelming the reader with an excessive number of bibliographic references, I have restricted my choice to the main contributors, mentioning in passing a few references of a more personal nature. Post-Freudian developments show how the psychoanalytic ideas outlined by Freud have later been taken up by one or another school of thought and enhanced by these innovative approaches. With this in mind, I have preferred to adopt an international approach with the aim of highlighting the diversity in contemporary thinking among psychoanalysts who are members of the International Psychoanalytical Association (IPA) (which, of course, was founded by Freud).

A seminar on the chronological reading of Freud's texts

An approach which is chronological, correlative and interactive

I would like briefly to present this seminar so as to give the reader some idea of the work we accomplished over the fifteen or so years it has been running, because this was what laid the groundwork for my writing *Reading Freud*. I must however insist on the fact that the blueprint we adopted for this seminar is only one of many possible approaches. Since there is no one way of familiarizing oneself with Freud's texts, it is up to each of us to discover the method with which he or she feels most comfortable.

The adventure began in 1988, when the idea was floated by a group of candidate members of our Psychoanalytic Society who were looking for training psychoanalysts who might like to lead a seminar on the chronological reading of Freud's texts. I found the challenge extremely interesting; I thought that in heading a seminar like that, I myself would probably learn a great deal. Until then, I had read Freud carefully, but in a selective and unsystematic manner. However, the usual way in which such a seminar functions – each participant reads a text then informally shares his or her thoughts with the other members of the group – did not appeal to me. I had the idea that all participants should contribute to shedding light on the text which we were studying by looking at it from different perspectives – biographical, the history of ideas, post-Freudian developments, etc. I felt that working along these lines would enable us to supplement our reading of Freud's texts thanks to this twofold method: a chronological study of his writings, allied to a correlative, interactive and non-linear approach. The project itself pleased me, and I felt that it was worthwhile taking up the challenge, as long as the potential participants were willing to accept the general approach which I was proposing.

The importance of the seminar setting

I gradually came to understand the importance of the setting in which a seminar on chronological reading takes place, as I began to realize that the success of the seminar partly depended on it. For example, I think it crucially important that, in the very first seminar session, participants are informed of the programme for the 3 years to come so that they have an idea of the commitment expected of them and how long the work will take. I divided Freud's major texts into three groups, to be read over a three-year period; it is this template that I have adopted also for this book. The seminar met once a fortnight, so that we had about fifteen sessions per year, each of which lasted for an hour and a half. There were about sixteen to eighteen participants at each session; the seminar was a "closed" group, i.e. no new members were accepted while the seminar was ongoing. The inaugural session, with the presentation of the programme, enabled prospective participants to see what they were letting themselves in for and to estimate whether or not they were ready to devote the necessary time and effort into reaching such an important goal and take pleasure in doing so.

The active participation of each member

Another crucial point was for participants in the seminar to feel directly involved in what was taking place – it would not be a series of *ex cathedra* lectures, and my role would be limited to helping them in their work over a predetermined period of time (3 years). That kind of participation implied both individual work and sharing thoughts and discoveries with the other members. As we travelled together on our journey, I came to realize that the more the group was asked to participate actively in constructing the seminar, the more they appreciated it and benefited from it. This was highlighted by the fact that the level of absenteeism was practically negligible: whenever someone really could not attend, he or she let me know at once and tried to find some other member who could communicate to the group the work which that participant had been due to share with the others.

Individual work implied the following:

- *Reading the chosen text*: before the seminar session, each participant read the scheduled text so as to be able to share with the others his or her own thoughts on it during the discussion period.
- *Freedom of choice as far as translation was concerned*: each participant could choose his or her preferred language or translation. Some participants read Freud in the original German, many used one of the available French translations, some read the text in English, Italian or Spanish. The great variety of translations meant that we could highlight the complex nature of the questions which Freud's translators have to cope with.
- *Writing a short commentary*: each participant wrote a short (one-page) commentary of about 300 words relative to one of the following headings:
  1 "Biographies and history": a short presentation of Freud's life at the time he wrote the paper under discussion, thereby placing it in its historical context.
  2 "Development of Freud's concepts": showing how, in the paper, Freud gradually introduced new ideas, so as to highlight the history of how his thinking developed.
  3 "Post-Freudians": selecting the main post-Freudian developments based on the text being discussed from a historical and international perspective.
  4 "The Minutes of the Seminar": drawing up a summary of what was discussed in the seminar so as to distribute these "Minutes" at the following meeting.

The sharing of each participant's individual work took place during the seminar session itself. Usually a session would begin with news items and with the distribution of the commentaries relating to the various headings I have just described. One participant would then read to the others the material relating to Freud's biography, and this would be briefly discussed. Then another participant would read out the material relating to Freud's concepts, following which the discussion would be thrown open. This would last for approximately three-quarters of an hour and was usually quite lively. If the discussion had difficulty in getting off the ground, I would ask each of the participants to raise some question or other that had come to mind concerning the relevant text; this generally helped to relaunch the debate. In the final part of the seminar session, one participant would read out the material concerning post-Freudian contributions; this too would be followed by a discussion which was thrown open to all. Elsewhere (J-M. Quinodoz 1997b), I have described in detail a seminar session devoted to Freud's "A Child is Being Beaten". The fact that sessions lasted for only a very short time was, paradoxically, really quite stimulating, since before the actual meeting each participant had to think about the various issues involved and prepare a brief statement of the ideas he or she wanted to share with the group.

The high standard expected was a dynamic factor

I am well aware that it was asking a lot of the participants not only to read personally most of Freud's writings, but also to share their own thoughts on these and do any research required in order to write a commentary relating to one of the headings. Preparing for the seminar sessions demanded that they devote quite some time to this activity, even though their workload was usually heavy enough and they were already short of time for their personal and family life. It was possible for them to do this only if, in return, the seminar meetings were an occasion for sharing pleasant moments. In addition, in order to get to know one another better, at the end of each year we had a "potluck buffet", a festive occasion to which spouses and partners were invited.

The requirement that each participant play an active role proved to be a decisive factor in the group dynamics which gradually became established as the seminar went on. This "additional" participation in the service of constructing the seminar created a friendly momentum during the fixed period of time we spent together – each of us knew from the outset that the seminar would last 3 years. In fact, the seminar gave us much more than an increase in knowledge, because working together in this way enabled participants to listen to what each person (including him- or herself) was trying to say, and this furthered personal development in all of us. It was a way of being more open both to what Freud was trying to express and to the great variety of possible points of view.

I had proof of the stimulating role of this high level of personal involvement for the proper functioning of the seminar group when, as I was setting up the second three-year cycle, I decided not to impose these rules. At the first meeting of this second three-year cycle, one of the participants objected to the work-plan I was outlining, criticized it in no uncertain terms and refused to take part in any such "marathon" (his word). At that time, I was not yet convinced of the validity of the seminar requirements; I took a vote on the question. The objections of that one participant were enough to rally to his cause the great majority of the seminar members; I thus agreed, with regret, to do away with the individual work of writing a short commentary on one or other of the headings. The only written document which I succeeded in maintaining was the "minutes" of each seminar meeting. I decided nonetheless that the seminar would proceed on that basis. During the 3 years the seminar lasted, it was the general discussion which suffered most, because it became difficult to get it off the ground. Even though the participants had read Freud's texts carefully, I could feel that something was missing in the group spirit: a certain way of organizing one's thinking which is built up over time, thanks in particular to the personal effort that goes into writing a one-page commentary and sharing it with the other participants. With hindsight, I would no longer give in on this point as I did then, through sheer lack of experience.

Acknowledgements

My thanks must go in the first place to the participants in the "Seminar on a chronological reading of Freud's writings". The material in the highlighted features "Biographies and history" and "Post-Freudians" is to some extent based on their active participation in the discussions and the individual comments they have made over the past fifteen or so years. I mention them by name in an Appendix to the main body of this book in order to show how grateful I am to them. I must also thank Hanna Segal, André Haynal, Augustin Jeanneau, Christoph Hering, Juan Manzano and Paco Palacio, who were good enough to comment on the initial typescript of this book, as well as Maud Struchen, who drew up the Bibliography. As far as this translation into English is concerned, I would like to say how grateful I am to David Alcorn, who found the words to express both the style and the spirit in which I wrote this book. My gratitude goes also to Dana Birksted-Breen, general editor of the "New Library of Psychoanalysis" series at Routledge, to Anne-Marie Sandler and to the three anonymous readers who studied *Reading Freud* so attentively and made suggestions which I have found most helpful.

And *last, not least*, I dedicate *Reading Freud* to Danielle, who was the first to encourage me to embark on this adventure.

In conclusion, let me wish you, the reader, a pleasant journey – though I must point out that reading a guidebook is no substitute for actually making the trip oneself!

Jean-Michel Quinodoz
Cologny (Geneva)
September 2004

I
THE DISCOVERY OF PSYCHOANALYSIS (1895–1910)

STUDIES ON HYSTERIA

(Freud and Breuer 1895d)

A significant discovery: hysterical symptoms have meaning

We shall begin with *Studies on Hysteria*, the foundation text upon which the whole of psychoanalysis was built, the one in which Freud and Breuer tell of their successful treatment of hysterical symptoms and the first hypotheses they drew from that achievement. Hysteria was a very common disorder at the end of the nineteenth century and questions were being asked about the causes of the affliction: organic or psychological? Faced with the impossibility of discovering the true cause of that illness, physicians were very much at a loss. Hysterical conversion phenomena were an undeniable challenge to medical science, because the symptoms did not correspond to any identifiable anatomical lesion; further, they tended to appear or disappear in a completely random fashion. The impossibility of understanding these often spectacular symptoms irritated doctors, who ended up rejecting these patients – most of them were women – whom they saw either as mad or as malingerers.

From 1882 on, Freud, encouraged by the success of his Viennese colleague Josef Breuer, began to take an interest in the part played by suggestion and hypnosis in the treatment of patients suffering from symptoms attributed to hysteria. In their *Studies on Hysteria*, a book which represents the outcome of more than 10 years of clinical work, the two practitioners describe in detail the treatment of five patients, and each author adds a theoretical chapter containing his own hypotheses. Freud's chapter, "The Psychotherapy of Hysteria", has gone down in history not only because of its historical value but also because in it Freud lays the clinical and theoretical foundations of a new discipline: psychoanalysis, itself derived from the cathartic method. In use from 1880 to 1895, the "cathartic method" was invented by Breuer; it was a kind of psychotherapy which enabled the patient to recall memories of past traumatic events, when the hysterical symptoms first appeared. Breuer, then Freud, noted that those symptoms disappeared as the patient gradually managed to recall the memory and to re-experience, in all their intensity, the emotions which had accompanied the original event. Freud tells us that, at first, like Breuer, he had recourse to hypnosis and suggestion in order to help the patient make contact with those pathogenic memories. He soon abandoned that technique, however, and changed his approach radically: he noticed that if he asked the patient to say out loud everything that came into his or her mind – the method which came to be known as free associations – the paths taken spontaneously by the patient's thoughts enabled Freud not only to work his way back to the pathogenic memories which up till then had been repressed, but also to identify the resistances which stood in the way of the patient's getting in touch with those memories in order to resolve them. This new technical approach brought in its wake an increasing awareness of the part played by resistance, transference, the symbolic nature of language and the processing that goes on in the mind – all elements which are typical of every psychoanalytic treatment and which were already being outlined by Freud in Chapter IV of *Studies on Hysteria*. Though abreaction was gradually abandoned, release of emotional tension has remained a significant feature of every psychoanalysis.

Are the hypotheses Freud put forward in 1895 outmoded nowadays? To those who raise that objection, I would reply that psychoanalysis has known the same fate as other significant discoveries: as the nineteenth century drew to a close, all sorts of inventions appeared at the same time as psychoanalysis; they too have been improved over time but, at the time of writing, no new revolutionary discovery has come to replace them. Hence the considerable interest in beginning our study of Freud's writings with the major work in psychoanalysis that is still *Studies on Hysteria*, because the therapeutic approach described therein has even today lost none of its value when applied within its own domain.

Biographies and history

Freud's life up to the publication in 1895 of *Studies on Hysteria*

In 1895, Freud was 39 years of age. He was married, had several children and was already well established in his medical career both in research (neuropathology) and in clinical practice as a neurologist. He was born in 1856 in Freiberg, a small town in Moravia, of Jewish parents; though he declared himself to be liberal-minded and atheist, Freud remained emotionally attached to Judaism. In his family, generation issues were somewhat complicated. When Jakob, Freud's father, was 40 years old, he married his second wife – a young woman of 20, Amalia Nathanson, who was thus more or less the same age as the two grown-up sons born of Jakob's first wife. This was a source of some confusion for the young Sigmund, who at that time imagined himself to be the son of a young couple – his mother and one of his half-brothers – rather than the son of an elderly father. The eldest of eight children, Freud was always his mother's favourite, which no doubt strengthened his conviction that he would be successful in life. In 1860, the family moved to Vienna. There Sigmund studied medicine and worked under some eminent professors, such as the physiologist Ernst Brücke, a positivist physician. It was he who introduced Freud to Josef Breuer, a prominent Viennese physiologist and physician, who was 14 years older than Freud and who for some time had been interested in the treatment of hysteria.

From a scientific point of view, the freshness of Freud's outlook had already proved its worth in various research projects which had brought him to the attention of his peers. His pioneering work on the morphological and physiological unity of brain cells and nerve fibres made of him the unacknowledged inventor of the neuronal theory which Walder was to put forward in 1891. As for Freud's articles on aphasia and infantile paralysis, published in 1891, their merit is still acknowledged today, and in particular his functional conception of aphasia, which broke away from the then current theory of cortical localization. He also studied the pharmacological effects of cocaine, including on himself, but the fame and recognition of his discoveries went to one of his colleagues. He obtained the honorary title of *Privatdozent* in 1885.

Sigmund fell in love with Martha Bernays in 1882; he was 26, and she 20. Their engagement lasted 4 years, during which time they wrote to each other almost every day. In this correspondence, Freud shows himself to be an often anxious, passionate and tyrannical fiancé; Martha appears solid and discreet, a "normal" woman, as Ernest Jones, who liked her very much, was later to describe her. They married in 1886, shortly after Freud had set up in private practice, and had six children. In 1891, the Freuds moved house and went to live at no. 19 Berggasse, in Vienna; they would stay there until their departure for and exile in London in 1938, fleeing the Nazi persecutions.

Freud and Breuer: a decisive collaboration

It was while listening to his Viennese friend and colleague, Josef Breuer, tell him in 1882 of his success in treating the hysterical symptoms of a young patient, Anna O., that Freud had his attention drawn for the first time to the possible use of hypnosis in treating hysterical patients. Born in 1842, Breuer played a decisive role in the birth of psychoanalysis. Himself of Jewish descent, Breuer was an eminent physiologist and a brilliant specialist in internal medicine, and was also a highly cultivated person. He was both friend and family doctor to many celebrities of Viennese society such as the philosopher Franz Brentano and the composer Johannes Brahms. Freud was introduced to Breuer by his mentor, Ernst Brücke, an eminent physiologist for whom Freud had done some research work on neurophysiology from 1876 to 1882. After setting up in private practice, Freud applied Breuer's technique to several patients and was impressed by the fact that Breuer's observations were confirmed with his own patients. Freud's spirit of investigation, however, was always on the lookout for new discoveries, and soon he would be ready to follow his own path.

Freud learns from the pioneers: Charcot and Berheim

In order to learn more about these topics, Freud decided to spend some time in Paris under Jean-Martin Charcot (1885–1886), then in Nancy under Hippolyte Bernheim in 1889. Freud attended Charcot's lectures for several months; Charcot had become famous through his attempts to resolve the problem that hysteria posed to medical science. Abandoning the hypotheses dating from antiquity and the Middle Ages according to which hysteria was caused by some irritation or other in the uterus or could be attributed to malingering, Charcot gave this condition the status of a well-defined nosological entity and turned it into a topic of study and research. He classified hysteria as one of the functional nervous diseases or neuroses, thus distinguishing them from psychiatric disorders of organic origin. He established this distinction after observing that hysterical paralysis could appear randomly in many shapes and forms, quite different from the radicular distribution observed in neurological paralysis. In order to prove that hysterical disorders were psychological in nature and not organic, Charcot used hypnotic suggestion both to produce hysterical symptoms and to remove them. His hypothesis was that "dynamic brain damage", traumatic in nature, was probably the cause of hysteria in men as well as in women.

Charcot, however, used hypnotic suggestion mainly for purposes of demonstration, not as a means of treatment. Accordingly, in 1889, Freud decided to improve his own technique and went to study under Bernheim in Nancy. Bernheim had shown that hypnosis was a suggestion which used language as a vehicle, not the magnetism of the physician's staring eyes, thereby transforming that approach into a genuine psychotherapeutic technique that Freud put into practice as soon as he returned to Vienna.

Studies on Hysteria: 15 years in the making

It took Freud several years before he could persuade Breuer to gather together in a single volume the clinical observations which they had made from 1881 on, together with their respective hypotheses. They began by publishing their interim conclusions on the results of the cathartic method in their "Preliminary Communication" (1893). This paper is reprinted in *Studies on Hysteria* (1895d), where it constitutes the opening chapter.

The publication of *Studies on Hysteria* was, however, to mark the end of their collaboration; from 1896 onwards, Freud, disappointed by Breuer's lack of ambition, continued his investigations on his own. One of the reasons for the growing distance between the two men was the fact that Breuer was not convinced of the importance of sexual factors as a cause of hysteria, whereas Freud was laying increasing emphasis on these. Nonetheless, Breuer continued to show interest in Freud's developing ideas – but from a safe distance. Freud was surprised to learn of this after Breuer died in 1925, when Breuer's son Robert replied to Freud's letter of condolence: according to Hirschmüller (1978), Robert Breuer told Freud that his father had always kept himself informed of Freud's work.

Discovering the text

Page numbers are those of *The Standard Edition of the Complete Psychological Works of Sigmund Freud*, vol. **2**, 1–309.

● "ON THE PSYCHICAL MECHANISM OF HYSTERICAL PHENOMENA" (BREUER AND FREUD)

This opening chapter is the "Preliminary Communication" which was published in 1893. In it, the authors describe the successive stages of their clinical procedure and put forward their preliminary hypotheses. In general, they say, it was chance observation which enabled them to discover the cause or, more exactly, the event which provoked the first occurrence, often many years earlier, of the hysterical symptom. No simple clinical examination is enough to reveal the point of origin, for the patient has lost all memory of it. As a rule it is necessary to hypnotize the patient to awaken any memories of the time at which the symptom made its first appearance: "*When this has been done, it becomes possible to demonstrate the connection in the clearest and most convincing fashion*" (Freud and Breuer 1895d: 3). Quite frequently, it is some event in childhood which triggers more or less severe pathological manifestations in the years that follow.

Observations such as these show that there is an analogy between the pathogenesis of hysteria and that of the traumatic neuroses, so that the cause of hysterical symptoms could be said to be a "*psychical trauma*". Later, the psychical trauma and the memory of it "*act like a foreign body which long after its entry must continue to be regarded as an agent that is still at work*" (ibid.: 6). According to Breuer and Freud, the disappearance of the symptoms which follows on from recollection of the traumatic memory confirms that hypothesis. I shall let them describe in their own words their new therapeutic method:

> *We found, to our great surprise at first, that each individual hysterical symptom immediately and permanently disappeared when we had succeeded in bringing clearly to light the memory of the event by which it was provoked and in arousing its accompanying affect, and when the patient had described that event in the greatest possible detail and had put the affect into words.* (ibid.: 6)

They add that it is vital that the patient re-experience the original affect for the recollection to have a therapeutic effect: "*Recollection without affect almost invariably produces no result*" (ibid.: 6). These repeated observations led Freud and Breuer to their henceforth famous statement: "Hysterics suffer mainly from reminiscences" (ibid.: 7).

They go on to say that language plays a decisive role in the "*cathartic*" effect, because the erasing of a pathogenic memory implies a reaction of emotional discharge, whether it be tears or an act of revenge.

> *But language serves as a substitute for action; by its help, an affect can be "abreacted" almost as effectively. In other cases speaking is itself the adequate reflex, when, for instance, it is a lamentation or giving utterance to a tormenting secret, e.g. a confession. If there is no such reaction, whether in deeds or words, or in the mildest cases in tears, any recollection of the event retains its affective tone to begin with.* (ibid.: 8)

Freud and Breuer observe too that the patient's memory has no trace of the original event and that in most cases it is a question of something which "*the patient wished to forget and therefore intentionally repressed from his conscious thought*" (ibid.: 10). Hysterical phenomena are the result of a "*splitting of consciousness*"; in other words, a "*dual consciousness*" linked to the presence of a "*hypnoid state*" is the basic phenomenon of hysteria. Put briefly, hysterical symptoms are the result of severe trauma – such as occurs in a traumatic neurosis – or a laborious suppression (in which sexual affect plays a part) which brings about a "splitting-off" of groups of pathogenic representations. How then, ask Freud and Breuer in concluding their paper, does the psychotherapeutic procedure they describe have a curative effect?

> *It brings to an end the operative force of the idea which was not abreacted in the first instance, by allowing its strangulated affect to find a way out through speech; and it subjects it to associative correction by introducing it into normal consciousness (under light hypnosis) or by removing it through the physician's suggestion, as is done in somnambulism accompanied by amnesia.* (ibid.: 17)

- **"CASE HISTORIES":**
  FIVE PATIENTS TREATED SUCCESSFULLY BY THE CATHARTIC METHOD

The authors go on to present reports on five clinical observations, only the first of which was written by Breuer, the other four involving patients who were treated by Freud. Here, in broad outline, is a brief reminder of each case; my aim is to highlight the successive stages that the thinking of the two physicians went through in their respective investigations.

- *"Fräulein Anna O." by J. Breuer: the paradigmatic case*

When Breuer met "Anna O." for the first time – her real name was Bertha Pappenheim – she was 21 years old and suffered from a severe cough ("*tussis nervosa*") and several other hysterical symptoms: moodiness, disturbances of vision, paralysis of her right side, "*absences*" filled with hallucinations, various speech disorders, etc. In the course of his frequent and lengthy discussions with her, Breuer noticed that some symptoms disappeared when the young woman gave him a detailed account of the memory linked to their original appearance and at the same time re-experienced the intense emotions she had felt at that moment. After these chance observations, Breuer repeated the experiment in a more systematic fashion with other symptoms, and he began to realize that when he asked Anna O. about the circumstances in which they first appeared, they would disappear as the patient answered his questions. To quote Breuer himself:

> *Each individual symptom in this complicated case was taken separately in hand; all the occasions on which it had appeared were described in reverse order, starting before the time when the patient became bedridden and going back to the event which had led to its first appearance. When this had been described, the symptom was permanently removed.* (ibid.: 35)

Breuer observed also that this phenomenon occurred when the patient was in a state of diminished consciousness resembling self-hypnosis, a state he described as a "*hypnoid state*". Later, Breuer improved his technique by hypnotizing the patient himself, instead of waiting for her to go into a self-hypnotic state, thereby saving time. Anna O. herself called this curative procedure the "*talking cure*" and described as "*chimney-sweeping*" (ibid.: 30) the recollection of memories linked to the appearance of her symptoms which enabled abreaction.

Breuer goes on to quote a long list of symptoms which were eliminated thanks to their having been "*talked away*" (ibid.: 35). The most important therapeutic success was undoubtedly the one involving the paralysis of Anna O.'s right arm. Anna was sitting at the bedside of her seriously ill father, when she suddenly had a kind of hallucination in which she saw a black snake coming to bite the sick man; at the same time she noticed that she could not move her right arm which, over the back of her chair, had gone to sleep. After that initial occurrence, the anxiety-provoking hallucination was frequently repeated, together with the paralysis of her right arm; in addition, she could speak no other language but English. Breuer tells us that at the end of her treatment, Anna O. gave him a full account of the circumstances in which the snake hallucination had first appeared. Once she had succeeded in recollecting what she had felt on that dramatic night when she had stayed by her sick father's bedside, the paralysis of her right side disappeared and she was able to speak again in German:

> *immediately after its reproduction she was able to speak German. She was moreover free from the innumerable disturbances which she had previously exhibited. After this she left Vienna and travelled for a while; but it was a considerable time before she regained her mental balance entirely. Since then she has enjoyed complete health.* (ibid.: 40–41)

Post-Freudians

How did Anna O. end her treatment?

Breuer concluded his report on an optimistic note, saying that though the patient had needed some time before regaining her mental balance entirely, since then "*she has enjoyed complete health*" (ibid.: 41).

More recent research casts doubt on that conclusion. Freud himself gave different accounts of the end of Anna O.'s analysis. Some time afterwards, he said that the treatment had been interrupted because Breuer, finding it impossible to tolerate his patient's transference love, made his escape. As Freud wrote in a letter to Stefan Zweig: "*With all his [Breuer's] great mental endowment he had nothing Faustian about him. In conventional horror he took to flight and left the patient to a colleague*" (Letter, 2 June 1932). In his biography of Freud, Ernest Jones (1953–1957) quotes one of these accounts: on the final day of her treatment, Breuer was called to Anna O.'s bedside and found her having a full-blown hysterical attack, mimicking giving birth to a baby she claimed was Breuer's. It seems that Breuer made good his escape and the very next day left for Venice with his wife; there they conceived a baby daughter.

Recent historical research, however, has established that the account widely disseminated by Jones is in fact a retrospective reconstruction by Freud himself, and one that does not correspond to reality. Albrecht Hirschmüller (1978) shows that Breuer in fact did continue to treat Anna O. after the cathartic treatment had been brought to a close. Some manifestations of her illness persisted and in addition, she suffered from neuralgic pains in the trigeminal nerve that Breuer treated with morphine – to which Anna O. became addicted. In July 1882 he sent the patient to Ludwig Binswanger, the director of Kreuzlingen sanatorium, asking him to continue the treatment; her health having improved, Anna O. left the sanatorium in October of that year. She then lived in Vienna where on several other occasions she had medical treatment, before leaving for Frankfurt. In Germany, she had a very active career as a writer, and she did a great deal of charity work. With this recent research in mind, Britton (2003) has put forward some highly convincing hypotheses as to the nature of hysterical conflict, based on a reassessment of this paradigmatic case.

Some critics of psychoanalysis have used the fact that the patients described in *Studies on Hysteria* were not completely rid of their symptoms to question the validity of psychoanalysis, accusing Freud and Breuer of deception and Anna O. of malingering. It is true that, in their enthusiasm, Breuer and Freud did somewhat embellish the reports of their clinical cases; the very act of publishing them was, at least in part, aimed at proving that their research predated that of Pierre Janet. One should not, however, fall into the trap of not seeing the wood for the trees, because even though this treatment may have had only a limited success, Anna O.'s therapy will remain in the annals as the first successful treatment by the cathartic method as it was then called and as the one that launched Freud on the road to discovering psychoanalysis.

- ## "Frau Emmy von N." by S. Freud
  ## *Freud uses the cathartic method for the first time*

Just as we attribute the discovery of the cathartic method to Breuer's treatment of Anna O., Freud's treatment of "Emmy von N." is the one in which he decided to abandon hypnosis in favour of free association as the preferred method of treatment. This 41-year-old patient – her real name was Fanny Moser – was the widow of a rich manufacturer with whom she had had two daughters; she suffered from severe animal phobias. In this treatment, which began on 1 May 1889 and lasted six weeks, Freud's discussions with the patient had a cathartic purpose; she had massages, too, and hypnosis in order to stimulate memory recall. However, in the course of their discussions, Freud observed that if the patient talked spontaneously, she could recall significant moments, so that the cathartic effect followed on from the simple fact of her unburdening herself without being asked to. As Freud puts it: "*It is as though she had adopted my procedure and was making use of our conversation, apparently unconstrained and guided by chance, as a supplement to hypnosis*" (ibid.: 51). A few days later, irritated by Freud's questions, she asked him to stop interrupting her all the time and "*to let her tell [him] what she had to say*" (ibid.: 63). Freud fell in with the suggestion and observed that he could still obtain the necessary recall of memories, even without hypnosis (though he did go on using that technique with Frau Emmy von N.). The patient often told Freud not to touch her when she felt terrified as she recalled certain memories: " '*Keep still! – Don't say anything! Don't touch me*' " (ibid.: 51), she would say, before calming down somewhat. For Freud, Frau Emmy von N.'s case was not so much one of conversion hysteria as one in which the symptoms of hysteria were above all psychological: anxiety, depression and phobias. As for the origins of her hysteria, Freud believed that the repression of the sexual element played a decisive role since it is "*more liable than any other to provide occasion for traumas*" (ibid.: 103).

- **"Miss Lucy R." by S. Freud**
  Freud gradually abandons hypnosis in favour of suggestion

In December 1892, Freud treated over a period of nine weeks a young English governess who suffered from a loss of the sense of smell and olfactory hallucinations, one of which was a pervasive smell of burning; these disorders were considered to be symptoms of hysteria. After trying in vain to hypnotize her, Freud abandoned that procedure and applied the method of "*free association*", sometimes placing his hand lightly on the patient's forehead whenever she had difficulty in recalling memories.

> *I placed my hand on the patient's forehead or took her head between my hands and said: "You will think of it under the pressure of my hand. At the moment at which I relax my pressure you will see something in front of you or something will come into your head. Catch hold of it. It will be what we are looking for . . . Well, what have you seen or what has occurred to you?"* (ibid.: 110)

That treatment confirmed Freud's hypothesis that it is the reminiscence of an incident – though forgotten, it has been accurately stored in memory – which lies at the origin of the pathogenic effect of hysterical symptoms. There is a conflict in the mind, usually of a sexual nature, and the pathogenic effect is due to the fact that some incompatible idea "*must be* intentionally repressed from consciousness *and excluded from associative modification*" (ibid.: 116). In the present case, the symptoms disappeared after Freud discovered that Miss Lucy R. had secretly fallen in love with her employer; she acknowledged that she had repressed her love for him because there was no hope of fulfilment.

- **"Katharina" by S. Freud**
  An account of a brief psychoanalytic therapy

In this report, Freud gives a brief but brilliant demonstration of the role played by sexual trauma in the aetiology of hysterical symptoms. The treatment took the form of a conversation which lasted for a few hours between Freud and this young (18-year-old) woman. The consultation was an impromptu one which took place in August 1893, during a mountain walk while Freud was on holiday. Katharina was the innkeeper's daughter and, knowing that he was a doctor, she asked him if he could help her with her shortness of breath accompanied by the sight of an awful face which looked at her in a dreadful way. During their conversation, which Freud later noted down as accurately as he could, Katharina remembered that her symptoms had begun 2 years earlier, when she had witnessed sexual intercourse between her "uncle" and her cousin Franziska; she had been deeply shocked at the sight. That memory reminded Katharina of the fact that her "uncle" had also made sexual advances to *her* on several occasions, when she was 14 years of age. Freud observed that, after recounting these incidents, the young woman felt relieved because, as he puts it, her hysteria "*had to a considerable extent been abreacted*" (ibid.: 132). For Freud, this strengthened his thesis: "*The anxiety from which Katharina suffered in her attacks was a hysterical one; that is, it was a reproduction of the anxiety which had appeared in connection with each of the sexual traumas*" (ibid.: 134). In a footnote added in 1924, Freud reveals that the man in question was not the young woman's "*uncle*" but her father (ibid.: 134, note 2).

- **"Fräulein Elisabeth von R." by S. Freud**
  The first complete analysis of a case of hysteria

The fourth case described by Freud is that of a young 24-year-old woman of Hungarian origin, "Elisabeth von R." (her real name was Ilona Weiss), whom he treated from the autumn of 1892 until July 1893. She had been suffering for more than 2 years from pains in her legs and had unclassifiable difficulties in walking. These disorders had appeared for the first time as she was looking after her father, who was ill. Shortly after her father's death, the patient's sister fell ill and died; these two deaths played a decisive role in her symptomatology. Freud tells us that there were three phases to her treatment. The first was dominated by the fact that it proved impossible to establish with the patient any connection between her actual symptoms and a precipitating cause. She was resistant to hypnosis, so that Freud simply asked her to lie down with her eyes closed, though allowing her to move as she wished. In spite of his efforts, the expected therapeutic effect did not occur. He then had recourse to his technique of lightly pressing his hand on her forehead while asking her to tell him what came into her mind. The first thought she had was the memory of a young man with whom she had fallen in love just as her father's state of health was deteriorating. Given the seriousness of her father's illness, she had once and for all relinquished her love for the young man. She remembered that it was when this internal conflict appeared that she first felt pain in her legs – an instance, says Freud, of the mechanism of conversion in hysteria. Recalling this setback in her love life led Fräulein Elisabeth von R. herself to discover the reasons for this first conversion:

The patient surprised me soon afterwards by announcing that she now knew why it was that the pains always radiated from that particular area of the right thigh and were at their most painful there: it was in this place that her father used to rest his leg every morning while she renewed the bandage around it, for it was badly swollen. (ibid.: 148)

During this period of "*abreaction*", the patient's condition improved dramatically. This gave Freud confidence in the pressure method he was using in an attempt to bring about the recall of images and ideas; he was no longer reluctant to insist on the patient's telling him what was going through her mind whenever she claimed that – because of resistances – she could think of nothing. "*In the course of this difficult work I began to attach a deeper significance to the resistance offered by the patient in the reproduction of her memories*" (ibid.: 154).

It was only during the third phase of the treatment that a complete cure was obtained. A chance occurrence enabled Freud to discover the "*secret*" which lay behind Fräulein Elisabeth von R.'s pains. During one session, she asked Freud to break off for the day because she had heard her brother-in-law in the next room inquiring about her. When she returned after the interruption, she was again feeling severe pains in her legs. Freud therefore determined to get to the root of the mystery. The arrival of the brother-in-law reminded her that the pains first appeared around the time when her sister had died; as she walked into the room where her dead sister's body was laid out, a shameful thought had passed through her mind: the death of her sister meant that her brother-in-law was free again and that she could become his wife! Her love for her brother-in-law was resisted by her whole moral being, which was why she had "*repressed*" that intolerable idea and banished it from consciousness. Upon that basis, the mechanism of conversion was free to operate: "*her pains had come on thanks to the successful conversion*" of psychical excitations into something physical (ibid.: 157). This insight led to a complete cure. Freud was able to see this for himself when, a year later, he saw his former patient taking part in a lively dance at a private ball. The success of the treatment did not, however, prevent her from bearing a terrible grudge against Freud for having revealed her secret.

"THEORETICAL" BY J. BREUER

In his theoretical chapter, Breuer develops a certain number of hypotheses already outlined in the "Preliminary Communication". His main contribution has to do with "hypnoid states" and on the splitting of the mind that comes about because certain unconscious representations which cannot become conscious thereby acquire pathogenic potentiality. For Breuer, hysterical disorders appear in people who are particularly excitable and present a tendency to self-hypnosis – what he calls "*absence of mind*" – thereby facilitating suggestion. He notes also that these patients have an innate disposition to reject anything which is sexual in nature, particularly in cases of conversion hysteria: "*The most numerous and important of the ideas that are fended off and converted have a sexual content*" (ibid.: 245). Breuer, however, contented himself with applying the cathartic method which he had invented, without any attempt to improve on it; in the final chapter of the book, Freud shows how he developed that method. It is because of this that Breuer's chapter is of historical rather than theoretical interest.

- **"THE PSYCHOTHERAPY OF HYSTERIA" BY S. FREUD**

From hypnosis to free association

Starting from his own clinical experience, Freud shows how he was gradually led to modify the cathartic technique and adopt an innovative therapeutic approach, different from that of Breuer, the advantages and disadvantages of which he goes on to describe. As we read this highly significant chapter, we see Freud outlining in more and more detail what was to become the psychoanalytic method with its constitutive principles already sketched out. In this paper, written in 1895, we find new notions such as the unconscious, resistance, defence mechanisms, transference and many others.

Freud begins his chapter by reminding the reader that it was the difficulties and limitations of the cathartic method which led to his search for more effective ways of facilitating recall of pathogenic memories, as well as to his exploration of these new techniques which would soon replace his earlier approach. In the manner in which it was put into practice, the cathartic method demanded a considerable length of time and, if hypnosis was to be successful, the patient had to have complete confidence in the physician. Not all patients had that required degree of confidence. Far from being discouraged by this, Freud overcame the obstacle by finding a way for the patient to recall pathogenic memories without having to be hypnotized. This was one of Freud's brilliant ideas. He had observed that by making the patient lie down on the couch and asking her to close her eyes and concentrate, he succeeded – sometimes after a great deal of insistence on his part – in bringing new memories to the forefront. But since this procedure too demanded a quite considerable effort on his part and since results were slow in coming, he felt that this could be an indication that the patient was putting up "*resistance*". The physician thus had to overcome these new obstacles which hindered the emergence of representations.

In this way, Freud discovered the part played by *resistance* and by the *defences*, psychological mechanisms which try to prevent pathogenic representations from reaching the "*ego*" (ibid.: 269). He realized that their objective was to force "*out of consciousness and out of memory*" (ibid.: 269) any incompatible ideas, by a process he called censorship: "*Thus a psychical force, aversion on the part of the ego, had originally driven the pathogenic idea out of association and was now opposing its return to memory*" (ibid.: 269). According to Freud, the pathogenic representation provoked on the part of the ego a repelling force which he associated with *repression* (ibid.: 269). However, if the undischarged emotion is too powerful for the patient to tolerate, the psychical energy is converted into its physical counterpart, thereby giving rise to a hysterical *symptom*, in accordance with the mechanism of *conversion*.

Freud had based his approach on the fact of the therapist's "*insisting*" on the patient's need to overcome his or her resistance. He then added the "*small technical device*" (ibid.: 270) of applying pressure to the patient's forehead with the aim of facilitating the emergence of pathogenic memories. However, he shortly afterwards discovered the free association approach, and abandoned this technical gesture too. The discovery of the free association method was a gradual one; it developed at some point between 1892 and 1898, but it is difficult to be more precise than that. Freud, all the same, says that he was applying it in his treatment of "Frau Emmy von N.", where he gradually allowed the patient to express herself more spontaneously.

Studies on Hysteria – and in particular Freud's contributions to the book – are full of clinical, technical and theoretical comments which open up new paths and constitute the foundation on which psychoanalysis was about to be constructed. Among the new concepts Freud introduced in that book, three notions are worth looking at in more detail: sexuality, symbolism and transference.

The part played by sexuality

Although Freud had observed almost from the beginning that sexual trauma was a regular feature of what patients said about the circumstances in which their hysterical symptoms first appeared, he was at first reluctant to admit to a causal link between them: "*I had come fresh from the school of Charcot, and I regarded the linking of hysteria with the topic of sexuality as a sort of insult – just as the women patients themselves do*" (ibid.: 260). But the more he observed the presence of sexual trauma in his patients' reports of their illness, the more he was forced to recognize that the sexual factor played a decisive role as a precipitating cause of their symptoms. He was later to realize that this factor played a part not only in hysteria but also in all the neuro-psychoses, which is why he called them "*sexual neuroses*" (ibid.: 261).

Though Freud had little to say about that revolutionary point of view in *Studies on Hysteria*, he goes into more detail about it in several papers he wrote at that time. He repeatedly maintained that in the neuroses – and in hysteria above all – the original trauma is always linked to real sexual encounters which have been experienced in early childhood, and at any rate before puberty. These experiences, which could be anything from simple sexual advances to actual sexual activity of one sort or another, says Freud, "*are to be described as sexual abuses in the narrowest sense*" (Freud 1897b: 253). With the idea of an actual sexual trauma having occurred in the patient's early childhood, Freud introduced a hypothesis which he was to maintain for only a short period, from 1895 until 1897. It should be pointed out that with this notion of actual sexual trauma, Freud made no mention of infantile sexuality – the fact that children have sex drives – as Richard Wollheim (1971: 38) observes. Freud was soon to change his mind on this point as his clinical observations increased in number. From that point on, he began to doubt whether the sexual scenario which the patient recounted had actually occurred in reality: perhaps it had been imagined rather than actually experienced? From then on, he considered that the decisive traumatic factor depended more on fantasy and on the instinctual drives than on the reality of the sexual scene. I shall come back to this question later.

• *Symbols and hysterical symptoms*

Freud observed also that there was a symbolic determinism in the form adopted by the hysterical symptom, of which conversion by means of the mechanism of symbolization constitutes the clearest expression. He gives several examples of this "*determination through symbolism*". In one of these, a girl felt a penetrating pain in her forehead between her eyes; the pain disappeared when she recalled that her grandmother had given her a look so "*piercing that it had gone right into her brain*" (Freud and Breuer 1895d: 180). Breuer observes that "*what unites the affect and its reflex is often some ridiculous play upon words or associations by sound*" (ibid.: 209). Freud suggests that hysteria restores "*the original meaning of words*" in depicting feelings and innervations because "*in all probability the description was once meant literally*" (ibid.: 181). Freud, however, did not at that point pursue his investigation of "*mnemic symbols*" any further; this he left for a later date.

• *An outline of the idea of transference*

It is not without surprise that we discover that, in these early writings on hysteria, Freud was already describing transference phenomena and actually using the term. He begins by referring to it indirectly, from the point of view of having to ensure that the patient trusts the physician. For example, in his description of the cathartic method, he notes that for hypnosis to be successful, the patient has to have complete confidence in the doctor as well as "*complete consent*" (ibid.: 265). When he raises the question of how to eliminate resistance, Freud argues that the doctor's personality plays a major role, since "*in a number of cases the latter alone is in a position to remove the resistance*" (ibid.: 283).

Freud mentions the idea of transference explicitly when he examines more closely the reasons for the patient's resistance, particularly in cases where the technical device of applying pressure failed to bring any modification. He sees two obstacles which prevent awareness of resistance: personal estrangement with respect to the physician, an obstacle which is not too difficult to surmount; and the dread of becoming over-attached to the physician, an obstacle which is more difficult to eliminate. Freud then adds a third obstacle which can prevent resistance from reaching consciousness:

> *If the patient is frightened at finding that she is transferring on to the figure of the physician the distressing ideas which arise from the content of the analysis. This is a frequent, and indeed in some analyses a regular, occurrence. Transference on to the physician takes place through a* false connection. (ibid.: 302)

Freud reports briefly the case of a woman patient who had wanted a male friend to take her in his arms and kiss her. On one occasion, at the end of a session, a similar wish came up in her with respect to Freud – she wanted him to take her in his arms and kiss her. She was horrified at the idea. After Freud discovered the obstacle and removed it, the work of the therapy could proceed. Freud calls this phenomenon "*mésalliance*" or "*false connection*".

> *Since I have discovered this, I have been able, whenever I have been similarly involved personally, to presume that a transference and a false connection have once more taken place. Strangely enough, the patient is deceived afresh every time this is repeated.* (ibid.: 303)

Post-Freudians

Hysteria one hundred years on

How do psychoanalysts see hysteria nowadays? Has it disappeared? Do we still know how to diagnose it today? These were the questions asked by Edward Nersessian, from New York, one of the participants in a panel called "Hysteria 100 years on" at the International Psychoanalytical Congress held in San Francisco in 1995. According to Joana M. Tous's (1996) report, the debate highlighted the various points of view which are current today. Here is a brief summary of that account.

Nowadays most psychoanalysts would agree that hysteria involves a wide range of pathological conditions, from the neuroses to the psychoses and including severe borderline and narcissistic pathologies. However, from the point of view of therapeutic procedure, there are two main lines of thought, one of which is represented by French psychoanalysts, the other by the British school.

For Janine Chasseguet-Smirgel (Paris), the psychoanalyst must not lose sight of the sexual dimension of hysteria and be content with the idea that it is based solely on a primitive, pregenital pathology. She accepts that the psychoanalyst is often disconcerted by the sheer abundance of clinical phenomena which this kind of patient presents, giving the impression of a great variety of primitive pathological states. Chasseguet-Smirgel argues that we should not play down the importance of interpreting the Oedipal conflicts and guilt feelings which have to do with destructive attacks against the mother. If we focus our attention exclusively on the primitive aspects, we run the risk of watering down hysteria as a clinical entity closely related to sexual identity and Oedipal phenomena. She goes on to say that she is not alone in thinking along these lines; other psychoanalysts of the French school – André Green and Jean Laplanche, for example – have voiced the same concern. Further, for Chasseguet-Smirgel, hysteria belongs to "the kingdom of the mothers" in the sense that the uterus and pregnancy are very much involved, both in fantasy and in reality. It is for this reason that she insists on the role played by biological factors in hysteria: these ought not to be underestimated, because hysteria is a pathology of the mind that is played out in the theatre of the body. By her insistence on the role played by the body, Chasseguet-Smirgel distances herself from those psychoanalysts who give priority to linguistic considerations and ignore the importance of the body.

Eric Brenman (London) has a very different theoretical and clinical point of view, which is representative of the manner in which British psychoanalysts look at these issues. For Brenman, in his or her earliest object relations, the infant very quickly sets up defences against anxiety, and these defences determine how anxiety will be dealt with in adulthood. Brenman of course acknowledges the importance of the role played by sexuality in hysteria, but for him the dominant factor is the hysterical patient's struggle to overcome primitive anxieties. He shows how, in the transference, patients act on the psychic reality of the analyst, and describes how they cope with primitive anxieties – these, he says, are experienced both as catastrophic anxiety and as non-existent danger. We often find in such patients splitting mechanisms which give rise to states of mind which divide up their mental life into various strata. For example, hysterical patients want a relationship with idealized objects yet they are immediately disappointed as soon as they are in contact with them – which is why they continually go from one extreme state to another. For Brenman, hysteria is above all underpinned by severe psychotic disorders. That said, psychoanalysis has evolved over the past 100 years relative to its capacity to contain psychotic anxiety and to process it; as a result, patients nowadays have improved means of overcoming their anxieties and coping with the ups and downs of daily life.

"Ruby abhors red"

That is the title which Jacqueline Schaeffer (1986) chose for her paper in which she describes the relationship between hysteria and sexuality; her metaphor was inspired by the mineralogist's definition of the ruby: "The ruby is a precious stone which abhors red. It absorbs and holds on to all the other colours of the spectrum. It rejects red, yet that is what it presents to our eyes." Just like the ruby, hysteria "glistens", says Schaeffer (1986: 925):

> *How better to describe what the hysteric presents to our eyes – her horror of anything red, of sexuality, the exhibition of her trauma? ... The ego cunningly pushes to the fore the most threatening of aspects as well as those which are under the greatest threat, displaying them for all to see, those which are foreign, hated and hurtful – and cunningly attacks with what is doing the actual attacking. Perhaps, like the ruby, something extremely precious has to be kept very well hidden.*

New concepts

Abreaction – actual sexual trauma – cathartic method – censorship – conversion – defence – fantasy – free association – repression – resistance – trauma – unconscious

LETTERS TO WILHELM FLIESS

(1950a [1887–1902]) AND (1985c [1887–1904])

A testimony to Freud's initial researches and to his self-analysis

The letters that Freud wrote to his friend Wilhelm Fliess during the seventeen years between 1887 and 1904 are an invaluable source of information. Not only do we learn a great deal about his everyday private and professional life, but also they show how his thinking was developing throughout this particularly fertile period and they give us a glimpse of how his self-analysis was progressing. Of these numerous letters, only Freud's have survived; they were bought in 1936 by Princess Marie Bonaparte from a Viennese antique dealer. In 1950, she, together with Anna Freud and Ernst Kris, published a carefully edited version of 168 letters (out of a total of 284) under the title *The Origins of Psychoanalysis*; this was accompanied by "A Project for a Scientific Psychology", a text that Freud had always refused to publish. It was only in 1985 that all of these letters were finally published, after Anna Freud's death and once sufficient time had elapsed to remove any issues of confidentiality.

Biographies and history

The passionate friendship between Freud and Fliess

Freud was introduced to Wilhelm Fliess in 1887 by Breuer. Fliess was an ear, nose and throat specialist who had set up practice in Berlin; he was very keen on somewhat audacious biological and mathematical theories and incredibly self-assured as to his own hypotheses. All this time, Freud was very much an outsider as far as Viennese medical circles were concerned because of his theories on the sexual aetiology of neurosis, and he found in Fliess someone reassuring, someone to whom he could talk openly. His friendship with Breuer gradually gave way to that with Fliess who, for several years, was to be Freud's most intimate confidant. In addition to their exchange of letters, the two friends met from time to time to have what Freud called a "*congress*", a discussion session in which they would reflect on their hypotheses and work out more theoretical avenues to explore. In this way Freud's "*dear Wilhelm*" became a participant observer with respect to his discoveries and scientific contributions as they were being made, all through the period which ran from the preparation of *Studies on Hysteria* to the publication of *The Interpretation of Dreams* in 1900. However, from 1897 on, the spell began to break; Freud gradually began to de-idealize his friend and to be less dependent on the powerful relationship they had established – later, he would acknowledge the homosexual dimension implied in their friendship. As he progressed with his self-analysis, Freud discovered the hatred he had felt towards his father – as well as the disguised hatred he felt for Fliess. They had their final disagreement at a congress held in 1900: Freud criticized Fliess's theory of periodicity, and Fliess blamed Freud for reading his own thoughts into his patient's material. Their relationship deteriorated, their exchange of letters became more and more

> sporadic, and the final break-up took place in 1906. Thereafter, Freud destroyed all of Fliess's letters, though he did later acknowledge that Fliess's ideas on bisexuality were of great assistance to him.

Discovering the text

> Page numbers are those of (i) Freud, S. (1985c [1887–1904]) *The Complete Letters of Sigmund Freud to Wilhelm Fliess 1887–1904*, translated and edited by J. Masson, London & Cambridge, MA, 1985 and (ii) *The Standard Edition of the Complete Psychological Works of Sigmund Freud*, vol. **1**.

At first sight, reading Freud's letters to Fliess is not of any great interest, but for anyone who is already familiar with Freud's ideas, they are an invaluable source of information. We see Freud's germinating questions on hysteria, on the neuro-psychoses, on paranoia, on depression (which he called "melancholia"). As we follow – step by step – the everyday issues he was trying to deal with, the comments he made on his patients, the family problems he had to cope with, we suddenly stumble upon an intuition which was to prove decisive, for example when he mentions for the first time the Oedipus complex. Though I would really like the reader to discover these letters at his or her own pace, I feel I must point out three decisive moments: when Freud discovered the impact of seduction fantasies; when he intuitively recognized the Oedipus complex in his self-analysis; and when he finally gave up any idea of elaborating a theory which could have given psychoanalysis a "scientific" basis.

• *Actual seduction and fantasies of seduction*

As I pointed out in the previous chapter, when Freud listened to what his (women) patients had to tell him about their recollections of actual seduction that had occurred in their childhood (when the initial symptoms of hysteria appeared), he felt sure that the origins of hysteria lay in the fact that an adult close to the patient had actually seduced her. Constructed in 1893, this hypothesis – the "seduction theory" – was Freud's main tenet until 1897. In the meantime, he was expanding his hypothesis beyond hysteria in order to account for the neuro-psychoses in general. In so doing, however, he was not claiming that there was a simple causal relationship between actual seduction and the presenting symptoms – his theory was aimed at explaining how repression came about, as Laplanche and Pontalis (1967) quite rightly point out. That is why Freud suggested that the process took place in two stages separated by puberty: in the initial phase, the individual cannot experience any sexual arousal since sexual maturity is as yet inadequate – the scene is therefore not repressed. In the second phase, which, for Freud, occurs after puberty, a new event revives the memory of the earlier incident, thereby giving rise to a traumatic impact which is much more important than the earlier event, by reason of the individual's newly acquired sexual maturity; this is the point at which the memory is repressed, "retrospectively" or as a "deferred action", a concept which would play a crucial part in psychoanalysis thereafter.

As he accumulated more and more clinical material, however, Freud began to have doubts concerning the authenticity of the seduction scenes about which his patients were telling him. In his famous letter to Fliess dated 21 September 1897, he announced: "*And now I want to confide in you immediately the great secret that has been slowly dawning on me in the last few months. I no longer believe in my neurotica*" (Freud 1985c [1887–1904]: 264). Freud puts forward several reasons for his change of mind. In the first place, he doubts whether perverse acts against children are as widespread as would seem to be the case. He goes on to suggest quite explicitly that the fantasy of seduction more than any actual event of this nature plays the decisive role: "*Accordingly, there would remain the solution that the sexual fantasy invariably seizes upon the theme of the parents*" (ibid.: 264–265). Finally, he comes to the conclusion that it is difficult to decide which of the two, reality or fantasy, should be given more weight: *"there are no indications of reality in the unconscious, so that one cannot distinguish between truth and fiction that has been cathected with affect"* (ibid.: 264).

The role of infantile sexuality

What brought Freud to the conclusion that fantasy rather than reality plays the decisive role, forcing him to abandon to a considerable extent his initial hypotheses? As he listened to what his patients reported in their memories and dreams – and by analysing his own – Freud discovered that children too have feelings, sensations and thoughts which are sexual in content and that they often find it difficult to distinguish between reality and fantasy. *"And now, from behind the fantasies, the whole range of a child's sexual life came to light"* (1914d: 18). Contrary to what had been thought until then, that domain was not the exclusive prerogative of adults and adolescents. Nevertheless, though the discovery of the importance of infantile sexuality in the aetiology of the neurosis led Freud to abandon his earlier theory, he never failed to emphasize, throughout his life, that any seduction experienced in reality by children does have a pathogenic effect and that any resultant neurosis could not be attributed to fantasy alone. As matters stand at present, the question remains very much an open one because in many cases it is difficult – for both patient and psychoanalyst – to differentiate between what actually occurred in reality and what belongs to the patient's imagination.

What do we mean by the term "infantile sexuality"? It is a concept which should be clearly defined from the outset, because it is often misunderstood. What psychoanalysts mean by the term "infantile sexuality" is not limited to the various kinds of erotic activity that can be observed in young children, including the thoughts and desires which they express from infancy onwards; "infantile sexuality" also comprises the whole series of transformations in mind and body which continue until puberty and adolescence. The process begins with the first awakening of the senses as the infant sucks the mother's breast during a feed, and it continues stage by stage, becoming more and more organized as it does so, until it attains the genital maturity characteristic of adulthood and the gender determination as man or woman. It is this entire process, throughout which sexuality plays the decisive organizing role, which we call infantile sexuality, with the term "sexuality" being understood in its broadest sense. Some years later, Freud would synthesize the various strands of thought already contained in his exchange of letters with Fliess and publish *Three Essays on the Theory of Sexuality* (1905d).

Freud's self-analysis and his discovery of the Oedipus complex

Shortly after his father's death in 1896, Freud embarked upon his own psychoanalysis, in a period that ran approximately from 1896 to 1899. His *"self-analysis"* – as he called it in his letters to Fliess – was based for the most part on the analysis of his own dreams; thanks to these, he was able to realize not only the part which dreams play in mental life but also the importance that sexuality had had in his own childhood:

> *later (between two and two and a half years) my libido toward* matrem *was awakened, namely, on the occasion of a journey with her from Leipzig to Vienna, during which we must have spent the night together and there must have been an opportunity of seeing her* nudam. (Freud 1985c [1887–1904]: 268)

He goes on, in the same letter (dated 3–4 October 1897): *"I greeted my one-year-younger brother (who died after a few months) with adverse wishes and genuine childhood jealousy, and [...] his death left the germ of [self-]reproaches in me"* (ibid.: 268).

One week after this, he wrote for the first time that in his self-analysis he had discovered what, more than ten years later, he would call the *"Oedipus complex"* (1910h: 171):

> *My self-analysis is in fact the most essential thing I have at present and promises to become of the greatest value to me if it reaches its end. [...] I have found, in my own case too, [the*

phenomenon of] being in love with my mother and jealous of my father, and I now consider it a universal event in early childhood [. . .]. If this is so, we can understand the gripping power of Oedipus Rex, *in spite of all the objections that reason raises against the presupposition of fate.* (Freud 1985c [1887–1904]: 270 & 272)

In that letter, Freud refers only to the direct form of the Oedipus complex as it occurs in boys, with the desire to replace the father in his relationship with the mother. Freud would later describe the direct form of the Oedipus complex in girls – with the desire to take over the mother's role in her relationship with the father – and, later still, the inverted form of the Oedipus complex in both boys and girls. The discovery that in every individual there coexists the direct form of the Oedipus complex, the basis for identification with the same-sex parent, and the inverted form of the complex, the basis for identification with the opposite-sex parent, enabled Freud (in *The Ego and the Id* (1923b)) to apply to fantasy material the idea of psychical bisexuality which he had borrowed from Fliess. The latter had drawn Freud's attention to the part played by bisexuality in masculine and feminine gender identity, not only at the anatomical and biological levels but also as far as the psychological dimension is concerned.

Even though Freud's self-analysis had enabled him to explore some decisive issues in his attempt to know himself and to investigate as thoroughly as he could the workings of the human mind, he realized that this kind of introspection came up against intrinsic limitations which could not be surmounted. He felt it indispensable that any prospective psychoanalyst should initially have recourse to some other psychoanalyst in order to overcome his or her unconscious resistance and have the experience of working through a transference relationship. Freud went on to say that once this analysis had ended, every psychoanalyst should then embark on an ongoing process of self-analysis, one that would last all through life.

• THE "DRAFTS"

Several of Freud's letters are accompanied by what he calls "*Drafts*", each of which is followed by a capital letter. In these short papers, he presents his initial thoughts on topics to which he would later return in a more detailed fashion – sometimes several decades later, in fact. For example, in "*Draft E*" (Freud 1950a [1887–1902]: 189), he discusses how anxiety originates, saying that it is a question of "an accumulation of physical sexual tension" (ibid.: 191) that cannot be discharged. This was his first theory of anxiety, but he quickly came to the view that there is another mechanism involved which, when tension becomes too great, brings into play the mind's inability to "*bind*" anxiety, as he shows in 1926 in *Inhibitions, Symptoms and Anxiety*. "*Draft G*" deals with melancholia; Freud suggests that the affect involves mourning and has to do with the longing for something lost. This can be attributed to a "*loss of libido*" (Freud 1985c [1887–1904]: 99). He goes on to say that "*there may come about an* in-drawing, *as it were*, into the psychic sphere" (ibid.: 103), a process which could be likened to "*an* internal haemorrhage" (ibid.); he would come back to this topic in "Mourning and Melancholia" (1917e [1915]). "*Draft H*" deals with projection as a mechanism of defence.

Post-Freudians

The controversy over Freud's seduction theory

In 1984, Jeffrey M. Masson, who had access to the Freud Archives and published in 1985 all of Freud's letters to Fliess, wrote *The Assault on Truth: Freud's Suppression of the Seduction Theory*, a controversial book about the so-called "true" reasons behind Freud's abandonment of the seduction theory. According to Masson, Freud's only aim in so doing was to disguise the truth; by inventing a theory of fantasized seduction, he could protect fathers from being rightfully accused of seducing their own daughters.

Setting the record straight: a salutary clarification

In his critical review of Masson's controversial book, Charles Hanly (1986) shows not only that the latter's arguments are tendentious but also that Freud never completely abandoned his seduction theory – he referred to it throughout his life and emphasized that it was often difficult to distinguish between what may actually have occurred in reality, and fantasy representations of the event in question.

Hanly's clarification in fact corresponds to the opinion held by most contemporary psychoanalysts: (1) a particularly powerful infantile fantasy may have as much impact on mental development as a real event; (2) real events may have little or no effect at the time when they actually occur – in general, before puberty – but acquire a powerful feedback effect from adolescence on, given the fact of intervening sexual development; (3) in the course of an analysis, it is sometimes difficult to decide whether a reconstruction based on the patient's associations and on the transference corresponds to a highly cathected fantasy or an infantile hallucinatory experience; (4) an analyst may well believe that fragments of events, residues of dreams, etc. correspond to real events, whereas in fact they are part of hallucinations or of defences against dangerous infantile wishes; (5) it may be that a patient who has omnipotent infantile wishes and aggressive fantasies had also experienced actual situations of pathogenic seduction; (6) the analyst's task is to help the patient to clarify what, in the past, belongs to fantasy and what actually occurred in reality.

New concepts

Actual seduction – anxiety – bisexuality – melancholia (depression) – psychic bisexuality – seduction fantasies – seduction theory – self-analysis

"PROJECT FOR A SCIENTIFIC PSYCHOLOGY"

(1950c [1895])

An attempt to build psychoanalysis on a foundation of quantifiable scientific data

Among the letters Freud wrote to his friend Fliess was discovered this unpublished manuscript which bore witness to Freud's intention to *"furnish a psychology that shall be a natural science"* (1950a [1887–1902]: 295), an ambition that he was never to abandon. The "Project" is by no means a major work, but it has two main claims to interest. First, the reader discovers the early stages of Freud's innovative and fundamental intuitions concerning the workings of the mind; these original hypotheses were later to give rise to a fair number of significant developments in psychoanalysis. Second, writing the "Project" proved to Freud that any intention to provide psychoanalysis with a scientific basis led to an impasse, which is why he always refused to publish this paper. However, the text did leave its mark on the development of his ideas because, in abandoning this particular approach, Freud, in what can only be called a stroke of genius, established psychoanalysis as a discipline in its own right.

Discovering the text

Page numbers are those of *The Standard Edition of the Complete Psychological Works of Sigmund Freud*, vol. **1**, 283–397.

- **Some inspired intuitions scattered throughout an unfinished manuscript**

In his "Project for a Scientific Psychology", Freud places side by side ideas borrowed from neurophysiology, such as neurones (discovered in 1892) and synaptic transmission, and clinically observed data drawn from his recent experience of treating hysteria, from which he deduced some audacious ideas. This in itself lends significant interest to this manuscript from the point of view of the development of Freud's ideas. Admittedly, many sections of this paper – which Freud was never to complete – are obscure or outdated, but the reader can also take pleasure in discovering some fundamental intuitions, which a hundred years later are still as fresh as ever.

- ### *The search for an integrated model of the workings of the mind*

Still very much under the influence of his training in research, Freud takes as his starting-point what was then known in neurophysiology about neurones and nerve impulses; his intention is to construct an integrated model of the workings of the mind based on quantifiable data. Consequently, the conception he proposes in the "Project" is built essentially on the idea of quantities of energy circulating among networks of neurones; this allows him to translate in terms of energy the observed psychological data which he had accumulated up till then. For example, Freud thinks that in pathological states, the quantities of physical energy circulating in the organism can choose different means of discharge, mental or somatic, in accordance with the degree of resistance or facilitation existing in the various networks. That hypothesis can thus explain conversion hysteria and obsessive-compulsive behaviour in terms of the resultant discharge into the body of an excessive quantity of excitation which has become uncontrollable.

Freud goes on to establish a series of equivalences between physiological and psychological processes. On the physiological level, for example, he defines the fundamental principle of the function of neurones as the "*principle of inertia*"; neurones tend to divest themselves of any excess of energy, which therefore becomes freely available. Transposed to the way the mind works, the inertia principle is equivalent to the idea of the *primary process*, a mental process which is characterized by the free and uninhibited flow of psychic energy. The mind, however, cannot function solely according to the principle of discharge, because it is required to tolerate a certain quantity of excitation. For this reason, Freud postulates the existence of a regulatory system in the mind which is able to resist discharge of excess psychic energy and has the property of transforming primary processes into secondary ones. The latter are characterized by their ability to bind energy and inhibit the primary processes. This whole regulatory system is based on the "*principle of constancy*", the function of which is to organize the "*secondary processes*". For example, in hysteria, it is the "secondary process" which enables the patient to maintain the emotional potential in his or her mind, thanks to the possibility of recalling the traumatic memory and putting it into words; as a result, the excess of excitation no longer requires to seek an outlet via somatic conversion and symptoms. Employed by Freud as early as 1895, the notions of primary and secondary processes would remain fundamental to his conception of the workings of the mind.

- ### *Outlining the function of the "ego"*

What role does the individual person play in this process? Freud has the idea of calling *the* "*ego*" an agency that functions simultaneously on two levels: on the one hand, the "ego" functions on the physiological level as a group of neurones which are constantly cathected and maintain their "*bound energy*"; and, on the other, the "*ego*", functioning on the psychological level, is the agency whose task it is to establish the predominance of secondary processes over the primary ones. Another essential function of the "*ego*" is that of "*reality testing*", thanks to which the person distinguishes between perceptions coming from outside and hallucinations or memories coming from within the self. The "*ego*" as Freud had described it in 1895 (in *Studies on Hysteria*) is a conscious ego; it did not at that point take on the meaning which he would give it in *The Ego and the Id* (1923b), with the unconscious interactions between ego, id and superego taking place inside the mind.

- ### *A closer look at "the experience of satisfaction"*

Let us focus our attention for a moment on one particular issue, the one that Freud calls "*the experience of satisfaction*"; this will enable us to follow step by step Freud's scientific approach. What does he mean by "*the experience of satisfaction*"? For Freud, it is the complex process which begins with the internal state of tension generated by an instinctual need – for example, hunger in an infant or sexual desire in an adult. He begins by describing the attendant phenomena in terms of tension and discharge occurring in a reflex arc, with the idea that neurophysiological phenomena (φ) have their psychological equivalent (ψ). As the need intensifies, physical and mental tension increase, leading to the expectation of discharge as a way of obtaining satisfaction. This can happen only with the help of someone extraneous to the individual, alerted by the infant's cries of distress: "*this intervention calls for an alteration in the external world (supply of nourishment, proximity of the sexual object)*" (1950a [1887–1902]: 318). Once that person has done what was required, the path of discharge then becomes particularly important on two levels: on the one hand, a connection is established in the person's mind between the suppression of unpleasure and the intervention of the helper, thus creating a feeling of "*communication*" (ibid.); on the other, the person carries out on the physical level what the suppression of the unpleasure requires, by means of the motor functions. "*Thus, as a result of the experience of satisfaction, a facilitation comes about between two mnemic images*" (ibid.: 319), in other words, between that of the desired object and that of the reflex movement. However,

> *when the state of* urgency *or* wishing *re-appears, the cathexis will also pass over on to the two memories and will activate them. Probably the mnemic image of the object will be the first to be activated by the* wishful activation. (ibid.: 319)

Freud calls the whole of this process an "*experience of satisfaction*" and argues that it plays a decisive role in establishing in the individual a capacity to cope with his or her instinctual needs. It is here that the "*ego*" intervenes, says Freud; its role is to ensure that tensions are removed and that satisfaction is obtained, as well as to oppose the repetition of painful experiences and affects by means of inhibiting mechanisms.

- ***The links between pleasure/unpleasure, affects, ego and objects***

Freud goes on to complete his survey by examining "*the experience of pain*". He shows that the need-related increase in tension which produces unpleasure does not simply call to mind the image of the person who had brought satisfaction; unpleasure also triggers hostile feelings towards that person experienced as frustrating and "*excit[ing] the pain*" (ibid.: 320). Similarly, he adds, when satisfaction occurs, pleasure is attributed to the person who is the reason for that satisfaction:

> *The emergence of another object in place of the hostile one was the signal for the fact that the experience of pain was at an end, and the* ψ *system, taught* biologically, *seeks to reproduce the state in* ψ *which marked the cessation of the pain.* (ibid.: 322)

By highlighting the link between aggressive or affectionate feelings and the person to whom is attributed frustration or satisfaction, Freud introduces an affective dimension into object relations which complements the pleasure/unpleasure principle.

Briefly, Freud shows that from the very beginning of life, the experience of pain and that of satisfaction are not isolated experiences; they are closely linked to the intervention of the object and determine a primary distinction between negative and positive affects. In 1915, in "Instincts and their Vicissitudes" (1915c), Freud comes back to the idea that from the outset there is a fundamental division between the affects, and introduces the idea of the "*purified pleasure-ego*"; there too he continues his investigation into the vicissitudes of love and hate with respect to feelings of pleasure and unpleasure in an object relations context.

- ***The idea of deferred action and proton pseudos***

Finally, mention must be made of the fact that in the "Project" Freud also introduces the concept of "*deferred action*" when he asks why, in hysteria, repression has mainly to do with sexuality. With the help of a clinical example, that of Emma, he shows that repression is a two-stage process. The initial phase is the result of a sexual seduction which occurred when she was a child – at 8 years of age she had gone into a small grocery store and the shopkeeper had grabbed at her genitals through her clothes – but that incident did not carry with it any traumatic sexual significance for her at the time. The second phase occurred later and did trigger sexual arousal due to the onset of puberty; this reawakened the memory of the initial incident, which thereupon took on traumatic sexual significance. Five years later, when she was 13, Emma went into a shop to buy something and saw the two shop-assistants laughing together: Emma ran off. Since the ego could not defend itself against these intolerable affects, it had recourse to repression. Thus it is the second incident that determines the pathogenic nature of the first; Freud calls this phenomenon "*deferred action*". "*We invariably find that a memory is repressed which has only become a trauma by* deferred action. *The cause of this state of things is the retardation of puberty as compared with the rest of the individual's development*" (1950a [1887–1902]: 356). For Freud, the claim that his patient did not have any knowledge of the sexual nature of the initial trauma is the hysteric's first false message, describing it as a *proton pseudos* (which does not mean "initial falsehood" as is sometimes thought; the meaning of the term is closer to "false premises" or "preceding falsity").

• *An example of Freud's scientific approach*

Reading the "Project" enables us to follow step by step the meticulous scientific approach which is typical of Freud: he starts from observed neurophysiological and psychological data and then goes on to draw conclusions which have a much wider significance. We shall encounter this attitude time and again as we progress through our reading of his texts, and especially in his Papers on Metapsychology (1915–1917). But there is one difference: after writing the "Project", Freud abandoned once and for all any idea of basing psychoanalysis on neurophysiology. The fact that he was bold enough to give up that idea enabled him to establish psychoanalysis in a domain of its own, as Green (1992) has pointed out. As for the indissoluble link between mind and body, Freud went on supporting that point of view though he did adopt a different perspective.

Post-Freudians

Contemporary scientific models and psychoanalysis

What if, one hundred years after the "Project", psychoanalysts were to use the scientific models of the end of the twentieth century and adopt an approach similar to that of Freud in 1895? Some contemporary psychoanalysts have attempted to do just that: this is what they have to say.

Mark Solms trained both as a neuropsychologist and as a psychoanalyst; he is therefore particularly well qualified to examine in detail any correlations between psychoanalysis and the neuro-sciences (Solms and Kaplan-Solms 2000). His research is based on the use of psychoanalysis as a method of investigation in patients who present neuro-anatomical lesions. For him, mental phenomena involve a functional system located within a network of anatomical structures in the brain. Solms's work, which has attracted a great deal of attention, does not give preference to neuro-anatomical models over psychological ones, in contrast to much contemporary research which seeks to bring psychoanalysis closer to the neuro-sciences, with the risk that each of these disciplines loses its specificity.

Solms's studies have the advantage of not "reifying" the mind, in that they do not reduce its workings to a mere function of the brain, as Jean Roiphe (1995) points out. For Solms, neurones are no more real than thoughts or feelings; as a result, the concept of the Unconscious transcends the Cartesian dualism between mind and body. For example, for both Solms and Freud, consciousness is a sense organ which possesses two perceptual surfaces, one of which is oriented towards the outside world, the other towards the inner world. If we take as our starting-point the Freudian model, our subjective consciousness is produced by the unconscious mind in a way that is similar to the process which results from the perception of objects in the external world; the unconscious is also "*affected by experiences originating from external perceptions*" (Freud 1915e: 194). For Solms, these two perceptual surfaces register unknowable reality which is located below the threshold of conscious perception in two ways which are *qualitatively different* but *hierarchically equivalent*. In other words, what we perceive as subjective psychic reality, i.e. our consciousness, is correlative to the way in which we perceive our physical body as if it were seen from outside. Thus there are two kinds of perceptions that reach our consciousness: those which come from concrete external objects, including the bodies of other people – these are perceptions of external reality; and those which come from subjective internal experience, including the minds of other people – these are perceptions of psychic reality. Solms's innovative research thus leads in the direction of a unitary psychoanalytical conception of mind and body, thereby opening up new and highly interesting horizons.

Pragier and Faure-Pragier (1990) have adopted a different approach. Leaving aside the models derived from classical physics, they base their approach on more recent research in physics and biology and propose "new metaphors" which, in their view, could be an appropriate description of how the mind works as it can be observed through psychoanalysis. For example, they have suggested several highly evocative parallels between phenomena related to the emergence of something "new" – on the one hand in the evolution of a self-structured biological system in sequential phases and, on the other, in the free associations which arise in the course of psychoanalytic treatment. In addition, they suggest interesting lines of convergence between the unpredictable nature of the phenomena which are observed within complex systems and the unpredictability of mental phenomena. In complex systems there may be a very great number of variables – which is the case also of the human mind – so that classical linear causality is not an adequate model; chaos theory has shown that in so-called complex systems any prediction may quickly be proved wrong because of the inevitable emergence of minor events.

If we apply these new theories to the situation created by psychological trauma, for example, we can better understand why it is impossible to predict whether a given trauma will have a long-term impact on the mind, simply a minor impact, or no impact at all. We can know this only *a posteriori*. Pragier and Faure-Pragier take the precaution of saying that the comparisons they make should be looked on as *metaphors*, thereby placing them on an unequivocally linguistic plane; in my view, this would tend to limit the value of their comparisons. I think that they correspond more to "analogical models"; if we want them to account for the fact that the workings of the mind are based on biophysiological functions, we need only include the idea of *anaclisis* introduced by Freud (1905d:181–182) in 1905 (J-M. Quinodoz 1997a). This point of view is compatible with the unitary conception of psyche and soma as put forward recently by Solms.

Post-Freudians

Have the neuro-sciences replaced psychoanalysis?

Throughout his life, Freud maintained that, at some point in the not-too-distant future, developments in biology and in the neuro-sciences would shed more light on the workings of the mind as psychoanalysis sees them, thereby accomplishing what he had failed to do in his "Project for a Scientific Psychology". "*It is probable that some time in the future there will really be a 'bio-analysis'*" (1933c: 229). He even foresaw psychotropic medication: "*The future may teach us to exercise a direct influence, by means of particular chemical substances, on the amounts of energy and their distribution in the mental apparatus*" (1940a [1938]: 182).

What is the position one hundred years after the "Project"? The discovery of psychotropic medication in the 1950s and the unbridled enthusiasm which accompanied research developments in biology and the neuro-sciences have undoubtedly contributed to the decline of psychoanalysis in the modern world. After having won for itself an important place among psychotherapeutic methods and university courses, in particular in the United States, psychoanalysis has come under constant pressure. Not only have there been overall changes in mentality – the demand for treatment methods which act ever more quickly and for outcome assessments based on quantifiable results – but also social, political and economic pressures have come together to impose treatment procedures which rely on medication rather than on the various psychotherapeutic approaches. To these factors we must add the promises made by the scientific establishment claiming that current research into brain functioning and memory were already pushing into oblivion any approach based on a psychotherapeutic relationship – even though this research is still far from being able to propose procedures which could be applicable in clinical practice.

In 1998, Nancy Andreassen, a scientist whose work is known world-wide, sent out a cry of alarm to call attention to the severe shortage of psychotherapists in the United States – where the general population is discovering that treatments based on medication also have their limitations:

> *Therefore, we need to make a serious investment in training a new generation of real experts in the science and art of psychopathology. Otherwise, we high-tech scientists may wake up in 10 years and discover that we face a silent spring.* Applying technology without the companionship of wise clinicians with specific expertise in psychopathology will be a lonely, sterile, and perhaps fruitless enterprise.*
> (Andreassen 1998: 1659)

*A reference to *Silent Spring*, a novel by Rachel Carlson (1962), in which, one spring morning, humanity awakens – but not to the sound of birds singing, because they have disappeared from the face of the earth.

New concepts

Deferred action – experience of satisfaction – primary process, secondary process – principle of constancy – principle of inertia – "proton pseudos" – reality-testing – science – scientific models

"THE NEURO-PSYCHOSES OF DEFENCE"
(1894a)

"ON THE GROUNDS FOR DETACHING A PARTICULAR SYNDROME FROM NEURASTHENIA UNDER THE DESCRIPTION 'ANXIETY NEUROSIS' "
(1895b[1894])

"FURTHER REMARKS ON THE NEURO-PSYCHOSES OF DEFENCE"
(1896b)

"SEXUALITY IN THE AETIOLOGY OF THE NEUROSES"
(1898a)

"SCREEN MEMORIES"
(1899a)

A new way of looking at psychopathology

In several papers written between 1895 and 1899, Freud went into more detail concerning a certain number of concepts which he had already outlined in his writings on hysteria. The third of the papers mentioned above follows on from the first; both are an excellent demonstration of how Freud was developing his thinking on the mechanism at the origin of hysterical symptoms, phobias and obsessions; the second paper identifies "anxiety neurosis" – what today we would call "panic attacks" – as a specific disorder, differentiating it for the first time from neurasthenia; the fourth aimed to convince medical circles in Vienna of the validity of his hypothesis on the sexual aetiology of the neuroses, and the fifth paper introduces the idea of "screen memories", childhood memories which, in all their apparent banality, mask others which, having undergone repression, retain their pathogenic potentiality in the unconscious.

Discovering the texts

- **"THE NEURO-PSYCHOSES OF DEFENCE" (1894a)**
- **"FURTHER REMARKS ON THE NEURO-PSYCHOSES OF DEFENCE" (1896b)**

Page numbers are those of *The Standard Edition of the Complete Psychological Works of Sigmund Freud*, vol. **3**, 41–61 and 157–185.

In the article published in 1894, Freud was already able to describe in some detail the mechanism which lay behind hysterical symptoms, phobias and obsessions; he further developed what he had to say on the subject in the paper he wrote in 1896, and in 1915 he put the finishing touches to his ideas in a metapsychological paper he called "Repression" (1915d).

- **Hysterical symptoms: somatic conversion of psychical energy**

In "The Neuro-Psychoses of Defence" (1894a), Freud takes hysteria as his model and goes further than any of his predecessors, who had contented themselves with describing the dissociative state which they considered to be the primary cause of hysterical symptoms. Janet had called this "*splitting of consciousness*", and Breuer "*hypnoid state*". Freud put forward his own hypotheses, showing that this splitting of consciousness is not spontaneous – it is the result of a voluntary act on the patient's part; in other words, this splitting of the content of consciousness is initiated by "*an effort of will*" (1894a: 46). Hysterical splitting may occur in people, who up till then "*had enjoyed good mental health*" (ibid.: 47), whenever they have to deal with intolerable representations which arouse "*such a distressing affect*" that they "*decide to forget about it*" (ibid.: 47). "*The subject decided to forget about it because he had no confidence in his power to resolve the contradiction between that incompatible idea and his ego by means of thought-activity*" (ibid.: 47). How does the ego manage to "forget" these intolerable ideas? For Freud, the ego tries to turn the powerful idea into a weak one in an attempt to defend itself – hence the term "*neuro-psychoses of defence*" – because it cannot be completely eradicated. The residual excitation emerges in the shape of pathological symptoms; in the case of hysteria, it is transformed into a somatic symptom: "*The sum of excitation [is] transformed into something somatic. For this I should like to propose the name of conversion*" (ibid.: 49).

In putting matters thus, Freud shows that the symptoms which emerge in the neuro-psychoses are well and truly a manifestation of some disorder or other which involves the mind; they have nothing to do with individual or hereditary "degeneracy" as had been thought until then. That hypothesis also explains why the process is reversible, thanks to the work of therapy:

The operation of Breuer's cathartic method lies in leading back the excitation in this way from the somatic to the psychical sphere deliberately, and in then forcibly bringing about a settlement of the contradiction by means of thought-activity and a discharge of the excitation by talking. (ibid.: 50)

- **Transformation of pathogenic thoughts into phobias, obsessions or hallucinations**

Freud then turns to exploring his hypotheses as to how phobias, obsessions and hallucinatory psychosis are produced. In the neuro-psychoses characterized by phobias and obsessions, the somatic conversion typical of hysteria no longer holds, so that the weakened idea is still left in consciousness in the shape of obsessional thoughts which have replaced the pathogenic thoughts:

The idea, now weakened, is still left in consciousness, separated from all association. But its affect, which has become free, attaches itself to other ideas which are not in themselves incompatible, and, thanks to this "false connection", those ideas turn into obsessional ideas. (ibid.: 52)

In hallucinatory psychosis, the same mechanism which operates in the neuro-psychoses is at work here too; however, in this case the splitting of consciousness allies itself with a much more energetic and successful kind of defence:

Here, the ego rejects the incompatible idea together with its affect and behaves as if the idea had never occurred to the ego at all. But from the moment at which this has been successfully done the subject is in a psychosis, which can only be classified as "hallucinatory confusion". (ibid.: 58)

This shows that, from his earliest attempts at theorization, Freud was exploring simultaneously the mechanisms at work in neurosis and in psychosis, as he was to do from then on.

Two comments should be made here. First, though Freud speaks of "*an effort of will*" on the patient's part in order to "*forget*", "*suppress*" or "*repress*" incompatible ideas, he seems to realize intuitively that this process occurs without the patient's being conscious of it; he does not as yet however use the term "*repression*" in the strict sense of the word: "*These are processes which occur without consciousness*" (ibid.: 53). He introduced the idea of repression in his 1896 paper. Second, Freud claims that there was no option but to have recourse to "*psychological abstractions*" (ibid.: 48) in order to account for his observations in general terms – what in later years he would call the "metapsychological" point of view.

- ## *The role of "deferred action"*

In "Further Remarks on the Neuro-Psychoses of Defence" (1896b), Freud develops his earlier hypotheses, in particular one which he presented in *Studies on Hysteria* (1895d), published a year earlier; there he argued that pathogenic hysterical representations were linked to a sexual trauma which had occurred in childhood. The nucleus of hysteria has to do with the fact that the individual "*forgets*" the traumatic experience by "*repressing*" it with the help of an unconscious mechanism. But the impact of the trauma cannot in itself explain repression, he says, and introduces the idea that the process is a two-stage one, which acts in a "*deferred fashion*" (1896b: 166–167, n. 2), a notion already mentioned in "A Project for a Scientific Psychology" (Freud 1950a [1887–1902]). Obsessional ideas also involve the process of repression followed by the return of the repressed, then by the formation of compromise-ideas. Freud concludes this paper by applying these points of view to a case of chronic paranoia which he regards as a "*psychosis of defence*" (1896b: 175) and which is subjected to the same process as the neuro-psychoses of defence.

Twenty years later, in his paper on "Repression" (1915d), Freud defines the term "*repression*" as dealing specifically with representations, while "*suppression*" refers to affects.

- ## "ON THE GROUNDS FOR DETACHING A PARTICULAR SYNDROME FROM NEURASTHENIA UNDER THE DESCRIPTION 'ANXIETY NEUROSIS' " (1895b [1894])

> Page numbers are those of *The Standard Edition of the Complete Psychological Works of Sigmund Freud*, vol. **3**, 85–115.

The syndrome known as "neurasthenia" was identified in the 1880s as a disorder characterized by great feebleness and lassitude, the symptomatology of which could vary considerably. The originality of Freud's approach to the question lies first in what he had to say about the root cause of neurasthenia: he argues that, as with all other "nervous" disorders, the underlying cause involves some sexual problem or other. A further original perspective is the fact that he gathers together under the heading "anxiety neurosis" a group of symptoms, and argues that this type of neurosis deserves to be looked upon as a specific entity within the broader nosological concept of neurasthenia, which covers a wide variety of clinical syndromes. In anxiety neurosis, the principal symptom is anxiety, together with its somatic equivalents such as trembling, palpitations, disturbances of respiration, etc., as well as vertigo which, he says, is a major equivalent of anxiety:

> "Vertigo" occupies a prominent place in the group of symptoms of anxiety neurosis. In its mildest form it is best described as "giddiness"; in its severer manifestations, as "attacks of vertigo" (with or without anxiety), it must be classed among the gravest symptoms of the neurosis. (1895a: 95)

At the time when Freud was classifying these various symptoms under a single heading, he did not think that the symptoms of anxiety neurosis and its equivalents, including these different sorts of vertigo, could be attributed to a psychological cause (D. Quinodoz 1994). His idea at that time was that manifestations of anxiety had exclusively to do with physical forces which were not accessible to symbolic meaning or to psychoanalysis – unlike hysteria, in which psychical energy can be converted into a somatic symptom (such as paralysis) so that the situation is reversible once the symbolic meaning of the symptom is brought to the patient's consciousness and thus can be analysed.

What, then, causes anxiety neurosis? Observing that in these patients a decrease in libido accompanies their anxiety symptoms, Freud thought that this neurosis was due to an excessive accumulation of unsatisfied sexual excitation – such as occurs in *coitus interruptus* – a purely physical state of tension which is directly transformed into anxiety given that it cannot be processed by the mind. That theory, known as Freud's "first theory of anxiety", lasted for some thirty years, until he replaced it with his "second" theory of anxiety: from 1926 onwards, he argued that anxiety is due above all to a fear of losing the object and being separated from it, thus placing the origin of anxiety firmly in the psychological sphere.

- **"SEXUALITY IN THE AETIOLOGY OF THE NEUROSES" (1898a)**

> Page numbers are those of *The Standard Edition of the Complete Psychological Works of Sigmund Freud*, vol. **3**, 259–285.

This paper was read at a conference and shocked medical circles in Vienna. In it, Freud brings together several trains of thought on which he had been working during the previous year, and argues clearly for the first time for the existence of infantile sexuality as a phenomenon in its own right. He had begun revising his seduction theory in 1897 after writing the famous letter to Fliess in which he acknowledged the fact that he had been mistaken ("*I no longer believe in my neurotica*", Letter 69, 21 September 1897): what he had initially taken to be the actual sexual seduction of a child by an adult was no more than the expression of a fantasy of the child's incestuous wishes involving the parents. With that discovery in mind, Freud felt it was important to inform his medical colleagues that the aetiology of the neuro-psychoses was not simply a matter of precipitating factors such as actual sexual abuse but also of fantasy experiences linked to instinctual drives which emerged during childhood and puberty. In this paper he elaborates on the idea of *deferred action*: the pathogenic effect of a traumatic event occurring in childhood may be manifested not at the time it actually took place but retrospectively, when the child reaches a subsequent phase of sexual development (puberty, adolescence).

Freud read this paper in 1898 to the Viennese medical association; it shocked his colleagues in spite of the scientific rigour with which he developed his thinking and illustrated it by means of clinical examples. Already in 1896, Richard von Krafft-Ebing, though himself an expert in sexual psychopathology, called Freud's ideas "a scientific fairy-tale". Freud had hoped, thanks to this paper, that his discoveries would be given official recognition; he was bitterly disappointed and even more pessimistic than before. Among other consequences, the hostility his ideas encountered further delayed his appointment as professor in the university.

- **"SCREEN MEMORIES" (1899a)**

> Page numbers are those of *The Standard Edition of the Complete Psychological Works of Sigmund Freud*, vol. **3**, 299–322.

The concept of screen memory had up till then been unheard of: a childhood recollection remains engraved in the memory with exceptional clarity, in spite of the fact that the content of that recollection seems unimportant. How can such a paradox be explained? Taking the example of a recollection he attributes to one of his patients – it is in fact an autobiographical one – Freud makes a detailed analysis of a screen memory which, once adequately processed, helped to relieve him of a slight phobia. The scene takes place somewhere in the countryside; the protagonist is between the ages of 2 and 3 and there are other children present, one of whom is a pretty girl-cousin of his, of about the same age. The scene stayed in his memory without being particularly meaningful until he recollected that, when he was 17, he fell in love with a young woman. That new recollection shed fresh light on his childhood memory and awakened a whole series of other repressed recollections, which he describes with some literary talent. The recall of the unconscious pathogenic potentiality contained in these repressed memories enabled (the patient) to be relieved of his phobia. This clinical example, a piece of literature in itself, shows convincingly that a screen memory is the result of a *compromise* between two psychical forces, one of which maintains the banal event in memory while the other sets up a resistance which hides the unconscious pathogenic meaning: these two opposing forces do not cancel each other out but generate a compromise which condenses both memories. This condensation plays upon the polysemous nature of the words used: "*What provides the intermediate step between a screen memory and what it conceals is likely to be a verbal expression*" (1899a: 319). Freud would later describe the same phenomenon when he studied slips of the tongue and bungled actions.

In a later paper, he again discussed the importance of screen memories which condense a considerable number of elements, both real and fantasy, dating from childhood:

> *Not only* some*, but all of what is essential from childhood has been retained in these [screen] memories. It is simply a question of knowing how to extract it out of them by analysis. They represent the forgotten years of childhood as adequately as the manifest content of a dream represents the dream-thoughts.* (Freud 1914g: 148)

The concept of screen memory has important repercussions, because it implies a challenge to the validity of childhood memories: these can no longer be taken at face value. Freud concludes his paper with the following statement: "*Our childhood memories show us our earliest years not as they were but as they appeared at the later periods when the memories were aroused*" (1899a: 322). In other words, he says with not a little humour, we should not put too much trust in memory, because the conscious recollections we have *from* our childhood are perhaps simply memories *relating to* our childhood, ones which have been worked over many times in the interval.

New concepts

Affect – anxiety neurosis – compromise – deferred action – first theory of anxiety – infantile sexuality – neuro-psychosis – neurosis – representation – repression – screen memory – traumatism – vertigo

THE INTERPRETATION OF DREAMS
(1900a)
ON DREAMS
(1901a)

"The interpretation of dreams is the royal road to a knowledge of the unconscious activities of the mind" (1900a: 608)

In *The Interpretation of Dreams*, Freud proposes some innovative ideas which were not only to revolutionize the manner in which dreams were understood up till then, but also to throw new light on how thought and language operate. According to Freud, dreaming is an organized mental activity distinct from those of waking life and one which obeys its own laws; in so doing, he takes the opposite point of view from both conventional wisdom and scientific opinion. Thus he distances himself on the one hand from the classical and popular methods of dream interpretation in use since ancient times, which, based on deciphering dream material with the help of culturally symbolic codes, aimed to foretell the future. He distances himself also from the men of science of his day for whom dreams had no psychological significance – they were simply disorganized productions generated by mental stimuli (this opinion still holds sway even today in some scientific circles).

In *The Interpretation of Dreams*, Freud introduces another innovative point of view, according to which the dream is created by the dreamer: it does not come from some external source or other as if it were imposed from outside. For long it had been thought that the dream was either a benevolent or a hostile message addressed to the dreamer and sent by some superior power, god or demon. It was the psychoanalytic method of free association which led Freud to discover the aim and the meaning of dreams – hence his famous and often-quoted claim: "*The interpretation of dreams is the royal road to a knowledge of the unconscious activities of the mind*" (1900a: 608). This fundamental text, which, for the rest of his life, Freud maintained was the most important of all his writings (according to Jones, his biographer), thus goes far beyond the explanation of nocturnal dreaming. By proposing in *The Interpretation of Dreams* a general model of the way the mind works, under normal as well as pathological conditions, Freud laid the foundations of psychoanalysis in all of its aspects – clinical, technical and theoretical.

Although more than a hundred years have elapsed, the conception of dream life which Freud established in 1900 is still today *the* essential reference in its own field, that of psychoanalysis. From 1900 right up to the present day, post-Freudian developments in psychoanalysis, as well as scientific advances in many domains – and in particular in that of the neuro-sciences – have expanded our knowledge of the mechanisms involved in dream formation, but no new theory has managed to supplant Freud's approach to the interpretation of dreams in the context to which it applies: psychoanalysis. And if that had been the case, would not psychoanalysts themselves have been the first to notice the fact?

Biographies and history

"The book of the century"

Based on the study of his own dreams

Freud seems to have been interested in his dreams ever since he was a child, and in a letter dated 18 July 1883 to his fiancée Martha, he mentions a notebook in which he wrote down his thoughts on the topic. But his interest in the scientific study of dreams dates from the time when he applied his free association method to the treatment of hysteria, because that approach enabled him to discover the close relationship between dreams, fantasies and symptoms. Freud discovered also that his own dreams and those of his patients had a lot in common; this showed him just how important a role dreams played not only in psychopathology but also in the normal workings of the mind. In July 1895 he did the first complete analysis of one of his own dreams, "*Irma's injection*", a paradigmatic dream which he examines in detail in *The Interpretation of Dreams*.

Full of enthusiasm for these new horizons opened up by his study of dreams and by the recent discovery of neurones, Freud tried to synthesize these two modules – in 1895 he began writing his "Project for a Scientific Psychology". He had, all the same, a strange feeling that this particular line of approach would lead him nowhere; he therefore abandoned his idea of founding a general theory of mind based on quantifiable data, and decided not to publish that text. Quite deliberately turning his back on neurophysiology, he decided in favour of a point of view which situated mental phenomena within the field of subjective experience – in other words, what was later to be known as psychoanalysis. It is for these reasons that we can say that psychoanalysis was born between 1896 and 1899 – a period that coincided both with Freud's self-analysis and with the gestation of *The Interpretation of Dreams*.

The death of Freud's father and the beginning of his self-analysis

Though Freud's ideas on dreams were already in his mind in 1895, the actual writing of the book took him almost four years. It was after his father Jakob's death in 1896 that he began his systematic exploration of this domain; in particular, he began analysing his own dreams, and the work he did on these served as a catalyser for his self-analysis. His father's death and the many memories that Freud had of his father were recurrent themes in his dreams during the months which followed. It was a difficult time for him, and we may well feel that writing this book not only had a scientific aim but also was an attempt to overcome the internal crisis into which the death of his father had precipitated him. At the same time, it was a very productive period for him, because it was thanks to his self-analysis and the interpretation of his dreams that Freud discovered the technique of interpretation which was to prove specific to psychoanalysis.

His relationship with Fliess also played a significant role throughout this period of his life. On the one hand, the letters which Freud wrote on a regular basis to his friend are an invaluable *a posteriori* testimony to the different phases of Freud's self-analysis – for example, when he informs Fliess that the motive force behind dreams is the fulfilment of a wish: "*The day before yesterday, a dream gave me the most amusing proof that the reason for dreaming is indeed to fulfil a wish*" (Letter from Freud to Fliess, 23 September 1895). Fliess was not only *the* person who could bear witness to Freud's endeavours, but also someone on whom Freud could project his fantasies and transference affects. However, this unconscious transference/counter-transference relationship which was played out without either of them realizing what was going on – Freud, all the same, did have a vague idea – could lead only to deadlock, because it did not take place in circumstances which would have enabled it to be analysed and worked through (in other words, with the help of an external analyst). That is probably one of the reasons for the break-up of the relationship between Freud and Fliess which occurred shortly afterwards, as Freud's self-analysis was drawing to a close.

The Interpretation of Dreams (1900a)

Freud finished writing the book in September 1899. There were periods of inhibition and moments of elation – when, for example, he wrote the famous Chapter VII on the psychology of dreams in just two weeks in August 1899. The book was published on 4 November 1899, but the publisher post-dated it "1900". Freud expected a great deal of this published text, in particular some recognition of the value of the discoveries he had made, but it took eight years for the 600 copies of the initial print run to sell. Gradually, however, success came, and the study of dreams remained one of his keen interests for the rest of his life. Freud made many changes to his original text in the course of the eight editions in German which were published in his lifetime, the last appearing in 1930.

This *chef-d'oeuvre*, *The Interpretation of Dreams*, runs to more than 700 pages in its final form. Freud analyses almost 200 dreams, 47 of which are his own, the others reported by members of his immediate circle as well as by some of his colleagues. Yet although the sheer number of dreams analysed and the diversity of the hypotheses which Freud puts forward in this weighty volume mean that no psychoanalyst even today could do without it, these very qualities mean that the reader who is not particularly familiar with the subject will find the book difficult. Didier Anzieu (1988a) has given probably the best description of the impact that *The Interpretation of Dreams* may have on the novice reader; this is what he has to say:

> Die Traumdeutung *is an inspired book, full of energy, intrepid, but made difficult by the sheer originality of the ideas it contains, by the complexity of its architecture, by the precision and the multiplicity of its theoretical ramifications, by the novelty of its concepts, by the abundance of examples, by the concise manner in which these are studied (or, a contrario, by the fact that their exploration is spread over several different chapters), by the tangled web of observations (some from Freud's own dreams, many from those of others), by the author's hesitation over what kind of book he was writing: a scientific treatise, a diary, a confession, a diviner's handbook, an imaginary journey, an initiatory quest, an essay on the human condition, and, perhaps above all, a wide-ranging panorama of the Unconscious.* (Anzieu 1988a: 10)

On Dreams (1901a)

In order to make the innovative ideas contained in *The Interpretation of Dreams* accessible to a wider audience, the publisher asked Freud to condense and summarize that text. Though at first reluctant to do so, in the end Freud did agree to write *On Dreams*, a short work aimed at the "*educated and curious-minded reader*" (1900a: xxv), written in a style close to that of a conversation and bringing the reader into the search for the meaning of dreams in a manner reminiscent of a detective novel. Freud added several new dreams, the two best known of which are the *table d'hôte* and another dream which reveals his unconscious aggressive feelings towards Fliess, thus foreshadowing the break-up of their relationship that was soon to follow.

As Anzieu correctly points out, Freud's first two books raise the problem of how to write about psychoanalysis; these very different books are already proof that the style of psychoanalytic literature inevitably fluctuates between two opposing poles: at the one extreme, that of *The Interpretation of Dreams* – an "open" text, in Umberto Eco's sense of the word, written in the "baroque" style – the writing is "inspired", whereas *On Dreams*, an essay written for teaching purposes, written in a much more "classical" style, has a more didactic tone (Anzieu 1988a: 34).

Discovering the texts

I would recommend that the novice reader begin by reading *On Dreams* (1901a) before *The Interpretation of Dreams* (1900a), even though the latter was the first of the two to be published. Reading *On Dreams* first will make it easier for the reader to find his or her bearings in the much more complex *Interpretation of Dreams*.

- **ON DREAMS (1901a)**

> Page numbers are those of *The Standard Edition of the Complete Psychological Works of Sigmund Freud*, vol. **5**, 633–686.

- ## *The meaning of a dream is discovered thanks to the dreamer's free associations*

Freud observes that it is only in recent times that dreams have been thought of as being the dreamer's own psychical creation, rather than as a benevolent or hostile message from *"higher powers, daemonic and divine"* (1901a: 633) as in mythological times. Nevertheless, he adds, many of his contemporaries in the scientific field still believed that dreams have an exclusively biological function and that their actual content has no psychological meaning whatsoever.

It is true, he adds, that if we try to understand the content of any one dream on its own, we will not succeed very often in discovering its meaning. But if we apply the new method of investigation which Freud had developed, that of "free association", things will be quite different. That method enabled Freud to discover that dreams are meaningful, just as he had discovered that hysterical symptoms, phobias, obsessional ideas and delusions were also meaningful and could be interpreted.

In *On Dreams*, Freud makes a detailed analysis of the *"table d'hôte"* dream he had in October 1900. He begins by reporting what he remembers of the dream: a woman is sitting beside him and lays her hand on his knee in an intimate manner; Freud removes her hand and she says that he has beautiful eyes. On awakening, Freud is surprised by this dream, for it seems obscure and meaningless – all the more so since he had not seen the woman involved for a long time. He then tries to set down the thoughts which come spontaneously to his mind as he recalls every detail of the dream, relying on his associations to it: *"table d'hôte . . . debt . . . for the sake of your beautiful eyes . . . without paying for it . . . etc."* Starting with these scattered fragments, Freud informs us of the connections he was able to make between images, thoughts and memories which followed on from one another and began to make sense to him. Step by step, he invites the reader to share with the dreamer the firm belief that this dream – incomprehensible at first – does in fact have meaning and that only the dreamer's associations can reveal that meaning: *"By following the associations which arose from the separate elements of the dream divorced from their context, I arrived at a number of thoughts and recollections, which I could not fail to recognize as important products of my mental life"* (ibid.: 639). Freud, however, does not follow through on his demonstration, arguing that every time he analyses one of his dreams there are intimate thoughts which come to the surface, ones which are difficult to admit, even to himself. No dream can escape this, he says; for that reason, whenever he reports a dream – his own or that of someone else – he feels obliged to respect the confidential nature of what is thus revealed.

- ## *Manifest content and latent content of the dream*

Freud then introduces a distinction between the *"manifest content of the dream"* – the dream as the dreamer reports it, that content usually being somewhat obscure – and the *"latent content of the dream"*, the meaning of which becomes clear only once the dream has been deciphered in the light of the patient's associations. Manifest content and latent content are closely connected by reason of the secret meaning which links the one to the other, a meaning which can be revealed only by analysis. Freud then explores the nature of the mental process which transforms latent content into manifest content and makes it unrecognizable, and the reverse operation which analysis of the dream carries out in deciphering the manifest meaning in order to discover the latent meaning of the dream. He terms *"dream-work"* the mental processes which transform the latent content into manifest content with the aim of making the former unrecognizable, and *"work of analysis"* as follows: *"the task of dream-interpretation is [. . .] to unravel what the dream-work has woven"* (ibid.: 686).

• *Dreams are unconscious wish-fulfilments*

Freud's second fundamental thesis can be summarized in a sentence taken from his *Interpretation of Dreams* (1900a: 160): "a dream is a (disguised) fulfilment of a (suppressed or repressed) wish". From that point of view there are simple dreams in which the wish appears as having already been fulfilled; this is particularly the case with children's dreams, more rarely with those of adults. Freud quotes examples which have now become classics of their kind, such as that of the little girl who dreams of the strawberries she had not been allowed to eat the day before or that of the little boy and the basket of cherries:

> *The day before, he had been obliged to present his uncle with a gift of a basket of fresh cherries, of which he himself, of course, had only been allowed to taste a single sample. He awoke with this cheerful news: "Hermann eaten all the chewwies!"* (1901a: 644)

More often than not, however, dream content seems incoherent and meaningless, so that the wish-fulfilment is heavily disguised; in these cases, the *dream-work* has transformed the dream-thoughts in such a way that the fulfilment of the wish no longer appears in the dreamer's account of the dream – only the *work of analysis* can accomplish the reverse operation and uncover the meaning behind the dream-thoughts.

• *The mechanisms employed in the dream-work*

What means does the dream-work use in order to disguise the wish-fulfilment, so that no trace of this is left in the manifest content of the dream? Freud says that, in the main, the following five mechanisms are used in dreams in order to attain that aim.

Condensation

Condensation consists in bringing together several elements – images, thoughts, etc. – belonging to different chains of association into a single one. The analysis of a dream highlights the phenomenon of "*compression*" or "*condensation*" which the dream-work accomplishes in order to gather all the scattered fragments into a single unit:

> *If in any particular instance we compare the number of ideational elements or the space taken up in writing them down in the case of the dream and of the dream-thoughts to which the analysis leads us and of which traces are to be found in the dream itself, we shall be left in no doubt that the dream-work has carried out a work of compression or* condensation *on a large scale.* (ibid.: 648)

When we make a detailed analysis of a dream, we can see that the process of condensation applies to every element in the dream, so that each element looked at on its own derives in turn from a series of elements which may belong to different domains – in this way, every element of a dream is *overdetermined*. It is the mechanism of compression which makes it difficult to understand the manifest content of the dream. Condensation is one of the fundamental mechanisms of dream-work, and we find it also in symptom formation, slips of the tongue and jokes. In the latter, condensation creates a common representation between different thoughts by drawing them together in an unexpected way, through a play, for example, upon certain similarities between words, thereby giving rise to "*intermediate thoughts [. . .] which are often highly ingenious*" (ibid.: 650).

Displacement

The mechanism of displacement enables the dream-work to substitute incidental thoughts for the more meaningful dream-thoughts, in such a way that the crucial content of the dream is moved off centre-stage and conceals the wish-fulfilment. For example, the impression that a dream is showing a highly significant element may be replaced by a contrary impression such as indifference. Condensation and displacement may combine to create a compromise, as in the "*Irma's injection*" dream, which Freud mentions in this context. In this dream, there was a question of an injection with *propyl*; Freud found a meaningful connection between *amyl* and a memory of the *Propylaea* which he had seen in a museum. This is an example of compromise formation, created by means of simultaneous condensation and displacement.

Representability (Darstellbarkeit)

This is the process by which the dream-work transforms the dream-thoughts into pictures, and in particular visual ones. Freud describes the process thus:

> *If we imagine ourselves faced by the problem of representing the arguments in a political leading article or the speeches of counsel before a court of law in a series of pictures, we shall easily understand the modifications which must necessarily be carried out by the dream-work owing to considerations of representability in the content of the dream.* (ibid.: 659)

He goes on to mention the various means employed by the dream-work to transform thoughts into the visual mode of expression which is specific to dreams.

Secondary revision of dream-content

Thanks to this procedure, the dream-content is presented as a coherent and intelligible scenario. This mechanism accompanies each stage of dream formation, but its effects are more visible once the dreamer wakes up and tries to recollect the dream or to report it. As we gradually come to remember a dream, we tend to distort its content so as to make it more coherent and give it a rational facade. The distortion which this secondary revision brings about, however, is by no means insignificant, because we can always find in it the scenario marked by the fulfilment of a repressed wish, which is the real motive behind the dream.

Dramatization

In 1901, Freud added the mechanism of dramatization which consists in transforming a thought into a situation. This process is similar to the work done by the director of a play who transforms a written text into a theatrical representation.

• *Residues of the previous day*

Dream formation obeys another fundamental principle: the dream scenario always involves events which occurred the day before the dream; Freud calls these "*the day's residues*":

> *If we seek the help of analysis, we find that every dream without any possible exception goes back to an impression of the past few days, or, it is probably more correct to say, of the day immediately preceding the dream, of the "dream-day".* (ibid.: 655)

The day's residues have a more or less close connection with the unconscious desire which is fulfilled in the dream.

• *The role of censorship*

For Freud, the main reason behind any distortion of a dream has to do with *censorship*. This is a specific agency which lies at the frontier between consciousness and the unconscious and which allows only what is agreeable to it to pass through, holding back everything else: what is rejected by the censorship is in a state of *repression* – these are the *repressed* elements. Under certain conditions, of which the state of sleep is one, there is a relaxation of the censorship. When this happens, it becomes possible for what has hitherto been repressed to make its way into consciousness by means of a dream. Since, however, the censorship is never completely eliminated, even in dreams, the repressed material must submit to certain alterations in order to avoid offending the censorship; this leads to the formation of *compromises*. Repression, followed by relaxation of the censorship and then by the formation of a compromise is not exclusive to dreams; it occurs in many other psychopathological states in which condensation and displacement also play a part.

Given that the sudden emergence of uncensored unconscious wishes could well waken the dreamer up, it follows that dreams are also a fulfilment of the wish to sleep. For this reason, Freud considered that dreams also have the function of safeguarding sleep. "*It is commonly said that sleep is disturbed by dreams; strangely enough, we are led to a contrary view and must regard dreams as* the guardians of sleep" (ibid.: 678).

- ## *Dream censorship applies to repressed infantile sexual wishes*

If we explore dream-analysis further, says Freud, we often discover that dreams' latent content has to do with the fulfilment of erotic wishes. This observation confirms the role of censorship as regards sexual material, and more specifically infantile sexual wishes which have been repressed: "*repressed infantile sexual wishes provide the most frequent and strongest motive-forces for the construction of dreams*" (ibid.: 682). But in spite of the part played by sexuality, Freud goes on, it is only very rarely that the manifest content of a dream reveals as such the fulfilment of a wish which is sexual in nature; usually it is disguised and only the work of analysis can unmask it. In *On Dreams*, Freud does not mention the Oedipus complex, even though he had already written of it one year previously in *The Interpretation of Dreams*, when he described "*typical*" dreams that involve the "*death of persons of whom the dreamer is fond*" (1900a: 248).

- ## *The role of symbols in dreams*

The creation of symbols plays a crucial role in dream-formation, because symbols enable the dreamer to circumvent censorship by stripping sexual representations of all intelligibility. Freud distinguishes between two types of symbol: the universal kind which belong to the "dream-book" category of "a key to dreams" and which have been used from time immemorial, and individual symbols, those which are constructed out of the dreamer's own ideational material in the way that Freud showed. As to universal symbolism, Freud lists a whole series of items which bear a single meaning:

> *The majority of dream-symbols serve to represent persons, parts of the body and activities invested with erotic interest; in particular, the genitals are represented by a number of often very surprising symbols, and the greatest variety of objects are employed to denote them symbolically.* (1901a: 683)

At first sight, we may think that all that is required is to have a fair knowledge of universal symbolism in order to interpret a dream, without any need for the dreamer's associations. But, as Freud had already pointed out in *The Interpretation of Dreams*, this is not enough; if the psychoanalyst is to avoid arbitrary interpretations, a twofold approach is necessary, one which takes into account both universal symbolism and the dreamer's associations.

> *We are thus obliged, in dealing with those elements of the dream-content which must be recognized as symbolic, to adopt a combined technique, which on the one hand rests on the dreamer's associations and on the other hand fills the gaps from the interpreter's knowledge of symbols. We must combine a critical caution in resolving symbols with a careful study of these in dreams which afford particularly clear instances of their use, in order to disarm any charge of arbitrariness in dream-interpretation.* (1900a: 353)

- **THE INTERPRETATION OF DREAMS (1900a)**

> For didactic purposes, I have reversed the chronological order in which these two books were published. I have presented *On Dreams* (1901a) first, so that this shorter work may serve as an introduction to *The Interpretation of Dreams* (1900a); indeed shortage of space means that I shall present only an outline of this latter book.

> Page numbers are those of *The Standard Edition of the Complete Psychological Works of Sigmund Freud*, vols **4–5**.

- *A work in three parts*

In Chapter I, which constitutes the first part of the book, Freud gives an overview of the most significant scientific writings on dreams which had been published until then. This synthesis makes for heavy going, and Freud was reluctant to set it all down on paper; but in the end it did help him prove that none of his predecessors had managed to discover the meaning of dreams.

The second part comprises Chapters II to VI inclusive. Freud begins Chapter II by describing the method of dream interpretation which he devised in the course of his self-analysis and he illustrates his hypotheses with a detailed analysis of the now-famous dream of "*Irma's injection*". He applies to the interpretation of this dream the procedure that he employs for analysing the many other examples of dreams which he reports in the book. First of all, he makes a careful note of the dream material as it appears to the dreamer on awakening; then he breaks it down into its component parts; he notes the associations which emerge spontaneously concerning each fragment of the dream; on that basis, he makes connections between the different sequences and in so doing constructs the possible interpretations of the dream. In Chapter III, he develops his central thesis according to which dreams are the expression of the fulfilment of a frustrated wish. On very many occasions, however, wish-fulfilment appears in the dream content only because it has been subjected to distortions of various kinds; it is thanks to the work of analysis that the wish-fulfilment aspect of the dream is discovered. In Chapter V, Freud examines the sources of dreams in order to find out whether their content might help to find solutions to the puzzles which still remain. In Chapter VI, he shows how the dream-work is carried out by means of condensation, displacement, representability, reversal, secondary revision and representation by symbols.

The third part stands as an essay in its own right: the famous Chapter VII, in which Freud constructs a general model of the mind and its workings. This is an ambitious project, the aim of which is to explain mental functioning in both normal and pathological states, starting from his clinical observations on dreams and neuroses. Here again we see Freud-the-scientist, but this time a scientist who has quite definitely moved on from the neurophysiological perspective of the "Project" and is proposing a topographical model of the psychical apparatus. For the first time, he defines the Unconscious, the Preconscious and the Conscious as specific *loci* (in Greek, *topos*) in which mental phenomena are located; this model is designated as the "first structural theory", the first topographical division of the mind. There operates between the Unconscious and the Preconscious what Freud at that time called *censorship*, the forerunner of the concept of the superego, which controls what may be allowed to move between Unconscious, Preconscious and Conscious. Among other fundamental hypotheses that Freud introduces in this ground-breaking chapter, which heralds what he would say in his metapsychological papers, he develops his ideas on the opposition between *primary* and *secondary processes* as well as on *repression*, a notion adumbrated in his *Studies on Hysteria*. Because of regression, the repressed wishes which are deposited in the Unconscious join up with *repressed infantile scenarios*, which is why their content is able to re-emerge in dreams, where censorship is less strong, or in the shape of *compromise formations* expressed as neurotic symptoms.

- *Developments in Freud's ideas on dreams after 1900*

Freud remained faithful to his conception of dream theory as formulated in 1900; in contrast to other aspects of his theories, he would make only slight changes to it. Among the major additions he made to *The Interpretation of Dreams*, it is worth noting that, with the introduction in 1923 of his "second structural theory", he replaced the idea of dream "*censorship*" with that of the *superego*. From then on, dreams were seen as having to reconcile the demands of the id and of the superego (Freud 1933a [1932]). Nevertheless, though his second theory of the instinctual drives was introduced in 1920, Freud did not develop the idea that the work of the dream has as its aim not only to reconcile a prohibited wish with the superego or the ego, but also to find a compromise or other solution to the fundamental conflict between the life and death drives, as some contemporary psychoanalysts argue (Segal 1991; J-M. Quinodoz 2001).

Post-Freudians

A psychoanalytic study of Freud's self-analysis

In his book, *Freud's Self-Analysis*, Didier Anzieu (1988b) adopted an innovative approach: he used the psychoanalytic method itself to explore the circumstances surrounding the creative work which led Freud to the discovery of psychoanalysis between 1895 and 1902. In order to accomplish that task, Anzieu based his investigation on the abundant documentary evidence which Freud himself left, in which – sometimes explicitly, sometimes in spite of himself – he revealed a great many of the products of his unconscious which could be analysed: dreams, childhood memories, bungled actions, lapses of memory and slips of the tongue. Anzieu's meticulous investigation of these documents meant that he could put a date on most of the dreams which Freud reports in *The Interpretation of Dreams* and, with the help of many self-analytic papers, to study them in chronological order. Anzieu's investigation enabled him to emphasize the highly personal and intimate work Freud did all through those decisive years during which he discovered in turn the meaning of dreams, the Oedipus complex, the primal scene fantasy and castration anxiety (Anzieu 1959, 1988b).

The Interpretation of Dreams in modern clinical practice

The Interpretation of Dreams generated – as indeed it still does – a considerable number of psychoanalytic and non-psychoanalytic papers and books; there are in fact too many published works for me to do justice to them all here. That said, in spite of their richness and diversity, none of these post-Freudian publications has ever pushed Freud's fundamental text into the background. As André Green puts it: "Of all Freud's discoveries, dreams are probably the one in which the contributions of those psychoanalysts who have continued to explore this field after *The Interpretation of Dreams* have been the least significant" (1972: 179). It is true that when future psychoanalysts are being taught the technique of dream interpretation, this is the first book we turn to – and not for historical reasons but because it is unique, the only one even today which presents such a complete overview of the issues involved. That said, as far as general writing on the topic is concerned, I must mention Ella Freeman Sharpe's *Dream Analysis*; this introduction to dream interpretation in psychoanalytic treatment is still highly relevant today, even though it was published in 1937. There are very few wide-ranging texts; most post-Freudian contributions to dream interpretation concern only part of his general theory and technique – most, indeed, have been published in the various reviews or journals. Some of the more significant articles have been reissued in book form, such as *Essential Papers on Dreams* (Lansky 1992), *The Dream Discourse Today* (Flanders 1993) and *Dreaming and Thinking* (Perelberg 2000). These different selections reflect the points of view of psychoanalysts from different schools of thought in contemporary psychoanalysis.

It must be said, however, that if we look back on the whole corpus of psychoanalytic writings published since the 1960s or 1970s, relatively few of them have to do with dream analysis. According to Flanders (1993), this is due to a gradual shift in psychoanalytic technique. In the 1920s and 1930s, the very first psychoanalysts tended to focus on the analysis of their patients' dreams, whereas from the 1950s on, psychoanalysts have tended to attach more and more importance to the analysis of the transference. Flanders has an elegant way of summarizing this evolution: "the transference to the analyst has become the royal road to the understanding of the patient's emotional and mental life" (1993: 13). In spite of the diminishing number of theoretical publications on the topic of dreams, it is heartening to note that, in psychoanalytic practice, dream interpretation has lost none of its value – proof of this being the fact that most of the clinical illustrations published in psychoanalytic papers nowadays contain the analysis of at least one of the patient's dreams.

New concepts

Censorship – compromise solution – condensation – day's residues – displacement – dramatization – dream-symbols – dream-work – manifest content, latent content – overdetermination – representability (or means of representation) – secondary revision – work of the analysis

THE PSYCHOPATHOLOGY OF EVERYDAY LIFE
(1901b)

Parapraxes: manifestations of the unconscious in the daily life of normal people

In writing this book, Freud aimed to inform the general public of the existence of the unconscious, as it is revealed through those "failures" of repression that are parapraxes or "bungled actions". What, then, *is* a parapraxis? An unintentional event which occurs in the life of every normal person, not simply in that of neurotics. Freud declares that, in order to belong to the category of bungled actions, this kind of event ought not to go beyond what "*we characterize by the expression 'within the limits of the normal'*" (1901b: 239); "*it must be in the nature of a momentary and temporary disturbance*" and "*the same function must have been performed by us more correctly before*". In German, the idea of parapraxis has a much wider meaning than in some other languages; it includes a wider range of phenomena, apparently insignificant, such as bungled actions, slips of the tongue, forgetting, negations or misunderstandings; it is not limited to acts such as the loss or breakage of a significant object, as is the case for example in French. In addition, all these failures of the unconscious begin in German with the prefix "Ver", which has the advantage of bringing them all together under a common denominator: *das Vergessen* (forgetting), *das Versprechen* (slip of the tongue), *das Verlesen* (misreading), *das Verschreiben* (slip of the pen), *das Vergreifen* (bungled action), *das Verlieren* (mislaying) (Laplanche and Pontalis 1967 (1973: 300–301)).

In *The Psychopathology of Everyday Life*, Freud describes different forms of parapraxes, and gives many examples to illustrate them. In spite of their diversity, all of these phenomena are the result of one psychological mechanism similar to that which underlies dreams: they are the manifest expression of a wish which until that point had been repressed into the unconscious; the nature of that wish can be discovered thanks to the free association method. The success of this book went far beyond what Freud expected, and the psychoanalytic ideas he developed in it are without a doubt among the best known even today. Who nowadays has never smiled at a slip of the tongue or a bungled action, thereby showing that he or she fully realizes that the "accident" in fact expresses a secret intention and as such comes directly from the unconscious?

Biographies and history

Freud's most popular and most widely read book

In 1899, when Freud finished writing *The Interpretation of Dreams*, he began gathering data that would form the basis of three other books which extended the discoveries he had made about dreams to other fields: *The Psychopathology of Everyday Life* (1901b), *Jokes and their*

Relation to the Unconscious (1905c) and *Three Essays on the Theory of Sexuality* (1905d). His self-analysis had enabled him to overcome his own inhibitions and meant that he was in better shape emotionally. He thus began to make a systematic analysis of his own parapraxes – forgetfulness and slips of the tongue – just as he had analysed his own dreams. It was in a letter to Fliess dated 26 August 1898 that Freud first mentioned "*failures*" of the unconscious – the forgetting of the poet Julius Mosen's name; in a subsequent letter, dated 22 September 1898, he mentions his forgetting of Signorelli's name – the names Botticelli and Boltraffio were those that came to his mind – and this incident is developed to a much fuller extent in the first chapter of *The Psychopathology of Everyday Life*. That book is full of personal anecdotes culled from the breeding-ground that was Freud's family and professional life; it also seems to be closely related to the deterioration of his relationship with Fliess – the break-up occurred in 1902, though Freud did testify to the part his friend had played up till then in his life: "*It [The Psychopathology of Everyday Life] is full of references to you, manifest ones, for which you supplied the material, and concealed ones, for which the motivation goes back to you*" (Letter from Freud to Fliess, 7 August 1901 [Freud (1985c [1887–1904]: 447]).

The book first appeared as a series of articles in 1901, then, in 1904, these were gathered together and published in book form. The ideas Freud develops therein were roundly criticized by psychologists, but this did not prevent the general public from being won over by them, to such an extent that *The Psychopathology of Everyday Life* was immediately able to spread psychoanalytic ideas to a wider audience, something that *The Interpretation of Dreams* had proved much less able to accomplish. The book ran through ten editions during Freud's lifetime and was gradually expanded to include more material from Freud himself as well as items from some of his pupils. The 1904 edition contained 66 parapraxes, 49 of which came from Freud's own observations; the latest (1924) edition contains 300, half of which were provided by people other than Freud, thereby multiplying fourfold the size of the original edition. In 1909 during his voyage to the United States, Freud realized just how popular *The Psychopathology of Everyday Life* was when he had the good fortune to see one of the stewards reading it on board the ship.

Discovering the text

Page numbers are those of *The Standard Edition of the Complete Psychological Works of Sigmund Freud*, vol. **6**.

- **The example par excellence:** *forgetting the name "Signorelli"*

The first chapter of the book is devoted to the detailed study of forgetting a proper name – that of the artist Signorelli, who painted the frescoes of the "*Four Last Things*" in Orvieto Cathedral. This event had already been described by Freud in a short paper ("The Psychical Mechanism of Forgetfulness", Freud 1898b). Freud tells us that in the course of a conversation, he could no longer recall the name Signorelli, and that the names of two other painters, Botticelli and Boltraffio, came into his mind (he realized that neither of those was the one he was looking for). By going back through what he did remember and the associations which had led to these two names, in accordance with the method adopted in dream analysis, he was able to discover the reason behind the repression of what he had forgotten. Deduction leading to fresh deduction, the name *Bo*tticelli reminded him of *Bo*snia, and Bol*traffio* brought to his mind the town of *Trafoï*; these two geographical locations were closely linked to distressing memories involving sexuality and death. Freud then realized that sexuality and death were major themes in Signorelli's frescoes of the "*Four Last Things*". Forgetting Signorelli's name was thus the result of a compromise formation which enabled Freud to forget an unpleasant memory partly but not entirely, because it re-emerged under the disguise of the names Botticelli and Boltraffio:

The substitute names no longer strike me as so entirely unjustified as they did before the matter was elucidated: by a sort of compromise they remind me just as much of what I wanted to forget as of what I wanted to remember, and they show me that my intention to forget something was neither a complete success nor a complete failure. (1901b: 4)

• *A systematic study of different kinds of parapraxis*

After the chapter devoted to the forgetting of proper names, Freud gives an overview of other kinds of forgetting, such as forgetting foreign words, names and sets of words, forgetting impressions and forgetting intentions. He explores the question of childhood memories and "screen memories", which are generated in much the same way as are parapraxes: when the content of a childhood memory comes up against resistance, it is repressed and can no longer appear as such – it re-emerges in substitute form as a "screen memory" with the distressing affects removed. Chapter V is devoted to an extensive study of slips of the tongue, a well-known phenomenon in which one word is substituted for another. I shall quote the following example – there are many more – taken from an article which was published in the Viennese newspaper *Neue Freie Presse*. The newspaper reported a slip of the tongue made by the President of the Lower House of the Austrian Parliament who had ceremoniously "*opened*" the sitting by declaring it "*closed*":

His attention was drawn only by the general merriment and he corrected his mistake. In this particular case the explanation no doubt was that the President secretly wished *he was already in a position to close the sitting, from which little good was expected.* (ibid.: 59)

In the following chapters, Freud examines misreadings and slips of the pen, bungled actions, symptomatic and chance actions, as well as combined parapraxes. The final chapter is devoted to determinism, belief in chance and superstition. Freud develops the idea that parapraxes are not due to chance or to absent-mindedness, as the person concerned tends to think; they are generated by the intervention of a repressed idea that distorts the speech or the behaviour which the individual is usually able to accomplish without mishap. This point of view leads Freud to argue that there are two kinds of chance: "external chance" linked to causes that have nothing to do with the psychological field as such, and "internal chance" in which mental determinism plays a crucial role, given that the parapraxis is the result of an *unconscious* intention which replaces a *conscious* one.

• *How is a parapraxis generated?*

In spite of their infinite variety, parapraxes are all based on one mechanism: they are all the expression of a wish that has been repressed into the unconscious, access to which requires the work of psychoanalysis. According to Freud, a parapraxis is the result of a compromise formation between the person's *conscious* intention – in the earlier example, "*opening*" the parliamentary sitting was the conscious intention of the President of the Lower House – and the *unconscious* wish associated with it ("*closing*" the sitting), which imposed itself on the manifest level of what the President was saying, and there was nothing he could do about it. From that point of view, every parapraxis has two sides to it, as Laplanche and Pontalis point out: "it transpires that what appear to be bungled actions turn out in fact – on another level – to be quite successful ones, and that unconscious wishes are fulfilled by such behaviour in a manner that is often very plain to see" (1967 [1973: 300]).

The mechanisms involved in creating a parapraxis are thus the same as those which apply to dreams and symptom formation, those which Freud described in *The Interpretation of Dreams*: condensation, displacement, substitution and substitution of opposite. In addition, just as in the analysis of dreams or of symptoms, free associations will help us discover the hidden meaning of a parapraxis. As to the relationship between the intended word and that which is substituted for it, substitution is facilitated by several procedures: contiguity, for example – "*closing*" rather than "*opening*" the sitting – or by sound – the name Signorelli has a phonetic resemblance to Botticelli and Bosnia, Boltraffio and Trafoï. At other times this relationship may be established thanks to associations which refer to a person's own history.

• *What are the sources of parapraxes?*

According to Freud, our minds are constantly being crossed by thoughts and associations of which, generally speaking, we have no knowledge; they constitute a series of disruptive complexes which are destined to be repressed into the unconscious – but they may suddenly emerge in the shape of parapraxes. Internal resistance works against elucidating them, and though sometimes repressed ideas are obvious enough and can be interpreted directly, more often than not they can be deciphered only after detailed analysis. It ought to be said too that, if parapraxes often betray us, Freud describes some situations in which they may prove useful:

> [*This example*] *may also present us with a somewhat unusual case in which the forgetting ranges itself on the side of our good sense, when the latter threatens to succumb to a momentary desire. The parapraxis thus comes to serve a useful function. When we have sobered down once more we appreciate the rightness of this internal current, which had previously only been able to express itself in a failure to function – a forgetting, a psychical impotence*. (1901b: 19)

In the closing pages of the book Freud shows that there is a certain degree of continuity between the phenomena observed in normal mental life and in psychopathological states:

> *If we compare them [parapraxes] to the products of the psychoneuroses, to neurotic symptoms, two frequently repeated statements – namely, that the borderline between the normal and abnormal in nervous matters is a fluid one, and that we are all a little neurotic – acquire meaning and support*. (ibid.: 278)

I think that the ideas – and, even more so, the many examples – presented in *The Psychopathology of Everyday Life* cannot be summarized any more than I have done here; I am sure the reader will discover them with pleasure in the book itself.

Post-Freudians

Parapraxes and the transference relationship

Are forgetfulness, slips of the tongue and other forms of parapraxis simply manifestations which belong to the everyday life of ordinary people, or do they really have something to do with the psychoanalytic treatment of neurotic patients? Even though in his conclusion Freud claimed that there is a close connection between parapraxes and disorders of neurotic origin, he said nothing about how he would interpret them in a psychoanalytic setting. Yet he did approach the question – albeit indirectly – when he pointed out the similarities that exist between the mechanisms that underlie parapraxes and those which involve dream-formation. Thus by demonstrating that parapraxes are the expression of an unconscious repressed wish and that the work of analysis enables the latent meaning to be elucidated, Freud opened the way to interpreting parapraxes in the transference relationship, just as dreams and symptoms require interpretation.

For contemporary clinical psychoanalysts, the interpretation of parapraxes which emerge in the transference/counter-transference is crucial, whether they take the form of "mistakes" in the patient's behaviour, forgetfulness, slips of the tongue or other so-called "blunders". These "bungled actions" reveal, sometimes in a spectacular fashion, the patient's unconscious repressed wish – not to mention that of the psychoanalyst, aspects of whose counter-transference feelings may well be highlighted in this manner too. "Acting-in" is the term generally used to designate the parapraxes which occur within the session itself – the patient may be late, or fall asleep on the couch . . . – whereas the term "acting-out" refers to bungled actions which occur outside the session; these are to be understood as displacements which have to do with the transference. Anxiety over separation from and loss of the object gives rise to situations in which parapraxes occur most often in the analyst/analysand setting (J-M. Quinodoz 1991). For example, if a patient unwittingly experienced an emotional reaction towards the analyst, he or she may well fail to turn up for the following session: once that bungled action is elucidated, different repressed feelings, some hostile, towards the analyst may be easier to see – a disappointment, for instance, may surface as turning up late for the session. The patient's free associations are the only way to get in touch with the true reasons for a parapraxis of this sort – to act otherwise would be to interpret in an inappropriate and arbitrary fashion. Jacques Lacan highlighted the slips of the tongue which occur in the course of an analysis: in other words, the relationship between the structure of language and that of the unconscious. These parapraxes are a means of understanding the *hic et nunc* unconscious transference.

Perhaps psychoanalysis should be reserved for people who have access to symbolic meaning?

Insight as regards the unconscious meaning of a parapraxis or slip of the tongue is not for everyone: a parapraxis or slip of the tongue may be meaningful for the individual's immediate circle, but not necessarily for that person him- or herself. That, in itself, is a definition of the unconscious – everything which lies outside his or her consciousness. Sometimes it takes several months of analysis before the analysand can discover the true meaning of a parapraxis or slip of the tongue, and integrate that with the emotions linked to the relationship with the psychoanalyst.

Of course, the capacity to integrate the meaning of a parapraxis – or of any other phenomenon directly related to the unconscious – depends in part on the strength of the resistance against any form of insight; but it depends also on the person's ability to access the symbolic meaning of what he or she says or does in a symptomatic manner. The capacity to access symbolic meaning varies quite considerably from one person to another – is it possible, in other words, for *everybody* to engage in psychoanalysis? Is everybody receptive to interpretation? And, to extend the question as far as possible: can everybody be receptive to interpretation of the transference relationship? Different psychoanalysts take different views on the subject, especially in France, where the classical psychoanalytic treatment is more or less reserved for those who, from the outset, are open to the symbolic meaning of what they may have to say – in other words, for those whose mind structure is fundamentally neurotic (Gibeault 2000). On the other hand, for psychoanalysts who are more attuned to the Kleinian approach, there are two levels of symbolization: the primitive level dominated by concrete thinking – the mind operates in terms of "symbolic equations" – and a more advanced level at which the capacity for symbolic representation is dominant, the level which corresponds to neurotic organizations. For these psychoanalysts, there is a continuous to-and-fro movement between the primitive and the more sophisticated levels of symbolization, such that they feel able to offer psychoanalytic treatment not only to neurotic patients but also to those who are borderline or psychotic – not to mention the archaic aspects which have to be coped with in every neurotic or normal analysand (Jackson and Williams 1994).

New concepts

Condensation – displacement – forgetting names – parapraxes – slips of the tongue – substitution

JOKES AND THEIR RELATION TO THE UNCONSCIOUS

(1905c)

What makes us laugh at a joke?

Freud collected jokes – *Witz* in German – including Jewish ones, and he had a strong sense of humour; it is hardly surprising, then, that he tried to discover the hidden motivations that make us laugh at jokes. In this book, he makes a systematic exploration of many different forms of comical material which come under the heading of jokes, and suggests that they reveal the unconscious influence which, in a covert way, dominates speech and language. To that extent, the mechanisms which produce a comic effect are very similar to the work that the mind accomplishes through dreams: we find *condensation*, in other words saying little in order to express much; *displacement*, which enables prohibitions to be circumvented, particularly those which censorship places on repressed aggressive or sexual content (while still allowing them to return in some other shape or form); and finally the process of *representability*, which modifies the form of words, creating double meanings or plays upon words, transforming thinking by creating something nonsensical or replacing one thought by its opposite. However, unlike dreams, which Freud considered to be a-social products, jokes are the most social of all the mind's activities: a joke is a sophisticated game which aims at an increase in pleasure, so that the mechanism of regression is not active in this domain in the way as it is in dreams. The pursuit of pleasure exists also in dreams, of course, but there pleasure is obtained through regression to hallucinatory satisfaction in order to avoid unpleasure.

> **Biographies and history**
>
> ### Similarities between dreams, parapraxes and jokes
>
> *Freud: a man with a strong sense of humour*
>
> Fliess was probably the impetus for this book because, when he read the proofs of *The Interpretation of Dreams*, which Freud had sent him, he observed that plays upon words were a recurrent feature of dreams. Freud wrote back to him, saying: "*All dreamers are equally insufferably witty, and they need to be because they are under pressure and the direct route is barred to them [. . .] The ostensible wit of all unconscious processes is intimately related to the theory of the joke and the comic*" (Letter from Freud to Fliess, 11 September 1899 [Freud 1985c (1887–1904): 371]). In *Studies on Hysteria*, Freud had for the first time noted the part played by symbolization and polysemy in one of Frau Cäcilie's dreams (Freud and Breuer 1895d: 181) and in *The Interpretation of Dreams* he gives a considerable number of examples. The publication in 1898 of Theodor Lipps's *Komik und Humor* was also a factor in Freud's decision to write a book on the topic. Writing a volume like this, with so much detail and in

many respects highly complex, was very time-consuming – all the more so, in fact, because he was writing both the book on jokes and *Three Essays on the Theory of Sexuality* at the same time, the manuscripts being placed in separate piles on the same table. Both books were published simultaneously in 1905.

Freud's interest in jokes was not merely scientific; he himself had a strong sense of humour, and amusing anecdotes of one kind or another are scattered throughout the letters he wrote. Many of his contemporaries have emphasized his ability to find something amusing in most situations. When he left Austria in 1938 to take refuge in London, the comment he wrote on the declaration demanded by the German authorities, certifying that he had not been mistreated, bears witness to the fact that even then he could be amusing: "*I can heartily recommend the Gestapo to anyone.*"

"*Witz*" *do not travel particularly well*

More than any other of Freud's books, *Jokes and their Relation to the Unconscious* creates problems for the translator; this explains why it is one of his least known works outside of the German-speaking world. The very word "*Witz*" – the sound of which, in German, brings to mind "*Blitz*", a flash of lightning – does not have an exact equivalent in most other languages. In French, for example, it was translated as "*mot d'esprit*" by D. Messier, who writes: "The word designates either a witticism (*mot d'esprit*) or wittiness, the ability to 'be witty'." The French translators of the more recent *Complete Works of Sigmund Freud* think that the earlier translation is incorrect and prefer "*trait d'esprit*", which is closer to the idea of "flash of wit". Lacan suggested this translation of the German word *Witz*: the idea of "*mot*" does not exist in *Witz*, so that "*mot d'esprit*" could cause confusion with *Wortwitz* and *Gedankenwitz* (Bourguignon et al., 1989: 150). Also, how can we translate plays upon words which make the German-speaking reader laugh when the equivalent words do not exist in other languages – a great deal of the *Jokes* book remains untranslatable. Most translators have decided to put any necessary explanations in footnotes, so as to make Freud's original thoughts as accessible as possible because they are, in German, so delightfully expressive.

Discovering the text

Page numbers are those of *The Standard Edition of the Complete Psychological Works of Sigmund Freud*, vol. **8**.

The book itself is divided into three parts: the first deals with the technique of jokes, i.e. with the different processes used by the mind to produce a comic effect; the second part explores the motives behind jokes, and in particular the role played by pleasure from the point of view of psychic economy; and the third part begins by investigating the relationship between jokes and dreams in the light of the idea of "wish-fulfilment", and ends with a short essay on the different species of comic.

- **THE TECHNIQUES WHICH UNDERLIE THE COMICAL EFFECT OF JOKES**

The comical effect of a joke is obtained by two distinct techniques, according to Freud: the first is based on the actual *words* themselves and depends on verbal expression; the second has to do with the *thought* contained in the joke, this technique being independent of the verbal expression employed.

- ## Techniques based on the words used

As regards jokes which are based on the actual words used, Freud draws a distinction between three processes which all use the same technique, that of *condensation*, a mechanism typical of dream-work.

The first technique consists in *condensing two words or two fragments of words*, thus creating a neologism that is at first sight absurd; the amalgamated word, however, has a comic effect on those to whom the joke is told. Freud, for example, quotes the joke built around the word "anecdotage", an invented word borrowed from the English author Thomas De Quincey, according to whom "*old people are inclined to fall into their 'anecdotage'*" (Freud 1905c: 21–22). In this example, the comic effect comes from the actual *word* that is pronounced; the technique used is the abbreviation or compression of two partly overlapping words, "anecdote" and "dotage", which in themselves are not particularly funny when considered separately. The words are *condensed* in order to fabricate a mixed word, a neologism – "anecdotage" – that would in itself be incomprehensible. The readers, however, who are aware of the context, immediately grasp the meaning behind it, and this is what makes them laugh. Freud gives other examples of comic effect associated with the technique of condensation followed by the formation of a substitute – the word *Cleopold*, for example, which he decomposes thus: "*The voice of Europe once made the cruel joke of changing a potenate's name from Leopold to Cleopold, on account of the relations he had at one time with a lady with the first name of Cleo*" (ibid.: 20). Another example is that of the word "famillionairely", an invented word pronounced by a character in one of Heine's novels. In this novel, a quite ordinary person is boasting of his relations with the wealthy Baron Rothschild. In boasting to the poet, the ordinary man says: "*I sat beside Salomon Rothschild and he treated me quite as his equal – quite famillionairely*" (ibid.: 16).

The second technique consists in using a single word twice over. Freud gives an example based on the homophony between the name "*Rousseau*" and the two words "*roux*" and "*sot*". A hostess of a Parisian *salon* made the following joke after being introduced to a young man whom she had invited but who had behaved in a decidedly awkward manner. The impolite young man was red-haired, and a distant relative of Jean-Jacques Rousseau. The hostess said to the person who had introduced him: "*Vous m'avez fait connaître un jeune homme roux et sot, mais non pas un Rousseau*" ("*You have made me acquainted with a young man who is roux [red-haired] and sot [silly], but not a Rousseau*") (ibid.: 29–30). Here the joke-technique consists in the fact that a single word – "Rousseau" – is used twice over, the first time broken down into its component syllables, then as the whole word, much in the same way as in charades.

The third technique used in jokes is that of the *double meaning* or multiple use of the same word, as we find in plays upon words. Plays upon words are considered by Freud to be the ideal case of multiple use of the same material: "*Here, no violence is done to the word; it is not cut up into its separate syllables [. . .] Exactly as it is and as it stands in the sentence, it is able, thanks to certain favourable circumstances, to express two different meanings*" (ibid.: 37). Freud illustrates this technique with several examples, including that of the physician examining a woman patient:

> *A doctor, as he came away from a lady's bedside, said to her husband with a shake of his head: "I don't like the look of her." "I've not liked her looks for a long time," the husband hastened to agree. The doctor was of course referring to the lady's condition; but he expressed his anxiety about the patient in words which the husband could interpret as a confirmation of his own marital aversion.* (ibid.: 37)

According to Freud, it is an economy of means that is uppermost in the use of condensation in these three techniques, as in the example I have just quoted: "looks" means not only physical condition but also general appearance. "*Has no condensation and economy been made? Most certainly. There has been a saving of the whole of the second thought and it has been dropped without leaving a substitute*" (ibid.: 43). He concludes the discussion thus: "*All these techniques are dominated by a tendency to compression, or rather to saving*" (ibid.: 42), in other words to economy of the means of expression.

As for puns, though they may be the most common form of jokes, they "*pass as the lowest form of verbal joke, probably because they are the 'cheapest' [and] can be made with the least trouble*" (ibid.: 45).

- ### *Techniques based on thought processes*

Freud continues his detailed investigation into the different techniques employed with a review of jokes based on thought, in other words those which do not depend on the actual wording of the joke but on the thought processes behind it; they are therefore independent of verbal expression. In such cases, the joke-work – Freud uses this term to highlight the analogy with dream-work – makes use of thought processes which diverge from normal reasoning as the technical means of producing an amusing witticism. He mentions several processes, such as *displacement*, which uses logic to disguise an error of reasoning, and the use of *nonsense* in the construction of a joke. What turns nonsense into a joke? Freud's amusing way of putting it is that "*there is sense behind joking nonsense [. . .] and it is this sense that makes the nonsense into a joke*" (ibid.: 57). The technique used here consists in putting forward something silly or nonsensical, the sense of which is to bring out something else which is also silly and nonsensical.

- ### *Innocent and tendentious jokes*

We could divide jokes into *innocent* and *tendentious*, according to the reaction which they provoke in those who hear or read them. The innocent joke is an end in itself and has no other specific aim. On the other hand, the tendentious joke is in the service of an intention which may comply with all kinds of motive such as hostility (aggressiveness, satire, cynicism), obscenity (with the aim of exposing), bawdiness which emphasizes sexual matters, and scepticism – this being, for Freud, the worst of all motives.

- ### JOKES AS A SOURCE OF PLEASURE AND AS A SOCIAL PROCESS

In this second part, Freud discusses the role played by pleasure in the mechanism of joking. The mechanisms which underlie the pleasurable effect are easier to perceive in tendentious jokes than in innocent ones, because in the former case a tendency is satisfied: that satisfaction is a source of pleasure. The tendency, of course, comes up against obstacles which the joke can circumvent, whether these obstacles be external (fear of the person at whom the hidden insult is aimed) or internal and linked to one's upbringing. In both of these cases in which a tendentious joke is made, a yield of pleasure is obtained because it corresponds to an "*economy in expenditure on inhibition or suppression*" (ibid.: 119). In the case of innocent jokes, the technique employed is itself the source of pleasure, as in plays upon words.

Tendentious jokes have a social dimension which something merely comic does not possess, because jokes need at least three persons: the first makes the joke, the second is the target of the hostile or sexual aggression and the third hears the joke and takes pleasure in the content of the underlying intention. Why is the presence of some third person so necessary? According to Freud, a joke aims to have a pleasurable effect both on the person who makes it and on the third person, who hears it: "*A joke is thus a double-dealing rascal who serves two masters at once*" (ibid.: 155). The pleasure felt by the author of the joke is veiled in obscurity because, generally speaking, no one laughs at his or her own jokes – "*we laugh, as it were, 'par ricochet [on the rebound]'*" (ibid.: 156), via the person who laughs at the joke.

- ### JOKES, DREAMS AND SPECIES OF COMIC

The third part of the book compares dreams and jokes, and ends with an essay on the comic effect, humour and jokes.

- ***Dreams, jokes and the return to the infantile unconscious***

In comparing dreams and jokes, Freud begins by making a list of the similarities and differences between them. The dream is above all the expression of a wish-fulfilment and has as its aim the avoidance of unpleasure, while the purpose of jokes is to obtain pleasure. Jokes manage to find pleasure not only through the various techniques employed, but also in going back to the infantile unconscious which is their primary source. As children begin to use speech, we see them playing with words and assembling them with no heed for their meaning, because they are seeking the pleasure which is associated with the sounds of the words. That pleasure will soon be prohibited by the emergence of internal criticism – censorship – and the only constructions which will be allowed to continue are those which are meaningful. Later, adults will resort to plays upon words in order to get back in touch with their infantile pleasure and circumvent censorship in a movement of rebellion against the constraints imposed by thinking and by reality.

- ***Species of comic***

Freud then goes on to discuss the different forms of the comic such as mimicry, parody, caricature, etc. He attributes the source of pleasure in certain forms of the comic to the comparison between the other person and one's own ego. The book ends with an essay on humour, which Freud distinguishes from irony; this essay was to be developed further some twenty years later in a short paper called "Humour" (1927d), where he introduced the idea of the superego.

Post-Freudians

Lacan: jokes and "flashes" of insight

A "return" to Freud's early writings

At the beginning of the 1950s, Jacques Lacan called on psychoanalysts to "return to Freud". What did this "return" imply? In fact, it had nothing to do with going back and reading all of Freud's writings; the idea was to return to Freud's first theoretical texts which gave a pivotal role to language in matters relating to the unconscious: *The Interpretation of Dreams, The Psychopathology of Everyday Life* and *Jokes and their Relation to the Unconscious*. Written between 1900 and 1905, these three books published more or less at the same time lay particular stress on language as a disguised expression of the unconscious. It was from this trilogy that Lacan drew his main concepts – and in particular from jokes, to which he granted "the status of an authentic psychoanalytic concept" (Roudinesco and Plon 1997).

There were several stages to Lacan's undertaking. In 1953, in his "Rome Discourse", he began by recommending the return to meaning: "The meaning of a return to Freud is a return to Freud's meaning," he declared, in a witty turn of phrase (Lacan 1955: 405 [2004: 110]). By his insistence on meaning, Lacan was aiming to re-establish the psychoanalytic experience of the unconscious in what he considered to be its most Freudian originality; Lacan maintained that his contemporaries in the psychoanalytic world had abandoned "the foundation of speech" (1953: 243 [2004: 37]).

The unconscious is structured like a language

As early as 1956, Lacan focused the experience of the unconscious on its symbolic dimension in the light of contemporary linguistic science, in particular as regards the distinction between the notion of "signifier" and "signified" which the Swiss linguist, F. de Saussure, had developed. Those contributions enabled Lacan to highlight the "supremacy of the signifier over the signified", a postulate which appeared to him to be one of the main lessons to be learned from *The Interpretation of Dreams*. Applying the free association method brings us closer and closer to sequences of thought which, in turn, lead back to sequences of words; that technique enables the analyst to identify the track somewhere along which the signifier became lost: "beyond [. . .] speech, it is the whole structure of language that psychoanalytic experience discovers in the unconscious" (Lacan 1957: 494–495 [2004: 139]). Adopting a structural approach, Lacan also re-examined the notion of condensation as it appeared in both dreams and jokes – Lacan preferred to use the term "flash of wit" to translate the German *Witz* – and argued that the joke was a signifier which would reveal, through the play of language, an unconscious truth which the person concerned was trying to conceal.

Lacan's reappraisal of the notions of condensation and displacement led him to formulate his famous dictum according to which "the unconscious is structured like a language". As Joël Dor (1985: 17 [2004: 3]) points out, Lacan's central hypothesis is condensed into that one proposition: the mechanisms which shape the unconscious are exactly similar to those which give meaning to language: "We may even consider this to be the most fundamental hypothesis in all of Lacan's theoretical work, if only because it both presupposes and embodies the meaning of the *return to Freud* that Lacan ceaselessly advocated throughout his career."

Differences of opinion concerning technique, theory and training

Lacan's psychoanalytic writings, and in particular those which concern language, have aroused (and to this day still arouse) a degree of interest which goes well beyond psychoanalytic circles. However, differences of opinion on certain fundamental issues soon arose between Lacan and other analysts who belonged to the International Psychoanalytical Association (IPA). These disagreements led to a split in 1953 and, in 1964, Lacan founded "all by himself" the *Ecole Freudienne de Psychanalyse* – which in 1980, shortly before his death, he decided to dissolve. From that point on, the Lacanian movement split up into a large number of smaller groups.

From a technical point of view, I think that the "return to Freud" advocated by Lacan in 1953 focused attention particularly on the neuroses and on verbal communication, to the exclusion of Freud's post-1915 writings – those in which Freud discusses whether psychoanalytic treatment is appropriate for patients who have disorders of verbal communication and symbolization, such as we find in depressive and psychotic states (J-M. Quinodoz 2000, 2002).

In addition, Lacan thereafter paid more and more attention exclusively to what the analysand actually said, going almost as far as to take into account only the "flashes" of insight into the patient's symbolic discourse – when there are sudden breakthroughs from the unconscious that Lacan saw as having the impact of a Signifier. (In German, there is an amusing play upon words when *Blitz* (flash) and *Witz* (joke) are brought together via condensation and displacement.) The danger with this technique is that such plays upon words and their supposed value as interpretations can be used to fit any and every occasion; it encouraged Lacan to shorten the length of sessions and to ignore the time required for the transference and counter-transference to be processed. On this crucial point, my own opinion is that not everybody can have immediate insight into meaningfulness – far from it, indeed. It is a slow and gradual process which more often than not necessitates the strict conditions of the classic psychoanalytic setting if it is to go on unfolding at a rhythm which needs to be respected throughout.

The technical issue concerning shortened sessions is far from being the only point of divergence between Lacanian psychoanalysts and those who belong to the International Psychoanalytical Association (IPA). As D. Widlöcher (2003) has pointed out, many other differences which are impossible to ignore still remain, particularly as regards use of the counter-transference, a technique which Lacan rejected with the utmost vigour, as do those who follow his outlook today (Duparc 2001).

As regards the training of candidate psychoanalysts, Lacan was completely and utterly opposed to the manner in which the IPA organized this. In particular, he was against any form of "preselection" and did not accept the requirement that the candidate have had a previous personal analysis (the so-called "training analysis"). In his view, assessment of candidates at different stages in the programme, as well as the overall hierarchical organization, meant that colleagues remained in a state of perpetual subjection. When he founded his own school in 1964, he laid down the principle that it would neither authorize nor ban anyone who wished to practise psychoanalysis; for Lacan, the responsibilities involved in analytic treatment are personal to each analyst – hence his statement: "A psychoanalyst needs no authorization from anybody other than him- or herself." The refusal to contemplate any assessment other than one's own meant that very many people began calling themselves "psychoanalysts", with reference to Lacan but without specifying what kind of training they had had.

Some psychoanalysts who belong to the Lacanian movement would like to rejoin the International Psychoanalytical Association (IPA), which was founded by Freud himself. There are still wide divergences, in my opinion, as to certain theoretical and technical issues.

The British school: from primitive symbolism to symbolic representation

Widening the scope of psychoanalysis beyond the neuroses

Psychoanalysts belonging to the British school also discussed the question of symbolism, but from a different perspective. This approach enabled them to offer psychoanalytic treatment to patients with difficulties in verbal communication, verbalization being a highly developed form of symbolism. In their view, psychoanalytic treatment was not the exclusive province of neurotic patients able to communicate with themselves and with other people by means of words; it could help patients in whom concrete thinking predominates but who, thanks to the opportunity for working-through that analysis offers, can develop their symbolic function and capacity to communicate verbally.

As early as 1916, Jones had explored the question of symbolism with reference to the point of view that Freud had expressed in *The Interpretation of Dreams* (1900a). For Jones, there is a distinction between conscious and unconscious symbolism; the formation of a symbol is the result of intrapsychic conflict, and the symbol itself is a representation of what has been repressed.

Shortly after this, Melanie Klein introduced a novel approach to the question of symbolism, based on her work with children and her understanding of their play in the therapy session in terms of the symbolic expression of unconscious conflict. In her paper "The Importance of Symbol-Formation in the Development of the Ego", based on her observation of Dick, a 4-year-old autistic boy, Klein (1930) shows that symbol formation may be inhibited specifically, and that this kind of inhibition has serious consequences for the future development of the ego. Her conclusion is that if the processes of symbol formation cannot begin to operate, all ego development is halted; she attributes this inhibition to excessive anxiety brought about by the infant's aggressive fantasies involving the mother's body and to a resultant increase in guilt feelings.

The transition between primitive and more developed forms of symbol formation

The fact that the process of symbol formation may be inhibited during infant development led Hanna Segal and W. R. Bion to investigate more closely the issues raised by Klein. As a result, they drew a distinction between a primitive and a more developed form of symbolism and shed light on the transition processes between these two, with reference to the concept of the paranoid-schizoid and depressive positions. I shall discuss in more detail these points of view later, when I examine the developments that followed on from Freud's study of the specific features of schizophrenic speech, which he included in his paper on "The Unconscious" (1915e).

The developments initiated by Segal and Bion, in addition to those of Herbert Rosenfeld on the narcissistic transference, meant that it became possible to offer psychoanalysis to psychotic, narcissistic and borderline patients; there are many more of these nowadays on the analytical couch than there are neurotic patients.

New concepts

Dream mechanisms (condensation, displacement, wish-fulfilment) applied to jokes, to the comic and to humour

THREE ESSAYS ON THE THEORY OF SEXUALITY

(1905d)

The discovery of infantile sexuality: a revolution and a scandal

Published in 1905, *Three Essays on the Theory of Sexuality* is often considered to be Freud's second most important book, ranked just after *The Interpretation of Dreams* (1900a), and his most outstanding work on sexuality. In it, Freud openly challenges popular opinion and the then current assumptions about sexuality. On the one hand, he expanded the idea of sexuality beyond the narrow limits within which that notion was conventionally defined, and on the other he argued that the beginnings of sexuality are to be found in early childhood, in other words at a much earlier period than had been thought up till then. He showed that sexuality does not begin with the onset of puberty but in early childhood and that it develops through successive stages before adult sexuality is reached. In addition, he built bridges between abnormal and so-called normal forms of sexuality.

With simple words of everyday language, Freud put forward a certain number of hypotheses on sexuality which people were simply unwilling to take on board. Yet he said nothing in that book which was not already known – and in particular he said nothing new to parents, educators and writers who, almost from time immemorial, had observed and described various manifestations of infantile sexuality. In addition, the descriptions of sexuality which Freud presents in the book are much less provocative than the obscene images which had been published a few years earlier by sexologists whom Freud mentions, Krafft-Ebing or Havelock Ellis, for example, but their writings did not give rise to such an uproar. There was a public outcry when people began reading the *Three Essays*, to such an extent that, as Jones puts it, Freud became "universally unpopular". The book was to damage relations between Freud and the general public for quite some time to come. He was considered to be a man with an evil and obscene mind, all the more so when he published in the same year his case-study of *Dora* without the patient's permission, a fact which shocked the Viennese medical establishment. Why was there so much hostility? Freud – a middle-class physician and family man – was of course going down a very risky road indeed when he turned ethics on their head by refusing to make a moral judgement on the perversions. Deaf to criticism, Freud was more determined than ever to see scientific knowledge triumph over obscurantism.

Biographies and history

The moment when the significance of infantile sexuality was discovered

Even as he was working on his earlier discoveries, in the 1890s, Freud suspected that factors of a sexual nature which went back to childhood could be the cause of hysterical symptoms. Also, he had thought at first that it was only after seduction by an adult that sexual impulses could be prematurely aroused in children. But when he discovered the Oedipus complex in

1897, in the course of his self-analysis, Freud came to the conclusion that sexual impulses were present very early on in life in all children and that they were manifested independent of any arousal initiated by an adult. Early in 1900, he told Fliess that his next book would be about a theory of sexuality and that all he was waiting for was "*some spark [that] can set what I have collected ablaze*" (Letter to Fliess, 26 January 1900). Freud no doubt had to overcome strong internal resistance before admitting that infantile sexuality is a universal phenomenon; he finished the book more or less at the same time as *Jokes and their Relation to the Unconscious*, which was also published in 1905.

This was a very productive time for Freud, and it was also the point at which he finally broke off all relations with Fliess. His private practice was taking up almost all of his time, with most of his patients coming from Eastern Europe. He spent 3 years lecturing at the university, and more colleagues were attending his Wednesday Society meetings; 1905 was also the year in which international recognition of Freud's work began to grow. Accompanied by his sister-in-law, Minna Bernays, or his brother, Alexander, Freud travelled abroad each summer, visiting Italy and Greece on several occasions.

Was Freud a pan-sexualist?

In his *Three Essays*, Freud declares that infantile sexuality is of crucial importance, arguing in particular that repressed drives in neurotic people are sexual in nature and that adolescent and adult sexuality is based on infantile sexuality. This gave rise to misunderstandings, to such an extent that he was accused of being "pan-sexualist" – in other words, of advocating a simplistic theory according to which all human behaviour was to be explained in sexual terms: sexuality in the narrowest sense of the word. Though he did emphasize the importance of sexuality in human beings, he did not accept the accusation of pan-sexualism which was being levelled against him. In a letter to Professor Claparède in Geneva, Freud protested against this accusation – which was aimed not only at his theory of sexuality but also at his conception of dreams: "*I have never claimed that every dream expressed the fulfilment of a sexual wish, and I have often asserted the contrary. But this produces no effect, and people continue to repeat the same thing*" (Letter from Freud to Claparède, 25 December 1920 [1921e: 214–215]).

Discovering the text

> Page numbers are those of *The Standard Edition of the Complete Psychological Works of Sigmund Freud*, vol. **7**, 123–243.

The book is divided into three parts. The first deals with perversions under the heading of "The Sexual Aberrations", the second with infantile sexuality and the third with the transformations of puberty.

- **FIRST ESSAY: THE SEXUAL ABERRATIONS**

- ## *The infantile origins of perversion*

In this first essay, Freud criticizes both popular opinion and the belief, widespread in scientific circles at the time, according to which perversions such as homosexuality were the result of degeneracy or of some innate characteristic. He argues that the true cause is to be found in the individual's childhood, in other words that it is a question of psychosexual development. He begins by reviewing the sexual deviations which sexologists of the time, such as Krafft-Ebing and Havelock Ellis, had classified, and discusses them from an entirely new perspective – that of their relationship with accepted norms, i.e. of so-called "normal" sexuality.

Basing his argument on the notions of *"instinctual drives"* and *"objects"* – concepts which were later to prove decisive for psychoanalysis – Freud introduces a distinction within the category of perversions: he differentiates between *"deviations in respect of the sexual object"* (i.e. as regards the *person* who is felt to be sexually attractive) and *"deviations in respect of the sexual aim"* (i.e. as regards the *act* towards which tends the drive). It may be worth pointing out that in psychoanalysis the term *"object"* is used not to mean a "thing", but in the classical sense of "person" – cf. Shakespeare, who, in his *The Two Gentlemen of Verona*, has Valentine proclaim: "Upon a homely object / Love can wink", or as Sylvia Plath in her *Journals* (1982: 73) writes: "respect and admiration must equate with the object of my love".

- ## *The role of bisexuality*

Freud classifies under the heading *"deviations in respect of the sexual object"* the various forms of homosexuality, as well as paedophilia and zoophilia. For him, these perversions are due to an acquired characteristic of human sexuality, not to something innate or constitutional as had been thought up till then. But if homosexuality is the result of some development of the individual's psychosexuality, we would be justified in asking under what conditions do some people make a homosexual object choice, while others tend towards a heterosexual object choice. Freud answers that question by bringing in the idea of *bisexuality*, a universal tendency which had been postulated by Fliess, based on the development of the human embryo. However, though Fliess had emphasized biological bisexuality, Freud was the first to apply the notion to the mental sphere by postulating that masculine and feminine dispositions coexist in everybody from childhood on, so that the final choice of an object depends on the predominance of one of these tendencies over the other.

- ## *Component instincts*

Freud goes on to discuss matters relating to *"deviations in respect of the sexual aim"*, in which the sexual drive breaks up into its various parts which he called *"component instincts"*: the component instincts have as their source of sexual arousal the erotogenic zones. This implies that the perversions are under the domination of a component instinct of infantile origin. Among the types of perversion which are linked to component instincts, some use parts of the body or fetishistic objects as a means of obtaining sexual satisfaction; these replace the body zones which are normally meant for sexual intercourse. In other forms of perversion, there is a fixation with respect to preliminary sexual aims – for example, erotic practices involving the oral zone (fellatio, cunnilingus), touching, looking at, or even sadism and masochism. In these cases, says Freud: *"The tendency [lingers] over the preparatory activities and [turns] them into new sexual aims that can take the place of the normal one"* (1905d: 156). If we were to summarize Freud's point of view, we could say that in the perversions the sexual drive breaks up into its various parts, called the *"component instincts"*, while in normal sexuality the component instincts come together and work towards genital maturity.

- ## *Perversions, neurosis and normality*

From all this, Freud draws two conclusions which particularly shocked the general public. First, he maintains that neurotic symptoms are not created exclusively at the expense of the normal sexual drive but in part also at the cost of abnormal sexuality. He summarizes his point of view in a phrase which has become famous: "neuroses are, so to say, the negative of perversions" (ibid.: 165). The metaphor is borrowed from photography and means that what is *enacted* by perverts through their deviant sexual behaviour is *imagined* by neurotics in their fantasies and dreams. Second, Freud argues that the predisposition towards perversion is not an exception but fully belongs to the so-called normal constitution, already outlined in childhood: *"This postulated constitution, containing the germs of all the perversions, will only be demonstrable in* children, *even though in them it is only with modest degrees of intensity that any of the instincts can emerge*" (ibid.: 172).

SECOND ESSAY: INFANTILE SEXUALITY

Infantile amnesia: forgetting the earliest years of one's childhood

In this second essay, Freud turns even more on its head the popular belief according to which the sexual drive is absent in childhood and appears only at puberty; at the same time, he upset the scientific circles of his day, who ignored the existence of infantile sexuality. He attributes this lack of awareness to what he calls "*infantile amnesia*", i.e. to the fact that, generally speaking, adults have very few memories of their earliest childhood years. For Freud, the forgetfulness of both infantile amnesia and hysterical amnesia is caused by repression: the hysteric represses sexual drives related to seduction, while the adult keeps well away from conscious awareness the beginnings of sexual life in childhood.

According to Freud, the sexual life of children usually emerges in a form accessible to observation around the third or fourth year of life, but manifestations of the sexual drive come up against external obstacles such as one's upbringing, a feature of the culture in which one lives, as well as internal obstacles such as disgust, modesty and moral standards, these being the expression of repression. During the latency period, the sexual impulses turn away from directly sexual aims and are directed towards other ends, in the form of cultural achievements, thanks to the process which Freud calls *sublimation*. He does accept that, sometimes, the sexual drive may break through during the latency period either occasionally or in a more durable manner which may continue until puberty.

The manifestations of infantile sexuality

Freud takes *thumb-sucking* as his model of the manifestations of infantile sexuality; this activity appears in early infancy and may persist all through life. For him, the child who indulges in thumb-sucking is driven by a search for some pleasure which has already been experienced based on "*the child's first and most vital activity, his sucking at his mother's breast, or at substitutes for it*" (ibid.: 181). During the breast-feed, the child's lips behave like an erotogenic zone, the source of pleasurable sensation. "*To begin with, sexual activity attaches itself to functions serving the purpose of self-preservation*" (ibid.: 182); it is only later that sexual satisfaction can separate from the need for food and become independent. However, according to Freud, this erotogenic quality is not limited to the oral zone; it may attach to any other part of the body which then becomes as excitable as the genitals.

It follows that the main feature of the sexual drives in childhood is their essentially *masturbatory* nature. Among the manifestations of infantile sexuality, Freud includes not only oral masturbatory activity but also the masturbatory activities which are linked to the anal zone (pleasure in retention or in expulsion linked to the intestinal function, etc.), as well as the urethral activities which involve the pleasure of urinating (in both boys and girls) and those linked to the genital zones. These observations led Freud to describe three distinct phases of infantile masturbation: the first is that of the young infant's onanism linked to the feeding situation, the second belongs to the third or fourth year of life, while the third phase corresponds to pubertal masturbation, which for a long time was the only kind taken into account.

The polymorphously perverse disposition

The discovery of the part played by the erotogenic zones in early childhood led Freud to the conclusion that children have a "*polymorphously perverse disposition*". What does he mean by that?

The term "*perverse disposition*" means that the various regions of the infant's body present from the very beginnings of life a particularly strong sensitivity to eroticization; it is only later that the erotogenic zones are subjected to a genital organization which aims to unify sexuality. The term "*polymorphously*" emphasizes the great diversity of erotogenic zones which can be sexually aroused in early childhood. The existence of a polymorphously perverse disposition in infants enables Freud to explain the fact that an organized perversion such as we find in adults derives from the persistence of a component part of infantile sexuality which has remained fixated at an early stage of psychosexual development.

Even today, Freud's notion of the "*polymorphously perverse disposition*" often creates a scandal, because it generally goes misunderstood. The fact that a child can obtain sexual pleasure from erotogenic zones does not mean that he or she is a "pervert" in the sense in which the word is used of an adult. For Freud, the term meant that the infantile stage of the polymorphously perverse disposition is an early phase in the individual's psychosexual development, which has not yet reached the stage of genital sexuality, before a hierarchy is established between the erotogenic zones and places them under the sway of the reproductive function. Perversion in adults is a different matter altogether; here there is a highly organized kind of behaviour in which component satisfaction is obtained at the expense of the full development of the individual's genital sexuality, and sexual pleasure is obtained either with same-sex objects, as in homosexuality, or through particular kinds of demand, as in fetishism. It can happen, of course, that a child may present a genuinely perverse fixation, but such cases are very much the exception.

- ## *Infantile sexual theories*

Among the manifestations of infantile sexuality, Freud includes the intense curiosity that children express via their unrelenting questions on sexual matters: where do babies come from? How do daddy and mummy do it? These questions, repeated in all shapes and forms, give us a glimpse of the particular theories which children invent on the subject of sexuality – for example, that there is only one organ which determines the difference between the sexes: boys have a penis, girls are deprived of one. Other infantile sexual theories concern the ideas children have about birth (are babies born through the bowel like a discharge of faeces?) or about sexual intercourse between the parents (impregnation via kissing, sadistic view of sexual intercourse, etc.). Yet whatever their nature, the conscious fantasies of children are above all a reflection of their unconscious sexual organization and of the way in which they imagine, in fantasy, relationships between the people in their immediate circle.

- ## *The phases of development of the sexual organization*

The book went through six editions, and Freud continued to introduce new and fundamental concepts – the finished work, starting from a mere 80 pages in 1905, numbered some 120 pages in the sixth and final edition published in 1925 (which included all of the updates). In the 1915 edition, Freud introduced the idea of an organization of the libido in successive stages, each of which corresponds to the primacy of a given erotogenic zone. Freud goes on to describe the oral phase, the anal-sadistic phase and the genital phase. He suggests that libidinal development goes through successive phases, each of which corresponds to the dominant erotogenic zone. In 1923, he added to the three stages already described "the phallic stage of organization" which he placed between the anal and genital phases; the phallic stage knows only one kind of genital: the penis in boys and its equivalent in girls, the clitoris. The development of sexuality would thus seem to follow a path which runs from the pregenital stages of libidinal organization – oral, anal-sadistic and phallic – to the genital organization which is inaugurated at puberty. Though Freud describes infantile psychosexual development in evolutionist terms, he does point out that the trajectory is not a completely linear one and that some overlapping may easily occur, because each stage leaves permanent marks even when the individual has moved on to the following one.

THIRD ESSAY: THE TRANSFORMATIONS OF PUBERTY

The contrast between infantile auto-eroticism and post-pubertal object choice

In the 1905 edition of the book, Freud sharply contrasts infantile sexuality, which for him functions in an auto-erotic manner, with that of the post-pubertal period, focused on "object choice", in other words on the person who is chosen as a love-object. In the original version, the early stages of sexuality have as their sole object the individual's own body, whereas post-pubertal sexuality is based, Freud says, on the choice of an object, i.e. on the person who is loved and desired once the individual has reached physical and psychological maturity.

That said, as early as the first edition of the *Three Essays*, Freud described part-object and whole-object relations. When, in 1905, he wrote for example, "*a child sucking at his mother's breast has become the prototype of every relation of love*" (1905d: 222) and describes it as "*the first and most significant of all sexual relations*" (ibid.: 222), he was obviously referring to an early part-object relation, since the maternal breast is taken by the infant as a substitute for the mother. He described also the way in which the infant, having relinquished the breast – nowadays we would talk of a part-object relation – discovers the mother as a whole being: this shift occurs "*at the time [. . .] when the child is able to form a total idea of the person to whom the organ that is giving him satisfaction belongs*" (ibid.: 222). That is a description of the movement from a part-object to a whole-object relation, one which Freud was to complete in 1915 in his papers on metapsychology with the introduction of the concept of "component instincts".

The role of affects in object relations

As Freud continued to add material to successive editions of the *Three Essays*, he tended to tone down the contrast between infantile auto-eroticism and post-pubertal object choice. When in 1915 he introduced the idea of libidinal phases, he described for each of these a corresponding type of object. With the onset of puberty, the component instincts become gradually more integrated and lead to an object choice – in contemporary language, a "whole" object – typical of the genital phase: "*the whole of the sexual currents have become directed towards a single person in relation to whom they seek to achieve their aims*" (ibid.: 199).

Later, Freud would gradually take more account of the part played by the affects of love and hate in object relations in the course of an individual's development. In 1912, he introduced the concept of ambivalence in "The Dynamics of Transference" (1912b); from that point on, he argued that the ambivalence between love and hate was characteristic of pregenital object relations. He emphasized also the contrast between the *affectionate* current, typical of infantile component instincts, and the *sensual* one, a feature of pubertal object choice. For the sensual current of object choice to operate, the child has to give up the early incestuous love-objects represented by the father and mother because of the barrier against incest, and direct his or her object choice towards other people. These new object choices, however, are still under the influence of the early choices, so that there remain similarities between the desired objects chosen after puberty and the child's earliest object choices, the parents. In other words, says Freud, none of us can escape the impact of our earliest incestuous object choices made in infancy, for these remain influential all through life: "*Even a person who has been fortunate enough to avoid an incestuous fixation of his libido does not entirely escape its influence*" (1905d: 228). Freud subsequently went on to show how the affectionate current and the sensual one become integrated when the genital phase develops; in the case of neurotic disorders, however, these two currents do not succeed in coming together: "*Two currents whose union is necessary to ensure a completely normal attitude in love have [. . .] failed to combine*" (1912d: 180).

Finally, Freud considers object-love from a developmental point of view. Children learn to love other people on the basis of the sexual love they felt for the people who took care of them from the latency period onwards. If we were to summarize the sequence of psychosexual development in children, we could say that the sexual drive begins by targeting part-objects which are essentially pregenital in nature; there then follows a gradual process of development which leads to a synthesis between the libidinal and affective currents in the choice of a love-object. Freud used the term "object choice" to describe the love relation directed towards someone experienced as a whole object; this kind of relationship introduces another pair of opposites, love and hate, as he describes them in 1915 in "Instincts and their Vicissitudes": "*the [terms] of love and hate cannot be made use of for the relations of instincts to their objects, but are reserved for the relations of the total ego to objects*" (1915c: 137). Freud did recognize, however, that sexual maturity as he described it was only rarely attained; stressing the decisive role played by infantile sexuality in normal and pathological development, he wrote: "*Every pathological disorder of sexual life is rightly to be regarded as an inhibition in development*" (1905d: 208).

Development of Freud's concepts

The Oedipus complex: discovered in a succession of stages

The idea of the Oedipus complex as such does not figure in the first (1905) edition of Freud's *Three Essays on the Theory of Sexuality*; it appears only with the additions he made in later editions. I shall, however, at this point outline the main stages of this development. The notion itself was gradually worked on all through Freud's writings; no one text is devoted to the Oedipus complex as a whole.

It was one of the most significant of Freud's discoveries. The Oedipus complex emerges in the course of the child's development and constitutes the central organizer of mental life, around which the individual's sexual identity is structured. For Freud, the complex is a universal one, as he makes plain in the *Three Essays*: "*Every new arrival on this planet is faced by the task of mastering the Oedipus complex*" (1905d: 226). The Oedipus complex is not limited to normal development; it lies also at the heart of psychopathology, forming "*the nuclear concept of the neuroses*" (ibid.).

The simple (or positive) form of the Oedipus complex

It was in the course of his self-analysis that Freud came to acknowledge the love towards his mother and the jealousy towards his father that he had felt as a child. He associated this conflict in his feelings to the myth of Oedipus:

> *I have found, in my own case too, [the phenomenon of] being in love with my mother and jealous of my father, and I now consider it a universal event in early childhood. [. . .] If this is so, we can understand the gripping power of* Oedipus Rex. (Letter from Freud to Fliess, 15 October 1897)

He took up the same theme again in *The Interpretation of Dreams*: "*King Oedipus, who slew his father Laïus and married his mother Jocasta, merely shows us the fulfilment of our own childhood wishes*" (1900a: 262). In the years that followed, Freud constantly referred to the idea of the Oedipus complex in his clinical work, as in the "Dora" case in 1905 and in that of "Little Hans" in 1909. But it was not until 1910, in "A Special Type of Choice of Object Made by Men" (1910h), that the notion of the "*Oedipus complex*" emerges for the first time, the term "*complex*" being borrowed from Jung.

At first, Freud discovered the simple form of the Oedipus complex (also called positive or direct) and described how it evolved in the course of the young boy's psychosexual development. The boy's first object of affection is his mother, whom he desires to possess exclusively, but from ages 3 to 5, the love he feels for her brings him into rivalry with his father, whom he begins to hate. He therefore fears that his father will castrate him – deprive him of his penis – because of the incestuous wishes he feels for his mother and the hate he has towards his father. Under the impact of the anxiety aroused by the threat of castration, the boy finally gives up the idea of fulfilling his incestuous sexual wishes for his mother, and enters into the latency period.

Freud thought initially that there was total symmetry as regards psychosexual development in both boys and girls. As the boy fell in love with his mother and began to hate his father, so the girl fell in love with her father and hated her mother. Later he came to understand that the girl's developmental trajectory is different from that of boys.

In 1913, in *Totem and Taboo*, Freud attempted to explain the universal nature of the Oedipus complex and in particular the structuring role it played in the personality development of all human beings. He tried to establish this through the hypothesis of the killing of the father of the primal horde by the sons, who wanted to possess the women whom the father kept for himself. According to Freud, this original crime is handed down from generation to generation via phylogenesis, and the guilt associated with this first murder emerges in each of us in the shape of the Oedipus complex.

The complete form of the Oedipus complex: a much later discovery

Many years later, in *The Ego and the Id* (1923b), Freud added to the idea of the positive (or direct) Oedipus complex that of its negative (or inverted) form, a notion based on the existence of the bisexual constitution, physical and mental, of all human beings from infancy onwards. In the positive Oedipus complex, the boy wants to marry his mother and kill his father, but in the negative or inverted complex he wants to marry his father and eliminate his mother, experienced as a rival. Unlike the positive form of the Oedipus complex, in which the boy identifies with his rival and wants "to be *like*" his father, in the negative or inverted form, he wants "to *be*" his mother by means of a regressive identification which, for Freud, is the earliest form of love for the object. The passive feminine wishes which the boy feels towards his father leads him to relinquish his heterosexual desires for his mother as well as his masculine identification with the paternal rival – as Freud shows in his case-study of "Senatspräsident Schreber" in 1911 and of the "Wolf-Man" in 1918. For Freud, both forms of the Oedipus complex coexist in the mental life of every human being; as a result, the complete form of the Oedipus complex involves four people: on the one hand the father and the mother, and, on the other, the masculine and feminine tendencies of the child (boy or girl) based on the "psychic bisexuality" which exists in all human beings. The relative proportion of these two tendencies varies, and the sexual identity of any given individual depends on which of the two prevails over the other; so-called normal psychosexual development is the result of the predominance of the positive Oedipus complex over the negative one.

In 1923, in "The Infantile Genital Organization" (1923e), Freud added a fourth pregenital phase, the "phallic stage" to the three – oral, anal and genital – he had introduced in 1915 in one of his revised versions of the *Three Essays*. From then on, he considered that the child's psychosexual development focuses essentially on the primacy of the penis as the decisive erotogenic zone, and on the Oedipus complex as regards object relations. At the same time, he stated that the Oedipus complex reaches its climax between 3 and 5 years of age, during the phallic phase – precisely when sexual desire for the opposite-sex parent is at its height and castration anxiety at its most intense.

In 1924, in "The Dissolution of the Oedipus complex" (1924d), Freud described how the Oedipus complex "*dissolves*" or "*disappears*". However, unlike what the title of that paper might have us believe, what in fact disappears is the Oedipal conflict as it is observed in all of its acuity in the 3–5-year-old child. The Oedipal situation as such persists in its final form in the unconscious as the fundamental organizer of the individual's mental life, having lost, as it were, the pathogenic character associated with the idea of "complex".

In 1925, Freud reconsidered what he had written on the sexual development of girls in "Some Psychical Consequences of the Anatomical Distinction between the Sexes" (1925j). He had come to realize that, if both boys and girls have the same object at the beginning of life – the mother – subsequent development follows a different path for girls. The girl has to change her object and move from the love experienced for the mother towards love for the father. That said, as we shall see later on the topic of Freud's conception of femininity, he still believed that the girl's psychosexual development is crucially influenced by penis envy, for which the desire to have a child by the father is a substitute. Freud remained faithful to this theory, known as "phallic monism" – this could be seen as a residue of his own attachment to an infantile sexual theory. In an article entitled "Female Sexuality" (1931b), he reaffirmed what he had said about the importance of the girl's original tie to her mother and the resultant difficulty she has in changing her object and in moving from the mother to the father in the course of her psychosexual development.

New concepts

Anaclisis – auto-eroticism – bisexuality – developmental phases: oral, anal, phallic, genital – drive – erotogenic zone – infantile amnesia – infantile sexual theories – object – object choice – Oedipus complex – perversions – polymorphously perverse disposition – psychosexual development (in boys and in girls) – whole-object, part-object

"FRAGMENT OF AN ANALYSIS OF A CASE OF HYSTERIA" (DORA)

(1905e [1901])

The discovery of transference

The account of Dora's psychoanalytic treatment is particularly interesting in that this is where Freud tells us how he discovered the transference. When Dora began her analysis, Freud thought that she would confirm the correctness of his views as to the sexual origins of hysterical symptoms and the part played by dreams in representing these symptoms: it was quite a shock to him when he could do nothing to stop her abandoning the treatment after only eleven weeks. Freud was intuitive enough, however, to turn this therapeutic failure to some advantage – he realized afterwards that a resistance connected with the transference process had been in operation without his having been aware of it. Freud concluded that, had he managed to identify this obstacle in time, he would have been able to interpret it and thus prevent the interruption of the analysis by his patient: "*Transference, which seems ordained to be the greatest obstacle to psychoanalysis, becomes its most powerful ally, if its presence can be detected each time and explained to the patient*" (1905e: 117). That was not, however, the end of things with Dora, because more than twenty years later Freud made a significant modification to his view of the transference as outlined in 1905, when he realized that the interruption of the analysis was not due simply to Dora's paternal transference but involved also her maternal transference, i.e. the persistence of the young girl's powerful homosexual attachment to her mother.

Though it can be said that Freud discovered the transference in 1905 thanks to his analysis of Dora, the notion itself was developed over several decades in many of his writings. The idea of the counter-transference, which Freud mentions on only two occasions, has been the subject of much important work by post-Freudian psychoanalysts, who have opened up fresh perspectives on the inseparable links between transference and counter-transference.

Biographies and history

Freud's genius: putting a therapeutic failure to good use

In 1900, Freud had just published *The Interpretation of Dreams* and was about to begin writing *The Psychopathology of Everyday Life* when Dora, a young woman of 18 – her real name was Ida Bauer – consulted him on the advice of her father. Freud began the analysis in October 1900, but Dora put an abrupt end to her treatment only three months later. Freud was very disappointed at first, but he overcame that reaction and immediately afterwards wrote this fundamental text on transference phenomena; it took him barely two weeks.

He told Fliess that this brief analysis had given him the opportunity of making two significant discoveries: the first had to do with the importance of the part played by the erotogenic zones, and in particular the oral zone at the origin of Dora's nervous cough (eroticization of the oral cavity); the second concerned the part played by psychic bisexuality in Dora's conflict, torn as she was between her attraction for men and the feelings she had towards other women. This was the first occasion on which Freud applied, in a clinical setting, the notion of bisexuality, which he borrowed from Fliess. On the other hand, as far as the interruption of the analysis was concerned, Freud admitted to his friend that he had been unable to control the transference, because he had failed to recognize it in time and therefore could not interpret it. But the lessons he was able to learn from that failure make this brilliant clinical observation one of his most significant writings on the topic of transference phenomena. For reasons of confidentiality, Freud deferred publication until 1905; this did not stop his adversaries from severely admonishing him for publishing a case report without the patient's consent.

What became of Dora in subsequent years? In 1903, she married Ernest Adler, by whom she had a son, Kurt-Herbert, who became Director of the San Francisco Opera. In 1923, she suffered from numerous anxiety attacks, as well as from feelings of persecution with respect to men; she then consulted the psychoanalyst Felix Deutsch, who recognized her as Freud's former patient. Afterwards, she lived in Vienna until the end of the 1930s, and became a great friend of Peppina's, alias "Frau K.", who is one of the characters in Freud's 1905 clinical paper on "Dora"! Interrogated by the Nazis who were searching for her brother, a politician known for his Marxist ideas and a former prime minister of Austria, Dora emigrated to the United States. She died in New York in 1945.

Discovering the text

Page numbers are those of *The Standard Edition of the Complete Psychological Works of Sigmund Freud*, vol. 7, 1–122.

- *From a real attempt at seduction . . .*

Dora consulted Freud after her father had had an affair with Frau K. This took place in Merano, a holiday resort in which two middle-class Viennese couples had met: Philip and Katherina Bauer, Dora's parents, and Hans and Peppina Zellenka, alias Herr K. and Frau K. (the "K" coming from "Zellen*ka*"). Suffice it to say that Dora's father had begun having an affair with Frau K., and her husband, furious at having been deceived in this way, began flirting with Dora, his rival's daughter. But Dora was anyway secretly in love with Herr K. because he reminded her of her father. One day, taking Dora by surprise, Herr K. took her in his arms and kissed her on the lips. Shocked, Dora slapped him and pushed him away. In the course of her analysis, Dora admitted to Freud that she had felt sexually aroused by her physical contact with Herr K. because of "*the pressure of his erect member against her body*" (1905e [1901]: 30); this upset her and filled her with shame. From that moment on, Dora began to feel shock and disgust whenever she was in the company of men; Freud considered these signs to be typically hysterical in nature. Shortly after the incident with Herr K., Dora had tried to discuss the matter with her father, but he and Herr K. accused her, quite unjustly, of having invented this attempted seduction. Dora then left the holiday resort before the scheduled date, without saying anything about the true reasons for her departure. Noticing that Dora's nervous condition was worsening, that she was suffering from depression and that she even threatened to commit suicide, her family made an appointment for her with Freud.

- ***... to the unconscious fantasy of seduction in the transference***

Freud's account of Dora's sessions is a good indication of the interest he took in this case, which brought such clear confirmation of his hypotheses on the sexual origins of hysterical symptoms, as well as on the role of dreams as revealing unconscious conflicts. With undisguised enthusiasm, Freud threw himself into a detailed analysis of Dora's neurotic problems and reports the interpretations he made to her as their work progressed. Determined to have his patient concur in the validity of his deductions, he spoke to her in a tone of hitherto-unsuspected self-confidence, especially when we compare this attitude with the hesitant and prudent approach he adopted in his *Studies on Hysteria* in 1895.

At the time of Dora's analysis, Freud's interpretative technique was aimed mainly at reconstructing the chain of events which had led to the emergence of the neurotic symptoms, and was based on the associations, dreams and childhood memories as reported by the patient. Here Freud adopts the same approach with Dora when, for example, he analyses the first dream, in which she escapes from a house on fire. Freud shows her the various unconscious aspects of her fantasies, including her flight to her father when she became frightened by the man who tried to seduce her, and her attraction towards her father when the dream reveals her unconscious wish to substitute him for the seducer. With this step-by-step approach, Freud was trying to make available to the patient's consciousness the unconscious chain which underlies the formation of her symptoms. But deeply involved in the search for Dora's memories and his own subsequent reconstructions, Freud did not see the underlying resistance which his "*explanations*" awakened in his patient. That was when he realized that it was not enough to share with Dora his reconstructed representations; she would have to experience the related affects in the *hic et nunc* relationship with him.

It was therefore much to his surprise that Dora interrupted the analysis after only three months of treatment. With the help of his notes, Freud began writing an account of the analysis; as he did so, he discovered in the session material many signs which foreshadowed the subsequent interruption. For example, taking as his starting-point the smell of smoke which had appeared in Dora's dreams, he realized that Dora's father, Herr K. and Freud himself were inveterate smokers; he drew the following conclusion as an *a posteriori* reflection on the transference which he had failed to notice:

Taking into consideration, finally, the indications which seemed to point to there having been a transference on to me – since I am a smoker too – I came to the conclusion that the idea had probably occurred to her one day during a session that she would like to have a kiss from me. (ibid.: 74)

He blamed himself for having failed to interpret the transference in good time:

But when the first dream came in, in which she gave herself the warning that she had better leave my treatment just as she had formerly left Herr K.'s house, I ought to have listened to the warning myself. "Now," I ought to have said to her, "it is from Herr K. that you have made a transference on to me. Have you noticed anything that leads you to suspect me of evil intentions similar [. . .] to Herr K.'s?" (ibid.: 118)

It seems as though Dora had unconsciously experienced not only disturbing affectionate and erotic feelings towards Freud, as she had felt with respect to Herr K., but also the wish to take revenge on Freud just as she had wanted to take revenge on her seducer.

- ***The transference: displacement of some person from the patient's past on to the psychoanalyst***

It was in this manner that the power of the transference revealed itself to Freud. Transference could be described as a drama which, in the course of an analysis, is enacted with respect to a significant person in the patient's past who is projected into the present and on to the psychoanalyst. In Dora's case, it was not just one important person from her past who was transferred on to Freud, but two: Freud represented not only Herr K. but also an earlier seducer, Dora's father, who in turn had been relayed by Herr K. Thus in the course of the analysis, a real event which had recently taken place in Dora's life echoed something from her childhood: the fantasy of being seduced by her father when she was a little girl. That fantasy event linked to the Oedipal situation had taken on so much more importance in Dora's childhood for the structure of her psyche than had the actual and more recent incident with Herr K.

• *A later modification: Dora's homosexual transference*

When he published this case history in 1905, Freud attributed Dora's resistance to her affectionate feelings and sexual desires for men, as represented by Herr K., her father and Freud himself. At that time, Freud took into account only the heterosexual dimension of the transference; he imagined therefore that Dora would see in him nothing but a man, i.e. a substitute for Herr K. or for Dora's father: "*At the beginning it was clear that I was replacing her father in her imagination*" (ibid.: 118). However, in a footnote he added in 1923 – more than twenty years after the end of the analysis – Freud acknowledged the fact that he had played down the strength of Dora's homosexual attachment to Frau K.: "*I failed to discover in time and to inform the patient that her homosexual (gynaecophilic) love for Frau K. was the strongest unconscious current in her mental life*" (ibid.: 120). He ends the footnote thus: "*Before I had learnt the importance of the homosexual current of feeling in psychoneurotics, I was often brought to a standstill in the treatment of my cases or found myself in complete perplexity.*"

The interesting conclusion to this discussion is that, in Dora's analysis, Freud thought in 1905 that he was involved only as a masculine figure, a replacement for Herr K. and for Dora's father. When, however, in his 1923 footnote, he highlighted Dora's attachment to Frau K., he did not see himself as a feminine figure in the transference – in other words, as a replacement for Frau K. or for Dora's mother. It would seem, therefore, that Freud had even then not fully understood that, whatever the actual gender of the analyst, he or she may represent, in the transference, a male or female character. In other words, a male analyst may, in the transference, represent either a man or a woman, just as a female analyst may represent either a woman or a man – and this depends on the transference situation at any given moment. That feature of the transference/counter-transference relationship is particularly difficult to understand when one is at the beginning of one's practice as a psychoanalyst.

Development of Freud's concepts

The transference in Freud's later writings

Just as for the Oedipus complex, the idea of the transference developed stage by stage in Freud's writings over several decades. Though "transference" itself is present as early as 1895, in *Studies on Hysteria*, it was only with the analysis of Dora in 1905 that Freud really began to understand how significant it could be. He was later to refine his ideas on the topic in several short papers devoted to different aspects of transference. Here, in chronological order, is an outline of the principal phases of Freud's thinking on this topic.

"Anna O." and Breuer's supposed flight

Transference undoubtedly has its own myth of origins in Freud's statement, published some years after the event, of how Breuer terminated Anna O.'s treatment in 1881. Freud's report lent credence to the belief that Breuer suddenly interrupted the treatment because Anna O. had fallen in love with him and that, faced with the sexual nature of her transference, Breuer took flight: "*In conventional horror he took to flight and left the patient to a colleague*" (Letter from Freud to Stefan Zweig, 2 June 1932, 1987c [1908–1938]). Recent historical research, however, would seem to indicate that Breuer's supposed flight, as Freud reported it, has less to do with actual events than with Freud's later memories, probably modified by the difficulties he had with Breuer – a colleague, all the same, from those pioneering days – over the role of sexuality in hysteria.

When Freud first used the term "transference" – in 1895 in *Studies on Hysteria* – he believed it to be a form of resistance just like any other, and did not at that time attach to it the importance he was later to see in the phenomenon. He saw it then as limited in scope and as an obstacle to the relationship of trust necessary for the treatment to be properly carried out. He gave as examples the grievances or the excessive attachment which the patient may unwittingly manifest as regards the physician. His advice was to bring out into the open the unconscious motives behind this resistance so that the patient might be helped to overcome it, just as any other symptom is dealt with in psychoanalysis.

Discovery of the transference after Dora's departure

Transference took on its full significance with Freud's treatment of Dora in 1905, when he realized that she had put an end to her treatment because of the affectionate and erotic feelings she had unconsciously transferred on to Freud. This enabled Freud to define the transference as a displacement on to the analyst of feelings, wishes, fantasies or perhaps even whole scenarios which in fact reproduce experiences already gone through with significant persons in the patient's past and in particular during childhood. But even though Freud realized *a posteriori* that transference had played a major role in Dora's decision to interrupt the treatment, he did not yet consider it to be the real motive force behind the whole dynamics of the psychoanalytic process. This is how he defined the phenomenon at that time:

> *What are transferences? They are new editions or facsimiles of the impulses and phantasies which are aroused and made conscious during the progress of the analysis; but they have this peculiarity, which is characteristic for their species, that they replace some earlier person by the person of the physician. To put it another way: a whole series of psychological experiences are revived, not as belonging to the past, but as applying to the person of the physician at the present moment.* (1905e [1901]: 116)

Freud gives more details as regards the nature of this transference, saying that "*there is no means of avoiding it*" and that it "*has to be detected almost without assistance*" (ibid.: 116).

Talking to Freud, he said "Captain"

In "Notes upon a Case of Obsessional Neurosis" (1909d), Freud gives a fine example of transference displacement on to him, which is also a picture of the stereotyped nature of the phenomenon: the patient – known as the "Rat Man" – began having obsessional ideas while he was in the army, when he heard a captain describe, with a note of delectation in his voice, a Chinese torture in which rats burrowed their way into the victim's body through the anus. After listening to the patient's account, Freud, in the second session of the treatment, was about to explain in some detail that the symptoms were sexual in origin, when he heard the "Rat Man" repeatedly address him as "*Captain*".

Projections on to the psychoanalyst of figures from the patient's childhood

"The Dynamics of Transference" (1912b) is the first article Freud wrote exclusively devoted to the transference; in it he uses the term "*imago*" – an idea of Jung's – to describe the internal figures from the patient's past which are displaced on to the person of the psychoanalyst. Freud also takes into account the role of the transference affects of love and hate highlighted by Ferenczi in 1909, after the latter had observed that patients were inclined to force the physician into adopting the role of parental figures who were simultaneously loved and feared. It is not enough to think simply in terms of "*transference*", writes Freud; the psychoanalyst has to take into account the affective qualities inherent in the transference: he therefore distinguishes the "*positive*" transference, where affectionate feelings are dominant, from the "*negative*" one in which feelings are predominantly hostile. He goes on to argue that the tender feelings linked to the positive transference always have an erotic basis, partly conscious and partly unconscious, because the earliest object relations which the infant establishes always involve sexual objects. As a result, the transference on to the analyst always has a twofold aspect, positive and negative; when the transference is accompanied by hostile feelings or repressed erotic elements, it is transformed into resistance. This twofold current of affects led Freud to adopt Bleuler's (1911) notion of *ambivalence*. Though, as he says, ambivalence may be a perfectly normal phenomenon, when it becomes excessive, especially in the psychoses, it may induce in the patient a negative transference towards the analyst which could go as far as to prevent a successful outcome of the treatment.

Transference and repetition

In "Remembering, Repeating and Working-Through" (1914g), Freud goes even further: he emphasizes the repetitive dimension of the transference and shows that the greater the patient's resistance, the greater the tendency to repeat the core problem situation through enactment rather than through memory recall.

> *For instance, the patient does not say that he remembers that he used to be defiant and critical towards his parents' authority; instead, he behaves in that way to the doctor.* [. . .] *He does not remember having been intensely ashamed of certain sexual activities and afraid of their being found out; but he makes it clear that he is ashamed of the treatment on which he is now embarked and tries to keep it a secret from everybody. And so on.* (1914g: 150)

In that paper, Freud makes a more successful attempt than before at showing how "*the transferences*" met with in everyday life, and especially in one's love life, are different from the transference *stricto sensu* which emerges in psychoanalytic treatment and has to do with the person of the analyst: he calls this latter type of transference the "*transference neurosis*" and describes it as "*an artificial illness*" (ibid.: 154) which is generated in and by the analytic situation. The psychoanalytic setting as Freud recommends it offers, he adds, sufficient security for the patient to give free rein to his or her transference fantasies, which the therapeutic work will cure: "*The main instrument* [. . .] *for curbing the patient's compulsion to repeat and for turning it into a motive for remembering lies in the handling of the transference*" (ibid.: 154).

Transference love: a stubborn form of resistance

In another technical paper, "Observations on Transference-Love" (1915a [1914]), Freud discusses what the analyst should do if a woman patient becomes enamoured of him. Putting an end to the treatment is no solution, he says, because the phenomenon has to do with her transference, and therefore will inevitably tend to be reproduced with the second analyst, then with the third, and so on, given the fact of repetition. But the therapist has to recognize that this is not true love on the patient's part, and that "*it is* [. . .] *just as disastrous for the analysis if the patient's craving for love is gratified as if it is suppressed*" (1915a [1914]: 166). When such a situation arises, Freud warns the therapist to be wary of his possible "*counter-transference*" (ibid.: 160). In other words, the love which the (woman) patient feels for her therapist is the expression of a resistance which opposes the development of the transference, which is why it is important to uncover its unconscious origins. Freud argues that this love is simply a new edition of certain past situations and infantile reactions; it is this infantile origin which gives it its compulsive and pathological character, and turns it into a source of resistance which has to be analysed. Faced with transference love, the analyst must adopt an attitude of reserve and abstinence:

> *it is quite out of the question for the analyst to give way. However highly he may prize love he must prize even more highly the opportunity for helping his patient over a decisive stage in her life.* (ibid.: 170)

It is only thus, adds Freud, that the analyst can help his patient "*to acquire the extra piece of mental freedom which distinguishes conscious mental activity* [. . .] *from unconscious*" (ibid.: 170).

Transference, the compulsion to repeat and the death drive

In 1920, in *Beyond the Pleasure Principle*, Freud observes that in some patients the repetitive nature of their transference seems to be impossible to overcome; instead of making progress, these patients go on and on repeating their failures or reproducing their symptoms because apparently they find it impossible to recall memories and process them adequately. Pointing out that the behaviour of these patients contradicts his first theory of the instinctual drives – according to which the human mind has as its essential goal the pursuit of pleasure and the avoidance of unpleasure – Freud began to call into question that initial conception. He suggested that a relentless psychical force obliges some patients to go from distress to distress, from failure to failure, so that they never succeed in surmounting them. In order to distinguish this clinical phenomenon from simple "*repetition*", he calls it "*the compulsion to repeat*", because the patient appears to be utterly incapable of breaking free of this compulsive drive-related force which Freud describes as "*daemonic*" (1920g: 21). Freud went as far as to postulate the existence, beyond the pleasure principle, of a more fundamental conflict – that between two sets of instinctual drives: the life drive and the death drive. This new idea enabled him to account for the difference between neurotic patients, who manifest "*transference neurosis*" and follow the principle of pleasure/unpleasure, and those who suffer from depression, perversion or psychosis and who present a "*narcissistic neurosis*" and a hostile transference based on the fundamental conflict between the life and death drives.

Freud and counter-transference

The concept of counter-transference rarely figures in Freud's writings. He defined the term in 1910, in "The Future Prospects of Psycho-Analytic Therapy", as "*a result of the patient's influence on* [*the analyst's*] *unconscious feelings*" (1910d: 144); for the physician to "*recognize this counter-transference in himself and overcome it*", Freud recommends not only a prior analysis but also the continuation of the practitioner's self-analysis (1910d: 145). In a letter to Binswanger written on 20 February 1913, Freud (1992 [1908–1938]) states that the counter-transference counts as one of the most complicated technical problems of psychoanalysis. Analysts, he writes, should resist any temptation to convey their immediate feelings to the patient; what is much more important is the analyst's efforts to elucidate the counter-transference experience and to work on it. Freud goes on to say that what analysts give back to their patients should never be the instantaneous affect, but always one that has been consciously worked over before being restored to them, more or less according to the necessities of the moment. Though in certain circumstances, he adds, analysts may well have a lot to give back, they should never divulge anything that they may have dug up from their own unconscious. That, to a very real extent, was Freud's way of putting it: the analyst's counter-transference had both to be acknowledged as such and overcome.

Freud did not explore the question any further. For him, the counter-transference was essentially the psychoanalyst's unconscious response running "counter" to the patient's transference; in other words, it is a reaction which, when it has not been sufficiently processed and integrated by the analyst, opposes the unfolding of the transference. It was left to post-Freudian psychoanalysts to explore in more detail the issues involved in this notion and to turn it into an indispensable tool for working with the transference within the psychoanalytic relationship.

Post-Freudians

Counter-transference developments after Freud

Paula Heimann and Heinrich Racker: fresh perspectives

From the 1950s on, the concept of counter-transference was developed to such an extent that it is now regarded as a fundamental instrument for understanding how patient and analyst communicate, at least as we conceive of that communication today. Paula Heimann in London and Heinrich Racker in Buenos Aires were the first to emphasize the fact that the analyst's counter-transference gives valuable clues as to how the patient is experiencing the analytical situation. It should be pointed out that the impetus for these fresh perspectives was undoubtedly Klein's description of projective identification in 1946, even though Klein herself did not go along with the way in which her concept was later put to use in the analysis of the counter-transference in the session.

In 1950, Paula Heimann drew attention to the importance of the analyst's emotional response to the patient in her article "On Counter-Transference" and showed that it could be a first-class research tool for exploring the patient's unconscious. She differentiated between this use of the counter-transference in the analytical setting and the analyst's unconscious reaction associated with his or her personal neurosis. At the same moment, Racker was arguing that the analyst's counter-transference feelings could be an important clue as to how the patient is experiencing the situation. Racker made a distinction between two types of counter-transference: the "concordant counter-transference", on which empathy is based – the analyst consciously identifies with certain aspects of the patient's personality – and the "complementary counter-transference" – the analyst unconsciously projects his or her own internal objects into the patient, thereby establishing a transference directed towards the patient (Racker 1953). At about this time, several other psychoanalysts who were working with a more or less Kleinian approach – Winnicott (1947) and Little (1951), for example – were also exploring the counter-transference and its importance. Neyraut (1974) too is worth mentioning in this context: he included in his conception of the counter-transference not only feelings but also the analyst's personal psychoanalytic references and metapsychological outlook.

The "normal" counter-transference and projective identification: Wilfred R. Bion

Towards the end of the 1950s, Bion also contributed to thinking about the counter-transference. He identified what he called the "normal" counter-transference – based on the distinction he made between pathological and normal projective identification (Bion 1959). These various developments meant that what transpired between patient and analyst could henceforth be seen in the light of new concepts, particularly that of the "container" with its reference to the capacity to tolerate and transform anxiety. From that point on, transference and counter-transference were looked upon as an inseparable couple; Betty Joseph, indeed, used the term "total situation" (1985).

Projective counter-identification: Leon Grinberg

Basing his own developments on Racker's dichotomy and Bion's contribution, Leon Grinberg (1962) postulated the existence of what he called "projective counter-identification" – the analyst's specific unconscious response to the patient's projective identification: the analyst unconsciously identifies with what has been projected into him or her. Projective counter-identification, says Grinberg, arises independently of the analyst's own internal conflicts – hence the difference with Racker's complementary counter-transference. When an analyst has to put up with excessive projective identification, he or she may well "passively" succumb to the patient's powerful projections, believing that these are in fact the analyst's own fantasies. If the analyst manages not only to contain but also to differentiate and to identify the projected emotions as belonging to the patient, projective counter-identification can be a highly useful technical instrument for making contact with the deepest levels of the analysand's fantasy material.

The manner in which the concept of counter-transference has developed since the 1950s has had an enormous influence on analytical technique – not only within Kleinian and post-Kleinian analysis, but also as regards most analysts who belong to one or other of the various schools of thought linked to the International Psychoanalytical Association (IPA). That said, there are many divergent opinions as to the manner in which counter-transference should be used in everyday clinical practice – each psychoanalyst would seem to have his or her own view on that issue.

Contrasting points of view as regards counter-transference

I cannot conclude this brief overview without at least mentioning the fact that the concept of counter-transference has given rise to two positions which are poles apart.

The first has to do with what is known as "counter-transference self-disclosure": the analyst reveals (divulges, uncovers . . .) to the patient what he or she is feeling, so as to highlight the difference between the analyst's experience and that of the patient. As Cooper (1998) says, this technique can operate for better or for worse – especially when the analyst has not adequately processed the counter-transference material which is given back to the patient. In the United States, several psychoanalysts have transformed "self-disclosure" into a genuine technique. In my opinion, this implies an entirely different view of what communication between patient and analyst is all about – one that has little to do with the classic approach to counter-transference in the psychoanalytic relationship.

The other point of view is diametrically opposed to this: the absolute refusal to take any account whatsoever of the counter-transference. Most psychoanalysts who follow Lacan's teaching go along with this point of view: counter-transference is not simply one form of resistance, it is *the* ultimate resistance of the analyst. This is one of the major theoretical and technical differences between contemporary Lacanian psychoanalysts, as J-A. Miller pointed out in his discussion with D. Widlöcher:

> *If we want to discover what separates Lacanians from the rest, we find this: dealing with the counter-transference has no place in the Lacanian way of practising psychoanalysis, nor is it considered to be a topic worthy of investigation. This is consistent with the adoption, by Lacanian psychoanalysts, of "shortened" sessions and with Lacan's view of the unconscious.* (Miller 2003: 14)

New concepts

Heterosexual transference – homosexual transference – maternal transference – paternal transference – transference

DELUSIONS AND DREAMS IN JENSEN'S "GRADIVA"

(1907a)

A clinical study of psychosis based on a character in a short story

This is Freud's first published analysis of a work of literature; other texts, on literature and art, would follow, thus marking the beginnings of what today we call applied psychoanalysis. In publishing this book in 1907, Freud was trying to reach a wider audience – in the hope that psychoanalysis would be more warmly welcomed – and in so doing demonstrate that a work of literature such as "Gradiva" could confirm many of his clinical observations. This short story lends itself particularly well to that kind of demonstration, because the adventures which the hero, an archaeologist called Hanold, experiences in his dreams and delusions can be looked upon in much the same way as a psychoanalyst would study the development of a clinical condition as observed in a patient. In addition, there is an interesting analogy between Hanold's actions all through the story and the psychoanalyst's work of exploration into the deepest layers of the unconscious – an exploration which Freud himself often likened to that of an archaeologist.

In this book, we also discover Freud's highly developed gift for observation. In 1907, he saw at work in Hanold a certain number of psychopathological phenomena such as denial of reality and splitting of the ego, even though he did not then realize that these mechanisms are specific to psychosis and perversion. It was only twenty years later that he would argue that these defence mechanisms – denial (or disavowal) of reality and splitting of the ego – are typical of psychosis, differentiating them from repression, which from then on he would see as an exclusively neurotic mechanism.

Biographies and history

Freud, Pompeii and "Gradiva"

It was Carl Gustav Jung who brought to Freud's notice the short story published by Wilhelm Jensen in 1903 and showed him how interesting it could be for psychoanalysis. After reading it with some enthusiasm, Freud set about writing his comments on it in the summer of 1906 while he was on holiday, and they were published in May 1907. With respect to "Gradiva", we should keep in mind the fact that Freud had visited Pompeii in 1902 with his brother Alexander, who was ten years younger than him, and that he claimed towards the end of his life to have read more books on archaeology than on psychology. In September 1907, shortly after the book was published, Freud travelled to Rome and visited the Vatican museum where he saw the sculpture which had inspired Jensen to write his novel. Freud bought a cast of it to hang in his consulting-room, at the foot of his couch; he took it with him to London when he emigrated in 1938.

The year 1907 was a particularly important one in the history of psychoanalysis, because it was then that Freud had three decisive encounters. The first was with Jung; the second with

Max Eitingon who, during their long walks together in Vienna, embarked on the very first training analysis; and the third was with Karl Abraham, who had just set up practice in Berlin after spending three years working with Bleuler in Zurich.

Carl Gustav Jung (1875–1961)

The Swiss psychiatrist Carl Gustav Jung was the founder of analytical psychology. He was born in 1875 into a Protestant family in Zurich; his father was a minister of religion. In 1895, he began his medical studies in Basel, and in 1900 he became an assistant doctor in the Burghölzli psychiatric clinic in Zurich, at the head of which was Eugen Bleuler. He became interested in spiritualism early on in his life, and in 1902 he published his dissertation under the title "On the Psychology and Pathology of So-Called Occult Phenomena". In that clinic, Jung developed a psychological test based on word-associations, and introduced the term "complex" to designate the set of images and fantasies which this test awakened in those who took it. He also used it with psychotic patients, and in 1906 published a book which is now regarded as a classic text: *The Psychology of Dementia Praecox*. This was also when he began corresponding with Freud, whom he met for the first time in February 1907.

From the outset, their relationship was of some considerable importance for Freud, for it meant that, in Jung, he had a spokesman within Bleuler's clinic in Zurich, one of the most prestigious psychiatric hospitals of the time. In addition, the presence of someone like Jung, coming as he did from a Protestant family in Zurich, highlighted the non-denominational aspect of psychoanalysis. Speaking of Jung, Freud wrote to Karl Abraham: "*It was only once he arrived that psychoanalysis escaped the danger of becoming a Jewish national affair* [. . .] *Our Aryan comrades are indispensable to us.*" Freud was very sympathetic towards Jung, sometimes calling him his "*son and heir apparent*", convinced as he was that Jung would one day be called upon to succeed him. He was perhaps partly transferring on to Jung his idealization of Fliess of a few years earlier. In 1909, invited by Clark University, Freud, accompanied by Jung and Ferenczi, visited the United States. Immediately afterwards, Jung was appointed the first President of the International Psychoanalytical Association (IPA) and became editor in chief of the *Jahrbuch*. In that same year, he set up in private practice in Küssnacht, near Zurich, where he would spend the rest of his life.

The conflict between Freud and Jung became particularly acute in 1912. The main points of disagreement had to do with the fact that Jung did not accept Freud's libido theory nor the role he assigned to infantile sexuality. Shortly after publishing *Psychology of the Unconscious* in 1913, Jung left the psychoanalytic movement for good and resigned from his position in Zurich University. He then had a breakdown, and for a time suffered from anxiety and hallucinations. He thereafter devoted all his time to an in-depth self-analysis which he called in his autobiography his "confrontation with the unconscious"; it was at this time that he developed most of the concepts which belong to his way of understanding mental life – the collective unconscious, archetypes, individuation, Jungian dream-interpretation – as well as his own therapeutic method, which he called "analytical psychology".

From then on, he followed his own path; during this post-Freudian period, he gradually gathered a certain number of followers around him and his work became more and more widely known internationally. In 1921, he published *Psychological Types*, in which he draws up a typological classification of psychological development based on the idea of individuation. However, his views on the psychology of different peoples led him at times to adopt a racist and even anti-Semitic ideology, so that his stance with respect to national-socialist dogma was somewhat ambiguous. During the Second World War, which he spent for the most part in an isolated tower he had built for himself in Bollingen, Jung concentrated on his psychotherapeutic practice and on writing various papers. His research touched on a wide variety of topics including alchemy, spirituality and mysticism; he tried to establish connections between these domains and his own phenomenological conception of the development of the mind through individuation. Jung died in Küssnacht in 1961.

How are we to define Jung's role and that of his thinking in our contemporary world? According to Taylor (2002), twentieth-century historians see Jung above all as an acolyte of Freud, and Jung's theory was regarded as a dissident voice in the psychoanalytical *corpus*. However, more recent research into the history of depth psychology tends to show that Jung was a genuine exponent of the "symbolic hypothesis", in continuity with nineteenth-century psychologies of transcendence, though the fact of his being indebted to Freud is still acknowledged. Taylor claims that that influence continues to be important in contemporary society:

> *To these earlier roots, we may attribute rising interest in Jungian ideas within the psychotherapeutic counterculture in Western countries. Meanwhile, credentialed Jungian analysts continue to identify their lineage as a variant of Freud and to seek legitimacy within the wider mainstream culture of psychology and psychiatry by their increased efforts to colonize the field of psychoanalysis, when they actually have an as yet unclaimed lineage of their own.* (Taylor 2002: 300)

Discovering the text

Page numbers are those of *The Standard Edition of the Complete Psychological Works of Sigmund Freud*, vol. **9**, 1–95.

• "Gradiva": *the narrative*

Hanold, the hero of the story, is an archaeologist with a passion for his work; he enjoys travelling and lives a more or less ordinary life, though from time to time he suffers from a *"temporary delusion"* (1907a: 72). As a child, Hanold dearly loved a little girl who lived close by, Zoë Bertgang (in German, "Bertgang" means *"someone who steps along brilliantly"* [ibid.: 37]). In adolescence, unsettled by his developing sexuality, he turned away from the young girl and from women in general, going as far as to ignore them completely. However, Hanold had seen in a museum a sculpture representing a young woman of ancient times, and he was fascinated by her elegant gait and in particular by the way she placed her foot. He bought a plaster cast of the bas-relief and hung it in his study; he gave the girl the name of "Gradiva" – "the girl who steps along". The attraction which this mysterious young Roman woman had for him grew and grew, so that he could think of little else. One night, he dreamt that he was in Pompeii shortly before the eruption of Vesuvius, and that he met Gradiva there; in the dream, he tried to warn her of the danger which was threatening her, but to no avail. When he awoke, impelled by a passionate unconscious wish, Hanold left for Pompeii.

Once there, he met in the ruins of the buried city a young woman whom he took to be Gradiva – but in fact it was Zoë, his childhood neighbour and friend, who also happened to be visiting Pompeii. The novelist gives us a very talented description of the ins and outs of the various encounters between the two protagonists, and skilfully brings his readers to a point where they too find themselves sharing Hanold's doubts and even delusion: can the young woman of whom from time to time he catches a glimpse really be the Gradiva who lived two thousand years ago? At that point it falls to Zoë, alias Gradiva, as Jensen describes her, to play a therapeutic role: just as a therapist might do, she begins to share part of Hanold's delusion, without being taken in by it. Her remarks have a double sense, so that she can talk to him carefully, make him face up to his delusional ideas and encourage him to relinquish them. At the end of the story, Hanold acknowledges that Gradiva was in fact Zoë, whom he loved without realizing the fact, and he no longer has to displace that love on to the woman represented in the antique bas-relief sculpture. Jensen concludes his narrative by allowing us to discover, with not a little surprise, a particularly significant detail from the psychoanalytic point of view: Hanold's quest was unwittingly determined by an infantile wish which was both earlier in time and hidden more deeply – the wish to seek out his mother who had died when he was a child, as though the last memory of his mother had been buried under layers of forgetfulness as a consequence of some psychological upheaval resembling the eruption of a volcano.

- *Fictional characters portrayed as in a clinical situation*

In his comments on Jensen's story, Freud studies the fictional characters as if they were in a clinical situation. He shows that Hanold's dreams, fantasies and delusion can be analysed using the same therapeutic procedure as for the dreams and fantasies of patients in analysis. For example, when Hanold dreams of meeting Gradiva in Pompeii, the content of the dream shows itself to be the fulfilment of an unconscious repressed wish to be in contact once more with the woman he loves and desires, just as Freud had suggested was the case in *The Interpretation of Dreams* (1900a). However, given that these sexual drives were consciously unacceptable and had to be repressed, Hanold turns away from the woman he loves in reality – Zoë – and towards a mythical figure, Gradiva. It is the return of these repressed sexual drives which compels him to set out on his pathological journey to Pompeii, to hallucinate the presence of Gradiva and to fail to recognize Zoë. In other words, the novelist's story reinforces Freud's thesis, because the narrative shows that what in fact determines Hanold's dreams and delusion has to do with the repression of his sexual drives. In addition, Freud shows that the dreams which novelists attribute to their protagonists can be interpreted in just the same way as those of patients in analysis. Freud emphasizes also the similarity between the psychoanalyst's therapeutic role and that which Jensen attributes to Zoë – she is the person who gradually helps Hanold to distinguish between hallucination and reality and to succeed in consciously accepting his desire for Zoë, a truly alive and lively young woman whose name means "life".

Development of Freud's concepts

Freud and literary or artistic creation

In 1907, for the first time, Freud examined a work of literature in the light of psychoanalysis. Let us think for a moment about his relationship to artistic creation. Art in all its forms and in particular works of literature have always been of great interest to Freud and other analysts, fascinated as they are by the artist's capacity to stir up emotions in the spectator or reader. In works of literature, the choice of themes such as Sophocles' *Oedipus Rex* or Shakespeare's *Hamlet* has enabled significant parallels to be drawn between the affairs of fictional characters and the conflicts we observe in patients who are in analysis. Those parallels have enabled psychoanalysts – beginning with Freud himself – to see fictional characters as potential clinical cases.

Freud gave considerable thought to what made an artist produce a work of art and to how an artistic creation could have such an emotional impact on the spectator or reader. He felt that the source of the artist's creativity lay in his or her own unconscious, with the artist's internal fantasy world being projected into the work of art – the painter on to canvas, the writer into the characters of the novel or play.

> *The author no doubt proceeds differently. He directs his attention to the unconscious in his own mind, he listens to its possible developments and lends them artistic expression instead of suppressing them by conscious criticism. Thus he experiences from himself what we learn from others – the laws which the activities of the unconscious must obey.* (1907a: 92)

That is what enables us to analyse not only the work of art itself but also its author.

As for the impact on the reader of a work of literature or on someone looking at a painting, Freud says that the effect is brought about through identification. Identification is the result of the artist's repressed wishes being hidden in the work of art as presented and of the artist's intention to awaken in the person looking at or reading it the same emotional quality which inspired it in the first place (Freud 1914b).

Freud's initiative has encouraged many psychoanalysts to contribute their thoughts to the study of works of art. Among recent writings on the subject, I would mention Hanna Segal's (1991) point of view, which goes deeper than Freud's. For Segal, the artist is not seeking simply to communicate an unconscious wish through the work of art; there is also the search for a *fantasy solution* to an unconscious problem, as well as the attempt to communicate the *need for reparation* which lies at the heart of the artist's creative impulse. Segal draws a parallel between dreams and works of art; yet, as she says, unlike dreams, works of art can be "embodied" in material reality. That is why their aesthetic impact depends in part on the way in which artists use the actual concrete medium with which they express symbolically their fantasies: "[The artist] is not only a dreamer, but a supreme artisan. An artisan may not be an artist, but an artist must be an artisan" (Segal 1991: 176).

Post-Freudians

Are neurosis and psychosis juxtaposed in "Gradiva"?

Delusions and Dreams in Jensen's "Gradiva" is interesting not only from the point of view of psychoanalysis applied to a work of literature, but also on the theoretical and clinical levels. As far as the clinical approach is concerned, Freud's remarkable gift for observation enables him to devise a whole range of symptoms which he ascribes to neurosis, such as Hanold's inhibition with respect to women and his temporary hallucinatory delusion. Freud, however, uses only the term "delusion" when writing of Hanold's hallucinations, never that of "psychosis". Could we nevertheless talk of psychosis in this case?

The comments of post-Freudian psychoanalysts vary widely on that question. For those who adhere strictly to Freud's text, Hanold's delusion has mainly to do with a temporary obfuscation of consciousness, non-psychotic, which can be observed from time to time in neurotic personalities (Jeanneau 1990). For other post-Freudian psychoanalysts who read "Gradiva" with an eye to Freud's later writings on the denial of reality and splitting of the ego, Hanold's hallucinations belong to that part of his ego which denies a reality that it finds unbearable, while the rest of his ego accepts it. From that point of view, Hanold is cured once the part that accepts reality for what it is dominates the part of his ego that denies reality. According to Ladame (1991), Hanold's delusion and hallucinations are typical of the kind of psychopathology which we encounter in adolescents; nowadays we would talk of a psychotic breakdown, the outcome of which may vary considerably from one individual to the other. Danielle Quinodoz (2002) has emphasized the way in which Freud offers psychoanalysts a model which shows "how to address the 'mad' part of our patients without neglecting the rest of their person" (D. Quinodoz 2002 [2003: 53]). She goes on to say that the fact that Hanold can be both delusional and capable of leading a more or less normal life implies a splitting of his ego – the kind of phenomenon which we often come across nowadays in patients she calls "heterogeneous". The situation in which, within the same individual, a delusional part and another part which takes reality on board coexist, requires the psychoanalyst to adopt a very specific technical approach. Although Zoë, for example, is not taken in by Hanold's delusion, she is very careful not to say this to him immediately; "her remarks have a double sense" such that they can be understood not only by Hanold's delusional part but also by that part of his personality that is perfectly aware of reality.

If we read what Freud had to say on this topic in the light of later comments, it seems obvious that in most of the clinical cases he describes he does juxtapose mechanisms typical of psychosis and those that have more to do with neurosis. Even though he makes no attempt to conceptualize this, we can observe this approach of his from *Studies on Hysteria* in 1895 all the way through to the "Wolf-Man" case in 1918. In *An Outline of Psycho-Analysis* (1940a [1938]), Freud argues that not only in psychotics but also in neurotics and in normal individuals there coexists – to a variable extent, perhaps – a part of the ego which denies reality and a part which accepts it.

Several writers have pointed out how the topic of fetishism is ubiquitous in this paper of Freud's – as Jean Bellemin-Noël (1983) has noted: from foot fetishism to Gradiva's gait.

New concepts

Hallucination – hallucinatory delusion – neurosis – psychoanalysis applied to a work of literature – psychosis

"ANALYSIS OF A PHOBIA IN A FIVE-YEAR-OLD BOY ('LITTLE HANS')"

(1909b)

The first ever child analysis

This case study is an account of the very first psychoanalytical treatment of a child. It was the little boy's father, Max Graf, who conducted the treatment of "Little Hans" (alias Herbert Graf), a quite common practice at the time. The analysis lasted from January to May 1908 and was supervised by Freud on the basis of the observations the boy's father noted down and communicated to Freud. Freud himself took an active part on only one occasion – a discussion with both father and son which was to prove decisive. Freud wrote an account of the treatment and, with the father's permission, published it in 1909. This article appeared in the first issue of the psychoanalytical review, the *Jahrbuch für Psychoanalytische und Psychopathologische Forschungen*, which the first Psychoanalytical Congress in Salzburg the previous year had decided to found. Though the review did not last long, it was published until the outbreak of the First World War.

What can we learn from this case study? First, "Little Hans" provided Freud with "proof" – which he very much needed – of the accuracy of his hypotheses concerning the existence of sexuality in children in general. Second, the ability to cure a case of phobia was an excellent illustration of how the therapeutic potential of psychoanalysis could be used not only with adults but also with children.

Biographies and history

"Little Hans": a brilliant career as director of opera

Little Hans's parents were no strangers to Freud because his mother, Olga Graf, had been analysed by Freud some years previously. Hans's father, Max Graf, was a composer and music critic; he had met Freud in 1900 and, passionately interested in the discoveries which psychoanalysis was making, regularly took part in the meetings of the "Psychological Wednesday Society" until 1913. From 1906 on, when Little Hans was not quite 3 years old, Max Graf began sharing with Freud the observations he was making of his son. In so doing, he was acceding to Freud's request that his closest followers should take notes on everything which had to do with infantile sexuality so as to buttress the hypotheses he had put forward in *Three Essays on the Theory of Sexuality* in 1905. Freud used some of the observations made by Little Hans's father in two articles, "The Sexual Enlightenment of Children" (Freud 1907c) and "On the Sexual Theories of Children" (Freud 1908c). The "Little Hans" case report published in 1909 gives us an account of the work of interpretation and processing which was required to resolve, at least in part, the conflicts underpinning the phobic symptom.

Afterwards Freud lost touch with both the boy and his parents, but in a Postscript he wrote in 1922, he tells us that in the spring of that year he had a visit from a young man who informed him that he was the "Little Hans" of whom Freud had written in 1909. Freud was glad to learn that the boy for whom "*a most evil future had been foretold*" (1909b: 148) was in perfect health and no longer suffered from inhibition. Freud learned also that Hans's parents had divorced and that each of them had remarried. Freud was nonetheless surprised to learn that the young man had no memory of his psychoanalytic treatment.

Herbert Graf, whose godfather was the composer Gustav Mahler, became a renowned director of opera. He was appointed stage manager of the Metropolitan Opera in New York, then returned to Europe to finish his career as director of the Grand Theatre in Geneva. Though he had a brilliantly successful professional career, his private life was marked by an unhappy marriage; as a result, he sought analysis with Hugo Solms in Geneva in 1970. He died in Geneva in 1973. Herbert Graf (1972) published four interviews with the journalist Francis Rizzo under the title "Memoirs of an Invisible Man" in which he states publicly that he was "Little Hans". Unlike his father, however, he was not interested in psychoanalysis; Max Graf was instrumental in publishing a paper of Freud's after the latter's death – in 1906 Freud had given to Max Graf the manuscript of his "Psychopathic Characters on the Stage" (Freud 1942a [1905–1906]).

Discovering the text

Page numbers are those of *The Standard Edition of the Complete Psychological Works of Sigmund Freud*, vol. **10**, 1–147.

- ## *Proof of the importance of sexuality in a young child*

Freud's account is divided into two parts: the first is a short introduction which brings together the observations made by the father of "Little Hans" when the boy was aged between 3 and 5, the period immediately before the outbreak of the phobia; the second is a narrative of how the treatment progressed and is followed by Freud's own comments.

Accurately written down by his father, Little Hans's thoughts on sexual matters clearly showed that the young boy was very preoccupied with the enigma of sexuality in all of its forms. In addition, what had been observed in this little boy could be applied more generally to all children however young they were, since there was nothing pathological about the case. The observations reported by Hans's father lent support to the hypotheses Freud had put forward in *Three Essays on the Theory of Sexuality* as regards the existence of infantile sexuality; these hypotheses had for the most part been deduced from memories which adult patients had communicated in the course of their analysis.

- ## *Early manifestations of infantile sexuality in "Little Hans"*

In the father's notes, Freud found proof of the particularly keen interest this little boy took in his own body and especially in his penis, which he called his "*widdler*". That particular organ became the object of his unflagging curiosity and was a source both of pleasure and of anxiety. He hardly stopped asking his parents about it. "*Daddy, have you got a widdler too?*", he asked his father, who answered in the affirmative. From time to time, however, the answers he obtained were ambiguous, especially when his questions related to his mother or to little girls. One day, as he watched his mother undressing, she asked him:

"*What are you staring at me like that for?*"
Hans: "*I was only looking to see if you'd got a widdler too.*"
Mother: "*Of course. Didn't you know that?*" (1909b: 9–10)

With that ambiguous reply, did Hans's mother simply mean that she too had an orifice for urinating, or was she implying that she too had a penis? For Freud the latter possibility is much more important in the little boy's eyes; this thought creates in his mind an *"infantile sexual theory"* according to which women have a penis just as men do. Freud was struck by how convinced the young child was of this; he was probably all the more convinced of it given his mother's answer, in spite of his father's saying the opposite – that girls do not have a penis. Here is an extract from this kind of conversation between father and son:

> *"Hans had promised to go with me to Lainz the next Sunday, March 15th,"* writes Hans's father. *"He resisted at first, but finally went with me all the same. [. . .] On the way I explained to him that his sister has not got a widdler like him. Little girls and women, I said, have no widdlers: Mummy has none, Hanna has none, and so on."*
> Hans: *"Have you got a widdler?"*
> I: *"Of course. Why, what do you suppose?"*
> Hans (after a pause): *"But how do little girls widdle, if they have no widdlers?"*
> I: *"They don't have widdlers like yours. Haven't you noticed already, when Hanna was being given her bath?"* (ibid.: 31)

Freud was surprised to discover that children very often have misperceptions on this matter and do not appear to integrate what they actually observe – for example, that little girls do not have "widdlers"; this is where feelings of castration anxiety begin. Hans's father notes that when the boy was 3½ years old, his mother saw him one day with his hand on his penis.

> *She threatened him in these words: "If you do that, I shall send for Dr A to cut off your widdler. And then what'll you widdle with?"*
> Hans: *"With my bottom"*. (ibid.: 8)

This, says Freud, was the occasion of his acquiring the "castration complex", which plays such a decisive role in the emergence of a neurosis.

As we read more and more of the report, we cannot fail to be surprised by the sheer relevance of Hans's questions and above all by his search for truth, especially when either his father or his mother give him answers which do not satisfy him. For example, the birth of his sister Hanna in October 1906, when he was 3½, was the great event of his life:

"April 14th. The theme of Hanna is uppermost," writes Hans's father in the notes he prepared for Freud.

> *As you may remember from earlier records, Hans felt a strong aversion to the new-born baby that robbed him of a part of his parents' love. This dislike has not entirely disappeared and is only partly overcompensated by an exaggerated affection. He has already several times expressed a wish that the stork should bring no more babies and that we should pay him money not to bring any more "out of the big box" where babies are.* (ibid.: 68)

Hans had understood that Hanna had been in there and that she had come out like a *"lumf"* (the word he had invented to designate faeces). In the months that followed the birth of his sister, Hans was not simply jealous: he several times went as far as to express the wish that she might die, at the same time openly declaring how fond he was of her.

- ### The Oedipal situation and the conflict of ambivalence with respect to the father

Freud was delighted to see that Hans *"confirms in the most concrete and uncompromising manner"* (ibid.: 111) what he had written in *The Interpretation of Dreams* and in *Three Essays on the Theory of Sexuality*: *"Hans really was a little Oedipus who wanted to have his father 'out of the way', to get rid of him, so that he might be alone with his beautiful mother and sleep with her"* (ibid.: 111). Hans's wish to sleep with her and *"coax with"* her had originated during the summer holidays, when his father was often away; the little boy expressed the wish that his father should *"go away"* and *"be* permanently *away*" – in other words, the wish that his father be "*dead*". For Freud, this death-wish aimed at the father is a feature of all little boys and is part of the normal Oedipal situation; however, when it becomes exacerbated it may lie at the origin of various symptoms, as was the case with Hans. In this way, the conflict of ambivalence between love and hate becomes a central focus of the Oedipal situation.

> *But this father, whom he could not help hating as a rival, was the same father whom he had always loved and was bound to go on loving, who had been his model, had been his first playmate, and had looked after him from his earliest infancy: and this it was that gave rise to the first conflict. Nor could this conflict find an immediate solution.* (ibid.: 134)

Freud also observes that at this age Hans showed his affection to little boys and girls indiscriminately. "*Hans was a homosexual (as all children may very well be), quite consistently with the fact, which much always be kept in mind, that* he was acquainted with only one kind of genital organ – *a genital organ like his own*" (ibid.: 110). In this paper, as in many of his later writings, Freud gives the penis a pivotal role in the psychosexual development of boys and girls alike. He does, however, mention here the possibility that little boys may be able to envisage the existence of the vagina:

> *But although the sensations of his penis had put him on the road to postulating a vagina, yet he could not solve the problem, for within his experience no such thing existed as his widdler required. On the contrary, his conviction that his mother possessed a penis just as he did stood in the way of any solution.* (ibid.: 135)

Though on several occasions in this paper Freud mentions fantasies which are specifically linked to female sexuality, he does not connect them explicitly to any particular conception of female sexuality which would be the counterpart of male sexuality: this challenge would later be taken up by his followers, and in particular by female psychoanalysts. Freud's conception of sexuality remained "phallocentric", that is, based on the idea that the difference between the sexes is essentially a matter of possessing or of not possessing a penis. In my view, that conception amounts to the persistence in Freud himself of an infantile sexual theory about the difference between the sexes, as I pointed out earlier.

• *The process of curing an infantile phobia by means of psychoanalysis*

Little Hans's analysis was motivated by the emergence of a major phobia: the boy began to refuse to leave his home and go outdoors in case he might be bitten or knocked over by a horse. Freud explains the establishment of this phobic symptom as being the result of a compromise: Hans's fear of being bitten by a horse was the consequence of displacing on to the animal his unconscious anxiety about being castrated by his father. But where did this castration anxiety spring from? The clinical material shows that this fear originated in Hans's inability to resolve the Oedipus complex: on the one hand, he felt a powerful incestuous attachment to his mother which went as far as to want to sleep with her and eliminate the father – wishes that the little boy experienced as intolerable; and on the other hand, he felt strongly attracted to his father yet at the same time hated him as a rival, standing in the way as he tried to reach his mother – and this experience was just as intolerable. For Freud, the combination of Hans's incestuous wish for his mother and the guilt feelings he experienced for hating his beloved father activated in the little boy the fear of being punished – by being castrated – for his forbidden desires.

But is this not the kind of Oedipal situation which every little boy finds himself in, as we can see if we pay some attention to what goes on in them? On what grounds are we to make a distinction between the normal Oedipal situation and a pathological one, between normal castration anxiety and one which will give rise to a phobic symptom? It may be that the birth of his little sister when he was 3½ fuelled Hans's Oedipus conflict by intensifying his jealousy towards his sister, as well as his anger against his mother and father, the genitors of the new baby.

For Freud, the pathogenic element which created the phobia is not to be found in Hans's death-wishes aimed at his sister, because the little boy was able to talk about them openly. The true cause of the phobia lies in the death-wishes aimed at his father, because these were repressed into the unconscious. To feel such hatred towards his beloved father could not be tolerated by the boy's consciousness: his aggressive impulses were repressed, and the anxiety about being castrated by his father was displaced, taking the form of a fear of being bitten or knocked over by a horse. This compromise-formation/symptom enabled Hans to go on loving his father consciously and to avoid feeling an intolerable hatred towards him, for such a situation implied a deadlock that he would never have been able to resolve.

After the therapy reached this crucial stage, no more progress was being made, which was why Freud himself decided to intervene. When Freud met Hans and his father together, he realized that certain details which the little boy had noticed in horses must have reminded him of his father – the eyeglasses and moustache; he pointed this out to the little boy. This was a turning-point in the treatment, which from then on was firmly on the road to a complete cure. Freud had in fact interpreted the little boy's transference on to his father; the explanation he gave helped Hans to become aware of the reasons for his displacing on to the animal both his death-wishes against his father and his fear of being castrated by the latter.

I should add that the analysis of this case enabled Freud to show that there was no fundamental difference between pathological manifestations of infantile sexuality and normal ones. For example, castration anxiety and incestuous libidinal or aggressive impulses are present both in children who suffer from phobic symptoms and in those whose development can be considered to be normal. The difference between normal and pathological depends above all on a quantitative factor: when the internal situation creates an excess of anxiety which cannot be processed, there appears a compromise-formation/symptom. For Freud, this infantile neurosis constitutes a model which is of general application, because it proves that neuroses in adults are closely related to the same infantile complex which we discovered in Little Hans's phobia. In *Inhibition, Symptoms and Anxiety*, Freud (1926d) reconsidered the case of Little Hans when he came to modify his theory of anxiety in the light of his introduction of the superego, a notion which had not as yet been conceptualized in 1909.

Post-Freudians

Little Hans's passive and active tendencies looked at in retrospect

The "Little Hans" case elicited a considerable number of comments, of which I shall discuss only a few.

Some psychoanalysts have quite correctly noted that Freud took account in his interpretations only of Little Hans's wish to identify with his father through becoming his mother's husband, and in so doing replace his father – in other words that he gave pride of place to the direct or positive Oedipus complex, neglecting the inverted or negative one. Nonetheless, according to Silverman (1980) and Frankiel (1991), Freud did have at his disposal certain indications which showed how Hans had also the wish to identify with his mother, with the aim of taking over her place. For example, the report of the case reveals Hans's eroticized attachment to his father, his wish to have babies like his mother, his identification with his pregnant mother as well as his anger and feelings of rivalry with respect to her. We may wonder why Freud did not make use of this material, even though he was beginning to understand the importance of bisexuality and the need to interpret not only the wishes and defences associated with the direct form of the Oedipus complex but also those connected with its inverted form, if the neurosis was to be resolved. Among the reasons which may have motivated Freud's abstention, we must remember that, at the time when "Little Hans" was being treated, Freud was still using the idea of constitutional bisexuality; it was only in 1923 that he would begin to talk both of psychic bisexuality and of the negative or inverted form of the Oedipus complex. In addition, we may assume that the fact that Freud had little to say about Hans's conflicts with his mother had also to do with reasons of confidentiality, because Hans's mother had previously been in analysis with Freud. It is true also that Freud often gives us a masterly description of clinical phenomena which will only later be conceptualized, either by Freud himself or by his psychoanalyst followers: this is why the contemporary reader always finds it interesting to return to Freud's writings and read them through again.

Mahony (1993) has made a close study of the notes Max Graf took of his son over a period of more than two years. He was the first to suggest that there must inevitably be distortions in the transcription of the clinical material. For Mahony, writing up these notes must have played a decisive transference role in the little boy's treatment; the turning-point came when "Little Hans" actively took upon himself the task of setting down what was to be transmitted to Freud, dictating his statements to his father. "*If I write everything to the Professor, my nonsense'll soon be over, won't it?*" (Freud 1909b: 61). With a play upon the polysemous nature of the words used, Mahony calls his paper "The Dictator and his Cure" in order to highlight in a condensed fashion both the authoritarian determination of the little boy and the active part he took in dictating what should be written down – the report thus becoming "his *own* activity" (Mahony 1993: 1250).

Biographies and history

Pioneers in the field of child psychoanalysis

Hermine Hug-Hellmuth (1871–1924)

Hermine Hug-Hellmuth is still relatively unknown, even though she was, historically speaking, the very first child psychoanalyst. In 1910, after beginning analysis with Isidor Sadger, she decided to stop working as a schoolteacher and concentrate wholly on child psychoanalysis. In 1913 she was admitted to membership of the Vienna Society and took part in the meetings of the Wednesday Society. She wrote several papers in which she argued that the intellectual and emotional development of children begins in the very first weeks of life, as do their earliest sexual feelings and masturbation. Hermine Hug-Hellmuth was also the first psychoanalyst to draw attention to the value of play in children, but simply as a means of observing their development; the use of play technique as such in psychotherapy was developed later by Melanie Klein, then by Anna Freud. At the Congress in The Hague in 1920, Hermine Hug-Hellmuth argued that in child psychoanalysis it was necessary to keep in mind the "pedagogical" and "educational" dimension (Geissmann and Geissman 1992). Hermine Hug-Hellmuth died in 1924, strangled by her nephew Rolf, whom she had taken into analysis because of his behaviour problems. Her murder was brandished by the detractors of psychoanalysis, who publicly denounced the dangers which this approach was creating for children and adolescents.

Melanie Klein (1882–1960)

Loss, mourning and depression

Born in Vienna in 1882, Melanie Klein had very early on in her life to cope with problems relating to mourning: she lost her older sister when she was 4 years old. Her relationship with her mother was highly ambivalent; her mother was said to be very possessive and intrusive, and Melanie had bouts of severe depression. In 1902, when she was 20, her brother Emmanuel, whom she loved very much, died. One year later, in 1903, she married Arthur Klein, an engineer, by whom she had three children: Melitta, born in 1904, Hans, born in 1907, and Erich, born in 1914, one year after the death of Melanie's mother. In 1914, Melanie began her first analysis with Sándor Ferenczi in Budapest; he encouraged her to develop her interest in early infantile fantasies and in child analysis. In 1919, she read a paper called "The Development of a Child" (Klein 1921), an account of her observations of a young infant (who was none other than her own son, Erich), and became a member of the Hungarian Psycho-Analytical Association. In that year too, she left Hungary because of the political unrest and the anti-Semitism which was rife there, and moved to Berlin, where she settled with her children, while her husband settled in Sweden. They divorced in 1923.

The technique of child psychoanalysis

It was while she was in Berlin that Klein put the finishing touches to her technique of infant observation from a strictly psychoanalytic point of view, as she put it. In addition, she began a second analysis, this time with Karl Abraham, whose thinking had an enormous influence on her; she always considered herself one of his followers and believed that her own work was a continuation of his (Segal 1979). The analysis ended when Karl Abraham died in December 1925. In that year, she was invited to give a series of lectures in London; she was made to feel very welcome there, which was no longer the case in Berlin now that Abraham was dead. When she was invited by Jones to stay for a while in London, she left Berlin in September 1926 and, shortly afterwards, decided to settle in London. In 1932 she published *The Psycho-Analysis of Children*, in which she discusses her new insights into the early stages of development in boys and girls.

Conflicts with Anna Freud

Melanie Klein was at first warmly welcomed by her British colleagues. But from 1927 on, Anna Freud was developing a different view of child analysis and began to criticize Melanie Klein more and more scathingly (Grosskurth 1986). Nonetheless, Klein was regarded as a key figure and a pioneer by her colleagues in the British Psychoanalytical Society, and she had a significant impact on the way they worked (Hinshelwood 2002). She had begun to write her key paper on depression (published in 1935) when she lost her son Hans at the age of 26 in a mountaineering accident in 1934. That was a particularly sad year for Klein, all the more so because she was bitterly criticized by Edward Glover (who analysed her daughter Melitta Schmideberg) and by Melitta herself. Among other grievances, Melitta accused her mother of being the cause of her brother's "suicide" (there is in fact no doubt that it was an accident). But the strongest opposition was yet to come when, in 1938, Anna Freud arrived in London with her father, fleeing the rise of Nazism in Austria. With the aim of debating the theoretical positions and conceptions of all concerned, the British Society organized in 1943 – the war was still on – a series of Scientific Discussions known as the "Controversial Discussions" which have left us with some remarkable texts (King and Steiner 1991). After reaching a gentleman's agreement, the protagonists decided to form three psychoanalytic groups under the aegis of the British Society: one school of thought was headed by Anna Freud, another by Melanie Klein and the third included the majority of the members of the society who did not adhere to one or the other of these – this was the "Middle Group", later known as the "Independents' Group" after Klein's death. These three distinct groups are still in existence, but the scientific differences between their members are nowadays much less pronounced (King and Steiner 1991).

Analysis through play: an innovative technique

Melanie Klein was the inventor of a new method of child psychoanalysis: the play technique, which she developed as the basic approach to child analysis (not simply as a method of observation).

> *Klein's stroke of genius lay in noticing that the child's natural mode of expressing himself was play, and that play could therefore be used as a means of communication with the child. Play for the child is not "just play". It is also work. It is not only a way of exploring and mastering the internal world but also, through expressing and working-through phantasies, a means of exploring and mastering anxieties. In his play the child dramatizes his phantasies, and in doing so elaborates and works through his conflicts.* (Segal 1979: 36)

In other words, with children, play can reveal the same fantasies as their dreams, but unlike the latter it includes an element of reality-testing.

For Melanie Klein, the child makes an immediate and very powerful transference on to the psychoanalyst; she maintained that the negative transference also had to be interpreted, unlike Anna Freud, for whom what was initially important was to prepare the child for analysis by creating a therapeutic alliance. In addition, Klein argued that the educational methods advocated by Hermine Hug-Hellmuth or Anna Freud had no place in the psychoanalytic approach to children and served only to confuse the young patient. For Klein, a true psychoanalytic situation can be created only by psychoanalytic means. Little by little, between 1919 and 1923, Klein put the finishing touches to her views on the specific setting required for child analysis, with its precise times of sessions, each child having his or her own box of toys – houses, dolls of both sexes and various sizes, animals, modelling clay, pencils, string, scissors . . . For Winnicott, that option marked "the most significant advance in child analysis" (Segal 1979: 42).

On the theoretical level, the expertise that Melanie Klein acquired through child analysis enabled her to put forward a certain number of hypotheses which have increased our knowledge in particular of the early stages of child development. From that point of view, we could say that if Freud discovered the child-in-the-adult, Melanie Klein was instrumental in discovering the infant-in-the-child.

A comparison between Freud and Klein

On a great number of topics, Melanie Klein is at one with Freud's thinking and in complete agreement with the basic psychoanalytic tenets he postulated: the existence of the unconscious, the part played by infantile sexuality, the Oedipus complex, the transference and other key aspects. That said, on a certain number of other issues, Klein's ideas are at variance with those of Freud; the conclusions she drew were disputed over many a long year, but a good number of contemporary psychoanalysts now treat several of her proposed hypotheses as going almost without saying.

Here are some of the issues on which Klein's opinion was at variance with that of Freud. She argued that the object is knowable from the very beginning of life, whereas, for Freud, it was much later that the infant discovered the existence of the object (his hypothesis of primary narcissism). Klein showed that the Oedipus complex was functional long before Freud had thought – she argued in favour of the "Early Stages of the Oedipus Conflict" (Klein 1928). She claimed that this primitive complex had its origin in the oral and anal drives, not only in the genital ones, and that it was constructed on the basis of part-objects (and not, at that stage, of whole-objects). In Klein's theory, the early stages of the Oedipus complex are a significant element in primitive object relations. She completed Freud's description of the psychosexual development of both boys and girls. She attached more importance than Freud did to the young boy's fixation on his mother – Freud was more concerned with the young girl's fixation. Her conception of female sexuality was also quite different from Freud's. It is not, she argued, the "castrated" equivalent of male sexuality; it has its own specific reality, based on the knowledge, in infants of both sexes, that the vagina exists *per se*. Klein went on to describe the fundamental anxiety which the little girl experiences: the fear of being robbed and emptied of the contents of her body (Klein 1932).

She hypothesized the existence of a primitive superego which is extremely severe. It is established *before* the Oedipus complex, not as a successor to it as in Freud's theory. In a paper he wrote in 1930, Freud refers explicitly to Klein's point of view: "Experience shows, however, that the severity of the superego which a child develops in no way corresponds to the severity of treatment which he has himself met with" (Freud 1930a [1929]: 130). Klein then went on to develop further original notions of her own, such as the depressive position (Klein 1935, 1940), then the paranoid-schizoid position and the concept of projective identification (1946); it was only gradually that these notions were fully understood and could gain acceptance.

It should be noted that Klein agreed with Freud when he postulated the existence of a death drive; her own important contribution was that of "primary envy", which predated jealousy (Klein 1957). The idea of envy is of significant help in clinical situations which result from the conflict between the life and death drives; that notion had remained basically theoretical before Klein and the post-Kleinians went on to develop some of its clinical aspects.

Anna Freud (1895–1982)

Analysed by her father

Anna Freud, Sigmund and Martha Freud's third daughter and the youngest of their six children, was also a pioneer of child psychoanalysis. As an adolescent, she was already interested in psychoanalysis, but trained first as a schoolteacher and practised that profession until 1920. At puberty, she began to have beating fantasies; that symptom was one of the main reasons for her having her first analysis, which lasted from 1918 until 1922, followed by another in 1924. In both cases, her analyst was her father. This was not a rare occurrence in those days, because psychoanalysts had not yet discovered the disadvantages to which this could give rise in the transference/counter-transference relationship. In 1922 she read a clinical paper on beating fantasies and was admitted to membership of the Vienna Psycho-Analytical Society at the age of 27.

Child psychoanalysis according to Anna Freud

In 1925, Anna Freud headed a seminar on child psychoanalysis in Vienna and in 1927 published an *Introduction to the Technique of Child Analysis* in which she presented her own ideas on child psychoanalysis. In her approach, she recommended using the child's dreams and drawings, and employing the play technique – but mainly with the aim of observing the child. She argued that the analyst should adopt an educational as well as a psychoanalytical attitude towards the child patient, although later she changed her opinion on this point when she discovered the role played by the defence mechanisms; it thereafter became possible to interpret the child's initial resistances. In her book, Anna Freud (1927a) was sharply critical of some of Melanie Klein's ideas. At that time, their differences of opinion had mainly to do with the transference: for Klein, this was a typical feature even in the early stages of the treatment, whereas Anna Freud argued that transference phenomena emerged much later. In addition, they disagreed over the implementation of the play technique and about the nature of the superego: for Klein, it was a primitive and harsh agency in infants, while for Anna Freud, given the immaturity of the child's ego, the superego could not be integrated at so young an age.

Towards the end of the 1920s, Anna Freud was becoming interested in the growth of the ego and in the problem of adaptation; she worked with Heinz Hartmann, one of the founders of *Ego Psychology*, before he left Vienna for the United States. It must be remembered, however, that Anna Freud always distanced herself somewhat from Ego Psychology; in her therapeutic practice, she called upon both of Freud's structural theories, choosing one or the other in accordance with what seemed beneficial for her young patient.

The Ego and the Mechanisms of Defence

In order to understand Anna Freud's contribution to psychoanalysis, we must take into account certain aspects of her personality which left a deep imprint on her professional life. Her work reveals her strong identification with her father – she was never to abandon that – as well as her capacity for developing her own original ideas (A-M. Sandler 1996).

In her book *The Ego and the Mechanisms of Defence* (1936), Anna Freud explored the manner in which the ego interacts with the id, the superego and external reality. She showed that, in pathological states, the excessive use of defence mechanisms may lead to an impoverishment of the ego and distort the perception of reality. In addition to the mechanisms of defence already known to psychoanalysis, she added two new ones: "identification with the aggressor" and "altruistic surrender", in which a person renounces his or her own wishes in order to experience them vicariously. In that book, Anna Freud drew a distinction between so-called primitive defences and those that are more developed, the latter requiring a higher degree of ego maturity.

Direct observation of children

Even in her earliest writings, Anna Freud attached great importance to the direct observation of children, as long as this were done from a psychoanalytic point of view. In her opinion, this kind of observation makes it easier to understand how even very young infants experience life events, and the results of these explorations can throw light on psychoanalytic theory and technique.

In addition, her unceasing concern for expanding the field of psychoanalysis laid the foundations for the creation of psychoanalytic institutions in which research and treatment could go hand in hand. In 1925 she set up in Vienna a nursery school for young underprivileged children with the help of Dorothy Burlingham, who was to remain a lifelong friend. Indeed, Burlingham's two children were the first cases of child analysis that Anna Freud undertook in 1923. In London, where she had taken refuge with her father and family in 1938, Anna Freud created – again with Dorothy Burlingham – the "Hampstead War Nurseries" for the care of children who had been separated from their parents. In parallel with John Bowlby, Anna Freud made an intensive study of the impact of mother–child separation; after the war, she campaigned in favour of allowing parents to visit their young children in hospital and, if the children were very young, of allowing mothers to stay with them on an ongoing basis. We may well feel that Anna Freud's obvious concern for underprivileged and neglected children had something to do with the fact that, as the youngest child in her family, she may have felt neglected by her older siblings. This was probably also one of the reasons for the importance she attached to preventive work with the child's parents and family circle.

The concept of "Lines of Development"

The heart of Anna Freud's theoretical and technical approach lies in a perspective which owes much to her concept of development, which is of wider scope that the one familiar to classical theory. For long the concept of development had been closely linked to that of libidinal phases as described by Freud in 1915; gradually it became necessary to include in the description of child development such factors as aggressiveness, object relations and the relationship between ego, id and superego, to name but a few. With this in mind, Anna Freud introduced an original notion – that of "lines of development" – in her book *Normality and Pathology in Childhood* (1965). The concept is based on the idea that someone who has been trained in psychoanalysis can make use of a detailed description of a child's behaviour to deduce valuable information about how his or her inner world functions.

Basing her work on the concept of lines of development, Anna Freud went on to describe ways of understanding the complexity of the phenomena which occur simultaneously throughout child and adolescent development until the onset of adulthood. Examples of such changes would be the age-related evolution of different kinds of anxiety, transformations associated with changes in bodily functions – feeding, toilet-training, etc. – and the shift from the newborn infant's dependence to the acquisition of autonomy. She emphasized the importance of examining each child's overall development; the main focus of psychoanalytic work, she argued, is to help the child find his or her way back into the normal developmental process.

Training prospective child psychoanalysts

In the aftermath of the Second World War, several of Anna Freud's "War Nurseries" colleagues wanted to follow a more structured course of training in order to become child psychotherapists. She therefore developed her own training programme in 1947, and in 1952 she founded the Hampstead Child Therapy Training Course and Clinic – nowadays known as "The Anna Freud Centre". Child observation concerns children under 5 years of age and plays a relatively small part in the training of future "psychoanalytically trained child therapists". In 1970 the British Psychoanalytical Society officially recognized the training programme developed in the Anna Freud Centre, which is open to candidates who wish to become child analysts.

New concepts

Castration anxiety – childhood phobia – infantile curiosity – infantile neurosis

"NOTES UPON A CASE OF OBSESSIONAL NEUROSIS (THE 'RAT MAN')"

(1909d)

Obsessional symptoms too have meaning and can be resolved by psychoanalysis

The psychoanalytic treatment of Ernst Lanzer, nicknamed the "Rat Man", convinced Freud that even severe obsessional symptoms can be cured by psychoanalysis, using the same technique as had proved successful in cases of hysteria. Obsessional neurosis – or "*doubting mania*" (Freud 1895b [1894]: 93) as it was also called – is characterized by inordinately compulsive phenomena which severely curtail the patient's freedom: rumination, obsessive ideas, compulsion to carry out undesirable acts, various rituals designed to struggle against these thoughts and acts, etc. Ernst Lanzer, for example, was terrified by the obsessive thought that the rat-torture might be inflicted on his father, hence the nickname given to him by Freud. Given the incapacitating nature of obsessional symptoms, the disorder had up till then been regarded as due to degeneracy or to some organic weakness of the mind. The successful outcome of this treatment enabled Freud to prove that obsessional neurosis is of psychological origin and that, just like hysteria, it derives from unconscious conflicts of a sexual and emotional nature; in addition, if the analysis succeeds in bringing to the patient's consciousness memories of significant conflicts which had occurred in childhood, the symptoms of the neurosis can be eliminated. Moreover, this treatment enabled Freud to highlight the decisive role of anal eroticism in obsessional neurosis as well as that of the conflict between love and hate which, from 1912 on, he was to call "conflict of ambivalence".

Many psychoanalysts have commented on this clinical case, especially now that the notes that Freud took have become available in their entirety. This has enabled us to learn significantly more about Freud's actual technique and compare its strengths and weaknesses with contemporary practice.

Biographies and history

Ernst Lanzer, the "Rat Man"

Ernst Lanzer, a 29-year-old lawyer, consulted Freud because he was suffering from so many obsessions that he was severely inhibited in everything he did in life. It took him ten years to complete his law studies at Vienna University, and he was finding it extremely difficult to adapt to professional work; as for his love life, he kept on postponing the idea of marriage. Ernst Lanzer had already consulted several eminent psychiatrists – to no avail – before beginning analysis with Freud on 1 October 1907. Freud realized at once the scientific interest which treating such a case could have, especially since the patient seemed to have a gift for the work. It seems also that Freud liked him a great deal: he even invited the patient one day to have lunch with Freud's family, a rare occurrence and one which ran counter to the ethical rules Freud himself advocated. On four occasions while the treatment was continuing, Freud presented to his colleagues in the Vienna Psycho-Analytical Society at their Wednesday meetings a report on the patient's progress. In 1908 he read a very highly thought-of paper about the case at the First International Psychoanalytical Congress in Salzburg; Freud's biographer, Ernest Jones, met Freud there for the first time and noted just how impressed he was by Freud's masterly presentation.

In addition to the report on the case published by Freud in 1909, we have available to us Freud's daily notes on how the treatment was progressing – this is quite exceptional, because Freud was in the habit of destroying his notes. These precious notes highlight Freud's talent as a writer – over and beyond the content, their literary quality enables the reader to make contact with the Rat Man's anxiety and to feel the empathy with which Freud approached his patient. Part of these notes were published in 1955 in the *Standard Edition* (1909d: 251–318, "Addendum: Original Record of the Case"); a complete version of Freud's original notes was published in German and translated into French by E. R. Hawelka in 1974.

Freud was very pleased with the outcome of the treatment; the patient was thereafter able to find employment, something that he had found impossible for several months before consulting Freud. In August 1914, Ernst Lanzer was called up for military service; taken prisoner by the Russian army, he died in November 1914, shortly after the outbreak of the First World War.

Discovering the text

Page numbers are those of *The Standard Edition of the Complete Psychological Works of Sigmund Freud*, vol. **10**, 151–249.

• *An astonishing series of obsessions*

When Ernst Lanzer consulted Freud, he described a whole range of obsessional symptoms which had gradually become worse and worse, to the extent that he had been quite unable to work for the previous two months: an irrational fear that something might happen to his beloved father and to a "*lady*" whom he admired; a fear that he might fall prey to a compulsive impulse to cut his own throat with a razor; and absurd prohibitions which invaded his mind more and more, to such an extent that his thinking and actions were completely paralysed.

Freud immediately made Ernst Lanzer promise to follow the rule of free association, which up to the present day remains the fundamental rule of psychoanalysis:

The next day I made him pledge himself to the one and only condition of the treatment – namely, to say everything that came into his head, even if it was unpleasant *to him, or seemed* unimportant *or* irrelevant *or senseless. I then gave him leave to start his communications with any subject he pleased.* (1909d: 159)

In that first session, Freud released the patient from his obsession to see women naked and from the idea that his father or the "*lady he admired*" might die. The patient told Freud that his voyeuristic obsession had begun around 6 or 7 years of age, when a pretty young governess would take him into her bed and let him caress her. These early sexual experiences were accompanied by intense excitation and an intolerable sense of guilt, thereby creating in the young boy's mind an insoluble conflict:

We find, accordingly: an erotic instinct and a revolt against it; a wish which has not yet become compulsive and, struggling against it, a fear which is already compulsive; a ditressing affect and an impulsion towards the performance of defensive acts. The inventory of the neurosis has reached its full muster. (ibid.: 163)

• *The great obsessive fear of rats*

It was the analysis of his patient's great obsessive fear of rats that enabled Freud to explore in depth the true causes of this obsessional neurosis and see how the symptoms could be eliminated. It had all started shortly before, the previous August, when the patient was in the army and had heard a captain describe a particularly horrible punishment used in the East. A pot was turned upside down and attached to the condemned man's buttocks; the pot contained rats, which burrowed their way into his anus. From the moment he heard this story, the patient was terrified at the obsessive idea that such a punishment might be inflicted on his father and on the lady he admired. In an attempt to drive away that intolerable idea, he would carry out a gesture of repudiation accompanied by the incantation "*Whatever are you thinking of*". Freud noticed that at each important point in the narrative, the patient had a strange look on his face which appeared to be "*one of* horror at pleasure of his own of which he himself was unaware" (ibid.: 167).

That narrative was the starting-point for the detailed analysis of the many obsessional thoughts and actions from which the patient suffered; the method systematically employed was that of the patient's free associations. At the end of this work of meticulous de-condensation, Freud succeeded in eliminating one after the other all of his patient's obsessive ideas and behaviour.

• *The relentless struggle between love and hate and anal eroticism*

In the Rat Man's analysis, Freud focused his interpretations mainly on his reconstruction of two fundamental conflicts: on the one hand, a triangular conflict between the patient himself, his father and the lady he admired – this conflict was seen mainly from the perspective of the Oedipal relationship with his father – and, on the other, the conflict between love and hate, given that the patient's obsessions were the consequence of an emotional imbalance associated with the fact that his hate was stronger than his love: "*A battle between love and hate was raging in the lover's breast, and the object of both of these feelings was one and the same person*" (ibid.: 191). In addition, the Oedipal conflict and that between love and hate were closely intertwined, so that together they formed the inextricable web which is typical of obsessional neurosis and its symptoms.

In the course of his report on the case, Freud shares with us the complex paths he had to follow in order to unravel this tangled web. With great patience, taking each obsessive idea or act in turn, he tries to discover its meaning – at first sight, absurd – and thereby make it comprehensible to his patient. Next, he tries to replace each element in network of wider meaning, a network which gradually expands as the work of the analysis progresses, so as to obtain an overall view of the psychopathology. Freud's reconstructions are based for the most part on the patient's free associations; he tries to convince the patient of the validity of his discoveries and in so doing creates a therapeutic alliance which was to prove extremely helpful for the success of the treatment. He does not, however, make very much use of the transference, even though on several occasions he does remark on the fact that transference elements are present – for example, when the patient dreams of Freud's daughter, when he insults Freud in his dreams, or when he addresses Freud as "*Captain*" during a session in which the transference is being explained.

• *Interpretation of compulsive symptoms and actions*

How did Freud analyse the patient's compulsive ideas and actions? I shall take a single example, that of the compulsion which seized hold of the Rat Man to remove a stone from the road along which the lady he admired was due to travel in order to protect her – then immediately to put the same stone back in its place. For Freud, the compulsive gesture of removing then replacing the stone is highly significant from a symbolic point of view, because by these contradictory actions the patient was expressing the doubts he had concerning the love he felt for her: removing the stone in order to protect her is an act based on love, while replacing it is based on hate, because by this gesture he recreates an obstacle which could cause the lady harm. Here Freud is giving a clinical description of what was later to be known as "undoing what has been done" – a two-stage compulsive action, the first part of which is cancelled out by the second.

According to Freud, the true meaning of this kind of action comes from the fact that the obsessional symptom juxtaposes two contradictory tendencies, love and hate, in such a way that both of them are simultaneously fulfilled. The patient, however, remains unaware of the hate component, and justifies his actions by means of rationalizations, i.e. hardly credible justifications which aim to hide the element of hate and keep it repressed into the unconscious. What characterizes this kind of neurosis, writes Freud, is the fact that

> *the love has not succeeded in extinguishing the hatred but only in driving it down into the unconscious; and in the unconscious the hatred, safe from the danger of being destroyed by the operations of consciousness, is able to persist and even to grow.* (ibid.: 239)

The theme of anal eroticism pervades the whole of this analysis, but here Freud does no more than mention it in passing; he does not yet give it the importance he would later attribute to it as a factor in obsessional neurosis. For example, he mentions it when he elucidates the patient's obsession with rats: it reawakened in the patient the memory of intensely erotic moments in his childhood, a pleasure which had been maintained over many years by an irritation of the rectum caused by worms. Freud mentions also the many symbolic meanings which involve money and anal eroticism and which determine the character traits typical of obsessional neurosis: for example, compulsive cleanliness associated with an obsessive fear of contamination, the equation between money and excrement, and between rats and children, the infantile sexual belief according to which babies are born *per anum*.

• *Neurotic and psychotic elements side by side*

Though Freud speaks of *"neurosis"* when discussing how to diagnose the Rat Man's disorder, on several occasions he notes elements which to my mind are more evocative of psychosis than of neurosis, yet they coexist side by side with their neurotic counterparts. For example, when the patient imagines that his parents can read his thoughts, Freud wonders if he is delusional: "*Indeed, something more is present, namely a kind of* delusion *or* delirium *with the strange content that his parents knew his thoughts because he spoke them out loud without his hearing himself do it*" (ibid.: 163–164). He again uses the term "*deliria*" (ibid.: 222) in describing the patient's compulsive action when, after working far into the night, he used to go to open the front door expecting his father to appear, although he knew that his father had died some nine years previously. That kind of belief is a denial of reality and as such is typical of psychotic thinking. Freud is reluctant to regard "*this idea [as] a delusion [. . .] that [. . .] oversteps the limits of obsessional neurosis*" (ibid.: 233), or as a relic of the old megalomania of infancy with the "omnipotence *which [the patient]* ascribed to his thoughts and feelings" (ibid.: 233). Freud mentions also the fact that Ernst Lanzer "*was to a high degree superstitious*" and that he believed in omens and premonitory dreams – though he goes on: "*Thus he was at once superstitious and not superstitious; and there was a clear distinction between his attitude and the superstition of uneducated people who feel themselves at one with their belief*" (ibid.: 229). In other words, Freud observes not only that the Rat Man simultaneously *believes and does not believe* in his superstitions, but also that he *believes and does not believe* in the death of his father.

Development of Freud's concepts

Freud's view of obsessional neurosis: thirty years of research

Freud was the first to identify obsessional neurosis as a specific psychopathological entity; this was in the period 1895–1896. However, in 1909, at the time of Ernst Lanzer, the Rat Man's analysis, Freud still had an incomplete picture of the psychopathology of the disorder. It took him about thirty years before the picture he drew was complete. I shall now briefly summarize the different stages in his thinking.

It was in 1895, in a letter to Fliess, that Freud first mentioned his feeling that the origin of the obsessive ideas and actions of these patients must involve some sexual trauma which occurred in their childhood. "*Have I revealed the great clinical secret to you, either orally or in writing? Hysteria is the consequence of a presexual* sexual *shock. Obsessional neurosis is the consequence of a presexual* sexual *pleasure, which is later transformed into* [*self-*]*reproach*" (Letter from Freud to Fliess, 15 October 1895 [Freud 1985c (1887–1904): 144]). In a series of articles published in 1895 and 1896, Freud presents his hypotheses on the mechanisms involved in obsessions and begins by showing that they originate in the mind (1894a); later, he gathers together under the heading "*obsessional neurosis*" a series of specific symptoms (obsessive ideas and actions, pathological doubting, etc.) which up till then had been ascribed to various other forms of pathology, ranging from degeneracy of the brain to neurasthenia (1895c, 1895h, 1896b). By introducing the concept of obsessional neurosis, Freud broke with the psychiatric tradition of his time – he attributed the origins of this syndrome to intrapsychic conflicts, just like hysteria, that other great clinical entity which he was the first to ascribe to psychological causes.

In 1905, when he introduced the revolutionary notion of infantile sexuality in *Three Essays on the Theory of Sexuality* (1905d), Freud mentioned the part played by anal eroticism in children's masturbation and showed that anal sadism was prevalent in pregenital organizations; both are closely linked to the conflict between love and hate which he would later designate as the "conflict of ambivalence".

It was the analysis of Ernst Lanzer, the Rat Man, carried out between 1907 and 1908, that enabled Freud to verify the accuracy of his hypotheses concerning the crucial importance of the conflict between love and hate in the psychogenesis of obsessional symptoms, thereby opening up new possibilities for treating this condition (1909d). In his narrative of that analysis, he describes the part played by anal eroticism in his patient's symptoms and overall personality. In two other papers dating from the same period, Freud explored other themes which he was able to relate to obsessional neurosis. In "Obsessive Actions and Religious Practices" (1907b), he made a link between the obsessional neurotic's compulsiveness and the practice of religion, both having the symbolic meaning of a protective ceremonial to guard against unconscious guilt feelings. In addition, in "Character and Anal Erotism" (1908b), he made a connection between anal eroticism – which emerges when the bodily functions associated with the anal region are powerfully eroticized in childhood – and the typical character traits observed in adults who suffer from obsessional neurosis: the need for order, meticulousness, obstinacy, and greed related to retention of the excrements.

In 1913, in an addendum to *Three Essays on the Theory of Sexuality* (1905d), Freud introduced a new developmental phase he called the "anal" stage, in which anal eroticism and the sadistic drives are dominant. This phase follows on from the oral stage and is in turn followed by the phallic stage; he argued that the anal stage constitutes the fixation point or regression level which is a feature of obsessional neurosis.

In 1917, in "On Transformations of Instinct as Exemplified in Anal Erotism" (1917c), Freud discussed what happens to the drives which are linked to anal eroticism when the primacy of the genital organization becomes established. For example, he argued that interest in money results from the pregenital interest in excrement, while both the wish to have a child and penis envy have their roots in anal eroticism – the patient creates a symbolic equivalence between the three terms faeces, baby and penis, such that the "*common symbol*" (1917c: 132) lives on in the mind at the genital stage.

Finally, in 1923, there appeared the concept of the superego which in its primitive form is extremely severe with the ego. This accounts for the excessive feelings of guilt which one finds in many patients, particularly those who suffer from obsessive symptoms; they often feel overwhelmed by the reproaches they heap upon themselves and by their need for punishment. Freud put the finishing touches to these hypotheses in 1924 with the development of the idea of erotogenic masochism, which he related to the fundamental conflict between life and death drives.

Post-Freudians

Neurosis or psychosis? Neurosis and psychosis?

Just as in the case of Hanold's "delusion" in "Gradiva" (Freud 1907a), we may ask ourselves whether Ernst Lanzer's symptomatology was at least in part psychotic rather than neurotic. Here, however, we have a real patient; this is not a case of psychoanalysis being applied to a work of literature. As I noted in my comments on "Gradiva", some psychoanalysts would see these symptoms as a temporary obfuscation of consciousness which is not psychotic and which can be observed in neurotic patients. Other psychoanalysts consider that in his account of the Rat Man, Freud describes typical neurotic mechanisms juxtaposed with others which are characteristic of psychosis, such as denial of reality, idealization and the omnipotence of thoughts. I would agree that there is a juxtaposition of these two kinds of mechanism in Ernst Lanzer's clinical material as reported by Freud; the same is true of other cases Freud presented –

from *Studies on Hysteria* (1895d) to "The Psychogenesis of a Case of Female Homosexuality" (1920a). Signs that Freud was already making the distinction can be found in his "Formulations on the Two Principles of Mental Functioning" (1911b), where he differentiates between the pleasure/unpleasure principle and the principle of reality; he continued in this vein right up to his final writings, in which he emphasizes the denial (or disavowal) of reality and splitting of the ego, as for example in "Fetishism" (1927e) and *An Outline of Psycho-Analysis* (1940a [1938]). Klein and Bion based their developments of the distinction which can be made between defence mechanisms associated with neurosis and those more typical of psychosis on these texts dating from the final period of Freud's life.

Freud's technique in the "Rat Man" case: criticism and comments

Blacker and Abraham (1982) point out that men are a dominant feature of the case as published by Freud, whereas, in his notes, women are ubiquitous. In their opinion, in addition to the conflict of ambivalence the patient experienced with respect to his father – highlighted by Freud – there lies in the background a conflict of ambivalence with respect to the patient's mother, an aspect which was never really taken into account in the analysis. Blacker and Abraham (1982) consider that certain counter-transference actings-out on Freud's part are indicative of the importance of the role played by this unacknowledged maternal transference – for example, when Freud invited the "Rat Man" to lunch with his family, a fundamentally maternal gesture linked to orality.

According to Mahony (1986, 2002), in spite of the obvious inadequacies which can in retrospect be noted in this analysis, it was a therapeutic success.

However, by his insistence and neglect of all possible transference reactions, especially negative ones, by ignoring the role of women in this analysis and mainly emphasizing the Oedipal relationship between the Rat Man and his father, [Freud] indeed succeeded in obtaining high quality therapeutic results. (Mahony 2002: 1435)

Examining the technique employed by Freud at the time of this analysis (1907), Lipton (1977) observes that the approach he adopted was what is now called "classical"; he would use this technique for the next thirty years, and his technical papers written between 1912 and 1914 would simply ratify this. For Lipton, the "classical" Freudian technique implicitly involves two separate elements: on the one hand, an instrumental approach which is intrinsic to the analytical situation and, on the other, a personal relationship which develops between patient and analyst and which is external to the analytical setting. The "modern" technique as practised by contemporary post-Freudian analysts differs from the classical technique because of the extensive use that is made of the transference and counter-transference; Lipton argues that the latter method involves the whole personal relationship between patient and analyst. In alluding to the "modern" technique, Lipton is explicitly referring to the psychoanalytic school associated with ego psychology and implicitly to the Kleinian and post-Kleinian current.

New concepts

Ambivalence – anal character – anal eroticism – anality – compulsive actions – conflict between love and hate – obsessions, obsessive ideas – omnipotence of thought – therapeutic alliance – undoing what has been done

LEONARDO DA VINCI AND A MEMORY OF HIS CHILDHOOD

(1910c)

Freud in Leonardo's mirror

Freud had long been fascinated by the enigma which represented for a psychoanalyst the life and work of the universal genius of the Renaissance that was Leonardo da Vinci. His study of Leonardo, written in 1910, enabled Freud to introduce several fundamental psychoanalytic concepts such as *sublimation* and *narcissism* and to describe a particular kind of homosexuality.

Freud takes as the starting-point of his analysis certain surprising kinds of behaviour mentioned by Leonardo's biographers: why, for example, the parallelism between the inordinate development of his passion for invention and the gradual relinquishing of his activity as an artist, culminating in his abandonment of painting altogether? For Freud, the impulse which drives us to acquire knowledge has its source in infantile sexual researches, i.e. in the wish shared by all of us to know where babies come from and what part in that is played by father and mother. However, when infantile sexuality is subjected to an excessive degree of repression, as was the case with Leonardo, the libido is transformed into intellectual curiosity devoid of all sexual content, thanks to a process which Freud calls *sublimation*.

Freud then goes on to analyse the only childhood memory which Leonardo reported – when a vulture opened his mouth by striking at it with its tail while Leonardo was in his cradle. That memory enabled Freud to elucidate an unconscious fantasy of fellatio which seemed to account for the early establishment of Leonardo's personality organization and of the specific modes of relationship which belong to it. Finally, with reference to the love the young artist showed towards the young men in his immediate circle, Freud described a particular species of homosexual object choice: according to this hypothesis, by surrounding himself with young boys whom he loved as would a mother, Leonardo was identifying with a loving mother while simultaneously loving himself through them. Freud calls this kind of self-love *narcissistic*; this was the first occasion on which he used the word.

Biographies and history

The affinities between two men of genius

It was in a letter to Fliess that Freud first expressed interest in Leonardo da Vinci (letter dated 9 October 1898); he began to develop the subject further in November 1909, after his return from the United States. Before he undertook this work, Freud gathered a great deal of information about Leonardo and read Dimitry Merezhkovsky's novel, written as though it were a diary kept by one of the master's young disciples, describing day after day the life of torment led by the creative genius that was Leonardo. Freud published his book in May 1910, but Ferenczi, who felt that nothing more shocking had been written since the "Little Hans" case history, was concerned about the reception it would be given. Even those sympathetic towards Freud's work were horrified that he had dared speak of fellatio and homosexuality. But Freud was well pleased with what he had written. The only concession he made was to replace the term "*homosexuality*" with "*inversion*" in the second edition of the book. The third edition was published in 1923; half of the copies were burned by the Nazis in 1938.

What were the reasons that led Freud to identify with Leonardo, a creator of genius with whom Freud had a strong sense of affinity? In the first place, Freud and Leonardo da Vinci shared the same passion for knowledge: both were untiring in their research endeavours, always on the look-out for new discoveries, never hesitating to explore a vast range of topics, and often at odds with their contemporaries. In addition, this particular period of Freud's life corresponded to inner developments which led him to a greater awareness of the unconscious homosexual and paranoid feelings he had harboured from time to time during his long friendship with Fliess; at the same time, these same tendencies were re-emerging in his relationship with new pupils of his, in particular Jung and Ferenczi. It should be noted that Freud's study of Leonardo was finished shortly before he turned to examine the Schreber case – one in which he would demonstrate that paranoia is to a great extent based on repression of homosexual tendencies. In Leonardo's past history, Freud discovered similarities between his own childhood and that of the artist: like Leonardo, at the time of his birth Freud's mother was very young and his father much older than she, so that the order of generations appeared to be turned upside-down. Unlike Freud, however, Leonardo was an illegitimate child and he suffered all through his life because of that. Also, Freud observed in Leonardo some psychopathological manifestations which reminded him of the obsessional neurosis he had recently studied in the "Rat Man" case: a fundamental ambivalence, ruminations which became obsessive, and the search for absolute perfection – to such an extent that Leonardo failed to complete some of his major works.

In 1910, Freud was 54 years of age. He was no longer an isolated figure; indeed, even though many of his ideas were still being challenged, his celebrity was growing. In that year he founded the International Psychoanalytical Association (IPA) (Jung was its first president). This was also a period when dissent was growing among his pupils; Freud had Adler appointed president of the Vienna Society with the aim of calming the situation, but to no avail. Freud's extraordinary creative potential was at its height at this point, and his family life gave him every satisfaction – later, he would look back on this period as the happiest years of his life.

Discovering the text

Page numbers are those of *The Standard Edition of the Complete Psychological Works of Sigmund Freud*, vol. **11**, 57–137.

• *A genius whose behaviour was enigmatic*

Freud begins the book by reminding his readers that Leonardo was known in the first place as a highly influential painter, because his contemporaries knew nothing of his talent for invention, as it appears in his scientific notebooks. He painted such works of art as the *Mona Lisa* and the *Last Supper*, but with a proverbial slowness; he rarely managed to bring to final completion the paintings he began, apparently oblivious as to what would become of them. He finished by abandoning painting completely – Freud sees in this a symptom of his inhibition. At the same time, he had an unquenchable thirst for knowledge – whatever the subject – and his inordinate activity of research finally overwhelmed him. Freud notes also that Leonardo liked to surround himself with handsome boys and youths; he named one of these as his heir, though he does not seem to have had a homosexual relationship with any of them. According to his biographers,

Leonardo never fell in love with a woman or had any sexual relationship with them. Freud was struck by the fact that a great artist such as Leonardo seems to have been more or less insensitive to eroticism, even though he painted the beauty of women with talent, and indifferent towards feelings of love and hate – his thirst for knowledge seems to have done without feelings of any kind.

• *Sublimation: "able to investigate instead of loving" (1910c: 77)*

Freud wonders how Leonardo's passion for research originated, so powerful was it that it stifled the artist in both his emotional and his sexual life. He suggests that the energy which Leonardo put into his craving for knowledge sprang from the persistence in him of the curiosity about sexual matters which can be observed in young children, who want to know where babies come from; their researches come to nothing because they are never satisfied. Freud argues that, when infantile sexuality is repressed to an excessive degree, as was the case with Leonardo, the adult exchanges the sexual aim of the instinctual drives for a non-sexual one, through the operation of *sublimation*. "*Thus a person of this sort would, for example, pursue research with the same passionate devotion that another would give to his love, and he would be able to investigate instead of loving*" (ibid.: 77). When repression is particularly energetic, the sexual drive has three possible issues open to it, says Freud: curiosity and sexuality bring about a generalized inhibition of thinking, typical of neurosis; or curiosity is itself "sexualized", such that eroticized thinking becomes the equivalent of sexual curiosity and ends up by replacing sexual satisfaction, as in obsessional neurosis; or, third, the libido is transformed into a craving for knowledge which avoids any kind of sexual theme – this, according to Freud, was the case with Leonardo da Vinci.

Freud then turns to the little we know of Leonardo's childhood and in particular to the only remaining early memory which is mentioned in Leonardo's scientific notebooks, in a passage about a flight of birds: "*for I recall as one of my very earliest memories that while I was in my cradle a vulture came down to me, and opened my mouth with its tail, and struck me many times with its tail against my lips*" (ibid.: 82). This memory, in Freud's opinion, sheds an important light on the manner in which Leonardo's personality developed from early childhood on. The memory evokes an act of fellatio and no doubt has its roots in an even earlier childhood experience, one which goes back to the very beginnings of life before the child is able to build up memories. For Freud it is the sensory trace of the experience the infant has when sucking at the mother's breast: "*The organic impression of this experience – the first source of pleasure in our life – doubtless remains indelibly printed on us*" (ibid.: 87). Freud goes on to say that this oral fantasy – penis and mouth – also implies a passive homosexual fantasy related to the idea that the mother possesses both kinds of sex organ. This would seem, in Freud's eyes, to be confirmed by the fact that Leonardo, who had not been legally recognized by his father, was brought up by his mother alone for the first few years of his life. Freud substantiates his argument with a reference to ancient Egyptian mythology: the Mother Goddess *Mut*, portrayed as bisexual – "*her body was female, as the breasts indicated, but it also had a male organ in a state of erection*" (ibid.: 94).

• *A type of homosexuality based on narcissistic identification*

Basing his argument on the fellatio fantasy which he discovered in Leonardo's childhood memory, Freud goes on to describe a particular type of homosexuality as manifested by the artist: in his early childhood, a powerful erotic relationship with his mother transformed his love for her into an identification – and that relationship was strengthened by the fact of his father's absence. In such a context, a man would take his mother's place and love himself through his love for young men. Freud calls this type of homosexual object-choice "*narcissistic*" – this is the first time he uses the term – because the model for it is Narcissus, who, in ancient Greek mythology, fell in love with his own image as it was reflected on the surface of the lake: he thought it was someone else. This particular kind of homosexual object choice seems indeed to have prevailed in Leonardo's case: he surrounded himself with young men, whom he loved as would a mother, without having sexual intercourse in the narrow sense of the term with any of them. It is important too to note that Freud associates narcissism with identificatory processes: Freud's first theory of narcissism does not simply refer to the fact of loving oneself, it implies identification with the mother and thus to love oneself as one's mother would do. Later, Freud tended to dismiss this aspect of "narcissistic identification", though it undoubtedly has its place here; the idea would all the same be further developed by Melanie Klein when she introduced the concept of projective identification in 1946.

- ## Mona Lisa*'s enigmatic smile*

Freud says that Leonardo's paintings express the intensity of his early relationship with his mother; witness, for example, *Mona Lisa*'s enigmatic smile, which some commentators have gone as far as to call a "Leonardesque smile". In another painting, representing the Madonna, Jesus and St Anne, Freud saw a representation of the two mothers Leonardo had had, his real mother Caterina who raised him in his youngest years, then his father's young wife who took care of him afterwards. It is in this painting that, in 1913, O. Pfister pointed out the image of a vulture in the folds of the robes worn by the Madonna, which Pfister interpreted as a "*picture-puzzle*" (ibid.: 115, note. See also Figure 3 on page 116). Freud did not, all the same, forget Leonardo's father. He drew attention to the artist's identification with his father – materialized, for example, in the fact that he was as unconcerned about his paintings as his father had been about him, according to the biographical data available to Freud at the time. In addition, Freud saw in the research scientist's boldness and independence of spirit the result of having had, very early on in life, to do without any paternal support, as well as an act of rebellion against his father (and authority figures in general) – in particular against the dogmatic teachings of the Catholic Church.

Post-Freudians

"Vulture" instead of "kite": the consequences of an error in translation

Is an error in translation enough to invalidate Freud's hypotheses? In 1923, a magazine correspondent was the first to draw attention to the fact that there was a mistake in the German translation of Leonardo da Vinci's childhood memory, and that, as a result, Freud wrote about a "*vulture*" rather than a "*kite*". Apparently Freud had used a translation of Leonardo's scientific notebooks in which the Italian word "*nibio*" had been translated into German as "*Geier*", a vulture. That mistake led the magazine correspondent to express doubts about the validity of Freud's interpretation. In 1956, Meyer Schapiro, an eminent art historian, published a well-documented study confirming the fact that Freud had made a mistake, and attributing it to a superficial reading of Leonardo's notebooks; in addition, he proved that the theme of the painting in which St Anne figures as a third person was a recurrent one in Renaissance art, whereas Freud had taken it to be an exception. This error of translation was later used – sometimes maliciously – by the detractors of psychoanalysis; they made use of it not only to cast doubt on Freud's interpretations of Leonardo but also to disparage the value of Freudian psychoanalysis in general. In a paper published in 1961, Kurt Eissler, the custodian of the Freud Archives, took pains to rehabilitate Freud's approach, claiming that it was in no way invalidated by the substitution of the word "vulture" for the original "kite".

After a careful reading of a note Freud added in 1919, I was surprised to discover that Freud himself had envisaged the possibility that the bird in question may not have been a vulture – and this was before the issue became public in 1923. In 1910, Havelock Ellis had criticized one of Freud's arguments in the book; Freud replied some years later in the following terms: "*the large bird in question need not of course have been a vulture*" (1910c: 82, note 2). In the same note, Freud discusses the true nature of Leonardo's "*memory*": was it a memory of an actual event, or the trace left in his memory by a story repeatedly told him by his mother that he might later have taken to be the memory of an experience of his own? Faced with this dilemma, Freud unreservedly maintains the preponderant role of fantasy over actual memory. Nowadays, after all the controversy that has surrounded Leonardo's childhood memory, the role of fantasy is considered to be more important than that of the memory of a real event, since anyway the latter is also subjected time and again to different modifications.

New concepts

Homosexuality – homosexual object choice – narcissism – sublimation

II
THE YEARS OF MATURITY
(1911–1920)

"PSYCHO-ANALYTIC NOTES ON AN AUTOBIOGRAPHICAL ACCOUNT OF A CASE OF PARANOIA (DEMENTIA PARANOIDES)"

(1911c)

After the neuroses, the study of psychosis

After concentrating on discovering the origin of the neuroses, and in particular of the hysterical and obsessional neuroses, Freud went on to look for a specific mechanism that might lie at the root of psychosis. He had been struck by the similarities between the psychosexual content of the delusions produced by paranoid patients and of the repressed psychosexual material of neurotic patients; it was as though the former were openly expressing the fantasies which the latter hid away in their unconscious. From 1907 on, Freud began investigating the potential connection between paranoia and dementia praecox (schizophrenia) and, in the course of his discussions with Karl Abraham and C. G. Jung, his attention was drawn to Daniel Paul Schreber's autobiography, *Memoirs of my Nervous Illness*, published in 1903. Freud discovered in that book a rich source of clinical material: a paranoid delusion described with not a little talent by the patient himself. This case study, based entirely on Dr Schreber's autobiography – Freud never met the patient – enabled him to demonstrate quite convincingly that persecutory anxiety and paranoid delusions are the result of a defence against repressed homosexual wishes. As for the mechanism underlying paranoia, Freud argues that it is the result of the transformation of (homosexual) love into hate, this hate being subsequently evacuated via projection on to an external persecutor.

Since the study of Senatspräsident Schreber constitutes Freud's main theoretical and clinical text on psychosis, I shall briefly examine the attempts he made over several decades to discover a mechanism specific to that disorder. Though he identified in Dr Schreber several psychological mechanisms which had to do with the psychotic structure, Freud believed that psychotic patients do not create a transference relationship and therefore are impossible to analyse. That point of view no longer holds today, particularly among Kleinian and post-Kleinian psychoanalysts who have greatly developed the analytical approach with such patients.

Biographies and history

What Freud knew of the history of Dr Schreber's illness

In his exploration of Dr Schreber's illness, the only material that was at Freud's disposal was the biographical information which the patient himself provided in his *Memoirs*; although he attempted to contact Dr Schreber's friends and relatives, Freud was not allowed access to any other information concerning the patient's childhood or his family background. Here in brief is what Freud knew of Dr Schreber.

Dr Schreber's first illness began in 1884 and took the form of depressive hypochondriasis, shortly after he had failed to win election to the Reichstag. He was at that time 42 years of age and the presiding judge of a lower court. He was treated in Professor Flechsig's clinic in Leipzig; Flechsig was a world-famous psychiatrist and neuro-anatomist who discovered the dorsal spinocerebellar fasciculus (later named after him). After spending a few months in Flechsig's clinic, Dr Schreber recovered completely. The second illness began some years later, in 1893, shortly after he was appointed to the important post of President of the Appeal Court in Saxony; he was then 53 years old. He suffered from an acute hallucinatory delusion, and was again admitted to Flechsig's clinic; six months later, he was transferred to another clinic in Dresden, the director of which was Dr Weber. He stayed there for all of eight years, securing his own discharge by applying to the court in Dresden. It was in the course of this procedure that Daniel Paul Schreber wrote his *Memoirs of my Nervous Illness* in which he described in detail the progress of his illness, his delusion and his hallucinations in order to support his application to the court for release: his intention was to demonstrate to the court that he had become socially well adjusted and that his illness was no longer a sufficient reason in law for continuing to keep him in a psychiatric institution. He was accordingly freed in 1902, the judge observing that, though he was still insane, Dr Schreber was no longer a potential danger to himself or to other people. Daniel Paul Schreber retired to Dresden, where he lived with his wife and their adopted daughter. Five years later, he had a relapse of his depressive psychosis and had to be admitted to the psychiatric asylum in Leipzig, where he remained until his death on 14 November 1911 – the same year in which Freud's case study was published.

In his report, Freud mentions in passing that Daniel Paul's father, Dr Daniel Gottlob Moritz Schreber was a physician who was famous for encouraging young people to keep their bodies healthy and for having written a handbook on therapeutic gymnastics. As for Daniel Paul's mother, no mention of her is made in the patient's *Memoirs* – and, strangely enough, Freud does not mention her either.

Discovering the text

Page numbers are those of *The Standard Edition of the Complete Psychological Works of Sigmund Freud*, vol. **12**, 1–79.

- ***From anxiety over being transformed into a woman to a mission of redemption***

In its acute phase, Daniel Paul Schreber's paranoid and hallucinatory delusion was fundamentally an anxiety-provoking persecutory delusion focused on the idea that he had to be emasculated and changed into a woman, and that there was no way he could avoid this sexual mistreatment. Initially his persecutor was Professor Flechsig, the physician who was treating him; he was the instigator of this "soul-murder" and of the plot to change Schreber's body into that of a woman so that it could then be "*surrendered to the person in question with a view to sexual abuse, and then simply 'left on one side' – that is to say, no doubt, given over to corruption*" (1911c: 19). Thereafter, God himself replaced Flechsig. Daniel Paul Schreber saw confirmation of this persecution in the voices which he heard speaking to him and in the experience of having various organs of his body destroyed (his stomach or his intestine, for example).

Later, this persecutory delusion with its sexual foundation was transformed into a delusion of redemption, such that the harrowing fantasy of emasculation became associated with the idea that he had a divine mission to fulfil: the obsessive idea of being transformed into a woman then became part of a mystical project in which he would be impregnated by divine rays in order to procreate a new race of men. This mission meant that he was allied with God, towards whom he felt a mixture of veneration and rebellion, particularly because God demanded of Schreber, a highly moral person, the kind of voluptuous sexual ecstasy that only a woman can experience.

Freud says of this transformation in the delusion that "the delusional formation, which we take to be the pathological product, is in reality an attempt at recovery, a process of reconstruction" (ibid.: 71).

• *Paranoia as a defence against repressed homosexual wishes*

Since Daniel Paul Schreber's illness began with a persecutory delusion, Freud concludes that the author of all these persecutions was no doubt Professor Flechsig; all through Dr Schreber's illness, Flechsig was the principal seducer, for God himself fell under his influence. Freud asks why Flechsig – who had cured Dr Schreber of his first illness and had as a result become the object of his patient's heartfelt gratitude – turned into a persecutor. Freud argues that it is precisely the person who was once so loved and admired and to whom is attributed such a powerful influence who becomes the persecutor as a result of love being transformed into hate. Why does such a reversal of feelings take place? Because Schreber's gratitude towards Flechsig was based on an intense erotic attachment to the professor; it was that attachment which had led Schreber to want to be the wife of such a wonderful person as Flechsig: "*it must be nice to be a woman submitting to the act of copulation*" (ibid.: 42). In other words, "*the basis of Schreber's illness was the outburst of a homosexual impulse*" (ibid.: 45). In a later transformation of the delusion, Flechsig the persecutor was replaced by God; this meant that the homosexual fantasy could be more readily accepted by Schreber, since being emasculated and transformed into a woman became part of a divine project thanks to the operation of "*rationalization*". "*By this means an outlet was provided which would satisfy both of the contending forces. His ego found compensation in his megalomania, while his feminine wishful fantasy made its way through and became acceptable*" (ibid.: 48).

Freud indeed goes even further, and attributes Schreber's friendly feeling towards Flechsig to "*a process of transference*" (ibid.: 47), with the idea that this transference on to the doctor was the result of a displacement of the intense love which Daniel Paul Schreber must have felt for his father or older brother. Although he had no biographical information on Schreber's family, Freud assumed that if the patient had cathected his father or brother so intensely, it was probably because the person in question was dead; this assumption of Freud's was later found to be correct.

• *The father complex*

At this point in his demonstration, Freud was able to emphasize the infantile nature of Dr Schreber's relationship with his father. "*Thus in the case of Schreber we find ourselves once again on the familiar ground of the father-complex*" (ibid.: 55). He argues that analysis of Schreber's conflicts with Flechsig and with God shows that they are based on an infantile conflict with his beloved father, so that what lies behind the delusion is a mechanism similar to that which generates a neurosis. Freud suggests that Schreber's father must have seemed to his son to be a harsh and imposing figure who interfered with the young boy's autoerotic sexual satisfaction and threatened him with castration as a punishment. In other words, the wish to be transformed into a woman which formed the nucleus of Daniel Paul's delusion was simply the product of his fear of being castrated by his father because of his infantile masturbation; this led the boy to adopt a passive homosexual attitude or "*feminine attitude*" in the father complex, an attitude based on a mixture of submission and rebellion.

• *The narcissistic stage of infantile development*

Freud notes that it is not the fantasy of a homosexual wish linked to the father complex that characterizes paranoia, because that complex exists also in a latent state in neurotic as well as in normal people such as Schreber in his periods of recovery. What is paranoiac in this case, says Freud, is the fact that the patient's reaction was to produce a persecutory delusion in order to defend himself against the fantasy of a homosexual wish, given that he was unsuccessful in maintaining it in his unconscious.

Freud goes on to suggest that homosexuality is found at a particular *stage* of infantile sexual development which he calls the *narcissistic stage*, half-way between auto-eroticism and object-love.

> *This stage has been given the name of narcissism. What happens is this. There comes a time in the development of the individual at which he unifies his sexual instincts (which had hitherto been engaged in auto-erotic activities) in order to obtain a love-object; and he begins by taking himself, his own body, as his love-object, and only subsequently proceeds from this to the choice of some person other than himself as his object.* (ibid.: 60–61)

As a result, says Freud, when the heterosexual object choice is made in the course of normal development, homosexual tendencies do not disappear altogether; they become "*attached*" (ibid.: 61) to social instincts and thus form the basis for friendship and comradeship with persons of the same sex.

On the other hand, in pathological cases, the narcissistic stage of infantile development may constitute a "*point of fixation*" or of "*regression*" (ibid.: 62) in some people; this "weak spot" in their personality makes them particularly sensitive to paranoia and its concomitant persecutory anxiety.

• *The mechanism of paranoia*

Freud concludes his investigation by bringing the various forms of paranoia down to the single proposition "*I (a man) love him (a man)*" (ibid.: 63). Since that proposition is unacceptable to the individual's consciousness, it is transformed into its opposite "*I do not* love *him – I* hate *him!*" This intolerable feeling of hate is repressed into the unconscious then is projected on to someone in the external world: "*I hate him*" thus becomes "He hates *(persecutes)* me, *which will justify me in hating him*" (ibid.: 63). In this way, the unconscious feeling of hate within the individual makes its appearance as though it were an external perception: "*I do not* love *him – I* hate *him, because HE PERSECUTES ME*" (ibid.: 63). Freud goes on to say "*observation leaves room for no doubt that the persecutor is someone who was once loved*" (ibid.: 63). Freud concludes his paper by applying this formula to all the possible kinds of delusion which come under the heading of paranoia: persecutory delusions, erotomania, delusions of jealousy in both men and women and megalomania.

Development of Freud's concepts

Freud's search for a mechanism specific to psychosis

Freud's study of the Schreber case was part of his ongoing attempt to discover a mechanism specific to psychosis. As a rule, he was less interested in drawing up descriptive criteria to enable a systematic classification of delusions than in clarifying the underlying mechanisms. Without going into detail as regards any complex distinctions, I feel all the same that I ought to point out how Freud's use of the term paranoia changed somewhat as his thinking developed.

What did Freud mean by "paranoia" or "paranoid delusion"?

At the end of the nineteenth century, the term "paranoia" was used in German psychiatry to describe delusions in general, and in his early papers on the subject, Freud too used the term in its widest sense. Later, Emil Kraepelin introduced a fundamental distinction between the various types of delusion, separating dementia praecox, the outcome of which is insanity, from the systematized delusions of paranoia, in which there is no mental deterioration. The term "dementia praecox" soon gave way to "schizophrenia" as a result of Eugen Bleuler's researches, which highlighted the crucial part played by "splitting" (*Spaltung*) in this disorder. Freud included in his use of the term "paranoia" not only persecutory delusions, but also erotomania, delusions of jealousy and megalomania. From 1911 on, he remained faithful to Kraepelin's distinction between dementia praecox (schizophrenia) and paranoia; however Bleuler, Kraepelin's pupil, did not accept this distinction – he argued that splitting was just as much a feature of paranoia as of schizophrenia. In his study of Schreber's paranoia, Freud came to the conclusion that there are indeed various possible combinations of these psychopathological states.

The role of projection

Freud had already discussed paranoia in his correspondence with Fliess (Draft H, 24 January 1894, and Draft K, 1 January 1896) and had studied the subject in his "Analysis of a Case of Chronic Paranoia" (Section III in Freud 1896b). In these early writings, he emphasizes the mechanism of projection as being characteristic of psychosis, seeing it as an immediate discharge into the external world of an intolerable internal perception, nothing more than a kind of evacuation, as it were. Gradually, however, and especially as he was studying Schreber's *Memoirs*, he came to realize that projection is not simply an evacuation into the external world of some repressed material or other; on the contrary – what comes back "from the outside" has its origin in what has been suppressed "inside". "*It was incorrect to say that the perception which was suppressed internally is projected outwards; the truth is rather, as we now see, that what was abolished internally returns from without*" (ibid.: 71). From his study of the Schreber case onwards, Freud considered that the various types of delusion in paranoia are based on a defence against repressed homosexual wishes and that projection is not the prerogative of psychosis.

From "de-cathecting reality" to "disavowal of reality"

In 1911, Freud had described the part played by de-cathexes of external reality in Schreber's paranoia; this was long before he introduced the notions of "loss of reality" in 1924, then "disavowal of reality" in 1927. The withdrawal of cathexis which Freud described in Schreber's case in 1911 involved not only people in the patient's immediate circle but also the real world as a whole. "*The patient has withdrawn from the people in his environment and from the external world generally the libidinal cathexis he has hitherto directed on to them. Thus everything has become indifferent and irrelevant to him*" (ibid.: 70). Schreber then had the feeling that the world was coming to an end; Freud attributes this to the internal catastrophe represented by the patient's extensive de-cathexis experienced as a loss of love. Freud goes on to argue that the delusion is an attempt to recover these lost external cathexes – this is another reason for seeing the paranoid patient's delusion as an attempt at cure; Freud would come back to this essential point several times in his subsequent writings. "*The delusional formation, which we take to be the pathological product, is in reality an attempt at recovery, a process of reconstruction*" (ibid.: 71).

Schreber: a masterly clinical description of psychotic phenomena

As on other occasions when he defined concepts for the first time, Freud discovered in psychopathology certain phenomena which he would later realize existed also in neurotic and normal individuals, though with less intensity. For example, long before he introduced the idea of "*splitting of the ego*" (1940a [1938]) – separating the ego into a part which denies reality and another part which accepts it – Freud described something similar in Schreber; there he speaks of a division of the patient's personality into two parts, one of which was delusional while the other remained well adjusted.

> *The fact was that, on the one hand, he had developed an ingenious delusional structure, in which we have every reason to be interested, while, on the other hand, his personality had been reconstructed and now showed itself, except for a few isolated disturbances, capable of meeting the demands of everyday life.* (1911c: 14)

Taking the delusion as a whole, Freud notes that the more the illness progresses, the more the persecutor is decomposed; he describes different ways in which this "*decomposition*" is illustrated – "*upper God*" and "*lower God*", "*Flechsig*" and "*God*", "*venerated father*" and "*hated father*". Freud is here talking explicitly of "*splitting*" as a mechanism specific to paranoid psychosis.

> *A process of decomposition of this kind is very characteristic of paranoia. Paranoia decomposes just as hysteria condenses. Or rather, paranoia resolves once more into their elements the products of the condensations and identifications which are effected in the unconscious.* (ibid.: 49)

That said, although Freud did put his magnificent talent for observation to good use in describing many of the mechanisms which operate in the psychoses (as in his essay on Dr Schreber), it fell to post-Freudian psychoanalysts to make a much finer differentiation between the mechanisms which, based on primitive defences, belong to the psychoses and those which, based on repression, are typical of the neuroses. When that distinction is kept in mind it becomes possible to treat psychotic patients – adults or children – by the psychoanalytic method and to obtain some degree of therapeutic success in spite of the difficulties linked to the very particular kind of transference which such patients establish.

Post-Freudians

A reassessment of Freud's hypotheses in Schreber's case

The translation into English in 1955 of Daniel Paul Schreber's *Memoirs* (by Ida Macalpine and Richard A. Hunter) enabled English-speaking psychoanalysts to have direct access to the text used by Freud in his case-study; this led to a reassessment of some of the ideas Freud had put forward in 1911. Some challenged the hypothesis according to which psychosis was exclusively the consequence of repression of homosexual wishes. Fairbairn (1956), for example, argues that homosexuality is linked above all to an aggressive rejection of the opposite-sex parent – in particular of the mother, who is not even mentioned in Schreber's *Memoirs*. Fairbairn adds that the child chooses the same-sex parent as persecutor in order to avoid an even more intense persecutory anxiety derived from the primitive relationship with the mother. Macalpine and Hunter (1955) argue that psychosis originates at an even earlier stage of development which they call "object-less", a regression point which lies at the very heart of the individual's sense of identity. In general terms, we could say that Kleinian psychoanalysts feel that Freud laid too great an emphasis on Schreber's father complex; for these analysts, the origins of psychosis have more to do with the infant's early relationship with the mother.

The father's influence on Daniel Paul's delusion: reality or fantasy?

Beginning in the 1950s, several authors made in-depth historical studies of Daniel Paul Schreber's childhood and family background. They discovered in particular that his father had invented a whole series of quite astonishing orthopaedic instruments designed to rectify slovenly postures in children; the illustrations published in several books are really quite extraordinary. On the basis of this new information, Niederland (1963) suggests, for example, that Schreber's persecutory delusion was no doubt the consequence of a childhood trauma suffered by him as a boy, when he was subjected to the sadism and seductiveness of a domineering, tyrannical father. Racamier and Chasseguet-Smirgel (1966) highlight the impact of the father's psychotic personality; the father seems to have completely taken over the mother's role and absorbed her to such an extent that she does not even rate a mention in the *Memoirs*. More recently, Israëls (1981) and Lothane (1992) have challenged the idea of the father's traumatic influence – attributed by several psychoanalysts to Schreber's father – on the grounds that these conclusions have no basis in historical fact. It seems to me, however, that even if we do not have sufficient biographical evidence to support the claim that Daniel Paul's father had indeed been tyrannical in his upbringing of his son, that argument does not in any way invalidate the hypotheses concerning the impact of the sadistic and seductive fantasies which were present in Daniel Gottlob Moritz Schreber's theories of education and in the paranoid delusion of his son, Daniel Paul Schreber.

The foreclosure of the Name-of-the-Father: a theoretical conception of psychosis

In 1955, Lacan made a study of Schreber's paranoia based on the English translation of the latter's *Memoirs*. In his 1955–1956 Seminar on *The Psychoses*, Lacan (1981) introduced two new concepts in his theoretical developments of the origins of psychosis: foreclosure ("*forclusion*") and the Name-of-the-Father. For Lacan, foreclosure is the primary repudiation of a fundamental signifier out of the "Symbolic" order; since it is thereafter impossible to integrate it into the individual's unconscious, it returns as a "Real" element in the form of a hallucination. According to Lacan, in psychosis, the Subject cannot become adequately structured because the father is excluded from playing the symbolic paternal role which is properly his in his relationship with the child – the function which entails handing down his name in order for the child to acquire an identity. The fundamental signifier that is the Name-of-the-Father is thus foreclosed – what ought to have been symbolized has failed to be so – and returns in the "Real" order in the form of a paranoid delusion. In other words, for Lacan, Schreber's persecutory delusion of being transformed into a woman is the result of the son's inability to perceive the symbolic character of the threat of castration coming from the father; consequently, that threat is seen as a danger originating in external reality, in other words in a "Real" order which is inaccessible to analysis. For Lacan, foreclosure is characteristic of the psychoses, but he never at any time indicated how, in his view, foreclosure could be reversed; as a result, his point of view concerning the treatment of psychosis remained a purely speculative one (Diatkine 1997).

Melanie Klein: laying the foundations for the psychoanalytic treatment of psychosis

With her background as a child psychoanalyst, Klein's decisive clinical and theoretical contributions enabled the psychoanalysis of psychotic patients to develop. On the one hand, with her introduction of such notions as the paranoid-schizoid and depressive positions, she differentiated between the primitive defence mechanisms associated with psychosis and the more advanced mechanisms which are found in the neuroses; on the other hand, contrary to what Freud believed, she felt that psychotic patients did establish a transference relationship which could be analysed. For Klein, psychotic functioning is based on a fixation at the paranoid-schizoid position and on excessive recourse to projective identification. She did not envisage the possibility that there could be both normal and pathological forms of the paranoid-schizoid position, nor that the same could be true of projective identification. It was left to those who came after her – Rosenfeld, Segal and Bion—to make a closer investigation of the psychopathology of the paranoid-schizoid position; these psychoanalysts made a distinction between, on the one hand, the normal and pathological forms of the paranoid-schizoid position and, on the other, the normal and pathological forms of projective identification. Unlike Klein, who saw psychosis as a fixation at the paranoid-schizoid position, these analysts consider the disorder to be a regression to a pathological form of the paranoid-schizoid position, a psychotic regression which is characterized by pathological projective identification. The developments made in Kleinian thinking on early object relations have had a considerable impact on psychoanalytic technique; they constitute an essential part of the way we look at how the mind processes certain phenomena not only in psychotic and narcissistic analysands but also in those who are less disturbed mentally.

New concepts

Delusion as a defence against homosexuality – narcissism, narcissistic stage of psychosexual development – paranoia – point of fixation – point of regression – projection – rationalization

PAPERS ON TECHNIQUE WRITTEN BETWEEN 1904 AND 1919
"Freud's Psycho-Analytic Procedure" (1904a)
"On Psychotherapy" (1905a)
"The Future Prospects of Psycho-Analytic Therapy" (1910d)
" 'Wild' Psycho-Analysis" (1910k)
"The Handling of Dream-Interpretation in Psycho-Analysis" (1911e)
"The Dynamics of Transference" (1912b)
"Recommendations to Physicians Practising Psycho-Analysis" (1912e)
"On Beginning the Treatment" (1913c)

"REMEMBERING, REPEATING AND WORKING-THROUGH" (1914g)
"OBSERVATIONS ON TRANSFERENCE-LOVE" (1915a [1914])
"LINES OF ADVANCE IN PSYCHO-ANALYTIC THERAPY" (1919a)

A series of recommendations for practitioners

Freud never brought to a successful conclusion his intention to write a memorandum wholly devoted to psychoanalytic technique; the idea was to help the growing number of persons interested in psychoanalysis who could not come to Vienna in order to have instruction directly from him. His fundamental ideas on technique, however, can be found in a series of short papers written between 1904 and 1919. Using everyday language, Freud writes, in no particular order and in the form of recommendations, of his long experience as a practitioner of psychoanalysis. With this practical approach, he presents the elements of what constitutes the general methodology of psychoanalysis as it is still practised today (at least by those psychoanalysts who are affiliated to the International Psychoanalytical Association (IPA), founded by Freud in 1910). By about 1903, Freud had already established the basic rules for initiating and conducting psychoanalytic treatment, bringing together into a consistent whole the couch/armchair setting, the number and rhythm of sessions and the psychoanalytic process itself. The method has developed considerably since those early days and its potential for therapeutic intervention has widened to include not only the neuroses but also the psychoses, as well as patients of all ages, from young children to adults who are already late on in life. In spite of recent discoveries in the neuro-sciences and psychopharmacology, it has to be acknowledged that no new ground-breaking discovery has as yet been able to replace psychoanalysis when it is applied to its own domain: indeed, had that been the case, would not psychoanalysts themselves have been the first to notice the fact and to draw the necessary therapeutic conclusions?

The present-day reader of Freud's papers on technique written between 1904 and 1919 will be surprised to discover that many of the questions raised by Freud almost a century ago have remained unanswered. For example: given the therapeutic tools which have become available in more recent times, could we do without psychoanalysis altogether? Are we any more able nowadays to "prove" scientifically the effectiveness of psychoanalysis? Are the therapeutic techniques which claim to be quicker and less expensive than psychoanalytic treatment as effective in the longer term? All these questions were already being asked by Freud – who at that time hoped that satisfactory answers would be found in what for him was the not-too-distant future.

> **Post-Freudians**
>
> **Only a very few treatises on psychoanalytic technique have ever been published**
>
> Post-Freudian psychoanalysts seem to have come up against the same difficulty that Freud encountered in his attempt to write a handbook which would deal with issues relating to the technique of psychoanalysis. The number of treatises on the subject is very small compared to the quantity of papers published on other psychoanalytic topics. Among the classic writings – though published some time ago now – those by Otto Fenichel (1941), Edward Glover (1955) and Ralph R. Greenson (1967) are perhaps the best known. The book written by R. Horacio Etchegoyen, *The Fundamentals of Psychoanalytic Technique* (1991), is undoubtedly a work of international standing, presented as it is in the form of a well-researched and well-documented handbook which is easy both to read and to consult. The author gives an overview of what has been published on the technique of psychoanalysis from Freud right up to contemporary practitioners, following closely the development of ideas on the question, a development to which Etchegoyen has been a witness and in which he himself has played a role. Etchegoyen also studies how psychoanalytic technique is influenced by the wide variety of theoretical points of view adopted by psychoanalysts throughout the world, from Klein to Lacan via other major European, Latin American and North American practitioners, and he emphasizes the advantages and disadvantages of these various approaches in the light of his own clinical experience.

Discovering the texts

- **PAPERS ON TECHNIQUE WRITTEN BETWEEN 1904 AND 1913**

  > Page numbers are those of *The Standard Edition of the Complete Psychological Works of Sigmund Freud*, as follows: "Freud's Psycho-Analytic Procedure" (1904a), *Standard Edition*, vol. **7**, 247–254; "On Psychotherapy" (1905a), *Standard Edition*, vol. **7**, 255–268; "The Future Prospects of Psycho-Analytic Therapy" (1910d), *Standard Edition*, vol. **11**, 139–151; " 'Wild' Psycho-Analysis" (1910k), *Standard Edition*, vol. **11**, 219–227; "The Handling of Dream-Interpretation in Psycho-Analysis" (1911e), *Standard Edition*, vol. **12**, 89–96; "The Dynamics of Transference" (1912b), *Standard Edition*, vol. **12**, 97–108; "Recommendations to Physicians Practising Psycho-Analysis" (1912e), *Standard Edition*, vol. **12**, 109–120; "On Beginning the Treatment" (1913c), *Standard Edition*, vol. **12**, 121–144.

- *The method and its indications*

Freud begins by stating what psychoanalysis is and argues that it is of some considerable scientific value. He highlights the difference between the various kinds of psychotherapy then being practised and his own, psychoanalysis, which is, he says:

> the one that penetrates most deeply and carries farthest, the one by means of which the most extensive transformations can be effected in patients. [. . .] I may also say of it that it is the most interesting method, the only one which informs us at all about the origin and inter-relation of morbid phenomena. (1905a: 260)

This was his way of explaining why he was particularly interested in his own approach as distinct from other kinds of psychotherapy, though he had no intention of denigrating these other methods.

> *I despise none of these methods and would use them all in appropriate circumstances. If I have actually come to confine myself to one form of treatment, to the method which Breuer called* cathartic, *but which I myself prefer to call "analytic", it is because I have allowed myself to be influenced by purely subjective motives.* (ibid.: 259)

As to indications, Freud argues that psychoanalysis is a particularly useful treatment for the psychoneuroses because *"these diseases are not cured by the drug but by the physician, that is, by the personality of the physician, inasmuch as through it he exerts a mental influence"* (ibid.: 259). A certain number of conditions must be met by the patient, such as *"a certain measure of natural intelligence and ethical development"* (1904a: 254). Freud considers it inadvisable to begin such a treatment if the patient is over 50 years old because, he says, *"near or above the age of fifty the elasticity of the mental processes, on which the treatment depends, is as a rule lacking"* (1905a: 264). An age limit of this kind would no longer be accepted nowadays; indeed the creativity of which Freud himself was capable at 83 years of age shows that advancing years do not necessarily entail a loss of psychological elasticity, as he imagined when, at the age of 48, he was writing this recommendation. In this paper Freud acknowledges that he used his therapeutic method *"only on severe, indeed on the severest cases"* (ibid.: 263), but that the treatment was successful, so that the patients concerned were able to become *"permanently* fit *for existence"* (ibid.: 263). In addition, Freud warns inexperienced therapists not to underestimate the difficulties that are met with in analysing the patient's resistances, before they have sufficient experience to deal with these, *"for it is not so easy to play upon the instrument of the mind"* (ibid.: 262).

• *Process and setting*

The setting of "classic" psychoanalytical treatment has remained fundamentally unchanged since Freud established it at the beginning of the twentieth century, with its "couch-and-armchair" layout, the analyst being seated in an armchair behind and out of sight of the patient, who is lying on the couch. Freud gave his patients one-hour sessions every day for five (or even six) days per week. In these papers, Freud does not dismiss techniques derived from psychoanalysis, such as psychoanalytically oriented psychotherapy or other approaches; he writes only of the so-called "classic" form of psychoanalytic treatment.

As far as the unfolding of the psychoanalytic process itself is concerned, Freud notes that, given its complexity, it is practically impossible to describe; he compares it to the game of chess.

> *Anyone who hopes to learn the noble game of chess from books will soon discover that only the openings and end-games admit of an exhaustive systematic presentation and that the infinite variety of moves which develop after the opening defy any such description.* (1913c: 123)

Freud goes on to describe his manner of working and the conditions under which psychoanalytic treatment is conducted. At the beginning of every analysis, he asks the patient to observe without hesitation *"the fundamental rule of psychoanalytic technique"* (ibid.: 134), in other words the patient must communicate to the analyst everything that comes to mind *"without criticism or selection"* (1912e: 112). At the same time, Freud advises the analyst to maintain an attitude of *"evenly-suspended attention"* (ibid.: 111) and to avoid taking notes during the actual session so as not to interfere with listening to what the patient has to say. In Freud's opinion, *"the keeping of a shorthand record"* (ibid.: 113) is of little value, since written notes must of necessity only possess an *ostensible* exactness, which is why they *"do not succeed in being a substitute for [the reader's] actual presence at an analysis"* (ibid.: 114).

• *Allow oneself to be taken by surprise*

As we follow Freud's attempts at improving his technique, we can see that he decided to rely more and more on the patient's spontaneous and natural thinking processes; he gradually gave up any idea of extracting those aspects of the patient's associations which he himself was interested in –

with the aim of trying, through interpretation, to piece together the psychological structure of the patient he was treating. This crucial turning-point seems to have emerged during Freud's analysis of the "Rat Man" in 1907, where he changed his point of view and gave up the "active" attitude (which imposed the analyst's reconstructions on the patient); henceforth he would place his trust in the way in which the psychoanalytic process as such unfolded. Freud's way of putting it is as follows:

> *[The] most successful cases are those in which one proceeds, as it were, without any purpose in view, allows oneself to be taken by surprise by any new turn in them, and always meets them with an open mind, free from any presuppositions.* (1912e: 114)

• *Give oneself sufficient time*

If we put our trust in the patient's ability to find his or her own way of solving the presenting conflicts, we may well appreciate the fact that "*psycho-analysis is always a matter of long periods of time [. . .] – of longer periods than the patient expects*" (1913c: 129) – Freud insists on this point all through his papers on technique. Though he admits that "*to shorten analytic treatment is a justifiable wish*", he has no hesitation in saying that "*unfortunately, it is opposed by a very important factor, namely, the slowness with which deep-going changes in the mind are accomplished – in the last resort, no doubt, the 'timelessness' of our unconscious processes*" (ibid.: 130).

Freud states quite clearly that, once the psychoanalytic process is set in motion, the psychoanalyst has no choice but to follow wherever it leads.

> *[On] the whole, once begun, it goes its own way and does not allow either the direction it takes or the order in which it picks up its points to be prescribed for it. The analyst's power over the symptoms of the disease may thus be compared to male sexual potency. A man can, it is true, beget a whole child, but even the strongest man cannot create in the female organism a head alone or an arm or a leg; he cannot even prescribe the child's sex. He, too, only sets in motion a highly complicated process, determined by events in the remote past, which ends with the severance of the child from its mother. A neurosis as well has the character of an organism.* (ibid.: 130)

Given the great expenditure of time and money that psychoanalysis requires, he adds, some patients would be satisfied with being rid of just one of their symptoms; but for Freud the psychoanalytic method has to be taken as a whole since it constitutes an inseparable unity.

> *The patients who are bound to be most welcome to [the psychoanalyst] are those who ask him to give them complete health, insofar as that is attainable, and who place as much time at his disposal as is necessary for the process of recovery. Such favourable conditions as these are, of course, to be looked for in only a few cases.* (ibid.: 131)

• *Establishing the psychoanalytic setting*

Some specific requirements have to be met so that the process can unfold under optimal conditions. This is what Freud proposed to his own patients: "*Each patient is allotted a particular hour of my available working day; it belongs to him and he is liable for it, even if he does not make use of it*" (1913c: 126). He would ask the patient to lie on the couch while he (Freud) sat behind and out of sight of the patient, the better "*to isolate the transference*" (ibid.: 134) and also because he did not like being stared at. Each patient was given one session per day, that is, as a rule, six sessions per week – though he did allow some exceptions to that rule.

> *For slight cases or the continuation of a treatment which is already well advanced, three days a week will be enough. Any restrictions of time beyond this bring no advantage either to the doctor or the patient; and at the beginning of an analysis they are quite out of the question.* (ibid.: 127)

As to the length of treatment, Freud felt that it was almost impossible to give any indication of that at the outset. Every patient is free to break off the treatment whenever he or she likes, though Freud does take care to point out that, if the analysis is interrupted in this way, the patient's condition may worsen. Freud mentions several times the pressures which come from all sides aiming at shortening the length of psychoanalytic treatment; the arguments put forward are many and varied. "*As the combined result of lack of insight on the part of patients and disingenuousness on the part of doctors, analysis finds itself expected to fulfil the most boundless demands, and that in the shortest time*" (ibid.: 128). The question of shortening the length of analyses was always being brought up, and Freud makes his own humoristic rejoinder to it:

> *No one would expect a man to lift a heavy table with two fingers as if it were a light stool, or to build a large house in the time it would take to put up a wooden hut; but as soon as it becomes a question of the neuroses [...] even intelligent people forget that a necessary proportion must be observed between time, work and success.* (ibid.: 128–129)

Concerning the confidential nature of the treatment, Freud says that "*the patient must [...] be advised to treat his analysis as a matter between himself and his doctor and to exclude everyone else from sharing in the knowledge of it, no matter how close to him they may be, or how inquisitive*" (ibid.: 136). Freud discusses also the payment of the analyst's fee and notes that, in the analyst–patient relationship, money often has an unconscious sexual meaning; he advises the analyst to make sure that he or she is paid at regular intervals, so that large sums of money do not accumulate. He broaches the subject of free treatment, which he himself had practised for several years; he emphasizes the fact that gratuitous treatment enormously increases some of the resistances. He discusses also the question of the accessibility of psychoanalysis to poor people and to those who belong to the lower classes.

• *Transference and counter-transference*

Freud notes that transference is not a phenomenon specific to psychoanalysis; it occurs in other situations in life, but it is only in the psychoanalytic context that it can be processed adequately. He describes two kinds of transference: *positive*, based on affectionate feelings, and *negative*, based on hostile feelings. "*If we 'remove' the transference by making it conscious, we are detaching only these two components of the emotional act from the person of the doctor*" (1912b: 105).

Freud then draws the analyst's attention to what he calls for the first time the "*counter-transference*" which arises in the physician "*as a result of the patient's influence on his unconscious feelings*" (1910d: 144). What does he mean by "counter-transference"? In this paper Freud uses the term in a much more limited way than that in which post-Freudian psychoanalysts would later develop the concept; for Freud, the notion refers above all to the analyst's unconscious feelings which run "*counter*" to the patient's transference, hence the term "*counter-transference*". These reactions depend on the analyst's personality and if they are not overcome will be an obstacle to processing the transference. For this reason, Freud demands that all analysts be aware of their counter-transference and control it – and this can be done only through a personal experience of analysis followed by self-analysis.

> *[We] have noticed that no psycho-analyst goes further than his own complexes and internal resistances permit; and we consequently require that he shall begin his activity with a self-analysis and continually carry it deeper while he is making his observations on his patients. Anyone who fails to produce results in a self-analysis of this kind may at once give up any idea of being able to treat patients by analysis.* (ibid.: 145)

In addition, it is advisable for all prospective psychoanalysts to undergo a "*training analysis*" (ibid.: 145 note).

Freud insists also on the fact that all prospective psychoanalysts should familiarize themselves with the technique, so as to avoid such errors as "*wild*" psychoanalysis, defined as, at the initial consultation, "*brusquely telling [the patient] the secrets which have been discovered by the physician*" (1910k: 226). Freud discusses also the temptation an analyst may feel to let the patient know of his or her own conflicts and defects, with a view to overcoming the patient's resistances.

Young and eager psycho-analysts will no doubt be tempted to bring their own individuality freely into the discussion, in order to carry the patient along with them and lift him over the barriers of his own narrow personality. It might be expected that it would be quite allowable and indeed useful, with a view to overcoming the patient's existing resistances, for the doctor to afford him a glimpse of his own mental defects and conflicts and, by giving him intimate information about his own life, enable him to put himself on an equal footing. (1912e: 117–118)

However, says Freud, experience shows that such an approach does not have the expected results – quite the opposite, in fact.

[The patient] would like to reverse the situation, and finds the analysis of the doctor more interesting than his own. The resolution of the transference, too – one of the main tasks of the treatment – is made more difficult by an intimate attitude on the doctor's part [. . .]. I have no hesitation, therefore, in condemning this kind of technique as incorrect. The doctor should be opaque to his patients and, like a mirror, should show them nothing but what is shown to him. (ibid.: 118)

Like any other medical technique, psychoanalysis has to be learned from "*those who are already proficient in it*" (1910k: 226). It was with the aim of protecting patients as much as possible from the dangers arising from practitioners of "*wild*" psychoanalysis that, in 1910, Freud, as he tells us in that paper, founded the International Psychoanalytical Association (IPA), an organization which has come to play an important role in current practice. "*[Its] members declare their adherence [to the IPA] by the publication of their names, in order to be able to repudiate responsibility for what is done by those who do not belong to us and yet call their medical procedure 'psycho-analysis'*" (ibid.: 227).

Post-Freudians
The psychoanalytic setting: a slow and gradual process

What do we mean by the psychoanalytic "setting"?

The psychoanalytic setting is the series of conditions which must be satisfied if the psychoanalytic process is to unfold in the best manner possible. These conditions are established by mutual agreement between patient and analyst, if possible during their preliminary discussions. In classic psychoanalysis the patient lies on the couch with the analyst sitting behind and out of sight; in this way the patient can look at his or her internal world rather than at the analyst as a real person. This arrangement helps the patient to follow the "fundamental rule" of psychoanalysis – everything that comes to mind is to be communicated to the analyst – and facilitates free associations, as well as projections on to the analyst of the various roles he or she comes to play in the patient's fantasy world. The usual duration of a session is 45 or 50 minutes, with the patient having four or five sessions per week (in some regions, frequency may exceptionally be reduced to three sessions per week). The duration and frequency of sessions constitute a factor of psychological stability for the patient insofar as, once decided upon, they cannot be changed at the whim or according to the mood of either protagonist.

Outside the sessions, social and personal contact between patient and analyst should be avoided. In addition, for reasons of confidentiality, the analyst gives no information to any third party nor makes any attempt to contact the patient's circle of family and friends, unless in exceptional circumstances and with the patient's permission. All things considered, there is something inherently paradoxical in the fact that, in the analytical situation, the strict ethical constraints which patient and analyst impose on each other in their relationship in reality guarantee the integrity of the situation to such an extent that they are completely free to go beyond these restrictions in thought and in fantasy. From that point of view, the setting is a kind of safeguard which, on the symbolic level, represents the prohibition against incest.

The result of a lengthy development

Though Freud very soon came to the conclusion that it was indeed necessary to establish a proper setting for psychoanalytic treatment and had worked out its essential elements by about 1903, it took many years before psychoanalysts fully understood the real significance of the setting and its relationship to the psychoanalytic process. In *Studies on Hysteria* (1895d), Freud describes how he came to replace suggestion by the method of free association, thereby laying the foundations of the analytical setting. Later, in spite of the recommendations he wrote in 1904 and his subsequent papers on technique, Freud often exempted himself from following the strict rules he had laid down; he was not at that point able to understand the disadvantages which such dispensations entailed. For example, he discussed his analysands by name in his correspondence, making no attempt to disguise their identity; he invited some analysands to have a meal with him and his family; and he analysed people close to him such as Ferenczi and, later, his own daughter Anna. This goes to show that for some considerable time the limits of the psychoanalytic setting remained imprecise; it was only after the Second World War, when the emphasis began to be laid more and more on the transference/counter-transference relationship, that psychoanalysts felt it necessary to maintain the strict limits of the setting so that the intensity of the emotions evoked in both analyst and patient could be adequately contained.

The inseparable ties which link setting and analytical process

In the early days, psychoanalysts laid particular emphasis on working through the psychoanalytic process – in other words on the patient's inner development – with the setting being taken into account only insofar as it concerned the material arrangements which enabled that process to unfold correctly. Towards the end of the 1950s the first attempts to place the analytical setting on a sound theoretical basis appeared. W. R. Bion's (1962) work enabled practitioners to see the analogy between the analyst–analysand situation in the session and the mother–infant relationship, and to understand that setting and process are on the same footing as "container" and "contained". José Bleger (1967) argues that there is a stage in development which is earlier than Klein's paranoid-schizoid position, composed of what he calls agglutinated nuclei between the ego and the object, creating a symbiotic link. According to Bleger, this link is expressed via the intimate relationship which patients establish with the psychoanalytic setting until such time as they succeed in differentiating themselves from it. Since then, several psychoanalysts have contributed to our thinking about the relationship between setting and process, including D. W. Winnicott with his idea of "holding" and Didier Anzieu with his notion of the "skin ego".

Understanding the setting from the inside

These studies have given us a better understanding of the significance of the psychoanalytic setting with respect to the process which develops therein. The setting is often misunderstood not only by people who are not involved in psychoanalysis and by certain patients, but also by psychoanalysts themselves. For example, the general public often has only a distorted picture of the setting, seeing it simply as the patient stretched out on the couch with the psychoanalyst sitting in an armchair – this caricature making the setting meaningless, the whole psychoanalytic situation seems to be absurd. It often takes time before patients come to understand the significance of the setting arrangements which are specified at the beginning of the treatment: for example, the need for sessions to be regular, the sizeable number of sessions each week, the payment of the analyst's fee – especially when it comes to understanding why the analyst demands that missed sessions be paid for whatever the reason for the patient's absence. At first sight, these conditions may seem nonsensical – until patients themselves discover their significance and come to understand in their inner experience that a strict definition of the setting is indispensable if the psychoanalytic process is to develop successfully.

One important aspect as far as training is concerned is to ensure that the prospective analyst succeeds in internalizing the significance of the psychoanalytic setting so that it becomes second nature. This process begins with the candidate's personal experience of analysis and continues through supervision by colleagues proficient in psychoanalysis; thanks to this, the setting is not experienced simply as a series of inflexible rules imposed arbitrarily by the psychoanalyst or by the institution.

From this point of view, the analytical setting is of value only insofar as each of its elements is meaningful within the context of the analytical situation. For example, clinical experience shows that the relationship which the patient establishes with the setting is very often a non-verbal means of communication between analysand and analyst – in particular, it may express unconscious transference resistances which can thereupon be interpreted and worked through. In this way, as the treatment progresses and with the analyst's help, the patient gradually discovers the significance of the different elements of the setting and their relationship to the transference process.

The foundations of the setting in classical psychoanalysis

Insofar as setting and process are inseparable elements of a whole, psychoanalytic treatment with a sizeable number of weekly sessions remains a reference marker for those psychoanalysts who belong to the IPA and practise psychoanalysis according to Freud's teachings. A high frequency of sessions facilitates insight and the processing of interpretations. The inseparable links between setting and process enable us also to draw a distinction between the psychoanalytic process and its psychotherapeutic counterpart; the difference between them cannot be demonstrated by means of quantifiable data as classic scientific criteria would wish. For my part, I often make use of metaphors such as the one suggested by Laplanche (1987) with his comparison between mental energy and atomic energy: do we want to see it liberated as an uncontrollable chain reaction or to canalize it by means of a cyclotron? I like too the comparison between photography and cinema. Both are based on the same technique – photographic images – but the outcome is different because of the frequency with which these images succeed one another: with a frequency of less than eighteen images per second, each image is perceived on its own, while with a higher frequency what we perceive is movement, a characteristic of cinema.

An "art" rather than a "technique" in the sense of deterministic science

Given the nature of the psychoanalyst's therapeutic work and its object, the human mind, there is no absolute guarantee, even though an appropriate setting has been established, that the psychoanalytic process will be successful. This fact is an argument employed by some critics of psychoanalysis to cast doubt on the validity of the method; they base their argument on a scientific model which is deterministic in its approach. The objection, however, has to be dealt with, and I propose to do just that.

I shall begin by arguing that, as far as the human mind is concerned, it would be too simplistic were we to see matters in terms of a sharp contrast between success and failure, because this does not take into account the fact that the mind is a complex system. In such a system, as we now know, we cannot expect a given action always to produce a specific result: the laws of linear determinism are no longer applicable. From a scientific point of view, it has to be remembered that, since a complex system is made up of an infinite number of variables, it behaves in the long run in an "unpredictable" manner. Even small disturbances may at any one time modify the way in which the system is developing, so that its evolution becomes impossible to predict. Thus if we consider that the human mind behaves like a complex system as described by deterministic chaos theory, we are quite entitled to argue that psychological phenomena are in the long run unpredictable and do not correspond to the "classic" scientific model according to which a given action always leads to a specific outcome (Pragier and Faure-Pragier 1990; J-M. Quinodoz 1997a).

As regards the impossibility of accurately predicting whether or not psychoanalytic treatment will be successful with any given patient, I think that here too the methodological point of view is a sufficient answer. According to Vassalli (2001), the Freudian method is not a "technique" as we understand that term today, but a *technè* in Aristotle's sense, in other words an "art". Consequently, the outcome of this kind of activity has nothing to do with "certainty" or "inevitability" – as linear determinism would have it – but with "probability" and "possibility". The psychoanalyst's occupation is therefore an art; an analyst does not work with proof, but with clues, deductions and intuitive ideas – a process which Freud called *erraten* when describing how a psychoanalyst operates (the word is usually translated into English as "to guess"). If we adopt that point of view and treat the practice of psychoanalysis as a *technè*, this implies, first, that the work of interpretative thinking is not carried out through logical reasoning but in a conjectural manner, and, second, that there is no way of being sure that the psychoanalyst's art in treating a given patient will necessarily prove successful. According to Vassalli, this is due to the very nature of the object of psychoanalysis, the complexity of which justifies a conjectural approach. It is true, is it not, that the technique of interpretation is the only means at our disposal for exploring – with legitimate hopes of success – an object which no one has ever managed to represent: the unconscious.

Biographies and history

Sándor Ferenczi (1873–1933)

It is impossible to discuss matters of technique without mentioning the pioneering role of Sándor Ferenczi, the Hungarian physician and psychoanalyst whose contribution to clinical, technical and theoretical matters was extremely important. Though he was for some time one of Freud's closest collaborators, towards the end of his life there was a rift between the two men because of the vexed question of Ferenczi's so-called "active" technique.

Born in Hungary where he spent all his life, Ferenczi studied medicine at Vienna University and was awarded his diploma in 1896. In 1907, he discovered *The Interpretation of Dreams* and met Jung, who introduced him to Freud in 1908. The following year Ferenczi accompanied Freud and Jung on their trip to the United States. From then on a complex relationship burgeoned between Freud and Ferenczi; the latter became, in turn, Freud's pupil, friend, close family friend and confidant, and was analysed by Freud. From his very first meeting with Freud in 1908, Ferenczi participated actively in expanding the psychoanalytic movement not only in Hungary but throughout the world; it was he who launched the idea of creating an International Psychoanalytical Association (IPA) with Jung as its first president, and the IPA was indeed founded in 1910. From 1912 onwards, Ferenczi was a member of the "secret committee", set up after Jung's departure with the aim of protecting Freud against being implicated in political manoeuvring.

As to his writings, Ferenczi's best known paper, "Introjection and Transference", was published in 1909; in it, he introduced the idea of introjection, which has since become a fundamental concept of psychoanalysis. He published several other papers which are remarkable for their originality and clinical insights. He shared with Freud an interest in telepathic transmission and in the phylogenetic hypothesis according to which traumatic memories dating from prehistoric times are inherited by successive generations and lay the foundation for neurotic disorders. In addition, Ferenczi's work on war neuroses contributed to the spreading of psychoanalytic ideas in the aftermath of the First World War.

Ferenczi was analysed by Freud, though he had to insist several times before being accepted as a patient (and even then Freud hesitated a great deal). The analysis was carried out in three stages, the first in 1914 and the other two in 1916; each lasted for about three weeks, and in one of these phases Ferenczi had two sessions per day. Ferenczi's main problem had to do with his ambivalence, in particular when at one point in his analysis he was involved in a sentimental imbroglio – he hesitated between marrying Gizella Pálos, his mistress, and Gizella's younger daughter, Elma. In the end, he married Gizella in 1919 but immediately regretted having done so; thereafter, he constantly blamed Freud for influencing him in his decision. In particular, he accused Freud of not adequately analysing his (Ferenczi's) negative transference; Freud replied to this accusation in "Analysis Terminal and Interminable" (1937c).

In 1918, at the Fifth International Congress held in Budapest, Ferenczi was elected president of the International Psychoanalytical Association (IPA). However, with the social and political unrest which was rife in Hungary at that time, he had to relinquish the presidency in favour of Jones. The following year, 1919, Ferenczi resigned from his position as professor of psychoanalysis in Budapest University and devoted all his time to his patients and his writings on the technique of psychoanalysis.

In the 1920s, Ferenczi began exploring the possibility of what he called the "active" technique, pushing the idea to its very limits. This approach was meant to stimulate the development of an affective dimension in the transference of patients presenting very deep regression linked to early childhood trauma (which brought their treatment to a standstill). In 1924, Ferenczi and Rank, who was also an advocate of the active technique, published *The Development of Psychoanalysis*, a book which contains some ideas which were ahead of their time. *Inter alia*, Ferenczi and Rank emphasized the importance of analysing the negative transference in the analyst–patient relationship, and highlighted the maternal aspect of the transference (Freud had laid particular emphasis on the paternal dimension). The means they suggested for shortening the length of psychoanalytic treatment were vigorously opposed first by Abraham and Jones, then by Freud himself. Ferenczi's researches led him to adopt a technical approach, the aim of which was to give to patients the love they had not been given in their childhood; this led him to accept physical contact between patient and analyst, including reciprocal caressing and kissing, and to propose "mutual analysis" of the two partners in the psychoanalytic relationship. Sensing the risk of transgressing the prohibition against incest in the transference relationship, Freud accused his pupil of going beyond the boundaries of ethics in his attempt to give the patient love through actual satisfaction, rather than, as the psychoanalytic method advocated, restricting the relationship to communicating fantasies and affects, with no physical contact between patient and analyst.

In the twenty-five years that their relationship lasted, Freud and Ferenczi exchanged more than 1200 letters; their correspondence ended with Ferenczi's death in 1933 and is a precious source of information on this decisive period in history of psychoanalysis. Towards the end of the 1920s their disagreements meant that they could not be as close as before, but they never broke off all contact with each other; in his tribute to Ferenczi after the latter's death, Freud (1933c) acknowledged just how much psychoanalysis owed to his former pupil.

The fierce debate which surrounded Ferenczi's active technique resulted in his being quite unjustifiably forgotten for many a long decade by the Freudian psychoanalytic community.

Recent publications, however, have restored him to his rightful place in the history of psychoanalysis and have revived interest – which he richly deserves – in his innovative ideas (Haynal 1986, 2001). Though Ferenczi himself may have been consigned to obscurity, his influence lasted throughout that period thanks to the famous psychoanalysts whom he analysed such as Jones, Klein, Rickman, Roheim, Balint and Groddeck. In addition, his research into the active technique had a considerable influence on later practitioners such as Balint, a pupil of Ferenczi's, as well as Winnicott, Masud Khan, Kohut and Modell.

- "REMEMBERING, REPEATING AND WORKING-THROUGH" (1914g)

Page numbers are those of *The Standard Edition of the Complete Psychological Works of Sigmund Freud*, vol. **12**, 145–156.

This technical paper is of crucial importance for understanding the analysis of the transference. Freud shows that some patients do not have the capacity to remember what occurred in their past and to communicate these experiences verbally. These apparently forgotten memories re-emerge in their behaviour and are repeated as acts in the patient's relationship with the psychoanalyst. Here is a brief example of what Freud means when he talks of repeating rather than remembering. A patient who was abandoned in childhood may not remember this and therefore not talk about it; but in adulthood, the patient seems regularly to break off relations with other people with whom he is involved – a girlfriend or employer for instance. The patient is not aware that he is doing something in the course of the relationship which leads to his being abandoned once again, without his realizing why. Being abandoned is a pattern which keeps repeating itself, but the patient is not consciously aware of the fact that these are repetitions of a situation already experienced early in life, and there is nothing to stop him repeating this pattern of events. What is this patient "repeating"? According to Freud,

he repeats everything that has already made its way from the sources of the repressed into his manifest personality – his inhibitions and unserviceable attitudes and his pathological character-traits. He also repeats all his symptoms in the course of the treatment. (1914g: 151)

This "*compulsion to repeat*" is linked both to the transference and to resistance: on the one hand, it is linked to the transference insofar as it is a repetition in acts of the patient's past played out via the analyst as a person – "*the transference is itself only a piece of repetition*" (ibid.: 151) – and, on the other, this repetition is linked to resistance, to such an extent that "*[the] greater the resistance, the more extensively will acting out (repetition) replace remembering*" (ibid.: 151). It follows that the psychoanalyst should treat the illness not as a past event about which the patient remembers nothing, "*but as a present-day force*" before the work of the analysis becomes able to link it up consciously with the patient's past experience.

Freud notes also that the intensity of repetition is proportional to the affective quality of the transference: when the transference is positive, the patient tends to remember, while if the transference is negative and resistance stronger, the tendency to repeat through actions becomes more pronounced. In extreme cases, the transference relationship itself becomes trapped in repetition: "*the bonds which attach the patient to the treatment are broken by him in a repetitive action*" (ibid.: 154). However, if the transference is handled properly, the analyst will be able to "*[curb] the patient's compulsion to repeat and [turn] it into a motive for remembering*" (ibid.: 154). It is not enough for the analyst to "*[give] the resistance a name*", for this does

not result in its immediate cessation. One must allow the patient time to become more conversant with this resistance with which he has now become acquainted, to work through *it, to overcome it, by continuing, in defiance of it, the analytic work according to the fundamental rule of analysis.* (ibid.: 155)

The need for the analyst to respect the length of time the patient requires in order to accomplish this working-through is a crucial element in the entire psychoanalytic process.

- **"OBSERVATIONS ON TRANSFERENCE-LOVE" (1915a [1914])**

> Page numbers are those of *The Standard Edition of the Complete Psychological Works of Sigmund Freud*, vol. **12**, 159–171.

When the analyst is confronted with transference-love, what attitude should he or she take in order to avoid interrupting the treatment? For example, how should an analyst respond when a female patient appears to fall in love with her therapist, this love being in fact a repetition of the love she felt towards her mother or father when she was a child? According to Freud, the analyst should neither take a high moral stance and condemn the patient's attitude, nor ask her to "*suppress [. . .] her instincts*" (1915a: 164), because these attitudes would run counter to the analytic approach; also, he advises against "*declaring that one returns the patient's fond feelings but at the same time [. . .] avoiding any physical implementation of this fondness until one is able to guide the relationship into calmer channels and raise it to a higher level*" (ibid.: 164). This attitude is not without danger, because "*[our] control over ourselves is not so complete that we may not suddenly one day go further than we had intended*" (ibid.: 164). The risk with such an attitude is that the patient's advances find an echo in the analyst; in consequence, "*[she will] have succeeded in acting out, in repeating in real life, what she ought only to have remembered, to have reproduced as psychical material and to have kept within the sphere of psychical events*" (ibid.: 166). That is why the treatment should be carried out in abstinence – a notion which Freud was to discuss at greater length in the article I shall be turning to shortly – while allowing the patient's need and longing to subsist, for they are the forces which impel him or her to make changes.

Post-Freudians

The ethical dimension of psychoanalysis

Issues which have to do with transgressing the psychoanalytic setting are extremely complex because they involve so many factors, as Gabbard and Lester point out in their book *Boundaries and Boundary Violations in Psychoanalysis* (1995). As the psychoanalytic process unfolds, there is the risk of encountering not only sexual transgressions as described by Freud in "Observations on Transference-Love" but also non-sexual violations which, argue Gabbard and Lester (1995), ought not to be played down. These violations come in many shapes and sizes; each constitutes a breach of the setting, linked to counter-transference actings-out: for example, if an analyst sets the fee too low or too high, demands that the patient give up too much time, remains at the patient's beck and call by day and by night, etc. On the psychoanalyst's side, the reasons for not maintaining the setting as agreed upon with the patient are many and varied; Gabbard and Lester have observed that when a psychoanalyst acts out, this can usually be linked to some personal crisis or other which he or she is going through.

They emphasize the fact that preventive measures of various kinds must be put in place. During a prospective psychoanalyst's training, attention must be paid to the manner in which the candidate's personal analysis was brought to a close, and the capacity to analyse his or her own counter-transference responses should be assessed. At the clinical level, supervision is a particularly useful tool for exploring technical problems linked to maintaining an appropriate setting, which alone guarantees the proper development of the psychoanalytic process. "The most effective and powerful gift we have to offer the patient is the analytic setting" (Gabbard and Lester, 1995: 147). In addition, these authors consider that the fact that psychoanalysts in private practice work in particularly isolated conditions is a risk factor; their advice is that, no matter how proficient an analyst may be, he or she should take time to discuss with an experienced colleague questions relating to the counter-transference. Finally, Gabbard and Lester (1995) suggest that every psychoanalytic association or society should set up an Ethics Committee independent of the institution itself. Such a committee would be able to hear in complete confidentiality not only any patient or third party who has something to communicate, but also any psychoanalyst who happens to be in difficulty. In their experience, issues involving violations of the boundaries of the psychoanalytic setting are usually considered from a moral point of view or else ignored; they feel that something must be done in order to offer therapeutic help to those who are in distress.

- **"LINES OF ADVANCE IN PSYCHO-ANALYTIC THERAPY" (1919a)**

> Page numbers are those of *The Standard Edition of the Complete Psychological Works of Sigmund Freud*, vol. **17**, 157–168.

In this paper, Freud discusses what he means by his statement "Analytic treatment should be carried through, as far as is possible, under privation – in a state of abstinence" (1919a: 162). It does not mean depriving the patient of all satisfaction whatsoever nor demanding that he or she refrain from sexual intercourse; but there are two kinds of danger that may threaten the progress of the treatment. The first concerns the patient's tendency to look for substitutive satisfactions such as fulfilling with some friend or other what should properly be undertaken by the analyst, because this kind of satisfaction runs the risk of taking over where the symptoms leave off. The other danger is when the patient looks for substitutive satisfactions in the transference relationship itself, in other words with the analyst. That is why the analyst must ensure that "*the patient [is] left with unfulfilled wishes in abundance*" (ibid.: 164); some degree of frustration must be imposed, even if from time to time "*the physician is bound to take up the position of teacher and mentor*" (ibid.: 165).

In concluding his paper, Freud considers the future prospects of psychoanalysis by imagining technical developments which would enable psychoanalytic treatment to be employed in cases of psychosis and not only neurosis. He mentions also the fact that the poorer sections of the community may also be able to have recourse to a modified form of psychoanalytic treatment, such treatments being free.

It is very probable, too, that the large-scale application of our therapy will compel us to alloy the pure gold of analysis freely with the copper of direct suggestion; and hypnotic influence, too, might find a place in it again, as it has in the treatment of war neuroses. But, whatever form this psychotherapy for the people may take, whatever the elements out of which it is compounded, its most effective and most important ingredients will assuredly remain those borrowed from strict and untendentious psycho-analysis. (ibid.: 167–168)

Post-Freudians

The present role of the International Psychoanalytical Association

In 1910, at the Nuremberg Congress, Freud founded the International Psychoanalytical Association (IPA) with the aim of safeguarding psychoanalysis as he had created it. With 240 members in 1920, the IPA now numbers a little over 10,000 members from some thirty countries, mainly in Europe, North America and Latin America. The IPA's role is to establish common directives concerning training, to organize conferences and international congresses, and to promote the development of clinical matters, training and research. It coordinates the international aspects of the professional life of psychoanalysts and supervises the creation of new groups, in particular in countries where renewed interest in psychoanalysis is becoming manifest – as is at present the case in Eastern Europe, for instance, as well as in many other countries.

From the 1920s on, given the increasing number of psychoanalytic centres of activity in the world, it was deemed necessary to set up international criteria so that psychoanalysis could be transmitted under optimal conditions. Training is left to the various constituent societies of the IPA and is ruled by a series of regulations internal to the association in order to avoid the obstacle of having prospective psychoanalysts assessed by some "external" agency. Training is based essentially on three complementary vectors: *personal experience* of psychoanalysis – what is referred to as the "training analysis"; *supervision* of the candidate's initial treatment cases by an experienced psychoanalyst; *learning the fundamental tenets* of psychoanalysis, pride of place being given to Freud's own writings.

Over time, the International Psychoanalytical Association (IPA) has attempted to promulgate minimal recommendations as regards the conditions which must be fulfilled by candidates seeking training in psychoanalysis, by those wishing to become members, and by those seeking accreditation as training members. At each stage, an assessment is usually made on the basis of a series of encounters between the individual concerned and experienced psychoanalysts who try to evaluate whether that person has the necessary qualities – either for conducting psychoanalytic treatment or, at the other extreme, for training prospective psychoanalysts. These recommendations are the result of a consensus reached between the various affiliated societies of the IPA. For example, according to the directives published at the end of the 1980s, the prospective psychoanalyst's personal analysis must have comprised a sufficient number of weekly sessions for the candidate to have had in-depth experience of what psychoanalysis is all about – Freud himself recommended this. Nowadays most societies require four or five weekly sessions (some, in exceptional cases, three); it is also recommended that the prospective psychoanalyst should have successfully conducted two psychoanalyses under the supervision of an experienced training analyst. Though these minimum recommendations are still applied by most societies, more and more pressure is being brought to bear – not only from sources external to the IPA but also from some of its own members – to have the length of training reduced and to make the criteria for admission to training less strict than they are at present. The idea behind these suggestions is to allow more psychotherapists to be able to train and subsequently to practise as psychoanalysts.

My own view is that it will never be easy to strike a balance between, on the one hand, the need to maintain the fundamental achievements of psychoanalysis – which are in themselves very demanding, given the nature of the psychoanalyst's work and the psychoanalytic process itself – and, on the other, the wish to open up psychoanalysis to even more people, without running the risk of losing its specificity.

New concepts

Abstinence – counter-transference – positive transference, negative transference – psychoanalytic process – psychoanalytic setting – psychoanalytic technique – remembering – repetition, compulsion to repeat – transference-love

TOTEM AND TABOO

SOME POINTS OF AGREEMENT BETWEEN THE MENTAL
LIVES OF SAVAGES AND NEUROTICS (1912–1913)

The work of a visionary – or already outdated?

In this major book, which deserves to be appreciated much more than is usually the case today, Freud develops a remarkable psychoanalytic view of human nature, and opens up fresh perspectives as compared to his earlier writings. Basing his study on the researches of ethnologists and anthropologists, he draws parallels with certain discoveries made by psychoanalysis, and in particular with certain elements involving the Oedipus complex such as the prohibition against murdering one's ancestors – the father or his representatives – and the barrier against incest – against marrying the father's wife. However, the Oedipus complex is not born afresh with each individual or each generation, and this idea led Freud to put forward a hypothesis so daring in its acumen that he was fiercely criticized for it: ancestral traces going back to the origins of humanity influence the constitution of the Oedipus complex. For Freud, these ancient traces can be discerned in the powerful ambivalent feelings which every individual has with respect to his or her father – Freud says nothing about the mother – and in the unconscious sense of guilt which is handed down from generation to generation. These guilt feelings, says Freud, are without doubt the residue of a wrong committed in time immemorial in the course of a totem meal when the brothers, united in their hatred for their father, killed and then ate him in order to succeed him as rulers. This ancestral act of cannibalism not only gave rise to an individual sense of guilt, but also generated the different developmental stages in the social organization of human beings, from the totemism of primitive peoples to the collective morality which enables social life to continue. Religion is also an expression of this, says Freud, and here again we can find traces which have been handed down from the totemic religion of ancient times to modern Christianity, based on the original sin committed by the first inhabitants of the earth against God the Father. The various hypotheses which Freud suggests in *Totem and Taboo* have given rise to much criticism from all quarters, but the fact remains that the book raises fundamental questions which "*disturbed the sleep of the world*" as he himself had predicted (Freud 1914d: 21). That may perhaps be the explanation for the lack of interest in *Totem and Taboo* in contemporary society.

> **Biographies and history**
>
> ### The enigma of the origins of religion
>
> The question of the origins of religion was constantly in Freud's mind, and even though he was a non-religious Jew, his interest in the subject was rekindled by Jung's studies of mythology and mysticism. From 1911 onwards, Freud devoted a great deal of time to studying the many writings that existed on religions and ethnology; he was particularly interested and

fascinated by what Frazer and Wundt had written. He spent almost all of the following two years writing the four essays that make-up *Totem and Taboo*; these were first published in 1912 and 1913 in the periodical *Imago*, then brought together in book form. Outside the psychoanalytic community, the book met with disdain, especially from anthropologists who claimed that Freud had wrongly interpreted certain facts and who questioned the universal nature of his hypotheses. Freud, however, never abandoned his ideas and saw no need to change anything in what he had written – quite the contrary, in fact: he advanced the same propositions in his later writings on group psychology and restated his position in 1939 in the same terms: "*Above all, however, I am not an ethnologist but a psychoanalyst. I had a right to take out of ethnological literature what I might need for the work of analysis*" (Freud 1939a: 131).

The break-up with Carl Gustav Jung

In 1911, the psychoanalytic movement was beginning to develop quite considerably. Within the Vienna Society, conflicts – some of them quite bitter – began to arise; they had to do with disagreements and feelings of jealousy which, for some members, grew fiercer by the day. Adler, whose theoretical development led him to abandon such notions as the unconscious, repression and infantile sexuality – all of them essential concepts in psychoanalysis – resigned in 1911. In 1912, Stekel left the society, much to Freud's relief. For Jung, who had long been considered to be Freud's "crown prince", the situation was somewhat different. They worked together for six years, but shortly after their first meeting in 1907 differences of opinion were already becoming manifest between the two. That did not prevent Jung from becoming the first president of the International Psychoanalytical Association (IPA) in 1910 and editor-in-chief of the *Jahrbuch*; also, he accompanied Freud in 1909 when the latter was invited to the United States to give a series of lectures at Clark University. At that time, Jung was beginning to study mythology. Their difference of opinion focused on the meaning that was to be given to the concept of "libido": for Freud, the libido was the expression of the sexual drives and no more, while Jung felt that the libido could not be restricted to sexuality alone – it must refer to the drives in general and include those involved in self-preservation. Jung published his essay "Symbols of the Libido" in 1912, in which he develops his ideas on the nature of the libido, on mythology and on the symbolic meaning of incest. It was the ideas contained in that book which decided Freud to ask Jung to leave the psychoanalytic movement: their scientific divergences were henceforth manifest. Several anecdotal events previous to this had already made it plain that each was about to go his separate way – several bungled actions on Jung's part and, in Munich, the time when Freud fainted in Jung's presence. That incident made Freud aware of his death-wishes against his former pupil, and awakened in him the memory of what had happened when he was 19 months old: he had experienced similar death-wishes against his younger brother. The final break-up between Freud and Jung took place in September 1913 at the Weimar Congress.

Discovering the text

Page numbers are those of *The Standard Edition of the Complete Psychological Works of Sigmund Freud*, vol. **13**, 1–161.

- ### *The horror of incest*

In this book, Freud's intention is to highlight a certain number of similarities between the psychology of primitive peoples as taught by ethnology and the psychology of neurotics as revealed by psychoanalysis. His starting-point is totemism as practised in particular by the Australian

Aborigines. Each Aboriginal tribe is named after its totem, which in general is an animal – the kangaroo, for example, or the emu. The totem is hereditary and its character is inherent in all the individuals who share the same descent. Wherever a totem exists, says Freud, there is also *"a law against persons of the same totem having sexual relations with one another and consequently against their marrying"* (1912–1913: 4). The violation of this prohibition is punished extremely severely, as though it were a question of averting some danger which threatened the whole tribe. These primitive peoples must have an unusually great horror of incest, and Freud gives other examples taken from social anthropology. To the fear of violating the prohibition is attached a series of *"customs"* the aim of which is to avoid any kind of intimate contact between individuals belonging to the same totem. By far the most widespread and strictest of these concerns the avoidance of all such contact between a man and his mother-in-law. From a psychoanalytic point of view, Freud sees this reciprocal avoidance as based upon an *"ambivalent"* relationship, that is on the reciprocal coexistence of affectionate and hostile feelings, closely connected with the horror of incest.

According to Freud, the horror of incest linked to the totem that we encounter in *"savages"* is manifested also in the mental life of neurotics, in whom it is essentially an infantile feature.

Psycho-analysis has taught us that a boy's earliest choice of objects for his love is incestuous and that those objects are forbidden ones – his mother and his sister. We have learnt, too, the manner in which, as he grows up, he liberates himself from this incestuous attraction. (ibid.: 17)

As a result, unconscious incestuous fixations or regressions of libido play a crucial role in neurosis, in such a way that the incestuous desire with respect to one's parents constitutes *"the nuclear complex of neurosis"* (ibid.: 17). The revelation by psychoanalysis of the importance of the horror of incest in the unconscious thinking of neurotics was received with universal scepticism; for Freud, such a reaction is proof of the fact that this factor generates a great deal of anxiety in every one of us.

We are driven to believe that this rejection is principally a product of the distaste which human beings feel for their early incestuous wishes, now overtaken by repression. It is therefore of no small importance that we are able to show that these same incestuous wishes, which are later destined to become unconscious, are still regarded by savage peoples as immediate perils against which the most severe measures of defence must be enforced. (ibid.: 17)

• *Taboo and emotional ambivalence*

Freud goes on to examine the notion of taboo, a Polynesian word which means two things: on the one hand, it contains the idea of *"sacred"*, *"consecrated"* and, on the other, it means *"uncanny"*, *"dangerous"*, *"forbidden"*. Prohibitions linked to taboos are not part of a religious or moral system, but impose themselves on their own account. The taboo is originally derived from the fear of diabolical powers, before itself becoming diabolical. Its source is a peculiar magical power inherent in persons who are in an exceptional state – kings, priests, menstruating women, adolescents, etc. – or in certain places; in all cases, the taboo gives rise to simultaneous feelings of respect and unease. In psychoanalysis we encounter people who subject themselves to taboos as these "savages" do – obsessional neurotics. These patients have the inner certainty and moral conviction that if they violate some enigmatic prohibition or other, unfortunate consequences will surely follow. The fear which is associated with the prohibition does not prevent – in both primitive peoples and in neurotics – the pleasure-cum-desire attached to violating the prohibition. Freud adds that the wish to violate the prohibition is a highly contagious one.

Freud then attempts to discover what is common to the taboos of primitive peoples and those of obsessional neurotics – and he finds it in the subject's ambivalent attitude. In primitive peoples there is a high degree of ambivalence in the many regulations which accompany taboos. This can be seen, for example, in the way enemies are treated – putting them to death is governed by a number of observances such as acts of expiation – or in the taboo upon rulers, in which the royal personage is both venerated and enclosed in a restrictive ceremonial system, a clear sign of ambivalence towards the privileged person who is simultaneously envied.

The regularity with which we find ambivalent feelings in taboos leads Freud to examine even more closely the part played in these phenomena by a certain number of fundamental psychological mechanisms. For example, he draws a parallel between the persecutory feelings a primitive man may have towards his king and the delusions suffered by paranoiacs: both are based on the ambivalence between affectionate and hostile feelings which the son feels towards his father, as Freud had already shown in his discussion of Schreber's father complex. As for the taboo upon the dead, Freud notes that the "*obsessive self-reproaches*" which overwhelm the survivor after someone has died arise because the survivor feels responsible for the death of the loved person – and this too involves powerful feelings of ambivalence.

> *In almost every case where there is an intense emotional attachment to a particular person we find that behind the tender love there is a concealed hostility in the unconscious. This is the classical example, the prototype, of the ambivalence of human emotions.* (ibid.: 60)

What then differentiates an obsessional neurotic from a primitive person? According to Freud, the obsessional neurotic's hostility against the dead person is unconscious, because it is the expression of an unmentionable satisfaction to which that person's death gives rise; in primitive peoples, the mechanism is different, since hostility is "*projected*" on to the dead person. "*The survivor thus denies that he has ever harboured any hostile feelings against the dead loved one; the soul of the dead harbours them instead and seeks to put them into action during the whole period of mourning*" (ibid.: 61). Freud notes the division which exists between ambivalent feelings – a topic which would later be developed in his writings on splitting.

> *In this respect taboo observances, like neurotic symptoms, have a double sense. On the one hand, in their restrictive character, they are expressions of mourning; but on the other hand they clearly betray – what they seek to conceal – hostility against the dead disguised as self-defence.* (ibid.: 61)

The explanation of taboos also throws light on such notions as "*conscience*" or "*sense of guilt*", which were beginning to become clearer in Freud's thinking. He defines "*conscience*" as the perception of the internal condemnation of particular wishes which are experienced by neurotic individuals; this terrifying feeling is no different from the savage's attitude towards taboo – it is a "*command issued by conscience*", any violation of which produces "*a fearful sense of guilt*" (ibid.: 68). For Freud, sense of guilt and fear of punishment are based on the ambivalence of feelings, in neurotics as in primitive peoples; what distinguishes the former, however, is that a taboo is not a neurosis but a social institution. These developments foreshadow the idea of the superego which Freud would define some ten years later, in 1923.

• *Animism, magic and the omnipotence of thoughts*

Animism is highly prevalent in primitive cultures, in which the world is peopled by innumerable spirits both benevolent and malevolent; these spirits are considered to be the causes of natural phenomena. According to Freud, in the course of history humanity went through three major phases in its vision of the world: animistic (mythological), religious and scientific. The first *Weltanschauung* was animism, which is a psychological theory; in addition, animism goes hand-in-hand with sorcery and magic. Sorcery is the art of influencing spirits, while magic is an essential part of animistic technique. Magic is used for subjecting natural phenomena to the will of humans, and for protecting the individual from his enemies and from danger; at the same time it gives him the power to injure his enemies. In this vision of the world, a general overvaluation of thought eclipses the perception of reality, such that the principle on which magic is based is the omnipotence of thoughts: "*the principle governing magic, the technique of the animistic mode of thinking, is the principle of the 'omnipotence of thoughts'* " (ibid.: 85).

In neurotics, psychoanalysis has revealed this primitive mode of mental functioning that is the omnipotence of thoughts, in particular in the case of obsessional neurosis, where over-valuation of thought processes takes over from reality, as in the Rat Man's obsession with rats. The over-valuation of the power one attributes to one's own mental processes is an essential element in "*narcissism*", writes Freud, the stage in development during which the sexual drives have already found an object – but this object is the person's own ego. It may therefore be said that the omnipotence of thoughts in primitive peoples corresponds to an early stage of libidinal development – that of *"intellectual narcissism"* – in which neurotic individuals also find themselves, either through regression or through a pathological fixation. In his conclusion, Freud comes back to the idea that in an animistic system, the spirits and demons which people the universe are simply *"projections"* of the individual's own emotional impulses and important figures; in this way the individual sees his internal mental processes as being external to himself, just as Schreber saw his mental processes in the context of his paranoid delusion as coming from outside himself.

• *The return of totemism in childhood*

Totem and Oedipus

Basing his discussion on the work of such authors as the ethnologist J. G. Frazer, who showed that the totem animal was generally felt to be the ancestor of the tribe and that the totem was handed down as an inheritance from generation to generation, Freud emphasizes the fact that totemism and exogamy are ancestral in origin; in this respect he agrees with Darwin's idea of the original existence of a primal horde in primates as well as in humankind. With this in mind, Freud draws a parallel between the totem animal and childhood phobias, since in the latter situation the object of the phobia is often an animal. Freud argues that both the totem animal and the object of the phobia represent the father who is both feared and revered, as we saw in Little Hans's phobia of horses. The presence of ambivalent feelings towards the father in both of these situations enables Freud to draw the conclusion that the totem and the Oedipus complex have the same origin.

> *If the totem animal is the father, then the two principal ordinances of totemism, the two taboo prohibitions which constitute its core – not to kill the totem and not to have sexual relations with a woman of the same totem – coincide in their content with the two crimes of Oedipus, who killed his father and married his mother, as well as with the two primal wishes of children, the insufficient repression or reawakening of which forms the nucleus of perhaps every psychoneurosis.* (ibid.: 132)

The totem meal and the killing of the father

In his exploration of other features of totemism – in particular of the supposed existence of a ceremonial "totem meal" in ancient times – Freud puts forward a bold hypothesis according to which the father of the primal horde was killed and eaten by his sons at one point, lost in the mists of time, in the course of a sacrificial meal.

> *One day the brothers who had been driven out came together, killed and devoured their father and so made an end of the patriarchal horde. United, they had the courage to do and succeeded in doing what would have been impossible for them individually.* (ibid.: 141)

The ceremony of the totem meal in primitive peoples would thus appear to be a commemoration of this event.

> *The totem meal, which is perhaps mankind's earliest festival, would thus be a repetition and a commemoration of this memorable and criminal deed, which was the beginning of so many things – of social organization, of moral restrictions and of religion.* (ibid.: 142)

Having satisfied their hatred, the sons began to feel a sense of guilt and remorse, which made them seek reconciliation with the outraged father. They therefore created out of their filial sense of guilt a totem religion which incorporated the two fundamental taboos of totemism: the prohibition against killing the totem animal, representing the father, and the prohibition against incest. According to Freud, this sense of guilt lies at the heart not only of the totem religion but also of all religions, of society and of ethics.

> *Society was now based on complicity in the common crime; religion was based on the sense of guilt and the remorse attaching to it; while morality was based partly on the exigencies of this society and partly on the penance demanded by the sense of guilt.* (ibid.: 146)

The totemic sacrifice is the origin of all religions

Freud then proceeds to argue that religion constitutes the acme of ambivalence with respect to the father: after the latter's elimination, followed by his incorporation by the brothers in order for them to become like their father, the dead father, idealized and exalted, is transformed into the tribal god. The memory of this first great sacrificial act thus proved indestructible, and the various later developments of religious thinking are a kind of rationalization of this. Freud shows how this becomes manifest in Christianity, where Christ sacrificed his life to redeem his brothers and deliver them from the hereditary sin: "*There can be no doubt that in the Christian myth the original sin was one against God the Father*" (ibid.: 154).

In his concluding remarks, Freud wonders how this sense of guilt connected with the killing of the father has managed to persist over so many thousands of years, without either individuals or successive generations being aware of the fact. He assumes the existence of a "*collective mind*" in which mental processes occur just as they do in the mind of an individual. These are handed down from generation to generation over and beyond "*direct communication and tradition*". How this process operates is still largely unknown.

> *Social psychology shows a very little interest, on the whole, in the manner in which the required continuity in the mental life of successive generations is established. A part of the problem seems to be met by the inheritance of psychical dispositions which, however, need to be given some sort of impetus in the life of the individual before they can be roused into actual operation. This may be the meaning of the poet's words: "What thou hast inherited from thy fathers, acquire it to make it thine" [Goethe, Faust, Part I, v. 682–683].* (ibid.: 158)

Freud concludes the book with a distinction between neurotics and primitive peoples:

> *[N]eurotics are above all* inhibited *in their actions; with them the thought is a complete substitute for the deed. Primitive men, on the other hand, are* uninhibited*: thought passes directly into action. With them it is rather the deed that is a substitute for the thought. And that is why [. . .] I think that in the case before us it may safely be assumed that "in the beginning was the Deed".* (ibid.: 161)

Post-Freudians

The work of a visionary and the criticism it provoked

As soon as the book was published, it provoked a storm of criticism – from psychoanalysts as well as from anthropologists. Even today the controversy has hardly abated; the following short extracts, culled from much more plentiful sources, will be sufficient proof of this.

Criticism of Freud's ethnological hypotheses

In 1920, the ethnologist Kroeber was one of the first to raise objections as regards *Totem and Taboo*. He challenged both the methodology which lay behind it and its theoretical conclusions, and rejected Freud's hypothesis of the social and religious foundations of civilization. Kroeber did, however, keep an open mind as regards the use of the discoveries of psychoanalysis in anthropological research. Other critics have attacked Freud as a person: Freeman (1967) argued that the theory of the original murder was essentially an expression of Freud's ambivalence as regards his own father. Generally speaking, Freud's opinions were attacked not only because of the "social Darwinism" which inspired them but also because most specialist writers rejected the ethnological and anthropological foundations of *Totem and Taboo*.

Phylogenesis: a controversial issue

One of the major criticisms levelled against Freud's hypotheses as developed in *Totem and Taboo* came from psychoanalysts themselves. It is worth our while to pause for a moment and examine their point of view because, having read all of Freud's published writings, I am convinced that in emphasizing the importance of phylogenetic transmission, he was both perspicacious and a forerunner. This controversial issue has to do with his hypothesis concerning the transmission from generation to generation of memory traces which go back to the origins of humanity; in a considerable number of his writings, Freud had recourse to this explanation. He draws a distinction between the process of individual development from infancy to adulthood – ontogenesis – and the developmental process which concerns the human species from its origins to the present day – phylogenesis. He argues that traces of traumatic events which have occurred in the history of mankind reappear in each individual and play a part in structuring the individual personality. For example, in *Totem and Taboo* he argues that the Oedipus complex and the sense of guilt which exist in all of us are based on personal elements which are linked to our family background, to which is added the "historical" trace of the killing of the father of the primal horde which goes back to the very origins of the human species.

Even today many psychoanalysts reject the hypothesis of phylogenetic transmission, implying as it does both biology and genetics. Some have recourse to technical arguments, saying that as far as their everyday work is concerned, the origin of instinctual drives and conflicts is not very important: whatever the balance between nature and nurture, the same interpretation will be proposed to the patient so that, in the opinion of these analysts, the distinction remains purely theoretical. Others have recourse to a more psychological argument, observing that Freud seemed to adopt a phylogenetic explanation whenever his attempt to account for a given phenomenon by ontogenesis came up against the "*bedrock of biology*", as he himself put it in his moments of doubt. However, I am convinced that phylogenesis does play a part in psychic causality, as Braunschweig (1991) also argues, even though as yet we do not possess sufficient knowledge of the biological foundations upon which phylogenetic transmission could operate. As far as I am concerned, Bion opened up new horizons in psychoanalysis with his idea of "pre-conceptions" which he describes as an innate ability to have psychological experiences. Pre-conceptions which have not yet been confirmed by experience have to await their realization, whereupon they become "conceptions".

In the past few decades, there has been an increasing interest in post-Freudian psychoanalytic writing concerning one particular aspect of transmission: transgenerational transmission, a phenomenon which is regularly encountered in clinical practice. This transmission takes place by means of unconscious identificatory processes which are handed down from generation to generation, following other paths than those thought to be operative in phylogenetic transmission.

I think it would also be useful were psychoanalysts to take into account the phenomena of transmission of instinct as observed in animals, as Freud suggested in 1939 in *Moses and Monotheism*. In the same way, I am sure that contemporary psychoanalysts would benefit from knowing more about recent discoveries in ethology; their acquaintance with these is too often sketchy. This new data could well contribute to bringing together complementary disciplines which share a common goal: learning more about human nature (Schäppi 2002).

Towards a psychoanalytic anthropology

In spite of its controversial aspects, *Totem and Taboo* may quite justifiably be looked upon as the starting-point of an authentic psychoanalytic anthropology and ethno-psychoanalysis. Many books now bear witness to the usefulness of these developments. Abram Kardiner, an American psychoanalyst, tried to bring together psychoanalysis and social anthropology, and conceived the idea of the "basic personality" which he saw as the integration of social norms at a subconscious level (Kardiner and Linton 1939). Roheim (1950), the Hungarian anthropologist and psychoanalyst, was the first to do actual fieldwork, introducing into his anthropological studies not only the concept of the Oedipus complex but also the whole theoretical basis of psychoanalysis as it then stood. He analysed the dreams of the local population, their play, their myths and their beliefs. He was a true pioneer in that discipline. For Roheim, the universality of psychological mechanisms in all cultures was never in doubt; others such as Münsterberger (1969), Hartmann, Kris and Lowenstein (1969), as well as Parin and Morgenthaler (1969), came to share that view. On the other hand, some anthropologists – Malinowski and Mead, for example – were not convinced of the universality of the Oedipus complex; the topic remains a controversial one. Devereux (1972) took a "complementarist" standpoint: psychoanalysis and anthropology have different but complementary points of view on any given reality, the one looking at phenomena from the inside, the other from the outside. Devereux's theoretical developments gave rise to ethno-psychoanalytic clinical work which succeeded in taking into account the specific counter-transference feelings evoked in the practice of trans-cultural psychoanalysis.

New concepts

Ambivalence – animism – conscience – incest taboo – killing of the father – love/hate – magic – omnipotence of thoughts – phylogenetic transmission – sense of guilt

"ON NARCISSISM: AN INTRODUCTION"

(1914c)

A concept that has many implications

The word narcissism was brought into psychoanalysis to designate self-love, in reference to the Greek myth of Narcissus. Narcissus fell in love with what he thought was another person, though it turned out to be his own image reflected in a pool of water. It is important to note that Narcissus drowned without realizing that he was looking, not at someone else, but at the reflection of his own face. Freud used the term for the first time in 1910 to describe the type of object choice made by homosexuals who choose a partner who resembles them, and in so doing "*take* themselves *as their sexual object*" (1905d: 144 [note added in 1910]). Shortly after this, Freud showed that narcissism was an intermediate stage in the child's psychosexual development, between auto-eroticism (the model for which is masturbation) and the more advanced stage characterized by object-love (1911c [1910]; 1912–1913).

In 1914, when he wrote the paper discussed in this chapter, Freud in fact goes much further than a simple "introduction" to narcissism: he makes a general survey of the issues raised by this notion for the whole of psychoanalytic theory. This makes the paper difficult to read, all the more so because the term narcissism – and in particular primary narcissism – is used in several different ways by Freud and post-Freudian psychoanalysts. In this text, Freud states once again that the libido is primarily sexual in nature, and he describes a primitive or early form of narcissism which he calls *primary narcissism*; infants take themselves as their love-object and feel that the whole world revolves around them, before going on to choose some external object. The capacity to love other people for what they are, perceived as being separate and different from the self, is a progress in relationship terms, because it means that, in loving some other person, the individual can in turn love him- or herself: it is this turning-around of cathexis on to the self that Freud calls *secondary narcissism*. In normal development, secondary narcissism lays the foundations for self-esteem and coexists with object-love. Pathological forms of narcissism do exist, however; these take the shape of personality disorders of varying severity which, in psychosis, may go as far as delusions of grandeur. In addition, narcissism has considerable implications for the individual's relationships; Freud describes two main types of object choice: *anaclitic*, in which the object as such is loved and acknowledged as being distinct from the self, and *narcissistic*, based essentially on the love the individual has for him- or herself. Freud gives various examples of these.

The withdrawal which is characteristic of narcissistic personalities led Freud to believe that such persons were not suitable for analysis because, unlike neurotics, they cannot establish a transference relationship. Post-Freudian psychoanalysts, on the other hand, have shown that the narcissistic transference can in fact be analysed, thereby opening the way to some highly significant developments in psychoanalysis.

Development of Freud's concepts

Narcissism: a concept that is difficult to define in Freud's writings

The terms "narcissism", "primary narcissism" and "secondary narcissism" are very difficult to define, because they are used in many different ways both by Freud himself and in psychoanalytic literature as a whole. As Laplanche and Pontalis (1967) point out, Freud's use of the expression "secondary narcissism" is less problematic than that of "primary narcissism". Freud defines secondary narcissism as "a turning round upon the ego of libido withdrawn from the objects which it has cathected hitherto"; primary narcissism, for Freud, denotes "an early state in which the child cathects its own self with the whole of its libido" (Laplanche and Pontalis 1967 [1973: 337]). These authors note that, in attempting to ascertain the exact moment of the establishment of this state, we are faced – even in Freud's writings – with a variety of views. In the 1910–1915 period, he placed the narcissistic phase between those of auto-eroticism and object-love; later, in the years 1916–1917, he used the term "primary narcissism" to mean rather a first state of life, prior even to the formation of an ego, which is epitomized by life in the womb. Laplanche and Pontalis point out also that this definition of primary narcissism often denotes in psychoanalytic theory "a strictly 'objectless' – or at any rate 'undifferentiated' – state, implying no split between subject and external world" (ibid.: 338). In their discussion of the various psychoanalytic points of view on narcissism, they note that this conception of primary narcissism loses sight of the reference to an image of the self or to a mirror-type relation – a reference to the kind of relationship described by Lacan in his work on the "mirror stage" of development.

For Freud, narcissistic patients do not establish a transference relationship

Given their tendency to withdraw into themselves and turn away from relationships with people in the external world, Freud thought that patients who presented a *"narcissistic neurosis"* could not be analysed because, in his view, they did not establish a transference. He placed patients incapable of establishing a transference, for example those presenting a psychosis or a manic-depressive state, in the category of "narcissistic neuroses", as opposed to neurotic patients who establish a *"transference neurosis"* which can then be analysed.

With hindsight, we could say that the manner in which Freud saw the transference probably prevented him from entertaining the idea of analysing the negative transference. Although he had described both forms of transference, positive and negative, he saw in the latter only a kind of resistance that stood in the way of the positive transference; for that reason, he could not conceive of analysing this resistance as an integral part of the transference itself. The work of post-Freudian psychoanalysts has meant that it is now possible to envisage the whole transference; in their clinical practice, psychoanalysts work with the transference situation in accordance with their own theoretical and technical references.

Discovering the text

Page numbers are those of *The Standard Edition of the Complete Psychological Works of Sigmund Freud*, vol. **14**, 67–102.

- ## *From primary to secondary narcissism*

Freud begins by defining the idea of narcissism as it appears in the clinical descriptions that were made a few years previously by sexologists:

> *the attitude of a person who treats his own body in the same way in which the body of a sexual object is ordinarily treated – who looks at it, that is to say, strokes it and fondles it till he obtains complete satisfaction through these activities.* (1914c: 73)

Psychoanalysis, however, he adds, has shown that this sexual cathexis of the individual's own body is encountered not only in psychopathological cases but also in the course of normal psychosexual development; with this statement, Freud opened up a much wider domain for the exploration of narcissism.

Psychoanalytic practice, writes Freud, has shown that some patients – schizophrenics in particular – have a kind of "narcissistic attitude" towards the analyst. They have withdrawn their interest from people and things in the external world; as a result, they become inaccessible to analysis, as Abraham had pointed out as early as 1908. What then happens to the libido in schizophrenia? According to Freud, when the libido is withdrawn from the external world, it takes refuge in the megalomaniac's delusions of grandeur. *"The libido that has been withdrawn from the external world has been directed to the ego and thus gives rise to an attitude which may be called narcissism"* (1914c: 75). Delusions of grandeur are not, however, some new creation *ex nihilo*; they are a magnification of a condition which had previously existed – this is the state which Freud proposes to call *primary narcissism*. The narcissism which results from the drawing in of object-cathexes back to the ego is *secondary narcissism*. *"This leads us to look upon the narcissism which arises through the drawing in of object-cathexes as a secondary one, superimposed upon a primary narcissism that is obscured by a number of different influences"* (ibid.: 75).

In the schizophrenic's delusions of grandeur, psychoanalysis finds features similar to those it discovered in the thought processes of young children, such as omnipotence of thoughts, magic and megalomania. Freud goes on to suggest that in very young infants there may be an original libidinal cathexis of the ego – primary narcissism – from which some is later given off to objects, i.e. directed towards people in the external world. However, he notes, this libidinal cathexis of the ego essentially persists all through life *"and is related to object cathexes much as the body of an amoeba is related to the pseudopodia which it puts out"* (ibid.: 75). In contrasting in this way ego–libido and object–libido, Freud says that these two orientations of cathexes are in a state of equilibrium: *"The more of the one is employed, the more the other becomes depleted"* (ibid.: 76).

In asserting once more that the libido is always sexual in content, Freud emphasizes his controversy with Jung; the latter, in Freud's view, emptied the concept of all substance in declaring that it was no more than ordinary mental interest. To support his hypotheses concerning the crucial role played by the libido in mental life, Freud argues at some length that his theory of the libido is essentially based on biology, even though science as it existed in his day gave him little in the way of endorsement.

Since we cannot wait for another science to present us with the final conclusions on the theory of the instincts, it is far more to the purpose that we should try to see what light may be thrown upon this basic problem of biology by a synthesis of the psychological *phenomena*. (ibid.: 79)

• *The many manifestations of narcissism*

The chief means of access to the psychoanalytic study of narcissistic phenomena – and of primary narcissism in particular – remains the investigation of the psychoses; it is not, however, the only means. Other approaches are open to us, says Freud: the study of organic illnesses, of hypochondriasis and of erotic life.

It is a well-known fact that persons who are suffering from some organic pain or discomfort withdraw all interest from the external world, including their libidinal cathexes of their love-objects; these libidinal cathexes are restored once the individual concerned has recovered. Sleep gives rise to a similar pattern of withdrawal: *"The condition of sleep [implies] a narcissistic withdrawal of the positions of the libido on to the subject's own self, or, more precisely, on to the single wish to sleep"* (ibid.: 81). Hypochondriacs too withdraw their interest and libido from things of the external world, concentrating it on the organs which engage their attention and which are causing them pain. Narcissistic libidinal cathexis of a part of the body is not a feature of hypochondriasis alone; it occurs also in the neuroses by virtue of the fact that any part of the body may find itself given the quality of erotogenic zone and behave as a substitute for the genitals. *"For every such change in the erotogeneity of the organs there might then be a parallel change of libidinal cathexis in the ego"* (ibid.: 84). In this view, to every libidinal cathexis of an erotogenic zone corresponds a libidinal cathexis of the ego and has therefore to do with primary narcissism.

The parallel which Freud draws between hypochondriasis and schizophrenia enables him to go further and introduce a new idea, that of the *"damming-up of the libido"* as a result of its *"introversion"* in the process of pathological regression (ibid.: 84). Damming-up of the libido would thus be the root cause of organ delusions in hypochondriasis and delusions of grandeur in schizophrenia. With this quantitative idea of damming-up of the libido, Freud adds an *economic* dimension to the nature of narcissism, which is different from the concept of narcissism as a *developmental phase* which he had introduced in his study of Senatspräsident Schreber in 1911; this completes the contrast between ego–libido and object–libido.

The erotic life of human beings offers many examples of libidinal cathexes based on narcissism. The infant's earliest sexual satisfactions are experienced in connection with those vital functions which serve as a support for them – being fed, being cared for, etc.; later, this supportive aspect becomes manifest through the fact that the primary caregivers are also the child's first sexual objects – in the first instance, the mother or some substitute for her. Freud proposes to call "*anaclitic*" this kind of object-choice which, in adults, is based on the earliest object-choices of their childhood. Other individuals, such as perverts and homosexuals, do not model their choice on their mother but on their own self – Freud calls this kind of object-choice "*narcissistic*". That said, as Freud himself immediately points out, the difference is not as sharp as might at first appear between these two types of object-choice: "*We assume rather that both kinds of object-choice are open to each individual, though he may show a preference for one or the other*" (ibid.: 88). Consequently, says Freud, "*a human being has originally two sexual objects – himself and the woman who nurses him – and in doing so we are postulating a primary narcissism in everyone, which may in some cases manifest itself in a dominating fashion in his object-choice*" (ibid.: 88).

Freud then goes on to outline several kinds of object-choice. Complete object-love of the anaclitic type is characteristic of men. He remains faithful to his idea that being in love is a pathological condition because falling passionately in love displays an over-valuation of the woman involved and is evocative of a "*neurotic compulsion*" which entails "*an impoverishment of the ego as regards libido in favour of the love-object*" (ibid.: 88). As for object-choice in women, Freud thinks that many women base their relationships on the pattern of a narcissistic object-choice. In support of this hypothesis, he notes that, with the onset of puberty, the maturing of the sexual organs "*seems to bring about an intensification of the original narcissism*" (ibid.: 88), so that more often than not the charm that women have for men is of a narcissistic kind. "*Strictly speaking, it is only themselves that such women love with an intensity comparable to that of the man's love for them. Nor does their need lie in the direction of loving, but of being loved*" (ibid.: 89). Freud does add, however, that he is prepared to admit that there are quite a number of women who love according to the masculine type and who develop the sexual over-valuation typical of that kind of object-choice. Other narcissistic women tend to turn away from men yet manage to find a road which leads indirectly to complete object-love – the love they have for the child to whom they give birth. Freud explores in a very perceptive manner why narcissistic personalities have so great an attraction for those around them; he infers that those who let themselves be fascinated by such personalities "*have renounced part of their own narcissism and are in search of object-love*" (ibid.: 89). Freud concludes this section of his paper with an evocation of the primary narcissism of children, which is easy to deduce from the attitude of the parents: they overvalue their child, ascribe every perfection to him or her, and expect that their child's life will be much better than their own – a true example of "*His Majesty the Baby*" (ibid.: 91).

- ### *From infantile narcissism to the formation of ideals in adulthood*

Freud goes on to discuss what happens to the excessive self-love which is characteristic of the infant's primary narcissism once the child, now an adult, has had to cope with frustration in the external world. No human being can forego the wish for narcissistic perfection which prevailed in childhood; this indeed does not disappear – it is replaced by the formation of an intrapsychic agency which Freud at times calls "*ideal ego*" [Idealich] and at others "*ego ideal*" [Ichideal]. He would later employ these notions in a more precise sense. In other words, "*[what] the adult projects before him as his ideal is the substitute for the lost narcissism of his childhood, in which he was his own ideal*" (ibid.: 94).

The formation of an ideal against which the individual is constantly measuring his or her own thoughts and deeds entails a corresponding increase in the demands made upon the ego. This is the role of what Freud calls "*conscience*", which is often a factor favouring repression.

> *It would not surprise us if we were to find a special psychical agency which performs the task of seeing that narcissistic satisfaction from the ego ideal is ensured and which, with this end in view, constantly watches the actual ego and measures it by that ideal.* (ibid.: 95)

This kind of demand made upon the ego is encountered not only in the pathological form of a delusion of being watched – in which patients imagine that their thoughts are known and their actions observed – but also in normal individuals, who have this idea somewhere in their mind. "*A power of this kind, watching, discovering and criticizing all our intentions, does really exist [. . .] in every one of us in normal life*" (ibid.: 95). The institution of conscience is at bottom an embodiment of parental criticism with respect to the child, then that of educators and finally that of society as a whole. The "*dream-censor*" Freud described in 1900 is another of the forms this may take. In addition to its individual aspect, this ideal has a social side; it is also the common ideal of a family, a class or a nation. Freud would later develop this topic much more fully in his detailed exploration of the mechanisms involved in group psychology.

Post-Freudians

Narcissistic transference phenomena are analysable

Towards the end of the 1920s, a certain number of psychoanalysts proved beyond any doubt that patients whose condition, for Freud, belonged to the category of "narcissistic neuroses" did in fact manifest transference phenomena, contrary to what Freud had thought. These analysts – among whom were Ruth Mack Brunswick, Melanie Klein, Harry Stack Sullivan and Paul Federn – argued that though with such patients the negative transference tended to prevail over the positive one, they were nonetheless accessible to analysis. The work of these pioneers later made possible a psychoanalytic approach to a wide variety of psychopathological conditions which, before then, had been thought unsuitable for analysing the transference. Out of these early attempts there grew the psychoanalysis not only of the psychoses in children and adults but also of manic-depressive states and the perversions – together with newer pathologies which for the time being are classified as borderline states and narcissistic personality disorders. Generally speaking, Freud's distinction between narcissistic neuroses and transference neuroses has been abandoned, now that it has become clear that patients who used to be thought of as purely neurotic do in fact present some narcissistic troubles, and vice versa. Contemporary psychoanalysts thus often have to deal with "heterogeneous" patients (D. Quinodoz 2002), whose transference is made up both of more developmentally-advanced elements which are neurotic in nature and of primitive elements which are a mixture of psychotic, perverse and narcissistic components in varying proportions.

Psychoanalytic treatment of narcissistic disorders: two main trends

Two different conceptions of narcissistic disorders

There is at the moment a wide range of points of view concerning the manner in which psychoanalysts think of narcissism from both theoretical and technical standpoints; as a result, the therapeutic approach to these conditions varies considerably. I cannot go into any great detail about all of these trends – their terminology differs significantly, as do the clinical techniques employed. There are, however, two main therapeutic tendencies among psychoanalysts, depending on which conception of narcissism they take as their reference. Some follow Freud's conception of primary narcissism, with the idea that there exists a phase at the beginning of life in which the infant has as yet no knowledge of the object: for these psychoanalysts, this phase is part of normal child development. Others feel that object relations exist from the very beginning of life, and adopt Klein's approach: there is no primary narcissistic phase in Freud's sense, only "narcissistic states". These different models give rise to contrasting technical approaches to the psychoanalytic treatment of narcissistic disorders.

Those who hold that there is an "objectless" phase at the beginning of life

From a technical point of view, those psychoanalysts who see primary narcissism – "objectless" – as a normal phase of development tend to consider the narcissistic phenomena which appear in the course of an analysis as relatively normal, which is why they would not pay particular heed to the conflictual aspects of the narcissistic transference when making their interpretations, as Palacio Espasa (2003) has pointed out. Typical figures of this school of thought are Anna Freud, Margaret Mahler, D. W. Winnicott, Michael Balint and Heinz Kohut.

Adopting her father's point of view, Anna Freud (1965) considered that in new-borns and young infants there is at the beginning of life an undifferentiated narcissistic state in which the object does not exist; she called this first stage of the child's mental development a "symbiotic phase". Later, as infants develop, their interest comes more and more to focus on the object; this process unfolds through a series of different stages.

Margaret Mahler's conception is somewhat different. For her, object relations develop from the phase of symbiotic or primary infantile narcissism onwards, and evolve in parallel with what she calls the "process of separation-individuation" (Mahler et al. 1975). She also introduced the notion of "symbiotic psychosis" after observing the states of panic which emerge in psychotic children when they perceive a sense of separateness. Drawing on this concept, she describes a "normal symbiotic phase" in the mental development of all children. Margaret Mahler's ideas were adopted by psychoanalysts belonging to the Ego Psychology school of thought and applied to the psychoanalytic treatment of children and adults.

For his part, Winnicott (1955–1956) also held that primary identification was prevalent at the beginning of life – the infant believes that mother-and-child are completely merged with each other – but he rarely used the term primary narcissism. During this phase, the baby has the illusion of having created the object and the mother's function is to maintain that illusion until her infant is ready to abandon it. If something goes wrong at this stage, disorders of "primitive emotional development" will ensue. With such patients, the aim of psychoanalytic treatment is to allow them to regress to a stage of early infantile dependence, in which the analysand and the setting merge together in a state of primary narcissism out of which the "true self" will be able to grow. For Balint (1952), the need for physical contact which some analysands present corresponds to the need to return to "primary object-love" which is, in his view, the equivalent of a return to primary narcissism: in allowing the patient to return to this state, the psychoanalytic process enables "progression by means of regression".

Among the supporters of an objectless narcissistic phase, I must mention the points of view of both Béla Grunberger and Kohut. For Grunberger (1971), narcissism is a psychic agency in its own right; he argues that the "narcissistic analytical relationship" gives an impetus to the treatment. Kohut (1971) has an original approach to the psychoanalytic treatment of narcissistic disorders, and he identifies two phases in the treatment of patients who present an idealizing transference: an initial phase of regression to primitive narcissism, followed by a phase in which this kind of transference can be processed or worked through once the initial state of equilibrium begins to collapse.

Those who hold that the object is perceived from the very beginnings of life

Those psychoanalysts who argue that the newborn's ego perceives the object from the outset consider narcissistic phenomena to be the expression of aggressive or libidinal drives and of defences which are set up as soon as the object is perceived as separate and different from the self. As a result, psychoanalysts who belong to this group tend to think that narcissistic phenomena can be interpreted in a detailed manner in the *hic et nunc* of the transference relationship; they set great store by interpreting the anxiety involving differentiation and separation which emerges in the relationship with the analyst (J-M. Quinodoz 1991). Among the main figures in this group, I would mention Melanie Klein and the post-Kleinian psychoanalysts such as Rosenfeld and Segal, whose work has been continued at least in part by André Green and Otto Kernberg.

For Klein, the primary narcissistic phase does not exist; the newborn perceives the object immediately after birth – this is probably Klein's greatest difference of opinion with respect to Freud. The idea of narcissism is still present in her writings, but it appears in 1946 along with that of projective identification and again in 1957 with that of envy: these notions have thrown fresh light on the part played by narcissism as a defence against perceiving the object as separate and different. This point of view led Kleinian analysts to talk of narcissistic "states" rather than of a narcissistic "phase". It was on the basis of these ideas that Bion (1957, 1967), Rosenfeld and Segal began, towards the end of the 1940s, to analyse psychotic patients, with the traditional psychoanalytic setting being rigorously maintained. Subsequently, their clinical work enabled the development of a specifically Kleinian approach to the psychoanalytic treatment of the narcissistic dimension of the transference.

I feel it important to discuss in some detail Herbert Rosenfeld's contributions; they were particularly influential as regards the possibility of analysing the narcissistic transference. For Rosenfeld, the phenomena which Freud described in terms of primary narcissism, preceding the perception of the object, ought really to be seen as genuine object relations of a primitive type. Narcissism, argues Rosenfeld, is based on omnipotence and idealization of the self obtained via introjective and projective identifications with the idealized object. Identification with the idealized object results in the denial of any difference or of any frontier between self and object. That is why, says Rosenfeld (1965: 171), "in narcissistic object relations, defences against any recognition of separateness between self and object play a predominant part." Rosenfeld ascribes also a crucial role to envy in narcissistic phenomena. Continuing his exploration in the light of the conflict between the life and death drives, Rosenfeld introduced in 1971 a distinction between libidinal narcissism and destructive narcissism. He notes that when the narcissistic position with respect to the object is abandoned, hate and contempt for the object become inevitable, because the patient feels humiliated as soon as the external object is perceived to possess certain qualities. When this resentment is analysed, the patient can then overcome his or her hostile transference: "it is then that [the patient] becomes aware of the analyst as a valuable external person" (1971: 173). But when these destructive aspects predominate, envy appears as a wish to destroy any progress made in the analysis and to attack the analyst, as representing the object who is the true source of life and goodness. According to Rosenfeld, whatever the strength of the destructive impulses, it is clinically essential to gain access to the dependent libidinal part of the self in order to attenuate the impact of hate and envy, thereby allowing the patient to establish good object relations. This can be achieved through a detailed analysis of the constant switching between narcissistic positions in which the object is denied and object-related positions in which it is acknowledged.

Segal's (1986) views on narcissism are close to those of Rosenfeld; in her opinion, the concept of life and death drives is useful for resolving the problem raised by Freud's hypothesis of primary narcissism. According to Segal, in some patients narcissism may take the form of idealizing death and hating life – hence their wish to annihilate not only the object but also their own self; this wish appears as a defence against perceiving the object. Segal takes up the question of how the individual emerges from narcissism. She says that it is only through "negotiating" the depressive position that one can emerge from narcissistic structures and establish stable non-narcissistic object relations.

Green discusses some of Rosenfeld's ideas and develops them in his own way, particularly in *Life Narcissism, Death Narcissism* (1983). Green highlights the "unbinding" which the death drive generates in every kind of relationship with the object; he calls this effect the "de-objectalizing function" of the death drive (Green 1986). He shows also how, in psychosis, the death drive may bring about an extinction of projective activity and a de-cathexis which cause "blanks" in thinking. I shall conclude this brief overview with a word or two about Kernberg's (1975) position. In his theoretical approach to narcissism, Kernberg tries to reconcile Freud's views with those of the object relations school such as Klein and Bion. Kernberg sees in pathological narcissism a specific pattern which has become fixed in the patient's childhood; narcissistic personality disorders, he writes, are similar to those we encounter in borderline states, though varying degrees of severity do exist. Narcissistic personalities have a grandiose self which is more cohesive than that of borderline personalities, he says, but the self remains pathological and masks the fragmenting of the person's sense of identity.

New concepts

Anaclitic object choice – damming-up of the libido – ego ideal – narcissism – narcissistic object choice – primary narcissism – secondary narcissism

PAPERS ON METAPSYCHOLOGY WRITTEN BETWEEN 1915 AND 1917
"Instincts and their Vicissitudes" (1915c)
"Repression" (1915d)
"The Unconscious" (1915e)
"A Metapsychological Supplement to the Theory of Dreams" (1917d)
"Mourning and Melancholia" (1917e [1915])
"A Phylogenetic Fantasy: Overview of the Transference Neuroses" (1985a [1915])

INTRODUCTORY LECTURES ON PSYCHO-ANALYSIS
(1916–1917 [1915–1917])

When an epilogue is also a prologue . . .

What is "metapsychology"? It is a word invented by Freud to denote his theory of mental functioning based on an experience of psychoanalysis which had lasted for over thirty years. As he himself put it, metapsychology is to the observation of psychological phenomena what metaphysics is to that of phenomena in the physical world. Freud thus went from a clinical and descriptive level to one of abstract theory; he put forward models of the way in which the human mind works which were intended to be generally applicable. Consider, for example, the idea of "drive". Freud introduced the term in order to describe what impels human beings to eat and to procreate; he calls the first of these "self-preservation drives (or instincts)" and the second group "sexual drives (or instincts)". Given that "drives" are an abstract idea, they are never encountered as such, but are perceived indirectly via the effects to which they give rise or the means by which they are represented. Thus a sexual drive may be manifested in several different ways – the turmoil generated by an erotic desire for someone, the words used to express that desire, or the scenario of a dream. In these Papers on Metapsychology, Freud writes for the most part in general and abstract terms; this makes these texts somewhat difficult to understand for the reader who has little or no clinical experience. It should not be forgotten, however, as we follow Freud in his reflections, that the link between clinical matters and theory was constantly on his mind.

From the point of view of how Freud's thinking was developing, the Papers on Metapsychology are first and foremost the result of a gradual evolution which led him to propose a synthesis of the way in which the mind works under both normal and pathological conditions. This is known as his "first topographical (or structural) model" based on the distinction between unconscious, preconscious and conscious, and runs parallel to his first theory of the instinctual drives based on the pleasure/unpleasure principle. At the same time, these papers on metapsychology are the starting-point for fresh perspectives which would involve taking into account object relations, identifications, affects of love and hate, and unconscious feelings of guilt. These new avenues would lead, a few years later, to his "second topographical model" and an accompanying second theory of the instinctual drives.

> **Biographies and history**
>
> ### A difficult but productive period
>
> *The war years, 1914–1918*
>
> In the years between the outbreak of the First World War and its immediate aftermath, Freud went through a difficult time which nonetheless proved to be extremely productive from a scientific point of view. At the outbreak of hostilities in August 1914, Anna found herself stuck in England for a time; she was able to return to Vienna thanks to the efforts of Ernest Jones. The family were very worried about what might happen to Freud's two sons, who had been called up for military service – Martin in Russia, Ernst in Italy. In November 1915, Freud was very moved by the death of his half-brother Emmanuel, who was 81 years old, the same age as was their father when he died. The following year, 1916, Freud's son Oliver was called up. Given the difficulties caused by the war, few patients were able to seek treatment, letters could not be sent and received on a regular basis, and there were very few visitors; the survival of the psychoanalytic periodicals was in jeopardy and Freud himself had to take responsibility for them. He was, however, able to correspond on a regular basis with Karl Abraham, in particular about melancholia, as well as with Sándor Ferenczi and Lou Andreas-Salomé.
>
> *Taking stock as he was nearing 60*
>
> Freud began writing the twelve theoretical texts which comprise his Papers on Metapsychology in 1915, as though in an attempt to take stock of his work up to that point. He was then almost 60 years old, and he felt that he had only a few more years to live. The war and the misfortunes it brought in its wake served only to strengthen his concerns about death. He had originally planned to publish these texts after the war in book form under the title *Zur Vorbereitung einer Metapsychologie* (*Preliminaries to a Metapsychology*). In the meantime, he published the first three separately in 1915 – "Instincts and their Vicissitudes", "Repression" and "The Unconscious" – and, in 1917, the following two – "A Metapsychological Supplement to the Theory of Dreams" and "Mourning and Melancholia". We learn from his correspondence that he had in fact written the following seven papers; he never published them, however, and as a result the planned book never saw the light of day. However, in 1983, among Ferenczi's papers was found a copy of the twelfth (unpublished) essay entitled "A Phylogenetic Fantasy: Overview of the Transference Neuroses", together with a letter from Freud asking Ferenczi for his opinion on it (Freud 1985a [1915]). It seems probable that Freud himself destroyed the remaining texts.

Discovering the texts

- **"INSTINCTS AND THEIR VICISSITUDES" (1915c)**

> Page numbers are those of *The Standard Edition of the Complete Psychological Works of Sigmund Freud*, vol. **14**, 109–140.

- *General characteristics of the instincts (or drives)*

The *Standard Edition* translates the German word "*Trieb*" by the English "instinct". The choice of this English equivalent rather than possible alternatives such as "drive" or "urge" is discussed in the General Preface to the first volume of the *Standard Edition* (**1**, xxiv–xxvi). Keeping to the point of view he had developed in *Three Essays on the Theory of Sexuality* (1905a), Freud defines the instinct as a dynamic pressure which has a *source*, an *aim* and an *object* and he describes the implications of these. An instinct operates as a constant force and is comparable to a "*need*" which can be done away with only through a "*satisfaction*" which corresponds to the aim of the drive. Models for what Freud means by instinct are the need for food and the search for sexual satisfaction, which are present in all human beings. Though the *aim* of an instinct is in every instance satisfaction, the *object* – the element in regard to which or through which the instinct is able to achieve its aim – is what is most variable: it may be an external object, someone in the person's immediate circle for example, or part of the subject's own body. In general, the object is incidental – it is not specific to any given instinct and can easily be replaced. "*It may be changed any number of times in the course of the vicissitudes which the instinct undergoes during its existence*" (1915c: 122–123). Finally, "*by the source [*Quelle*] of an instinct is meant the somatic process which occurs in an organ or part of the body and whose stimulus is represented in mental life by an instinct*" (ibid.: 123). In fact, we can know the source of an instinct only indirectly: "*in mental life we know them [i.e. the instincts] only by their aims*" (ibid.: 123).

It is up to the nervous system to master instinctual excitation. "*The nervous system is an apparatus which has the function of getting rid of the stimuli that reach it, or of reducing them to the lowest possible level*" (ibid.: 120). The mental apparatus, writes Freud at this point in his theoretical developments, is governed by the pleasure principle and its workings are regulated automatically by feelings belonging to the pleasure/unpleasure series. "*Unpleasurable feelings are connected with an increase and pleasurable feelings with a decrease of stimulus*" (ibid.: 120–121). On these premises, Freud redefines what he means by the concept of instinct (or drive):

> an "instinct" appears to us as a concept on the frontier between the mental and the somatic, as the psychical representative of the stimuli originating from within the organism and reaching the mind, as a measure of the demand made upon the mind for work in consequence of is connection with the body. (ibid.: 121–122)

• *Self-preservative instincts and sexual instincts*

There are many different kinds of instinctual drive, but Freud proposes to group them under two headings: the *ego*, or *self-preservative*, instincts – the model for which is hunger and the ingestion of food – and the *sexual* instincts. At their first appearance, the sexual instincts are attached to the instincts of self-preservation which provide them with an organic source, direction and object; it is only once the external object is abandoned that the sexual drives become independent. For example, in the pleasure the infant derives from sucking at the mother's breast, the satisfaction of the erotogenic zone – the mouth – is an erotic pleasure linked to feeding; it is only later that the sexual pleasure associated with sucking will detach itself from that. For Freud, the opposition between self-preservative and sexual instincts is the source of the conflicts which emerge in the transference neuroses, as he had previously argued: conflict results from the fact that sexual drives, which can obtain satisfaction through fantasy and thus follow the pleasure/unpleasure principle, come up against the reality principle represented by the self-preservation instincts which cannot obtain satisfaction other than through a real object: "*An essential part of the psychical disposition to neurosis thus lies in the delay in educating the sexual instincts to pay regard to reality*" (1911b: 223). Freud would later attach less importance to the distinction between these two groups of instinctual drives and to the resultant conflict which arises in neurotic individuals.

• *The gradual synthesis of the instinctual drives*

Among the general characteristics of the sexual drives, adds Freud, is the fact that they are numerous, they emanate from a great variety of partial somatic sources and only through a gradual process do they achieve synthesis and sexual maturity.

> They [. . .] act in the first instance independently of one another and only achieve a more or less complete synthesis at a late stage. The aim which each of them strives for is the attainment of

"organ-pleasure"; only when synthesis is achieved do they enter the service of the reproductive function and thereupon become generally recognizable as sexual instincts. (1915c: 125–126)

- ### What are the vicissitudes of the sexual drives?

Freud begins by defining what he means by the "*vicissitudes*" of the various kinds of defence which are raised against the instinctual drives in order to oppose their being carried through. A sexual drive may undergo the following vicissitudes: reversal into its opposite, turning round upon the subject's own self, repression and sublimation. Reversal of an instinct into its opposite and turning back on to the subject's own self are two distinct processes, but they are impossible to describe separately, he claims. The first vicissitude concerns the aim of the drive, which can be transformed into its opposite, the second involves the object which can be either some extraneous person or the subject's own self. In reversal of sadism into masochism, for example, we see that masochism implies a change from activity to passivity as well as a role reversal between the person who inflicts pain and the person upon whom it is inflicted. As he conceives of the genesis of this pair in 1915, Freud sees sadism as preceding masochism in the course of development; he did not, at that time, believe in the existence of primary masochism, as he was later to do (see his 1924 footnote in 1915c: 128). In his 1915 paper, he defines sadism as the exercise of violence upon another person without there being any concomitant sexual pleasure; it is only in the masochistic phase that pain is accompanied by sexual excitation. If a sadist does experience sexual pleasure in causing pain, this is due to identification with the suffering object.

> *For while these pains are being inflicted on other people, they are enjoyed masochistically by the subject through his identification of himself with the suffering object. In both cases, of course, it is not the pain itself which is enjoyed, but the accompanying sexual excitation – so that this can be done especially conveniently from the sadistic position.* (1915c: 129)

Freud then goes on to explore the similar changes which occur in voyeurism-exhibitionism.

- ### Love and hate: their relationship to the instinctual drives

Freud takes up the topic of love and hate from the point of view of ambivalence. He had gradually come to realize that this complex affect played a decisive role in the psychological conflicts his patients found themselves having to deal with: "*Since it is particularly common to find both [love and hate] directed simultaneously towards the same object, their coexistence furnishes the most important example of ambivalence of feeling*" (ibid.: 133). He then goes on to raise an important objection: since love and hate are *feelings* and not *drives*, what is their status with respect to the latter? And what processes lie behind the development of love and hate? How do primitive forms of love lead to "*loving as the expression of the* whole *sexual current of feeling*" (ibid.: 133)? Attempting to answer these questions led Freud to some of his most inspired writing; extracting a few sentences from these pages must of necessity interrupt the links between them, but I shall try nevertheless to outline his demonstration as best I can.

- ### Love and hate at the beginning of life

According to Freud, if we examine the vicissitudes of love and hate, we will see that there are three polarities which govern our mental life as a whole: (1) the polarity *ego–non-ego* (or *subject–object*), depending on whether the stimuli which reach the ego are internal or external in origin; (2) the polarity *pleasure–unpleasure* depends on the quality of feelings; (3) the polarity *active–passive*, which for Freud underlies the antithesis masculine–feminine. How are these three polarities organized at the very beginning of mental life?

Originally, the ego is cathected with instincts and is to some extent capable of satisfying them by itself. This makes for a primary state of narcissism in which the ego has no need of the external world because it is auto-erotic. "*During this period, therefore, the ego-subject coincides with what is pleasurable and the external world with what is indifferent (or possibly unpleasurable, as being a source of stimulation)*" (ibid.: 135). Later, when the ego cannot avoid feeling unpleasurable internal stimulation – such as hunger and the need to be fed by means of some external agency – it has to emerge from auto-eroticism and move in the direction of external objects. The impact which these have on the ego generates a new organization in terms of the pleasure–unpleasure polarity. "*Insofar as the objects which are presented to it are sources of pleasure, it takes them into itself, 'introjects' them (to use Ferenczi's term); and, on the other hand, it expels whatever within itself becomes a cause of unpleasure*" (ibid.: 136).

- *A fundamental division made by the "purified pleasure-ego"*

As a result, a fundamental division in the ego occurs which is no longer simply a matter of internal (ego/subject) and external (indifferent/unpleasurable), but involves on the one hand a "*pleasure-ego*" which includes objects that bring satisfaction and, on the other, the external world which becomes a source of unpleasure because it is perceived as being foreign.

> *Thus the original "reality-ego", which distinguished internal and external by means of a sound objective criterion, changes into a purified "pleasure-ego", which places the characteristics of pleasure above all others. For the pleasure-ego the external world is divided into a part that is pleasurable, which it has incorporated into itself and a remainder that is extraneous to it.* (ibid.: 136)

In other words, in the primary narcissistic stage, the object creates an opposition between "hating" and "loving".

> *At the very beginning, it seems, the external world, object, and what is hated are identical. If later on an object turns out to be a source of pleasure, it is loved, but it is also incorporated into the ego; so that for the purified pleasure-ego once again objects coincide with what is extraneous and hated.* (ibid.: 136)

- *Love is the expression of the whole sexual current*

Consequently, when the object is a source of pleasure, we say that we "love" that object; conversely, when it is a source of unpleasurable feelings we "hate" it. Freud then asks whether we can rightly say of an instinctual drive that it "loves" the object; he points out that to say that a drive "hates" the object strikes us as odd. He therefore argues that "*the [terms] of love and hate cannot be made use of for the relations of instincts to their objects, but are reserved for the relations of the total ego to objects*" (ibid.: 137). As far as objects which serve the interests of self-preservation are concerned (food, etc.), the most we can do is to use such terms as "being fond of", "liking", etc.

What then is the status of the word "love" when it is fully developed? For Freud, there is no doubt that love belongs to the genital stage of development, once the component instincts have been synthesized within the total ego.

> *[The] relation of the ego to its sexual object [is] the most appropriate case in which to employ the word "love" – this fact teaches us that the word can only begin to be applied in this relation after there has been a synthesis of all the component instincts of sexuality under the primacy of the genitals and in the service of the reproductive function.* (ibid.: 137–138)

As regards the use of the word "hate", there is no such intimate connection with sexual pleasure; the relation with *unpleasure* seems to be the decisive factor. "*The ego hates, abhors and pursues with intent to destroy all objects which are a source of unpleasurable feeling for it, without taking into account whether they mean a frustration of sexual satisfaction or of the satisfaction of self-preservative needs*" (ibid.: 138). For Freud, the origin of hate lies in the ego's struggle for self-preservation; hate, in other words, has more to do with the object which does not satisfy self-preservative needs than with sexual life. It is the self-preservation level which gives rise to the conflict of ambivalence, and this is particularly evident in the neuroses.

- ## *The genesis of love and hate in the course of development*

At first, writes Freud, the ego is able to satisfy some of its auto-erotic impulses – love is therefore originally narcissistic. It then directs itself towards objects. "*[Love] is originally narcissistic, then passes over on to objects, which have been incorporated into the extended ego, and expresses the motor efforts of the ego towards these objects as sources of pleasure*" (ibid.: 138). Freud goes on to describe the preliminary stages of love, the original aim of which is to *incorporate* or *devour* – this phase is ambivalent *par excellence*; the subject does not know whether the object is being destroyed by love or by hate. The next stage is that of the pregenital sadistic-anal organization, which will be followed by the genital stage. "*Not until the genital organization is established does love become the opposite of hate*" (ibid.: 139). From this, Freud concludes that hate is older than love, since the latter appears only once the ego becomes a "*whole ego*".

This explains also the nature of ambivalence, in which hate is combined with love towards the same object.

> *The hate which is admixed with the love is in part derived from the preliminary stages of loving which have not been wholly surmounted; it is also in part based on reactions of repudiation by the ego-instincts, which, in view of the frequent conflicts between the interests of the ego and those of love, can find grounds in real and contemporary motives. In both cases, therefore, the admixed hate has as its source the self-preservative instincts.* (ibid.: 139)

Freud goes on to point out that, if a love-relation with a given object is broken off, feelings of hate often emerge, so that "*we get the impression of a transformation of love into hate*" (ibid.: 139); he does not, however go into any detail about what he means by this "*transformation*". The paper ends with an evocation of the possibility for hate to acquire an erotic character whenever there is regression to the sadistic stage; Freud would later develop this idea in terms of sadomasochism and the fundamental conflict between life and death drives.

- ## "REPRESSION" (1915d)

Page numbers are those of *The Standard Edition of the Complete Psychological Works of Sigmund Freud*, vol. **14**, 141–158.

- ## *The role of repression*

Above all, the instinctual drive seeks the pleasure of satisfaction, as Freud put it in his "first theory of the instincts" in 1915. In this search for pleasure, however, the drive may meet with resistances which try to make it inoperative. Among these resistances, repression is of particular importance in that it is a compromise between flight – which is of no avail since the drive comes from within the subject – and condemnation. Why should an instinctual drive be repressed, when its sole aim is to find the pleasure of satisfaction? The reason is that, whereas satisfaction gives rise to pleasure in one part of the mind, that pleasure seems to be irreconcilable with the demands of another part of the mind; it is then that "*judgement by condemnation*" appears, and triggers repression. "*The essence of repression lies simply in turning something away, and keeping it at a distance, from the conscious*" (1915d: 147). As a defence mechanism, repression therefore does not exist from the very beginning; it is only when conscious and unconscious separate from each other that repression can be established. Before that differentiation, writes Freud, other defence mechanisms may be in force, such as reversal into the opposite or turning round upon the subject's own self.

• *The fate of representations*

Without explicitly saying so, Freud takes up some of the hypotheses he had put forward in his papers in 1894 and 1896 on the neuro-psychoses of defence. According to this point of view, there are two aspects of the psychical representative of an instinctual drive which may undergo repression, the representation and its affect, each of these having a different outcome. As far as the representation is concerned, Freud assumes that there must exist a primal repression, "*a first phase of repression, which consists in the psychical (ideational) representative of the instincts being denied entrance into the conscious*" (ibid.: 148). For example, in the case of "Little Hans", the anxiety over being bitten by a horse masked the unconscious anxiety of being castrated by the father, with the idea of "father" being the repressed representation. The second stage of repression, repression proper, "*affects mental derivatives of the repressed representative, or such trains of thought as, originating elsewhere, have come into associated connection with it*" (ibid.: 148). Thus repression concerns not only representations as such but also the *derivatives* of the unconscious, in other words productions which are more or less loosely connected with what is repressed; in turn, these derivatives too are subjected to defence mechanisms. From that point of view, symptoms are also derivatives of what has been repressed. Repression, however, does not prevent the instinctual representative from continuing to exist in the unconscious – it organizes itself still further and continues to produce derivatives: it "*proliferates in the dark, as it were*" (ibid.: 149). This ongoing process means that, in the strict sense of the term, repression is always a deferred action. For example, Little Hans's anxiety over horses, his inability to go out of doors and the memory of his friend's falling off a horse, and so on, are derivatives of the repressed.

These unconscious derivatives can have free access to consciousness if they are sufficiently far removed from the repressed representative; the patient's free associations enable the psychoanalyst to identify them.

• *The characteristics of repression*

According to Freud, repression is "*individual in its operation*" (ibid.: 151) and it deals with mental derivatives one by one. It is also highly *mobile* and demands an uninterrupted expenditure of energy; maintaining the repressed mental derivatives of an instinctual drive in the unconscious (or, alternatively, allowing it to emerge into consciousness) therefore depends on this *quantitative* factor. "*The quantitative factor proves decisive for this conflict: as soon as the basically obnoxious idea exceeds a certain degree of strength, the conflict becomes a real one, and it is precisely this activation that leads to repression*" (ibid.: 152).

• *The destiny of the affects*

Having shown what becomes of the representation, Freud now turns his attention to the destiny of the affects – or more precisely to the "*quota of affect*" (ibid.: 152): this is the quantitative element of the instinctual drive which is subjected to repression.

> *It corresponds to the instinct insofar as the latter has become detached from the idea and finds expression, proportionate to its quantity, in processes which are sensed as affects. From this point on, in describing a case of repression, we shall have to follow up separately what, as the result of repression, becomes of the* idea, *and what becomes of the instinctual energy linked to it.* (ibid.: 152)

If we go back to Little Hans, the affect which was subjected to repression was the boy's hostile impulses towards his father, the wish to kill him which belongs to the Oedipus complex.

The vicissitude of the *idea* which represents the instinct is that it should be kept away from consciousness, as we have seen above. The *quantitative* factor of the instinctual representative has three possible vicissitudes: the instinct may be altogether suppressed, so that no trace of it can be found, or it can appear as a qualitatively coloured affect, or it can be transformed into anxiety. Given that the purpose of repression is to avoid unpleasure, "*it follows that the vicissitude of the quota of affect belonging to the representative is far more important than the vicissitude of the idea, and this fact is decisive for our assessment of the process of repression*" (ibid.: 153). Freud goes on to say that repression creates substitutive formations and symptoms; in his view these are the direct result of the return of the repressed and owe their existence to quite different processes. Freud concludes the paper with a highly illuminating and detailed description of how, in clinical practice, repression operates in the three major forms of psychoneurosis. In anxiety hysteria (or phobia) such as an animal phobia, repression is unsuccessful – all it does is replace one representation by another, so that anxiety is not done away with at all. In true conversion hysteria, repression brings about a total disappearance of the quota of affect, hence the "*belle indifférence*" of hysterical patients. The price to pay is the creation of major substitutive formations which, by condensation, draw the whole cathexis on to them. Lastly, in obsessional neurosis, the hostile impulses against someone who is loved is repressed; but the repression cannot be maintained and the affect comes back as unlimited self-reproaches.

Development of Freud's concepts

What is affect?

When we try to define what we mean by the term "affect", we quickly find ourselves dealing with complex issues insofar as, in psychoanalysis, the word has several different meanings. We come across the term at the very beginning of Freud's work, and he uses it mainly in two ways: in its wider sense, "affect" refers to emotional states in general, of varying quality and intensity; in its narrower sense, it constitutes the quantitative aspect of an instinctual drive, in accordance with the theory that takes into account the quantity of instinctual force. Affect plays a major role in Freud and Breuer's *Studies on Hysteria* (1895d): Freud attributes the origins of hysterical symptoms to a "*strangulated affect*" which cannot be discharged. The aim of therapy is to allow the emotion to be discharged via the recall of a forgotten traumatic event, the discharge constituting catharsis. For Freud, representations and affects have different vicissitudes, and he emphasizes the economic dimension of affect when he writes of "*quota of affect*" in his 1915 papers on metapsychology.

The idea of affect was later to take on somewhat wider connotations and include a broad range of phenomena such as anxiety, mourning, guilt feelings, love, hate, etc. This was particularly the case after *Inhibitions, Symptoms and Anxiety* (Freud 1926d). Only a few of these affects would be studied in detail by Freud; he established a close connection between them and the development of the ego, because, for Freud, the ego is the true *locus* of affect. However, though the idea of affect is much wider in scope than the simple energy-based meaning comprised in the term "quota of affect", it remains relatively ill-defined even in contemporary psychoanalytic theory.

- **"THE UNCONSCIOUS" (1915e)**

Page numbers are those of *The Standard Edition of the Complete Psychological Works of Sigmund Freud*, vol. **14**, 159–215.

- ***Justification for the concept of the unconscious***

In this opening chapter, Freud demonstrates the existence of the unconscious and claims that psychoanalysis has revealed mental processes which are in themselves unconscious; when they are perceived by consciousness, this can be likened to the perception of the external world by means of the sense organs. He points out also that the process of repression does not put an end to the idea which represents an instinct – repression prevents it from becoming conscious. When this happens, the idea continues to produce effects which may reach consciousness while itself remaining unconscious.

• The topographical point of view

Until then, Freud had focused mainly on the "dynamic" point of view – in other words on the nature of the conflicts which give rise to the neuroses, for example, when he attributed Little Hans's phobia to the unconscious anxiety about being castrated by his father. By introducing a distinction between the unconscious, preconscious and conscious systems, he adopts a different point of view as regards mental processes – that of their localization in distinct topographical *loci* of the mind (hence the term "topographical", from the Greek *topos*, meaning "place", in the geographical sense of the word, for example). Freud emphasizes, however, that these various mental *loci* have nothing to do with anatomy as such.

It is the fact that a *"psychical act"* goes through two phases before becoming fully conscious that led Freud to introduce the idea of the *preconscious* (Pcs). He notes that between these two phases there is *"interposed a kind of testing (*censorship*)"* (1915e: 173). The first censorship takes place between the unconscious and consciousness and may prevent the psychical act from becoming conscious; if it passes this first test and enters consciousness, it has to undergo a second censorship before it is allowed to become fully conscious. This is where Freud localizes the preconscious. *"[The psychical act] is not yet conscious, but it is certainly* capable of becoming conscious" (ibid.: 173).

Freud then attempts to describe how a representation can pass from the state of being unconscious to that of consciousness. He argues that this is a two-stage process. Clinical experience shows us that, for the effects of a previously repressed representation to be done away with, it is not enough merely to bring it into consciousness.

> *If we communicate to a patient some idea which he has at one time repressed but which we have discovered in him, our telling him makes at first no change in his mental condition. Above all, it does not remove the repression nor undo its effects, as might perhaps be expected from the fact that the previously unconscious idea has now become conscious. On the contrary, all that we shall achieve at first will be a fresh rejection of the repressed idea.* (ibid.: 175)

For Freud, the patient now has the same idea in two different forms – an auditory trace which becomes conscious thanks to the analyst's interpretations, and an unconscious one, the unconscious memory of the patient's experience. As a result, *"there is no lifting of the repression until the conscious idea, after the resistances have been overcome, has entered into connection with the unconscious memory-trace. It is only through the making conscious of the latter itself that success is achieved"* (ibid.: 175–176). Yet Freud felt that to make a distinction between conscious and unconscious representations on that basis alone was unsatisfactory.

• Unconscious feelings

Freud begins this section by reminding the reader that an instinctual drive can never become an object of consciousness. It can become conscious only in one of two ways: by attaching itself either to a representation or to an affect. *"If the instinct did not attach itself to an idea or manifest itself as an affective state, we could know nothing about it"* (ibid.: 177).

Freud goes on to discuss whether feelings, emotions and affects can be unconscious, in the way that ideational representations can. If we consider that the essence of feelings, emotions and affects is that they can be perceived, Freud argues that they therefore cannot be *"unconscious"*. Yet in psychoanalytic practice we are accustomed to speak of unconscious love, hate, anger, as well as unconscious feelings of guilt, while at the same time we seem to be arguing that feelings can only be conscious. Freud attempts to resolve this contradiction by saying that only the *idea* of the affective impulse is made unconscious by repression, while feelings, emotions and affects are subjected to variations which are essentially quantitative in nature. If an affect or a feeling disappears, he says, what happens is that it is transformed or *"suppressed"* or *"prevented from developing at all"*, but it is not *"repressed"* (ibid.: 178).

When we talk of affects becoming unconscious, what we really mean is that some other operation has occurred: either the affect has become attached to another idea which can be repressed, or it has been transformed into anxiety. Although Freud states quite clearly *"strictly speaking, then, [. . .] there are no unconscious affects as there are unconscious ideas"* (ibid.: 178), he does go on to say:

> [but] there may very well be in the system Ucs. affective structures which, like others, become conscious. The whole difference arises from the fact that ideas are cathexes – basically of memory-traces – while affects and emotions correspond to processes of discharge, the final manifestations of which are perceived as feelings. (ibid.: 178)

Freud's standpoint as to the nature of affects remains hesitant in 1915; he would later acknowledge that affects play a major role in the unconscious.

- ***Topography and dynamics of repression***

In this section, Freud explores the mechanism which maintains in the unconscious the cathexis of the repressed idea. In repression, there is a withdrawal of cathexis from the idea, yet the repressed idea remains capable of action. How are we to explain the fact that this unconscious idea does not once again return to the preconscious or to consciousness? In order to make a full description of this complex process, it is not enough simply to take into account the displacement of cathexis; a multifocal approach is needed, one which includes the system to which the withdrawal takes place as well as the one to which the cathexis belongs – unconscious, preconscious or conscious. Freud assumes that a new factor must be at work, one which (ibid.: 181) he calls *anticathexis* (or counter-cathexis), by means of which the system Pcs. protects itself from the pressure exerted upon it by the unconscious idea. For example, Little Hans's phobic fear of horses was a conscious counter-cathexis which replaced his anxiety concerning his father, the cathexis of that idea remaining repressed. In the case of repression proper ("*after-pressure*"), the aim of the counter-cathexis is to maintain the idea in its repressed state, while primal repression ensures the establishment as well as the continuation of repression.

It is this multifocal approach that Freud calls "*metapsychology*"; the psychoanalyst examines psychological phenomena from a triple point of view: topographical, economic and dynamic. In the case of counter-cathexis, the *topographical* point of view has to do with the system in which the cathexes originate (unconscious, preconscious or conscious); the *economic* point of view takes into account the quantity of mental energy which is being deployed; and the dynamic point of view explores the conflict between, on the one hand, the pressure of the instinctual drive – the wish – which forces the representative idea to emerge from the unconscious, and, on the other, the defence set up by the ego to oppose the emergence of the repressed idea. Freud then goes on to show how these hypotheses can be applied to phobic, hysterical and obsessional neuroses, in a way that is highly instructive for clinical practice.

- ***The special characteristics of the system Ucs.***

In the unconscious there are "*no negation, no doubt, no degrees of certainty*" (ibid.: 186), and the great mobility of cathexes produces the phenomena of *displacement* and *condensation* which are characteristic of the *primary process*. In addition, unconscious processes are timeless and are subject to the pleasure principle, so that they take no heed of reality and are exempt from mutual contradiction. In the system Pcs., the *secondary process* is dominant, characterized by the inhibition of discharge of cathected representations. Freud also distinguishes between *conscious memory*, which depends wholly on the Pcs. system, and the *memory traces* in which the experiences of the Ucs. are fixed.

- ***Relationships between Ucs., Pcs. and Cs.***

The three systems, Ucs., Pcs. and Cs. are not isolated; there is a close relationship between them and the influence of each on the other two is constant. Freud examines these relationships, describes what belongs specifically to the unconscious and remains repressed, and highlights the two levels at which censorship operates. "*The first of these censorships is exercised against the Ucs. itself, and the second against its Pcs. derivatives*" (ibid.: 193). The process of becoming conscious, he says, is not simply a matter of moving from Ucs. to Cs.; true awareness of what emerges in the Pcs. system would seem to imply *hypercathexis*: "*The existence of the censorship between the Pcs. and the Cs. teaches us that becoming conscious is no mere act of perception, but is probably also a* hypercathexis, *a further advance in the psychical organization*" (ibid.: 194). He adds two important comments on this point: the first concerns communication from unconscious to unconscious, a phenomenon which he claims, "*descriptively speaking*", to be "*incontestable*". "*It is a very remarkable thing that the Ucs. of one human being can react upon that of another, without passing through the Cs.*" (ibid.: 194). The second observation concerns the difficulty for the Cs. to influence the Ucs. in the course of psychoanalytic treatment, since this process demands a very high deployment of time and energy.

• *Assessment of the unconscious*

The unconscious can be approached along a path which leads even more directly to it than that of the neuroses – the approach which schizophrenia places at our disposal, because here the unconscious is unveiled without any of the obstacles created by repression. Freud notes that schizophrenics have a "*stilted*" and "*precious*" way of expressing themselves, in a language which is peculiarly disorganized: the frequent reference to bodily organs borders on "*organ-speech*" (ibid.: 198). He notes, too, that in schizophrenia, words are subjected to a mechanism of condensation which is similar to the primary process which produces dream-images. "*The process may go so far that a single word, if it is specially suitable on account of its numerous connections, takes over the representation of a whole train of thoughts*" (ibid.: 199). Further, in these patients, *words* are more important than the *things* which they denote. To put it another way, in schizophrenia, there is a predominance of what has to do with words so that any similarity between verbal expressions is felt to be more important than any relationship to actual things. For example, one of Victor Tausk's patients, mentioned by Freud, was inhibited by the idea that there were "holes" in the knitting of his socks; even though the word "hole" represents two different things – the apertures in the knitting and the female genital aperture – the mere evocation of the word "hole" became a source of terror because it condensed both meanings. Thus schizophrenic patients express without any resistance the unconscious symbolic meaning of their inhibitions, so that the psychoanalyst has direct access to their unconscious. This is not the case with hysterical or obsessional patients, in whom access to unconscious meaning is made more difficult because of the operation of repression. To put it another way, we could say that what characterizes the schizophrenic's mode of thought is that "*he treats concrete things as though they were abstract*" (ibid.: 204).

Freud goes on to discuss why, in schizophrenia, word-presentations are treated as though they were thing-presentations, as when the word "hole" becomes the equivalent of the thing itself – "the female genital aperture" in the case of Tausk's patient. As regards the conscious presentation of the object, Freud introduces a further distinction between word-presentations and thing-presentations: the latter are fundamentally visual, while the former are fundamentally auditory. Word-presentations are thus integrated within a conceptualization that associates verbalization with conscious awareness. Unconscious representation, he says, is made up simply of thing-presentations, which precede the development of speech; as a result, verbal language has a particularly important role to play in permitting access to conscious awareness during psychoanalytic treatment. As Freud puts it: "*The conscious presentation comprises the presentation of the thing plus the presentation of the word belonging to it, while the unconscious presentation is the presentation of the thing alone*" (ibid.: 201). The specific properties of language make it possible for the primary process to be succeeded by the secondary process and establish the Pcs. system, which Freud describes as "*a higher psychical organization*" (ibid.: 202). In the transference neuroses, repression rejects word-presentations, so that the psychoanalytic process has to substitute words for acts; that is why verbal thought is the instrument *par excellence* of the psychoanalytic experience.

Referring again to schizophrenia, Freud says that the dominant cathexis of word-presentations in such patients is in fact the result of an attempt at recovery. Instinctual cathexis is withdrawn from the unconscious presentation of the object – a feature of the narcissistic neuroses – and the patient gives a more intense cathexis to word-presentations. These processes are "*directed towards regaining the lost object*" (ibid.: 204); in order to do so, "*they set off on a path that leads to the object via the verbal part of it*" – and this is an attempt at recovery or cure. All the same, adds Freud, schizophrenics "*then find themselves obliged to be content with words instead of things*" (ibid.: 204). Freud concludes this paper with a warning against allowing our thinking to become too abstract.

> When we think in abstractions, there is a danger that we may neglect the relations of words to unconscious thing-presentations, and it must be confessed that the expression and content of our philosophizing then begins to acquire an unwelcome resemblance to the mode of operation of schizophrenics. (ibid.: 204)

Post-Freudians

Freud's first topographical theory and first theory of the instinctual drives: a French speciality?

The psychoanalytic school of thought in the French-speaking world is undoubtedly the one that has taken much of its inspiration from Freud's earlier writings, of which these first three "papers on metapsychology" represent a culmination. It is for this reason that this school of thought is characterized by an approach to psychoanalysis based principally on Freud's first structural theory – the Ucs., Pcs. and Cs. systems – and on his first theory of the instinctual drives based on the pleasure/unpleasure principle. This particular emphasis can be seen in the many writings which follow on from Freud's metapsychological papers, most of which carry the mark of the abstract style which Freud himself adopted. There is a marked contrast here between French and British psychoanalytic schools of thought: in the former, reference to actual clinical practice tends to be implicit, while it is usually explicit in the latter. Probably a whole philosophical tradition has influenced the way in which French-speaking psychoanalysts tend to think, with the risk at times of leaving clinical experience behind and focusing on more speculative issues. As Pierre Luquet (1985) puts it: "Psychoanalysis is the fruit of the everyday work of acknowledging facts and not of speculation. It is only then that implementation and philosophizing come into their own."

There are several reasons for the importance which French psychoanalysts attach to Freud's first structural theory and theory of the instinctual drives. Probably one of the main explanations stems from the fact that Freud's earlier writings – or at least some of them – were the first to be translated into French, while his subsequent works did not appear in translation until much later. Also, this preference for his metapsychological papers was strengthened by Lacan's (1955) plea for a "return to Freud". As I have pointed out, this return to Freud did not concern all of Freud's writings but simply his early work, which focused mainly on the neuroses: *The Interpretation of Dreams* (1900a) and *Jokes and their Relation to the Unconscious* (1905c) spring to mind. Focusing selectively on part of Freud's work has had both advantages and disadvantages: on the one hand, it encouraged the study of Freud's earlier writings, but on the other it tended to play down the importance of his later work, and in particular his papers on depression, psychosis and perversion. Yet these innovative perspectives were discernible as early as 1915, particularly in "Instincts and their Vicissitudes" and "Mourning and Melancholia". These fresh ideas, indeed, would lead Freud to draw up a new theory of the instinctual drives and a second structural theory of the mind.

From the 1970s on, a growing number of French psychoanalysts felt the need to expand the applications of psychoanalysis beyond the neuroses; they began to show interest in treating "difficult" patients whose fundamental problems had to do with narcissistic issues. As a result, these psychoanalysts began gradually to show more interest in what Freud had written after 1915 – his second theory of the instinctual drives, the second structural theory of the mind, primitive defence mechanisms – without, however, ignoring Freud's earlier contributions. Among the best known of these internationally, I would mention Green's work on borderline states, Anzieu's on the skin-ego, McDougall's and Chasseguet-Smirgel's on the perversions, and Racamier's on the psychoses.

Affect is inseparable from representation

Towards the end of the 1960s, Green reacted vigorously against the way in which Lacan was developing his ideas: by eliminating the role of affect and of the body from his psychoanalytic conceptualization, Lacan appeared to be turning psychoanalysis into an intellectual game of linguistic signifiers. Green published *Le Discours vivant* [*The Fabric of Affect in the Psychoanalytic Discourse*] in 1973 in an attempt to reinstate the affective and bodily dimensions of experience in their rightful place, not only in psychoanalytic theory but also in the actual experience of the psychoanalytic process.

In that book, Green begins by re-reading Freud's writings chronologically and in so doing he highlights the crucial role that affect plays alongside representation in Freud's theory. Green contrasts this point of view with that of Lacan, who played down the role of affect and went as far as to suggest that affect had no place in the unconscious – only representations and verbal signifiers are found there – completely ignoring the role played by transference and counter-transference affects. Green agrees that, at the time he was writing his "Papers on Metapsychology", Freud was still unsure of the exact nature of unconscious affects. In his subsequent writings, however, Freud himself removed all doubt on that point; he concluded that unconscious affects do exist – the unconscious sense of guilt is one example – though they do not have the same status as repressed representations. In his development of Freud's ideas, Green argues that the "representation-representative" should be differentiated from the "affect-representative" of the instinctual drive. In addition, he claims that affects have two dimensions: on the one hand, they are closely linked to the body – "the affect is gazing into the moved body" (Green 1973 [1999: 164]) – and have an economic part to play in discharge; on the other, they have a psychological dimension and possess some "quality" or other linked to pleasure/unpleasure – "the body is not the subject of an action but the object of a passion" (ibid.: 164). Green draws a distinction between *language* in the purely linguistic sense of the term – which "refers only to itself", he says (ibid.: 177), paraphrasing Lacan – and *discourse*, which Green describes as "the return of the corporeal raw material into language" (ibid.: 178). This discursive aspect brings together thoughts, representations, affects, acts and states of the individual's body. Green did not go on to elaborate further on his point of view concerning affects; as a result, the conception he puts forward in *Le Discours vivant* is to all intents and purposes a development of Freud's first structural theory.

Nevertheless, that book represents a turning-point in French psychoanalysis because Green's ideas enabled many psychoanalysts who would otherwise have been tempted to embrace wholeheartedly Lacan's points of view not only to oppose the latter's implementation of variable-length sessions but also to regroup within a more developed theoretical and clinical movement that was part of the Freudian tradition.

"A METAPSYCHOLOGICAL SUPPLEMENT TO THE THEORY OF DREAMS" (1917d)

Page numbers are those of *The Standard Edition of the Complete Psychological Works of Sigmund Freud*, vol. **14**, 217–235.

Written in 1915 and published in 1917, this fourth paper is an attempt to integrate Freud's more recent theoretical developments within his theory of dreams. For example, he elaborates on the differentiation he put forward between *temporal regression* (regression in developmental history) which restores primitive narcissism – as in dream wish-fulfilment – and *topographical regression*, which "*goes back to the stage of hallucinatory satisfaction of wishes*" (1917d: 223). But if the dream-wish is a regression to hallucination and to belief in the actual fulfilment of the wish, how are we to distinguish between dreams and other forms of hallucination, Meynert's acute hallucinatory confusion and the hallucinatory phase of schizophrenia? Freud introduces at this point what he calls "reality-testing", which gives the ego the ability to differentiate between perception and representation, internal and external. He then goes on to explore how reality-testing is abolished in pathological states and in dreams. In dreams, the state of sleep brings about a withdrawal of cathexis from the Cs., Pcs. and Ucs. systems and leads to the abandonment of reality-testing; as a result, the way is open for innervation to regress to a "*hallucinatory wishful psychosis of the dream*". This paper sheds fresh light on the theory of dreams which Freud put forward in *The Interpretation of Dreams* (1900a), but does not contribute anything fundamentally new to that theory.

Biographies and history

Karl Abraham (1877–1925): a pioneer of psychoanalytic research

The hypotheses which Freud presents in "Mourning and Melancholia" owe much to the pioneering work of Karl Abraham, who was an important figure in the early history of psychoanalysis. Born in Germany, Abraham trained as a psychiatrist in Berlin, before travelling to Zurich in 1907 in order to have further training under Eugen Bleuler, who was director of the Bürghölzli clinic, where Jung was senior registrar. It was while he was in Switzerland that Abraham first learned of Freud's work. That same year, he began private practice in Berlin and travelled to Vienna in order to meet Freud. That meeting was the start of a long-lasting friendship between the two men, who discussed many scientific questions over the ensuing years as we can tell from the numerous letters they exchanged between 1907 and 1925. Rivalry quickly broke out between Jung and Abraham, a conflict partly fuelled by Freud, who at that time preferred Jung, whom he regarded as his heir apparent; Freud thought that Jung would give psychoanalysis a wider audience in international psychiatric circles and among non-Jews. The relationship between Freud and Jung soon deteriorated, however, because Jung rejected Freud's libido theory while Abraham defended it with conviction. From then on, Freud trusted Abraham wholeheartedly; Abraham was to play a major role in the development of psychoanalysis, in particular as the founder of the Berlin Psycho-Analytical Society in 1910. Later, he succeeded Jung as president of the International Psychoanalytical Association (IPA) and as editor-in-chief of several psychoanalytic periodicals, including the *Jahrbuch für Psychoanalyse*. He was also the training analyst of several distinguished psychoanalysts, such as Hélène Deutsch, Edward Glover, James Glover, Karen Horney, Melanie Klein, Sándor Radó and Theodor Reik. His early death from a pulmonary illness occurred when he was 48; the loss to the psychoanalytic movement was felt throughout the world.

Abraham immediately embraced Freud's ideas, though he opened up new paths and did sometimes have disagreements with his mentor. The hallmark of his many papers is their cogency and clarity of expression; I would like to draw the reader's attention in particular to Abraham's seminal work on manic-depressive disorders and on the stages of libidinal development. He was the first psychoanalyst to treat manic-depressive patients and, in a paper written in 1911, he showed that depressive patients suffer from a paralysis of their capacity to love because of the violent nature of their sadistic fantasies and the "over-strong sadistic component of [their] libido" (Abraham 1911 [1988: 139]). According to Abraham, depression arises from repression of the patient's sadistic tendency; melancholia and manic states are dominated by the same complexes, and it is only the patient's attitude towards these complexes which is different. He suggested also that depression in adults probably has its roots in a basic depression of childhood; though he was unable to prove this, Melanie Klein did provide him with a clinical demonstration of his hypothesis, and he shared this discovery with Freud (Letter 423A from Abraham to Freud, 7 October 1923).

In 1924, Abraham published a wide-ranging synthesis of his points of view, in which he attempted to locate the fixation points of different mental disorders with respect to the stages of libidinal development. In order to accomplish this, he took as his basis Freud's classic theory of the stages of the libido (Freud 1905a), adding to it some innovative ideas. He distinguished in particular two sub-stages in the anal-sadistic phase and two in the oral phase of libidinal development. According to Abraham, the anal-sadistic stage can be divided into an *early anal phase* linked to evacuation and destruction of the object – the fixation point of depression – and a *later phase* linked to retaining and controlling the object – the fixation point of obsessional neurosis. It may happen in depression that the fixation point is even earlier than the early sadistic sub-stage of expulsion: in such cases, according to Abraham, the fixation point involves the oral stage of libidinal development. Here too there are two sub-phases: an early oral phase of pre-ambivalent sucking, and a later oral-sadistic phase which corresponds to primary dentition and generates ambivalence between sucking and biting. At the same time, Abraham described the development of feelings of love and hate in terms of object relations up to the time when love for the whole object is established in the course of the genital stage of development: "a complete capacity for love is only achieved when the libido has reached its genital stage" (1924: 425).

Abraham's work had a major influence in particular on his pupil, Melanie Klein, "whose theories cannot be properly understood without the basis laid down by Abraham – incidentally, with Freud's knowledge and approval", as Haynal and Falzeder (2002: xxviii) point out.

- **"MOURNING AND MELANCHOLIA" (1917e [1915])**

Page numbers are those of *The Standard Edition of the Complete Psychological Works of Sigmund Freud*, vol. **14**, 237–258.

- ## *Normal and pathological mourning processes*

In "Mourning and Melancholia", Freud explores the individual's reaction to an actual loss or disappointment connected with a loved person, or to the loss of an ideal: why do some people respond with the affect we call mourning, which will be overcome after a certain time, while others sink into depression? What in Freud's day was called "melancholia" would nowadays be called "depression", the term "melancholia" being reserved for the most severe, psychotic form of depression (Bonaparte et al. 1956; Strachey 1957; Laplanche 1980). Freud notes that, unlike normal mourning in which the process involves consciousness, pathological mourning has more to do with the unconscious because the depressed patient "*cannot consciously perceive what he has lost*" (1917e [1915]: 245). In normal and pathological mourning, the inhibition and loss of interest common to both can be accounted for by the work of mourning in which the ego is absorbed. In melancholia, however, there is an additional element: an extraordinary diminution in self-esteem. "*In mourning it is the world which has become poor and empty; in melancholia it is the ego itself*" (ibid.: 246). In pathological mourning, the loss of self-regard is uppermost, expressed as self-reproaches and self-abasement. How are we to explain these accusations against the self, accusations which may lead to a delusional expectation of punishment?

- ## *In melancholia, "I am incapable!" really means "You are incapable!"*

Freud's ingenious idea was the realization that the self-accusations of the depressive individual are in fact reproaches against some important person who has been "lost", usually someone in the patient's immediate circle. Thus, he says, "*the woman who loudly pities her husband for being tied to such an incapable wife as herself is really accusing her* husband *of being incapable, in whatever sense she may mean this*" (ibid.: 248). In other words, when this woman blames herself, saying "*I* am incapable!", this self-reproach is in fact an accusation unconsciously directed towards her husband: "*You* are incapable!" As Freud puts it so succinctly in German, talking of such patients: "*Ihre Klagen sind Anklagen*", i.e. "*Their complaints are really 'plaints' in the old sense of the word*" (ibid.: 248) – there is a condensation here between *Klagen* ("complaints" in the sense of "to complain") and *Anklagen* ("complaints" in the judicial sense of "to lodge a complaint against someone").

Following his intuition, Freud realizes that the words used by the melancholic patient when expressing self-accusations – when, for example, the patient says "I am incapable!" – are an accurate description of his or her inner conflict. "*The point must rather be that he is giving a correct description of his psychological situation*" (ibid.: 247). Given that the actual linguistic structure of these self-accusations derives from the organization of the melancholic's inner conflict, Freud makes a systematic exploration of the different elements involved, breaking each step down into its component parts: he describes in turn the oral introjection of the lost object, the identification with this object via regression from object-love to narcissism, the turning back upon the subject of the hate originally aimed at the object, etc. I shall examine these concepts one by one – for a proper understanding of these processes, the reader will have to pay close attention to my description, especially since the clinical material on which Freud bases his theorizations remains more implicit than explicit. I shall however attempt an overview of all these aspects.

- ## *The break with the outside world and narcissistic withdrawal*

Freud begins by explaining the process which underlies the "You"/"I" substitution in the melancholic's explicit self-accusation "*I* am incapable!" when what is really – implicitly – meant is "*You* are incapable!" What mental processes correspond to the transformations which are given verbal expression in this way? Freud explains that when the object is lost, there is a fundamental difference between normal and pathological mourning, one which originates in the change of direction taken by libidinal cathexes. In normal mourning, the individual is able to give up the "lost" object, and withdraw libido from it, so that this libido, now free, can attach itself to a new object. In melancholia, however, the individual does not withdraw libido from the lost object, the ego "devours" the object in fantasy in order not to separate from it, in order to be as one with it – this is the path to narcissistic identification.

> *Thus the shadow of the object fell upon the ego, and the latter could henceforth be judged by a special agency, as though it were an object, the forsaken object. In this way an object-loss was transformed into an ego-loss and the conflict between the ego and the loved person into a cleavage between the critical activity of the ego and the ego as altered by identification.* (ibid.: 249)

It is this change of direction from object-cathexis to cathexis of the ego amalgamated with the object which explains the melancholic's loss of interest in those who belong to his or her immediate circle and the consequent "narcissistic" withdrawal on to the self: melancholic patients are so preoccupied with themselves that it is as though they are sucked into a whirlwind of self-reproaches.

In addition, the turning back of accusations on to the individual implies a split in the ego – one part merges with the lost object while the other criticizes the patient and sets itself up as an agency which Freud calls "conscience". "*We see how in him one part of the ego sets itself over against the other, judges it critically, and, as it were, takes it as its object*" (ibid.: 247). This criticizing agency is the forerunner of what would later become the superego.

- ### *Love regresses to narcissistic identification and hate turns back against the subject*

The depressive patient's powerful self-destructive tendency, writes Freud, is the result of an intensification of the ambivalence between love and hate as regards both the object and the ego; these affects then separate, with each following its own path. On the one hand, the subject continues to love the object, but at the cost of a return to a primitive form of love – identification – in which "loving" the object implies "being" that object. "*The narcissistic identification with the object then becomes a substitute for the erotic cathexis, the result of which is that in spite of the conflict with the loved person the love-relation need not be given up*" (ibid.: 249). The libido regresses to the cannibalistic oral phase of development in which the ego incorporates the object into itself by devouring it. Also, because of the ego's narcissistic identification with the loved object, the subject's hate aimed at the object in the external world is henceforth turned against the ego, now merged with that object.

> *If the love for the object – a love which cannot be given up though the object itself is given up – takes refuge in narcissistic identification, then the hate comes into operation on this substitutive object, abusing it, debasing it, making it suffer and deriving sadistic satisfaction from its suffering.* (ibid.: 251)

- ### *Manifest self-reproaches are latent reproaches against other people*

Freud notes a further decisive element when he points out that the melancholic's self-accusations are at the same time an attack on the object – in other words, the patient's narcissistic withdrawal does not exclude the fact that an unconscious object relation still exists. He shows that, like the obsessional patient, the melancholic finds it "*enjoyable*" to exercise simultaneously the sadistic and hate-filled tendencies both against him- or herself and against some other person, usually belonging to the patient's immediate circle.

> *In both disorders the patients usually still succeed, by the circuitous path of self-punishment, in taking revenge on the original object and in tormenting their loved one through their illness, having resorted to it in order to avoid the need to express their hostility to him openly.* (ibid.: 251)

In arguing that the melancholic patient's self-criticisms are a way of attacking the object and exacting revenge on it, Freud shows that, in addition to their narcissism, these patients manage nonetheless to maintain an object relation with their immediate circle, one which is based on hate and aggressiveness. It was probably the fact that he emphasized the narcissistic withdrawal of manic-depressive patients which led him to conclude that these patients were unable to establish a transference relationship and were therefore inaccessible to analysis – hence the designation "narcissistic neuroses". Post-Freudian psychoanalysts have shown that these patients do establish a transference relationship and that this relationship can be analysed, even though, in this kind of transference, hostility towards the analyst is uppermost.

Development of Freud's concepts

The developments which Freud subsequently brought to "Mourning and Melancholia"

Freud's description of the psychological mechanisms which underlie depression are easier to understand when we take into account the major developments he later brought to bear on his initial hypotheses. For the record, I shall simply mention a few points and come back to them in more detail when I discuss the relevant papers in which Freud elaborates on them.

The introduction of the conflict between life and death drives (1920)

The crucial role played by self-destructive impulses in depressive patients was one of the factors which led Freud to revise his first theory of the instinctual drives based on the pleasure/unpleasure principle as he had formulated it in 1915. If the aim of every drive is above all to obtain satisfaction, how are we to explain what may lead the depressive patient to commit suicide? It was in reply to this kind of question that, in 1920, Freud put forward a new theory of the instinctual drives, based on the fundamental conflict between life and death drives; he would apply this conception to several different psychopathological conditions, including melancholia.

The conflict between ego, id and superego (1923)

In 1915, in "Mourning and Melancholia", Freud attributed the melancholic's self-accusations to the "criticism" which one part of the ego addressed to another – the "conscience" or "voice of one's conscience" in the moral sense of the term. In 1923 this "criticism" would become an agency in its own right; he called it the *superego* and described its close connections with two other newly defined agencies, the *ego* and the *id*. Under normal conditions, the *superego* has a regulatory role with respect to the *ego*, and the latter has to cope with the drive-based demands of the *id*. In melancholia, however, Freud noted that the superego is overly sadistic towards the ego, because in this illness, he writes:

> *[the superego] rages against the ego with merciless violence, as if it had taken possession of the whole of the sadism available in the person concerned. [. . .] What is now holding sway in the superego is, as it were, a pure culture of the death instinct, and in fact it often enough succeeds in driving the ego into death, if the latter does not fend off its tyrant in time by the change round into mania.* (1923b: 53)

Splitting of the ego (1927)

The idea of splitting of the ego was already present in "Mourning and Melancholia", either expressed explicitly as *"cleavage"* or as one part of the ego being *"split off"* from the rest, when he describes in melancholic patients the severity with which *"conscience"* criticizes the ego. Subsequently, in his paper on "Fetishism" (1927e), he went on to complete his ideas on splitting of the ego by arguing that, in depression, this split is the result of denial of the loss of the object. He illustrates his argument with the analysis of two brothers who had *"scotomized"* the death of their father while they were still children, yet neither of them had developed a psychosis.

> *It was only one current in their mental life that had not recognized their father's death; there was another current which took full account of that fact. The attitude which fitted in with the wish and the attitude which fitted in with reality existed side by side. In one of my two cases this split had formed the basis of a moderately severe obsessional neurosis.* (1927e: 156)

In other words, in pathological mourning, the idea of splitting of the ego shows how one part of the ego can deny the reality of the loss while another part can accept it. In some of his last papers, Freud would attach more and more importance to phenomena such as denial ("disavowal") of reality and splitting of the ego.

Post-Freudians

Kleinian and post-Kleinian developments based on Freud's metapsychological papers

Before she introduced her own specific ideas, Klein based the developments of her hypotheses on classic Freudian theory. Among the fundamental Freudian concepts on which she based her work, several are to be found in Freud's Papers on Metapsychology and in particular in "Instincts and their Vicissitudes" (1915c), "The Unconscious" (1915e) and "Mourning and Melancholia" (1917e [1915]).

Klein herself never spoke of "metapsychology", preferring to present her concepts in clinical terms; she laid particular emphasis on structural notions such as the paranoid-schizoid and depressive positions, as well as on projective identification. I shall begin with a quick overview of these concepts.

A structural conception of the workings of the mind and of change

By introducing the idea of "position", Melanie Klein was able not only to identify two distinct and fundamental states of the structure of the mind – the paranoid-schizoid position and the depressive position – but also to account for the structural changes which occur during the psychoanalytic process. The idea of "position" is different from that of a chronological "stage" of libidinal development (such as the oral stage or the phallic stage), because it is a structural concept which aims to reflect the present state of the organization of the mind and the transitions which take place between these two states.

Many factors come into play in the constitution of the paranoid-schizoid and depressive positions, as well as in the shifts from one to the other. Here are a few of them: the degree of cohesiveness of the ego (fragmented or integrated?), the nature of object relations (part-object or whole-object?), the level of defence mechanisms employed (primitive or more advanced?). In the transition from the paranoid-schizoid position to the depressive position, there is a concomitant shift from the early stages of the Oedipus complex – which, according to Klein, is a feature of the initial phase of infant development – to the later form of the complex as described by Freud. In other words, with her structural concept of "position", Klein demonstrated that the transition from the paranoid-schizoid to the depressive position represents a fundamental shift from psychotic functioning to one which is psychologically healthy.

From the "purified pleasure-ego" to integrating love and hate

Klein took as her model the "purified pleasure-ego" described by Freud in 1915 in "Instincts and their Vicissitudes", as well as the notions of projection and introjection which are associated with it. She described the development of affects in very young infants starting with their earliest part-object relations and proceeding through to the relation with a whole-object experienced as separate. Here is what Freud said of the "purified pleasure-ego": "*Insofar as the objects which are presented to [the ego] are sources of pleasure, it takes them into itself, 'introjects' them (to use Ferenczi's [1909] term); and, on the other hand it expels whatever within itself becomes a cause of unpleasure*" (Freud 1915e: 136). Taking that as her basis, Klein went on to describe the infant's early relationships, showing that they are established with a part-object, the mother's breast, which is split into an ideal breast, source of all expectations, and a persecutory one, the object of hate and of fear – this situation is what she called the paranoid-schizoid position. She went on to describe the evolution which followed on the gradual integration of the ego and its objects, when the infant begins to perceive and to love the mother as a whole person – this change marks what she called the beginning of the depressive position.

If we read what Freud wrote in 1915 in the light of Klein's conceptions, we can see that Freud felt intuitively that a change did indeed occur in the quality of affects and object relations; he did not, however, explicitly conceptualize that transition in terms of integrating love and hate and moving from a part-object to a whole-object relation. Freud described the change in the following terms:

> *We might at a pinch say of an instinct that it "loves" the objects towards which it strives for purposes of satisfaction; but to say that an instinct "hates" an object strikes us as odd. Thus we become aware that the attitudes [= terms] of love and hate cannot be made use of for the relations of* instincts *to their objects, but are reserved for the relations of the* total ego *to objects.* (1915c: 137)

Klein was later to add her own contribution to Freud's picture of the vicissitudes of love and hate, thus making possible their application to clinical practice.

Mourning and manic-depressive states

The ideas which Freud had put forward in "Mourning and Melancholia" were also an inspiration for Klein as she constructed her own theory of manic-depressive states (Klein 1935). She discovered that the conflicts between aggressiveness and libido, as Freud had described them in 1917 in adult depressive states, were very early in origin and that the fixation point of depression was to be found in early childhood. Developing what Freud had said about the role played by aggressiveness and guilt feelings in depressive affect, Klein argued that the idea of reparation was particularly significant in this context – the wish to restore/repair the object damaged by aggressive and destructive fantasies. She pointed out that there were two kinds of reparation – normal, creative reparation, which arises from the depressive position and is linked to love of and respect for the object, and pathological reparation which can take several forms – for example, manic reparation based on a triumphant denial of depressive feelings, or obsessional reparation based on the compulsion to eliminate depressive anxiety in a magical way.

Defence mechanisms which are more primitive than repression

Klein was forced to revise Freud's ideas on repression when she realized that some defence mechanisms were already in operation before repression *stricto sensu* could be set up. She then drew a distinction between primitive defence mechanisms, which affect the structure of the ego by fragmenting it, and repression, which operates on psychical content without altering the structure of the ego. Primitive defence mechanisms have recourse to a form of suppression which has a particularly violent effect on external reality and on psychic reality – and in this they are quite different from repression. Five of these primitive defence mechanisms have particular relevance to Klein's theory: denial, splitting, projection, introjection and omnipotence. In 1946, Klein added to these the mechanism which she called projective identification, a derivative of primitive projection: in projective identification it is not only the instinctual drive which is projected, but also parts of the ego which, in fantasy, can be projected into the object. Projective identification involves the expulsion not only of bad and undesirable aspects of the self in order to control the object, but also of good parts. W. R. Bion (1959) would later distinguish between pathological and normal projective identification, thus making this concept one of the central tenets of Kleinian psychoanalysis (as well as in other currents of thought).

Transitions between pathological and normal symbolism

Taking Freud's ideas on the schizophrenic's language, outlined in "The Unconscious" (Freud 1915e), as a basis and following Klein's (1930) early work on symbolism, Hanna Segal and W. R. Bion developed their own point of view on the symbolic function and on the transitions between pathological and normal symbolism.

Hanna Segal: from symbolic equation to true symbolism (symbolic representation)

In 1957, Segal drew a distinction between two kinds of symbol formation and symbolic function: "symbolic equation" and true symbolism or symbolic representation. She pointed out that symbol formation is very dependent on the transition from the paranoid-schizoid to the depressive position, as well as on the strength of projective identification. When schizoid disturbances occur in object relations and projective identification increases, part of the ego identifies in a very concrete manner with the object; as a result, the symbol becomes equated with the symbolized object to such an extent that both are experienced as being identical – hence the term "symbolic equation".

Symbolic equations are what underlie schizophrenic thinking; they are a feature also of the process of identification with the lost object which is characteristic of pathological mourning. It is only when the depressive position arises, with its concomitant experience of separateness, that the symbol can represent the object without being its exact equivalent: the way is henceforth open for true symbolism (or symbolic representation). It should be pointed out that Segal first saw concrete symbolism as a regression to the paranoid-schizoid position; later, however, along with Rosenfeld and Bion, she differentiated between a normal and a pathological form of the paranoid-schizoid position and stated that concrete symbolism belonged in fact to the pathological paranoid-schizoid position.

Segal (1991) goes on to argue that the process of symbol formation is crucial, given that the symbol determines our capacity to communicate and that every communication we make is carried out with the help of symbols – not only as regards external reality but also when we communicate with our inner world.

W. R. Bion – creating an apparatus for thinking thoughts

In 1962, Bion introduced a distinction between alpha-elements and beta-elements. In so doing, he brought a new approach to symbolism and to the transition between pathological and normal symbolism; though Bion's perspective was different, it complemented what Segal had been saying. The idea of alpha-function arose from Bion's research into the schizophrenic's difficulty in making his or her experiences meaningful and in communicating them; Bion's aim was to show how raw data coming from our sense organs are converted into mental content which can thereupon become meaningful for the mind, be thought about and dreamt of. According to Bion, if a thought is to be thinkable by the mind – in a process similar to symbolization – there has to be a "pre-conception" which meets up with a "realization": it is this encounter which creates a "conception". This integration of two elements in order to create a third one lies at the very basis of forming thoughts and constructing theories. Like Segal, Bion saw thinking as being closely connected to emotions; these processes can be expressed in terms either of the paranoid-schizoid or of the depressive position. When alpha-function is distorted, sense-data can no longer be adequately processed – they remain in our mind as undigested beta-elements which can only be evacuated by projective identification.

- ## "A PHYLOGENETIC FANTASY: OVERVIEW OF THE TRANSFERENCE NEUROSES" (1985a [1915])

Biographies and history

An unpublished manuscript discovered in 1983

This paper is in itself highly significant in that it was discovered purely by chance in 1983 by Ilse Grubrich-Simitis among a series of papers which Ferenczi had entrusted to Balint; included in these was a letter by Freud dated 28 July 1915, in which he asked for Ferenczi's comments on certain ideas of his. It is a first draft of what ought to have been Freud's twelfth essay for his Papers on Metapsychology, in Freud's own handwriting – the only paper that has survived of the seven which were never published in the book he had envisaged. Of those twelve papers which were destined to be published as chapters of a book, only five were published by him between 1915 and 1917 as separate articles. His correspondence, however, shows that he did in fact write the other seven; it seems probable that he subsequently destroyed them. The discovery of his "Overview of the Transference Neuroses" was thus all the more surprising.

In this paper, which bears witness to his close collaboration with Ferenczi, Freud has more to say about phylogenesis, a topic which he had broached in *Totem and Taboo* (1912–1913) and which was to be a major theme in all of his subsequent writings. Freud argues that the mental life of human beings today carries indelible traces of our archaic heritage. What we see as the primal fantasies of psychic reality are in fact the traces left by real traumatic events which took place in prehistoric times such as the Ice Age.

Discovering the text

Page numbers are those of Freud, S. (1985a [1915]) "A Phylogenetic Fantasy: An Overview of the Transference Neuroses".

The first section of the paper, written in telegraphic style, is a brief reminder of the principal mechanisms at work in the three "transference neuroses": anxiety hysteria, conversion hysteria and obsessional neurosis. Freud mentions the part played by repression, counter-cathexis, formation of substitutes and of symptoms, etc. The second section of the paper has less to do with what the title would have us believe, because Freud goes into much more detail here than elsewhere about his phylogenetic hypothesis, which at times he calls his phylogenetic "*fantasy*". Unlike the first section, this part of the paper is written out more or less in full. Freud attempts to draw some parallels between the factors which produce neuroses – narcissistic neuroses as well as transference neuroses – and the history of the development of humankind, with reference to an earlier exploratory work by Ferenczi (1913) on the topic. Freud states that his only means of investigation is what he is able to observe in the neuroses:

One thereby gets the impression that the developmental history of the libido recapitulates a much older piece of the [phylogenetic] development than that of the ego; the former perhaps recapitulates conditions of the phylum of vertebrates, whereas the latter is dependent on the history of the human race. (1985a [1915]: 11–12)

Freud is here thinking about the impact that the trauma experienced by men in prehistoric times may have on the neuroses, in combination with those factors which are linked to the instinctual drives. For example, he feels that *"a portion of the children bring along the anxiousness of the beginning of the Ice Age and are now induced by it to treat the unsatisfied libido as an external danger"* (ibid.: 14). Freud mentions also in this paper his theory of the killing of the primal father by the primal horde, seeing in that event the root cause of guilt feelings and of civilization – a theme already explored in *Totem and Taboo* (1912–1913).

- **INTRODUCTORY LECTURES ON PSYCHO-ANALYSIS (1916–1917 [1915–1917])**

During two successive winter terms, 1915–1916 and 1916–1917, Freud gave a series of lectures which were attended by a very large audience and later published as *Introductory Lectures on Psycho-Analysis*. The book is written as though Freud was conversing interactively with the reader and it includes many anecdotes and illustrative clinical examples. It was an immediate success and remains, together with *The Psychopathology of Everyday Life* (1901b), probably the most widely read of all Freud's writings. Since these *Introductory Lectures* recapitulate the salient points of the discoveries made by psychoanalysis from its beginnings up to 1915, I shall say no more about this book as such. With the exception of a few addenda which clarify certain points of interest mainly for exegetes, its subject-matter is already dealt with in my presentation of several other texts of Freud's. It does not contain any new psychoanalytic ideas.

New concepts

Affects – ambivalence – conscience – criticism, criticism of the ego – depression – derivatives of the unconscious – ego instincts – feelings – guilt feelings – hate – identification with the lost object – incorporation – instinctual drives – introjection – love – mania – masochism – melancholia (depression) – metapsychology – narcissistic identification – normal mourning – organ-speech – pathological mourning – phylogenesis – preconscious – primal instincts – "purified pleasure-ego" – representation – representative-representation – repression – sadism – self-reproaches – symbolism – temporal regression – thing-presentation – topographical regression – unconscious – word-presentation

"FROM THE HISTORY OF AN INFANTILE NEUROSIS" (THE "WOLF-MAN")

(1918b [1914])

Zooming in on the primal scene at the heart of an infantile neurosis

This fascinating narrative is an account of the longest psychoanalytic treatment that we have by Freud. It is the story of the analysis of a young man of 23 who suffered from severe psychological problems which had been judged incurable; Freud felt that, after four-and-a-half years of a particularly difficult analysis, the patient was completely cured. In his account, Freud has little to say about the transference, but what he wrote to Ferenczi at the beginning of the analysis says a great deal about the sheer violence of the negative transference with which he was faced: "*A wealthy young Russian, whom I am treating for compulsive and passionate feelings of love, confessed to me, after the first session, the following transferences: Jewish swindler, he would like to use me from behind and shit on my head*" (Letter from Freud to Ferenczi, 13 February 1910). Even though the psychotic aspects of Sergueï Constantinovitch's personality had not escaped his notice, Freud focuses his narrative mainly on the patient's infantile neurosis; his aim was to demonstrate, with the help of this case, the fact that neuroses in adulthood are based on an infantile neurosis and that sexuality plays a decisive part in this. Freud invites the reader to follow him as he makes his discoveries one after the other, exploring Sergueï Constantinovitch's past history layer by layer.

He begins with a general view of the protagonists who played a role in one or other of the many scenes of seduction scattered throughout Sergueï Constantinovitch's childhood; these bring to the patient's mind a dream full of phobic anxiety, the famous dream of the wolves which he had when he was 4 years old. Freud interpreted this dream as a deferred reactivation of a primal scene – *a tergo* coitus between the parents – which the patient had witnessed when he was 18 months old. Continuing his investigation, Freud examines through a series of close-ups the various aspects of that primal scene, and finally focuses on the encounter between the child and the father's penis inside the mother's body. For Freud, this primal scene, as it appears in the child's unconscious fantasies, is the starting-point of the disorders which would subsequently determine the young man's neurosis in adulthood. Through a detailed analysis of Sergueï Constantinovitch's infantile sexual theories, Freud highlights the conflict between the little boy's passive feminine tendencies, corresponding to the inverted Oedipus complex, and his masculine tendencies, corresponding to the positive or direct form of the Oedipus complex. Once these masculine tendencies could be worked through, they succeeded in dominating the patient's unconscious homosexual impulses, thereby leading to recovery and cure. The psychotic aspects of Sergueï Constantinovitch's personality, however, did not lie dormant for very long. They re-emerged in 1926, when he had a hypochondriacal delusional breakdown, but were worked through after he had further analysis with Ruth Mack Brunswick, so that he recovered his health once again. Until the end of his life, however, Sergueï Constantinovitch remained identified as "Freud's famous patient", better known as the "Wolf-Man".

Biographies and history

Sergueï Constantinovitch Pankejeff (1887–1979): the "Wolf-Man"

His first analysis with Freud

Sergueï Constantinovitch Pankejeff, who was later to be known as the "Wolf-Man", was 23 years old when he consulted Freud for the first time in January 1910. The young man, who came from a very wealthy aristocratic Russian family, had no longer any hope of recovery. The illness which led him to consult Freud had begun a few years earlier: he had become depressed after a gonorrhoeal infection contracted when he was 18. His depression worsened after his father's suicide in 1906, and again in 1908 after his sister Anna, who had played a major role in his life, also committed suicide. His mental ill-health was such that he was entirely incapacitated and dependent on other people, to such an extent that he could no longer travel anywhere on his own; he had constantly to be accompanied by a manservant and by his personal physician. He had consulted the most eminent psychiatrists of the time and had been hospitalized in psychiatric units in Germany on several occasions, but all to no avail. Freud immediately began the analysis in February 1910, with the patient having five sessions per week; the treatment lasted four-and-a-half years. It was brought to a halt in July 1914, the date at which it was due to be ended having been fixed beforehand by Freud. A few days after the end of the analysis, the First World War broke out. Sergueï Constantinovitch returned to Odessa, married Teresa and completed his legal studies. In Freud's view, the patient had made a complete recovery.

In the service of a brilliant demonstration

Satisfied by this therapeutic success, Freud wrote his narrative of the treatment in November and December 1914, focusing his account exclusively on the patient's infantile neurosis and the part played in it by sexuality; he made it perfectly clear that he had no intention of writing a full report of the analysis. "*Only this infantile neurosis will be the subject of my communication*" (1918b [1914]: 8), he writes at the beginning. Why did Freud make that choice? Because he intended to use the case as a demonstration in support of his hypotheses. He wanted to show its detractors proof of the effectiveness of psychoanalysis; he was thinking in particular of those psychiatrists who had declared Sergueï Constantinovitch to be a hopeless case – including Theodor Ziehen in Berlin and Emil Kraepelin in Munich, who were among the most eminent of the time. In addition, Freud wanted to show his pupils how decisive was the part played by infantile neurosis and sexuality in the neurotic adult, for some of them were beginning to question that aspect – in particular Jung and Adler, who both disagreed with Freud over this issue, which he considered to be fundamental.

The beginning of the Wolf-Man's misfortunes

The Bolshevik revolution broke out in October 1917 and left Sergueï Constantinovitch completely destitute. He left Russia with his wife and settled in Vienna, where he would spend the rest of his days in some poverty. Depressed, penniless and out of work, he again consulted Freud, who took him back into analysis from November 1919 until February 1920. He at last found work as a clerk with an insurance company, and was supported financially by Freud and his Viennese colleagues. But Sergueï Constantinovitch's troubles were by no means over. After a breakdown in 1926 – acute paranoia – Freud referred him to Ruth Mack Brunswick, one of his pupils, who was interested in the psychoanalysis of the psychoses, and she began to treat him (see the section on "Post-Freudians", pp. 163–164).

Discovering the text

> Page numbers are those of *The Standard Edition of the Complete Psychological Works of Sigmund Freud*, vol. **17**, 1–122.

- ## *A lengthy course of treatment, the end of which was fixed in advance*

In his preamble, Freud reveals some of his thinking with the benefit of hindsight. He comments first of all on the fact that taking such a severely ill patient into analysis was something of a challenge; psychiatrists had diagnosed "manic depressive insanity" and had judged the patient incurable. Unable to detect any elements in favour of such a diagnosis, Freud thinks *a posteriori* that the patient was probably suffering from an obsessional neurosis which had appeared during his childhood and disappeared when he was around 8 years of age; he was therefore able to lead a fairly normal life until age 18, at which point he again became ill. Freud makes it plain that he intends to concentrate on the patient's infantile neurosis, without making any attempt to write up a complete account of his illness. "*My description will therefore deal with an infantile neurosis which was analysed not while it actually existed, but only fifteen years after its termination*" (1918b [1914]: 8).

The treatment lasted for four-and-a-half years and was a success. Freud has two important technical comments to make about this. The first concerns the length of the psychoanalytic treatment which, of necessity, is proportional to the severity of the case:

> *Something new can only be gained from analyses that present special difficulties, and to the overcoming of these a great deal of time has to be devoted. Only in such cases do we succeed in descending into the deepest and most primitive strata of mental development and in gaining from there solutions for the problems of the later formations.* (ibid.: 10)

In the end, the psychoanalyst's patience is rewarded by the revelations which the patient finally makes. "*And we feel afterwards that, strictly speaking, only an analysis which has penetrated so far deserves the name*" (ibid.: 10). The second technical comment concerns the necessity that Freud found himself in to fix a date for the ending of the analysis, which is not the usual procedure: he had been struck by the patient's lack of cooperation. "*He listened, understood, and remained unapproachable*" (ibid.: 11), so that "*the first years of the treatment produced scarcely any change*" (ibid.: 10). Freud then took the unusual step of fixing a date for the end of the analysis one year in advance, and decided, come what may, to keep to that date. He was delighted to discover that, as the date approached, the patient's resistances gave way. "*[In] a disproportionately short time the analysis produced all the material which made it possible to clear up his inhibitions and remove his symptoms*" (ibid.: 11). Freud says that he was himself very surprised at the success he thereby obtained, and that he can well understand the disbelief of any of his readers who themselves have no personal knowledge of such an experience, which alone can carry conviction.

- ## *The successive transformations of an infantile neurosis*

Freud begins by describing the situation as the patient had presented it at the beginning of his treatment, summarizing the childhood illness and establishing the main protagonists. He continues his narrative in the same manner in order to let us share in his discoveries, step by step, maintaining the suspense as he does so. The young man had lived until he was 5 years old in a magnificent country estate with his parents and his sister Anna, who was two years older. Thereafter, the family moved to a town house. His father was depressive and his mother was in weak health – though the patient fully realized this only in the course of his analysis. He remembered that he was looked after by a nanny, whom he called Nanya, who cared for him with much tenderness in his early years.

The first significant incident which impressed Freud was a sudden change in the patient's character when he was a little boy of 3½. Up till then, he had been very good-natured, but he became irritable, violent and even sadistic towards those close to him and towards animals; this change coincided with the arrival of an English governess. When he was about 5 years old, another transformation took place: he began to develop symptoms of anxiety and phobias – first a fear of being devoured by a wolf (a fear which his sister exploited), then a fear of caterpillars and of other animals. A third transformation took place, when the phobic symptoms were replaced by manifestations of an obsessional neurosis of a religious kind, with prayer rituals accompanied by blasphemous thoughts. However, these obsessions gradually diminished in intensity and had disappeared by the time he was 8 years old, so that he could thereafter lead a practically normal life. It is thus the analysis of this infantile neurosis, to the exclusion of all else, that Freud is about to describe.

- ## *The domino effect of a seduction scene*

Since the first change in the little boy's character had coincided with the arrival of the English governess, Freud was immediately suspicious of her. The patient then recalled two memories which appeared to confirm the hypothesis of seduction having taken place while he was still very young. The first memory had to do with verbal threats of castration made by the governess, while the second had to do with sexual play with his sister, who would toy with Serguei Constantinovitch's penis. Continuing his investigation, Freud then analyses in minute detail the consequences of these two events and concludes that the change in the little boy's character may well have been the immediate outcome. He goes on to analyse the whole series of events which followed on from these, showing how the little boy turned away from his sister, his first seducer, and towards Nanya, their nanny. One day, as he was showing off his penis to her, she scolded him and told him that children who did that kind of thing got a "*wound*" in that place – that threat triggered the fear that he might lose his penis. The castration anxiety was intensified when the idea came into his mind – after seeing his sister and another little girl urinate – that girls do not possess a penis.

However, the domino effect of the initial seduction did not come to an end with the fear of castration. It continued to have an ever more pervasive impact, leading to regression to the anal-sadistic stage for which his as yet insufficiently developed genital sexuality could not compensate. Freud draws an impressive picture of the "passive feminine attitude" which the young boy adopted, associated with the anal-sadistic stage; he adopted that position first with women, his earliest seductresses, then with his father.

> *It looks as though his seduction by his sister had forced him into a passive role, and had given him a passive sexual aim. Under the persisting influence of this experience he pursued a path from his sister via his Nanya to his father – from a passive attitude towards women to the same attitude towards men – and had, nevertheless, by this means found a link with his earlier and spontaneous phase of development.* (ibid.: 27)

Freud adds that in the period when Serguei Constantinovitch's behaviour problems were particularly difficult to put up with, the whole aim of his "*naughtiness*" was to force his father to punish him, so that his screaming fits were simply attempts to seduce his father and draw him into a sadomasochistic relationship. Freud takes advantage of this situation to warn parents and educators against falling into the trap laid by some children whose behaviour problems may mask an unconscious wish to be punished. The transformation in Serguei Constantinovitch's character may therefore be explained by a regression to the anal-sadistic stage; but what of the change which then occurred, when anxiety and phobias began to emerge?

- ## *The wolf dream and the primal scene*

The incident which coincided with the first appearance of anxiety when Serguei Constantinovitch was about 4 years old was not an external event but a distressing dream.

> *I dreamt that it was night and that I was lying in my bed. [...] Suddenly the window opened of its own accord, and I was terrified to see that some white wolves were sitting on the big walnut tree in front of the window. There were six or seven of them. The wolves were quite white, and looked more like foxes or sheep-dogs, for they had big tails like foxes and they had their ears pricked like dogs when they pay attention to something. In great terror, evidently of being eaten up by the wolves, I screamed and woke up.* (ibid.: 29)

The patient maintained that the dream referred to an incident which had occurred early in his childhood, when he was too young to remember it. As the young man associated more and more to his dream, Freud gradually managed to draw a parallel between the dream-content and the nature of the event which the patient could no longer remember. Here are the pieces of the puzzle he succeeded in placing side by side at this stage of the analysis, with the hope of discovering their meaning. "*A real occurrence – dating from a very early period – looking – immobility – sexual problems – castration – his father – something terrible*" (ibid.: 34).

Freud goes on to describe in detail the sequence of deductions which led him to think that the boy had probably witnessed sexual intercourse between his parents even earlier, when he was only 18 months old, and that copulation must have taken place from behind, so that the boy would have been able to see both his mother's genitals and his father's organ. According to Freud, witnessing this primal scene did not have a pathogenic effect at the time, i.e. when Serguëi Constantinovitch was 18 months old, but only later, when he was 4 years of age – at a time when the boy's sexual development enabled it to be reactivated as a deferred effect.

How then are we to explain the fact that the dream had generated so much anxiety? For Freud, this excessive anxiety was probably due to repudiation of the wish to be penetrated from behind by his father in order to take his mother's place; this passive attitude towards the father was repressed, while the anxiety he felt with respect to his father was displaced on to the wolves in the shape of a phobia. Freud puts it briefly thus:

> *His anxiety was a repudiation of the wish for sexual satisfaction from his father – the trend which had put the dream into his head. The form taken by the anxiety, the fear of "being eaten by the wolf", was only the (as we shall hear, regressive) transposition of the wish to be copulated with by his father, that is, to be given sexual satisfaction in the same way as his mother. His last sexual aim, the passive attitude towards his father, succumbed to repression, and fear of his father appeared in its place in the shape of the wolf phobia.* (ibid.: 46)

But in identifying with his mother, the boy identified with a castrated mother, the other danger against which his masculinity rebelled. Freud interprets this aspect thus: "'*If you want to be sexually satisfied by Father', we may perhaps represent him as saying to himself, 'you must allow yourself to be castrated like Mother; but I won't have that.' In short, a clear protest on the part of his masculinity!*" (ibid.: 47).

• *A scene which actually took place, or an imagined one?*

Could such a primal scene have really been witnessed by a child so young, or was it imagined in the course of a retroactive fantasy? After considering this fundamental question from a whole series of angles – "*This is the most delicate question in the whole domain of psycho-analysis*" (ibid.: 103, note) – Freud decides that if an analysis goes into sufficient depth, the analyst will end up being convinced that witnessing such a scene at 18 months of age is perfectly possible. At so young an age, however, the child does not have the means to understand what he or she perceives, so that those first impressions will have to undergo "*deferred revision*" (ibid.: 48), once the child's psychosexual development has progressed somewhat. From a technical point of view, Freud adds that, in the course of an analysis, the analyst may take such fantasies to be true. "*The difference would only come at the end of the analysis, after the phantasies had been laid bare*" (ibid.: 50). In other words, the analyst must wait until the patient is able to distinguish reality from fantasy. But whatever the relative weights of reality and fantasy, Freud appears to uphold the idea that the scene really does belong to the individual's past, ontogenetic or phylogenetic, and that it predates any meaning it may take on through deferred revision. In addition, he says that we cannot talk of "*memories*" or "*recollections*" with respect to such scenes; it is better to avoid the term altogether when they emerge during analytic treatment because they are fundamentally the product of constructions.

> *All that I mean to say is this: scenes, like this one in my present patient's case, which date from such an early period and exhibit a similar content, and which further lay claim to such an extraordinary significance for the history of the case, are as a rule not reproduced as recollections, but have to be divined – constructed – gradually and laboriously from an aggregate of indications*. (ibid.: 51)

• *From phobia to obsessional neurosis*

The third change – the transformation, when the patient was 4½ years old, of the phobic symptoms into obsessional ones with a religious theme – was the result of the intervention of an additional factor. According to Freud, the religious theme which was so much a feature of Sergueï Constantinovitch's obsessional neurosis was no doubt taken from the Bible stories which his mother used to read to him; the boy displaced on to the relationship between Christ and God the Father the masochistic and ambivalent relationship he had had with his own father. When he was 10 years old, he had a German tutor who had considerable influence over him. This tutor paid very little heed to his pupil's obsessions, which thereupon began to diminish in scope, before disappearing completely. Repression of his homosexual attitude did, however, leave traces which prevented him from establishing sublimations and from developing his intelligence during adolescence. When his analysis with Freud enabled him to eliminate the repression, these inhibitions were lifted, so that the patient became able to sublimate his homosexual drives and put them to use in his social life which up till then had been very restricted.

• *Anal eroticism, money and feminine identification*

In this chapter, Freud explores two issues: the first involves the relationship between money and anal eroticism, while the second concerns various aspects of the patient's passive feminine attitude and their relationship to disturbances of his intestinal function.

Freud begins by making several connections between the way the patient dealt with money matters and his eccentric behaviour as regards his bowel movements. For instance, this extremely wealthy patient had a paradoxical attitude towards money. He was at times a spendthrift, at others a miser, and this contradictory behaviour coincided with an intractable constipation which required him constantly to have enemas. This behaviour towards his bowels and stools was mirrored in his character: he was in a constant state of doubt, particularly as regards his psychoanalytic treatment. Freud says of doubt that "*it is the patient's strongest weapon, the favourite expedient of his illness*" (ibid.: 75).

Freud goes on to give a excellent description of how, as a little boy, Sergueï Constantinovitch built up a deformed image of adult sexuality as well as of his own, seeing it through the distorting lens of his infantile sexual theory marked by anal eroticism.

First, the patient recalled his fear of contracting dysentery when he was a child, since from time to time blood was found in his faeces. Freud interpreted this fear as the expression of a wish to identify with his mother, by equating the blood in his faeces with that of his mother's periods. His subsequent associations led the patient to make another link between the position adopted by the woman in the primal scene and the intensity of the anal-erotic fixation which was expressed through his intestinal disorders:

> *The organ by which his identification with women, his passive homosexual attitude to men, was able to express itself was the anal zone.* [writes Freud] *The disorders in the function of this zone had acquired the significance of feminine impulses of tenderness, and they retained it during the later illness as well.* (ibid.: 78)

Second, Freud notes that, as far as his patient was concerned, women were castrated and that the function of the vagina was equivalent to that of the intestine. In other words, as a child he had acquired a conception of the primal scene which was based essentially on the *"cloacal theory"* (ibid.: 79), because he had at that point insufficient knowledge of the difference between the sexes and of the role of genital sexuality in women. The idea that women could be castrated intensified in the little boy the fear of castration as regards his own penis, which in turn reinforced his identification with women and his passive feminine attitude towards men. His homosexual tendency was then repressed, but re-emerged in another form, that of his highly eroticized intestinal disorders.

His feminine attitude towards men, which had been repudiated by the act of repression, drew back, as it were, into the intestinal symptoms, and expressed itself in the attacks of diarrhoea, constipation, and intestinal pain, which were so frequent during the patient's childhood. (ibid.: 80)

Third, Freud goes a step further and equates three elements: faeces, gifts and children. Proceeding cautiously – *"The patient accepted this concluding act when I had constructed it"* (ibid.: 80) – Freud put forward the hypothesis that, as he witnessed the primal scene at 18 months of age, the little boy was filled with excitement and interrupted his parents' intercourse by passing a stool, which gave him an excuse for screaming. Producing a stool at that moment was not simply a sign of aggressiveness towards the parental couple, it had also the meaning of a gift – indeed of a child-gift offered to the father, for in ordinary speech "gift" and "child" are often felt to be equivalent. In addition, letting go of the stool may have been experienced as the prototype of castration, says Freud, the price to pay in order to obtain the father's love. This fantasy is reminiscent of Senatspräsident Schreber's delusion, in which he was willing to accept castration in order to become the wife of God the Father.

After discussing at some length his patient's unconscious homosexual tendencies, Freud ends this chapter by emphasizing his concomitant heterosexual tendencies. He shows that in fact the threat of castration comes from the father, and that it is a source both of unconscious hostility towards the father (which goes as far as to wish him dead) and of guilt linked to the affection he felt for his father. The path the young boy follows here is quite simply that of the positive Oedipus complex, says Freud, one which is common to all neurotics.

• *One seduction scene may well mask another*

After a date had been fixed for the end of the analysis, the final months of work brought fresh elements which completed the clinical picture, as is often the case when an analysis is drawing to a close. The patient recalled a seduction scene which he had never before mentioned; it had occurred apparently before he was 2 years old, and had involved Grusha, the nanny he had had before Nanya. He recalled that he saw Grusha kneeling on the floor to scrub it clean; her buttocks were towards him, he urinated, and she threatened him with castration. For Freud, this incident established a connection in his patient's mind between a young woman in a kneeling position and that adopted by the woman in the intercourse scene; in this way, the nanny became a substitute for the mother, and the boy identified with his father: *"He was seized with sexual excitement owing to the activation of this picture; and, like his father (whose action he can only have regarded at the time as micturition), he behaved in a masculine way towards her"* (ibid.: 93). According to Freud, that memory and the fantasies which accompanied it might well have laid the groundwork for the young man's particular attraction for his partner's buttocks and for his tendency to debase his love-objects, whom he invariably chose among women of humble origin.

Basing his remarks on the fact that the patient was convinced that he would be cured if only he could return inside his mother's womb and be reborn, Freud concludes this cinematographic tracking shot with a magnificent close-up of the primal scene, even going as far as to visualize the inside of the maternal womb. Freud goes as far as to suggest that the wish to return inside the maternal womb has as its aim not only that of being reborn, but also that of having intercourse with the father.

He wished he could be back in the womb, not simply in order that he might then be re-born, but in order that he might be copulated with there by his father, might obtain sexual satisfaction from him, and might bear him a child. (ibid.: 101)

Examined here as under a powerful magnifying glass, the protagonists of the primal scene are not whole objects as was the case previously, but part-objects – the paternal penis inside the maternal womb – as they appear in early childhood fantasies.

> *There is a wish to be inside the mother's womb in order to replace her during intercourse – in order to take her place in regard to the father. . . . There is a wish to be back in a situation in which one was in the mother's genitals; and in this connection the man is identifying himself with his own penis and is using it to represent himself.* (ibid.: 101–102)

The desire to be inside the mother's womb has to do with psychic bisexuality, says Freud, and is directed towards both the father and the mother. "*Thus the two phantasies are revealed as each other's counterparts: they give expression, according as the subject's attitude is feminine or masculine, to his wish for sexual intercourse with his father or with his mother*" (ibid.: 102). Freud thinks, in fact, that "*the two incestuous wishes*" are united in the patient's mind. After a detailed analysis of the various modalities which these two tendencies imply in the patient, Freud shows that the heterosexual tendency will win through: the boy's identification with his father leads to the dissolution of the positive Oedipus complex, while the lifting of repression as regards his homosexual tendencies enables their sublimation, thus setting the patient on the road to recovery.

- ### *Just a word or two about the transference*

Freud's whole account up to here had focused on a series of constructions and reconstructions, and it is only at this point that he explicitly mentions the transference. He notes that whenever some difficulty arose in the course of the analysis, the patient would threaten first to eat Freud up, then with all kinds of other ill-treatment. Freud feels that this wish has to do with the unconscious desire to devour the analyst as an expression of both love and hate, the effect of ambivalence – though he says no more about his patient's transference. In addition, he puts forward a few ideas concerning what causes repression, for in his view the conflict between the patient's masculine and feminine tendencies is not by itself a satisfactory explanation. Freud comes to the conclusion that repression has probably more to do with a conflict between the "*ego*" and the "*sexual tendencies*", i.e. the libido.

In a general conclusion to this case-history, Freud returns once more to his phylogenetic hypothesis: perhaps repression is the sign of the return to a primitive and instinctive kind of knowledge that has no means of representation, one which corresponds to "*some sort of hardly definable knowledge, something, as it were, preparatory to an understanding, [which] was at work in the child at the time*" (ibid.: 120). "*we have nothing at our disposal but the single analogy – and it is an excellent one – of the far-reaching* instinctive *knowledge of animals*" (ibid.: 120). Freud pursues this line of thought. "*If human beings too possessed an instinctive endowment such as this, it would not be surprising that it should be very particularly concerned with the process of sexual life, even though it could not be by any means confined to them*" (ibid.: 120). If we push this hypothesis a little further, "*repression would be the return to this instinctive stage*" – hence the possible existence of earlier, instinct-like, preliminary stages. Freud is, however, well aware of the reservations which surround these phylogenetic hypotheses.

> *I consider that they [phylogenetic hypotheses] are only admissible when psycho-analysis strictly observes the correct order of precedence, and, after forcing its way through the strata of what has been acquired by the individual, comes at last upon traces of what has been inherited.* (ibid.: 121)

Post-Freudians

The Wolf-Man's subsequent analyses

A period of analysis with Ruth Mack Brunswick: 1926–1927

In 1926, after some years of respite, Serguëi Constantinovitch had an acute attack of paranoia. He again consulted Freud, who referred him to Ruth Mack Brunswick, a psychoanalyst of American origin who was in analysis with Freud at the time. The analysis lasted five months, ending in February 1927. "Thereafter the Wolf-Man was well and relatively productive in a small bureaucratic capacity" (Mack Brunswick 1928b [Gardiner 1989: 263]). Ruth Mack Brunswick (1928a) published an account of this psychoanalytic treatment in close collaboration with Freud. She described the state of despair of the man whom she was the first to call "the Wolf-Man" – the nickname remains to this day – when he consulted her in October 1926. "During the analytic hours he talked wildly in terms of his fantasies, completely cut off from reality. He threatened to shoot both Freud and me" (in Gardiner 1989: 290). He was suffering from a hypochondriacal *idée fixe* as a result of an injury caused by a dermatologist – he was convinced that he had a hole in his nose and would therefore remain disfigured for the rest of his life. In spite of the difficulties with which she had to contend in this analysis – with the emergence of a persecutory delusion and delusional hypochondriasis – Ruth Mack Brunswick succeeded in analysing the psychotic component of the patient's personality, something that Freud had failed to investigate in his 1918 report. Moreover, she enabled the patient to work through his unresolved transference with respect to Freud, as well as his ambivalence towards his former analyst whom, of course, he admired – claiming indeed to be his "favourite son" – but whom he also hated and accused of having ruined him. She also analysed the Wolf-Man's negative transference, and in particular his contempt for her when he compared her – as he constantly did – unfavourably with Freud. In his paranoia, he believed that it was quite right for him not to have to pay for his current analysis – just as he felt that the financial help he received regularly from Freud and other psychoanalysts was no more than what he was owed.

Little by little, Ruth Mack Brunswick managed to analyse his persecutory delusion, thanks in particular to a dream the patient had in which the wolves reappeared in the guise of persecutors threatening to kill him. In one final dream, a connection was made between the patient's present illness and the gonorrhoeal infection which had triggered his neurosis when he was 18 years old; the link between his castration anxiety and his father was henceforth clear. It was after this dream, she adds, that "the patient actually and completely relinquish[ed] his delusion" (ibid.: 296). In a note she added in 1945, Ruth Mack Brunswick says that this analysis continued somewhat irregularly over a period of several years after 1928, and that the therapeutic results were excellent and long-lasting, despite major personal crises in the patient's life, crises which resulted only in a small measure from events linked to the Second World War (ibid.: 263–264).

Ruth Mack Brunswick had specialized in the study of the psychoses, which is no doubt one of the reasons for Freud's referring Serguei Constantinovitch to her. In addition, she was particularly interested in early mother–child relationships, and was one of the first psychoanalysts to employ the term "pre-Oedipal" in her writings, a term which Freud was later to adopt. Though her own mental health left a great deal to be desired, it was her professional experience with psychotic patients which enabled her to rescue the Wolf-Man once again, as her 1928 account of the treatment clearly shows.

Muriel Gardiner and the Wolf-Man

In 1926, Muriel Gardiner, an American psychoanalyst who was also in analysis with Ruth Mack Brunswick, met Serguei Constantinovitch and befriended him; her interest in him continued until the Wolf-Man died. In 1938, another misadventure struck Serguei Constantinovitch: his wife committed suicide at about the time when Austria was annexed by Nazi Germany. From 1945 on, Serguei Constantinovitch, who identified more and more with Freud's historic patient, was helped not only by Muriel Gardiner (1971), who encouraged him in 1971 to publish his *Memoirs*, but also by the psychoanalytic community throughout the world – and in particular by Kurt Eissler, custodian of the Freud Archives. Serguei Constantinovitch died in Vienna in 1979. After the Wolf-Man's death, Gardiner (1983) published an account of her final meetings with him, and in an appendix she cast doubt on the picture – in her view, distorted – which the journalist Karin Obholzer had drawn of him in 1980 (Obholzer and Pankejeff 1982).

New concepts

Ambivalence between love and hate – anal eroticism – castration (anxiety) – deferred action – end of an analysis – infantile neurosis – infantile sexual theories – passive feminine attitude – phobias – primal scene – religious obsessions – scenes of seduction – transference – unconscious homosexuality

"THE 'UNCANNY'"

(1919h)

The thousand and one aspects of a paradoxical feeling

In German, the term "*das Unheimliche*" carries many connotations which are unknown to other languages. The adjective *unheimlich* in everyday use evokes paradoxical feelings, combining what is familiar (*heimlich*) with what is unfamiliar (*un-heimlich*), in other words strange, foreign. Even though no translation could do full justice to the poetry of this paper, with its inspiration drawn from several works of literature, the reader cannot escape the intoxicating effect of the infinite variety of emotions which *unheimlich* evokes and of the range of interpretations which Freud suggests. Moreover, it is in this paper that Freud writes of the "compulsion to repeat". He was at that time working on the clinical implications of the concept with respect to the fundamental conflict between life and death drives; that notion was to play an increasingly important role from *Beyond the Pleasure Principle* (1920g) onwards.

Biographies and history

The First World War and its aftermath

A period of deprivation and isolation for Freud

The war years meant great hardship for Freud and his family. He suffered a great deal from the food shortages and the cold, to such an extent that in winter – as he wrote to his correspondents – he was unable to hold his pen properly, and he greatly missed his tobacco. He was worried whenever he had no news from his sons, who had been called up to serve in the army, and there were fewer and fewer patients; indeed, from time to time, he had only one patient. All the same, he refused to emigrate to London, as Jones had suggested he do. Though his brother in the United States was able to give him some financial help – Freud made a point of reimbursing every penny as soon as the war was over – his whole energy was applied to the task of managing to support his family's basic needs. The war years were not particularly productive as far as scientific advances were concerned; Freud had little or no energy for struggling on and he seemed to be resigning himself to death in the near future. Hope, however, was rekindled when Anton von Freund, a rich brewer from Budapest and a former patient of Freud's, arranged to subsidize a publishing house specializing in psychoanalytic publications and donated a considerable sum of money with this aim in mind. Thus was born the *Internationaler Psychoanalytischer Verlag* which in the years that followed published five scientific journals, more than one hundred and fifty books and Freud's *Complete Works* in eleven volumes. In September 1918, Freud and Ferenczi organized an International

Congress in Budapest, which attracted the attention of several official representatives of the Austro-Hungarian regime, mainly because of their interest in what psychoanalysis could do about the war neuroses.

Reunion in the difficult post-war years

After the Armistice in 1918, life remained difficult for the Viennese, almost as difficult in fact as it had been during the war years. The Versailles Treaty of 1919 led to the break-up of the territories which had belonged to the old Austro-Hungarian empire, and the Bolshevik revolution had completely upset the political geography of Eastern Europe. The frontier between Vienna and Budapest was closed, so that communication with Ferenczi was brought to a halt. Galloping inflation meant that Austrian crowns were of little or no value, and Freud decided to accept only patients who could pay him in foreign currency, mainly American and British analysands. In September 1919, after five years of separation because of the war, Jones was once more able to visit Freud. In 1919, too, Freud's son Martin married, and Freud visited his daughter Sophie Halberstadt-Freud in Hamburg when she gave birth to a son – the future "*Fort-Da*" boy. Unfortunately, Sophie died in 1920: an epidemic of influenza which ran rife in the post-war years carried her away; her death grieved Freud immensely. In September 1920 took place the Sixth International Congress in The Hague. Fifty-seven members were present, and Jones was elected president of the International Psychoanalytical Association (IPA).

Discovering the text

Page numbers are those of *The Standard Edition of the Complete Psychological Works of Sigmund Freud*, vol. **17**, 217–252.

- ### *The search for a specific form of anxiety*

Freud says that for some time now he has been intrigued by the kinds of feeling which lie behind the term *unheimlich*. At first sight, they seem to be related to something which is frightening, something which arouses anxiety and dread. Nevertheless, he adds, it is not only anxiety that is involved here, but also a "*special core*" of feeling which no doubt lies somewhere in the unconscious. Freud searches for this "*core*" in two directions: first in etymology, then in the different kinds of situation which arouse the feeling. He notes that the term is in common use in German and that it has no exact equivalent in other languages.

In German, from an etymological point of view, as Freud points out, *unheimlich* is the opposite of *heimlich*, meaning what is familiar, intimate, known, homely. But the word *heimlich* also means concealed, secret, kept from sight, doing something behind someone's back, and even dangerous – so that this meaning of *heimlich* becomes almost identical with that of its opposite, *unheimlich*: everything that is *unheimlich* ought to have remained secret and hidden but has come to light. Everyday language, then, shifts almost imperceptibly from *heimlich* to its opposite *unheimlich*. "*Thus* heimlich *is a word the meaning of which develops in the direction of ambivalence, until it finally coincides with its opposite*, unheimlich. Unheimlich *is in some way or other a sub-species of* heimlich" (1919h: 226).

- ### *From the uncanny to castration anxiety*

Freud then reviews the things, persons and situations which are able to arouse in us a feeling of the uncanny. One particularly good example occurs when we do not know whether the person we are dealing with is dead or alive, and many fictional narratives are based on this disquieting feeling. For example, Hoffmann's "The Sand Man" is particularly illustrative of this point of view: the hero, Nathaniel, falls in love with Olympia, a wax doll, though he is not sure whether she is alive or an inanimate figure. This theme was taken up by Offenbach in his opera *Tales of Hoffmann*. In addition, Nathaniel feels the same kind of anxious uncertainty with respect to Coppelius: he is not sure whether Coppelius is also the dreaded Sand Man. When the figure of Coppelius returns later, Nathaniel is thrown into a fit of madness; in his terror, he jumps to his death from a high tower. However, says Freud, the strongest impression of the uncanny in this fantastic tale has to do with the Sand Man, who threatens to tear out children's eyes. The fear of losing one's sight makes not only for an intellectual impression; from a psychoanalytic point of view it has more to do with the recollection of a terrifying infantile anxiety linked to castration anxiety. In other words, for Nathaniel, the Sand Man represents the dreaded father at whose hands castration is expected. We see here the connection with the Oedipus myth in which the hero inflicts punishment on himself by gouging out his eyes.

- ## *From narcissistic doubling to the ego's double, forerunner of the superego*

The paradox contained in the *unheimlich* feeling is also made use of by Hoffman with no little talent; the idea of the double is expressed in its diverse modalities. For example, Freud notes that, in Nathaniel, the paternal imago undergoes a whole series of "*doublings*" and "*divisions*" into pairs of opposites – and in particular between a terrifying father who threatens to castrate him, and a "*good*" father who protects him (ibid.: 232 note 1). These doublings and splittings, as we know from psychoanalysis, says Freud, occur in many kinds of mental state – for example, in the shape of the "narcissistic double", one of the aims of which is to ensure that part of the self can escape death. The idea of the double appears in all shapes and sizes, in particular in phenomena such as the immediate transmission of mental processes from one person to another. This is very reminiscent of telepathy, which, for Freud,

> *is marked by the fact that the subject identifies himself with someone else, so that he is in doubt as to which his self is, or substitutes the extraneous self for his own. In other words, there is a doubling, dividing and interchanging of the self. And finally there is the constant recurrence of the same thing – the repetition of the same features or character-traits or vicissitudes, of the same crimes, or even the same names through several consecutive generations.* (ibid. 234)

Freud then goes on to describe another kind of "*double*" – that which results from the formation of a specific agency which censors the mind and which we call our "*conscience*". This agency "*is able to treat the rest of the ego like an object [so that] man is capable of self-observation*" (ibid.: 235). In 1923, Freud would grant specific status to this agency, which he then designated as the "*superego*".

- ## *From "repetition of the same features" to the "compulsion to repeat"*

The idea of the double which generates the feeling of uncanniness is also at work in phenomena linked to "*repetition of the same features*", i.e. in disquieting situations which are simultaneously strange or foreign and yet familiar. It is the same kind of anxiety that we feel when, caught in a mist, we think we have wandered away from our starting-point only to find ourselves back in the same spot; we then realize with some anxiety that we have been going round in circles without noticing the fact. But there is another form of repetition which arouses even more anxiety: that which arises from what Freud calls the "*compulsion to repeat*".

> *For it is possible to recognize the dominance in the unconscious mind of a "compulsion to repeat" proceeding from the instinctual impulses and probably inherent in the very nature of the instincts – a compulsion powerful enough to overrule the pleasure principle, lending to certain aspects of the mind their daemonic character, and still very clearly expressed in the impulses of small*

children; a compulsion, too, which is responsible for a part of the course taken by the analyses of neurotic patients. (ibid.: 238)

Freud is here simply outlining one of the principal topics on which he was at that time working and which would be the major theme of his *Beyond the Pleasure Principle* (1920g).

Towards the end of this paper, Freud examines a certain number of psychopathological situations which may give rise to the paradoxical feeling of being both familiar and unfamiliar. Examples of these would be the incapacity to differentiate between reality and fantasy, madness and mental health, etc. Such phenomena have to do with a belief in the magical omnipotence of thoughts which similarly exaggerates the power of psychic reality over that of material reality. For Freud, the *unheimlich* feeling is one of the characteristic features of the repressed: the repressed content which is experienced as uncanny can be traced back to the revival of an infantile complex which was once familiar. Indeed, creative literature is based on the repressed material personal to each individual; when it succeeds in using all of the means upon which the author's imagination can call, it creates in the reader an effect which is both fascinating and uncanny.

Post-Freudians

"Dichotomization" of the parental imagos in the Oedipus complex

So prolific and varied are the literary and psychoanalytic themes which Freud discusses in "The 'Uncanny' " that it is hardly surprising that the paper has inspired many post-Freudian psychoanalysts to develop his thinking on these issues.

In my view, one of these is the dichotomization of the parental imagos: this is one aspect of the Oedipus complex which often goes unnoticed. When we think of the Oedipus complex with reference to Sophocles's *Oedipus Rex*, generally speaking only one parental couple comes to mind – that formed by the King and Queen of Thebes, Laïus and Jocasta. We tend to forget that when he was abandoned by them, Oedipus was taken in and adopted by another couple, the King and Queen of Corinth, Polybus and Merope, as D. Quinodoz (1999, 2002) points out. In the Oedipal myth, then, the hero has in fact two sets of parents – biological and adoptive – hence the dichotomization of the parental imagos in terms of "parents who abandon" and "parents who adopt". Consequently, if we analyse the Oedipal myth as if it were a dream brought to us by a patient, as D. Quinodoz suggests, it becomes clear that one result of this dichotomization is that Oedipus does not handle his complex very well. When he learns of the natural death of Polybus, his adoptive father, he thinks that what the oracle said no longer concerns him – "Thou shalt kill thy father and marry thy mother". It is only later that he learns that Polybus and Merope are his adoptive parents, while Laïus and Jocasta are his birth parents.

It is precisely because his parental couple was dichotomized that Oedipus managed to fulfil his unconscious wishes, for there was nothing to prevent him from enacting them: he could kill Laïus and marry Jocasta since they were not the father and mother he knew and was fond of. By dichotomizing the parental imago into two separate parental couples, Oedipus escaped the complexity of the triangular relationship – but, by thereby not stating the terms of his complex, he failed to negotiate it and work it through. (D. Quinodoz 2002 [2003: 72])

D. Quinodoz notes that some patients unconsciously double their parental imagos in order to avoid facing up to certain forms of anxiety such as castration anxiety, ambivalence or loneliness – but this only hinders the dissolution of their Oedipus complex.

Biographies and history

Ernest Jones (1879–1958)

As someone who was a close associate of Freud's and the author of the authoritative biography on him, Jones played a major role in the development of psychoanalysis, particularly in the English-speaking world. For many years president of the International Psychoanalytical Association (IPA), Jones founded the British Psychoanalytical Society and the *International Journal of Psycho-Analysis*. He helped Melanie Klein settle in Britain, and was later to act as a go-between in the "Controversial Discussions" which opposed Klein and Anna Freud.

Jones was born in 1879 in Wales and studied medicine in London. He discovered Freud's work in 1906 and stayed for a time in Munich in order both to further his knowledge of neurology and to learn German so as to be able to read *The Interpretation of Dreams*. In 1908, he met Freud in Vienna and corresponded with him on a regular basis until Freud's death in 1939. At the Salzburg Congress in 1908, Jones presented the now-classic psychoanalytic notion of "rationalization", the defence mechanism in which the subject puts forward a logically consistent explanation of some attitude or opinion or other, though he or she remains unaware of the true motivation behind it. In 1909, a complaint was lodged against him by the brother of one of his female patients; though he was cleared of all charges by the courts, his medical career was at an end. He left London with his common-law wife Loe Kann, and settled in Toronto for the following five years. From Canada, he contacted several American psychoanalysts and founded the American Psychoanalytic Association. In 1913, when he returned to Europe, he went first of all to Budapest, where he had a short spell of analysis with Ferenczi, then returned to Britain. At the same time, Freud had began analysing Loe, but she soon left Jones and married someone else in Budapest in 1914; Freud was one of the guests at her wedding. In June 1914, Anna Freud, who was 18 at the time, visited London, where Jones began to date her. When Freud heard of this, he wrote to Anna telling her to put an end to the relationship; he said that Jones would not make a good husband for her, and Anna complied with her father's wish. In 1916, Jones married a young artist who died two years later.

During the First World War, Jones practised psychoanalysis in London and, thanks to the papers he read at various symposia, he made Freud's work known both to physicians, who were very reserved about it, and to a wider audience. Since he continued to publish articles in German-language reviews, he was accused by *The Times* of collaborating with Germany and with the Austro-Hungarian empire; after an official inquiry exonerating him, he was granted permission to receive scientific publications in German – this meant in particular that he could remain in contact with Freud. In 1919, he married Katherine Jolk, who was from Vienna; they had four children. In that year too, Jones founded the British Psychoanalytical Society and in 1920 created the International Psychoanalytical Press publishing house in association with the Hogarth Press. In 1920 he was elected for the first time president of the International Psychoanalytical Association (IPA), a position he held for four years, and he launched the *International Journal of Psycho-Analysis*; he was its editor-in-chief until 1939. Jones was the instigator of the *Standard Edition* of Freud's complete works.

He was instrumental in helping Melanie Klein settle in Britain in 1926. He defended her point of view against the criticisms which were being levelled against her by Freud and by Anna Freud, yet at the same time he managed to stay on good terms with Freud and to continue working with him (Steiner 2002). In 1932 Jones was again elected president of the IPA and remained in that post until 1949. Towards the end of the 1930s, he helped a considerable number of Jewish psychoanalysts from Berlin, Vienna and Budapest to emigrate to Britain and North America; when Freud and his family fled Vienna to escape the Nazis, it was Jones, together with Princess Marie Bonaparte, who organized their departure and helped them settle in London. During the Second World War, at the time of the "Controversial Discussions" which took place within the British Psychoanalytical Society, Jones acted as go-between in the divergence of views between Anna Freud and Melanie Klein.

In 1946, Jones retired and spent the final ten years of his life writing an exhaustive biography of Freud, *The Life and Work of Sigmund Freud* (Jones 1953–1957), and his own autobiography entitled *Free Associations* (Jones 1959). In the course of his career, Jones published a considerable number of theoretical and clinical papers on psychoanalysis; the most important of these concern "The Theory of Symbolism" (1916), "The Early Development of Female Sexuality" (1927) and "Early Female Sexuality" (1935). It was thanks to Jones that a debate on female sexuality took place at the Berlin Congress in 1922; that debate created dissension between those who favoured the British school of psychoanalytic thought and the Viennese school. It was Jones who introduced the psychoanalytic notion of "aphanisis" to describe the disappearance of sexual desire in both sexes, a fear which is even more basic, he argues, than castration anxiety (Jones 1927). Ernest Jones died in London in 1958.

New concepts

Compulsion to repeat – doubling – repetition, repetition of the same features – splitting – the double – the narcissistic double – the uncanny

"A CHILD IS BEING BEATEN (A CONTRIBUTION TO THE STUDY OF THE ORIGIN OF SEXUAL PERVERSIONS)"
(1919e)
"THE PSYCHOGENESIS OF A CASE OF FEMALE HOMOSEXUALITY"
(1920a)

The first exploration of perversions and sadomasochism

These two studies enabled Freud to demonstrate that the Oedipus complex plays a crucial role in the perversions, as it does in the neuroses. In them, he shows that, like the neuroses, the origin of the perversions lies in an infantile neurosis. In addition, he highlights the prominent role played by psychic bisexuality, i.e. the presence of both masculine and feminine components in the minds of normal people as well as in pathological cases.

In "A Child is Being Beaten", Freud notes that, in beating fantasies, the sexual pleasure which is evoked by pain – a typical feature of masochism – is intimately linked to the eroticization of incestuous objects. For Freud, the girl's fantasy of being beaten constitutes a substitute for her unconscious incestuous wish for the father; moreover, with respect to beating fantasies, Freud describes in men a "*feminine attitude*" which is the substitute for a passive erotic relationship with the father, a typical feature of masochism in men.

In "The Psychogenesis of a Case of Female Homosexuality", Freud describes the treatment (interrupted) of a girl of 18 who was in love with an older woman. This is Freud's final published clinical case; for reasons of confidentiality, he no longer thought it advisable to publish case-reports. This case gave him the opportunity of studying female homosexuality, a subject hitherto much neglected by psychoanalytic research, no doubt because it is "*much less glaring*" (1920a: 147) than male homosexuality even though it is no less common. The analysis did not last for very long because the patient listened to what Freud had to say without really feeling herself personally involved. When Freud realized that her resistance was due to a hostile transference towards him – she was reproducing in the transference situation with Freud her wish to take revenge on her father – he put an end to the treatment and advised the patient to continue the analysis with a female psycho-analyst. In the genesis of the patient's homosexuality, Freud puts particular emphasis on the positive Oedipus complex, i.e. on the conflict with respect to her father, hardly mentioning the decisive part played by the girl's pre-Oedipal love for her mother; this is something he would take into account in the 1930s.

At the end of this chapter, I shall examine the different stages of Freud's developing conception of femininity.

> Biographies and history

Anna Freud's analyses with her father

Anna Freud and beating fantasies

Though Freud himself was very discreet on this point, there is hardly any doubt in the minds of their biographers that his daughter Anna was one of the cases he discusses in "A Child is Being Beaten" (Young-Bruehl 1988). Anna suffered from such fantasies, and this was one of the symptoms which led to her having a first analysis between 1918 and 1922 – with her father as analyst. It was by no means anomalous to do this in those days; the detrimental consequences had not at that time been identified. When that analysis ended, in 1922, Anna wrote a clinical dissertation in which she described beating fantasies in a 15-year-old girl; this was her presentation paper enabling her to become a member of the Vienna Psycho-Analytical Society. She later had it published under the title "The Relation of Beating Fantasies to a Daydream" (1923). Her own beating fantasies, however, were far from over. In 1924, a fresh outbreak of these fantasies led her to go back into analysis, again with her father. This is what she wrote to Lou Andreas-Salomé on 5 May 1924: "The reason for continuing [. . .] [were] the occasional unseemly intrusions of the daydreams combined with an increasing intolerance – sometimes physical as well as mental – of the beating fantasies and of their consequences (i.e., masturbation), which I could not do without" (quoted by Young-Bruehl 1988: 122).

Repercussions on Freud's conception of femininity

The fact that Freud analysed his own daughter no doubt had a considerable influence on his way of thinking about female sexuality. Anna's first analysis was closely linked to the publication by Freud of "A Child is Being Beaten", and her second analysis with him probably inspired him to write "Some Psychical Consequences of the Anatomical Distinction between the Sexes" (Freud 1925j), though for the latter we have no direct proof to support the claim (Young-Bruehl 1988: 125). In his 1925 paper, Freud takes as the crux of the young girl's development her penis envy; he observes that in normal development, relinquishing the father leads to the wish for a child, representing a substitute for the penis of which she feels dispossessed. If penis envy is too strong, however, and abandoning her attachment to her father fails, "*it may give place to an identification with him and the girl may thus return to her masculinity complex and perhaps remain fixated in it*" (1925j: 256). Falling back on identification with the father echoes not only the conclusions which Freud had reached in "A Child is Being Beaten", but also those of Anna in her "The Relation of Beating Fantasies to a Daydream"; moreover, identification with her father seems to have been a feature of Anna's life – her strong masculine identification, her asceticism, her renunciation of active sexual life as a woman, her difficult relationships with men and her long friendship with Dorothy Burlingham all bear witness to this.

Lou Andreas-Salomé (1861–1937)

A close friend of Freud's and of his family, Lou Andreas-Salomé was very involved with them at the time of Anna Freud's analysis with her father. Freud often wrote to her, telling her of the difficulties he was encountering in analysing Anna, while Anna was confiding in her as they were preparing together the admission dissertation on beating fantasies and daydreams.

Before she devoted herself entirely to psychoanalysis, Lou Andreas-Salomé's love life was, shall we say, eventful. She was born in 1861 in St Petersburg; her family was of German and French extraction, and her father was a general in the tsar's army. Lou was still very young when she broke away from her family; at 19 years of age, she left for Zurich to study philosophy and the history of art. When she was 21, she met in Rome two philosophers with whom she formed a passionate trio, Paul Rée and Friedrich Nietzsche. She had several affairs after this, including one with the young poet Rainer Maria Rilke. As Freud put it: "*she had acted alike as Muse and protecting mother to* [. . .] *the great poet*" (Freud 1937a: 297). In 1887, Lou married a German orientalist, Friedrich-Carl Andreas, who was a professor in the University of Gottingen.

> Lou Andreas-Salomé had met Freud in 1911, at the Weimar Congress. She immediately became interested in psychoanalysis and was herself an assiduous practitioner – thus becoming one of the first female analysts of all time. The following year, 1912, she settled in Vienna, was welcomed into Freud's family and became a very close friend of Anna's. She began corresponding regularly with Freud from 1912 on; by this means, Freud was able to supervise her analytic cases. Lou regularly attended the Wednesday meetings, and Freud soon had her admitted as a member of the Vienna Psycho-Analytical Society. Later, as a mark of her loyalty towards the cause of psychoanalysis, Freud gave her one of the rings which were attributed only to members of the "Secret Committee". When she began practice as a psycho-analyst, Lou Andreas-Salomé gradually gave up the career as a novelist and essay writer that she had followed until then, and gave pride of place to writing on psychoanalytic topics. She was particularly interested in the relationship between body and mind, highlighted the complementarity between men and women, and introduced a woman's point of view into psychoanalytical thinking. In spite of the rise of Nazism in the 1930s, she did not leave Germany and died in Gottingen in 1937.

Discovering the text

- **"A CHILD IS BEING BEATEN (A CONTRIBUTION TO THE STUDY OF THE ORIGIN OF SEXUAL PERVERSIONS)" (1919e)**

> Page numbers are those of *The Standard Edition of the Complete Psychological Works of Sigmund Freud*, vol. **17**, 175–204.

• *An obsessive fantasy with compulsive masturbation*

In this paper, Freud analyses an obsessive erotic fantasy in six of his patients, four women and two men. In its climactic phase, the fantasy is accompanied by an irrepressible and compulsive masturbatory satisfaction, as well as disorders of sexuality in adulthood. Freud notes that it is only with hesitation that this fantasy is confessed to, and the psychoanalytic treatment of the topic is met by unmistakable resistance because of the patient's feelings of shame and guilt. The "child is being beaten" fantasy appears early in childhood, usually before school age, and it is heightened when the child witnesses actual scenes of beating, at school for example, or when, later, he or she takes pleasure in reading books which describe such scenes. Adults who suffer from the fantasy have usually never been beaten as children, or only infrequently; in addition, more often than not they are unable to give any details as to the actual content of the fantasy: who is the child who is being beaten? By whom? And so on.

• *Infantile fixation, adult perversion*

A beating fantasy, particularly when it is accompanied by auto-erotic satisfaction, becomes structured as an "*infantile perversion*" (1919e: 181) and constitutes a fixation at an early stage of development, so that the child's future psychosexual development will be to some extent hampered. This fixation at a pregenital stage need not necessarily persist; it may develop in any one of several directions, including that of normal psychosexual development. It may however be repressed and re-emerge as a reaction-formation – several of the patients in Freud's study suffered from obsessional neurosis – or perhaps even be transformed by sublimation. Freud notes that the "child is being beaten" fantasy is very difficult to bring out into the open during therapy; he describes how the mind pushes this fantasy to one side, far from conscious awareness, in order to defend itself.

> *[The analytic physician] is obliged to admit to himself that to a great extent these fantasies subsist apart from the rest of the content of a neurosis, and find no proper place in its structure. But impressions of this kind, as I know from my own experience, are only too willingly put on one side*. (ibid.: 183)

Later, in 1927, he will attribute this phenomenon to a "*splitting of the ego*" and describe it as a major feature in perverse structures.

On the technical level, Freud insists on the need for the analyst to take as much time as may be required for the lifting of infantile amnesia, so that the patient may rediscover the memories of events which took place when he or she was between 2 and 4 or 5 years of age, the period when this kind of fantasy appears. He takes this opportunity to warn psychoanalysts against not allowing enough time for proper treatment. "*It would be desirable to obtain practical results in a shorter period and with less trouble*" (ibid.: 183). He emphasizes the importance of the earliest experiences, without implying any underestimation of the influence of later ones. "*[Anyone] who neglects childhood analysis is bound to fall into the most disastrous errors*" (ibid.: 183).

Freud goes on to examine in detail the beating fantasy in the course of infantile development, pointing out that this particular fantasy representation undergoes many transformations. He begins by studying the fantasy in his four female patients, then makes a more succinct exploration of it in his two male patients. Freud points out that the comments he makes in this paper remain somewhat tentative and concern only those cases which he himself treated.

- ## *The beating fantasy in girls*

In its initial phase, the girl's fantasy is "*My father is beating the child*". It is presented as a conscious daydream which appears in childhood, and little detail is given as to the protagonists. The author of the fantasy is not the child who is being beaten – it is usually one of her brothers or sisters who is at the receiving end – and no particular sexual quality is attached to the scene. Freud infers that "*My father is beating the child*" means, from the point of view of the affect involved "*My father is beating the child whom I hate*" (ibid.: 185); if we continue to analyse the fantasy, it turns out to mean "*My father does not love this other child, he loves only me*" (ibid.: 187).

The content of the second phase is "*I am being beaten by my father*": this is, for the patient, an unconscious fantasy and results from a reconstruction in the course of the analysis. After this transformation, the author of the fantasy is the child who is being beaten, while the person who is doing the beating remains the father. For Freud, "*I am being beaten by my father*" is the result of repression of the girl's incestuous Oedipal wish as regards her father (the direct or positive form of the Oedipus complex). In other words, the pleasure which accompanies the beating corresponds to a masochistic fantasy. The pleasure which is hidden within the suffering has a double meaning: in the first place, it ensures that the girl will be punished for her reprehensible desires with respect to her father – "*a sense of guilt appears*" (ibid.: 188); second, it is a regressive substitute for the incestuous erotic relationship with the father, through a return to the pregenital anal-sadistic stage of psychosexual development. "*This being beaten is now a convergence of the sense of guilt and sexual love. It is not only the punishment for the forbidden genital relation, but also the regressive substitute for that relation*" (ibid.: 189).

In its third and final phase, the content of the fantasy is: "*A substitute for the father (a teacher) is beating a child (who, generally speaking, is a boy)*". This fantasy carries with it a strong sexual excitation which leads to compulsive masturbatory satisfaction. Here, the girl who produces the fantasy is not the child being beaten, she is the spectator of a sadistic scene (voyeurism); and the person doing the beating is no longer the father. In the fantasy, the girl tends to identify with the boy, thereby reinforcing her masculine tendencies to the detriment of her feminine ones.

> *When they turn away from their incestuous love for their father, with its genital significance, they easily abandon their feminine role. They spur their "masculinity complex" [Van Ophuijsen (1917)] into activity and from that time forward only want to be boys*. (ibid.: 191)

- ### *The beating fantasy in boys*

In the clinical material of his two male patients, Freud was surprised not to find the three phases he had observed in the girl's fantasy. In the first place, boys have nothing which corresponds to the conscious fantasy in girls – "A child is being beaten" – which occurs in the first phase. In the second phase, the boy's unconscious fantasy, after analysis, turns out to be *"I am being beaten by my father"* and not, as expected, *"I am being beaten by my mother"*. In other words, in this phase, boys have the same unconscious fantasy as girls. Finally, in the third (conscious) phase, which is accompanied by masturbatory excitation or masochistic sexual intercourse, the boy's fantasy becomes *"I am being beaten by my mother (or mother-substitute)"*. According to Freud, this masochistic fantasy is a reversal of the boy's incestuous fantasy, transforming it into a masochistic one: abandoning an active attitude, the boy adopts a passive attitude towards the person doing the beating; this is what Freud calls the boy's *"feminine attitude"*.

Freud attempts to account for the difference he observes between girls and boys in the following way: though in both sexes the starting-point of the beating fantasy is the Oedipus complex, in girls the fantasy proceeds from the *"direct"* or *"positive"* form of the complex, because the fantasy *"I am being beaten by my father"* is a substitute for a (heterosexual) incestuous relationship with him. In boys, on the other hand, the fantasy *"I am being beaten by my father"* proceeds from the *"inverted"* or *"negative"* form of the Oedipus complex; it is the substitute for a (homosexual) incestuous relationship with the father, in which the boy takes the place of the (pregenital) mother and identifies with her. Freud emphasizes the fact that, in boys, both phases of the fantasy are passive in nature; the fantasy *"is derived from a feminine attitude towards his father"* (ibid.: 198), in spite of the change in sex of the person doing the beating – *father* in the unconscious fantasy and *mother* in the conscious one. In short, this is a masochistic fantasy common to both sexes. *"In the case of the girl the unconscious masochistic fantasy starts from the normal Oedipus attitude; in that of the boy it starts from the inverted attitude, in which the father is taken as the object of love"* (ibid.: 198–199).

- ### *Oedipus complex, perversion and masochism*

This study enables Freud to further his understanding of the psychogenesis of the perversions and of masochism and to show *"for the first time"*, he says, that perversions in adulthood have their roots in infantile sexuality and that they are *"brought into relation with the child's incestuous love-object, with its Oedipus complex"* (ibid.: 192). In other words, the Oedipus complex lies at the origin not only of the neuroses but also of the perversions. As regards the genesis of masochism, Freud goes back to the hypotheses he had developed in *Three Essays on the Theory of Sexuality* (1905d), according to which masochism is the result of the sadistic impulse being turned back on the self. Here, however, in "A Child is Being Beaten", he shows that this transformation occurs because of the impact of the sense of guilt which participates in the act of repression and *"compels [the genital] organization to regress to the earlier sadistic-anal stage"* (ibid.: 194). Where does this sense of guilt come from? According to Freud, *"we should assign it to the agency in the mind which sets itself up as a critical conscience over against the rest of the ego"* (ibid.: 194); he goes on to describe this critical function which he would later call the superego. Freud shows that the second phase of the fantasy, the unconscious fantasy, is by far the most important: *"I am being beaten by my father"*. This creates in the person concerned, boy or girl, an attitude in which they present themselves as victims of those in their immediate circle who represent the father: *"[I]n that way (to their own sorrow and cost), [they] bring about the realization of the imagined situation of being beaten by their father"* (ibid.: 195). The detailed analysis of the various aspects of the beating fantasy highlights the part played by psychic bisexuality, i.e. the masculine and feminine components which are present in all individuals, whatever their sex.

Post-Freudians

The girl's feelings of guilt as regards her mother

Some post-Freudian psychoanalysts claim never to have encountered the "child is being beaten" fantasy in their patients, whereas others say that they have come across it exactly as Freud described it. Ruth Lax (1992) is one such psychoanalyst; she studied beating fantasies in four female patients she had in analysis in whom the unconscious fantasy "I am being beaten by my father" corresponds to the second phase described by Freud. Unlike the latter, however, Lax observes that feelings of guilt as regards the mother play a much more important role in the case of her patients than guilt feelings involving the father. The mother is experienced as an extremely harsh judge who prohibits her daughter's incestuous wish for the father and threatens to deprive her of her female genital organs – a threat equivalent to the castration anxiety produced by the paternal superego in boys. This thought-provoking article describes the evolution of the maternal superego in these patients as their heterosexual tendencies gradually become stronger and their masochistic masturbatory fantasies diminish in intensity in the course of the analysis. To my mind, however, the four cases Lax presents seem to be neurotic organizations with moderate perverse and masochistic aspects, rather than highly structured perverse organizations like the one we see in the following case.

A perverse mirror fantasy as a defence against a psychotic breakdown

In a remarkable clinical paper, Ruth Riesenberg Malcolm (1988) describes a decisive turning-point in the analysis of a female patient who presented a severe masochistic perversion. From age 20 on, the patient's sex life had been dominated by perverse sadomasochistic fantasies and compulsive masturbation, and by constant changes of male partner. On several occasions, she had had to be hospitalized for a psychotic breakdown; in the end, she began an analysis (which lasted for some considerable time). For many years, the patient never even mentioned to her analyst either her perverse fantasies or her masturbatory activity. It was the analyst who discovered these elements thanks to her counter-transference. She noticed that the patient often talked about scenes from everyday life which fascinated the analyst and excited her curiosity, to the extent that the analyst herself felt a desire to participate in these scenes.

Gradually becoming aware of the intense curiosity which was overwhelming her, Riesenberg Malcolm interpreted it in terms of the consequence of the patient's desire to stimulate her analyst's curiosity. That interpretation made the patient think about her own curiosity as regards the analyst – which was particularly intense during weekend breaks – and she finally admitted, full of shame, that she spent a lot of time masturbating, with the concomitant feeling of being excluded by the parental couple (represented by the analyst); for the first time, she spoke of her mirror fantasy. In this fantasy, the patient saw a mirror inside which took place a series of violent, sadistic and humiliating sexual scenes. The protagonists were incestuous homosexual and heterosexual couples, and their intercourse lasted for hours on end. The patient imagined herself to be one or other of the partners in these brutal sex scenes. At the same time, while this mirror fantasy was going on, the patient imagined that spectators were watching the scenes and at the same time struggling against their sexual excitation – because, if they succumbed to it, they would fall into the mirror.

The analyst's interpretation concerning curiosity meant that the situation became much more mobile and could thus be transformed, so that instead of being enacted unconsciously in the transference, with the risk of coming up against a dead-end, it could be put into words and worked through. In the course of the analysis, the mirror fantasy was seen to have two functions: to prevent the patient making any progress by working through the Oedipal situation, while at the same time to prevent her regressing even more and risking a psychotic breakdown (as had often been the case before she began her analysis). In her discussion of this treatment, Hanna Segal (1995a) makes clear just how important in this case was the fact that the analyst could help her patient transform her *perverse voyeurism* into *normal infantile curiosity*; that transformation became possible as soon as the analyst was able to transform her own counter-transference voyeurism into an acceptable form of curiosity with respect to the patient. As a result, the patient became able to set in motion a process of identification with the analyst which could lay the foundations of psychic bisexuality, the guarantee of access to a more integrated form of female psychosexuality.

Discovering the text

- **"THE PSYCHOGENESIS OF A CASE OF FEMALE HOMOSEXUALITY" (1920a)**

Page numbers are those of *The Standard Edition of the Complete Psychological Works of Sigmund Freud*, vol. **18**, 145–172.

Therapeutic success depends in part on motivation

The young girl had been brought along by her parents, who were worried because she had fallen in love with a *"lady"* of doubtful morals, who was ten years older, lived with a married woman and had numerous male lovers. In spite of her parents' opposition, the young girl continued to pursue the lady in question, who remained indifferent to her attentions. One day, while she and the lady were walking arm in arm, they happened to meet the girl's father; he passed them by with an angry glance, and his daughter immediately threw herself on to the railway line. After recovering from her attempted suicide, the young girl's passionate love for the lady became even more intense; as a last resort, her parents sent her to consult Freud. The young girl seemed to have little motivation for treatment, which she had obviously accepted simply to please her parents and not out of any personal desire; Freud therefore begins his paper with a general discussion of the conditions required if psychoanalytic treatment is to have any chance of success. In particular, says Freud, patients must feel that they really do need the help of a psychoanalyst, because, for example, the suffering they feel is too great and they want to be able to overcome their problems. In the case of homosexual patients, adds Freud, the psychoanalyst has to see whether their heterosexual tendencies are sufficiently strong to counterbalance the impact of their homosexual tendencies; this is the case with both male and female homosexual patients.

From heterosexuality to homosexuality

Freud then proposes to reconstruct the course of the young girl's libidinal development from her childhood onwards. She said, however, that she could remember nothing in particular – except that, when she was 13 or 14, she seemed to have a strong desire to be a mother and to have a child. In Freud's opinion, she must have had a normal feminine Oedipus complex. Soon after this, the young adolescent began to be attracted towards mature women; in the course of the analysis, it appeared that these homosexual tendencies occurred while her own mother was again pregnant with the patient's third brother. Freud gives the following explanation: when she was 16, her mother was pregnant, and the young girl had herself felt a conscious desire to have a child. This corresponds to the unconscious wish to have a child by her father, and if possible a male child.

> *And what happened next? It was not she who bore the child, but her unconsciously hated rival, her mother. Furiously resentful and embittered, she turned away from her father and from men altogether. After this first great reverse she forswore her womanhood and sought another goal for her libido.* (1920a: 157)

Among the possible outcomes mentioned by Freud, the young girl's unconscious choice was to adopt a masculine identification. "*She changed into a man and took her mother in place of her father as the object of her love*" (ibid.: 158), and then became passionately attached to a mother-substitute: the *"lady"*. This attitude was strengthened when she discovered how much her passion for the lady displeased her father; forcing her attentions upon the lady, "*she realized how she could wound her father and take revenge on him. Henceforth she remained homosexual out of defiance against her father*" (ibid.: 159). Freud adds that her attraction towards a masculine kind of woman contributed to satisfying her bisexual tendencies. "*Her latest choice corresponded, therefore, not only to her feminine but also to her masculine ideal; it combined satisfaction of the homosexual tendency with that of the heterosexual one*" (ibid.: 156).

• *Masculine identification and melancholic identification*

Going more deeply into the analysis of the case, Freud draws a parallel between the kind of masculine identification adopted by the young girl with respect to the lady she adored, more or less as a man might do, and the particular type of object choice made by some men who choose as their love-objects women of easy virtue (Freud 1910h). Freud sees in his patient a tendency to want to "*rescue*" the lady from the disreputable life she was leading, just as in these men there is a tendency to "*'rescue' [their] beloved from these ignoble circumstances*" (1920a: 161).

As to what motivated her suicide attempt, Freud sees one reason in the fact of the young girl's despair at the idea that her father might force her to give up her beloved. But on a deeper level, her attempted suicide was both a "*punishment-fulfilment*" (self-punishment) and a wish-fulfilment. "*As to the latter it meant the attainment of the very wish which, when frustrated, had driven her into homosexuality – namely, the wish to have a child by her father, for now she 'fell' through her father's fault*" (ibid.: 162). The translator adds a note in which he explains "*In the text there is a play on the word* 'niederkommen', *which means both 'to fall' and 'to be delivered of a child'* " (ibid.: 162, note 1). With respect to her attempted suicide as a form of self-punishment, this is what Freud has to say:

> *From the point of view of self-punishment the girl's action shows us that she had developed in her unconscious strong death-wishes against one or other of her parents – perhaps against her father, out of revenge for impeding her love, but more probably against her mother too when she was pregnant with the little brother.* (ibid.: 162)

Among the motivations behind her suicide attempt, Freud sees in this young girl the same mechanism which operates in the suicide of depressed people, as he had described it earlier (Freud 1917e [1915]).

> *For analysis has explained the enigma of suicide in the following way: probably no one finds the mental energy required to kill himself unless, in the first place, in doing so he is at the same time killing an object with whom he has identified himself, and, in the second place, is turning against himself a death-wish which had been directed against someone else.* (Freud 1920a: 162)

If I may make just a comment here in passing: in cases of female homosexuality like that of Freud's patient, the homosexual woman's envy and hate are aimed at the genital parental couple, i.e. at the *genital* mother figure and the *genital* father figure. This implies that, when the homosexual woman says that she "loves women", it is not the *genital* mother figure whom she loves *via* these other women but the *pregenital* one. At the same time, she wants to eliminate the *genital* father in order to take possession of his penis and identify with it in terms of a *pregenital part-object* (J-M. Quinodoz 1989).

• *The hostile transference on to Freud: repetition of revenge against the father*

During her treatment with Freud, the young girl was not consciously aware of the role her father played in the conflict. Freud points out the fact that, unconsciously, "*he played the principal part*" (1920a: 163), both in the course and in the outcome of the analytic treatment. Behind the apparent submissiveness of the young girl with respect to her father was concealed an attitude of defiance and revenge against him. That attitude was expressed in two different ways in the course of the analysis. In the initial phase, the analysis seemed to progress almost without any resistance, and the patient participated actively; Freud soon realized, however, that she did not feel the least bit concerned by his reconstructions and that her progress in analytic understanding did not bring about the expected change in her. In the second phase, Freud understood that the patient's "*cool reserve*" had to do with her revenge against her father, transferred on to him as the analyst.

> *In reality she transferred to me the weeping repudiation of men which had dominated her ever since the disappointment she had suffered from her father. Bitterness against men is as a rule easy to gratify upon the physician; it need not evoke any violent emotional manifestations, it simply expresses itself in rendering futile all his endeavours and by clinging to the illness.* (ibid.: 164)

When he became aware of the patient's negative transference towards him, Freud broke off the analysis and advised her to continue treatment with a woman doctor; nowadays, of course, we would analyse the negative aspects of the transference just as we do the positive ones.

Freud observes also that the young girl's positive transference became manifest on only one occasion, not long after the treatment had begun. It was expressed through dreams which "*anticipated the cure of the inversion through the treatment*" and indicated her nostalgic longing for a man's love and for children. In waking life, however, the young girl consciously expressed the wish to marry, but only in order to escape from her father's tyranny and manage to have sexual relations with a man and a woman at one and the same time. Freud came to the conclusion that these dreams were "*lying*" (ibid.: 165), because they involved to some extent an attempt at seduction: betraying and pleasing the father originated in the same complex. We can see here that Freud's tone is indicative of the somewhat superego attitude he had towards this patient, something which contemporary psychoanalysts would avoid.

• *Homosexuality, heterosexuality and psychic bisexuality*

The psychoanalytic study of this clinical case enables us to reconstruct *a posteriori* the path which her psychological development had followed, beginning with a normal Oedipal situation which then led to homosexuality. However, though it may be possible to trace the development from its final stage backwards, it is not possible to follow the opposite direction and foretell the nature of the outcome.

> *[We] never know beforehand which of the determining factors will prove the weaker or the stronger. We only say at the end that those which succeeded must have been the stronger. Hence the chain of causation can always be recognized with certainty if we follow the line of analysis, whereas to predict it along the line of synthesis is impossible.* (ibid.: 168)

In other words, for Freud, it would be a mistake to infer from this case study that every girl who experiences an Oedipal disappointment at puberty may turn out to be homosexual.

This case shows also that homosexual friendships and strong attachments "*are common enough in both sexes during the first years after puberty*" (ibid.: 168). In the case of this young girl, her homosexual impulses were conscious, while those corresponding to the normal Oedipus complex remained unconscious. This leads Freud to infer that her homosexual libido was the more superficial of the two and that this current "*was probably a direct and unchanged continuation of an infantile fixation on her mother*" (ibid.: 168). Freud, however, simply mentions the part played by the mother–daughter relationship, he does not expand on it in this paper. He notes also that, in her childhood, the girl had suffered from a powerful "*masculine complex*", which he links to her intense penis envy – hence her disparagement of her own femininity and desire to be a mother. It is possible to draw these conclusions because they are based on what psychoanalysis has taught us about psychic bisexuality: "*[In] addition to their manifest heterosexuality, a very considerable measure of latent or unconscious homosexuality can be detected in all normal people*" (ibid.: 171).

Development of Freud's concepts

The development of Freud's conception of femininity

Freud's "phallic monism"

In "A Child is Being Beaten" and "The Psychogenesis of a Case of Female Homosexuality", Freud continues to refer to his initial conception of child development. The girl's psychosexual development is symmetrical to that of the boy, and belongs to the direct or simple form of the Oedipus complex; the boy wishes to marry his mother and eliminate his father, while the girl wishes to marry her father and eliminate her mother.

For Freud, the girl's psychosexual development turns for the most part on the infantile sexual theory that is common to both sexes "*[which] consists in* attributing to everyone, including females, the possession of a penis, *such as the boy knows from his own body*" (Freud 1908c: 215). Accordingly, when the girl reaches the phallic stage, which constitutes the turning-point, she shows great interest in the penis, just as boys do. But when she actually sees a boy's penis, she soon realizes that she herself does not possess one; this generates in her a "*castration complex*" rather than "*castration anxiety*" because, as Freud was later to emphasize (1933a: 87), she cannot be afraid of losing something she does not have. This complex creates in girls "*penis envy*": she feels disadvantaged with respect to boys, she would rather be a boy and she infers, from the difference in size between clitoris and penis, that she has already been castrated. The over-valuation of the male organ, combined with the idea that the mother possesses a penis like men do, has the additional consequence that it prevents both girls and boys from discovering the existence of the vagina, which "*makes it easier for him to reject and forget*" it (1908c: 219). Freud bases the subsequent destiny of the girl on the vicissitudes of her castration complex, because it may well lead to the wish to have a child. However, if they are unable to overcome this complex, little girls

> *feel greatly at a disadvantage owing to their lack of a big, visible penis, [...] they envy boys for possessing one and [...], in the main for this reason, they develop a wish to be a man – a wish that re-emerges later on, in any neurosis that may arise if they meet with a mishap in playing a feminine part.*
> (1916–1917 [1915–1917]: 318)

It is this conception of psychosexual development which has been called Freud's "phallic monism", because it essentially focuses psychosexual development, in girls and in boys, on the fact of possessing or not possessing a penis, and because he considered the libido to be purely masculine in nature.

The Oedipus complex was already implicitly present in Freud's work before he referred to it explicitly in 1910. In his first papers on the subject, he sees it as symmetrical in boys and girls, namely, the boy feels affectionately attached to his mother and wants to eliminate his father in order to take the father's place by her side, while the girl feels affectionately attached to her father and wants to eliminate her mother in order to take the mother's place by his side.

At that time too, Freud emphasizes the clear difference between masculine-active and feminine-passive, though he would later qualify his initial statements. "*I can well imagine the difficulties that the reader must find in the sharp distinction (unfamiliar but essential) which I have drawn between 'active' and 'masculine' and between 'passive' and 'feminine'*" (1918b: 111). Also, when he describes the "*feminine attitude*" and "*feminine masochism*" in men, as in "A Child is Being Beaten" (1919e), Freud appears to be describing the essential nature of masochism as a perversion, but his words are often ambiguous when they refer to the specific nature of femininity. On several occasions he states quite clearly that femininity is essentially masochistic – for example, when he describes masochism as "*an expression of the feminine nature*" (1924c: 161).

The part played by the early mother–daughter relationship

Though at first Freud thought there was strict symmetry in the development of the Oedipus complex, he began to change this initial position from about 1920 onwards, particularly as regards the following points.

Already in 1919 ("A Child is Being Beaten", followed by "The Psychogenesis of a Case of Female Homosexuality"), Freud hinted at the possibility that the little girl might become fixated in her relationship with her mother, but he did not pursue the idea any further at that point. Later, in a footnote added in 1923, almost twenty years after he had published his report on "Dora" in 1905, he acknowledged that he had interpreted only the patient's paternal transference, completely ignoring her maternal transference – in other words, the "*homosexual love*" that Dora felt for Frau K. Once again putting to excellent use the failure of that analysis, Freud began to realize the full importance of the little girl's early attachment to her mother; he describes Dora's homosexual attachment as "*the strongest unconscious current in her mental life*" (1905e: 120, note added in 1923). Freud goes on: "*Before I had learnt the importance of the homosexual current of feeling in psychoneurotics, I was often brought to a standstill in the treatment of my cases or found myself in complete perplexity.*"

In that same year, Freud describes, in *The Ego and the Id* (1923b), the two forms which the Oedipus complex may take on. Given the fact of psychic bisexuality, there exists in both boys and girls a direct or positive form of the Oedipus complex, corresponding to their heterosexual impulses, and an inverted or negative form, corresponding to their homosexual impulses.

In 1925, Freud realized that the Oedipus complex as he had described it up until then had a "*prehistory*": the pre-Oedipal love which both boys and girls have for their mother makes her their first love-object, and it is this that forms the preliminary stage of the Oedipal situation. Acknowledging the importance of this love relationship with the mother early in life led Freud to draw a distinction between boys and girls as to their psychosexual development. Unlike girls, the boy does not have to change the nature of the object when he relinquishes his pre-Oedipal love for his mother and turns towards a woman who will be a substitute for the mother. When the girl, however, gives up her pre-Oedipal love for her mother and turns towards her father – then, later, towards a man who will be a substitute for the father – she has an additional task to deal with: she has to change her love-object and this complicates the movement which takes her from loving her mother to loving her father.

What enables the little girl to detach herself from her mother and turns towards her father? Here again, Freud returns to his "phallic monism" theory to find an explanation: it is penis envy which encourages the girl to turn towards her father – but with an additional element: the child she wants to have by her father is a substitute for the penis. This substitution of child-for-penis occurs by means of what he calls a *"symbolic equation 'penis-child'"* (1925j: 256) ("*längst der vorgezeichneten symbolischen Gleichung Penis=Kind*": *G.W.* 14: 27). Thanks to this equation "*[she] gives up her wish for a penis and puts in place of it a wish for a child: and* with that purpose in view *she takes her father as a love-object*" (1925j: 256). This fresh point of view leads Freud to a somewhat paradoxical conclusion: "*Whereas in boys the Oedipus complex is destroyed by the castration complex, in girls it is made possible and led up to by the castration complex*" (1925j: 256).

In his paper "Female Sexuality" (1931b), Freud again emphasizes the importance he attaches to the early relationship with the mother and to the part it plays in the movement from mother to father, i.e. in the change of object which occurs in the development of girls. It should be noted, however, that he still makes no distinction here between the "pregenital" mother and the "genital" one, the one who forms a couple with the "genital" father. Also, Freud continued all through his work to emphasize the fundamental role of penis envy in women and the impossibility for both girls and boys to acquire, in their early development, any knowledge of the vagina or of the female genitalia (1940a [1938]). It is for this reason that Freud considers that a woman cannot have any specific anxiety about losing her own genital organs – that is to say, an anxiety that would be the equivalent of castration anxiety in men; in women, that anxiety is replaced by the fear of loss of love, "*which is evidently a later prolongation of the infant's anxiety if it finds its mother absent*" (1933a: 87).

As far as these statements of Freud's concerning female sexuality are concerned, I think it is important not to lose sight of the fact that the primacy he attaches to the penis is only one aspect of the psychosexual development of both girls and boys. It has above all to do with an infantile sexual theory which has to be surmounted in order to attain adult genital sexuality. Freud himself admitted that his knowledge of female sexuality was incomplete: "*If you want to know more about femininity, inquire from your own experiences of life, or turn to the poets, or wait until science can give you deeper and more coherent information*" (1933a: 135). It would be left to post-Freudian psychoanalysts to add to Freud's views a more positive description of femininity.

A questionable point of view – which has been well and truly called into question . . .

As early as the 1920s, Freud's ideas on the development of girls and femininity were being subjected to much criticism. Some psychoanalysts followed his lead – Hélène Deutsch, for example, and Princess Marie Bonaparte, who wrote "all masochism is female in nature" (1951: 71). Some others, however, such as Karen Horney, Ernest Jones and Melanie Klein, tried to highlight what was specific to the development of feminine identity. Horney (1922) was the first to voice disagreement with Freud's notion of penis envy and masochism being characteristic of femininity, but her ideas were ignored for quite some time. Over the years, however, the theory of phallic monism was gradually abandoned in favour of an attempt to highlight the perception of the feminine sex organ as a basis for defining femininity. Jones's (1927) description of the sexual development of girls is based on the idea that there exists a specifically feminine libido; he introduced the notion of *aphanisis*, the disappearance of sexual desire in both males and females. Aphanisis, for Jones, gives rise to a form of anxiety which is even more basic than castration anxiety which, according to his point of view, focuses too exclusively on the male organ.

Melanie Klein (1928, 1932) made two major discoveries. The first concerns the ferocity of early fantasy attacks on the mother's body in children of both sexes; these attacks give rise to the fear of losing the mother and, in girls, the fear that the mother will retaliate by attacking her daughter's genital organs. The girl's fear of having her womb emptied of everything it could contain is comparable, says Klein, to the boy's anxiety about being deprived of his penis. Her second discovery is a consequence of the intensity of the aggressiveness the little girl feels towards her mother; this causes the daughter to turn to another object, the father, and to adopt a feminine attitude towards him. When the girl's aggressiveness combines with her love for the mother, her development leads her in the direction of a feminine identification. According to Klein, the dynamic impulse which drives the infant to look for new objects enables the child to create symbols and to replace his or her primary objects, the source of primitive anxiety, with symbols; this is a crucial stage in infant development.

In the 1960s and 1970s, feminist movements came to the fore, particularly in the United States and in France; for these groups, psychoanalysis was one of the factors which led to the oppression of women, and their firm intention was to promote a reappraisal of the relationship between mothers and daughters. Psychoanalysis did, however, manage to recover some of the ground it had lost; according to Rosine Perelberg (2002), this reconquest began with the publication in 1972 of Juliet Mitchell's *Psychoanalysis and Feminism*, a book which highlighted the revolutionary approach of psychoanalysis to the feminine question.

Since then, there have been a considerable number of psychoanalytic writings on femininity involving so many different lines of approach that to give an overall view of these developments would go far beyond the scope of this book. Dana Birksted-Breen has nevertheless managed to identify two main trends in this "new explosion" (Breen 1993: 17): the French approach on the one hand, and its North American counterpart on the other. In France, the book edited by Janine Chasseguet-Smirgel et al. (1964) gave a new impetus to the study of the controversial question of femininity in psychoanalysis. These writers challenged Freud's conception of penis envy as the primary organizer of femininity, arguing that female sexuality has, from the very beginnings of life, its own unique characteristics. Those psychoanalysts who are followers of Lacan have to some extent remained faithful, like Lacan himself, to Freud's phallic monism. As a result, French psychoanalysis is quite eclectic as far as this question is concerned. In the United States, controversy over femininity broke out once more in psychoanalytic circles in 1966 when Sherfey published an article which took as its starting-point the ideas of Masters and Johnson (1966) on the physiology of the orgasm. Though Sherfey's (1966) arguments were much criticized at the time, they did give rise to a great deal of discussion, the main tenets of which were developed in a book edited by Blum (1976).

What, then, is the position at present? For Birksted-Breen, the debates which took place among North American psychoanalysts on the subject of femininity have not in any way exhausted the topic. "Nothing was resolved; if anything, they engendered greater diversity even if at first glance one aim was united around doing justice to women" (Breen 1993: 17). Chasseguet-Smirgel (1976) argues that, if Freud's theories on female sexuality still give rise to controversy in spite of all the accumulated clinical data, the reason is probably that there are internal obstacles – linked in particular to infantile distress – which prevent their acceptance and hinder any advance in our knowledge.

I would like to conclude this overview of Freud's ideas on femininity with a quote from R. J. Stoller, a psychoanalyst renowned for his work on sex and gender identity: "If Freud had worked with a woman without a vagina, I think he would have seen that the only thing a woman wants more than a penis is a vagina" (Stoller 1968: 51).

New concepts

Eroticization of the incestuous objects of the Oedipus complex – female homosexuality – feminine attitude in men – feminine masochism in men – heterosexuality – hostile transference – identification – infantile mother-fixation – infantile neurosis – masculine identification in girls – perverse fantasies – perversion – sadomasochistic fantasies

III
FRESH PERSPECTIVES
(1920–1939)

BEYOND THE PLEASURE PRINCIPLE

(1920g)

1920: a turning-point in Freud's thinking

The year 1920 was a decisive turning-point for the way Freud envisaged how the mind functions. Until then, the model he had adopted was that of the pleasure/unpleasure principle as we see it at work in the neuroses: neurotics suffer from their symptoms, and in order to avoid unpleasure they ask the psychoanalyst for help in making these disappear, so that they may once again find pleasure in life. It has to be admitted, however, that clinical practice all too often contradicts the pleasure principle: how are we to explain the fact, for example, that some patients cannot bear to be freed of their symptoms and have a relapse just when they ought to be feeling better? Why do others compulsively reproduce traumatic experiences, with their attendant suffering? How are we to explain masochism or sadism, i.e. the pleasure taken in suffering pain or in inflicting pain? And the sheer destructiveness which is sometimes carried to extremes in depressive patients, drug addicts, perverts and psychotics – where does that come from?

In *Beyond the Pleasure Principle*, Freud puts forward a new hypothesis according to which the workings of the mind are governed by a more basic conflict than that of the pleasure/unpleasure principle: the fundamental conflict between the life instinct (or drive) and the death instinct (or drive). Freud suggests that the death drive comes from the biological need of every organism to return to its original inorganic state. This death drive or destructive instinct is opposed by the life drive – Eros – of which the libido is part. The pleasure/unpleasure principle remains valid, but if it is to come into its own, the life drive must have succeeded in dominating the death drive, at least to some extent. In 1920, Freud presented this hypothesis as though it were mere speculation on his part, but he was soon to attach more and more importance to it and go on to develop other implications which it involved. In 1923, for example, he showed that when the death drive gains the upper hand in this conflict, the destructive component of the mind dominates, as in sadism and masochism; on the other hand, when the life drive is more powerful, the destructive component is neutralized to some extent and aggressiveness is in the service of the ego.

The "turning-point that was 1920" is not simply a reference to the year in which Freud introduced the fundamental conflict between the life drive and the destructive one; it refers also to the series of innovative ideas which would come to fruition in his mind in the years which followed. Among these, we could highlight the importance he would thereafter attach to the affects of love and hate, to ambivalence, to object relations and to identificatory processes, as well as to unconscious guilt feelings, to anxiety and to mourning processes. In addition, in 1923, when he introduced a new division of the mind into ego, id and superego – his "second structural theory" – Freud took into account his new theory of the instinctual drives, and thus completed his "first topographical theory", i.e. the division into Ucs., Pcs. and Cs. systems. The innovative ideas which Freud put forward after 1920 have been accepted in part by most psychoanalysts, though the division of the drives into two groups remains to this day one of the most contentious issues in the whole of his writings.

> **Biographies and history**
>
> ### The shadow of death hangs over Freud
>
> Freud presented an outline of *Beyond the Pleasure Principle* to the Vienna Society on 16 June 1920, and the book was published the following December. The highly speculative nature of this difficult text, in addition to the doubts Freud himself expressed as to the validity of his hypotheses, mean that these ideas have aroused substantial reservations. Those who challenged their validity were strongly tempted to see them simply as an expression of Freud's own anxiety as regards death; this was the opinion in particular of Freud's own personal physician, Max Schur (1972).
>
> Among the events which marked this period in history, the First World War was still very present in people's minds, with its daily hardships and the constant presence of death. In 1919, Freud had had to deal with the suicide of the psychoanalyst Victor Tausk, though he gave the impression of taking it in his stride (Gay 1988). On the other hand, Freud was very affected when Anton von Freund fell ill with cancer; von Freund was the rich Hungarian who gave considerable financial support to psychoanalytic ventures, and Freud visited him every day during his illness. In 1920, too, Freud's daughter Sophie died: she contracted Spanish influenza and died barely five days later; she was pregnant at the time with what would have been her third child. Freud had other dark thoughts running through his mind at that time too – including anxiety about his own death. Taking a superstition as the basis for his calculations – the recurrence of the number 62 at different periods – he had long been convinced that he would die in 1918 or 1919, when he reached the age of 62.
>
> ### The second theory of the instinctual drives: Freud becomes more and more convinced of its validity
>
> Though the shadow of death weighed heavily on Freud in the aftermath of the First World War, it should all the same be acknowledged that it was the development of his own thinking which, when all is said and done, led him to introduce these somewhat daring new hypotheses. Though he may have expressed some hesitation in 1920, for the rest of his life he stated quite clearly that the conflict between life and death drives had always to be taken into account. To all those who insisted that his preoccupation with death and the tragic events of that period, in particular the death of Sophie, were the reason for his introducing the idea of the death drive, Freud was quite adamant in his refusal to accept their arguments. As a psychoanalyst, he acknowledged the relevance of the interpretation, but he did not accept it as applying to himself in this particular instance. For example, in order to forestall this kind of objection, Freud asked Max Eitingon to bear witness to the fact that he had already finished writing about half of the book by 1919, a year before Sophie died, though he did not publish it until much later.

Discovering the text

> Page numbers are those of *The Standard Edition of the Complete Psychological Works of Sigmund Freud*, vol. **18**, 1–64.

• *The pleasure principle and its limitations*

Freud begins by reminding the reader of the reasons which led him to introduce the idea of the pleasure/unpleasure principle, which he developed more specifically in his Papers on Metapsychology in 1915. For example, processes such as hunger or sexual desire create in the mind a series of increasing tensions followed by discharge; increase in tension is accompanied by unpleasure, while discharge leads to pleasure. We may therefore quite justifiably describe mental processes in terms of a variation in quantities of energy, and we may hypothesize that there exists somewhere in the mind a regulatory principle the function of which is to deal with these variations in tension – this is what Freud calls the *"pleasure principle"*. The final aim of this principle is *"the avoidance of unpleasure or a production of pleasure"* (1920g: 7). The tendency towards stability which governs mental processes is derived from another principle, the *"principle of constancy"*, the aim of which is to maintain at as low a level as possible the quantity of excitation present in the mind (ibid.: 9).

Does the pleasure principle really govern all mental processes? No, says Freud. If that were the case, he argues, the majority of our mental processes would have to lead to pleasure – but experience shows that this is not the case.

> *The most that can be said, therefore, is that there exists in the mind a strong* tendency *towards the pleasure principle, but that that tendency is opposed by certain other forces or circumstances, so that the final outcome cannot always be in harmony with the tendency towards pleasure.*
> (ibid.: 9)

What are these forces that oppose drive satisfaction? They are two in number, says Freud. First, the *"reality principle"*, which enables satisfaction to be postponed and unpleasure to be tolerated temporarily *"as a step on the long indirect road to pleasure"* (ibid.: 10). Second, the *"ego"*, which also can oppose the obtaining of pleasure; unpleasure may result from the fact that certain individual drives, in the course of their development, may be experienced as incompatible with the ego: this is the case, for example, of neurotic unpleasure, *"pleasure that cannot be felt as such"* (ibid.: 11). In both of these eventualities, unpleasure results from the *perception* of painful internal or external pressures which give rise to a feeling of *"danger"*. When the mental apparatus reacts appropriately to the perception of an internal or external danger, it could be said to be obeying both the pleasure principle and the reality principle. There are situations, however, with which the pleasure principle cannot cope adequately: this is the case with traumatic experiences, a topic Freud discusses in the following section.

• *Traumatic neuroses and children's play: two sources of repetition*

Freud goes on to describe two situations in which repetition is an attempt to make a painful experience controllable. The first of these is the *"traumatic neurosis"*, which occurs as a result of some unexpected event that could put the individual's life at risk; its manifestations are anxiety, symptoms of various kinds, and recurrent dreams. A significant feature of the dreams of these patients is the repeated reproduction of the traumatic situation, which contradicts the classic theory according to which dreams are wish-fulfilments: *"The function of dreaming [. . .] is upset in this condition and diverted from its purposes"* (ibid.: 13).

The second situation in which we can observe the phenomenon of repetition is that of children's play. Freud reports an observation he made of his grandson aged 1½: the little boy never cried when his mother left him for a few hours. The boy had a wooden reel with a piece of string attached to it, and Freud noticed that time after time he would throw the reel out of his sight then pull it back in again with the string. For Freud, the meaning of the game was to make the mother disappear and then reappear; the game was a substitute for the cries and protests which his grandson never uttered. *"He compensated himself for this, as it were, by himself staging the disappearance and return of the objects within his reach"* (ibid.: 15). Freud saw that these repetitions had several consequences. They enabled the child to transform a passive unpleasurable situation into one in which he took an active part; and, by throwing the object far away, he could satisfy a suppressed impulse, namely to revenge himself on his mother for going away from him. Freud draws a general conclusion from this observation, arguing that play allows children to reproduce in a repetitive fashion experiences which have made a great impression on them, and thereby helps to give them more control over the situation. From that point of view, the wooden-reel game shows that repetition may lead to working-through, while still remaining subject to the pleasure principle. *"[E]ven under the dominance of the pleasure principle, there are ways and means enough of making what is in itself unpleasurable into a subject to be recollected and worked over in the mind"* (ibid.: 17).

- *The compulsion to repeat and the transference*

Freud next turns to the vicissitudes of what is repeated in the psychoanalytic transference. He shows that transference consists in the reproduction of repressed fragments belonging to childhood experiences, and says that what is *repeated* in this way has then to be *worked-through*, as he had argued in "Remembering, Repeating and Working-Through" (Freud 1914g). With some patients, however, the process of working-through proves unsuccessful, so that what was simply repetition turns into a "*compulsion to repeat*"; this is much more serious and may even compromise the successful outcome of the treatment. According to Freud, the resistances which go to make up the compulsion to repeat do not derive from a conflict between the unconscious and conscious systems, in the sense of the unconscious pushing for discharge in the conscious system – that kind of explanation is based on the classic model of neurosis in the context of his first topographical theory. The compulsion to repeat has to do with a conflict "*between the coherent* ego *and the repressed*" (1920g: 19), a conflict which implies, says Freud, the intervention of the unconscious repressed.

What, then, is the relationship between the compulsion to repeat and the pleasure principle? When we examine this relationship, we observe that the compulsion to repeat recalls past experiences which include no possibility of pleasure, whether from the psychoanalytic point of view or in ordinary life. In the course of their psychoanalytic treatment, these patients, under the compulsion to repeat, inevitably reproduce situations of unpleasure in the transference.

> *Patients repeat all of these unwanted situations and painful emotions in the transference and revive them with the greatest ingenuity. They seek to bring about the interruption of the treatment while it is still incomplete; they contrive once more to feel themselves scorned, to oblige the physician to speak severely to them and treat them coldly.* (ibid.: 21)

Similarly, in the lives of some ordinary people, we may come across phenomena involving the compulsion to repeat which echo those that occur in the transference of neurotic patients. "*The impression they give is of being pursued by a malignant fate or possessed by some 'daemonic' power*" (ibid.: 21). At first sight, such a person seems to experience this "*perpetual recurrence of the same thing*" (ibid.: 22) in a passive manner, but analysis shows that the person's behaviour is in fact active, but unconsciously so.

In concluding this section, Freud observes that both transference phenomena and the fate of some individuals prove to us that "*there really does exist in the mind a compulsion to repeat which overrides the pleasure principle*" (ibid.: 22). A similar kind of phenomenon is to be found in the recurrent dreams of the traumatic neuroses, as well as in children's play. In the manifestations which accompany these phenomena, the pleasure principle and the compulsion to repeat seem to be in close partnership. It is, however, easier, says Freud, to detect the participation of the pleasure principle than that of the compulsion to repeat, because it is only rarely that we can identify the pure effects of the latter. Even though the pleasure principle does play a part, it cannot in itself be a sufficient explanation for such phenomena: "*Enough is left unexplained to justify the hypothesis of a compulsion to repeat – something that seems more primitive, more elementary, more instinctual than the pleasure principle which it overrides*" (ibid.: 23).

- *The role of the protective shield against stimuli: to control the sudden irruption of a traumatic impact*

Freud then describes the function of the "*protective shield against stimuli*": to protect the mind against an overload of excitation coming both from inside the self and from the external world. This protection is necessary in order to avoid the risk of a traumatic irruption.

The protective shield against stimuli thus has to protect the mind from destructive internal and external energies and to transform them. As regards external excitation, the sense organs take in this excitation and sample it in small quantities. The underlying cortical layer constitutes the sensitive cortex which becomes the system Cs. This system also receives excitations from within, against which there is no protective shield similar to the one which deals with external stimuli. As a result, there is nothing to absorb internal excitations, which pass directly into the system and generate a whole range of pleasurable/unpleasurable sensations. In addition, as a mode of defence, internal excitations are treated as though they are operating from the outside – this is the mechanism of projection.

With these preliminary clarifications in mind, it is easier to see that excitations which have a *traumatic* effect are those which manage to break through the protective shield and provoke disturbances in the organism as a whole. For this reason, the pleasure principle is initially inoperative, whereupon another issue arises:

> *There is no longer any possibility of preventing the mental apparatus from being flooded with large amounts of stimulus, and another problem arises instead – the problem of mastering the amounts of stimulus which have broken in and of binding them, in the psychical sense, so that they can then be disposed of.* (ibid.: 29–30)

Faced with this irruption, the individual's entire mental energy is mobilized in order to set up an "*anticathexis*", in a manner similar to what happens in cases of physical pain. In this way, the surplus of energy is converted into a "*quiescent cathexis*" which can control the excitation, in other words to "*bind it psychically*".

Traumatic neurosis is therefore the consequence of an extensive breach having been made in the protective shield against stimuli. What causes the traumatism is not the mechanical violence of the shock but "*fright and the threat to life*" (ibid.: 31). This leads Freud to outline a new theory of anxiety, one which he would develop much more fully in future writings. For the moment, in 1920, Freud points out that in cases of traumatism there is a "*lack of any preparedness for anxiety*" (ibid.: 31); the outcome of the traumatic event thus depends on the state of preparedness of the system, particularly as regards manifestations of anxiety. This is the forerunner of the distinction he would later make in *Inhibitions, Symptoms and Anxiety* (Freud 1926d [1925]) between "*automatic anxiety*" and "*anxiety as a signal*".

As regards the compulsion to repeat and its relationship to the pleasure principle, the aim of recurrent traumatic dreams is to control the excitation retroactively; this function is more *primitive*, as it were, than the search for pleasure and the avoidance of unpleasure. In other words, these dreams constitute an exception to the classical theory according to which dreams are fulfilments of wishes. When traumatic dreams bring back into memory the mental traumata of childhood, they are obeying the compulsion to repeat rather than the pleasure principle – even though it is true that there is also at work the wish to conjure up what has been forgotten and repressed. "*If there is a 'beyond the pleasure principle', it is only consistent to grant that there was also a time before the purpose of dreams was the fulfilment of wishes*" (1920g: 33).

- ## "*The aim of all life is death*" (ibid.: 38)

The protective shield which shelters the mind against stimuli from the external world affords no protection against those that come from within – which is why external and internal excitations produce similar effects: "*[Excitations from within] often occasion economic disturbances comparable with traumatic neuroses*" (ibid.: 34). What are the sources of this internal excitation? They are what Freud calls "*instincts*" which originate in the interior of the body; if they cannot be "*bound*" mentally, they will cause as much disturbance as when external excitations overwhelm the mental apparatus in the traumatic neuroses. Consequently, just as in the case of external stimuli, the mental apparatus has above all to control and to bind the excitations that come from within: it is here that the compulsion to repeat operates; only thereafter can the pleasure principle come into play. Sometimes, however, in the course of psychoanalytic treatment, the compulsion to repeat which is in opposition to the pleasure principle takes on a "*daemonic*" appearance; consequently, repressed infantile experiences which are repeated in the transference cannot be "*bound*" mentally to the pleasure principle – they are therefore "*incapable of obeying the secondary process*" and cannot be adequately worked through (ibid.: 36).

Observing that, when a patient is dominated by the compulsion to repeat, the instinctual drives frequently lead to failure of the analysis, Freud puts forward a general hypothesis as to the true nature of the drives. Their aim would seem to be the restoration of an initial state – the inorganic state that preceded life.

It seems, then, that an instinct is an urge inherent in organic life to restore an earlier state of things which the living entity has been obliged to abandon under the pressure of external disturbing forces; that is, it is a kind of organic elasticity, or, to put it another way, the expression of the inertia inherent in organic life. (ibid.: 36)

For Freud, the organic drives are conservative by nature and aim to restore an earlier state; consequently any progress or development in the organism which results from external influence only distracts the drives from their ultimate goal. Freud says quite clearly that this "*ancient goal*" implies a return to the very beginning of things. "*[This aim] must be an old state of things, an initial state from which the living entity has at one time or other departed and to which it is striving to return by the circuitous paths along which its development leads*" (ibid.: 38). Consequently, says Freud, "*[if] we are to take it as a truth that knows no exception that everything living dies for* internal reasons – *becomes inorganic once again* – *then we shall be compelled to say that* 'the aim of all life is death' *and, looking backwards, that* 'inanimate things existed before living ones' " (ibid.: 38). The upshot of all this is: "*These circuitous paths to death, faithfully kept to by the conservative instincts, would thus present us today with the picture of the phenomena of life*" (ibid.: 39).

Germ-cells appear to escape this process and work against the death of the living substance, but their immortality is deceptive "*and may mean no more than a lengthening of the road to death*" (ibid.: 40). According to Freud, the instincts which watch over the germ-cells belong to the group of the sexual drives and are the "*life instincts*".

They operate against the purpose of the other instincts which leads, by reason of their function, to death; and this fact indicates that there is an opposition between them and the other instincts, an opposition whose importance was long ago recognized by the theory of the neuroses. (ibid.: 40)

This opposition between groups of instincts creates in the life of the organism "*a vacillating rhythm*" (ibid.: 41).

Freud goes on to speculate about the possible existence of "*an instinct towards perfection*", which some scientists had postulated, a kind of tireless thrust in the direction of progress. He rejects the hypothesis as unfounded, since there are always obstacles – resistances – on the road to full satisfaction. That role belongs to "*the efforts of Eros to combine organic substances into ever larger unities*", so that the life drive is a substitute for this "*instinct towards perfection*" (ibid.: 42–43).

- **Does the dualism between life and death drives have any other equivalent?**

Freud now turns to biology (as it stood in his day) to see whether there could be anything to confirm or to invalidate his hypothesis according to which "*all living substance is bound to die from internal causes*" (ibid.: 44). He does not in fact find any biological argument which contradicts his dualistic conception of instinctual life, but he does discover in other scientific research a similar postulate to his own: in living organisms, there are two sorts of contradictory processes, "*one constructive or assimilatory and the other destructive or dissimilatory*" (ibid.: 49). He reminds the reader that the philosopher Schopenhauer had already suggested that "*death is the 'true result and to that extent the purpose of life'* " (ibid.: 50) while the sexual drive is the embodiment of the will to live.

Taking his argument a step further, Freud discusses whether what occurs in cells can be applied to the libido theory: in each cell, there are life instincts or active instincts which neutralize the death instincts, while other cells sacrifice themselves in order to maintain life. In order to answer the question, Freud goes back to his theory of the instinctual drives, showing how they develop through their successive stages (ibid.: footnote on p. 60). His dualistic conception begins with the opposition between ego drives and sexual drives, from which he infers the opposition between life and death drives. Is it possible to go further, he asks, and draw a parallel between, on the one hand, the opposition between life and death drives and, on the other, that between love (affection) and hate (aggressiveness)? He evokes the part played by sadism and masochism, as well as that of the self-preservative sexual instincts, and comes to the conclusion that masochism – the aggressive and destructive drive which turns against the subject's own ego – may well regress to a much earlier phase, thus implying the existence of a "*primary masochism*". In accordance with the pleasure principle, the dominant tendency of mental life is the effort to reduce tension and to obey the principle of constancy – the "*Nirvana principle*"; Freud therefore draws the conclusion that this "*is one of our strongest reasons for believing in the existence of death instincts*" (ibid.: 56). He gradually comes to realize that the life and death drives cannot be dissociated from each another, yet he concludes this section with the admission that he is not entirely convinced by his own arguments in favour of that daring hypothesis; developments in biology will no doubt clarify the questions which remain, he says. In his subsequent writings, however, Freud's faith in these hypotheses would become stronger and stronger.

• *A paradox: the pleasure principle in the service of the death drive*

In the final section of the book, Freud tries to "*solve the problem of the relation of the instinctual processes of repetition to the dominance of the pleasure principle*" (ibid.: 62). He restates the fact that one of the earliest and most important functions of the mental apparatus is to "*bind*" the instinctual impulses which impinge on it, in order to replace the primary process by the secondary process, and to convert freely mobile cathectic energy into a mainly quiescent (tonic) cathexis. While these transformations are taking place, binding of the impulses is a preparatory act which introduces and ensures the dominance of the pleasure principle. Though the struggle for pleasure is far more intense at the beginning of mental life, the pleasure principle is not the prerogative of the primary process alone; it is present also in the secondary process. In conclusion, Freud argues that life is made up of a constant succession of tensions – he calls them "*breakers of the peace*" – "*whose release is felt as pleasure*", while the death drives operate in silence: "*The life instincts have so much more contact with our internal perception – emerging as breakers of the peace and constantly producing tensions whose release is felt as pleasure – while the death instincts seem to do their work unobtrusively*" (ibid.: 63).

Development of Freud's concepts

Post-1920 developments in Freud's theory of the conflict between life and death drives

Having in 1920 postulated the existence of a fundamental conflict between life and death drives, Freud went on to develop the idea in the years that followed. In 1923, when he introduced the distinction between ego, superego and id (*The Ego and the Id*, 1923b), his hypothesis then was that the melancholic (i.e. depressive) patient's superego had attracted the whole of his or her sadism and destructive component. "*What is now holding sway in the superego is, as it were, a pure culture of the death instinct*" (1923b: 53). In order to explain this self-destructive brutality, particularly when it leads to suicide, Freud suggested that the erotic component of the life drive is no longer strong enough to "*bind*" the whole of the destructiveness, so that this now becomes "*free*" and is expressed as an inclination towards aggressiveness and destruction. The introduction of the theoretical notions of "*binding*" (or "*fusion*") and "*defusion*" of the life and death drives enabled Freud to clarify more precisely the phenomena observed in clinical practice.

In "The Economic Problem of Masochism", Freud (1924c) says that in 1920, in *Beyond the Pleasure Principle*, he confused the Nirvana principle with the pleasure principle, thereby giving the impression that the pleasure principle was entirely in the service of the death drive. Going back on that statement, he now makes a clear distinction between the two principles and considers the Nirvana principle to be an expression of the death drive – *requiescat in pace* would perhaps be an appropriate analogy – while the pleasure principle is a demand of the libido. He adds the fundamental idea that the death drive, when influenced by the libido, is diverted outside of the self with the help of the muscular apparatus.

> *The libido has the task of making the destroying instinct innocuous, and it fulfils the task by diverting that instinct to a great extent outwards [. . .] towards objects in the external world. The instinct is then called the destructive instinct, the instinct for mastery, or the will to power.* (1924c: 163)

Freud adds that, though the main portion of the death drive is deflected outwards in the form of sadism projected on to objects, there remains inside a residue of it, turned against the self; this residue constitutes the "*original, erotogenic masochism*". In addition, the sadism diverted outwards by projection may once more be introjected and thus regress to its earlier situation; this is "*secondary masochism*".

In 1937, in "Analysis Terminable and Interminable", Freud restates the notion of which he personally is convinced, though he knows that very few people, even among his pupils, agree with him.

> *I am well aware that the dualistic theory according to which an instinct of death or of destruction or aggression claims equal rights as a partner with Eros as manifested in the libido, has found little sympathy and has not really been accepted even among psychoanalysts.* (1937c: 244)

Post-Freudians

Why are psychoanalysts so reluctant to accept the idea of a death drive?

As soon as Freud put forward the idea in 1920, the concept of the death drive gave rise to a great deal of controversy among psychoanalysts; few of them agreed with Freud on this point, and even his closest colleagues – Jones, for example – remained hesitant. There are several reasons for this, two of which I shall now discuss. In the first place, I feel that a certain number of objections which are presented as being theoretical appear to be based on a refusal of the role played in mental life by the aggressive and destructive drives; this attitude is often the product of unconscious defences of different kinds. I have often observed that the concept of the death drive becomes mixed up with the idea of death itself, with the result that the conflict between life and death drives turns into one between life and death as such. The truth is that what we are talking about is a conflict between two groups of instinctual drives which are at work in every single one of us.

A second difficulty arises from the fact that Freud expressed his point of view mainly in theoretical terms, only rarely mentioning what this implied in clinical practice. For instance, he wrote that the death drive works unobtrusively, but he did not illustrate what this could mean via clinical examples or show how he would have interpreted it. On the other hand, he tried on several occasions to substitute for the conflict between life and death drives that between love and hate; he was largely unsuccessful in that venture, as we shall see shortly when we study *The Ego and the Id* (1923b).

The dualism of the drives in the Kleinian approach

Melanie Klein was one of the first psychoanalysts to accept the concept of the death drive and to apply it in her clinical work. For her, the ego exists at birth and from the beginning has to cope with the anxiety generated by the innate polarity of the drives. In order to defend itself, the ego deflects the death drive and projects part of it on to the external object – as Freud had said – with another part being transformed into aggressiveness: "Instead of dying, killing" (Segal 1979: 20). Klein takes this a step further. In her view, this defensive process creates a split which divides the ego, and is followed by a projection which splits the primary object (the breast), which is then perceived both as persecutory and as ideal. On the one hand, the death drive is projected into the breast, thereafter experienced by the ego as persecutory and threatening; on the other, the libido also is projected, thereby creating an idealized breast, an object which is perceived as protecting life. When there is excessive idealization of the love-object, the aim of splitting is to keep it as far away as possible from the persecutory object. As a result, in this early stage of development, the main anxiety arises from the fact that persecutory objects might penetrate the ego and annihilate both the ideal object and the self; this phase was called by Klein the paranoid-schizoid position.

From the very beginning of life, says Klein, there is another disposition in which the gradual integration of self and object becomes stronger and stronger. When developmental conditions are favourable, the self can feel that the ideal object and its own libidinal impulses gradually become stronger than the dangerous object with its aggressive and destructive drives. In this way, the self has the experience of acquiring a growing capacity to defend both itself and the ideal object, and of possessing greater tolerance towards the death drives at work internally. As a result, paranoid anxiety is reduced, and splitting and projection diminish; there is a gradual movement towards integration of the self and of the object, i.e. towards working through the depressive position.

According to Klein, there is in the mind a constant oscillation between these two poles. On the one hand the internal situation is dominated by a lack of integration and a split between the idealized object and the persecutory one; here, hate is stronger than love. On the other, the situation is characterized by a tendency towards integration, and here love is stronger than hate.

From a technical point of view, the approach adopted by Klein and Kleinian psychoanalysts is based on the manner in which the individual deals with early infantile anxieties and attempts to process these. Without going into too much detail, I would say that, in any given session, the psychoanalyst will try to identify the twofold current – libidinal and aggressive – within the constant to-and-fro movement of transference projections and introjections between patient and analyst. If, in the counter-transference, the psychoanalyst agrees to represent not only the idealized, admired object but also the dangerous, hated one and can interpret this split to the patient, this will help the patient distinguish between the libidinal current and the aggressive one. The patient will thus be able to "bind" them, and in this in turn will facilitate integration.

The death drive today: a wide range of views

What of the death drive today? Unlike most of Freud's fundamental hypotheses, the dualism of the instinctual drives remains a highly controversial theory for many psychoanalysts, with the exception of those who belong to the Kleinian school, who accepted the hypothesis from the outset. As far as the rest of the psychoanalytic community is concerned, there is a wide range of divergent opinions; indeed, we could almost say that they are as many opinions as there are psychoanalysts.

In 1984, the European Psychoanalytical Federation devoted its inaugural scientific symposium to this controversial question, and a report on the symposium was published under the title *The Death Instinct* (*La Pulsion de mort*, 1986). Laplanche argued that the death drive is a drive in its own right, and he puts forward several arguments to show that it belongs to the realm of the sexual drives. For Hanna Segal, from the very beginning of life there are two kinds of response possible when the infant experiences a need: the first is the thirst for life, which leads to a search for the object; the second is the tendency to annihilate the self which perceives and experiences, together with everything which is perceived. Green has developed the idea that the aim of the death drive is to accomplish a "de-objectalizing" function; the specific manner in which the destructiveness of the death drive manifests itself is through "de-cathexis". As Widlöcher pointed out, the symposium debates highlighted a certain number of convergences and divergences; general agreement was reached on the fact that the dualism of the drives has to do with the psyche, so that it seems inadvisable to have recourse to the biological arguments put forward by Freud. This does not mean, however, added Widlöcher, that psychoanalysts refuse to acknowledge any biological or somatic basis for the concept.

Apoptosis: a biological model of regulation

Freud had looked in vain to the scientific research of his time for any biological observations which could reflect the dualism of the drives that he had postulated on the psychological level; very few scientists had ventured to speculate in this domain. It was only in the early 1970s that the mechanism of apoptosis was discovered: this is a particular kind of cell death, the function of which is to destroy cells in the course of development, organogenesis and tissue growth – but the process may also be triggered by pathological stimuli. Apoptosis is the end-point of a whole series of molecular events, and it is regulated by positive and negative signals issued by hormones, growth factors and cytotoxins: these signals can either inhibit cell-destruction or trigger apoptosis (Robbins et al. 1974).

Can a parallel be drawn between apoptosis and the conflict between life and death drives? It is not possible of course to make a simple transposition from the model of biological regulation that is apoptosis to that of mental regulation as postulated by Freud. On the other hand, I think that we can make use of an analogical model of functioning together with the psychoanalytic notion of anaclisis – mental functioning draws support from biological functioning (J-M. Quinodoz 1997a). From this point of view, the two systems do not function in isolation; psychological and biological elements have a reciprocal influence on one another. For example, in some cases of object loss which lead to pathological mourning, there are repercussions at the somatic level – the individual falls ill or has some accident or other. Could it not then be the case that the predominance of the death drive over the life drive in mental conflict has repercussions at the biological level by distorting the ongoing regulation carried out by apoptosis?

New concepts

Compulsion to repeat – death drive – life drive – Nirvana principle – primary masochism – recurrent dreams – repetition – repetitive play in children (wooden reel) – transference – traumatic neurosis – traumatism

GROUP PSYCHOLOGY AND THE ANALYSIS OF THE EGO

(1921c)

Love, identification and the ego ideal

Can we transpose what we know, thanks to psychoanalysis, of individual mental life to the domain of group psychology? And does the psychoanalytic study of group phenomena further our knowledge of how the individual mind works? Freud found unsatisfactory the explanations of those of his predecessors who saw in suggestion and hypnosis either the essential determinants of the cohesion or disunion of groups, or the fascination which the leader exerts on the other members of a given group. He made use of his libido theory to explore these phenomena in much more depth and came to the conclusion that only an emotional tie – love – can overcome the individual narcissism and hatred which make for divisions among human beings. It is the strength of that libidinal connection which ties individuals to the group leader – in the Christian Church, the love for Christ; in the Army, the love for the commanding officer – and, to a somewhat lesser extent, that same connection links individual members of the group to one another. This libidinal tie, however, is not a fully mature form of sexual love; it is the archaic kind of love which, inhibited as to its sexual aims, we call identification: "*identification is the earliest and original form of emotional tie*" (1921c: 107), writes Freud. Consequently, the identification of each individual with the group leader and that of the members with respect to one another are what creates the cohesiveness of the group; loss of this emotional tie leads to the break-up of the group, as we see whenever a state of panic arises. The tie with the leader is based also on idealization, so that, as any one group member is attracted to this ideal, his or her own personality tends to fade into the background: the "*ego ideal*" represented by the group leader takes precedence over the "*ego*" of each person in the group.

Can the interactions observed in the macrocosm between group members and group leader be transposed into the microcosm of the individual psyche? Freud made a thorough study of that question in his exploration of different aspects of the concept of identification, and outlined a new way of looking at intrapsychic relationships which "*may possibly be repeated upon this new scene of action within the ego*" (1921c: 130). The fact that the ego ideal can take over the ego's place enabled Freud to describe in detail not only the vicissitudes of being in love but also the normal and pathological identificatory processes. For example, a young boy's identification with his father leads him to grow and to *be* like his father in the positive form of the Oedipus complex; if, on the other hand, he identifies with his mother, this leads to the inverted form of the Oedipus complex. Freud saw more and more clearly that there was a state of tension between the ego ideal and the ego; in normal psychological structures, the ego ideal represents the demands which the parents make on the individual, while in pathological states this tension might become so extreme that it leads to such phenomena as the oscillation between melancholia and mania. With reference to what he had written in *Totem and Taboo* (1912–1913), Freud felt that the relationship between the group and its leader was a reactivation of the analogous relationship between the sons and the father of the primal horde:

after the father had been killed, he was replaced by the Hero as glorified in the imagination of the epic poets.

> **Biographies and history**
>
> ### Towards a better understanding of conflict in society and in groups
>
> After investigating masochism and the death drive, Freud decided to explore how groups function, and for this he turned again to sociology and the writers he had so much enjoyed reading as a young man. He wrote to Romain Rolland about what he was trying to achieve in this study: "*I do not think that this book is much of a success, but it does show the way which leads from individual analysis to an understanding of society*" (Letter from Freud to Romain Rolland, 4 March 1923, mentioned in Vermorel and Vermorel 1993: 219). He was particularly interested in understanding, with the help of psychoanalysis, the factors which make for social cohesiveness: when people come together to form a group, they gain in cohesion and security, but why do they lose their freedom of thought and their ability to judge things properly? Why are crowds more intolerant, more irrational and more immoral than the individual members themselves? Why do inhibitions break down, leading to outbreaks of murderous hatred?
>
> There were probably two main reasons which made Freud feel he had to undertake a study of group phenomena. In the first place, the First World War was still fresh in people's minds, and several of Freud's writings dating from this period had to do with his attempt to understand the destructive aspects of human beings. Second, in the 1920s psychoanalysis was being criticized from all sides, and the psychoanalytic movement itself was rocked by a series of violent conflicts. Freud was upset by the particularly bitter anti-German feelings which were rife in England at the time – his own work of course was written in German. As Jones puts it (1957: 49): "Psychoanalysis [. . .] was vilified as a typical product of German decadence and general beastliness." Jones was doing as much as he could to have Freud's writings translated into English, and, in 1920, founded the *International Journal of Psycho-Analysis* so as to encourage the spread of psychoanalytic ideas throughout the English-speaking world. This was also the time when Jones and Rank were at each other's throats. Freud supported first one, then the other, depending on the arguments which each presented to him. These conflicts made it plain almost from the outset that psychoanalysts were just as likely as anybody else to fall prey to the mechanisms of group functioning; it is probable that this was another reason which prompted Freud to explore the kind of phenomena to which such situations give rise. It seemed to be the case, for example, that as the psychoanalytic movement developed, it was by then reaching the stage of an organized group, the leader of which – Freud – had created an ideal which corresponded all too closely to his followers' ego ideal.

Discovering the text

Page numbers are those of *The Standard Edition of the Complete Psychological Works of Sigmund Freud*, vol. **18**, 65–143.

- ### *The characteristics of group psychology*

Freud begins his study with the comment that, although psychoanalysis may have focused on the individual as a single being, it takes also into account that person's relationship with those in his or her immediate circle. He therefore considers individual psychology to be also a social psychology, though the latter tends somewhat to forget about individuals.

He continues by making extensive reference to Gustave Le Bon's *Psychologie des foules* (1895) in order to give a rapid overview of the wide range of phenomena involved, and in so doing, to show on what particular points psychoanalysis can shed some light. Le Bon describes how, in groups, people think and act very differently from the way they behave in isolation, because, as each conscious personality fades into the background, the unconscious personality comes to the fore. The individual acquires a sense of invincible power to such an degree that notions such as individual responsibility and moral conscience are lost. In groups there is a kind of contagion, which can lead an individual to sacrifice – quite readily – his or her personal interest to that of the group as a whole, and to become as suggestible as the hypnotized individual in the hands of the hypnotist. For Freud, however, the crucial element here is the person who replaces the hypnotist in a group context. Le Bon shows that another feature of groups is regression: individuals behave in a way similar to primitive peoples or children. In isolation, any one individual may be well educated, but in a group that person falls victim to his or her instinctual drives and turns into a barbarian: "*He [the individual] possesses the spontaneity, the violence, the ferocity, and also the enthusiasm and heroism of primitive beings*" (Freud 1921c: 77). In addition, the only thing which a group respects is force; it regards kindness as a form of weakness.

> *What it demands of its heroes is strength, or even violence. It wants to be ruled and oppressed and to fear its masters. Fundamentally it is entirely conservative, and it has a deep aversion to all innovations and advances and an unbounded respect for tradition.* (ibid.: 78–79)

According to Freud, Le Bon's (1895) description of the group mind is very similar to what psychoanalysis had discovered in the minds of neurotics, of children and of primitive people. Le Bon argues that as soon as human beings are gathered together they require a leader; the group then becomes an obedient herd which has a thirst for obedience and submissiveness. Le Bon attributes the power of the group leader to a mysterious and irresistible force which he calls "*prestige*". This, for Freud, is an unsatisfactory explanation. In his conclusion, Freud is somewhat critical of Le Bon's hypotheses: they amount to little more than a descriptive picture of group psychology and do not provide us with satisfactory explanations – only psychoanalysis can do this properly.

• *Affects play a decisive role*

Freud then turns to another book on the topic, *The Group Mind* by William McDougall (1921). According to this writer, it is in the simplest form of a group, which he calls a "crowd", that we can observe some fundamental facts of group psychology. There are two decisive factors which lead to the forming of a group: on the one hand, each individual must have something in common with all the others – a common interest or a similar emotional bias; and on the other, members of the group must show some capacity for influencing one another. McDougall (1921) notes the crucial role of the affects in forming a "crowd": emotion is intensified and thinking inhibited.

> *It is a pleasurable experience for those who are concerned, to surrender themselves so unreservedly to their passions and thus to become merged in the group and to lose the sense of the limits of their individuality.* (ibid.: 84)

McDougall goes on to say that the organization of a crowd is characterized also by self-effacement on the part of each individual in favour of the group as a whole: "*The problem consists in how to procure for the group precisely those features which were characteristic of the individual and which are extinguished in him by the formation of the group*" (ibid.: 86). In other words, adds Freud, as it becomes organized the aim is "*to equip the group with the attributes of the individual*" (ibid.: 87).

• *The power of love*

How are the exaltation of the emotions and inhibition of thinking, so characteristic of group psychology, to be explained? Most of those who have written on the subject evoke some form of suggestion. For Freud, that explanation is unsatisfactory; he decides to use the psychoanalytic concept of libido – all the drives that may be comprised under the word "*love*" – to shed light on the question. He means by this, "*love*" in a wider sense, including the sexual drives, the Eros of which Plato wrote and the kind of love the apostle Paul described in his epistle to the Corinthians. Taking love as his starting-point, Freud suggests that "*love relationships (or, to use a more neutral expression, emotional ties)*" (ibid.: 91) form the essence of what brings a group together. In other words, it is love that constitutes the power which holds the group together; the individual gives up his or her distinctiveness and opens up to the influence of the other members mainly through "*ihnen zu Liebe*" (ibid.: 92).

• *The Church and the Army*

Freud then illustrates his hypotheses with reference to two groups which are highly organized – the Church and the Army – which he sees as artificial groups in the sense that a certain external force is employed to ensure their cohesiveness. The Church – and in particular the Catholic Church – has a supreme head, Christ, just as an army has its Commander-in-Chief. The head "*loves all the individuals in the group with an equal love. Everything depends upon this delusion; if it were to be dropped, then both Church and army would dissolve, so far as the external force permitted them to*" (ibid.: 94). In the Church, it is the love which Christ has for the faithful in the Christian community that brings the believers together; they call themselves brothers in Christ – hence the fact, says Freud, that Christ is their substitute father. The same is true of the army: "*The Commander-in-Chief is a father who loves all soldiers equally, and for that reason they are comrades among themselves*" (ibid.: 94). The army has a hierarchy which is organized pyramid-fashion much more than is the case with the Church; the latter however takes more care of its individual members.

As a result, "*in these two artificial groups each individual is bounded by libidinal ties on the one hand to the leader (Christ, the Commander-in-Chief) and on the other to the other members of the group*" (ibid.: 95). Given that each individual member establishes an emotional tie in both directions, this fact explains the limitation observed in that individual's personality when he or she is part of the group. Proof of this can be found in the phenomenon of panic, when the libidinal tie is lost – for example, in a military group which becomes disintegrated. Here, fear of some danger or other dissolves the emotional ties within the group; Freud draws a parallel between panic in a group and the origins of neurotic anxiety, which is essentially based on "*the cessation of emotional ties (libidinal cathexes)*" (ibid.: 97). Freud will come back to this topic in 1926 in *Inhibitions, Symptoms and Anxiety*. Religious groups have ambivalent feelings, but their hostile impulses are held back "*owing to the equal love of Christ*" (ibid.: 98). Hostility does make its appearance, however, via religious intolerance: "*Fundamentally indeed every religion is in this same way a religion of love for all those whom it embraces; while cruelty and intolerance towards those who do not belong to it are natural to every religion*" (ibid.: 98). This intolerance persists if the religious tie is replaced by some other – this is the danger which faces the communist movement, for example: "*The socialistic tie seems to be succeeding in [replacing the religious one, so that] there will be the same intolerance towards outsiders as in the age of the Wars of Religion*" (ibid.: 99).

• *Love and hate as factors of cohesion*

Continuing his exploration of the nature of the link which binds the group and its members together, Freud argues that it is not only love that makes for unity – hate can do this too. The behaviour of groups, therefore, is also characterized by ambivalence, that is by feelings of hostility which are directed against people who are otherwise loved. Within any one group, however, hostile feelings between individual members paradoxically vanish for as long as group cohesion is maintained. Further, individual members are perfectly able to relinquish any personal interest in favour of those of the group as a whole. Freud attributes this limitation of narcissism to the emotional nature of the libidinal tie which binds them together. This renunciation of personal interests for the good of the majority is, says Freud, one of the foundations of civilization. "*And in the development of mankind as a whole, just as in individuals, love alone acts as the civilizing factor in the sense that it brings a change from egoism to altruism*" (ibid.: 103).

- ***Identification as the earliest expression of an emotional tie with another person***

Having discussed love as a factor of cohesion, Freud now takes up the topic of identification, another factor which may give rise to emotional ties within a group. In one incisive sentence, he reminds us of the link between love and identification: "*Identification is known to psychoanalysis as the earliest expression of an emotional tie with another person*" (ibid.: 105). It plays a part in the early history of the Oedipus complex, and Freud describes how the young boy reacts as regards his father: "*He would like to grow like him and be like him, and take his place everywhere. We may say simply that he takes his father as his ideal*" (ibid.: 105). As he identifies with his father, the young boy develops an object-cathexis towards his mother; this is quite clearly libidinal and sexual in nature. He then has to deal with what psychoanalysis calls the normal Oedipal situation, in which his masculine identification takes on a hostile colouring with respect to his father-as-rival; he would like to take his father's place in regard to his mother. This means of course that his identification is ambivalent in nature. The subsequent history of this identification with the father "*may easily be lost sight of*" (ibid.: 106).

It may happen that the Oedipus complex becomes inverted and that the young boy identifies with the object desired by his father – his mother; the boy adopts a feminine attitude, and the father becomes the object of his sexual drives. The Oedipus complex may become inverted in girls too, with the corresponding substitutions. What difference is there between identification with the father in the direct Oedipus complex and that in the inverted complex in which the father is chosen as an object? Freud's reply is simple but highly illuminating: "*In the first case one's father is what one would like to* be, *and in the second he is what one would like to* have" (ibid.: 106).

Freud goes on to describe several kinds of identification; any one symptom may be linked to three kinds of identification. In symptom formation, for instance, there is hysterical identification, one example being the little girl who contracts the same cough as her mother. "*The identification may come from the Oedipus complex; in that case it signifies a hostile desire on the girl's part to take her mother's place, and the symptom expresses her object-love towards her father*" (ibid.: 106). In this situation, the symptom is that of the hated rival, in which the little girl's identification expresses both her aggressiveness towards her mother and her love for her father. Another form of identification which is involved in symptom formation is illustrated by Dora's cough – which she took from her father. Here the symptom is similar to that of the loved object: "Identification has appeared instead of object-choice, and [...] object-choice has regressed to identification. [...] *It often happens that [...] object-choice is turned back into identification – the ego assumes the characteristics of the object*" (ibid.: 106–107). There is a third kind of identification, based on a common quality with other people who are not the object of the sexual drives. In this case, the identification is partial and creates a new bond. The example Freud gives is that of a fit of hysterics in a girl's boarding school: other pupils may also have a fit of hysterics – through mental infection, as it were. To summarize, these three forms of identification have taught us

> [*first, that*] *identification is the original form of emotional tie with an object; second, [that] in a regressive way it becomes a substitute for a libidinal object-tie, as it were by means of introjection of the object into the ego; and third, [that] it may arise with any new perception of a common quality shared with some other person who is not an object of the sexual instinct*. (ibid.: 107–108)

According to Freud, it is this third form of identification that underpins the tie between group members and leader.

Freud goes on to describe another kind of identification – identification with an object which is renounced or lost – and gives two examples of this. The first involves identification by introjection into the ego of the fantasy of the renounced or lost object which then becomes a substitute for it. This is Freud's explanation of Leonardo da Vinci's homosexuality (Freud 1910c). In this case, Leonardo identified with his mother and loved young men in the way his mother used to love him. The second kind of identification with a renounced or lost object occurs in melancholia (depression), in which part of the ego identifies with the absent object. Freud refers again here to the intrapsychic conflict in melancholia: one part of the patient's ego is bitterly reproachful towards another part. He calls "*ego ideal*" this criticizing agency – which may become implacable and relentless – the functions of which are "*self-observation, the moral conscience, the censorship of dreams, and the chief influence of repression*" (1921c: 110). He notes that this inner criticism is a consequence also of the demands made upon the child's ego by superior powers, and above all by the parents. From 1923 on, he would call this criticizing agency the "*superego*".

• *The constitution of the ego ideal*

Since identification is a form of love, Freud goes on to examine what is common to being in love and the ego ideal, then draws a parallel between the attraction which the hypnotist has for the person hypnotized and that which the group leader has for the other members.

As far as being in love is concerned, Freud describes the vicissitudes of feelings of love throughout the child's development and their links with the sexual drives. He says that there are two distinct currents in love, one of which is "*affectionate*" while the other is "*sensual*"; these have to be brought together in order to constitute genital love. Sometimes these two currents remain separate, in which case dissociation between the affectionate current and the sensual current is the outcome; this is the case, for example, of some romantically inclined men who are impotent with women they admire but perfectly potent sexually with women whom they do not love at all. In another vicissitude of being in love, the man sexually over-values the loved object through a tendency towards idealization; this feeling, which brushes aside any criticism which could be levelled at the object, has to do with narcissism:

> *The object serves as a substitute for some unattained ego ideal of our own. We love it on account of the perfections which we have striven to reach for our own ego, and which we should now like to procure in this roundabout way as a means of satisfying our narcissism.* (ibid.: 112–113)

In extreme cases of passion and fascination, the object is so idealized that the ego quite literally hands itself over to the object, which has "*so to speak, consumed the ego*" (ibid.: 113) and all criticism is abolished. In other words, "[the] object has been put in the place of the ego ideal" (ibid.: 113). The difference between identification and being in love can thus be expressed as follows. In a successful identification the ego has enriched itself with the qualities of the object and has "*introjected*" the object, as Ferenczi (1909) put it. In the case of being in love, according to Freud, the ego "*is impoverished, it has surrendered itself to the object, it has substituted the object for its own most important constituent*" (1921c: 113); in other words, the ego has put itself in the place of the ego ideal. We should note here that Freud draws no distinction between being in love and idealization of the object. He argues that there is a price to pay in every idealization of an object – that of losing the ego; it is for this reason that Freud considers being in love to be primarily a pathological state.

As regards the relationship between hypnosis and being in love, Freud points out a certain number of similarities. There is the same subjection, the same absence of criticism towards the hypnotist as towards the loved object: "*No one can doubt that the hypnotist has stepped into the place of the ego ideal*" (ibid.: 114). The hypnotic relationship seems to be the unlimited devotion of someone in love, but with sexual satisfaction excluded; as for being in love, this kind of satisfaction is regarded as a possible aim for some point in the future. In other words, the hypnotic relationship can be seen as "*a group formation with two members*" (ibid.: 115); what brings people together in a group is a series of tendencies which do not have a sexual aim, "*those sexual impulsions that are inhibited in their aims*" (ibid.: 115). In concluding this section, Freud proposes the following definition of a group which has a leader, taking into account the part played by the ego ideal: "A primary group of this kind is a number of individuals who have put one and the same object in the place of their ego ideal and have consequently identified themselves with one another in their ego" (ibid.: 116).

• *The father of the primal horde, the leader and the hypnotist*

After concluding that Wilfred Trotter's idea of a specific "*herd instinct*" could not be sustained, Freud goes on to examine the similarities he observed between group psychology and the organization of the primal horde, the group being for Freud a revival of the primal horde. The group leader is thus the equivalent of the feared primal father, while the submissive attitude of the group members corresponds to a regression to the primitive mental state of the organized horde. In the horde, the primal father dominates his sons by preventing them from having any sexual satisfaction, so that the emotional tie which brings the brothers together originates in their inhibited sexual drives, just as in groups. At first, the dead leader is replaced by a young son who claims for himself all power and sexual satisfaction; this put an end, as far as he was concerned, to the importance of the sexual impulses which had been inhibited as to their aim. As we have seen in both the Church and the Army, all the members are under the – idealistic – illusion that the leader loves each and every one of them equally and justly. In the primal horde, on the other hand, it is hate which brings them together, because all of the sons "*knew that they were equally* persecuted *by the primal father, and* feared *him equally*" (ibid.: 125).

Freud goes on to discuss the nature of the mysterious power which emanates from kings and tribal chiefs, and which is similar to that of the hypnotist's gaze. The hypnotist wants all the individual's attention to be focused on the hypnotist's own person to the exclusion of the outside world; this unconscious hypnotic *rapport* is similar to the transference. From a psychoanalytic point of view, the hypnotist who gives the command to sleep is putting him- or herself in the place of the subject's parents, as Ferenczi (1909) pointed out. In this kind of relationship, the hypnotist awakens in the subject a portion of his archaic heritage, thereby reactivating the terrifying relationship with the feared primal father; this "*passive-masochistic*" attitude is similar to that adopted towards the group leader, who "*is still the dreaded primal father*" (Freud 1921c: 127). Given the group's thirst for authority and need to be dominated, Freud draws the conclusion that "*the primal father is the group ideal, which governs the ego in the place of the ego ideal*" (ibid.: 127).

- ## *The ego ideal in normal and in pathological states of mind*

Once again, it was his observation of pathological phenomena that led Freud to discover how normal individuals operate. Here, after introducing a distinction between ego and ego ideal, this new conception of the way the mind works enables him to see that the interactions between the ego as a whole (the "*whole ego*") and external objects may be repeated in the internal world, i.e. "*upon this new scene of action within the ego*" (ibid.: 130).

Freud outlines the consequences of this in both normal and pathological states of mind. As far as normal organizations are concerned, the division between ego and ego ideal entails a heightening of the "*tension*" between two opposite polarities in this object relationship: this heightened tension is difficult to endure and efforts are always being made to reduce it. For example, in sleep, there is a periodical return to the state of avoiding the object, in other words, a narcissistic regression. As for pathological states, the "*separation*" between ego and ego ideal may not be tolerated for long either and has to be temporarily undone. In such cases, the ego may either rebel against prohibitions and allow itself to transgress them – as in the various festivals of primitive peoples or our modern carnivals – or submit to the prohibitions of the ego ideal, which "*comprises the sum of all the limitations in which the ego has to acquiesce*" (ibid.: 131).

These oscillations may perhaps explain the psychogenic component that precipitates the mood swings which can be observed in melancholic depression and mania. Since the manic patient is no longer bound by inhibitions, Freud suggests that the change from melancholia to mania may be attributable to a resolution of the ego ideal into the ego (whereas, in the melancholic state, the ego ideal is particularly harsh). It could be argued too that the reversal from melancholia to mania arises from the ego's periodic revolt against the ego ideal: "*The ego would be incited to rebellion by ill-treatment on the part of its ideal – an ill-treatment which it encounters when there has been identification with a rejected object*" (ibid.: 133).

- ## *The myth of the hero: a step towards individual psychology*

The distinction between ego and ego ideal gives Freud the opportunity to make a few additional comments. The first of these concerns the advance, somewhere in the mists of time, from group psychology to individual psychology, which followed the killing of the father of the primal horde. Returning to the ideas he had put forward in *Totem and Taboo*, Freud suggests that the conflicts which broke out between the brothers prevented them from finding a successor to the primal father. The first person who crossed this barrier and went from deeds to words was the first epic poet: he made this advance in his imagination, inventing as he did so the myth of the Hero – the man who, by himself, had killed the father and become his successor through the mythical story. "*The myth, then, is the step by which the individual emerges from group psychology*" (ibid.: 136). The real hero, says Freud, is the poet himself who, in recounting the legend, identifies with the hero whose deeds he relates to the rest of the group. The next step is that of the deification of the hero, the precursor of the return of the primal father as a deity.

Freud goes on to discuss in some detail the relationship between love on the one hand and, on the other, directly sexual drives and those which are inhibited as to their aims. The latter correspond to the sublimation of the sexual drives. Directly sexual impulsions are unfavourable to the formation of groups, as we can see when two people in love avoid the group and prefer each other's company. If directly sexual impulsions are expressed in a group context, they tend to make the group split up. In the great artificial groups such as the Church or the Army, writes Freud, "*there is no room for women as a sexual object*" (ibid.: 141), and the difference between the sexes plays no part. Neurosis is fundamentally asocial because it tends to make the neurotic person withdraw from any group formation. "*It may be said that a neurosis has the same disintegrating effect upon a group as being in love*" (ibid.: 142).

Post-Freudians

Psychoanalysis and groups

Group analysis can quite justifiably be looked upon as a development of Freud's work on group psychology. In the narrower sense, the term refers to a therapeutic technique based on psychoanalytic theories concerning individuals and on various points of view as to how groups function. In the wider sense, the term refers to psychoanalytic studies of groups of various sizes. Siegmund H. Foulkes and Wilfred R. Bion were two of the pioneers in this field.

Foulkes: group-analytic psychotherapy

Foulkes was a psychoanalyst who trained in Germany and, after emigrating to Britain, began practising group psychotherapy in the 1930s. He called his approach "group-analytic psychotherapy"; his basic idea was that the therapeutic ability of the group members should be developed in order for them to become co-therapists for the other participants in the group. The role of the group therapist is to facilitate these processes and to emphasize the quality of communication as a therapeutic instrument. In Foulkes's approach, only the group transference on to the analyst is taken into consideration, not the lateral transferences which exist between the group members themselves. He defined group-analytic psychotherapy as an attempt to treat the whole network of troubles, either at their point of origin in the original – primary – group or by placing the disturbed individual under transference conditions in an unfamiliar group (Foulkes 1964).

Bion's work on groups

Bion's approach was somewhat different, in particular because of the fundamental distinction he established between individual and group mentality. In the 1940s, he worked with rehabilitation groups for British Army officers, and that experience made him realize that an observer who knew something about psychoanalysis could pick up certain elements which would otherwise have gone unnoticed. For example, when several people are brought together with the aim of accomplishing some task or other, two tendencies come to the surface within the group: the one tends towards accomplishing the prescribed task, while the other seems to be working against this. In other words, the work activity is counteracted by regressive activity. In order to describe these phenomena, Bion invented his own terminology (Bion 1961; Grinberg et al. 1973).

The regression which takes place among members of a group can be explained by the fact that a "group mentality" is created; this expresses the group's opinion and the will of its members, but unconsciously and without their realizing it. The group thus becomes structured around certain "basic assumptions" – the group operates as though it had shared expectations, but these remain implicit and are never put into words. For Bion, there are three kinds of basic assumption – "*dependency*", in which the group expects the leader to satisfy all its needs and desires, while the group itself adopts a passive attitude without any discernment; "*fight/flight*", in which the group is convinced that there is an enemy who must be destroyed through fighting or avoided through taking flight – this kind of group chooses as its leader a paranoid character; and "*pairing*", where the group awaits some future event which is messianic in nature, with this unconscious irrational expectation often being placed in the child born to one of these pairs or couples. Any group which is built on one or other of these Basic Assumptions finds itself in a highly charged primitive emotional state which expresses the group's unconscious fantasy. It then begins to operate in a completely chaotic manner and its activity is hindered, because what a group wants above all is the immediate satisfaction of its omnipotent desires; as a result, it tends not to take reality into account.

Distinct from the "Basic Assumption" group, there is another level of group functioning which Bion calls the "work-group". In this kind of group, each participant is expected to cooperate in the achievement of the group task through verbal communication and with due heed to reality.

Both these kinds of group – Basic Assumption and work-group – exist within any given group structure, hence the fact that there is always a conflict ready to emerge in the group. For Bion, Basic Assumptions are defensive and regressive group reactions against the psychotic anxieties which are reactivated in each individual member of the group; they correspond to the primitive defence mechanisms described by Klein. The work-group corresponds to a way of functioning which tends towards psychic integration. Bion's hypotheses have given those who work with groups a new instrument with which to enhance their understanding of the phenomena that occur in groups of which they are part; this is particularly the case of therapeutic groups.

New concepts

Army – Church – ego – ego ideal – group psychology – hypnosis, hypnotist – ideal – idealization – identification – individual psychology – love, being in love

THE EGO AND THE ID

(1923b)

A new division of the mind: ego, id and superego

The Ego and the Id is a particularly important book, because in it Freud presents a synthesis of the hypotheses he put forward since the "1920 turning-point". He begins by showing how his original model of the mind with its division into Unconscious, Preconscious and Conscious systems – his "first structural theory" with its topographical division of the mind – was no longer adequate for describing how the mental apparatus functions; the model would have to be developed further. Taking as his basis the fact that, in the course of psychoanalytic treatment, the "*ego*" shows resistance towards becoming aware of the real issues, Freud introduces a new division of the mental apparatus. Henceforth there are three agencies – the ego, the id and the superego; this model is known as his "second structural theory". The two models are not mutually exclusive; indeed, quite the contrary – they complement each other in the sense that they describe the same mental phenomena from two different perspectives, much as we could describe a house in terms of its general shape, its dimensions and its price.

In Freud's definition of the terms, ego, id and superego all have the quality of being both conscious and unconscious. The idea of the ego was present from the very beginning of Freud's work, though he uses it at first to designate the conscious personality or individual self. From 1923 on, the ego is conceived of as a regulatory agency with respect to mental phenomena, because it is always attempting to reconcile the demands of the id – the "*reservoir of libido*" – and those of the superego (which Freud had previously called the censor or conscience in the moral sense of the word). The unconscious conflicts and tensions thus created between ego, id and superego with their contradictory demands have a lasting influence on personality development – the outcome of the struggle between the different forces and of the dynamic equilibrium which is set up between them. If the aim of any analysis is to make the unconscious conscious (in terms of the first topographical model), this same aim can be expressed in terms of the second structural theory as "*Wo Es war, soll Ich werden*" ("*Where id was, there ego shall be*") (1933a [1932]: 80).

Developing the hypotheses he had discussed in 1921 in *Group Psychology and the Analysis of the Ego*, Freud comes to the conclusion that an individual's personality and character are the outcome of a series of identificatory processes. It is in this book too that he gives a full description of the Oedipus complex both in its positive form – the boy identifies with his father, the girl with her mother – and in its inverted form – feminine identification in boys and masculine identification in girls – thus taking into account the psychic bisexuality which is present in all of us. In *The Ego and the Id*, Freud shows just how convinced he now is of the decisive part played by the fundamental conflict between the life and death drives. This is illustrated in the analysis of patients who paradoxically become worse instead of getting better: they exhibit what he calls a "*negative therapeutic reaction*" (1933a [1932]: 49); in melancholic (depressive) patients, too, the superego is "*a pure culture of the death instinct*" (ibid.: 53). However, the superego is not simply an agency which treats the ego sadistically as in pathological states of mind, because the role attributed to the post-Oedipal superego in normal individuals is a protective and safekeeping one through identification with the father and mother.

Biographies and history

Georg Groddeck: *Das Buch vom Es* (1923) (*The Book of the It*)

The term "*das Es*" (*id* or *it*) was first used by Nietzsche and was taken up by Groddeck in a book he published, *Das Buch vom Es*, just weeks before Freud's own book appeared in print. Groddeck was one of Freud's most creative and resourceful followers; he was director of a clinic in Baden-Baden, and had started off by denigrating psychoanalysis before becoming passionately interested in it. Groddeck described himself as a "wild analyst"; he met Freud for the first time at the Congress in The Hague in 1920. Freud liked Groddeck's charm, liveliness and sharpness of mind and his freedom of thought – though this sometimes had a scandalous note to it, as when he published *The Soul Seeker* in 1921. This work of fiction, which narrates the trials and tribulations of a psychoanalyst, pleased many of his readers, including Freud, but others found it obscene and unscientific. Groddeck reached a much wider audience with the book which was to make him famous, *The Book of the It*, published in 1923. In that text, he writes of his work in psychosomatics and presents the id as "some wondrous force which directs both what [a man] himself does, and what happens to him." " 'Man is lived by the It' ", is for Groddeck a "fundamental principle" (Groddeck 1923 [1949: 11]). Though Freud's definition of the id is somewhat different from Groddeck's, he did acknowledge that his follower's contribution had had some influence on him. Groddeck was quite a controversial figure because of his lack of scientific rigour and his somewhat imprecise technique, but he is still considered to be the first to have highlighted the therapeutic potential of psychoanalysis in the field of somatic and psychosomatic illness.

Freud suffers from cancer

Freud wrote *The Ego and the Id* in 1922 and published it in April 1923. He was 67 years of age, and his fame was spreading – though this mattered little to him, because it interfered with his work. In February 1923, he discovered a growth on his jaw, which he had removed only after *The Ego and the Id* was published. He had the feeling that this leucoplastic tumour might well be malignant, but he said very little about it, fearing that his physicians might tell him to stop smoking. Instead of consulting a renowned specialist, he was treated by Marcus Hajek, who was not particularly competent as a surgeon. After having the tumour removed in the out-patient department, Freud almost died of a blood haemorrhage. In the following sixteen years, Freud underwent thirty-three operations for recurrent leukoplakia. After the initial operation in 1923, he had to have radiotherapy; this proved very painful, and he was unable to work for the following six months, so great was the pain he was in. For several months, both his physician and Felix Deutsch said nothing to Freud about the cancerous nature of the tumour, because they were afraid that he might commit suicide; indeed, they informed his close circle of followers only in September 1923. Another physician, Hans Pichler, who was a distinguished mouth surgeon, re-operated in October of that year; he removed the whole upper jaw and palate on the affected side and inserted a huge prosthesis which Freud referred to as "*the monster*" because it was so difficult to insert and to take out. From then on, talking and eating became difficult for Freud; his hearing on the right side was also affected, and in time he became completely deaf in that ear. Henceforth, whenever he was in pain, he would allow no one else to nurse him but his daughter Anna.

Emilio Rodrigué, one of Freud's biographers, has cast doubt on the true nature of the cancer from which Freud suffered. Rodrigué (1966) claims that the initial diagnosis was mistaken because, according to the histological tests carried out on the first series of samples taken in 1939 by Dr Lacassagne of the *Institut Curie*, this was a case of papillomatosis which was not malignant. This implies that Freud's cancer in fact began later than was thought to have been the case, as a consequence of the intensive radiotherapy he had undergone. Rodrigué argues that Freud's attitude towards his own health no doubt contributed to the many mistakes made by his physicians throughout those years, and goes on to say that, on this

> point, Freud himself was at fault: what role did he himself play in the midst of all this iatrogeny? The relationship with doctors, adds Rodrigué, had always been something of a problem for Freud.

Discovering the text

> Page numbers are those of *The Standard Edition of the Complete Psychological Works of Sigmund Freud*, vol. **19**, 1–59.

• *Towards the notion of the ego*

Developing the lines of thought he had opened up in *Beyond the Pleasure Principle*, Freud presents in this book a synthesis of the wholesale reorganization of psychoanalytic theory which was typical of his thinking from the 1920s on. In *The Ego and the Id*, however, he leaves to one side any biological considerations and concentrates solely on a strictly psychoanalytic point of view.

He begins by reminding the reader that psychoanalysis is based on a fundamental premiss: the distinction between what is conscious and what is unconscious. The unconscious can be approached from two different perspectives, one descriptive, the other dynamic. From the descriptive point of view, it means that there are representations which are not yet present in consciousness but which are capable of becoming conscious; we could say that they are "*unconscious*" while they remain in a *latent* state. From the dynamic point of view, however, some representations are "*unconscious*" because they have been *repressed*; these ideas are not capable of becoming conscious, because other forces – which we call *resistances* – stand in their way. The technique of psychoanalysis is one way of making them conscious. Therefore we can distinguish between two sorts of unconscious: the *latent unconscious*, which is what, descriptively speaking, we mean by unconscious – this corresponds to the *preconscious* (Pcs.); and the *unconscious stricto sensu* or *dynamic unconscious*, which is the one that we deal with in psychoanalysis.

Let us now turn to the ego. For Freud initially, the idea of the "*ego*" referred only to what was conscious; he soon came to realize, however, that the ego put up its own resistance against repressed material becoming conscious. He had therefore to accept that a part of the ego was unconscious in the dynamic sense of the term and that it was only through psychoanalysis that the repressed material could be made conscious. Already in 1915 (Freud 1915e), he had mentioned the fact that "*the Ucs. does not coincide with the repressed; it is still true that all that is repressed is Ucs., but not all that is Ucs. is repressed*" (1923b: 18). Consequently, though the relationship between conscious and unconscious is an essential fulcrum of analytic work, the idea of the unconscious is no longer by itself an adequate description of the human mind.

• *The ego and the id*

Freud next examines the relationship between the ego and the system which receives perceptions and ensures that the individual is aware of them; this is the system he calls perception-consciousness or Pcpt-Cs. From a spatial point of view, consciousness is the surface of the mental apparatus, which receives perceptions both from without and from within the organism. Perceptions which come from the sense organs – sight, hearing, etc. – are conscious from the start; what we call thought processes become conscious thanks to language, after having been transformed thanks to their connections with word-presentations. As for those internal perceptions which come from the deepest layers of the mental apparatus, they are more elementary than external perceptions and reach consciousness by means of sensations of pleasure/unpleasure.

The manner in which sensations "*become conscious*" is not, however, without its problems. Freud thinks that we are quite justified in speaking of "*unconscious feelings*" before they reach consciousness. But he introduces a distinction between the process through which ideas maintained in the unconscious by repression can be made conscious and the way in which sensations or feelings become conscious; in the latter case, transmission is direct.

> *Actually the difference is that, whereas with* Ucs. *ideas connecting links must be created before they can be brought into the Cs., with* feelings, *which are themselves transmitted directly, this does not occur. In other words, [. . .] feelings are either conscious or unconscious*. (ibid.: 22–23)

It should be noted here, it seems to me, that though Freud says that feelings cannot be repressed – repression is exclusively a neurotic mechanism – he does use the term "*repression*" to refer to the suppression of the perception of feelings and affects; nowadays, we would want also to include the defensive mechanism which is characterized by denial of psychic reality. Freud concludes this chapter with some remarks on the relationship between the ego and the body. For him, the ego is above all derived from bodily sensations given its special position at the junction between perception and feelings. "*The ego is first and foremost a bodily ego; it is not merely a surface entity, but is itself the projection of a surface*" (ibid.: 26).

For a fuller description of the complex relationships between the "*ego*" and various mental processes, Freud turns to a notion devised by Groddeck (1923): the "*id*". According to Freud, the "*id*" is the "*great reservoir of the libido*" and of the passions, and it is governed by the pleasure principle which, in the id, takes over from the reality principle. Disagreeing with Groddeck, Freud argues that the ego does not passively submit to the id's assaults on it – it tries to subjugate them, much as a man on horseback will try to hold the animal in check. "*Often a rider, if he is not to be parted from his horse, is obliged to guide it where it wants to go; so in the same way the ego is in the habit of transforming the id's will into action as if it were its own*" (ibid.: 25).

- ## *The superego (or ego ideal)*

There is another phenomenon which comes from the unconscious: the "*unconscious sense of guilt*" which is found in many of the neuroses; it is manifested through excessive self-reproaches and a harsh moral conscience. Freud calls the agency specifically responsible for such feelings the *ego ideal* or *superego*, which is in conflict with the ego.

Where do these two agencies – ego and ego ideal or superego – come from? Freud suggests that they have to do with identificatory processes; from this point of view, two kinds of identification can therefore be distinguished. At the beginning of life, as he had shown in *Group Psychology and the Analysis of the Ego* (1921c), identification and object-cathexis cannot be distinguished from each other, so that "*loving the object*" is the same as "*being the object*". In other words, these first identifications are narcissistic in nature, but with the sexual object being set up inside the ego – as happens in melancholia via the mechanism of introjection; this "*makes it possible to suppose that the character of the ego is a precipitate of abandoned object-cathexes and that it contains the history of those object-choices*" (1923b: 29). These early identifications come to act as a specific agency within the ego and, in their role as superego or ego ideal, oppose what the ego tries to do. When the ego gains in strength, a more advanced form of identification is established: the ego succeeds in distinguishing between love and identification, it becomes able to abandon its sexual aims, and, as it cathects its Oedipal objects with a sublimated narcissistic libido, it also identifies with certain of their character traits.

> *When the ego assumes the features of the object, it is forcing itself, so to speak, upon the id as a love-object and is trying to make good the id's loss by saying: "Look, you can love me too – I am so like the object."* (ibid.: 30)

In a note written on 12 July 1938, Freud summarizes the differences between these two identificatory processes:

> *"Having" and "being" in children. Children like expressing an object relation by an identification: "I am the object". "Having" is the later of the two; after loss of the object it relapses into*

"being". Example: the breast. "The breast is part of me, I am the breast". Only later: "I have it" – that is, "I am not it". (Freud 1941f [1938]: 299)

Freud then goes on to describe the relationship between identificatory processes and the Oedipus complex. He draws the conclusion that, in its complete form and given the psychic bisexuality of each individual, the Oedipus complex has two aspects, the one positive, the other negative. For example, the young boy's identification with his father consolidates his masculinity (this is his positive or direct Oedipus complex); his feminine identification, on the other hand, is a manifestation of the negative (or inverted) Oedipus complex. *Mutatis mutandis*, the same is true of the young girl: in her positive Oedipus complex she identifies with her mother, while in its negative version she identifies with her father. What, then, is the decisive factor which determines the child's final identification? Freud now realizes that, to his surprise, the process which occurs in melancholic (depressive) patients does not provide us with an adequate explanation. He therefore gives up any idea of putting forward a psychological explanation and prefers to fall back on constitutional factors; this, however, does not answer the real question – and in addition it pushes to one side the psychoanalytic element. "*It would appear, therefore, that in both sexes the relative strength of the masculine and feminine sexual dispositions is what determines [. . .] the outcome of the Oedipus situation*" (1923b: 33). Later, post-Freudian psychoanalysts – especially Jones and Klein – would see identification with the rival as the decisive element in the individual's final identification.

The child's ego ideal or superego is not simply a matter of identifying with the father – or with "*the parents*" as Freud points out in a footnote (ibid.: 31, note 1); it has also to do with identification with parental prohibitions which have stood in the way of accomplishing the child's incestuous Oedipal desires. In other words, the ego ideal/superego has a "*double aspect*" in its relationship with the ego. On the one hand, it is encouraging: "*You ought to be like this (like your father)*", but on the other, it comprises a prohibition: "*You may not be like this (like your father) – that is, you may not do all that he does; some things are his prerogative*" (ibid.: 34). Freud summarizes these complex processes thus: "*When we were little children we knew these higher natures, we admired them and feared them; and later we took them into ourselves*" (ibid.: 36). Thus an agency separates out from the ego, the harshness of which varies from one individual to another: "*the more powerful the Oedipus complex was [. . .] the stricter will be the domination of the superego over the ego later on – in the form of conscience or perhaps of an unconscious sense of guilt*" (ibid.: 34–35). In the end, "*the ego ideal is [. . .] the heir of the Oedipus complex*" (ibid.: 36). I would simply mention here the fact that Freud uses three different terms which he does not explicitly define (though he does not seem to think they are interchangeable): ideal ego, ego ideal and superego.

Religious feelings, individual moral conscience and social feelings ultimately derive from the existence of an ego ideal which makes considerable demands on human beings. Religious feelings lie at the heart of all religions: "*The self-judgement which declares that the ego falls short of its ideal produces the religious sense of humility to which the believer appeals in his longing*" (ibid.: 37). Moral conscience results from the internalization of injunctions and prohibitions which are issued by teachers and other authority figures; the tension between the demands of conscience and the actual performance of the ego is experienced as "*a sense of guilt*". Freud adds that "*social feelings rest on identifications with other people, on the basis of having the same ego ideal*" (ibid.: 37).

Freud concludes this chapter with an investigation into the primitive origins of the ego ideal or superego. He turns to the hypotheses he had put forward in *Totem and Taboo*, and argues that social feelings are to some extent the consequence of the killing of the father of the primal horde and of the moral restraints which derive from that event. Turning to the history of how the superego came into being and is handed down from generation to generation, Freud says that the phylogenetic imprints of ancient experiences are not transmitted by the ego but by the hereditary id.

> *Thus in the id, which is capable of being inherited, are harboured residues of the existences of countless egos; and, when the ego forms its superego out of the id, it may perhaps only be reviving shapes of former egos and be bringing them to resurrection.* (ibid.: 38)

• *The ego and the conflict between life and death drives*

What influence do the drives exert on the ego, and in particular the life and death drives which Freud described in *Beyond the Pleasure Principle* (1920g)? He suggests that these two classes of instinctual drives may unite and divide in varying proportions. It is difficult to imagine such a blending between these drives, though it can be surmised that the death drive is neutralized by the living organism and its destructive part, diverted on to the external world by means of a particular organ, is expressed as aggressiveness. "*This special organ would seem to be the muscular apparatus; and the death instinct would thus seem to express itself – though probably only in part – as an* instinct of destruction *directed against the external world and other organisms*" (ibid.: 41).

Once we accept the idea of fusion between the life and death drives, it becomes possible to imagine their more or less complete "*defusion*". In severe neurotic states and in the perversions, says Freud, the death drive plays the dominant role. "*We perceive that for purposes of discharge the* instinct of destruction *is habitually brought into the service of Eros; we suspect that the epileptic fit is a product and indication of an instinctual defusion*" (ibid.: 41). For Freud, regression from the genital to the anal-sadistic phase also involves defusion of the drives, while any move forward depends on the fact of the erotic component of the life drive taking precedence over the death drive.

Freud then discusses whether it is possible to see the opposition between the two classes of drives in terms of the polarity between love and hate. Love can easily be looked upon as the representative of Eros, while hate and the destructive impulse could be seen as representatives of the death drive. This, however, does not appeal to Freud, because clinical observation, he says, shows us that in a number of circumstances hate can change into love and love into hate. In paranoia, for example, the excessively strong homosexual attachment to a particular person leads to "*this person whom he loved most [becoming] a persecutor, against whom the patient directs an often dangerous aggressiveness*" (ibid.: 43). Unable to make much headway on this point, Freud prefers to leave the question open for the moment. He suggests that another factor, different in nature, may be at work so that there is no need to assume a direct transformation of love into hate and vice versa. There may be some kind of "*displaceable energy, which, indifferent in itself*" (ibid.: 44) is in operation; this energy has its source in "*the narcissistic store of libido*" and is therefore "*desexualized Eros*" (ibid.: 44). However, after deciding against any direct transformation between love and hate, Freud goes on to say in the following chapter that such a transformation does indeed occur, thus making no attempt to disguise his hesitations on this question.

In the light of his new way of looking at the structure of the mind, Freud redefines both primary and secondary narcissism.

> *At the very beginning, all the libido is accumulated in the id, while the ego is still in the process of formation or is still feeble. The id sends part of this libido out into erotic object-cathexes, whereupon the ego, now grown stronger, tries to get hold of this object-libido and to force itself on the id as a love-object. The narcissism of the ego is thus a secondary one, which has been withdrawn from objects.* (ibid.: 46)

• *The negative therapeutic reaction and the melancholic superego – "a pure culture of the death instinct"*

Freud next turns to the relationships between ego and id on the one hand, and ego and superego on the other. He compares the ego to a servant having to wait upon three masters: the ego has to cope with three sorts of danger – from the external world, from the libido of the id and from the severity of the superego. For instance, with respect to the superego, we often encounter patients who react in a paradoxical fashion to any improvement they may be making in the course of their analytic treatment – every improvement brings about an exacerbation of their illness. Freud calls this phenomenon "*a negative therapeutic reaction*" (ibid.: 49). What matters most to these patients is not the will to recover from their illness but the need to remain ill, because they unconsciously feel themselves to be guilty and thus refuse to give up the punishment of suffering. "*But as far as the patient is concerned this sense of guilt is dumb; it does not tell him he is guilty; he does not feel guilty, he feels ill*" (ibid.: 49–50). This kind of negative therapeutic reaction is found in most cases of severe neurosis; here the sense of guilt is unconscious, as opposed to the normal sense of guilt which is consciously felt.

How is it that the superego is so harsh and strict in certain disorders, such as melancholic depression? For Freud, the destructive component of the melancholic's superego has to do with the death drive.

> *What is now holding sway in the superego is, as it were, a pure culture of the death instinct, and in fact it often enough succeeds in driving the ego into death, if the latter does not fend off its tyrant in time by the change round into mania.* (ibid.: 53)

Freud asks himself how it is that, in melancholia, the superego becomes a kind of gathering-place for the death drive. He introduces the idea of "*instinctual defusion*" brought about by the fact that the erotic component no longer has the power to bind the whole of the destructiveness that was combined with it, so that "*this is released in the form of an inclination to aggression and destruction*" (ibid.: 54). It is from this defusion between life and death drives that the depressive patient's superego takes its harshness and cruelty towards the ego.

What is the situation in cases of obsessional neurosis? In this disorder, the superego is implacably harsh towards the ego but, unlike the depressive patient, the obsessional individual appears to be "*immune against the danger of suicide*" (ibid.: 53). The reason for this, according to Freud, is that in obsessional patients love has been transformed into hate: "*It has become possible, through a regression to the pregenital organization, for the love-impulses to transform themselves into impulses of aggression against the object*" (ibid.: 53). He repeats here his conviction that what takes place is "*an actual substitution of hate for love*"; this substitution shuts the door firmly on any possibility of maintaining a distinction between love and hate, such a distinction being necessary if we are to conceive of a binding–unbinding process between these affects similar to the fusion–defusion one which occurs between the life and death instincts. According to D. Quinodoz (1994) the difficulty Freud has with this question seems to be due to the fact that he fails to establish a clear distinction between *fusion* and *binding* of the affects. She argues that at an early stage in the child's development, love and hate can be so mixed up with each other that it is impossible to know whether we are dealing with one or the other; in a more advanced stage of development, however, the patient is able to distinguish between feelings of love and feelings of hate aimed at one and the same object. It then becomes possible to bind them: "We must be able to distinguish before we can combine. Without a prior distinction, we end up with confusion, not combination" (1994: 90).

Freud goes on to describe the characteristics of the ego, with its strengths and its weaknesses. In contact with perceptions coming from the external world, the ego subjects mental processes to "*reality-testing*", aided in this by its capacity for thinking which helps to secure a postponement of motor discharge. The experiences of life which come from outside enrich the ego, while at the same time it attempts to cope with the drive impulses coming from the id; this bears witness to the therapeutic effect of psychoanalysis. "*Psychoanalysis is an instrument to enable the ego to achieve a progressive conquest of the id*" (Freud 1923b: 56).

The introduction of the concept of the ego leads Freud also to lay the foundations of a new theory of anxiety, one that he would develop in 1926 in *Inhibitions, Symptoms and Anxiety*. But already in 1923 he shows how mental processes participate in generating anxiety, whereas beforehand this role was attributed exclusively to biological factors. Anxiety is henceforth to be regarded as an ego phenomenon. "*The ego is the actual seat of anxiety*" (ibid.: 57). Faced with the libidinal danger originating in the id, the ego fears "*being overwhelmed or annihilated*"; it is warned of this danger by the pleasure/unpleasure principle. When it is faced with other dangers – represented by its fear of the superego – the ego reacts with "*fear of conscience* [Gewissenangst]", which usually takes the form of castration anxiety. Anxiety concerning death, according to Freud, has no meaning in psychoanalysis "*for death is an abstract concept with a negative content for which no unconscious correlative can be found*" (ibid.: 58).

Freud concludes his text by highlighting the protective role of the superego as regards the ego, particularly when it attempts to manage the libidinal and aggressive drives associated with the Oedipal situation. It is the loss of this protective function of the superego in the melancholic patient which enables Freud to infer – by default, if I may put it thus – that the normal superego protects the ego.

> [In melancholia] *the ego gives itself up because it feels itself hated and persecuted by the superego, instead of loved. To the ego, therefore, living means the same as being loved – being*

loved by the superego. [. . .] The superego fulfils the same function of protecting and saving that was fulfilled in earlier days by the father and later by Providence and Destiny. (ibid.: 58)

On the other hand, when the ego is faced with a real danger, it feels itself to be deserted by all protecting forces and lets itself die. This feeling is the basis for our very first state of anxiety – that of birth – and is the source of infantile anxiety concerning separation from the protecting mother. The id, for its part, evinces neither love nor hate towards the ego; it is above all *"under the domination of the mute but powerful death instincts"* (ibid.: 59), locked in an interminable conflict with Eros.

Post-Freudians

Anna Freud: *The Ego and the Mechanisms of Defence* (1936)

In 1936, Anna Freud elaborated on her father's thinking on the subject in what has come to be regarded as a ground-breaking book, *The Ego and the Mechanisms of Defence*, in which she studied the defences that the ego develops with respect to the id, the superego and the external world. She argues that the ego has to cope with a whole series of conflicts which try to force their way into consciousness – those which derive from the demands of the drives, from the requirements of the superego, and the dangers which have their source in the external world. With the aim of preventing the emergence of anxiety, the ego employs a wide range of defence mechanisms. Anna Freud begins by listing those that Sigmund Freud had described – repression, regression, reaction formation, isolation, undoing what has been done, projection, introjection, turning against the self, reversal into the opposite and sublimation. She adds further mechanisms – identification with the aggressor and altruistic surrender – and makes it clear that the list is by no means closed. Anna Freud's work was the starting-point for a major current of psychoanalytic thought which began in Vienna at the end of the 1930s and grew in magnitude under her leadership in London and that of Heinz Hartmann in North America; Hartmann was one of the founders of what came to be known as the Ego Psychology movement.

Heinz Hartmann and "Ego Psychology"

It was in 1939, in his book *Ego Psychology and the Problem of Adaptation* published in Vienna, that Hartmann presented the ideas which were to form the basis of "Ego Psychology". After emigrating to the United States in 1941, he was joined by other European emigrants fleeing the Nazis, among them Ernst Kris and Rudolph Loewenstein, who shared his views. From then on, the ideas of Ego Psychology quickly spread throughout North America, so much so in fact that it became a major current of psychoanalytic thought there. In 1945 Hartmann founded the journal *The Psychoanalytic Study of the Child* with Kris and Anna Freud.

Though the basis for Hartmann's ideas was Freud's 1923 development of the ego, superego and id, his own contribution is sometimes quite remote from Freud's concepts. For Hartmann, the ego has two functions. One is to set up defences whenever the ego has to deal with a conflict; the other – the more important of the two according to Hartmann – is free of all conflict: this is what he calls the "autonomous ego". The autonomous ego is present from birth onwards and develops quite independently of the id. In Hartmann's view, behaviour problems in individuals are the result of their more or less pronounced inability to adapt to social conditions, an issue which as such does not involve the drives. It follows that the crucial role of the autonomous ego thus defined is "to adapt to" the external world. As for the libido, Hartmann sees it as desexualizing the aggressive drives via a process he calls "neutralization", one of the processes he ascribes to the ego: the stronger the ego is, the more capable it becomes of "neutralizing" libidinal energy, and vice versa. On the technical level, the Ego Psychology approach focuses above all on the analysis of the patient's resistances and defences and on reinforcing the conscious ego, to the detriment of the analysis of unconscious fantasies. This is where this approach finds itself in close agreement with the technique adopted by Anna Freud and her followers. In addition, this current of thought laid the foundations for a truly psychoanalytic sociology. In Ego Psychology, the autonomous ego's adaptive function with respect to the social environment is crucially important. This dimension was particularly elaborated on by Erik H. Erikson in his book *Childhood and Society* (1950), in which he describes the development of the social ego from childhood to old age.

It is therefore no surprise to learn that the theoretical and clinical approach adopted by the Ego Psychology school gave rise to fierce debates within the International Psychoanalytical Association (IPA); these led to deep differences of opinion, notably with Melanie Klein in Great Britain and Jacques Lacan in France. For Klein, the ego and the object are present from the very beginnings of life; as a result, the "Controversial Discussions" focused mainly on the progressive growth of the ego, on the relationship between the ego and the object, and on the importance of unconscious fantasy. Lacan drew a distinction between the "ego" and the "I", based on the mirror stage of development, the "I" being a forerunner of the concept of the "subject" which he was later to introduce. Though Lacan had been analysed by Loewenstein, he was always critical of the ideas adopted by the Ego Psychology school. In particular, he would have nothing to do with the idea of adaptation, declaring that the most that could be said of the notion was that it was an attempt by American psychoanalysts to make their patients comply with their ideals. As Alain de Mijolla puts it: "Lacan's irony could not have been more scathing than when he condemned the supporters of Ego Psychology; basing his argument on structuration by language, he claimed that the ego belonged above all to the domain of the Imaginary" (2002: 1024).

Heinz Kohut and Self-Psychology

In reaction to the ideas suggested by Hartmann and the Ego Psychology school, Kohut (1971) put forward a psychoanalytic theory focused on the *Self* and its metamorphoses. The idea of the Self had already been introduced by Hartmann in 1950, with the aim of distinguishing between "ego" and "self". On that basis, Kohut constructed the Self-Psychology current of psychoanalytic thought; over the years, this approach has grown in strength and is now one of the major contemporary schools of thought in the United States. Kohut's idea was to contribute to the development of Freud's thinking on the psychoanalytic treatment of narcissistic states, and he proposed a technique based on the empathic method he advocated.

New concepts

Death drive – ego – ego ideal – full form of the Oedipus complex – fusion/defusion of the drives – hereditary id – id – ideal ego – identification – life drive – melancholic superego – narcissistic identification – negative therapeutic reaction – reality-testing – superego – unconscious sense of guilt

"THE ECONOMIC PROBLEM OF MASOCHISM"

(1924c)

From perverse masochism to primary or erotogenic masochism, protecting the individual against self-destruction

In this paper, Freud continues his research into the nature of masochism, the perversion which consists in taking pleasure in suffering. He had already dealt with the question of masochism in earlier texts (1905d, 1915c), together with that of sadism. Once, however, he had introduced the fundamental conflict between the life and death drives, together with the concepts of ego, id and superego, an updated version of his hypotheses concerning masochism became necessary. All the more so, in fact, because masochism is in contradiction with the pleasure/unpleasure principle which Freud had earlier put forward – the idea there being that the mind operates in such a way as to avoid unpleasure and maximize pleasure.

Freud begins by redefining the pleasure principle on fresh grounds. Henceforth, there are three basic principles that regulate how the mind operates: the *Nirvana principle*, which tends to reduce all excitation to zero level; the *pleasure principle*, which links life and death drives together; and the *reality principle*, which enables pleasure to be postponed and unpleasure to be tolerated at least temporarily. He then goes on to explore two kinds of perversion in the strict sense of the term: *feminine masochism* in men, and *moral masochism*. These are characterized by regression to an earlier libidinal stage, in particular to the anal-sadistic stage, and by a re-cathexis of incestuous Oedipal objects – the re-sexualization of the Oedipus complex. This goes hand in hand with an erotic satisfaction which gives rise to an unconscious sense of guilt such that the ego feels a masochistic need to be sadistically punished by the superego. With the introduction of the notion of *primary* or *erotogenic masochism*, Freud expands the concept well beyond that of a masochistic perversion *stricto sensu*. He opens up new horizons with his idea that the conflict between life and death drives lies at the very heart of the processes of life, and this from the very outset: in other words, the pleasure we take in living has constantly to be recaptured from the tendency to self-destruction.

Biographies and history

Internecine conflicts and fears for the future of psychoanalysis

"The Economic Problem of Masochism" was written at the end of 1923 and published in April 1924 in the *Internationale Zeitschrift für Psychoanalyse*. At that time in his life, Freud had to cope with a series of highly distressing events, including the onset of his illness in February 1923 (which I mentioned in the previous chapter) and the atmosphere of dissension within the committee. Though he himself was by now world-famous, Freud was worried about the future of psychoanalysis, in particular because of the disagreements which had broken out between Rank and Jones; he felt they endangered the harmony which ought to reign in the committee – which was, after all, Freud's main hope of ensuring that his life's work would not die with him. Rank and Jones had not been seeing eye to eye for many a long year, even though they were supposed to be working together and co-editing various psychoanalytic publications. In the summer of 1923, Rank and Jones had a final meeting somewhere in the Dolomites; the conflict between the two men reached such a level of intensity that the committee had to be disbanded. It was also on that occasion that the members were informed of Freud's illness.

Discovering the text

Page numbers are those of *The Standard Edition of the Complete Psychological Works of Sigmund Freud*, vol. **19**, 155–170.

- ### *Another look at the pleasure principle*

Freud begins this paper by explaining the reasons for his wishing to revise what he had already written about the pleasure principle, and in particular about its relationship to the Nirvana principle with which he had equated it. In *Beyond the Pleasure Principle* (1920g), Freud had borrowed the term "*Nirvana principle*" to describe the tendency of the mental apparatus to reduce to zero any quantity of excitation which might arise; if this were indeed the case, the tendency to annihilate all excitation would seem to be the same as the death drive. In "The Economic Problem of Masochism", he reasserts his belief in the Nirvana principle, but acknowledges that this does create a specific difficulty: if the pleasure principle is truly the equivalent of the Nirvana principle as he had previously suggested, then we have no option but to conclude that it is in the service of the death drive – and that would be something of a paradox. "[*The*] *Nirvana principle (and the pleasure principle which is supposedly identical with it) would be entirely in the service of the death instincts, whose aim is to conduct the restlessness of life into the stability of the inorganic state*" (1924c: 160). There is a further contradiction here. The pleasure principle – which supposedly reduces the tensions which engender unpleasure – is also put in difficulty by the fact that some tensions are pleasurable, the most striking example being the state of sexual excitation. These contradictions lead Freud to the conclusion that the Nirvana principle, belonging as it does to the death drive, must have undergone some modification in living organisms, in order not to bring life back to an inorganic state (and so put itself in the service of the pleasure principle). This modification, says Freud, must be because of some intervention on the part of the libido which, in combining with the death drive, plays a part in regulating the processes of life.

Up till then, Freud had thought that pleasurable and unpleasurable sensations depended on a *quantitative* factor, related exclusively to an increase or decrease in amounts of stimulus. He now introduces a new dimension: feelings of pleasure and unpleasure do not depend exclusively on some *quantitative* factor but also on a *qualitative* factor – which he finds difficult to define. "*Perhaps it is the* rhythm, *the temporal sequence of changes, rises and falls in the quantity of stimulus. We do not know*" (ibid.: 160).

This leads Freud to the conclusion that three principles govern the regulation of the processes of life: the *Nirvana principle*, which represents the death drive through its tendency to reduce *quantities* of excitation to zero; the *pleasure principle*, which expresses the binding between life and death drives through the *quality* of libidinal excitation; and the *reality principle* which enables postponement of pleasure and temporary acquiescence in unpleasure. These three principles cannot avoid coming into conflict with one another, but they are obliged to put up with one another if the processes of life are to be preserved. In order to protect life from being destroyed, the pleasure principle has to accept that the death drive must be to some extent fused with the life drive. "*The conclusion to be drawn from these considerations is that the description of the pleasure principle as the watchman over our life cannot be rejected*" (ibid.: 161).

In the light of these theoretical considerations, Freud begins to investigate three kinds of masochism: feminine masochism in men, primary or erotogenic masochism and moral masochism.

• *Feminine masochism in men*

It is above all in men that feminine masochism can be observed. For Freud, it is truly a perversion the manifest content of which is expressed in fantasies dominated by the wish to be bound, beaten or whipped, etc.; these fantasies either lead to masturbation or represent sexual satisfaction in themselves. In these cases of perversion, we discover that the subject is placed "*in a characteristically female situation; [the fantasies] signify, that is, being castrated, or copulated with, or giving birth to a baby*" (ibid.: 162). It is for this reason that Freud calls this form of masochism "*the feminine form*", signifying that this passive attitude towards the object is the consequence of regression to infantile sexuality. In addition, in this perversion, the individual reproaches him- or herself with having committed some wrongful deed or other that has to be atoned for through pain and suffering. These self-reproaches are the expression of an unconscious sense of guilt which has to do with infantile masturbation. The unconscious sense of guilt in feminine masochism finds an echo in another sort of masochism – moral masochism.

• *Primary or erotogenic masochism*

Freud reminds the reader that in 1905 in his *Three Essays on the Theory of Sexuality*, he had already observed that, in a great number of internal processes, sexual excitation arises as soon as the intensity of those processes goes beyond a certain limit, and that this "*libidinal sympathetic excitation*" is frequently accompanied by feelings of pain and unpleasure. His intuition then was that "*nothing of considerable importance can occur in the organism without contributing some component to the excitation of the sexual instinct*" (1905d: 205, quoted in 1924c: 163). Henceforth taking into account the dualism between life and death drives, Freud can elaborate on the notion of libidinal sympathetic excitation: it appears to govern all of the processes of life – the libido renders innocuous the destructive and death drives which dominate organic life from the very outset, and in this way it prevents the organism being brought back to an inorganic state. With the aim of emphasizing the primary nature of this process of eroticization of the death drive, Freud calls it "*primary masochism*" or "*erotogenic masochism*".

How does the libido accomplish the task of rendering the death drive innocuous? It has two paths open to it, says Freud. First, it can divert the drive to a great extent outwards, on to external objects, with the help of the muscular apparatus – the drive is then called the destructive instinct, the instinct for mastery, the will to power. Part of the drive can be placed directly in the service of the sexual function: this is sadism proper. Second, part of the death drive may not be projected outwards, for it can be made innocuous inside the organism: "*It remains inside the organism and, with the help of the accompanying sexual excitation described above, becomes libidinally bound there. It is in this portion that we have to recognize the original, erotogenic masochism*" (1924c: 163–164). As Freud says, we know nothing of the ways and means by which this taming of the drives is carried out. From a psychoanalytical point of view, they are always fused and amalgamated with each other in varying proportions, so that we never encounter life or death drives in any pure form.

Freud goes on to list a certain number of phases in the development of the libido in which primary masochism plays a part – for example, in the fear of being eaten up by the totem animal (the father) at the oral stage, the wish to be beaten in the anal-sadistic stage, the fear of castration in the phallic stage, etc. In addition, part of the primary masochism which first enabled the death instinct to be tamed by the libido "*still has the self as its object*" (ibid.: 164), thus affording protection against self-destruction. Freud then discusses the possibility that the sadism and the destructive drive which had been projected on to the external world may be turned inwards again, thus producing a "*secondary masochism*" which is added to the original masochism.

- ## *Moral masochism*

The moral masochist seeks suffering but is not aware of the sexual satisfaction that he or she takes from the wished-for feeling of pain, which has to do with an unconscious sense of guilt; these patients do not appear to take any erotic pleasure in suffering. The extreme case of moral masochism can be found in patients who reject any improvement which may come their way in the course of their psychoanalytic treatment; in 1923, Freud had attributed this paradoxical behaviour to an unconscious sense of guilt and had given it the name "*negative therapeutic reaction*". For such patients, satisfying their unconscious sense of guilt constitutes the secondary gain from illness (hence their unwillingness to recover), so that this becomes one of the most serious resistances to psychoanalytic treatment. However, when the psychoanalyst speaks of an unconscious sense of guilt, this means nothing to the patient: he or she will begin to understand something if the analyst speaks instead of a "*need for punishment*" (ibid.: 166). To explain how this unconscious sense of guilt arises with such shattering force, Freud turns to the concepts he had introduced in 1923 in his second structural theory and in particular to the overwhelming tension which appears between ego and superego when the ego feels itself unable to meet the demands of its ideal, the superego, as a model to follow.

Freud reminds us also that the superego came into being thanks to the child's identification with the parental couple. When the Oedipus complex is dissolved, the relationship with the parental objects becomes desexualized, by being diverted from its direct sexual aims. In this way, the superego retains the characteristics of the internalized parents. In addition, the demands of the superego tend to be increased by external influences such as those exerted by teachers and other authority figures, thus contributing to its moral role. "*In this way the Oedipus complex proves to be [. . .] the source of our individual ethical sense, our morality*" (ibid.: 167–168).

- ## *The "re-sexualization" of the Oedipus complex*

After this digression concerning the origins of the superego, Freud returns to the question of moral masochism. He emphasizes the fact that such individuals appear to be morally inhibited to an excessive degree and behave as though they were dominated by an especially harsh conscience, though they seem not to be aware of this "*ultra-morality*".

> *It can hardly be an insignificant detail, then, that the sadism of the superego becomes for the most part glaringly conscious, whereas the masochistic trend of the ego remains as a rule concealed from the subject and has to be inferred from his behaviour.* (ibid.: 169)

Why does moral masochism remain unconscious? Freud attributes this to the fact that the unconscious sense of guilt expresses a need for punishment at the hands of a parental power. This gives him a clue as to the real-but-hidden meaning of moral masochism: it is closely related to a "*re-sexualization*" of the Oedipus complex. What does Freud mean by this? "*Re-sexualization*", he says, means that the moral masochist has made a regressive return to the Oedipal situation, and the revived incestuous desire brings in its wake the feeling of having committed some sexual misdemeanour or other – a "*sinful*" action – for which only chastisement by the great parental power of Destiny can suffice. In order to obtain this, moral masochists must act against their own interests and perhaps even destroy their own existence. As Freud puts it: "*The sadism of the superego and the masochism of the ego supplement each other and unite to produce the same effects*" (ibid.: 170). Drawing a conclusion from this internal conflict, Freud argues that moral masochism is undoubtedly proof of the fact that there is a fusion between the life and death drives.

> *Its danger lies in the fact that it originates from the death instinct which has escaped being turned outwards as an instinct of destruction. But since, on the other hand, it has the significance of an erotic component even the subject's destruction of himself cannot take place without libidinal satisfaction.* (ibid.: 170)

> **Development of Freud's concepts**

The idea of masochism and its ambiguities in Freud's writings

The question of "feminine masochism"

Freud tends to use the term "*feminine masochism*" in a somewhat ambiguous way. There is no doubt that, when he refers to "*feminine masochism in men*", he is quite clearly referring to what he sees as a masochistic perversion. However, the very term "**feminine** *masochism*" would seem to indicate that, for Freud, women are by nature masochistic. That ambiguity has been highlighted by, among others, Laplanche and Pontalis:

> By "feminine masochism" one is naturally tempted to understand a "masochism of women". Freud certainly used such terms to mean the "expression of the feminine essence", but in the context of the theory of bisexuality feminine masochism is an immanent possibility for any human being regardless of sex. (Laplanche and Pontalis 1967 [1973: 245])

Generally speaking, some degree of ambiguity concerning the masochistic nature of femininity runs all through Freud's writings; it begins with the contrast between active and passive/masculine and feminine mentioned in his *Three Essays on the Theory of Sexuality* (1905d) and it goes all the way through to his later writings in which he explicitly connects activity and masculinity on the one hand, passivity and feminine masochism on the other. However, in his *New Introductory Lectures on Psycho-Analysis* (1933a [1932]), this contrast between the two sexes is somewhat reduced.

Primary (or erotogenic) masochism is not a perversion

It should be pointed out that Freud's use of the term "*masochism*" to designate primary or erotogenic masochism may lead to confusion as regards the concept of perversion. By introducing the notion of primary or erotogenic masochism, Freud was attempting above all to expand the idea of masochism beyond that of perversion in the narrow sense of the term; his aim was to emphasize the fact that any link between pain and sexual pleasure was essentially based on a fusion between the life and death drives. In other words, as he himself put it, primary or erotogenic masochism "*would thus be evidence of, and a remainder from, the phase of development in which the coalescence, which is so important for life, between the death instinct and Eros took place*" (1924c: 164). As a result, he saw in this primary form of masochism a fundamental structure which plays the part – again, to use his own words – of "*the watchman over our life*".

> **New concepts**
>
> *Feminine masochism – feminine masochism in men – moral masochism – Nirvana principle – pleasure / unpleasure principle – primary or erotogenic masochism – reality principle – "re-sexualization" of the Oedipus complex – secondary masochism*

INHIBITIONS, SYMPTOMS AND ANXIETY

(1926d)

A new source of anxiety: the fear of separation from and loss of the object

As he neared 70 years of age, Freud proposed new hypotheses as to the origins of anxiety, hypotheses which had the effect of making his earlier explanations obsolete. For the previous thirty years, he had argued in favour of a biological conception of the anxiety-generating mechanism: unsatisfied libido achieved discharge by being directly transformed into anxiety, for example in *coitus interruptus*. "*Neurotic anxiety arises out of libido, [and] is thus related to it in the same kind of way as vinegar is to wine*" (1905d: 224, note added in 1920).

From 1926 on, with the publication of *Inhibitions, Symptoms and Anxiety*, Freud's conception of the origins of anxiety has more to do with the mind: anxiety is an affect experienced by the ego whenever it is faced with a danger – which, in the final analysis, always implies fear of separation from or loss of the object. Freud's thesis is based on the distinction between various kinds of anxiety: anxiety due to a real danger (*Realangst*); automatic anxiety (*automatische Angst*) triggered by a traumatic situation which overwhelms the helpless ego; anxiety as a signal (*Signalangst*) activated in a situation where the ego is able to respond to the threat of impending danger.

In this book, Freud takes a fresh look at the question of defence mechanisms. He had previously thought that repression provoked anxiety, but here he changes his mind and decides that in fact it is anxiety which provokes repression. He suggests also that the ego creates symptoms and builds up defences above all as a means of avoiding the experience of anxiety, which habitually implies for the ego some danger or other related to fear of becoming separated from or of losing the object.

This is a difficult book to read, because the topics with which it deals are wide-ranging and Freud seems to have found it unusually difficult to unify the work, as Strachey (1959) points out. The same topic is often discussed in more than one section and from different points of view. It is only at the end of the book, in the "Addenda", that we find the true essence of Freud's thinking on the subject. In 1933, in one of his lectures, Freud returns to the subject of anxiety as he had dealt with it in 1926, but this time his synthesis is much clearer (Freud 1933a: 32nd Lecture).

Biographies and history

Freud and Otto Rank

Inhibitions, Symptoms and Anxiety was Freud's response to *The Trauma of Birth*, written by his follower, Otto Rank (1884–1939), and published in Vienna in 1924. For Rank, all attacks of anxiety could be understood as attempts at "*abreacting*" this original trauma, the trauma of birth; he went on to argue that all the neuroses could be accounted for on the basis of this initial anxiety. This over-simplistic argument pushed into the background the essential role played by the Oedipus complex in neurotic conflicts. Freud was at first somewhat hesitant as regards Rank's ideas and seemed even to view them initially with favour; he himself had argued that birth was the very first kind of anxiety which human beings experience (Freud 1900a) – "*the first great anxiety-state of birth*" (1923b: 58), as Freud puts it. In the end, however, while he continued to acknowledge the fact that Rank's research into the origins of anxiety had been an important stimulus for him, Freud rejected Rank's views and went on to publish his own ideas on the question. Rank found it difficult to accept any criticism on this subject coming from Freud, with the result that there was a complete breakdown in their relationship. Freud regretted the defection of someone who had been one of his closest collaborators over the previous twenty years; he liked Rank, and did not realize that criticizing the theses put forward in the book would affect Rank so much on a personal level. Rank was only 22 when he was admitted to the Vienna Psycho-Analytical Society in 1906 and immediately appointed secretary. He edited the *Minutes of the Vienna Society* from 1906 until his army call-up in 1915, and became one of the first editors of *Imago* (in 1912) and of the *Zeitschrift* (in 1913). He wrote a vast number of papers and was particularly interested in the mother–child relationship – the importance of this subject, in Rank's view, had been neglected by most psychoanalysts – and in pre-Oedipal relationships.

Freud at 70 years of age

In June 1925, as he was writing *Inhibitions, Symptoms and Anxiety*, Freud learned of the death of Josef Breuer, with whom he had written *Studies on Hysteria* in 1895. The two men had not seen each other for some twenty-five years, and Freud was surprised to learn from Robert Breuer, the son of his former friend, that Josef Breuer had kept himself informed of Freud's work and had continued to show interest in the development of psychoanalysis. On 25 December 1925, Karl Abraham died in Berlin at the age of 48 from complications arising out of a pulmonary illness which was probably cancerous. His death was a terrible loss for psychoanalysis. Freud wrote:

> *We bury with him* – integer vitae scelerisque purus ["*He that is unstained in life and pure from guilt*", Horace, *Odes*, I, xxii, 1] – *one of the firmest hopes of our science, young as it is and so bitterly assailed, and a part of its nature that is now, perhaps, unrealizable*. (1926b: 277)

In February 1926, Freud had two attacks of angina pectoris while walking in the street; he attributed these to an intolerance of tobacco. Ferenczi was convinced that these attacks were due to anxiety and offered to spend some months in Vienna analysing him. Freud thanked his colleague, but refused the offer. On his seventieth birthday, on 6 May 1926, Freud received a considerable number of letters and telegrams from all over the world; special articles on Freud and psychoanalysis were published in all the Vienna newspapers and in several German ones.

Discovering the text

Page numbers are those of *The Standard Edition of the Complete Psychological Works of Sigmund Freud*, vol. **20**, 75–174.

- *Inhibitions are restrictions on the function of the ego*

Inhibition is not synonymous with symptom, says Freud, because an inhibition (i.e. a lowering of a sexual, motor, etc. function) may exist without necessarily having any pathological implication. Symptoms, on the other hand, are signs that a pathological process is taking place. Freud then gives an overview of the disturbances which might occur in various ego functions in cases of neurosis and reaches the following conclusion with its implications for ego participation:

"*inhibition is the expression of a* restriction of an ego-function" (1926d: 89). He goes on to differentiate between two types of inhibition: specific and generalized.

Specific inhibition can take on various forms. These neurotic forms of inhibition occur, for example, in people who play the piano, write or even go for walks, because the physical organs involved in these activities have become too strongly eroticized. In other words, the function of an organ may be impaired when its erotogenicity – its sexual significance – is unconsciously increased, as in the following example.

> *As soon as writing, which entails making a liquid flow out of a tube on to a piece of white paper, assumes the significance of copulation, or as soon as walking becomes a symbolic substitute for treading on the body of mother earth, both writing and walking are stopped because they represent the performance of a forbidden sexual act.* (ibid.: 90)

In this variety of inhibition, the ego renounces its functions in order to avoid any conflict with the id. Other forms of inhibition serve the purpose of self-punishment, especially in the case of professional activities: here, the ego avoids coming into conflict with the superego by not allowing itself certain possibilities and by giving up these activities.

The generalized inhibitions appear when the ego has a particular task to carry out, such as mourning, or when it has to contain a continual flood of sexual fantasies – the ego has to cut down on its expenditure of energy because its reserves are needed elsewhere. Freud draws the conclusion that inhibitions are restrictions on the functions of the ego either imposed as a measure of precaution or brought about as a result of an impoverishment of energy. Consequently, we are fully justified in making a distinction between inhibition and symptom, "*for a symptom cannot any longer be described as a process that takes place within, or acts upon, the ego*" (ibid.: 90).

- ### *A new theory of anxiety*

In this book, Freud puts forward some fresh hypotheses concerning the origins of anxiety, hypotheses which involve the ego, and abandons his earlier ideas on the subject in which the ego had no part to play. Henceforth, Freud considers anxiety to be an affect that is experienced by the ego when it is faced with danger – and this danger, in the final analysis, always has to do with the fear of losing the object, as he emphasizes in the chapters which follow. He reaches this conclusion on the basis of his definition of a symptom: it is the sign of and substitute for a drive satisfaction which has not occurred, and is a consequence of the process of repression. "*The ego is able by means of repression to keep the idea which is the vehicle of the reprehensible impulse from becoming conscious*" (ibid.: 91). How does the ego manage to achieve this? Thanks to a "*signal of unpleasure*" (ibid.: 92) which the ego sends out when it perceives a drive-related threat emerging from the id. The repression which follows on from this could be likened to an attempt at flight; it is during this process that the ego withdraws cathexis from the unwelcome representation and uses that energy for the purpose of releasing unpleasure in the form of anxiety. Freud draws the conclusion that "*we may legitimately hold firmly to the idea that the ego is the actual seat of anxiety and give up our earlier view that the cathectic energy of the repressed impulse is automatically turned into anxiety*" (ibid.: 93). Further, anxiety is reproduced as an affective state in accordance with an already existing mnemic image, so that these affective states are "*precipitates of primaeval traumatic experiences*" (ibid.: 93). Freud disagrees here with Rank's idea according to which every manifestation of anxiety is a reproduction of the anxiety which is experienced at birth. Freud acknowledges, *pace* Rank, that birth does indeed constitute the very first anxiety situation that we have to deal with, but he objects to the idea that it is merely reproduced in similar terms in every anxiety state. He notes that many writers have tended to lay too much stress on the weakness of the ego and to play down the power it exerts through the process of repression.

- ### *The ego's contradictory attitudes with respect to the symptom*

Repression not only proves how strong the ego is, but also illustrates its weaknesses, because the drive impulses of the id – which repression has turned into a manifest symptom – remain impervious to any influence and maintain their existence outside the organization of the ego. "*An analogy with which we have long been familiar compared a symptom to a foreign body which was keeping up a constant succession of stimuli and reactions in the tissue in which it was embedded*" (ibid.: 98). As a result, the struggle against the drive impulse is prolonged into a struggle against the symptom, and this secondary defensive struggle has two contradictory expressions. On the one hand, because the ego is characterized by a tendency to integrate and to unify, it tries to incorporate the symptom so as not to consider it a foreign body any longer. But the ego's tendency to incorporate the symptom may increase the latter's fixation, thus resulting in "*a (secondary) gain from illness*" – thereby reinforcing the resistances to treatment. The alternative is for the ego to continue to be troubled by the presence of the symptom.

> *The ego is an organization. It is based on the maintenance of free intercourse and of the possibility of reciprocal influence between all its parts. Its desexualized energy still shows traces of its origin in its impulsion to bind together and unify, and this necessity to synthesize grows stronger in proportion as the strength of the ego increases.* (ibid.: 98)

• *The motive for repression: castration anxiety*

Freud looks back at the case of "Little Hans" and draws a distinction between the presenting symptom (the little boy's unaccountable fear of horses) and the inhibition (his inability to go out into the street): this was a restriction which his ego had imposed on itself so as not to arouse the anxiety-symptom. But how is it that Hans's anxiety amounts to a neurosis and not simply to a fear? Freud replies: "*What made it a neurosis was one thing alone: the replacement of his father by a horse*" (ibid.: 103). This displacement was facilitated because the boy was so young and at that age the inborn traces of totemic thought can easily be reactivated. What means does the ego have at its disposal for fighting against an unwelcome drive impulse such as little Hans's aggressiveness towards his father? Freud says that the ego has at its disposal several defensive mechanisms in addition to reaction formation – excessive affection as a disguise for hostility – and transformation into its opposite – turning back against the self of the hostility directed against the father. The ego can also make the drive impulse regress, for example to the oral stage, and be expressed as anxiety about being bitten. The real motive force of repression, however, is castration anxiety, and Freud shows this quite clearly both in Little Hans's case and in that of the Wolf-Man.

> *[In] both patients the motive force of the repression was fear of castration. The ideas contained in their anxiety – being bitten by a horse and being devoured by a wolf – were substitutes by distortion for the idea of being castrated by their father. This was the idea which had undergone repression.* (ibid.: 108)

Freud goes on to modify his earlier thinking on the origins of repression: "*It was anxiety which produced repression and not, as I formally believed, repression which produced anxiety*" (ibid.: 108–109).

• *The formation of symptoms in obsessional neurosis*

A characteristic feature of obsessional neurosis is the great variety of symptoms that are presented. Freud explores how the fierce defensive struggle typical of this disorder gradually entails a restriction of ego functions, a restriction which is reinforced by an over-harsh attitude on the part of the superego. In this neurosis, the symptoms fall into two contrasting groups: they are either prohibitions or substitutive satisfactions which often appear in symbolic disguise. "*The symptom-formation scores a triumph if it succeeds in combining the prohibition with satisfaction so that what was originally a defensive command or prohibition acquires the significance of a satisfaction as well*" (ibid.: 112). This combination is due to ambivalence which may also operate during the two phases of the symptom, with the second stopping or undoing the first. Initially, in obsessional neurosis as in hysteria, defences are raised against the libidinal demands of the Oedipus complex, and the motive force of defence is also castration anxiety. In obsessional neurosis, however, the ego makes the genital organization regress to the anal-sadistic phase of development and turns to repression as its defence mechanism. In addition to repression – *"repression is only one of the mechanisms which defence makes use of"* (ibid.: 114) – and regression, the ego has recourse to reaction formation, which can take the shape of conscientiousness, pity and cleanliness, in obedience to the superego. During the latency period, the main task is to avoid the temptation to masturbate and, at puberty, the re-awakening of libidinal and aggressive impulses reactivates the defensive struggle against sexuality, which henceforth will be carried out *"under the banner of ethical principles"* (ibid.: 116). In obsessional neurosis the aggressive impulses remain unconscious and require a great deal of analytical work to make them conscious. It is as though the aggressive affect emerges in a quite different place, taking the form of a sense of guilt arising from the attitude of an implacably harsh superego towards the ego. From time to time, however, this sense of guilt is completely absent; it is expressed via symptoms such as penances or rituals of a self-punishing kind. These symptoms also represent a substitutive satisfaction of masochistic impulses.

- *Undoing what has been done and isolating*

Freud then mentions two other defensive techniques which are employed in obsessional neurosis: undoing what has been done, and isolating. Undoing what has been done – in German, *ungeschehenmachen* – literally means *"making unhappened"* some event or other. It is, as it were, negative magic which endeavours to *"blow away"* not merely the consequences of some event but the actual event itself. In the "Rat Man" case, for example, the patient put back a stone in the road which he had just removed in order to prevent the wheel on his beloved's carriage from running over it. Isolation also is typical of obsessional neurosis; it is a defensive technique which consists in separating-off a thought or an action – for example by interpolating an interval of time in the course of thinking processes. The experience is not forgotten but is deprived of its affect and its associative connections. *"The elements that are held apart in this way are precisely those which belong together associatively. The motor isolation is meant to ensure an interruption of the connection in thought"* (ibid.: 121). To isolation is added the taboo against touching; the avoidance of touching, contact or contagion plays a major role in this neurosis. The magnitude of these defence mechanisms is such that the obsessional neurotic finds it particularly difficult to obey the fundamental rule of psychoanalytic treatment.

- *Separation and loss: a new conception of anxiety*

Continuing his investigation into anxiety in phobias and in obsessional neurosis, Freud introduces a new way of looking at the origin of anxiety; he attributes it to a reaction to a situation in which the individual is faced with the danger of loss or separation – this goes beyond the kind of danger-situation which is derived directly from the threat of castration. Until then, Freud had thought that, in phobias, anxiety involving animals was an affective reaction of the ego when faced with the threat of castration, and that, in obsessional neurosis, anxiety arose from the punitive attitude of the superego towards the ego – again deriving from castration anxiety. In 1926, Freud goes a step further, moving from the fear of castration to a more general *"situation of danger"*, that of separation from and loss of the object. This has nothing to do with a fear of death, which for some was a sufficient explanation of the traumatic neuroses, because, in Freud's view, *"the unconscious seems to contain nothing that could give any content to our concept of the annihilation of life"* (ibid.: 129). On the other hand, each one of us experiences loss on a daily basis, an experience which prepares us for that of separation and loss in general – such as *"the daily experience of the faeces being separated from the body or [. . .] losing the mother's breast at weaning"* (ibid.: 129–130). This leads Freud to a new concept of anxiety. *"We have hitherto regarded [anxiety] as an affective signal of danger; but now, since the danger is so often one of castration, it appears to us as a reaction to a loss, a separation"* (ibid.: 130).

- *From loss of the object to fear of losing the object*

What is the true nature of the "*danger*" perceived by the ego which leads it to set in motion the affect we call anxiety? The act of birth, says Freud, is the prototype experience of anxiety, but there are other similar experiences, and the manifestations of anxiety in children are part of these: for example, when a child is left alone, or in darkness, or in the presence of an unknown person instead of someone with whom he or she is familiar (the mother). "*These three instances can be reduced to a single condition – namely, that of missing someone who is loved and longed for*" (ibid.: 136). Freud points out that this is not simply an instance of loss; the anxiety situation is an expression of the infant's feeling at his or her wits' end. According to Freud, the "*real essence of the 'danger'*" for the infant lies in the economic disturbance which results from non-satisfaction, in other words the increase in tension due to need. "*The reason why the infant in arms wants to perceive the presence of its mother is only because it already knows by experience that she satisfies all its needs without delay*" (ibid.: 137). Freud goes on to draw a fundamental distinction between the infant's physical and psychological distress; this leads to a distinction between anxiety involving *loss* of the object – automatic, involuntary anxiety – and that linked to the *fear* of losing the object – anxiety as a signal, which is psychological.

> *When the infant has found out by experience that an external, perceptible object can put an end to the dangerous situation which is reminiscent of birth, the content of the danger it fears is displaced from the economic situation on to the condition which determined that situation, viz., the loss of object. It is the absence of the mother that is now the danger, and as soon as that danger arises the infant gives the signal of anxiety, before the dreaded economic situation has set in.* (ibid.: 137–138)

The progress which the child makes in the course of his or her development means that the content of the danger-situation changes. In the phallic stage, fear of losing the maternal object is transformed into castration anxiety. In the following stage appears anxiety with respect to the superego and the fear of losing the love of the superego, while castration anxiety develops into moral and social anxiety. Freud points out that all these anxiety situations can persist side by side in later life and cause the ego to react to them with anxiety. He concludes this chapter by stating that castration anxiety is not the sole motive force behind neurosis; women, for example, have a castration *complex* but do not experience castration *anxiety*, because there can be no fear of losing something which one does not possess. In women, he says, the danger-situation which is the most effective in arousing anxiety is indeed loss of the object, though here a slight modification is required: "*It is no longer a matter of feeling the want of, or actually losing the object itself, but of losing the object's love*" (ibid.: 143).

- *The neurotic patient and the normal individual*

In the course of development, certain determinants of anxiety are relinquished, such as infantile anxiety about being left alone in the dark or in the presence of some unknown person. Some anxieties do persist, perhaps in a modified form, all through one's existence – such as castration anxiety or anxiety involving the superego. In these cases, neurotics differ from normal persons in that their reactions to the dangers in question are unduly strong and they behave as if the earlier danger-situations were still very much active. In addition, being an adult affords no absolute protection against a return of the original traumatic situation which proved conducive to arousing anxiety. "*Each individual has in all probability a limit beyond which his mental apparatus fails in its function of mastering the quantities of excitation which required to be disposed of*" (ibid.: 148).

- *Three factors at the origin of neurosis*

Freud goes on to discuss why some people manage to overcome the affect of anxiety while others fail to do so. He begins by rejecting two attempts to explain this, one suggested by Adler, the other by Rank. For Freud, Adler's explanation is too simplistic: failure to master anxiety is due to some organic weakness in the individual concerned. As for the theory expounded by Rank in *The Trauma of Birth* (1924), attributing the ultimate cause of anxiety to the experience of birth, Freud feels that it does not give a satisfactory explanation of the onset of neurosis, though he does appreciate the attempt that Rank made.

Freud concentrates next on showing that *quantitative* factors are what determine a possible neurotic outcome, even though these elements are not directly observable. Three main factors are prominent in the causation of the neuroses. The first is biological and has to do with the fact that the offspring of the human species has an initially long period of helplessness and dependence. For this reason, "*[the] biological factor [. . .] establishes the earliest situations of danger and creates the need to be loved which will accompany the child throughout the rest of its life*" (ibid.: 155). The second factor is phylogenetic and is due to the fact that, in human beings, sexual life does not develop in one movement from birth to maturity but in two phases, the second of which occurs at puberty. Freud attributes this to the fact that "*something momentous must have occurred in the vicissitudes of the human species which has left behind this interruption in the sexual development of the individual as a historical precipitate*" (ibid.: 155). This element seems to influence the ego into treating the drive-related demands of infantile sexuality as dangers – hence the risk of regression and repression. "*It is here that we come upon the most direct aetiology of the neuroses*" (ibid.: 155). The third factor is psychological and has to do with a defect in our mental apparatus: the ego can defend itself from the danger represented by drive impulses only "*by restricting its own organization and by acquiescing in the formation of symptoms in exchange for having impaired the instinct*" (ibid.: 156).

- ## *Addenda*

In the "Addenda", Freud deals with some complementary issues which remained to be clarified. In the first of these, he discusses the modifications he makes to his earlier views, in particular by the introduction of his new theory of anxiety in which the ego has a role to play in danger-situations. Thus it is not repression as such which generates anxiety; the ego sets up defences in order to avoid the emergence of anxiety. Also, Freud deems it helpful "*to revert to the old concept of 'defence'*" (ibid.: 163); this implies that repression no longer has pride of place, it is one defence mechanism among others. He notes also that "*the resistance that has to be overcome in analysis proceeds from the ego, which clings to its anticathexes*" (ibid.: 159).

However, it is in the second and third of these "Addenda" that Freud sheds a decisive light on anxiety. In "Addendum B", he discusses first the difference between realistic anxiety and neurotic anxiety, the latter being out of all proportion to the actual danger encountered. He distinguishes between physical helplessness (*Hilflosigkeit*) when faced with a real danger and psychological helplessness when the danger is drive-related. A state of helplessness may give rise to a *traumatic situation*, but this in turn has to be distinguished from a *danger-situation*. When the individual becomes able to foresee a danger-situation and to prepare for it, instead of waiting passively until it arrives, this denotes an important advance in the capacity for self-protection. In this situation of expectation – the danger-situation – the ego can send out a "*signal of anxiety*". "*The signal announces: 'I am expecting a situation of helplessness to set in,' or: 'The present situation reminds me of one of the traumatic experiences I have had before'*" (ibid.: 166). The shift from passivity to activity is similar to what children attempt to achieve through play – by reproducing distressing impressions, they try to master them. "*But what is of decisive importance is the first displacement of the anxiety-reaction from its origin in the situation of helplessness to an expectation of that situation, that is, to the danger-situation*" (ibid.: 167). It is on this basis that Freud moves from a biological theory of the origins of anxiety to one which involves what goes on in the mind.

In "Addendum C", Freud defines in more detail the differences between anxiety, pain and mourning. Starting with the anxiety an infant experiences when in the presence of a stranger, Freud notes that it is not only anxiety that the child feels but also pain.

> *Certain things seem to be joined together in [the infant] which will later on be separated out. It cannot as yet distinguish between temporary absence and permanent loss. As soon as it loses sight of its mother it behaves as if it were never going to see her again.* (ibid.: 169)

Repeated experiences of reassurance will enable the infant to learn that the mother's disappearance is usually followed by her reappearance, and this helps to diminish his or her anxiety. "*In these circumstances [the infant] can, as it were, feel longing unaccompanied by despair*" (ibid.: 170). Freud adds that the situation in which the infant feels anxiety at the mother's absence is a traumatic one if, at the time, there is some need or other which the mother ought to be satisfying. The situation turns into one of danger if that need is not present at the given moment. "*Thus, the first determinant of anxiety, which the ego itself introduces, is loss of perception of the object (which is equated with loss of the object itself). There is as yet no question of loss of love*" (ibid.: 170). Freud then goes on to summarize his argument: "*Pain is thus the actual reaction to loss of object, while anxiety is the reaction to the danger which that loss entails and, by a further displacement, a reaction to the danger of the loss of object itself*" (ibid.: 170). He argues also that at birth, the infant cannot experience absence of the mother, because, says Freud, no object as yet exists, so that none can be missed. He closes this chapter and the book with some thoughts on pain and mourning. He draws an analogy between the economic situation which arises when pain is felt at the loss of an object, and that created by physical pain concentrated on the injured part of the body. Mourning, he says, occurs under the influence of reality-testing; the pain which arises here comes from the individual's need to separate from an object which no longer exists.

Post-Freudians

Separation anxiety and anxiety over loss of the object in the clinical work of psychoanalysis

Innovative Freudian concepts which were not immediately accepted

Some of the ideas which Freud discussed in *Inhibitions, Symptoms and Anxiety* in 1926 were accepted, some were ignored, and some were quite simply rejected (Kris 1956; Bowlby 1973). Various reasons were put forward by those who played down the value of his new approach to the origins of anxiety. Laplanche (1980), for example, argues that Freud paid too much attention to reality in his attempts, from 1926 onwards, to modify his previous hypotheses on the origins of anxiety, and in so doing he more or less neglected the part played by drive-related impulses. For psychoanalysts of the Lacanian current of thought, separation anxiety, anxiety over object loss and the affect of mourning do not belong to what they call the "Symbolic" register but to the "Real" one. Consequently, as far as these psychoanalysts are concerned, such concepts cannot be analysed. Lacanian psychoanalysts feel that the modifications Freud introduced in 1926 are unhelpful, and they focus exclusively on castration anxiety; their work of reference on the subject is Freud's "The 'Uncanny' " (1919h). I would emphasize, however, that not too much should be read into the fact that Freud himself played down the value of *Inhibitions, Symptoms and Anxiety* just after the book was published: Freud always tended to be somewhat dismissive of any new text he wrote, usually in the immediate aftermath of its publication – he did the same, for example, with *The Ego and the Id* (1923b) just after it was published. Whatever doubts some psychoanalysts may have about *Inhibitions, Symptoms and Anxiety*, in my opinion the book amounts to much more than speculative theorizing: it is a significant attempt to think deeply about clinical phenomena which we encounter in our everyday psychoanalytic practice, phenomena which must undoubtedly have intrigued Freud himself.

Separation anxiety in various object-relations theories

In the course of the decades that followed, the ideas which Freud put forward in this book gave rise to a number of highly significant contributions, mainly from psychoanalysts interested in the early stages of infantile development and in the vicissitudes of anxiety concerning separation and loss in the context of object relations theory (Manzano 1989). Even though phenomena relating to anxiety concerning separation from and loss of the object occur in varying degrees in all analysands at one point or another in the course of their psychoanalytic treatment, the first psychoanalysts to evince any real interest in them were those who worked with children or with narcissistic or psychotic patients. Let us take a closer look at the more important of these developments.

For Klein, separation anxiety is to be understood in the context of her own conception of object relations and theory of anxiety. She argues that the infant's first anxiety is the fear of being annihilated by the death drive; it is for this reason that the drive is projected on to the external world and creates the fantasy of the bad object threatening the self from the outside. On this point, it should be noted that Klein's description of the fear of annihilation is not unlike the first danger-situation experienced by the ego in Freud's 1926 text: the fear of being overwhelmed by an excessively strong and uncontrollable excitation. Klein argues that, in the course of his or her development, every child experiences situations of separation and loss which may give rise to two kinds of anxiety: *persecutory anxiety*, in which the self feels threatened with annihilation by the bad object – this is typical of the paranoid-schizoid position; and *depressive anxiety*, characterized by the fear of having damaged the object and therefore of losing it – this kind of anxiety belongs to the depressive position. According to Klein, weaning is the prototype of all later losses. As the infant continues to develop, these losses are experienced less and less in terms of persecutory attacks and more and more in a depressive mode – so that, in later life, every loss reactivates depressive feelings. In the analytical situation, reactions to separation are seen by Klein to be a re-awakening of paranoid and depressive anxieties. Consequently, Kleinian and post-Kleinian analysts attach particular importance to a detailed analysis of the patient's fantasies as well as of the drive-related impulses and defences which emerge within the transference situation (J-M. Quinodoz 1991).

The connection between anxiety and separation does not appear in Anna Freud's initial work, but she dealt with the question as soon as she saw infants being separated from their parents during the war (A. Freud and Burlingham 1943). In her later writings, she discusses the problem of separation anxiety in children both theoretically and clinically, and describes the different ways in which anxiety can be expressed in the child's early years – for example, separation anxiety – each of these modalities being typical of a particular stage in the development of object relations (A. Freud 1965). Anna Freud was particularly interested in patients' responses to interruptions in their analysis, because they illustrated the developmental stage the child had reached, as well as the phase at which regression would be at its maximum; these responses also shed light on the patient's mental organization. For example, if the stage of object permanence has not been reached, the child cannot attribute any meaningful role to the analyst in his or her internal world.

René Spitz did a great deal of work on the consequences of separation, based for the most part on observing situations of loss and separation with respect to the actual object. The conclusions he drew for the mental development of both children and adults are close to the model proposed by Anna Freud. Spitz was particularly interested in the kind of anxiety which appears towards the eighth month of life – "stranger anxiety": the infant reacts to the absence of the mother when he or she perceives the face of an unknown person. He emphasized also what he called "anaclitic depression" which occurs whenever an infant is separated prematurely from his or her mother: deprived of the mother, the infant can no longer develop either physically or psychologically – sometimes in fact, the child may even regress to the point of letting him- or herself die (Spitz 1957, 1965).

For Winnicott (1958), any disturbance of "primitive emotional development" – such as a massive separation anxiety – would be an indication of some failure or other in the early mother–infant relationship during the first months of the infant's life. He argued that the primary development of infants depends entirely on mothering ("holding"), and went on to describe the maturational process which gradually enables the infant to acquire the "capacity to be alone". Progressively, the facilitating environment which supports the ego is introjected, so that the infant acquires a capacity to be truly alone, even though unconsciously there is always some internal presence which represents the mother and the care she gives to her child (Winnicott 1958).

For Margaret Mahler, separation anxiety occurs quite naturally in child development towards the end of the symbiotic period, i.e. quite late on in infancy when, at around twelve to eighteen months the struggle for individuation begins (Mahler et al. 1975). Mahler draws a distinction between biological and psychological birth; the latter, which she calls the process of separation-individuation, is a later development. Though the more decisive stages of separation-individuation take place in early childhood, that conflict situation is revived throughout life; every new life cycle reactivates anxiety involving the perception of separateness and calls into question one's sense of identity.

For every psychoanalyst who thinks deeply about the problem of anxiety – especially the kind of anxiety which involves separation from and loss of the object – John Bowlby's (1969, 1973, 1980) seminal writings remain an authoritative guide, even though the conclusions he drew may well be debatable from a strictly psychoanalytic point of view. His idea was to put aside all contradictions and controversies and to propose a new theory which, in his view, would serve as a common denominator for all the theories which he had himself consulted. For Bowlby, attachment is an instinctive behaviour: the infant becomes attached not necessarily to the person who feeds but to the one with whom he or she has most interaction; development of attachment towards the mother depends on whether or not mother and infant manage to achieve some kind of mutual understanding. It should not be forgotten, all the same, that some fundamental psychoanalytic concepts have no place in Bowlby's theorizations: drives, defences, unconscious fantasies, infantile experiences being reproduced in adult life in the transference situation, etc. That said, the questions Bowlby raised have at least had the merit of inciting other psychoanalysts to take interest in a major issue which, before he put forward any ideas of his own, had been insufficiently explored.

New concepts

Anxiety as signal – automatic anxiety – castration anxiety – danger-situation – defences – helplessness (Hilflosigkeit) – isolation – mourning (affect) – object loss – pain – repression – separation – separation anxiety – traumatic situation – undoing what has been done

THE FUTURE OF AN ILLUSION
(1927c)
THE QUESTION OF LAY ANALYSIS
(1926e)

A profession of faith in science

Between 1926 and 1930, Freud published three books in which he discussed, from a psychoanalytic point of view, various aspects of society and civilization.

In *The Future of an Illusion* (1927c), Freud, taking as his model Christianity as practised in the West, argues that religion is based on the need for illusion which is felt by all human beings in their attempt to protect themselves from the dangers of their existence. He again states that religion is "*a universal obsessional neurosis*" (1907b: 126) and as such ought to be given up, just as children relinquish their infantile neurosis as they progress in their development. Freud placed his hopes in the primacy of science as *the* factor which could facilitate humankind's evolution to maturity. In this book, he dialogues with an imaginary person – it is not difficult, however, to recognize Freud's Swiss friend and correspondent the Protestant clergyman Oskar Pfister – to whom Freud declares his unwavering faith in science: "*No, our science is no illusion*" (1927c: 56). Pfister plays an important role not only as a clergyman in *The Future of an Illusion* but also as a lay (i.e. non-medical) analyst in *The Question of Lay Analysis*.

The Question of Lay Analysis (1926e) constitutes Freud's contribution to the debate on an issue which, at the time, was causing considerable dissension in the psychoanalytic world: should the practice of psychoanalysis continue to be open to non-doctors – Freud's position from the very beginning, and the one he supports in this little book – or should it be restricted only to those practitioners who are also physicians?

I shall discuss in the next chapter the third book of Freud's trilogy, *Civilization and its Discontents* (1930a).

Biographies and history
Freud and Judaism

Freud was born into a Jewish family which, though not particularly observant, did follow certain Jewish traditions such as the main religious festivals. Very early on in life he found himself surrounded not only by many forms of culture and various languages but also by several religious influences. At birth, he had been given a Jewish first name, Shlomo, as well as a Christian one, Sigismund, later shortened to Sigmund. In addition, he was looked after, for at least some of the time, by his "Nanya", who was a devout Catholic. Throughout his life he remained faithful to his Jewish identity; in "An Autobiographical Study" (Freud 1925d [1924]: 7) he wrote: "*My parents were Jews, and I have remained a Jew myself*". For many years he was a regular attender at B'nai B'rith Society meetings. Although he saw himself as a non-religious Jew, like his parents, Freud acknowledged that there were close ties between Judaism and psychoanalysis, in particular as regards the Talmudic way of thinking. When C. G. Jung joined the psychoanalytic movement, Freud was relieved at the idea that, by welcoming non-Jews into its ranks, psychoanalysis could no longer be seen merely as an offshoot of Judaism in a society in which, at the time, anti-Semitism was pervasive.

The point of view of "an infidel Jew" psychoanalyst on religion

On several occasions, Freud, who described himself as *"an infidel Jew"*, discussed the question of the relationship between religion and psychoanalysis. His approach to religion, however, could well be seen as more anthropological than theological. This is Odon Vallet's opinion, for example; according to him, Freud considered the question of religion principally as a fact of civilization; the discussion of dogma was less important to him than the grip religion had on society and on individuals (Vallet 2002: 1432). However, though Freud refrained from taking a stand on theological issues, this could not prevent him from declaring on several occasions that he was an atheist, as in "A Religious Experience" (1928a) where he replies to a letter from a young American doctor recounting his mystical experience. In an earlier article on "Obsessive Actions and Religious Practices" (1907b), Freud had already drawn a parallel between the rituals of the obsessional neurotic and the ceremonial of religious rites. He again took up the question of religion in *Totem and Taboo* (1912–1913), then in *Group Psychology and the Analysis of the Ego* (1921c), in which he described the Church as one prototype of an artificial group. He would once more discuss the issue of religion in *Moses and Monotheism* (1939a [1934–1938]).

When Freud wrote *The Future of an Illusion* in 1927, he was no doubt driven by an internal need and by the wish to respond to the religious interrogations of the French writer Romain Rolland. In 1919, Rolland had written a poem called "Liluli" – an onomatopoeic rendering of "illusion" – which he dedicated "to the destroyer of illusions, Prof. Dr. Freud". Freud replied, choosing a title for his book which was evocative of "Liluli". Romain Rolland had written also about religious feelings which he likened to an *"oceanic feeling"*, a topic which Freud went on to discuss in *Civilization and its Discontents* (1930a). The impact of *The Future of an Illusion* was such that, as soon as it was published, it raised a storm of controversy. Freud's friend, the Protestant clergyman from Zurich, Oskar Pfister, wrote a strongly-worded rebuttal of Freud's arguments in "The Illusion of the Future" (Pfister 1928), in which he pointed out that Freud was confusing religion with faith.

Freud and the Rev. Pfister

Oskar Pfister (1873–1956) was a Protestant clergyman and educationalist who lived in Zurich. He was a faithful friend of Freud's for over thirty years, and the two men wrote regularly to each other. Pfister came across Freud's work in 1908 thanks to C. G. Jung and Eugen Bleuler, and he began immediately to apply psychoanalytic ideas to educational issues as well as to his role as spiritual adviser. In particular, he defended the idea that spiritual treatment could be enhanced by Freudian theories and that the role of a Minister of the Church who had felt his own thinking to have been enlightened by psychoanalysis was to help patients resolve their neurosis so that they might acknowledge the value of Christian beliefs. This is what Jones says about the close friendship between the two:

> *Freud was very fond of Pfister. He admired his high ethical standards, his unfailing altruism and his optimism concerning human nature. Probably it also amused him to think he could be on unrestrainedly friendly terms with a Protestant clergyman, to whom he could address letters as "Dear Man of God" and on whose tolerance toward "an unrepentant heretic" – as he described himself – he could always count.* (Jones 1953–1957, II: 48)

Pfister was one of the pioneers of psychoanalysis in Switzerland. He began by joining the Zurich Psychoanalytical Association founded by Jung, then took Freud's side in the quarrel which led to the latter's break-up with Jung in 1913. In 1919, he was one of the founder members of the Swiss Psychoanalytical Society.

Some years later, dissension broke out within the young society over the practice of psychoanalysis by non-doctors, as well as the question of shortened psychoanalysis in which the patient's transference and resistances were not worked through; this technique had been introduced by Pfister in the pioneering days (Weber 2002: 1662). Thereupon, a group of medical practitioners founded the Swiss Medical Society of Psychoanalysis, from which all non-doctors, including Pfister, were banned. He remained, however – in spite of of his somewhat unorthodox ways and Freud's disapproval of shortened analyses – a member of the Swiss Psychoanalytical Society. As to the close links between *The Future of an Illusion* and *The Question of Lay Analysis*, one could do worse than quote the following extract from the letter Freud wrote to Pfister on 25 November 1928 (Freud and Pfister [1963a]):

> *I do not know if you have detected the secret link between the* "Lay Analysis" *and the* "Illusion". *In the former I wish to protect analysis from the doctors and in the latter from the priests. I should like to hand it over to a profession of* "lay" *curers of souls who need not be doctors and should not be priests.*

Discovering the texts

- **THE FUTURE OF AN ILLUSION (1927c)**

Page numbers are those of *The Standard Edition of the Complete Psychological Works of Sigmund Freud*, vol. **21**, 1–56.

- *Ethical values for the protection of civilization*

In the first two chapters of the book, Freud shows how necessary it is for civilization to call upon high moral standards if it is to protect itself against the destructive tendencies of the individuals who compose it. Among these ethical standards – what he calls the *"mental assets of civilization"* (1927c: 10) – Freud includes psychological values, cultural ideals, art, and religious ideas. Before discussing the question of religion *stricto sensu*, Freud gives us a panoramic sketch of the stages in the development of civilization in order to demonstrate that, little by little, humans learned to dominate Nature and to organize the distribution of such wealth as came into human hands. Every civilization demands that its members suppress some of their instinctual needs and make sacrifices for the common good. As a result, at one point, it inevitably comes up against the hostility of its members; it is for this reason, writes Freud, that *"[it] seems [. . .] that every civilization must be built up on coercion and renunciation of instinct"* (ibid.: 7). In order to protect civilization from the rebellious and destructive tendencies present in all men, it is not enough to distribute society's wealth equitably and have recourse to coercion; it is necessary to use every possible means to reconcile individuals to civilization and provide some compensation for the sacrifices imposed on them. Among these means, the psychological advances of mankind have enabled external coercion gradually to become internalized, thanks in particular to the establishment of the superego. Though civilization may have succeeded in keeping more or less under control such primitive instincts as incest, cannibalism and killing, many more still remain untamed – and for these, coercion is the only way to keep them in check.

> *Here we observe with surprise and concern that a majority of people obey the cultural prohibitions on these points only under the pressure of external coercion – that is, only where that coercion can make itself effective and so long as it is to be feared.* (ibid.: 11)

As a result, it is impossible to rely solely on the moral standards of human beings. Other means of raising the ethical level of the members of any given society are the cultural ideals of that civilization: they serve as an example, and the satisfaction which they offer to participants in the culture is of a narcissistic nature – and this in turn counterbalances their hostility to the civilization to which they belong. Art is the third means suggested by Freud for reconciling human beings to the sacrifices they must make – art offers substitutive satisfactions for these, because it brings to mind in an impressive manner the ideals of the given culture. However, the moral values which are by far the most important for maintaining civilization, says Freud, are its religious ideas in the widest sense.

• *The birth of religious ideas*

In what does the particular value of religious ideas lie? Freud invites us to imagine the chaos which would ensue were we to remove all instinctual prohibitions and allow mankind to return to a state of nature. "*[The] principal task of civilization, its actual* raison d'etre, *is to defend us against nature*" (ibid.: 15). Yet civilization succeeds in doing this only to a limited extent; it does not afford us shelter from natural catastrophes or from the riddle of death, and this in itself brings to our mind our weakness and our helplessness. How did primitive humans react when faced with the forces of nature and destiny? The first step was to humanize natural phenomena and consider them to be supermen – by turning them into supernatural beings, into gods. According to Freud, this response has its source in the young infant's helplessness: the child sees in his or her parents (and especially in the father) omnipotent beings who are both protective and feared.

In the course of time, human beings came to realize that the gods could not be expected to protect them from the inevitable dangers which nature and destiny held in store for them. It became the task of the gods to attend to the sufferings of humankind and to preserve the precepts of civilization. Religious ideas, then, would seem to be born of the need to help human beings tolerate the distress they feel when faced with the dangers threatened by nature and destiny and with the damage which human society wreaks. "*Here is the gist of the matter. Life in this world serves a higher purpose; no doubt it is not easy to guess what that purpose is, but it certainly signifies a perfecting of man's nature*" (ibid. 18). Thus "*an intelligence superior to us*" looks after our destiny and a "*benevolent Providence*" watches over us. Life after death continues life on earth and brings us perfection and ideals. The idea of God, writes Freud, is based on the child's relationship with his or her father. Freud points out that for the moment he is exploring simply "*the final form taken by our present-day white Christian civilization*" (ibid.: 20), leaving aside all other kinds of religion.

• *The role of infantile helplessness*

Freud continues his investigation with the help of an unnamed "*opponent*" – it is not difficult to recognize the figure of Oskar Pfister – and the two men initiate an imaginary dialogue. Freud hears his opponent ask why he replaced the animal god at the origin of totemism by a god with a human face. In his reply, Freud uses the idea of the helplessness of the child, a notion he had introduced in 1926 in *Inhibitions, Symptoms and Anxiety*. It is his or her physical and mental helplessness which makes the infant turn for help and protection first to the mother, then to the father; as for the latter, however, "*[the child] fears him no less than it longs for him and admires him*" (ibid.: 24). For Freud, it is the child's feeling of helplessness and distress which lie at the heart of religion.

• *The lack of proof*

How are we to define religious ideas, asks Freud, i.e. assertions about facts concerning external or internal reality "*which lay claim to one's belief*" (ibid.: 25)? According to Freud, though religious ideas are of the highest importance for our cultural heritage, they are paradoxically founded on the shakiest of evidence: we can hardly accept as sufficient proof the argument according to which our ancestors believed in them or that they have been handed down from time immemorial. Nor can we have recourse to the *credo quia absurdum* of the Fathers of the Church, which carries the meaning that religious doctrine lies above reason and that its truth must be felt inwardly. Also, if it is dependent on a personal inner experience, what concern is that to the majority of people? "*If one man has gained an unshakeable conviction of the true reality of religious doctrines from a state of ecstasy which has deeply moved him, of what significance is that to others?*" (ibid.: 28). How then have religious ideas managed to exert such tremendous influence on humankind independently of reason and "*in spite of their incontrovertible lack of authentication*" (ibid.: 29)?

- ### *Religious ideas are illusions*

Freud draws the conclusion from all this that religious ideas are illusions, that is fulfilments of the strongest and most urgent wishes of humankind. These wishes are based on our helplessness as children and our anxiety when faced with the dangers of life: these fears are soothed by the idea that there exists a benevolent Providence, justice and life after death. Freud, however, has no intention of offending either his imaginary opponent or the reader; he makes it clear that an illusion is not the same thing as an error or a hallucination. An illusion is a distortion derived from human wishes and is not necessarily in contradiction with reality, as hallucinations are. In the last resort, it is one's personal attitude which decides whether any given belief is an illusion or a delusional idea. Freud makes it clear that "*[to] assess the truth-value of religious doctrines does not lie within the scope of the present inquiry*" (ibid.: 33), though he does indirectly express his doubts when he says that it is all the same surprising that the idea of a God who created the world, of benevolent Providence, of a moral order in the universe and of an after-life corresponds so closely to our own wishes as well as to those of our ancestors.

- ### *And if humankind were to lose its religious illusion . . . ?*

Freud's imaginary opponent counters these arguments by saying that if religious beliefs are really illusions, as Freud claims, it could be dangerous to reveal the fact to other people: it would rob them of this support and consolation without having anything to offer them in exchange. Freud retorts that there is no danger of a devout believer's being convinced by such arguments as Freud's. Indeed, says Freud, the one person who could be harmed by publishing such views is Freud himself – and, by the same token, psychoanalysis: " '*Now we see,*' they will say, '*where psycho-analysis leads to. The mask has fallen; it leads to a denial of God and of a moral ideal, as we always suspected*' " (ibid.: 36). Freud, however, is prepared to weather this particular storm. It is true, he admits, that religion has contributed much to preserve civilization over the centuries, but now that it no longer has such a powerful influence over people as it used to, civilization itself is in danger, particularly because of the increasing development of scientific thinking. That said, if there is a threat to civilization, it does not come from scientists or other educated people, but from the great mass of the uneducated and those who are dissatisfied with civilization. One day, of course, they will discover that people do not believe in God. "*Thus either these dangerous masses must be held down most severely and kept most carefully away from any chance of intellectual awakening, or else the relationship between civilization and religion must undergo a fundamental revision*" (ibid.: 39).

- ### *Religion: the universal obsessional neurosis*

In this section, Freud argues that religious ideas are not only wish-fulfilments but also historical reminiscences which have to do with the father of the primal horde who, after his killing, was transformed into the figure of God. Developing his phylogenetic hypothesis, Freud suggests that religion is the equivalent of the neurosis which can be observed in all children in the early years of life, a neurosis which usually disappears in the course of the child's development. From a historical point of view, religion is a residue of the neurosis of prehistoric times. "*Religion would thus be the universal obsessional neurosis of humanity; like the obsessional neurosis of children, it arose out of the Oedipus complex, out of the relation to the father*" (ibid.: 43). It is for this reason that, by analogy with the infantile neurosis which gradually disappears in the course of a child's development, religion also must inevitably fade away; this, adds Freud, is the developmental phase in which we find ourselves at present.

• *The harmful influence of religious teaching*

The doctrines of religion are taught to children while they are still very young, and it is to a considerable extent for this reason that their sexual – and, therefore, intellectual – development is weakened. Further, religious doctrines are imposed on children at an age when they themselves have no interest in such matters. This is particularly true of women who in general, according to Freud, *"are said to suffer from 'physiological feeble-mindedness' – that is, from a lesser intelligence than men"* (ibid.: 48). He is all the same careful to cast doubt on this assertion. *"The fact itself is disputable and its interpretation doubtful."* Nonetheless, because of the religious prohibitions against showing interest in sexual life, women do suffer from *"intellectual atrophy [. . .] of a secondary nature."* Freud wants to see the introduction of non-religious education in order to do away with psychological inhibitions. When his imaginary opponent asks him why he is publishing this book, Freud replies that it is to encourage human beings not to remain as children all their lives and dare to step out into *"hostile life"*. His hope is that science and the primacy of the intellect will help mankind to stand up to the test.

• *No, science is not an illusion*

In the final chapter of the book, Freud replies to the objections raised by his imaginary opponent: he is no mere dreamer, nor has he let himself be carried away by his own illusions. On the contrary, says Freud: he has high hopes in the primacy of the intellect and in scientific thinking, even though the day may yet be far off before such conditions prevail.

> *We believe that it is possible for scientific work to gain some knowledge about the reality of the world, by means of which we can increase our power and in accordance with which we can arrange our life. If this belief is an illusion, then we are in the same position as you. But science has given us evidence by its numerous and important successes that it is no illusion.* (ibid.: 55)

In his penultimate paragraph, Freud reasserts his faith in the constant evolution of science, before concluding: *"No, our science is not an illusion. But an illusion it would be to suppose that what science cannot give us we can get elsewhere"* (ibid.: 56).

Post-Freudians

The relationship between faith, religion and psychoanalysis: some controversial issues

As soon as it was published, *The Future of an Illusion* sparked off a heated debate which continues to this day, with points of view which are diametrically opposed to one another. I cannot deal with these issues in detail, but I shall at least give some indication of the controversy concerning the relationship between psychoanalysis and religion, a topic I shall come back to when I discuss *Moses and Monotheism* (Freud 1939a).

The first to object strongly to Freud's point of view as expressed in *The Future of an Illusion* was the Protestant (Lutheran) clergyman, the Rev. Oskar Pfister, from Zurich – no doubt Freud's *"imaginary opponent"* in the book, though Freud does not say so explicitly. The particular significance of the debate between Pfister and Freud lies in the fact that their arguments already contain the main topics which would continue to be discussed in the years to come. Pfister criticizes Freud for focusing exclusively on the pathological aspects of religious practices rather than on the phenomenon of religion as a whole. Both men have sharply opposing views on a number of issues; for Freud, psychoanalysis and religion are completely opposed to each other, while Pfister sees in psychoanalysis a possibility for believers to improve their faith. Freud sees in religion an expression of the immaturity of human beings, while, for Pfister, religion is one of the highest ideals humankind possesses.

The Roman Catholic Church was immediately suspicious of Freud's views and showed open hostility towards them; already in 1905, with the publication of *Three Essays on the Theory of Sexuality* (Freud 1905d), the Church condemned what it considered to be Freud's pan-sexualism. Later, after the Bolshevik revolution, the Church considered Freudianism to be every bit as dangerous as Marxism, since both doctrines represented a threat to the existence of the family. Though clearly hostile to Freud's ideas, especially after the publication of *The Future of an Illusion*, the Catholic Church did not issue any official ban on psychoanalysis; its disapproval was made known mainly by individual priests, such as the repeated criticism expressed by Father W. Schmidt in the 1930s, or through the condemnation of individual members such as that of Abbott Oraison in 1955 (one of whose books was placed on the *Index Librorum Prohibitorum*). After the Second Vatican Council, a more open spirit saw the light of day in the 1960s, though a psychoanalytic psychotherapy group experience in the Cuernavaca monastery in Mexico led to the monastery's being closed down; the majority of the monks had decided to get married. Though Pope Paul VI condemned the experiment, he nonetheless adopted an attitude of hostile neutrality towards Freudianism; this attitude was henceforth to be the credo of a Church which respected the secularization of knowledge (Roudinesco and Plon 1997: 241).

Are all psychoanalysts atheists?

Ever since *The Future of an Illusion* and in spite of the fact that the International Psychoanalytical Association (IPA) gives its members complete freedom as far as religious matters are concerned, there is a widespread belief that all psychoanalysts are atheists, as Freud was. Though it is no doubt true that this notion is one of the many preconceived ideas that people tend to have about psychoanalysts, the latter have done little to counteract that belief – on the contrary: it could be said that it is almost quite fashionable for a psychoanalyst not to deny the presumption even though he or she might not actually make an open display of being an atheist as Freud did.

Only very few psychoanalysts have dared to declare publicly that their Christian faith was compatible with Freud's discoveries and that they were in disagreement with Freud on this issue. In North America, in the 1930s, the Catholic psychoanalyst Gregory Zilboorg took a stand which was quite similar to that of the Rev. Pfister.

> *I venture to say that the time will come when good and courageous Catholics will study psychoanalysis seriously, as seriously as they study the Galilean optics and the heliocentric system, and will find nothing in clinical psychoanalysis that would contradict their religious faith.* (Zilboorg 1942: 419)

In France, Maryse Choisy and Françoise Dolto are among the few psychoanalysts known to have refused to hide the fact of their religious belief. Dolto wrote two books, *L'Evangile au risque de la psychanalyse* [*The Gospel at the Risk of Psychoanalysis*] (Dolto and Séverin 1977–1978) and *La Foi au risque de la psychanalyse* [*Faith at the Risk of Psychoanalysis*] (Dolto 1981), but she had to face much criticism from her colleagues, who felt that her religious faith was the residue of a personal analysis which had not gone deeply enough. "[Laforgue, her analyst] could not have confronted his patient with her desire for Omnipotence that was transformed into Word of God, Symbolic, Subject, Castration, Supreme Principle" (This 2002: 462). Sometimes psychoanalysts have taken it upon themselves to judge some other person's faith, thus failing to show sufficient respect towards the secret part we all of us have inside. I recall a comment made by the French psychoanalyst René Diatkine (Paris) about a Dominican monk at the end of a discussion session between psychoanalysts and Catholic priests: "Father Plé is undoubtedly convinced that he has faith, but he does not realize that, in his unconscious, he is not a believer!"

I think that these elements shed light on what I want to emphasize here, namely that even today it is difficult for psychoanalysts who have learned so much from Freud to put forward an opinion which is completely independent of his concerning their own religious beliefs and those of their patients. In my opinion, though religious faith may sometimes be the expression of a psychopathological disorder, it cannot be seen simply as a neurosis or as a psychosis, as Freud seemed to think; faith is on quite a different level from that of psychoanalysis, both for neurotics and for so-called "normal" people.

- **THE QUESTION OF LAY ANALYSIS: CONVERSATIONS WITH AN IMPARTIAL PERSON (1926e)**

Page numbers are those of *The Standard Edition of the Complete Psychological Works of Sigmund Freud*, vol. **20**, 177–250.

Freud published this little book in 1926 in defence of Theodor Reik who, though a psychoanalyst, was not a medical practitioner; Reik was being prosecuted for illegally practising medicine. From the very beginning, Freud had been in favour of lay analysis – in German, *Laienanalyse* – that is, analysis carried out by a non-medical person. The proceedings against Reik were dropped, but Freud went on to publish his views in the form of a dialogue with an "*impartial*" person. In this book, he argues that, in order to become a psychoanalyst, one must have already been analysed and undergo proper training. He says also that he is not in favour of any attempt to legislate on the issue, since in his view it was an internal question which fell to be dealt with by the profession itself. He goes on to discuss the kind of training most appropriate for a prospective psychoanalyst, arguing that the manner in which universities train doctors – be they general practitioners or psychiatrists – is certainly not suitable. He concludes the book by evoking the kind of psychoanalytic training he would ideally like to see – one which would be dispensed in special colleges of psychoanalysis: "*An ideal, no doubt. But an ideal which can and must be realized. And in our training institutes, in spite of all their youthful insufficiencies, that realization has already begun*" (1926e: 252).

The question of lay analysis, however, quickly became acrimonious because American psychoanalysts, influenced by Abraham Brill, insisted that nobody other than qualified medical practitioners should be allowed to practise psychoanalysis, while their Viennese counterparts, some of whom were not doctors of medicine, agreed with the point of view put forward by Freud.

In preparation for the Innsbruck Congress, Jones carried out a survey among the entire membership of the psychoanalytic community. Some twenty-eight articles by eminent psychoanalysts were received in reply, and these were published in the *Internationale Zeitschrift für Psychoanalyse* and in the *International Journal of Psycho-Analysis*. In his article, Freud reiterated his point of view in favour of psychoanalysis being practised by non-doctors. The Congress debate, which took place in 1927, could not resolve the issue, and it was decided that each society should be free to allow non-doctors to be admitted or to bar them from admission to that society. Many societies adopted Freud's standpoint, but in the United States only medical practitioners were admitted to the American Psychoanalytic Association (APA). It was only after lengthy proceedings were instituted in 1985 – the case was decided in their favour – that some institutes of non-medical psychoanalysts were accepted by the American Psychoanalytic Association and by the International Psychoanalytical Association (IPA).

At the same time as the question of lay analysis was being debated, other issues concerning how psychoanalysts should be trained were also being discussed; differences of opinion on these two highly controversial topics were such that the IPA almost fell apart as the 1920s drew to a close. In 1932, after some arduous discussion, the Wiesbaden Congress decided that each affiliated society should establish its own criteria for selecting prospective candidates, just as had been done for the question of lay analysis. Jones was pleased with the compromise, because he had put a tremendous amount of energy into safeguarding the unity of the psychoanalytic movement. It was a great disappointment for Freud, all the same, because he had hoped that, in his lifetime, he would see all parties reach agreement on the fact that IPA-affiliated societies should adopt the same criteria for selecting prospective candidates for psychoanalytic training.

New concepts

Civilization – helplessness in childhood – illusion – omnipotence of thoughts – religion, religious ideas – science – universal obsessional neurosis

CIVILIZATION AND ITS DISCONTENTS
(1930a)

NEW INTRODUCTORY LECTURES ON PSYCHO-ANALYSIS
(1933a [1932])

A pessimistic view of the human condition or a realistic one?

Civilization and its Discontents is the third and final book of the trilogy which Freud began with *The Question of Lay Analysis* in 1926 and continued with *The Future of an Illusion* in 1927. Freud again declares quite unambiguously that, in his view, the true source of religious feelings is purely secular and rooted in each individual's psychological make-up. After this clear restatement of his atheistic views, Freud embarks on a bold synthesis which takes a fresh look at the fragile equilibrium that human beings build for themselves in a civilization which is intended to protect them but which, paradoxically, may end up destroying them. This equilibrium is quite simply a reflection of the fundamental conflict between the life and death drives, of which Freud is more and more convinced as time goes by. Since civilization restricts the sexual and aggressive impulses of individuals in order to maintain the cohesion of society, it inevitably comes into conflict with individual members of that society; were these individuals to rise up in revolt, civilization could be destroyed. The crux of Freud's argument, however, is that the conflicts which can be observed in external reality between individuals and society have their counterpart in those which occur in the mind of each individual: the conflicts between the demands of the superego (now feared in the same way as external authority was) and the ego, which represents the interests of the individual. For Freud, the unconscious sense of guilt which results from these unconscious conflicts is the source of the "*discontents*" we find in civilized society. It is for this reason too that the human condition is so precarious – human beings have to grapple with the uncertainties of the conflict between their life and death drives and with their own illusions.

Biographies and history

The Great Depression of 1929 and the rise of Nazism in Germany

It was at the suggestion of Romain Rolland, who saw in the "*oceanic feeling*" the *fons et origo* of religion, that, in 1929, Freud began writing *Civilization and its Discontents* during his summer holiday in Berchtesgaden. The book is often seen as a sombre but perspicacious sociological legacy. The somewhat pessimistic tone at the end – especially in the closing paragraph in which Freud discusses the future of mankind now that technical progress makes it possible to exterminate one another to the last man – was soon to show just how right he was. Barely a week before he delivered the manuscript to the publisher on Tuesday, 29 October 1929, the New York Stock Exchange crashed, dragging the Western world into a Great Depression which lasted for several years and brought in its wake bankruptcy, unemployment and extreme poverty. Dated 1930, *Civilization and its Discontents* was an immediate success and without more ado was translated into several languages. One year later, in September

1930, the Nazi party won an overwhelming victory in the elections to the Reichstag, the German parliament, thus opening the way for Hitler's rise to power. These disastrous events prompted Freud to add a final sentence to the 1931 edition of the book; previously he had been suggesting that there might be some hope of a favourable outcome to the struggle between the life and death drives, but now his concluding sentence became: "*But who can foresee with what success and with what result?*" (1930a: 145). In a letter to Arnold Zweig, he made no secret of his pessimistic view: "*We are approaching dark times. I ought not to be concerned about this, with the apathy of old age, but I cannot help pitying my seven grandchildren*" (Letter to Arnold Zweig, 7 December 1930).

The topics Freud discusses in this book had already been outlined in " 'Civilized' Sexual Morality and Modern Nervous Illness" (Freud 1908d) and in "Thoughts for the Times on War and Death" (Freud 1915b), and would later be taken up again in "Why War?" (Freud 1933b [1932]).

"Kultur": civilization or culture?

The terms "*culture*" and "*civilization*", used indiscriminately by Freud in this book and by several of its translators, have given rise to much debate. The way the words are interpreted varies from one translator to another and from one era to another. To give the reader some idea of these discussions, I shall look more closely at the meaning which Freud ascribes to the word "*Kultur*" in this book, a word he uses much more frequently than "*Zivilisation*" (both words, of course, exist in German). Freud had already given a loose definition of what he meant by "*Kultur*" in *The Future of an Illusion*, where he states quite categorically "*I scorn to distinguish between culture and civilization*" (1927c: 6). In *Civilization and its Discontents*, he appears at first sight to use both words indiscriminately, but on closer inspection we see that he does draw a distinction as to the ways in which he uses the term "*Kultur*":

> It [*die Kultur* – translated in the *Standard Edition* as "human civilization"] *includes on the one hand all the knowledge and capacity that men have acquired in order to control the forces of nature and extract its wealth for the satisfaction of human needs, and, on the other hand, all the regulations necessary in order to adjust the relations of men to one another and especially the distribution of the available wealth.* (1927c: 6)

This difference between culture and civilization corresponds to the dictionary definitions of the terms – *culture*: "the arts and other manifestations of human intellectual achievement regarded collectively"; *civilization*: "an advanced stage or system of social development" (*Concise Oxford Dictionary*). The evolution of ideas, especially in philosophy and in the human sciences, has led to the gradual integration of what we used to designate as "culture" into the modern definition of "civilization"; Freud himself appears to have followed this trend. The French translators of the *Complete Works* of Freud have chosen a new title for the book we are discussing in this chapter – *Malaise dans la culture*, rather than the previous *Malaise dans la civilisation*. (See also the "Editor's Note" to *The Future of an illusion, Standard Edition*, vol. 21, 4.)

Discovering the texts

- **CIVILIZATION AND ITS DISCONTENTS (1930a)**

Page numbers are those of *The Standard Edition of the Complete Psychological Works of Sigmund Freud*, vol. **21**, 57–145.

• The "oceanic feeling": a residue of an infantile wish

After the publication of *The Future of an Illusion*, the French author Romain Rolland wrote to Freud saying that he regretted the fact that Freud had not taken into account the *"oceanic feeling"* which he (Rolland) considered to be the subjective source of religious energy and which he himself is never without. *"It is a feeling which he would like to call a sensation of 'eternity', a feeling as of something limitless, unbounded – as it were, 'oceanic'"* (1930a: 64). Freud begins by informing his friend that he himself has never experienced such a feeling, which would appear to correspond to *"a feeling of an indissoluble bond, of being one with the external world as a whole"* (ibid.: 65). It nonetheless gives Freud the opportunity of exploring the psychological origins of such a feeling. Freud discovers these in the infant's early emotional experiences: he says that at the beginning of life the infant cannot differentiate between his or her own ego and the external world; it is the periodic contact with the mother's breast which facilitates the gradual discovery of the existence of an *"object"* which is *"outside"* the infant's own ego. Early experiences of pain and non-satisfaction lead the infant to throw out everything that is a source of unpleasure and to keep inside everything that is a source of pleasure. A pleasure-ego [*Lust-Ich*] is thus created which obeys the pleasure principle and stands against the external world which is governed by the reality principle.

> *In this way, then, the ego detaches itself from the external world. Or, to put it more correctly, originally the ego includes everything, later it separates off an external world from itself. Our present ego-feeling is, therefore, only a shrunken residue of a much more inclusive – indeed, an all-embracing – feeling which corresponded to a more intimate bond between the ego and the world about it.* (ibid.: 68)

For Freud, the limitless sensation characteristic of the oceanic feeling is a survival in adults of the primitive feeling of union which we experience as infants. Can we really claim, he goes on to ask, that this oceanic feeling is to be regarded as the source of religious needs? Freud rejects this point of view, arguing that religious needs are a derivation of the infant's helplessness and the longing for a protective father. Thus in Freud's view the religious feeling described by Romain Rolland is not primary, but secondary to humankind's need to deny the dangers by which the ego feels threatened in the outside world and to the consequent attempt to seek some sort of consolation.

• The purpose of life: the search for happiness and the avoidance of suffering

Freud goes on to remind the reader that, in *The Future of an Illusion* (1927c), he pointed out that the aim of every religious system was to explain the riddle of the universe, to offer reassurance that a benevolent Providence was watching over our life, and to promise that there is indeed a life after death. According to Freud, this conception of the purpose of life is infantile in nature; he regrets the fact that most individuals are unable to go beyond this religious stage, which he sees as a childhood fixation. If we put the aim proposed by religion to one side, what *can* we say about the purpose of life? Freud states that it is the pleasure principle which governs the purpose of life. But if this programme consists simply in striving after happiness, there is no possibility whatsoever of its being carried through. If we do not succeed entirely in this endeavour, however, two avenues remain open to us in our quest for happiness: the search for pleasure, and the avoidance of suffering. The paths which lead there are many and varied, and Freud goes on to discuss a few of them: the quest for unlimited satisfaction of every need, the hermit's voluntary aloofness with respect to other people, intoxicating substances, controlling one's instinctual impulses as prescribed by the wisdom of the Orient, sublimation by means of science, art and the enjoyment of beauty. The result, however, is disappointing, because even love can be a source of distress and suffering. The ultimate refuge is that offered by neurosis or psychosis ... Freud draws the conclusion that the quest for happiness is above all a personal matter. *"There is no golden rule which applies to everyone: every man must find out for himself in what particular fashion he can be saved"* (ibid.: 83). Freud concludes this chapter with an even more severe judgement than he had done in 1927 in *The Future of an Illusion* on the harmful role of religion – in his view, it constitutes a major obstacle to the search for happiness and the avoidance of pain.

Its technique consists in depressing the value of life and distorting the picture of the real world in a delusional manner – which presupposes an intimidation of the intelligence. At this price, by forcibly fixing them in a state of psychical infantilism and by drawing them into a mass-delusion, religion succeeds in sparing many people an individual neurosis. But hardly anything more. (ibid.: 84)

• *Civilization fails to bring the happiness we expect from it*

Why is it so difficult for human beings to be happy? It would seem that civilization itself is one of the reasons for this, since it fails to prevent us from suffering even though it is supposed to protect us against such an eventuality. Civilization does not mean constant progress, because advances in culture and in modern technology have not kept their promises. That is the main reason for the discontent which modern civilized man feels: "*We do not feel comfortable in our present-day civilization*" (ibid.: 89). What, anyway, do we mean by "*civilization*"?

We shall therefore content ourselves with saying once more that the word "civilization" [Kultur in the German text] *describes the whole sum of the achievements and the regulations which distinguish our lives from those of our animal ancestors and which serve two purposes – namely to protect men against nature and to adjust their mutual relations.* (ibid.: 89)

There have been, of course, many advances in science and in culture which can be seen as conquests typical of civilization, but they have not necessarily made human beings any happier. Civilization did, however, take a decisive step forward when society succeeded in imposing on each individual member of it a restriction on his or her instinctive impulses, both sexual and aggressive, in order to preserve the cohesion of the group as a whole. Thus, for Freud, civilization is built upon a renunciation of drive-related impulses, and this "*cultural frustration*" (ibid.: 97) governs social relationships between human beings – while at the same time being the cause of the hostility which individuals feel towards civilization.

• *Family and sexuality: both for and against civilization*

Love, the prototype of happiness from time immemorial, is the foundation of civilization: love is at the origin of the family which unites man and woman and binds the child to his or her parents. The love which founded the family continues to operate in civilization by enabling both genital sexual satisfaction and "*aim-inhibited affection*" (ibid.: 102). This affection, says Freud, is the kind of love which unites members of a family, forms the basis of friendship and creates bonds within the community. But in the course of evolution, conflict inevitably arises between community and family: the former endeavours to bring people together, the latter will not give the individual up. Women play a decisive role in this conflict.

Furthermore, women soon come into opposition to civilization [...]. Women represent the interests of the family and of sexual life. The work of civilization has become increasingly the business of men, it confronts them with ever more difficult tasks and compels them to carry out instinctual sublimations of which women are little capable. (ibid.: 103)

Thus pushed somewhat into the background, women then become hostile towards the demands of civilization. Civilization imposes further important restrictions on sexual life: not only does it restrict the choice of object of the person who has reached genital sexual maturity to someone of the opposite sex, but it also prohibits most extra-genital sexual satisfactions and declares them to be perversions. All that remains is heterosexual genital love, but even this is restricted by further limitations – civilization accepts only monogamy and tolerates sexuality only "*as a means of propagating the human race*" (ibid.: 105). In other words, the sexual life of human beings is very badly treated by civilization, and this diminishes the value of love and sexuality as a source of happiness.

- *The role of aggressiveness: "man is a wolf to man"*

If human beings have so much difficulty in finding happiness, it is because civilization imposes on them the heavy burden of renouncing the satisfaction not only of their sexual drives but also of their aggressive impulses. As Freud points out, *"men are not gentle creatures who want to be loved, and who at the most can defend themselves if attacked"* (ibid.: 111), they are also aggressive creatures. Every human being has a strong tendency to aggress his or her neighbour and will certainly exploit that neighbour if given the chance. Freud reminds us that in Roman times there was a saying *"Homo homini lupus* ['*Man is a wolf to man*']" (ibid.: 111). There is no need to look far afield to observe this aggressive tendency; it lies within each of us.

> *The existence of this inclination to aggression, which we can detect in ourselves and justly assume to be present in others, is the factor which disturbs our relations with our neighbour and which forces civilization into such a high expenditure [of energy]*. (ibid.: 112)

That is why civilization has to put its utmost efforts into setting limits to human beings' aggressive impulses and promulgate ethical standards, if it is not to end up destroyed. For this reason, "*civilized*" morality establishes restrictions on sexuality and advocates an ideal, that of loving one's neighbour as oneself. In spite of these restrictions, however, civilization has never been able to impose an ideal society by law nor to eliminate the enmity that people feel towards their neighbour. Communism is no more than an illusion when it claims, for example, that humans are wholly good. Another illustration is given by the reciprocal hostility that we find in communities which on other levels are very close to each other – inhabitants of the same town, neighbouring countries. Freud calls this "*the narcissism of minor differences*" (ibid.: 114). We can of course hope that changes in civilization will continue to occur in such a way as to satisfy our needs more fully, but we must also realize that "*there are difficulties attaching to the nature of civilization which will not yield to any attempt at reform*" (ibid.: 115).

- *The evolution of civilization: a struggle between life and death drives*

The fact that no civilization can ever make human beings happy has therefore very much to do with human nature itself. In order to explain this, Freud goes back to his second theory of the instinctual drives, in which he emphasized the existence of a fundamental conflict between the life and death drives. Though at the time he put forward that hypothesis somewhat tentatively, he now says quite clearly that he is convinced of the validity of his views: "*in the course of time they had gained such a hold upon me that I can no longer think in any other way*" (ibid.: 119). Applying these views to the process of civilization, Freud draws the conclusion that, in human beings, aggressiveness is a primitive and self-subsisting instinctual disposition and that it constitutes one of the greatest impediments to civilization. The aggressive instinct is a representative of the death instinct which is always at work alongside of Eros.

> *And now, I think, the meaning of the evolution of civilization is no longer obscure to us. It must present the struggle between Eros and Death, between the instinct of life and the instinct of destruction, as it works itself out in the human species. This struggle is what all life essentially consists of*. (ibid.: 122)

- *The superego as the internalization of external authority*

If civilization is threatened by aggressiveness and destructiveness, what means does it have for inhibiting these impulses? According to Freud, the most effective way to do this involves the internalization of aggressiveness – it is sent back from whence it came, via what he calls the superego. The tension thus established between ego and superego is referred to as the "*sense of guilt*" and is expressed as a "*need for punishment*". The sense of guilt derives from two sources: anxiety with respect to the external authority, and anxiety involving the superego. The latter is experienced as a fear of being deprived of the love of the person who is protective. At first, the harshness of the superego has especially to do with the fear of external authority, but later, in the course of development, the external authority is internalized and in this way contributes to the establishment of an individual superego in the mind of the person concerned. Though it may still be possible to hide one's innermost thoughts from an external authority, no one can hide anything from his or her internalized superego. "*In this second situation bad intentions are equated with bad actions, and hence come a sense of guilt and a need for punishment. The aggressiveness of conscience keeps up the aggressiveness of the authority*" (ibid.: 128).

Why is the superego's aggressiveness towards the ego so harsh? According to Freud, the extreme harshness of the superego is the result of the turning back against the self of the child's aggressiveness towards his or her parents.

> *The relationship between the superego and the ego is a return, distorted by a wish, of the real relationships between the ego, as yet undivided, and external object. That is typical, too. But the essential difference is that the original severity of the superego does not – or does not so much – represent the severity which one has experienced from it [the object], or which one attributes to it; it represents rather one's own aggressiveness towards it.* (ibid.: 129–130)

This explains to some extent why there is no direct relationship between the parents' actual severity and that of the superego. "*Experience shows [. . .] that the severity of the superego which a child develops in no way corresponds to the treatment which he himself has met with*" (ibid.: 130). On this point, Freud refers explicitly to Melanie Klein and to other English writers (ibid.: 130, note 1). Both forms of aggressiveness coming from the superego – the fear of the father's punishment and the child's wish for revenge as regards the father – reinforce each other and are complementary. Freud adds that the phylogenetic factor must also be taken into account, because the sense of guilt is strengthened by the terror which the father of the primal horde awakened in his sons, as well as by the remorse the sons felt after killing their father. Subsequently, the original ambivalent conflict is reproduced not only as one between civilization and the individual but also within each individual as the ego's feeling of ambivalence towards the superego – an expression of "*the eternal struggle between the trends of love and death*" (ibid.: 132).

• *Can modern civilization avoid self-destruction?*

Freud's intention in this study is to show that the sense of guilt is the most important problem in the development of civilization; every advance in civilization has to be paid for through a loss of happiness and a heightening of the sense of guilt. This sense of guilt is generally not acknowledged as such: it remains to a large extent unconscious, or "*appears as a sort of* malaise, *a dissatisfaction, for which people seek other motivations*" (ibid.: 135–136). Just as there is an individual superego, there is also, says Freud, a cultural superego (*Kultur-Überich*) which sets up its own strict ideal demands; if these demands are not met, the punishment is "*fear of conscience*" (ibid.: 142). Often these demands are too harsh, particularly when they derive from the ethical code of the community, and produce rebellion or a neurosis in the individual, or make him or her otherwise unhappy. That is why we may wonder whether most civilizations – and possibly the whole of humankind – have become "*neurotic*" because of the process of civilization itself. As to the fate which awaits the future of the human species, Freud acknowledges that he has neither therapeutic solution nor comfort to offer. Leaving the question open, he concludes the book on a somewhat pessimistic note.

> *The fateful question for the human species seems to me to be whether and to what extent their cultural development will succeed in mastering the disturbance of their communal life by the human instinct of aggression and self-destruction. It may be that in this respect precisely the present time deserves a special interest. Men have gained control over the forces of nature to such an extent that with their help they would have no difficulty in exterminating one another to the last man. They know this, and hence comes a large part of their current unrest, their unhappiness and their mood of anxiety.* (ibid.: 145)

> **Post-Freudians**
>
> **From nuclear terror to international terrorism**
>
> *Civilization and its Discontents* was an immediate success and evoked many reactions both in psychoanalytic circles and in the general public. One consequence of its publication was to reopen the debate among psychoanalysts concerning the death drive. In this text, it is no longer simply a hypothesis; Freud speaks of it as something quite obvious and essential. Even some of his closest followers, however, still did not agree with him on this point. For Jones, the move from aggressiveness to the death drive appeared to be an unwarranted generalization, while for Pfister, it was simply a metaphor employed by Freud to designate a vital force.
>
> The possibility that the human species could exterminate itself to the last man evoked by Freud in the final paragraphs of his text has become particularly significant since the development of nuclear weapons. Given this heightened danger, a certain number of psychoanalysts have formed two organizations in order to make their voice heard. One of these is British – Psychoanalysis and the Prevention of Nuclear War (PPNW) – and the other international – International Psychoanalysts Against Nuclear War (IPANW). It is true of course that with the break-up of the Soviet Union and the end of the Cold War, things have changed – but not fundamentally. Among these psychoanalysts, I must mention the stance taken by Hanna Segal, which contributed to ending the silence surrounding the many dangers – not only that of a nuclear holocaust – which threaten our civilization. Her ideas take into account the contribution of psychoanalysis to our understanding of psychosis and of the way in which groups function. "If individuals behaved like groups they would be classified as mad," she writes (Segal 2002). She believes also that during the Cold War the "basic assumption" (in Bion's sense) was that war was impossible because all the protagonists were too afraid that the ensuing destruction would be total.
>
> Nowadays, the quasi-equilibrium which existed between the Soviet bloc and the Western world under the aegis of the United States has collapsed, and the myth of American invincibility was severely undermined on 11 September 2001; the extraordinary anxiety, fear and perhaps sense of guilt which resulted from that event are plain to see. This is what Segal says:
>
>> *I think September 11 was highly symbolic. We have been precipitated into a world of fragmentation, and at points total disintegration and psychotic terror – and also into total confusion: who are our friends? Who are our enemies? From what quarter do we expect aggression? [...] And are there enemies on the inside? [...] This is the most primitive terror in our personal development – not ordinary death, but some vision of personal disintegration imbued with hostility. And the situation is made much worse when God comes into the equation. The fundamentalist Christian longing for Armageddon is now matched by Islamic fundamentalism.* Our sanity is threatened by a delusional inner world of omnipotence and absolute evil and sainthood. Unfortunately, we also have to contend with the God Mammon.* (Segal 2002: 35)
>
> * "Armageddon is God's war to cleanse the earth of all wickedness, paving the way for a bright, prosperous new order" (Segal 1987).

- **NEW INTRODUCTORY LECTURES ON PSYCHO-ANALYSIS (1933a [1932])**

> Page numbers are those of *The Standard Edition of the Complete Psychological Works of Sigmund Freud*, vol. **22**, 1–182.

In 1932, two years after publishing *Civilization and its Discontents*, Freud wrote this supplement to the series of public lectures which he had delivered in 1916 and 1917 in the University of Vienna and which were published under the title *Introductory Lectures on Psycho-Analysis* (1916–1917 [1915–1917]). Just as that first volume of lectures had given Freud the opportunity to look back on psychoanalysis from its beginnings up to 1915, the *New Introductory Lectures* enabled him to bring psychoanalytic theory up to date in the light of the developments which had followed on from the "1920 turning-point". This book, written in 1932, was therefore Freud's way of turning the page – that of a life which was drawing to its close.

In order to emphasize the continuity between the 1916–1917 series of lectures and these new ones published in 1933, Freud carries on the chapter numbering begun in the earlier volume, so that the first chapter of the *New Introductory Lectures* is "Lecture 29". In his preface, Freud informs the reader that his illness had made it impossible for him to deliver the lectures in public as he had previously done; he thus addresses these to an imaginary audience. The 1933 book, however, was of interest to a different readership from that of 1916–1917. In 1932, Freud's readers were already informed of and familiar with his earlier psychoanalytic concepts. This is very similar to our present situation: in order to grasp what is new, the reader must already have a good idea of the chronological development of psychoanalysis, a specialized task which often amounts to making a highly detailed analysis of Freud's writings. Given the limits which I have imposed, I shall do no more than mention the following points. Lecture 29 deals with how Freud's recent concepts of ego, id and superego find their place in his view of the unconscious. From 1933 onwards, the unconscious is no longer an "*agency*" as it was before – the "*Ucs. system*" – but a particular quality: that of not being conscious. It is in this book too that Freud summarizes the aim of psychoanalytic treatment, in an expression which has remained famous: "*Where id was, there ego shall be*" (1933a [1932]: 80) ["*Wo Es war, soll Ich werden*" (*G.W.*, vol. 15, 86)]. In Lecture 33, on "Femininity", Freud emphasizes the role of the young girl's pre-Oedipal attachment to her mother and the importance of the physical (bodily) care which is part of the early relationship with the mother. Freud concludes his essay by admitting that women remain somewhat of an enigma for psychoanalysis.

New concepts

Aggression/aggressiveness – civilization – culture – oceanic feeling – religion, religious ideas – self-destruction – superego (its harshness in children) – superego and civilization

Papers on Denial of Reality and Splitting of the Ego Written between 1924 and 1938

"Neurosis and Psychosis" (1924b)
"The Loss of Reality in Neurosis and Psychosis" (1924e)
"Negation" (1925h)
"Some Psychical Consequences of the Anatomical Distinction between the Sexes" (1925j)
"Fetishism" (1927e)
"Splitting of the Ego in the Process of Defence" (1940e [1938])

AN OUTLINE OF PSYCHO-ANALYSIS
(1940a [1938])

Denial of reality and splitting of the ego: defence mechanisms typical of psychosis, of perversion . . . and even of neurosis

I have brought together in this chapter a certain number of papers written by Freud between 1924 and 1938 which all concern the same themes and bear witness to the development of his thinking on these issues. In this series of papers, Freud attempts to determine what defence mechanisms are specific to psychosis and in what way neurosis differs from psychosis. As his investigation proceeds, we see that, although Freud begins by emphasizing the differences, he subsequently moderates these contrasts. For example, in "Neurosis and Psychosis" (1924b), he says that the ego's relationship with perceived reality in psychosis is diametrically opposed to that in neurosis: in the former case, the perception of reality is rejected, while in the latter it is accepted. Yet in the very next paper he wrote (1924e), he moderates this view and comments that disturbances of the perception of the real world can be found in both disorders, though they are more pronounced in psychosis than in neurosis; it is for this reason that he introduces the idea of "denial of reality" as typically psychotic, thus distinguishing it from neurosis. In the following year, he draws a distinction between *negation* [*Verneinung*] – the refusal to acknowledge a wish which has already been expressed – and *disavowal* (or *denial*) [*Verleugnung*] – the refusal to acknowledge the perception of a reality experienced as traumatic (1925h). According to Freud, the mechanism of denial is particularly helpful when we try to explain the different attitude adopted by boys and by girls with respect to the perception that girls do not possess a penis: the extent of this denial will determine the orientation of the individual's psycho-sexual development (1925j). In a later paper on "Fetishism" (1927e), Freud makes a direct connection between the mechanism of *denial* of the perception that women do not possess a penis and the resultant *splitting of the ego* characteristic of the fetishist: denial and splitting of the ego are thereafter defined by Freud as typical features of the perversions and psychoses, as well as of pathological mourning processes. In 1938, in *An Outline of Psycho-Analysis*, Freud again modifies his position to some extent: although he continues to insist that denial of reality is characteristic of psychosis, he adds that even in this illness the denial is never total, and he argues that splitting of the ego is not specific to perversion and psychosis, because it can be found also in the neuroses and therefore in normal states of mind. In conclusion, we could say that in every individual there is a juxtaposition of two contradictory attitudes; the outcome – i.e. the predominance of a psychosis or of a neurosis – is above all a matter of proportion.

Discovering the texts

- **"NEUROSIS AND PSYCHOSIS" (1924b)**

> Page numbers are those of *The Standard Edition of the Complete Psychological Works of Sigmund Freud*, vol. **19**, 147–153.

In this short paper, Freud incorporates his recent notions of ego, id and superego into his conception of neurosis and psychosis. What differentiates these two pathologies and constitutes their pathogenic effect has to do with the fact that, in neurosis, "*the ego remains true to its dependence on the external world and attempts to silence the id*", whereas in psychosis "*[the ego] lets itself be overcome by the id and thus torn away from reality*" (1924b: 151). Let us examine this statement in more detail.

Taking the example of transference neurosis, Freud considers that the ego comes into conflict with the id because it refuses to accept an undesirable drive-related impulse – the ego defends itself against this impulse by repressing it into the unconscious. But the repressed material struggles against this and re-emerges as a symptom, a substitutive representation. The symptom is therefore the outcome of a compromise.

As for what occurs in psychosis, Freud says that here it is the relationship between the ego and the perception of the external world which is distorted. For example, in acute hallucinatory psychosis, not only is external reality no longer perceived at all, but also the internal world itself, made up of earlier perceptions stored in memory, loses its significance. As a result,

> *[the] ego creates, autocratically, a new external and internal world; and there can be no doubt of two facts – that this new world is constructed in accordance with the id's wishful impulses, and that the motive of this dissociation from the external world is some very serious frustration by reality of a wish – a frustration which seems intolerable*. (ibid.: 151)

For Freud, the precipitating cause of both neurosis and psychosis always involves frustration: "*a frustration, a non-fulfilment, of one of those childhood wishes which are forever undefeated*" (ibid.: 151). This frustration is usually an external one, but it may also derive from the superego, which in the last resort represents the demands of external reality.

Having thus established these points, Freud outlines a new psychopathological entity based on the conflict between ego and superego: the "*narcissistic psycho-neuroses*", the typical example of which is melancholia (depression). The narcissistic psychoneuroses lie half-way between transference neuroses and the psychoses. Neuroses and psychoses both involve conflicts between the ego and the other psychical agencies which come to dominate it – superego and id; it would be interesting to know how the ego can succeed in emerging from these conflicts without succumbing to illness. The outcome undoubtedly depends on some economic factor or other – the trends which are locked in the struggle. Freud goes further and suggests that the ego may be able to avoid collapse "*by deforming itself, by submitting to encroachments on its own unity and even perhaps effecting a cleavage or division of itself*" (ibid.: 152–153). He adds that the "*eccentricities and follies of men*" would thus be treated in the same way as their sexual perversions. What, then, is this mechanism, similar to repression, thanks to which the ego detaches itself from the external world? "*[Such] a mechanism, it would seem, must, like repression, comprise a withdrawal of the cathexis sent out by the ego*" (ibid.: 153). This is Freud's way of announcing the forthcoming arrival of the concepts of "*denial of reality*" and "*splitting of the ego*" which he would define in detail in "Fetishism" (1927e).

- **"THE LOSS OF REALITY IN NEUROSIS AND PSYCHOSIS" (1924e)**

> Page numbers are those of *The Standard Edition of the Complete Psychological Works of Sigmund Freud*, vol. **19**, 181–187.

In his preceding paper, Freud had indicated that what differentiated a psychosis from a neurosis was the fact that, in psychosis, the ego refuses to perceive external reality while, in neurosis, external reality is accepted as such. In this text, he moderates that position somewhat, considering that in both of these states there exists a distortion of the perception of reality; the difference between them lies in the nature of that distortion. He attempts, in this paper, to give a detailed account of this difference.

He begins by describing the two phases which are characteristic of the onset of neurosis on the one hand and of psychosis on the other. In neurosis, there is indeed in the first phase a loss of reality; this is followed by the formation of a compromise – the neurotic symptom. In that first phase, it is the fragment of reality that had to be avoided which produced the repression. He quotes the example of the young woman who was in love with her brother-in-law; as she stood by her sister's death-bed, she was horrified at the thought which came into her head: "*Now he is free and can marry me*". The scene was instantly forgotten, and the hysterical pains appeared. Freud notes that the repression of her love for her brother-in-law led to the fact that the young woman avoided any confrontation with reality as regards the thought that her brother-in-law would soon be free.

It is instructive precisely in this case, moreover, to learn along what path the neurosis attempted to solve the conflict. It took away from the value of the change that had occurred in reality, by repressing the instinctual demand which had emerged – that is, her love for her brother-in-law. The psychotic *reaction would have been a disavowal of the fact of her sister's death.* (1924e: 184)

Freud then examines what occurs in psychosis, and introduces the idea of "*denial* (or *disavowal*) *of reality*" as typical of the psychotic's refusal to perceive external reality. He argues that the onset of psychosis is also a two-stage process: in the first, the ego is cut off from reality because of the denial, and in the second a new reality is created – a delusion or a hallucination – in order to "*make good the damage done*" and compensate for the loss of reality. In other words, in neurosis a significant fragment of reality is avoided by a sort of flight, whereas in psychosis the denied fragment is remodelled: "*Neurosis does not disavow the reality, it only ignores it; psychosis disavows it and tries to replace it*" (ibid.: 185). "Normal" behaviour combines aspects of both reactions: as in neurosis, there is no disavowal of reality, but, as in psychosis, there is an attempt to bring about some modification in that reality.

Neurosis and psychosis share another feature – the anxiety reaction which accompanies the symptoms. In neurosis, anxiety is generated by the "*return of the repressed*", while in psychosis it comes from the fact that the denied reality constantly forces itself upon the mind. The "return of the repressed" is a classic Freudian concept, but this is the first time that Freud makes any mention of a similar kind of return as regards what had been disavowed in psychosis. "*Probably in a psychosis the rejected piece of reality constantly forces itself upon the mind, just as the repressed instinct does in neurosis, and that is why in both cases the consequences too are the same*" (ibid.: 186). These consequences are of course the emergence of anxiety.

Finally, Freud observes that, as regards the creation of a new reality, the distinction between neurosis and psychosis is not as clear-cut as one might think – neurosis, too, like psychosis, aims to find a substitute for an unacceptable reality. The difference lies in the fact that, in psychosis, the illness creates a new reality by means of a delusion or a hallucination, whereas in neurosis the patient attempts to replace a disagreeable reality through the world of fantasy. This fantasy world constitutes a kind of "*storehouse*" from which both neurotic and psychotic patients can draw their fantasy material. In the case of the neurotic patient, however, the ego is not completely cut off from reality as is the case with the psychotic patient. The latter also draws material from the storehouse, says Freud, but the neurotic uses the new world of fantasy like a child at play, giving it a "*symbolic*" meaning. In other words, the neurotic can distinguish between reality and fantasy, whereas the delusional or hallucinated psychotic patient is unable to do this.

- **"NEGATION" (1925h)**

Page numbers are those of *The Standard Edition of the Complete Psychological Works of Sigmund Freud*, vol. **19**, 233–239.

Freud defines negation as a technique used by patients when, in the course of a session, some thought, wish or feeling emerges which they deny belongs to them. "*We realize that this is a repudiation, by projection, of an idea that has just come up*" (1925h: 235). For example: "*'You ask who this person in the dream can be. It's not my mother.' We emend this to: 'So it is his mother.'*" (ibid.: 235). Thus negation is a means by which the content of a repressed wish, feeling or idea can make its way into consciousness – on condition that it be *negated*. A word as to terminology is required here. In German, the term *Verneinung* means both negation in the logical and linguistic sense of the word and negation in its psychological sense, i.e. the rejection of a statement which has already been made (Bourguignon et al. 1989).

Freud notes that negation is a way of becoming aware of what is unconscious but it is not an acceptance of what is repressed. Here, the intellectual function of judgement is separated from the affective process. When the patient negates something in a judgement, this at bottom means: this is something which I would like to repress. Thus the "no" is a hallmark of repression, "*a certificate of origin – like, let us say, 'Made in Germany'*" (ibid.: 236). The operation of the function of judgement is made possible by the "*symbol of negation*", which allows thinking some degree of freedom with respect to the consequences of repression.

The function of judgement has two other characteristics. The first is to decide whether such and such an attribute is possessed or not; this may be expressed in the language of the instinctual drives as "I should like to eat this" or "I should like to spit it out", that is, "it shall be inside me" or "it shall be outside me" – this is the task of the "*original pleasure-ego*". The second kind of decision made by the function of judgement is to determine whether a presentation really exists or not, and this has to do with reality-testing. These two functions are closely related. "*What is unreal, merely a presentation and subjective, is only internal; what is real is also there* outside" (ibid.: 237). Given that presentations all originate in previous perceptions, the existence of a presentation is a guarantee of the reality of what was presented. For this reason, "*[the] first and immediate aim, therefore, of reality-testing is, not to* find *an object in real perception which corresponds to the one presented, but to* refind *such an object, to convince oneself that it is still there*" (ibid.: 237–238). For Freud, judgement is the intellectual action which decides the choice of motor action, i.e. the decisive factor which "*leads over from thinking to acting*" (ibid.: 238). Finally, Freud makes a connection between the polarity "inclusion within the ego – exclusion from the ego" and the conflict between the life and death drives.

> *Affirmation – as a substitute for uniting – belongs to Eros; negation – the successor to expulsion – belongs to the instinct of destruction. The general wish to negate, the negativism which is displayed by some psychotics, is probably to be regarded as a sign of a defusion of instincts that has taken place through a withdrawal of the libidinal components.* (ibid.: 239)

- ## "SOME PSYCHICAL CONSEQUENCES OF THE ANATOMICAL DISTINCTION BETWEEN THE SEXES" (1925j)

> Page numbers are those of *The Standard Edition of the Complete Psychological Works of Sigmund Freud*, vol. **19**, 241–258.

The concept of denial is also at the forefront of this paper, which focuses for the most part on the consequences of the castration complex on the development of girls and boys. In his introduction to this investigation, Freud emphasizes how important it is to analyse infantile sexuality as it becomes manifest in the earliest period of childhood; he highlights also the time it takes in psychoanalysis before one obtains results. He does not agree with those who attempt to shorten the length of psychoanalytic treatments. "*An analysis of early childhood such as we are considering is tedious and laborious and makes demands both upon the physician and upon the patient which cannot always be met*" (1925j: 248).

- ### *Psychosexual development in girls and in boys*

Freud begins by outlining the main stages in the development of boys. He says that the Oedipal attitude in boys is at its height during the phallic phase and that its "*destruction*" – Freud's term – is brought about by the fear of castration. In addition, because of his psychic bisexuality, the little boy's Oedipus complex is both active and passive: he identifies with his father and wants to marry his mother, but at the same time he identifies with his mother and adopts a feminine attitude with respect to his father. Freud insists also on the importance of masturbation during the "*prehistory*" of the Oedipus complex, because it serves as a discharge for sexual excitation.

Having thus outlined the situation as regards boys, Freud goes on to examine the Oedipus complex in girls, and observes that they have one more problem than boys: girls have to change their object at one point in their early development. In both cases, the mother is the original love-object; boys retain their object in the Oedipus complex, while girls abandon it and take their father as a love-object. What brings girls to make this change of object?

Freud examines in detail what he calls the prehistory of the Oedipus complex in girls, i.e. what precedes the establishment of that complex. This has mainly to do with penis envy and the girl's capacity to overcome that envy in order to continue her development towards femininity. Freud situates the crucial point in the development of girls in the phallic phase, before the Oedipus complex, when

> *[they] notice the penis of a brother or playmate, strikingly visible and of large proportions, at once recognize it as the superior counterpart of their own small and inconspicuous organ, and from that time forward fall a victim to envy for the penis.* (ibid.: 252)

At that point the behaviour of little boys differs from that of little girls. When a boy first catches side of a girl's genital region, either he sees nothing or he disavows what he sees and thinks that he has seen a penis. It is only later, when the threat of castration has taken hold of him, that the observation retrospectively takes on its full meaning: from then on, the boy imagines that women are mutilated, castrated creatures. This explains why henceforth he has "*horror*" of girls and shows "*triumphant contempt*" for them (ibid.: 252).

The little girl behaves differently, says Freud. "*She makes her judgement and her decision in a flash. She has seen it and knows she is without it and wants to have it. Here what has been named the masculinity complex of women branches off*" (ibid.: 252–253). The way in which the little girl reacts to her masculinity complex will be decisive for her future development, depending on whether she overcomes it rapidly or gives way to it. And even if she does overcome it, "*[the] hope of some day obtaining a penis in spite of everything and of so becoming like a man may persist to an incredibly late age*" (ibid.: 253). If the little girl fails to overcome her masculinity complex, denial (or disavowal) of castration then emerges and she will behave in future as if she were a man.

> *Or again, a process may set in which I should like to call a "disavowal", a process which in the mental life of children seems neither uncommon not very dangerous but which in an adult would mean the beginning of a psychosis.* (ibid.: 253)

- ### *Penis envy in girls*

Penis envy has various psychological consequences for the little girl. It accounts for her sense of inferiority, which she experiences as "*a wound to her narcissism*" and "*a punishment personal to herself*", and she begins to share the contempt felt by men towards women. Penis envy also accounts for the jealousy particular to women and as such is connected to the masturbatory fantasy of a child being beaten (Freud 1919e). Another consequence "*seems to be a loosening of the girl's affectionate relation with her maternal object*" (ibid.: 254), because the mother is almost always held responsible for her lack of a penis. The most significant effect, says Freud, is the importance that clitoridal masturbation takes on as a masculine activity, because it hinders the development of femininity. Shortly after the penis envy phase linked to the phallic stage, the girl begins to rebel against clitoridal masturbation; her revolt against the fact of not being a boy is what points her in the direction of femininity. "*Thus the little girl's recognition of the anatomical distinction between the sexes forces her away from masculinity and masculine masturbation on to new lines which lead to the development of femininity*" (ibid.: 256). It is at this juncture that the Oedipus complex comes into the picture for little girls. As a result of the equation "*penis-child*" (in German: "*symbolische Gleichung: Penis=Kind*" (*G.W.* vol. 14, 27) – the *symbolic* equation "penis-child"), the girl

> *gives up her wish for a penis and puts in place of it a wish for a child: and* with that purpose in view *she takes her father as a love-object. Her mother becomes the object of her jealousy. The girl has turned into a little woman.* (ibid.: 256)

Here Freud makes one of the few explicit comments in the whole of his writings on the possible existence of specifically feminine sensations – no doubt in reaction to the opposition to which his "phallocentric" positions had given rise, not only from female psychoanalysts but also from some of his male colleagues. "*If I am to credit a single analytic instance, this new situation can give rise to physical sensations which would have to be regarded as a premature awakening of the female genital apparatus*" (ibid.: 256).

- ## *The Oedipus complex is different in girls and in boys*

Freud draws a series of conclusions from this. First, there is a fundamental contrast between the two sexes with respect to the Oedipus complex and the castration complex. In boys, the Oedipus complex is followed by the threat of castration which makes the complex disappear; in girls, castration precedes the Oedipus complex and makes its advent subsequently possible. "*Whereas in boys the Oedipus complex is destroyed by the castration complex, in girls it is made possible and led up to by the castration complex*" (ibid.: 256). This means that, for Freud, sexual development in men and women is a consequence of the anatomical distinction between the sexes and of the psychological effects which result from the question of castration. It corresponds to the difference between "*a castration that has been carried out*" – actual castration in girls – and "*one that has merely been threatened*" – i.e. a castration fantasy in boys (ibid.: 257). Once again, although it is true that lack of a penis is an important aspect of psychosexual development in girls as well as in boys, Freud does not take into account the other aspect which is just as important – the fact that there are specific factors linked to femininity, to the female genitalia and to the fantasies which involve these.

Finally, Freud describes how the Oedipus complex unfolds differently in boys and in girls. In boys, the Oedipus complex is not simply repressed, "*it is literally smashed to pieces by the shock of threatened castration*" (ibid.: 257), and the parental objects form the superego. In girls, the Oedipus complex is only slowly abandoned, as an effect of repression. It is for this reason, according to Freud, that the superego of women is never so inexorable as that of men; that fact leads to a certain number of character traits "*which critics of every epoch have brought up against women*" (ibid.: 257) – they show less sense of justice than men, they are less ready to submit to the great necessities of life, they tend to let their judgements be influenced by their emotions, etc. Freud nevertheless acknowledges the fact that, notwithstanding his criticism of women, most men also fall far short of the masculine ideal. Freud argues that sexual equality as demanded by feminists is unacceptable and that there exists in each one of us both masculine and feminine characteristics, "*so that pure masculinity and femininity remained theoretical constructions of uncertain content*" (ibid.: 258).

- ## "FETISHISM" (1927e)

> Page numbers are those of *The Standard Edition of the Complete Psychological Works of Sigmund Freud*, vol. **21**, 147–157.

- ## *The denial of perception of reality in fetishism*

In "Fetishism", Freud develops the concept of denial (disavowal), a defence which consists in refusing the perception of unacceptable reality; he links this to splitting of the ego which is one of the effects of the defence. The prototype of this kind of defence is the fetishist, who denies perception of castration in women, with the fetish being a substitute for the missing penis. Freud goes on to say that two contradictory attitudes coexist within the fetishist's ego, one of which denies the perception of women's lack of a penis while the other acknowledges the fact. The idea that there can exist a split in the ego which determines two contradictory attitudes in the mind leads Freud to modify some earlier points of view – on psychosis in particular – a topic he would continue to work on in two subsequent texts.

It was the analysis of several cases of fetishism which led Freud to the conclusion that the fetish – foot, shoe, fur, feminine lingerie, etc. – was a penis substitute – but not of just any penis: "*The fetish is a substitute for the woman's (the mother's) penis that the little boy once believed in and – for reasons familiar to us – does not want to give up*" (1927e: 152–153). (The translation, by Joan Riviere, published in the *International Journal of Psycho-Analysis* (1928), 9, 161–166, runs as follows: "The fetish is a substitute for the woman's (mother's) *phallus* which the little boy once believed in and does not wish to forgo – we know why" (italics added).) "*Phallus*" is a word which Freud rarely employs as a substantive; he usually employs the term "*penis*" (as in "*penis envy*", for example) or the adjective "*phallic*" ("*phallic phase*", etc.). Freud made no distinction between "phallus" and "penis" as do a certain number of post-Freudian psychoanalysts.

> *In contemporary psycho-analytical literature there has been a gradual tendency to use "penis" and "phallus" in distinct senses: the former denotes the male organ in its bodily reality, while the latter lays the stress on the symbolic value of the penis.* (Laplanche and Pontalis 1967 [1973: 312])

To return to the fetishist. In the fetishist's unconscious fantasies, the fetish is looked upon as representing the body of a woman, as a symbolic substitute for the penis. It follows that for the fetishist, women lose all sexual attraction; this is henceforth focused on the fetish, which becomes the only source of sexual excitation. Freud says that the establishment of a fetish is an attempt to set up a "*disavowal*" (*Verleugnung*) of castration in women in order to protect the fetishist from the anxiety to which that threatening perception would give rise: "*The horror of castration has set up a memorial to itself in the creation of this substitute*" (1927e: 154). The fetish thus has two roles to play, each of which is in contradiction with the other: to maintain the belief that women have a penis, while protecting the fetishist against perceiving the reality of castration in women. "*It [the fetish] remains a token of triumph over the threat of castration and a protection against it*" (ibid.: 154).

- ## *Denial of the perception of the loss of the object in pathological mourning*

Freud had observed this contradictory psychological attitude – here as regards perception of castration in women – in another context: that of pathological mourning processes. He gives the example of the attitude adopted by two young men after the death of their beloved father. He describes the "*split*" which occurred in the personality of each of them with respect to the loss of their object, and says that this split is analogous to the one he observed in his fetishist patients.

> *It turned out that the two young men had no more "scotomized" their father's death than a fetishist does the castration of women. It was only one current in their mental life that had not recognized their father's death; there was another current which took full account of that fact. The attitude which fitted in with the wish and the attitude which fitted in with reality existed side by side.* (ibid.: 156)

Freud describes the consequences for the ego of the disavowal of the reality of his father's death in one of the brothers. "*The patient oscillated in every situation in life between two assumptions: the one, that his father was still alive and was hindering his activities; the other, opposite one, that he was entitled to regard himself as his father's successor*" (ibid.: 156). This example shows that, in pathological mourning as in fetishism, the splitting of the ego which results from the introjection of the lost object sets up two contradictory attitudes with respect to the perception of the reality of the loss, one of which accepts it, while the other denies it. This observation enabled Freud to complete the hypotheses he had developed in "Mourning and Melancholia" (1917e [1915]). He ends the present essay with a statement to the effect that the same phenomenon occurs in psychosis, but here only one of the attitudes leads to withdrawal from reality, so that the withdrawal is not as complete as he had at first thought. "*I may thus keep to the expectation that in psychosis the one current – that which fitted in with reality – would have in fact been absent*" (ibid.: 156).

- **"SPLITTING OF THE EGO IN THE PROCESS OF DEFENCE" (1940e [1938])**

> Page numbers are those of *The Standard Edition of the Complete Psychological Works of Sigmund Freud*, vol. **23**, 271–278.

In this paper, Freud comes back to the idea that in childhood the ego may find itself having to deal with incompatible demands and may react to this conflict in two contradictory ways: on the one hand, the ego may reject reality and refuse to allow any prohibition of drive-related demands, and, on the other, it may acknowledge the danger coming from reality and deal with the fear of that danger by transforming it into a symptom. But this ingenious solution has to be paid for, and the split in the ego will increase as the years go by. "*[This] success is achieved at the price of a rift in the ego which never heals but which increases as time goes on. The two contrary reactions to the conflict persist as the centre-point of a splitting of the ego*" (1940e [1938]: 276). Freud adds that this kind of disorder of the ego seems strange to us, because we expect the ego to fulfil its synthesizing function. He concludes this paper with a discussion of the case of a young boy of between 3 and 4 years of age; this case confirmed Freud's point of view on splitting of the ego and the role of the fetish as a fantasy substitute for the woman's penis.

- **AN OUTLINE OF PSYCHO-ANALYSIS (1940a [1938])**

> **Biographies and history**
>
> **A legacy which opens on to the future**
>
> Since this book contains the final touches that Freud brought to this series of papers, I feel its rightful place is among these, even if it means taking slight liberties with the chronological order of his writings. The book was written between July and September 1938, shortly after Freud arrived in London; he was 82 years of age at the time. His work on it had to be interrupted because of a relapse of the cancer from which he suffered and the need to undergo an operation. The *Outline* was published in 1940, one year after his death.
>
> This sixty-six-page text, which for long was thought of as an unfinished manuscript, gave rise to some editorial problems. In fact, only the most recent and innovative ideas were written by Freud himself in a full and non-abbreviated manner. From that point of view, the third part, entitled "The Theoretical Yield", is the one which interests us most for the moment. In it, Freud discusses the relationship between the ego and the external world, and reports on his latest work on topics such as disavowal and splitting of the ego. By way of contrast, the first part of the book was hastily written; the original manuscript bears witness to the fact that Freud used a telegraphic style with many abbreviations. After Freud's death, his original text was worked on by the (German) editors of the time; though this undoubtedly changed part of the original, they left the third part exactly as Freud had written it (Grubrich-Simitis 1985).
>
> *An Outline of Psycho-Analysis* is much more than a summary or a simplified handbook for the general public. The text itself is not an easy one to read: it recapitulates the broad outline of the major themes of Freud's discoveries, and it opens the door to new explorations. Freud

says that *"for the time being"*, we should use psychoanalysis as a treatment procedure in spite of its limitations; but he envisages the discovery of other therapeutic procedures, in particular psychopharmacological treatment.

> *The future may teach us to exercise a direct influence, by means of particular chemical substances, on the amounts of energy and their distribution in the mental apparatus. It may be that there are still other undreamt-of possibilities of therapy. But for the moment we have nothing better at our disposal than the technique of psycho-analysis, and for that reason, in spite of its limitations, it should not be despised.* (1940a [1938]: 182)

As a result of what has just been said, the *Outline* is looked upon as a kind of testament addressed to psychoanalysts.

Discovering the text

Page numbers are those of *The Standard Edition of the Complete Psychological Works of Sigmund Freud*, vol. **23**, 139–207.

Parts I and II of the *Outline* are a condensed version of the main psychoanalytic discoveries as they then stood, while in Part III, entitled "The Theoretical Yield", Freud introduces fresh ideas concerning anxiety and splitting of the ego, together with the consequences the latter entails.

In presenting the role of the ego in mental life, Freud states that *"the ego is governed by considerations of safety"* (ibid.: 199). He goes on to describe the main points of his theory of anxiety, mentioning in particular the fact that anxiety is a signal which gives a warning of dangers that threaten the integrity of the ego; these dangers, therefore, have to do with fragmenting of the ego, a quite different mechanism from that of repression. *"[The] ego makes use of the sensations of anxiety as a signal to give a warning of dangers that threaten its integrity"* (ibid.: 199).

A little further on, Freud returns to his earlier point of view on psychosis, the main feature of which is detachment from reality; here again he argues that, contrary to what he had first thought, this detachment is not complete. He sees proof of this in the fact that some healthy part of the mind continues to exist even in the most severe cases of psychosis.

> *Even in a state so far removed from the reality of the external world as one of hallucinatory confusion, one learns from patients after their recovery that at the time in some corner of their mind (as they put it) there was a normal person hidden who, like a detached spectator, watched the hubbub of the illness go past him.* (ibid.: 201–202)

This observation, together with many other similar ones, was proof enough for Freud that, in psychosis, there occurs a splitting of the ego which gives rise to two contradictory attitudes as a consequence of the split mind. *"Two psychical attitudes have been formed instead of a single one – one, the normal one, which takes account of reality, and another which under the influence of the instincts detaches the ego from reality"* (ibid.: 202). These two attitudes coexist, and when the abnormal one gains the upper hand, the situation is ripe for the onset of psychosis.

Freud takes these points further. Whereas his earlier opinion was that the coexistence of two contradictory attitudes in the mind, one pathological and the other normal, was a feature of psychosis alone, he now argues that splitting of the ego occurs not only in non-psychotic states such as fetishism but also in the neuroses.

> *The view which postulates that in all psychoses there is a* splitting of the ego *could not call for so much notice if it did not turn out to apply to other states more like the neuroses and, finally to the neuroses themselves.* (ibid.: 202)

Freud draws the conclusion that normal and pathological states of mind are the consequence of a balance of power between these two contradictory attitudes which are independent of each other, one of them accepting reality while the other rejects it.

> *The disavowal is always supplemented by an acknowledgement; two contrary and independent attitudes always arise and result in the situation of there being a splitting of the ego. Once more the issue depends on which of the two can seize hold of the greater intensity.*
> (ibid.: 204)

Freud concludes this discussion with a reminder of how difficult it is to recognize the existence of such mental phenomena. "*In conclusion, it is only necessary to point out how little of all these processes becomes known to us through our conscious perception*" (ibid.: 204).

Post-Freudians

Splitting of the ego: differences in conception as between Freud and Klein

Splitting of the ego: Freud's view

In his earlier writings, Freud explained the onset of neurosis principally in terms of the mechanism of repression, but he soon came to realize that, at the same time, there existed pathological divisions in the mind. At first, he used various terms to designate these divisions, in particular that of *Spaltung* (splitting) or other closely related designations such as dissociation, dualism, separation, etc. In 1917, in "Mourning and Melancholia", he introduced the idea of introjection of the lost object into a "split-off part of the ego", and in 1923 he developed the notions of ego, id and superego. This enabled him to describe the role of disavowal of the perception of the reality of loss, together with the idea of splitting of the ego. It was in his paper on "Fetishism" (1927e) that he spoke of splitting of the ego as a true psychoanalytic concept. In his final papers written in the 1930s, Freud added that the two contradictory attitudes to which splitting of the ego gives rise exist to a varying degree in the mind of each individual, and in a wide range of conditions from psychosis to normality.

Splitting of the ego: Klein's view

The idea of splitting has been further developed and diversely understood by many psychoanalysts, in particular by those who belong to the Kleinian and post-Kleinian current of thinking. It is important to understand that the idea of splitting does not carry the same meaning for Freud and for Klein (Canestri 1990). For Freud, splitting of the ego is a consequence of the conflict which results from disavowal of reality – the ego finds itself *passively* split, as it were. For Klein and the post-Kleinians, on the other hand, splitting is an *active* defence mechanism which can operate in many ways.

Taking as their starting-point Freud's discussion concerning the introjection of the lost object (Freud 1917e [1915]), Karl Abraham and Melanie Klein based their conception of the development of the ego on the modifications to which it is subjected first as a result of introjection, then by the identification of parts of the ego with its internal objects. In her early texts, Klein writes about the *splitting of the object*. She describes how the object is perceived objectively, and how these perceptions are influenced by the affects of love and hate; as a result of this, the object is initially split into good and bad aspects. The gradual integration of these good and bad aspects, allied to a more realistic perception of the object as such, leads to the establishment of the depressive position and plays a decisive role in personality development. Given that the formation of the internal object and that of the ego are interdependent, splitting of the object corresponds to splitting of the ego.

From 1946 onwards, Klein further developed her ideas on splitting and began to describe the various ways in which it could operate. For example, in projective identification she speaks of "splitting off" to describe the process by which certain parts of the self, experienced as "bad", become detached from it and are projected into the object. In schizophrenia, she describes what she calls *minute splitting* – the object is divided up into tiny fragments; this leads to fragmentation of the ego ("falling to pieces"), and is the process which underlies the schizophrenic's annihilation anxiety. According to Robert D. Hinshelwood (1989: 435), four kinds of splitting can be clearly identified, among many other possibilities: "a coherent split in the object, a coherent split in the ego, a fragmentation of the object, and a fragmentation of the ego." These various kinds of splitting may coexist.

In his introduction to the French edition of *A Dictionary of Kleinian Thought*, Hinshelwood (2002) points out that the sheer variety of vocabulary in the English language makes it easy to make subtle distinctions in the different ways in which splitting operates (splitting up, splitting off, splitting apart . . .), and that there is often no equivalent term in French. He goes on: "I wonder whether the constraints of the French language, particularly in relation to this fundamental concept [splitting], have perhaps made Melanie Klein's thinking seem less subtle to the French-speaking reader, thereby leading to less interest in her ideas" (Hinshelwood 2002: 3).

New concepts

Anatomical distinction between the sexes – castration complex – disavowal (of castration) – disavowal (of reality) – narcissistic neuroses or psychoneuroses – negation – phallus – return of the repressed, return of split-off parts – splitting of the ego – symbolic equation

"ANALYSIS TERMINABLE AND INTERMINABLE"
(1937c)
"CONSTRUCTIONS IN ANALYSIS"
(1937d)

Final papers on technique

In "Analysis Terminable and Interminable", Freud begins by replying to Rank and Ferenczi who hoped that, by modifying certain aspects of psychoanalytic technique – for example, by shortening the duration of analyses – similar results could nonetheless be obtained. Freud, however, argues that it is impossible to eliminate an entire neurosis in the space of a few months, because experience shows us that the better the outcome we hope for in any given treatment, the less we are justified in shortening it. He goes on to outline the various resistances which work against the patient's recovery and set up limits for the analysis – some of these resistances may indeed turn the analysis into an interminable one. Two insurmountable obstacles prevent resolution of the transference, says Freud: a wish for the penis in women, and a passive attitude in men. Ferenczi thought that every successful analysis should allow these two complexes to be overcome in the course of the treatment, but Freud is more pessimistic than his pupil and considers these objectives to be too ambitious. For Freud, every analysis must in the end reach "*bedrock*" – penis envy in women and passive attitude in men, both of which are biological and psychological in nature. In addition, given the dangers which threaten psychoanalysts in their clinical work, Freud advises them to submit themselves periodically to further personal analysis.

In "Constructions in Analysis", Freud addresses his remarks first of all to those who accuse psychoanalysts of putting their own ideas into their patients' heads through their interpretations. He seizes the opportunity to examine the validity of the constructions and reconstructions which are made in the course of an analysis. The question of the reconstruction of childhood events had already come to the fore in the analysis of the "Wolf-Man" (Freud 1918b) with respect to the primal scene dream: was it purely a fantasy, or the revival of the memory of something which had actually been witnessed in the patient's childhood? Freud comes back to that question in 1937, and shows that the analyst's interpretations are hypotheses which are offered to the patient, who in the last resort decides whether they hold good or not: any such confirmation derives either from the return of the repressed infantile memory or from the patient's firm belief that the interpretation is an appropriate one.

Biographies and history

Hitler's rise to power and anti-Semitism

The Great Depression of 1929 led to dramatic consequences not only for the United States but also for Europe and the rest of the world. Unemployment rose to an alarming extent, particularly in Germany and Austria; the political situation deteriorated rapidly, and Hitler came to power in 1933 as Chancellor of the Reich. Anti-Semitism was transformed into persecution of the Jews, and Freud's writings, considered to be "Jewish literature", were burned on 10 May 1933 in the public squares of several German cities. Freud looked on in anguish at this descent into hell, oscillating between a wish to close his eyes to the reality of the Nazi peril and a clear-sighted judgement of what was taking place.

Freud and Romain Rolland

In 1936, Freud celebrated his eightieth birthday, although, because he had had to undergo two new operations, he abandoned any idea of having an official celebration. He did, however, have many visitors, among whom were famous writers and artists such as Romain Rolland, H. G. Wells and Stefan Zweig. For Romain Rolland's birthday – he was ten years younger than Freud – Freud sent him a congratulatory letter as well as a short paper entitled "A Disturbance of Memory on the Acropolis" (Freud 1936a). This short paper is a fragment of Freud's self-analysis in which he tells of the wonderment he felt when he visited the Parthenon for the first time: "it's too beautiful to be true" was mingled with a feeling of uncanniness. Though Freud had met Rolland only once, in 1924, they wrote regularly but intermittently to each other during the following thirteen years. There was a very strong rapport between the two, and they shared an interest in literature and mystical themes; Freud had used the "oceanic feeling" as described by Rolland as a basis for *The Future of an Illusion* (Freud 1927c).

Early in 1937, Lou Andreas-Salomé died. That same year, Freud learned that Princess Marie Bonaparte had bought from a Viennese antique dealer the letters he had written to Fliess; he asked her to destroy them, but she refused. In spite of the fact that his cancer was worsening, Freud managed to publish several more papers.

Princess Marie Bonaparte (1882–1962)

Freud and his family were very fond of Princess Marie Bonaparte. She was his main representative in the burgeoning world of French psychoanalysis and played a highly significant role in the development of the Société Psychanalytique de Paris (the Paris Psychoanalytical Society).

The direct descendant of one of Napoleon Bonaparte's brothers, Marie was born in St-Cloud (France) in 1882; one month after her birth, her mother died. Her childhood and adolescence were difficult. In 1907, she married Prince George of Greece and Denmark, and they had two children. According to René Laforgue, she suffered from an obsessional neurosis and was close to suicide; she consulted Freud in 1925 and began analysis with him. The treatment continued in short periodical phases until 1938. From her initial encounter with Freud onwards, Princess Marie Bonaparte devoted herself to defending psychoanalysis and proved to be a particularly generous patron. In 1926, she participated in the creation of the Paris Psychoanalytical Society, and was one of the founders of the *Revue Française de Psychanalyse*; in addition, she translated into French many of Freud's books and papers. She herself wrote several papers on applied psychoanalysis – for example on Edgar Poe's books and on social problems. Her point of view on female sexuality gave rise to much controversy – her basis was anatomical and typological rather than psychoanalytic – and she even suggested that the clitoris be operated on (she herself underwent the operation). The fact that her opinions on this point were so debatable enabled Janine Chasseguet-Smirgel et al. (1964) to highlight the features which are specific to feminine identity from a psychoanalytic point of view.

In 1939, with the help of the American ambassador, William Bullitt, and Ernest Jones, Princess Marie paid the ransom demanded by the Nazi authorities before they would permit Freud and his family to leave Vienna for London. In 1953, when Jacques Lacan inaugurated the first schism in the Paris Society, she sided with Sasha Nacht's group, and the following year she financed the creation of the Paris Institute of Psychoanalysis as well as its Library, rue Saint-Jacques. Princess Marie Bonaparte died in St Tropez in 1962.

Discovering the text

- **"ANALYSIS INTERMINABLE AND INTERMINABLE" (1937c)**

Page numbers are those of *The Standard Edition of the Complete Psychological Works of Sigmund Freud*, vol. **23**, 211–253.

- ***Psychoanalytic therapy is a time-consuming business***

This highly significant paper begins with an argument in favour of the defence, as it were: if someone is to be freed from his or her neurotic symptoms and inhibitions, psychoanalytic therapy cannot but be "*a time-consuming business*" (1937c: 216). Freud opposes the many attempts to shorten the duration of analyses, in particular that of Rank, who hoped that the after-effects of the trauma of birth and any subsequent neurosis could be got rid of after just a few months of analysis. As far as Freud is concerned, Rank is wrong to think that "*this small piece of analytic work would save the necessity for all the rest*" (ibid.: 216). Freud feels that Rank's argument is simply "*designed to adapt the tempo of analytic therapy to the haste of American life*" (ibid.: 216). Freud then recalls his own experience of fixing a time-limit for an analysis in which no more progress seemed possible, and of holding to that date once he had decided upon it, whatever the repercussions: this was in the "Wolf-Man" case (Freud 1918b). It was somewhat of a gamble, as Freud himself acknowledges; it did work at first, but the patient had a relapse some time later. Fixing a time-limit can be effective as long as one hits the right time for it, says Freud; there is, however, no general rule in the matter, so that we must above all trust our intuition.

- ***Is there such a thing as a natural end to an analysis?***

We often hear colleagues say: "*His analysis was not finished*" or "*He was never analysed to the end*" (1937c: 219), but what do we mean by "the end of an analysis"? An analysis may be ended, says Freud, on the one hand, when the patient no longer suffers from the symptoms, anxieties or inhibitions which brought him or her to analysis in the first place, and on the other, when a sufficient amount of repressed material has been made conscious; the upshot being that there is no need to fear a repetition of the pathological processes concerned. If that goal is not attained, the analysis is "*incomplete*" (ibid.: 219). In more favourable cases, the neurotic disorder can be completely eliminated and will not return. There is no doubt, says Freud, that an aetiology of the traumatic sort offers by far the most favourable field for analysis, because it succeeds in resolving traumatic situations which go back to the patient's early childhood, situations which the immature ego was unable to master. However, when the instinctual drives are excessively strong, they are recalcitrant to the ego's attempt at "*taming*" them; as a result, the analysis finds itself at a dead-end, because the strength of the drives leads to alterations in the ego. These modifications, says Freud, are acquired in the ego's defensive struggle "*in the sense of its being dislocated and restricted*" (ibid.: 221). The idea of "*dislocation*" and "*restriction*" are a reference to Freud's recent work on disavowal of reality and splitting of the ego: his discussion of these topics seemed, at that time, to have awakened but little interest in psychoanalytic circles.

> *And, indeed, it must be admitted that our knowledge of these matters is as yet insufficient. They are only now becoming the subject of analytic study. In this field the interest of analysts seems to me to be quite wrongly directed.* (ibid.: 221)

Freud then gives two clinical examples to show that, even though analytic treatment may well have a satisfactory outcome, later – and perhaps even several years later – a relapse may occur as a result of different factors. His first example is that of a man who was in analysis with Freud himself. Although Freud does not mention him by name, it is easy to identify Ferenczi as the analysand; the analysis was apparently successful. Several years later, however, the analysand became antagonistic towards Freud, reproaching him for having failed to analyse the negative transference.

> *The analyst, he [the patient] said, ought to have known and to have taken into account the fact that a transference-relation can never be purely positive; he should have given his attention to the possibilities of a negative transference. The analyst defended himself by saying that, at the time of the analysis, there was no sign of a negative transference.* (ibid.: 221)

The other example is that of a woman whose analysis was successful; she had a relapse as a result of several unfortunate events in her life and an operation, which remained inaccessible to analysis. A relapse can never be excluded, because "*we have no means of predicting what the later history of the recovery will be*" (ibid.: 223). The conclusion is therefore obvious: the more we demand a positive outcome, the less we are justified in shortening analytic treatment!

• *"Taming the instincts" has its limitations*

According to Freud, the success or otherwise of an analysis depends fundamentally on three factors: the effects of trauma, the constitutional strength of the drives, and the alteration of the patient's ego. As regards the strength of the drives, what means does the patient's ego have at its disposal for "*taming*" them, in order to resolve a drive-related conflict permanently and definitively? In order to explain this, says Freud, we must have recourse to the "*Witch Metapsychology*" – "*without metapsychological speculation and theorizing [. . .] we shall not get another step forward*" (ibid.: 225). For example, for normal individuals, solution of a drive-related conflict only holds good for a particular relation between the "*strength of the ego*" and the "*strength of the instincts*". If the strength of the ego weakens, or if the drives become excessively strong, the resultant imbalance will have a pathological effect. Considered from the point of view of the balance of power between these opposing forces, Freud notes the importance here of the *quantitative* or *economic* factor in the causation of illness. On this issue, Freud stakes a claim for the originality of analytic treatment, because it alone can enable the patient to take control over any strengthening that may occur in the instinctual drives. The process is not spontaneous; it is created only by means of the work of the analysis. Control over the instinctual drives, however, is by no means guaranteed, because it can never be either total or definitive. This uncertainty as to future outcome is an additional argument, writes Freud, for insisting that the work of the analysis should be truly "in-depth", in order to strengthen the ego's capacity for taming the drives. "*No doubt it is desirable to shorten the duration of analytic treatment, but we can only achieve our therapeutic purpose by increasing the power of analysis to come to the assistance of the ego*" (ibid.: 230).

• *The limits to psychoanalytic therapy*

Other questions arise in the course of an analysis. Can we protect a patient from future drive-related conflicts? As a preventive measure, should we stir up a conflict which is not at the time manifest? Freud says that these two questions are closely related, they have to do with the limits which are set to analytic therapy. He argues that, if a conflict is not currently active, the analyst can have no influence on it. We can treat an active conflict only if we can bring it into the transference, says Freud. If we try to produce artificially a new transference conflict as a preventive measure, this would have a damaging effect on the positive transference – which is essential if the work of the analysis is to proceed. Nor is it of any use to talk to the patient about such conflicts, with the hope of activating one of these in order to process it with the patient. He or she will simply answer: "*'This is very interesting, but I feel no trace of it.' We have increased his knowledge, but altered nothing else in him*" (ibid.: 233).

- ## *The ego's resistances against recovery*

Freud goes on to discuss the resistances against recovery which come from the ego. He deals first with the necessary alliance between the analyst and the patient's ego, then explores the ego's opposition to recovery.

As to the first point, Freud's opinion is that the analyst enters into an alliance with the patient's ego, one which "*is only normal on average*" he says, because the "*normal*" ego is "*an ideal fiction*". Seen from this point of view, the aim of analysis is to include "*in the synthesis of [the patient's] ego, the uncontrolled parts of the id*". This conception of working-through goes further than a mere lifting of repression; it implies a "*synthesis*" of the ego, bringing together parts of the ego which have in all probability been split off. For Freud there are two aspects which coexist within the ego, one which is close to being "*psychotic*" while the other is "*normal*".

> *Every normal person, in fact, is only normal on average. His ego approximates to that of the psychotic in some part or other and to a greater or lesser extent, and the degree of its remoteness from one end of the series and of its proximity to the other will furnish us with a provisional measure of what we have so indefinitely termed an "alteration of the ego".* (ibid.: 235)

The points Freud raises here would later be conceptualized in greater detail in *An Outline of Psycho-Analysis* (1940a [1938]).

As regards the ego's opposition to the analysis of resistance and to the patient's recovery, Freud reminds the reader of the role played by defence mechanisms. The mechanisms of defence described by Anna Freud (1936) aim to protect the ego against internal dangers, but if they become overdeveloped they may themselves become a danger for the ego and lead to damaging restrictions on its ability. To put it briefly, says Freud, the therapeutic effect of psychoanalysis depends on making conscious what is repressed; this is facilitated by the analyst's interpretations and constructions which weaken the patient's resistances. But in the course of this work it frequently happens that the patient no longer supports the effort to uncover resistances and defence mechanisms, and that the negative transference gains the upper hand, thereby threatening the success of the analysis.

> *The patient now regards the analyst as no more than a stranger who is making disagreeable demands on him, and he behaves towards him exactly like a child who does not like the stranger and does not believe anything he says.* (Freud 1937c: 239)

- ## *Resistances based on more fundamental conflicts*

There are many different kinds of ego, each of which is endowed with individual dispositions; some of them are acquired in the child's earliest years while others are innate and come from our archaic heritage. These dispositions go to make up each individual's personality, with its own resistances and defences which tend to be repeated in the analytical relationship. The more we take into account the complexity of the personality, the more difficult it becomes to localize the resistances: it is no longer possible simply to localize them in the ego or in the id, because other fundamental factors are at work within the individual mind.

One example of these deeper resistances, says Freud, is that of people who seem to have an excessive "*adhesiveness of the libido*", which slows down to a considerable extent the processes which the treatment sets in motion. There is also the opposite type of person, in whom the libido seems particularly mobile, going from one object to the next without cathecting any of them in depth. Again, other patients, in spite of the fact that they are still young, present a kind of "*psychical entropy*", the kind of inertia one expects to find more in very old people.

In another group of cases, the sources of resistance lie in the conflict between the life and death drives which we see at work in cases of masochism, negative therapeutic reaction and the sense of guilt found in neurotics.

> *These phenomena are unmistakable indications of the presence of a power in mental life which we call the instinct of aggression or of destruction according to its aims, and which we trace back to the original death instinct of living matter.* (ibid.: 243)

Recent experience showed Freud that the conflict between Eros and the destructive drive is not confined to pathological conditions; it is a factor of normal mental life too. Freud regrets that his ideas on this point have met with so little support.

> *I am well aware that the dualistic theory, according to which an instinct of death or of destruction or aggression claims equal rights as a partner with Eros as manifested in the libido, has found little sympathy and has not really been accepted even among psychoanalysts.* (ibid.: 244)

However, the Greek philosopher Empedocles of Acagras gave Freud unexpected support, for he taught that two principles which were constantly at war with each other govern events: Φιλια (love) and νειζοσ (strife); this dualism is quite similar to Freud's second theory of the instinctual drives.

- ### *An analyst must of necessity be analysed*

Freud next broaches the subject of psychoanalysts themselves, basing his remarks on a paper by Ferenczi (1928) in which the latter makes the point that, for an analysis to be successful, the analyst must have "*learnt sufficiently from his own 'errors and mistakes' and [. . .] got the better of 'the weak points in his own personality'*" (ibid.: 247). Of course, says Freud, analysts are human beings like anyone else, and "*[it] cannot be disputed that analysts in their own personalities have not invariably come up to the standard of psychical normality to which they wish to educate their patients*" (ibid.: 247). It is, however, legitimate, in the interest of patients, to demand that an analyst have "*a considerable degree of mental normality and correctness*" (ibid.: 248). It is for this reason that, in Freud's view, the psychoanalyst's personal analysis is a necessary condition for preparing for his or her future activity. Moreover, in order to avoid as much as possible the various dangers analysts themselves face in their work, Freud recommends that every analyst should periodically – at intervals of five years or so – submit to further analysis, "*without feeling ashamed of taking this step*" (ibid.: 249).

- ### *The end of an analysis and the underlying bedrock*

This final section is probably the best known of the whole paper. Freud describes two obstacles, which he considers to be insurmountable, to bringing an analysis to an end: penis envy in women, and the struggle against a passive attitude in men.

Although these two forms of resistance to ending an analysis are dissimilar, because of the difference between the sexes, what is common to both is the attitude of men and women with respect to the castration complex. For Freud, the castration complex does not carry the same meaning for both sexes. In men, striving to be masculine is in complete agreement with what the ego wishes; it is for this reason that the passive attitude, since it presupposes castration, is energetically repressed, so that often its presence is revealed only by excessive over-compensations. In women, on the other hand, the striving to be masculine is normal only during the phallic phase of her development, "*before the development to femininity has set in*" (ibid.: 251). The wish for a penis is thereafter repressed and the subsequent fate of her femininity depends on the outcome of this repression. If femininity fails to develop adequately, as in the case of the "*phallic*" woman, the masculinity complex takes the upper hand and exercises a permanent influence on her character; however, if this development does proceed favourably, the wish for a penis is replaced by the wish for a baby, writes Freud. He maintains all the same that the masculinity complex continues to disturb normal mental life in women: "*the wish for masculinity has been retained in the unconscious and, from out of its state of repression, exercises a disturbing influence*" (ibid.: 251).

Freud notes that, for Ferenczi, every successful analysis should have mastered these two complexes, the wish for a penis in women and the revolt against a passive attitude in men. Freud himself feels that such an objective is too ambitious, because analysts come up against insurmountable resistances whenever they try to encourage patients to work through these two phenomena.

At no other point in one's analytic work does one suffer more from an oppressive feeling that all one's repeated efforts have been in vain, and from a suspicion that one has been "preaching to the winds", than when one is trying to persuade a woman to abandon her wish for a penis on the ground of its being unrealizable or when one is seeking to convince a man that a passive attitude to men does not always signify castration and that it is indispensable in many relationships in life. (ibid.: 252)

In men, says Freud, arrogant masculine over-compensation produces one of the strongest transference-resistances. "*He refuses to subject himself to a father-substitute, or to feel indebted to him for anything, and consequently he refuses to accept his recovery from the doctor*" (ibid.: 252). With a woman patient, the wish for a penis does not produce an analogous transference, but the disappointment at not possessing a penis is "*the source of outbreaks of severe depression in her, owing to an internal conviction that the analysis will be of no use and that nothing can be done to help her*" (ibid.: 252). In Freud's opinion, that depression cannot but be the consequence of the failure of her hope to acquire, in spite of everything, a male organ, "*the lack of which was so painful to her*". It was this hope which was "*her strongest motive in coming for treatment*" (ibid.: 252). The idea never seems to cross Freud's mind that perhaps a woman patient may be depressed because she feels she is not accepted by her analyst in terms of what she possesses that is specifically feminine, and because of her anxiety at feeling amputated of her female organs; it is this that constitutes the equivalent of castration anxiety in men. Freud does not appear to realize that "*female sexuality*" may have positive connotations for a woman. As far as Ferenczi was concerned, access to femininity for women and access to masculinity for men are objectives which ought to be attained at the end of every analysis. Although Freud disagrees with his pupil's point of view, he does quote in full, in a footnote, the relevant extract from Ferenczi's paper.

Every male patient must attain a feeling of equality in relation to the physician as a sign that he has overcome his fear of castration; every female patient, if her neurosis is to be regarded as fully disposed of, must have got rid of her masculinity complex and must emotionally accept without a trace of resentment the implications of her female role. (Ferenczi 1928, quoted by Freud 1937c: 251, note 3)

To put it another way, Freud remains unwavering in his loyalty to "phallic monism", and implacably pessimistic when he reaches the conclusion that, as it draws to an end, every analysis necessarily comes up against a "*bedrock*" which Freud attributes to the biological field, the foundation of mental life.

This is probably true, since, for the psychical field, the biological field does in fact play the part of the underlying bedrock. The repudiation of femininity can be nothing else than a biological fact, a part of the great riddle of sex. (ibid.: 252)

Discovering the text

- **"CONSTRUCTIONS IN ANALYSIS" (1937d)**

Page numbers are those of *The Standard Edition of the Complete Psychological Works of Sigmund Freud*, vol. **23**, 256–269.

- *A task similar to that of the archaeologist*

Freud begins by observing that the work of the analysis consists in inducing the patient to give up the repressions which occurred in childhood and which are the source of his or her neurotic symptoms and inhibitions. In order to attain this therapeutic goal, the patient will have to recall the memory of early affective experiences; these can be glimpsed through free associations, dreams and the reproduction of certain affective states in the transference relationship. The analysand's task is to recollect what has been experienced and repressed, while that of the analyst consists in reconstructing, with the help of these clues, a picture that is as faithful as possible of the years about which the patient has forgotten. *"His task is to make out what has been forgotten from the traces which it has left behind or, more correctly, to* construct *it"* (1937d: 258–259). This work of construction – or, some would say, of reconstruction – resembles to some extent that of the archaeologist. There are two significant differences, however: on the one hand, *"psychical objects are incomparably more complicated than the excavator's material ones"*, and, on the other, *"for the archaeologist the reconstruction is the aim and end of his endeavours while for analysis reconstruction is only a preliminary labour"* (ibid.: 260).

- ### *What value should be attributed to our constructions?*

What guarantee do we have, asks Freud, that our reconstructions are accurate? For example, what happens if the analyst makes a mistake? Do such reconstructions operate solely thanks to suggestion? Freud refutes these objections. It is of course possible that the analyst presents to the patient an inaccurate construction as if it were the probable historical truth:

> *A single mistake of this sort can do no harm. What in fact occurs in such an event is rather that the patient remains as though he were untouched by what has been said and reacts to it with neither a "Yes" nor a "No".* (ibid.: 261)

Freud rejects also the accusation that, under the cover of constructions, the analyst might be making an abuse of suggestion.

Having dismissed these objections, Freud goes on to examine the patient's reaction when, in the course of an analysis, the analyst offers a construction. He acknowledges that there is some truth in the joke which says that psychoanalysts are always right, whatever the patient's answer: if the patient says "Yes", it means that the interpretation is accepted; if the patient says "No", that is only a sign of resistance, which again shows that the analyst is right! Freud makes it clear, however, that the analyst gives no more absolute value to a "Yes" than to a "No", for each of these replies is ambiguous. The analysand's "Yes" may imply acceptance of the construction – but it may also be the expression of a resistance. As for the "No" response, it is just as ambiguous as a "Yes" – though it may signify disagreement, more often than not it too expresses a resistance. How then is the analyst to make sense of all this? For Freud, there are indirect forms of confirmation which are completely trustworthy – those which derive from the patient's associations to the construction. *"An equally valuable confirmation is implied (expressed this time positively) when the patient answers with an association which contains something similar or analogous to the content of the construction"* (ibid.: 263). Other forms of indirect confirmation may be expressed as a parapraxis or a negative therapeutic reaction; in the latter case, if the interpretative reconstruction is correct, the patient reacts to it with an aggravation of his or her symptoms. In other words, contrary to what the critics of psychoanalysis claim, analysts do pay close attention to their patient's responses and often derive valuable information from them.

> *But these reactions on the part of the patient are rarely unambiguous and give no opportunity for a final judgement. Only the further course of the analysis enables us to decide whether our constructions are correct or unserviceable. We do not pretend that an individual construction is anything more than a conjecture which awaits examination, confirmation or rejection.* (ibid.: 265)

- ### *Delusion as the equivalent of a construction in analysis*

How does it come about that a conjecture of the analyst is transformed into the patient's conviction? The analyst's daily experience vouches for this, but one important issue does remain:

generally speaking, we expect that a construction offered to the patient in the course of analysis should lead to the recollection of the corresponding memory – that at least is the theory. However, in practice, it quite often happens that the patient does not recollect any meaningful repressed material. That is not important, says Freud, because when the patient becomes convinced of the accuracy of a construction, this achieves the same therapeutic effect as a recaptured memory. Why? For the moment this remains a mystery, and is a matter for further research.

Freud notes that in some cases the communication of a construction evokes in the patient a good number of lively recollections, very close to the material of the meaningful memory. Freud attributes this phenomenon to a resistance which succeeds in drawing consciousness away from the decisive memory and leading it towards memories of minor significance. He points out that, in spite of their liveliness, these recollections are not hallucinations. There are exceptions, however, which do lead Freud to draw some unexpected conclusions. He noticed that true hallucinations did occasionally occur – not only in the case of psychotic patients, but also "*in the case of other patients who were certainly not psychotic*" (ibid.: 267). This highly significant observation leads Freud to suggest that hallucinations may be the outcome of a forgotten childhood memory.

> *Perhaps it may be a general characteristic of hallucinations to which sufficient attention has not hitherto been paid that in them something that has been experienced in infancy and then forgotten returns – something that the child has seen or heard at a time when he could still hardly speak.* (ibid.: 267)

Going a step further, Freud suggests that even delusions, which are often accompanied by hallucinations, may be the outcome of "*the upward drive of the unconscious and the return of the repressed*" (ibid.: 267), following a mechanism similar to that involved in the formation of dreams, which mankind "*has equated with madness from time immemorial*" (ibid.: 267).

Taking this process of deduction even further, Freud suggests that madness itself may contain "*a fragment of historical truth*" and that the belief attaching to delusions takes its strength from some infantile source or other. If that were the case, the work of psychotherapy would aim to acknowledge the kernel of truth contained in the delusion and liberate it from its distortions. To put it differently, Freud comes to the conclusion that the delusions of patients are the equivalent of the constructions we build up in our analytical work; they are attempts at recovery and cure, as he had shown on many previous occasions. However, he adds, "*under the conditions of a psychosis, [delusions] can do no more than replace the fragment of reality that is being disavowed in the present by another fragment that had already been disavowed in the remote past*" (ibid.: 268). It would seem advisable, therefore, to clarify the relationship between disavowal and repression. "*It will be the task of each individual investigation to reveal the intimate connections between the material of the present disavowal and that of the original repression*" (ibid.: 268). Though Freud did not offer a definitive answer to the question, he must be given credit for having raised it.

Freud concludes this paper with an eloquent parallel between psychosis and hysteria.

> *Just as our construction is only effective because it recovers a fragment of lost experience, so the delusion owes its convincing power to the element of historical truth which it inserts in the place of the rejected reality. In this way a proposition which I originally asserted only of hysteria would apply also to delusions – namely, that those who are subject to them are suffering from their own reminiscences.* (ibid.: 268)

Post-Freudians

The end of an analysis: as many opinions as there are analysts . . .

As soon as it was published, in 1937, "Analysis Interminable and Interminable" gave rise to a considerable number of comments. In order to give the reader a true picture of the various opinions which have been expressed, I shall briefly summarize the points of view of a few psychoanalysts who belong to different schools of psychoanalytic thought and who come from various parts of the world. Their views were collated in 1991 by Joseph Sandler of London, and published as a Monograph of the International Psychoanalytical Association (IPA) entitled *On Freud's "Analysis Terminal and Interminable"*.

Jacob A. Arlow (New York) opens the discussion by insisting on the limits of the psychoanalytic approach; these limits are inherent not only to the technique but also to human nature, because conflicts are a fact of life. He warns against the illusion of creating a "perfect" human being thanks to psychoanalysis. Harald Leupold-Löwenthal (Vienna) observes that Freud quite clearly intended to avoid the trend which was beginning to emerge among some psychoanalysts of the time who wanted to codify the end of an analysis and subject it to strict technical rules and requirements. For David Zimmerman and A. L. Bento Mostardeiro (Porto Alegre), ending an analysis becomes possible once the patient has acquired a sufficient capacity for separateness and independence in the relationship with the analyst; these modifications have to do with the interaction between the psychoanalytic process and the developmental process. Terttu Eskelinen de Folch (Barcelona) writes that, although we acknowledge, as Freud did, that no analysis can ever really be complete, recent developments in theory and technique enable us nowadays to widen the field of psychoanalytic treatment and take on patients who, in Freud's day, would have been thought incapable of analysis. Arnold M. Cooper (New York) feels that the focus of contemporary psychoanalysis has shifted from the "taming of the instincts" which Freud wrote about in 1937 towards a more interpersonal standpoint involving object relations. He observes also that Freud was mistaken when he invoked biology to justify repudiation of femininity. André Green (Paris) examines the role attributed to the instinctual drives in Freud's final papers and argues that, as regards ending an analysis, it is a mistake to oppose drives and the object – the object reveals the drives because of its alternating presence and absence. In his conclusion, David Rosenfeld (Buenos Aires) highlights the many points of view held by psychoanalysts on such a complex set of problems as are involved in ending an analysis, and invites his colleagues to keep an open mind whenever fresh ideas are proposed.

New concepts

"Bedrock" – construction/reconstruction – delusion – ending an analysis – hallucination – passive attitude in men – penis envy in women – periodical analyses – the analyst's own analysis

MOSES AND MONOTHEISM

(1939a [1934–1938])

Freud's legacy: a work which raises more questions than it answers

Moses, the founder of Judaism, is one of the historical figures who most intrigued Freud. In 1914, he published "The Moses of Michelangelo" (1914b), a brief psychoanalytic study inspired by some unusual details of that famous statue. In the early 1930s, Freud had the impression that psychoanalysis was under threat both from within and from the rise of anti-Semitism; he decided to study the consequences of the surprising conclusion which he had drawn from his reading of certain books: Moses, the founder of Judaism, was not a Jew but an Egyptian who had forced the Hebrews to adopt the cult of Aten. The book, begun in 1934, was published in 1939, just a few months before Freud died. *Moses and Monotheism* is a development not only of *Totem and Taboo* – Freud attributes to the killing of Moses by the Hebrews a significance similar to the killing of the father of the primal horde – but also of *The Future of an Illusion*, for he sees in the murder of Moses the distant origin of the religion of Christ, with its sacrificial dimension. It is quite true that, from a historical point of view, the hypotheses discussed by Freud have a somewhat shaky foundation; those who have later commented on the book have no difficulty in acknowledging this. We should be careful, nonetheless, not to play down the importance of the questions Freud raises; they are also our own, be it in the field of religion or in that of science.

Biographies and history

Exile in London

In March 1938, Austria was annexed by Hitler's Germany. A few weeks later, the premises of the psychoanalytic publishing house – the inestimable *Verlag* – were raided and destroyed. All of Freud's friends, especially Ernest Jones and Princess Marie Bonaparte, insisted on his leaving the country. An international campaign, including in particular British and American diplomats, put considerable pressure on the German and Austrian authorities to allow him to leave Vienna. The greatest obstacle in fact was Freud himself: he did not want to leave his native country, for he felt that such a move would be tantamount to desertion. Jones tells us that he finally managed to convince Freud to emigrate by quoting the analogy of the second officer of the *Titanic*, who had been thrown off the sinking vessel by the explosion of a boiler; when the investigators asked him under what circumstances he had left the ship, he replied: "I did not leave her, she left me!" When the Austrian authorities finally agreed to allow Freud and his family to leave the country, the bureaucratic formalities began. Since Freud's bank accounts had been confiscated, it was Princess Marie Bonaparte who paid the considerable sum of money demanded by the authorities. These officials subjected Freud to one last humiliation: they required him to sign a declaration to the effect that he had not been in any way mistreated. According to Jones, Freud signed the requisite document, adding the ironic – but, given the circumstances, risky – comment: "*I can heartily recommend the Gestapo to anyone*". On 3 June 1938, Freud, his wife Martha and their daughter Anna left Vienna for London, travelling via Paris on the Orient Express. They spent a wonderful day in Paris at Princess Marie Bonaparte's house, and were very warmly welcomed on their arrival in London. Freud left behind in Vienna his four sisters, who had been unable to obtain exit permits; they died a few years later in a Nazi death camp.

Finishing *Moses* in freedom

Shortly after he settled in London, Freud began working on completing *Moses*; the third and final part was written in July 1938. The first two parts, which deal with Moses the Egyptian, had been published in 1937 in the psychoanalytic journal *Imago*, to which only a limited number of people subscribed. The idea of a book aimed at a much wider audience began to give cause for concern not only to his close friends, but also to the ever-widening circle of his acquaintances. Before his departure for England, Freud had given up the idea of publishing *Moses*, in order to avoid causing any irritation to the Catholic Church in Austria, which at the time was anti-Nazi. Settling in London, however, where he had come in order "*to die in freedom*" as he himself put it (Letter from Freud to Ernst Freud, 12 May 1938 [E. Freud 1975]), enabled him to develop his ideas to the full and to publish them as soon as possible. From both sides as it were – the Jews felt dispossessed of their ancestor, the Christians saw their belief in Christ treated by Freud as though it were a delusion – attempts were made to dissuade Freud from publishing *Moses*, but in vain. No argument could alter his resolve; indeed, each time he seemed even more determined to go ahead with his project. Freud could not understand why some people steadfastly refused to take into account the purely scientific character of his endeavour and demand that he censure his own writings. The book appeared in June 1939 simultaneously in Amsterdam (in German) and in New York (in an English translation).

23 September 1939: Freud dies

The year 1939 began on a sombre note – from Germany, there came news of looting and the arrest of thousands of Jews. In addition, Freud's health was deteriorating; a course of radium treatment gave him some temporary relief. In spite of his ill-health, he continued his analytical work until the end of July. In late September, he asked his doctor, Max Schur, to put an end to his suffering with the help of morphine, as Schur had agreed to do when he first became Freud's physician. Freud died with great dignity on 23 September 1939.

Discovering the text

Page numbers are those of *The Standard Edition of the Complete Psychological Works of Sigmund Freud*, vol. **23**, 3–140.

- **"MOSES WAS AN ARISTOCRATIC EGYPTIAN"**

When he argues that Moses, the liberator and law-maker of the Jewish people who look upon him as the greatest of their sons, was in fact of Egyptian origin, Freud is fully aware of the audacity of the claim he is making, especially for "*someone who is himself one of them*" (1939a [1934–1938]: 7). He begins by drawing our attention to the origin of Moses' name and puts forward a number of linguistic arguments in favour of the idea that the name is of Egyptian origin. Freud then finds support in Rank's work, and in particular in *Der Mythus von der Geburt des Helden* (Rank 1909) (*The Myth of the Birth of the Hero*), and compares the story of the birth of Moses with various myths which concern the origin of the Hero. This comparison shows that there is one significant feature common to all: the Hero is usually the child of the most aristocratic of parents – the son or daughter of a king – and is condemned to death by the father; the infant, however, is rescued and brought up by humble people, thereby escaping death. At some point in adolescence, the Hero takes revenge on the father and ends up triumphing over him. In the Moses myth, the child is of humble origin and is rescued by an Egyptian woman. Freud suggests that in fact Moses came from the Egyptian royal family; it was in order to comply with the myth that he was said to be of humble birth, and that it was these parents of low estate who set him adrift. Hence Freud's hypothesis:

> *then all at once we see things clearly: Moses was an Egyptian – probably an aristocrat – whom the legend was designed to turn into a Jew. [...] Whereas normally a hero, in the course of his life, rises above his humble beginnings, the heroic life of the man Moses began with his stepping down from his exalted position and descending to the level of the Children of Israel.* (Freud 1939a: 15)

- **"IF MOSES WAS AN EGYPTIAN..."**

- *The cult of Aten forced on the Hebrews*

What powerful motivation could have impelled an Egyptian of noble birth to put himself at the head of a group of foreign emigrants and leave his own land with them? For Freud, in all probability, Moses wanted to convert the Hebrews who had settled in Egypt to his own religion; this was no ordinary religion, all the same, it was monotheist. There was only one such religion at the time, that which had been introduced by the Pharaoh Akhenaten, who came to the throne in 1375 BCE. This young Pharaoh led the Egyptians away from the cult of Amun, too powerful in his view, and towards Aten, a Sun-God. Freud points out, however, that Akhenaten did not venerate the Sun as a material object but as the symbol of a unique and universal divine being. He left Amun-dominated Thebes for a new city which he named Akhetaten; the ruins of this royal capital were discovered in 1887, and it is now known as Tell el-'Amarna. We know nothing of how Akhenaten died, except that a rebellion among the oppressed priesthood re-established the cult of Amun, abolished that of Aten and removed all traces of the latter religion.

When we examine the cult of Aten more closely, says Freud, we notice that there are many elements which it has in common with the Jewish religion – for example, everything to do with magic is excluded from it, there is no representation of the Sun-God Aten, other than in symbolic form as a round disk with rays proceeding from it ending in human hands, and there is no mention of belief in a life after death. To these elements must be added the practice of circumcision, a typically Egyptian custom which no other people of the Middle East practised at that time; it would therefore seem that Moses forced the Hebrews to adopt this custom. In so doing, says Freud, Moses sought to emphasize the continuity with his Egyptian origins.

> *He wished to make them into a "holy nation", as is expressly stated in the Biblical text, and as a mark of this consecration he introduced among them too the custom which made them at least the equals of the Egyptians.* (ibid.: 30)

- *The cult of Yahweh: the return to a primitive god*

The biblical story continues to relate the history of the Hebrews, and tells us that at one point in time, after the Exodus from Egypt but before their arrival in the Promised Land, the people adopted a new religion. They chose to venerate the god Yahweh, a primitive and terrifying deity similar to the *Ba'alim*. This episode would thus imply a break in the continuity of transmission of Mosaic religion. Freud explains this with the help of a tradition which claims that the Egyptian

Moses was murdered by the Hebrews who rebelled against him and abolished the Egyptian religion which he had introduced. According to the historian Ernst Sellin (1922), from whom Freud borrowed the hypothesis, this tradition became the basis of all the later Messianic expectations.

• *The cult of Yahweh is eclipsed by the return of the Mosaic religion*

Basing his argument on the phenomenon known in psychoanalysis as *Entstellung* (distortion, displacement, putting something in another place), Freud shows that what we attempt to deny ends up re-emerging in a modified manner. He applies this concept to the reappearance of the old religion of Moses.

Moses, then, was killed by his people, and his murder was the result of a revolt against the authority which Moses himself had employed in order to force the Hebrews to adopt his religion. Proof of this can be found in the Biblical story of the adoration of the Golden Calf and the fury of Moses which resulted from that event. As Freud notes, the Egyptian Moses had given to some of the people a representation of God which was much more elevated spiritually than the primitive and terrifying god Yahweh; the Mosaic Egyptian religion had given to this highly spiritualized people "*the idea of a single deity embracing the whole world, who was not less all-loving than all-powerful, who was averse to all ceremonial and magic and set before men as their highest aim a life in truth and justice*" (Freud 1939a: 50).

In spite of the killing of Moses and the rejection of his God, Freud argues that the tradition of the Mosaic doctrine remained throughout the centuries that followed thanks to the Levites, who were probably the direct descendants of highly cultivated Egyptians who had accompanied Moses at the time of the Exodus; their teaching would have been handed down from generation to generation. Thus it was that the religion of Moses re-emerged and pushed the cult of Yahweh once and for all into the background.

• "MOSES, HIS PEOPLE AND MONOTHEIST RELIGION"

• *The return of the repressed in the emergence of religions*

Freud begins this section with a prefatory note: he states that initially he had no intention of publishing this third part of the book while he was still living in Austria, because he was afraid that he might lose the protection of the Catholic Church given the sheer audacity of his hypotheses; he feared that, as a result, psychoanalysis would find itself proscribed. Now that he is living in London, however, he feels free as to that point, all the more so in fact since the Catholic Church had proved itself a "*broken reed*" after the German invasion of Austria (ibid.: 57).

The latency period and tradition

How did it happen, asks Freud, that the Mosaic doctrines once again came to the fore? Psychoanalytic experience teaches us that there is a "*period of latency*" which can be observed clinically between the occurrence of a psychological trauma and the emergence of symptoms; Freud draws a parallel between this and, in the history of religions, the defection from the religion of Moses and the much later revival of Jewish monotheism. Freud explains this time interval in terms of the decisive role of "*tradition*" in handing down an event from generation to generation over the centuries.

> *And it was this tradition of a great past which continued to operate (from the background, as it were), which gradually acquired more and more power over people's minds and which in the end succeeded in changing the god Yahweh into the Mosaic god and in reawakening into life the religion of Moses that had been introduced and then abandoned long centuries before.*
> (ibid. 70)

The period of latency in neurosis

Psychoanalysis has taught us that a neurosis is caused by a traumatism which has occurred during the first five years of childhood. These traumatic experiences usually involve impressions of a sexual and aggressive nature. Afterwards, they are forgotten because we defend ourselves against becoming aware of them. After a certain length of time, however, they re-emerge in our adult life as a *"return of the repressed"*, and the neurosis becomes definitively established in one of several ways: compulsive constraints, inhibitions or phobias. Freud gives the brief example of a man who had been subjected to a psychosexual trauma in his childhood; the event itself was *"forgotten"* – i.e. repressed – but the subsequent outcome was sexual impotence, which appeared in adulthood, after a period of latency.

The period of latency applied to the history of humankind

Applying his hypotheses to the psychology of groups, Freud argues that a given population may have been marked by traumatic experiences of a sexual and aggressive nature which occurred far back in time and which were thereafter forgotten. After a period of latency, these collective traumatic experiences resurface and their effects are felt much later. This is also the case, says Freud, of religious phenomena. *"We believe that we can guess these events and we propose to show that their symptom-like consequences are the phenomena of religion"* (ibid.: 80).

Freud recalls that in *Totem and Taboo* (1912–1913) he had put forward the hypothesis of the killing of the father of the primal horde by his sons who rose up against him. The brothers banded together and, *"as was the custom in those days, devoured him raw"* (ibid.: 81). Later, a commemorative festival was established in order to venerate, in the totem animal, a substitute for the idealized dead father. Primitive peoples thus introduced totemic religion, the first form of religion in human history. In all religious teaching and rituals, adds Freud, we see emerging after lengthy intervals certain elements of the past history of our primitive forebears which had long been forgotten. A similar kind of phenomenon can be seen in the delusions of psychotics.

> *We must grant an ingredient such as this of what may be called* historical *truth to the dogmas of religion as well, which, it is true, bear the character of psychotic symptoms but which, as group phenomena, escape the curse of isolation.* (ibid.: 85)

It is on this pattern of the return of a forgotten historical past that Freud imagines the introduction of monotheism into Judaism and its continuation in Christianity. He argues that a growing sense of guilt – later designated as the "original sin" – led to a new religion which detached itself from Judaism, the religion of Christ, a man who himself belonged to the Jewish people. Since the original sin was a crime against God, it could be atoned for only by death. According to Freud, this crime was in fact the murder of the primal father.

> *In fact this crime deserving death had been the murder of the primal father who was later deified. But the murder was not remembered: instead of it there was a phantasy of its atonement, and for that reason this phantasy could be hailed as a message of redemption (*evangelium*). A son of God had allowed himself to be killed without guilt and had thus taken on himself the guilt of all men.* (ibid.: 86)

From this comes the famous saying: *"Judaism had been a religion of the father; Christianity became a religion of the son"* (ibid.: 88).

According to Freud, we can see in the Christian religion both the myth of the hero and a repetition of the ancient totem meal, represented by the ceremony of holy communion. Freud claims also that Christianity did not maintain the high spiritual level of Judaism, because it re-established the cult of *"the great mother-goddess"* and found room for *"many of the divine figures of polytheism"* (ibid.: 88) – an allusion to the Virgin Mary and to the Saints – and reintroduced magical and superstitious elements. In other words, for Freud, the arrival of Christianity was only partly an advance.

> *The triumph of Christianity was a fresh victory for the priests of Amun over Akhenaten's god after an interval of fifteen hundred years and on a wider stage. And yet in the history of religion – that is as regards the return of the repressed – Christianity was an advance and from that time on the Jewish religion was to some extent a fossil.* (ibid.: 88)

Following through his hypotheses all the way, Freud says that in retrospect the remorse arising from the killing of Moses no doubt provided the stimulus for the wishful fantasy of the Messiah. The Jewish people, however, continued to deny the father's murder, and anti-Semitism springs in part from the reproach addressed to them, in particular by the Christians: "*You killed our God!*" (ibid.: 90). Freud says that there should be an addition to this statement: "*We did the same thing, to be sure, but we have* admitted *it and since then we have been absolved*" (ibid.: 90).

Tradition: the main vehicle for transmission by phylogenesis

Archaic heritage: a constitutional factor

In this chapter, Freud asserts more firmly than ever before his belief in transmission through phylogenesis, a phenomenon he mentions all through his writings. According to Freud, a person's life is influenced not only by what has been experienced in the past and repressed into the unconscious, but also by innate factors, that is by "*elements with a phylogenetic origin – an* archaic heritage" (ibid.: 98), as is shown by the transmission of the religion of Moses. The questions which then arise are: Of what does this heritage consist? What does it contain? What is the evidence for it? For Freud, this archaic heritage corresponds to what in individuals we call "*the constitutional factor*": there are certain dispositions which are common to all human beings, and these are particularly obvious in the early years of life; these reactions, together with individual differences, can be attributed to the archaic heritage. Freud sees proof of this in the universality of symbolism in language – an original knowledge which transcends differences of language. He adds another argument in support of his hypothesis: the behaviour of children towards their parents in the Oedipus and castration complexes "*which seem unjustified in the individual case and only become intelligible phylogenetically – by their connection with the experience of earlier generations*" (ibid.: 99).

The role of the archaic heritage has been played down

Freud admits that he himself had not paid sufficient heed to the inheritance of traces left in memory through phylogenesis, tending to emphasize the acquired or learned influences.

> *On further reflection I must admit that I have behaved for a long time as though the inheritance of memory-traces of the experience of our ancestors, independently of direct communication and of the influence of education by the setting of an example, were established beyond question. When I spoke of the survival of a tradition among a people or of the formation of a people's character, I had mostly in mind an inherited tradition of this kind and not one transmitted by communication. Or at least I made no distinction between the two and was not clearly aware of my audacity in neglecting to do so.* (ibid.: 99–100)

In spite of the fact that it is impossible to bring any more tangible proof of the existence of an ancestral memory other than that observed in the work of analysis and ascribed to phylogenesis, Freud feels that he does all the same have sufficient evidence to support his theory.

Animal instinct: is this archaic heritage?

Perhaps an additional piece of evidence, says Freud, would be the parallel which can be drawn between, on the one hand, the instinct of animals, which is simply the memory of what was experienced by their ancestors, and, on the other, the archaic heritage of human beings. By making this assumption, says Freud,

> *[we] are diminishing the gulf which earlier periods of human arrogance had torn too wide apart between mankind and the animals. If any explanation is to be found of what are called the instincts of animals, which allow them to behave from the first in a new situation in life as though it were an old and familiar one – if any explanation at all is to be found of this instinctive life of animals, it can only be that they bring the experiences of their species with them into their own new existence – that is, that they have preserved memories of what was experienced by their ancestors. The position in the human animal would not at bottom be different. His own archaic heritage corresponds to the instincts of animals even though it is different in its compass and contents.* (ibid.: 100)

The killing of the father of the primal horde: an element which cannot be ignored

Fortified by the arguments he has just advanced, Freud asserts once again his firm belief that the killing of the father of the primal horde has been handed down from time immemorial through phylogenesis. "*After this discussion I have no hesitation in declaring that men must always have known (in this special way) that they once possessed a primal father and killed him*" (ibid.: 101). Two further questions now arise. First, how does an event such as the killing of the primal father enter the archaic heritage? For this to happen, the event must be important enough and repeated, so that it leaves a traumatic mark on memory, on the analogy of what happens in the neuroses. Second, in what circumstances can the event be reactivated? For Freud, the precipitating factor is the *real* repetition of the event in question; that is what revives the forgotten memory. Thus we can suppose that the murder of Moses, followed by the judicial murder of Christ, were the events which revealed the original cause. Moreover, there is another psychological argument, which involves repression followed by the return of the repressed.

> *A tradition that was based only on communication could not lead to the compulsive character that attaches to religious phenomena. It would be listened to, judged, and perhaps dismissed, like any other piece of information from outside; it would never attain the privilege of being liberated from the constraint of logical thought. It must have undergone the fate of being repressed, the condition of lingering in the unconscious, before it is able to display such powerful effects on its return, to bring the masses under its spell, as we have seen with astonishment and hitherto without comprehension in the case of religious tradition.* (ibid. 101)

• *Recapitulation and reassertion of atheistic convictions*

In the final part of the book, Freud recapitulates the broad outline of his argument and introduces some fresh thoughts to do with the genesis of certain character traits specific to the Jews as a people. In order to avoid unnecessary repetition – this is the second time that Freud summarizes his hypotheses in the course of the book – I shall do little more than mention some of this additional material. He attempts first of all to explain the fact that the Jews tend to consider themselves as superior to other peoples and indeed regard themselves as God's chosen people. Freud says that this self-esteem goes back to Moses, who did in fact state that they were God's chosen people. "*We venture to declare that it was this one man Moses who created the Jews*" (ibid.: 106).

The religion of Moses: an undoubted superiority

How was it possible for one man alone to have such an extraordinary influence on them? Freud sees in this a sign of the longing for the father which has lain within each of us since childhood; that is why "*all the characteristics with which we equipped the great man are paternal characteristics*" (ibid.: 109). Freud continues his recapitulation, reminding us that the religion of Moses brought the Jews a far greater conception of God; the prohibition against making an image of God encouraged the Jewish people to construct an abstract representation of their deity – and this implies a considerable advance in mentality.

> *For it (the prohibition) meant that a sensory perception was given second place to what may be called an abstract idea – a triumph of intellectuality over sensuality or, strictly speaking, an instinctual renunciation, with all its necessary psychological consequences.* (ibid.: 113)

The change from the matriarchal social order to the patriarchal one has, for Freud, similar implications.

> *But this turning from the mother to the father points in addition to a victory of intellectuality over sensuality – that is, an advance in civilization, since maternity is proved by the evidence of the senses while paternity is a hypothesis, based on an inference and a premiss.* (ibid.: 114)

The idea of a single God: the return of the memory of a repressed reality

Freud then states quite clearly that he does not believe in the existence of a single god, adding that such a belief derives from the fact that, in primeval times, there was indeed a single person who was elevated above all others. Afterwards, that person returned in the memory of human beings as a divinity. The phenomenon of the return of the repressed explains why the historical existence of that person had been forgotten, leaving nonetheless permanent traces in the human mind, comparable to a tradition. The idea of a single god would thus have re-emerged in the history of mankind in a way similar to the return of the repressed in neurotic individuals, in a compulsive manner; belief in a single deity is therefore no more than the revival of a memory of a long-forgotten historical truth.

> *One of these effects would be the emergence of the idea of a single great god – an idea which must be recognized as a completely justified memory, though, it is true, one which has been distorted. An idea such as this has a compulsive character:* it must *be believed. To the extent to which it is distorted, it may be described as a* delusion [In German *Wahn*, which can mean both illusion and delusion – author's note]; *insofar as it brings a return of the past, it must be called the truth. Psychiatric delusions, too, contain a small fragment of truth and the patient's conviction extends over from this truth on to its delusional wrappings.* (ibid. 130)

This second part of the book ends with an almost-verbatim repetition of the hypotheses Freud had developed earlier in his text.

Post-Freudians

The final challenge – and yet another outcry

When *Moses and Monotheism* was published, it caused a scandal, particularly in religious circles – Jewish and Christian alike. Freud's fellow Jews, furious at what they saw as his attempt to take their Moses away from them, were fearful of the long-term consequences which this might entail. The Christians responded all the more fiercely to his criticisms of Christianity because he went even further in this book than he had done in *The Future of an Illusion*: here he says not only that the Christian religion is the one which by far the most resembles a delusion, but also that he considers it to be a regression with respect to Jewish spiritual doctrine – a return to idolatry, in fact. This fierce debate, however, was soon pushed into the background by the declaration of war in September 1939. Moreover, for political reasons and in the light of the Nazi persecutions, Jewish circles attempted to play down the importance of Freud's thesis in order to leave the door open for a return to the tradition which had seen in Moses the founder of the Jewish religion.

What is left today of Freud's *Moses*?

With hindsight, Freud's text appears both complex and contradictory; it gave rise to a considerable number of different comments, many of which were impassioned. Recent research, however, enables us to read Freud's *Moses* with a rather more critical eye – and at the same time a more purposeful one. Of course Freud's thesis is questionable, particularly from the religious, historical and anthropological points of view – but it sheds a valuable light on Freud himself and asks fundamental questions to which as yet no satisfactory answer has been found. The following extracts from the major commentators may help the reader find his or her bearings.

For the psychoanalytic world, Freud's identification with Moses as a person was immediately obvious. Freud wrote the book in very particular circumstances: he was afraid that psychoanalysis would disappear and that he himself, as its founding father, would be threatened with death not only by the Nazis but also by his own followers, as had been the case with Moses. The book was in fact very well received by the authors of psychoanalytic psychobiographies, who saw in it a perfect example of its type. On the other hand, as regards the actual content of Freud's argument, contemporary psychoanalysts tend to see *Moses* in the same light as *Totem and Taboo* – a series of audacious hypotheses, the scientific validity of which is as yet far from being established. For example, it seems difficult to agree with the parallel Freud draws between the development of the individual and the historical development of the human species, with its appeal to group repression and the return of the repressed after a period of latency. It should however be acknowledged that the question of intergenerational phylogenetic transmission – Freud gives a clear account of his views on this towards the end of the book – has tended to be ignored by psychoanalysts; even today the question remains an open one.

Most contemporary anthropologists give little or no credit to Freud's hypothesis of the primal horde, though it must be said that some do adopt his point of view. From a historical point of view, recent research sees the Mesopotamian origins of the traditions of Judaism as more important than Egyptian sources; as a result, Freud's hypothesis according to which Moses was an Egyptian has been quite seriously called into question.

On the religious level, Freud's views have given rise to many and varied reactions. With respect to Freud's relationship with Judaism, *Moses* can be seen as a reflection on Jewish identity, on the character-traits which derive from it, and on the origins of anti-Semitism. Among the many studies which have explored these issues, Yosef H. Yerushalmi's (1991) book deserves a special mention. The author examines the manner in which Freud's text was so much part of his life at that point, and argues that through what he wrote, Freud turned Judaism into something "interminable" in the sense that it became god-less.

Freud was severely criticized also for what he said about the origins of religion and for the weakness of the arguments he put forward in support of his thesis. For example, when he states that obsessional symptoms and religious rituals are equivalent, this, for Meissner and Meissner (2002), is only a limited and in fact somewhat pathological aspect of religious expression; the impact of what Freud says is consequently very much reduced. "The analogy thus becomes reductionisic in the worst sense, and in the end contributes little to the understanding of authentic faith and religious practice" (2002: 475). Paul Ricoeur's view is similar: the psychoanalytic approach throws light only on that aspect of religion which has to do with idolatry (Ricoeur 1965). To put it in general terms, the reasons for Freud's hostility towards any form of organized religion – Christian or Jewish – involve many factors which I cannot go into here. However, if, as Emanuel Rice (2002) points out, we look beyond this figure of Freud "blinded by his hostility", we can see a very different picture emerge. Rice writes:

He [Freud] felt that Christianity was a return to premonotheistic pagan days, identical to the idol worship that predominated in Egypt prior to Akhenaton. It was prophetic religion that Freud pursued, and that was a worship based on the importance of individual responsibility and social justice. A theocentric conception of the universe would only interfere with its achievement. (Rice 2002: 297–298)

In conclusion, I would say that we must be careful not to underestimate the significance of what Freud had to say on the question of religion. In spite of the weakness of his arguments, of his own personal conflicts, and of his atheism, he raised many questions which still remain to be answered, as Meissner and Meissner (1984) pointed out. Ricoeur also disagrees with the preconceived idea according to which psychoanalysis is iconoclastic. For him, "destruction" of religion may quite simply be the critical expression of a faith which has been purified of all idolatry, independently of the psychoanalyst's opinion as regards religious belief. Moreover, from the point of view of religious faith, psychoanalysis has its limits; for Ricoeur, psychoanalysis ought not to make declarations on this topic at all.

Psychoanalysis is necessarily iconoclastic, regardless of the faith or nonfaith of the psychoanalyst, and this "destruction" of religion can be the counterpart of a faith purified of all idolatry. Psychoanalysis as such cannot go beyond the necessity of iconoclasm. This necessity is open to a double possibility, that of faith and that of nonfaith, but the decision about these two possibilities does not rest with psychoanalysis. (Ricoeur 1965: [1970: 230])

My own opinion is that psychoanalysis and religious belief belong to quite separate domains. Given, however, the inevitability of their interacting one with the other, I feel it is important to draw clear limits between each of these fields, in such a way that the existence of the one does not prevent that of the other.

New concepts

*Archaic heritage – displacement (***Entstellung***) – killing of the father – latency (period of) – monotheistic religion – phylogenesis – religion, religious ideas – tradition*

READING FREUD TODAY?

> *Man verstehet die Psychoanalyse immer noch am besten, wenn man ihre Entstehung und Entwicklung verfolgt.*
> Freud 1923a (1922): *G.W.* **13**: 211
>
> The best way of understanding psychoanalysis is still by tracing its origin and development.
> S.E. **18**: 235

Is Freud still relevant today? Have his ideas retained their universal value? As for the therapeutic method which derives from them – psychoanalysis as a treatment procedure – what is its significance in our day and age?

To those who ask such questions, I would reply that psychoanalysis is still very much alive: the "psychoanalytic revolution", as Marthe Robert (1964) put it, is still on the march. To demonstrate that fact, I imagined *Reading Freud* as an approach which would highlight the vitality of Freud's ideas and of psychoanalysis as a whole.

As far as I could, I have used the words of everyday language, as Freud did in German; this in no way diminished the complexity of his thinking. I feel it important to make Freud's writings and ideas easily accessible to the general reader, in such a way that reading one or other of his texts becomes meaningful to each of us and offers us something which will affect us on a personal level. If it finds an echo somewhere deep inside us, reading one of Freud's papers may be the starting-point for a deeper exploration of who and what we are.

From that point of view, Freud invites us to follow the road he himself took from the moment he discovered the unconscious in the course of his self-analysis. It was not just one discovery that he made – throughout his life, he made a series of discoveries, each leading on to the next. That is why reading Freud's texts chronologically is of more than just historical interest: it is the story of an exploration which we can use as a guide as we go deeper and deeper into ourselves and eventually find our own way forward.

As this book draws to a close, the reader will no doubt have realized that Freud left us a legacy which has an extraordinary potential for further development; it has been enhanced by the contribution of post-Freudian psychoanalysts. Its potential has not been used up – far from it, indeed, hence the question with which we find ourselves faced: what are *we* going to do with that inheritance? The answer to that question depends very much on the psychoanalyst concerned; the way in which we accept that inheritance depends on the process of mourning that we have to work through with respect to the death of Freud. For some, being faithful to one's inheritance means keeping it exactly as it is, with the risk of stultifying it, as Danielle Quinodoz pointed out, for example: "I may put Freud's precious texts away safely in a glass case, like the precious china dinnerware handed down from my ancestors, which would be ruined if I were I to put it in the dishwasher" (2002: 183–184). For others, being faithful to Freud means seizing hold of one part of the inheritance and developing it in isolation, to the detriment of the rest; the risk here is that of fragmenting psychoanalysis, with the result that there would be as many kinds of psychoanalysis as there are psychoanalysts.

With the passing of time, how are we to avoid the pitfalls which lie before us today? My own opinion is that the best way to keep Freud's legacy alive is to convey all of its dynamism by establishing a dialogue with him via what he bequeathed to us. I hope that *Reading Freud* will be for the reader not only an opportunity to meet Freud but also an invitation to go even further and dialogue with him through his own original texts.

Freud is no longer with us. Yet he remains alive not only through his writings but also through the psychoanalytic treatment he handed down to us. Reading Freud's writings and entering into analysis are two very different processes. It is true of course that, in the latter, a kind of dialogue is set up in continuity with Freud – through the transference/counter-transference relationship between analyst and analysand. But that, as they say, is another story . . .

APPENDIX

A seminar on the chronological reading of Freud's writings

As I wrote in the Introduction, I particularly want to thank by name everyone who participated in one or other of my seminars since 1988:

Adela ABELLA, Lolita ADLER, Anne-Sophie ARCHINARD, Viviane ARMAND-GERSON, Carole BACH, Jean-Pierre BACHMANN, Nourrédine BEN BACHIR, Éric BIERENS DE HAAN, Tiziana BIMPAGE, Marie-Luce BISETTI, Christiane BLANCHARD, Olivier BONARD, Marielle BOUCHACOURT-GUSBERTI, Évelyne BRENAS, Sylvie BURNAND, Jean-Marc CHAUVIN, Michèle DE RHAM, Bérangère DE SENARCLENS, Geneviève DEJUSSEL, Francis DELAITE, Marinella DESCLOUDS, Viviane DICHY, Marité GENOUD, Rino GENTA, Bernard GENTHIALON, Jacqueline GIRARD, Yvonne GITNACHT-KNABE, Françoise GOURMEL, Gilles GRESSOT, François GROSS, Céline GUR-GRESSOT, Franco GUSBERTI, José GUTIERREZ, Marie-Jeanne HAENNI, Rhéane HEMMELER, Manuela JACCARD-GOBBI, Nicolas JACOT-DES-COMBES, Marie-José JAUMAIN, Madeleine JOANES, Suzanna JOLIAT-DUBERG, Carole KAELIN, Dora KNAUER, Denise KOECHLIN, Bernard KRAUSS, Silvia KUEHNER-HELLMIGK, Alicia LIENGME, Luc MAGNENAT, Denise MATILE, Daniel NICOLLIER, Irène NIGOLIAN, Jérôme OTTINO (†), Berdj PAPAZIAN, Anna-Maria PARISI-GASTALDI, Claire PAYOT, Françoise PAYOT, Olga PEGANOVA, Ignacio PELEGRI, Maja PERRET-CATIPOVIC, Julia PREISWERK, Bernard REITH, Marion RIGHETTI, Nino RIZZO, Michel ROBERT, Anne-Lise ROD, Doriane RODITI-BUHLER, Marlyse ROHRBACH (†), Claire ROJAS, Andreas SAURER, Patricia SIMIONI, Joseph SNAKKERS, Benvenuto SOLCA, Branda STEINFELD-WALTHER-BUEL, Michel STEULET, Xavier VENTURA, Saskia VON OVERBECK-OTTINO, Christa VON SUSANI, Jean-Pierre WABER, Urs WALTHER-BUEL, Patricia WALTZ, Wolfgang WALZ, Nathalie ZILKHA, Stefan ZLOT.

BIBLIOGRAPHY

Abraham, K. (1908) "The Psychosexual Differences between Hysteria and Dementia Praecox", trans. D. Bryan and A. Strachey, in Abraham, K., *Selected Papers on Psychoanalysis*, London: Karnac (1927; reprinted 1988).
—— (1911) "Notes on the Psycho-analytical Investigation and Treatment of Manic-depressive Insanity and Allied Conditions", trans. D. Bryan and A. Strachey, in Abraham, K., *Selected Papers on Psychoanalysis*, London: Karnac (1927; reprinted 1988).
—— (1924) "A Short Study of the Development of the Libido, Viewed in the Light of Mental Disorders", trans. D. Bryan and A. Strachey, in Abraham, K., *Selected Papers on Psychoanalysis*, London: Karnac (1927; reprinted 1988).
Andreassen, N. C. (1998) "Understanding Schizophrenia: A Silent Spring?", editorial, *American Journal of Psychiatry*, 155: 1657–1659.
Anzieu, D. (1959) *L'Auto-analyse de Freud*, Paris: Presses Universitaires de France; trans. P. Graham (1986) *Freud's Self-Analysis*, Madison, CT: International Universities Press and London: Hogarth Press and The Institute of Psycho-Analysis.
—— (1988a) Preface to Freud, S. (1901) *Sur les rêves*, Paris: Gallimard.
—— (1988b) *L'Auto-analyse de Freud et la découverte de la psychanalyse*, Paris: Presses Universitaires de France.
Balint, M. (1952) *Primary Love and Psychoanalytic Technique*, London: Hogarth Press.
Bellemin-Noël, J. (1983) *Gradiva au pied de la lettre*, Paris: Presses Universitaires de France.
Bion, W. R. (1957) "Differentiation of the Psychotic from the Non-Psychotic Personalities", *International Journal of Psycho-Analysis*, 38, parts 3–4; also in Bion, W. R. (1967) *Second Thoughts*, London: Heinemann (reprinted London: Karnac, 1984).
—— (1959) "Attacks on Linking", *International Journal of Psycho-Analysis*, 40, parts 5–6; also in Bion, W. R. (1967) *Second Thoughts*, London: Heinemann (reprinted London: Karnac, 1984).
—— (1961) *Experiences in Groups and Other Papers*, London: Tavistock.
—— (1962) *Learning from Experience*, New York: Basic Books and London: Heinemann (reprinted London: Karnac, 1984).
—— (1967) *Second Thoughts*, London: Heinemann (reprinted London: Karnac, 1984).
Blacker, K. H. and Abraham, R. (1982) "The Rat Man Revisited: Comments on Maternal Influences", *International Journal of Psychoanalysis and Psychotherapy*, 9: 267–285.
Bleger, J. (1967) "Psychoanalysis of the Psycho-Analytic Frame", *International Journal of Psycho-Analysis*, 48: 511–519.
Bleuler, E. (1911) *Dementia Praecox oder die Gruppe der Schizophrenien*, trans. J. Zinkin (1950) *Dementia Praecox or the Group of Schizophrenias*, New York: International Universities Press.
Blum, H. P. (1976) "Masochism, the Ego Ideal, and the Psychology of Women", *Journal of the American Psychoanalytic Association*, 24 (5): 157–193.
Bonaparte, M. (1951) *La Sexualité de la femme*, Paris: Presses Universitaires de France; trans. J. Rodker (1953) *Female Sexuality*, New York: International Universities Press.
——, Freud, A. & Kris, E. (1956) Editor's note (note no. 5), in *La Naissance de la psychanalyse*, Paris: Presses Universitaires de France.
Bourguignon, A., Cotet, P., Laplanche, J. and Robert, F. (1989) *Traduire Freud*, Paris: Presses Universitaires de France.
Bowlby, J. (1969, 1973, 1980) *Attachment and Loss*, 3 vols, London: Hogarth Press and The Institute of Psycho-Analysis.
Braunschweig, D. (1991) "Fantasmes originaires et Surmoi: la phylogenèse", *Revue Française de Psychanalyse*, 55: 1251–1262.

Breen, D. (1993) *The Gender Conundrum: Contemporary Psychoanalytic Perspectives on Femininity and Masculinity*, London and New York: Routledge.
Breuer, J. and Freud, S. (1893) "On the Psychical Mechanism of Hysterical Phenomena: Preliminary Communication", in Freud, S. and Breuer, J. (1895d) *Studies on Hysteria, The Standard Edition of the Complete Psychological Works of Sigmund Freud*, vol. 2, London: Hogarth Press and The Institute of Psycho-Analysis.
Britton, R. (2003) *Sex, Death, and the Superego: Experiences in Psychoanalysis*, London and New York: Karnac.
Canestri, J. (1990) "Quelques réponses", in Amati-Mehler, J., Argentieri, S., and Canestri, J., *La Babel de l'inconscient: Langue maternelle, langues étrangères et psychanalyse*, Paris: Presses Universitaires de France; trans. J. Whitelaw-Cucco (1993) *The Babel of the Unconscious: Mother Tongue and Foreign Languages in the Psychoanalytic Dimension*, Madison, CT: International Universities Press.
Carson, R. L. (1962) *Silent Spring*, Boston, MA: Houghton Mifflin and Cambridge: Riverside Press.
Chasseguet-Smirgel, J. (1976) "Freud and Female Sexuality: The Consideration of Some Blind Spots in the Exploration of the 'Dark' Continent", *International Journal of Psycho-Analysis*, 57: 275–286.
——, Luquet-Parat, C., Grunberger, B., McDougall, J., Torok, M., and David, C. (1964) *Recherches psychanalytiques nouvelles sur la sexualité féminine*, Paris: Payot; *Female Sexuality: New Psychoanalytic Views*, London: Karnac Books (1991).
Cooper, S. H. (1998) "Counter-transference Disclosure and the Conceptualization of Analytic Technique", *Psychoanalytic Quarterly*, 67: 128–154.
Devereux, G. (1972) *Ethnopsychoanalysis: Psychoanalysis and Anthropology as Complementary Frames of Reference*, Berkeley, CA: University of California Press (2nd edn, 1978).
Diatkine, G. (1997) *Jacques Lacan*, Paris: Presses Universitaires de France.
Dolto, F. (1981) *La Foi au risque de la psychanalyse (Dialogue avec G. Séverin)*, Paris: Seuil.
Dolto, F. & Séverin, G. (1977–1978) *L'Evangile au risque de la psychanalyse*, Paris: J. P. Delarge; trans. Helen R. Lane as *The Jesus of Psychoanalysis: A Freudian Interpretation of the Gospel*, Garden City, NY: Doubleday.
Dor, J. (1985) *Introduction à la lecture de Lacan*, Paris: Denoël; ed. J. Feher-Gurewich, trans. S. Fairfield (1998) *Introduction to the Reading of Lacan: The Unconscious Structured Like a Language*, New York: Other Press and London: Karnac (reprinted 2004).
Duparc, F. (2001) "The Counter-transference Scene in France", *International Journal of Psycho-Analysis*, 82: 151–169.
Eissler, K. R. (1961) *Leonardo da Vinci: Psychoanalytic Notes on the Enigma*, New York: International Universities Press and London: Hogarth Press.
Erikson, E. H. (1950) *Childhood and Society*, New York: Norton and London: Imago (1951).
Etchegoyen, R. H. (1991) *The Fundamentals of Psychoanalytic Technique*, London and New York: Karnac.
European Psychoanalytical Federation (1986) *La Pulsion de mort: Symposium (Marseille, 1984)*, Paris: Presses Universitaires de France.
Fairbairn, R. D. (1956) "Considerations Arising out of the Schreber Case", *British Journal of Medical Psychology*, 19: 113–127.
Federn, P. (1943) "Psychoanalysis of Psychoses", in Federn, P. (1952) *Ego Psychology and the Psychoses*, New York: Basic Books and London: Imago.
Fenichel, O. (1941) *Problems of Psychoanalytic Technique*, trans. D. Brunswick, New York: Psychoanalytic Quarterly.
Ferenczi, S. (1909) "Introjection and Transference", in Ferenczi, S., ed. M. Balint, trans. E. Mosbacher and others (1955) *Final Contributions to the Problems and Methods of Psycho-Analysis*, London: Hogarth Press and The Institute of Psycho-Analysis (reprinted London: Maresfield, 1980).
—— (1913) "Stages in the Development of the Sense of Reality", in *Selected Papers of Sandor Ferenczi, Vol. 1*, New York: Basic Books.
—— (1928) "The Problem of the Termination of the Analysis", in Ferenczi, S., ed. M. Balint, trans. E. Mosbacher and others (1955) *Final Contributions to the Problems and Methods of Psycho-Analysis*, London: Hogarth Press and The Institute of Psycho-Analysis (reprinted London: Maresfield, 1980).
—— and Rank, O. (1924) *The Development of Psychoanalysis*, Madison, CT: International Universities Press (1986).
Ferro, A. (1996) *Nella stanza d'analisi: Emozioni, Racconto, Transformazioni*, Milan: Raffaello Cortina Editore; trans. P. Slotkin (2002) *In the Analyst's Consulting Room*, London and New York: Brunner-Routledge.
Flanders, S. (1993) Introduction, in *The Dream Discourse Today*, London: Routledge.
Foulkes, S. H. (1964) *Therapeutic Group Analysis*, New York: International Universities Press.
Frankiel, R. V. (1991) "A Note on Freud's Inattention to the Negative Oedipal in Little Hans", *International Revue of Psycho-Analysis*, 18: 181–184.
Freeman, D. (1967) "Totem and Taboo – a Reappraisal", in Münsterberger, W. (ed.) (1969) *Man and his Culture: Psychoanalytic Anthropology after "Totem and Taboo"*, London: Rapp & Whiting and New York: Taplinger.
Freud, A. (1923) "The Relation of Beating Fantasies to a Day-Dream", *International Journal of Psycho-*

Analysis, 4: 89–102; also in Freud, A. (1966–1980) *The Writings of Anna Freud*, vol. 1, New York: International Universities Press.
—— (1927a) *Einführung in die Technik der Kinderanalyse*, Vienna: Internationaler Psychoanalytischer Verlag; translated as *Introduction to the Technique of Child Analysis*, New York: Nervous and Mental Disease Publishing (1928) and as Parts I and II of *The Psycho-Analytic Treatment of Children*, London: Imago (1946).
—— (1927b) "Preparation for Child Analysis", in Freud, A. (1966–1980) *The Writings of Anna Freud*, vol. 1, New York: International Universities Press.
—— (1936) *The Ego and the Mechanisms of Defence*, London: Hogarth Press (International Library of Psycho-Analysis); also in *The Writings of Anna Freud*, vol. 2, New York: International Universities Press.
—— (1965) *Normality and Pathology in Childhood: Assessments of Development*, New York: International Universities Press; also in *The Writings of Anna Freud*, vol. 6, New York: International Universities Press.
—— and Burlingham, D. (1943) *War and Children*, New York: International Universities Press.
Freud, Ernst (ed.) (1975) *The Letters of Sigmund Freud*, New York: Basic Books.
Freud, Sigmund (1887–1902) *Extracts from the Fliess Papers*, edited by Marie Bonaparte, Anna Freud and Ernst Kris, *S.E.* 1: 175–280.
—— Draft G, in *Extracts from the Fliess Papers*, *S.E.* 1: 200–206.
—— Draft H, in *Extracts from the Fliess Papers*, *S.E.* 1: 206–212.
—— Draft K, in *Extracts from the Fliess Papers*, *S.E.* 1: 220–229.
—— (1894a) "The Neuro-Psychoses of Defence", *G.W.* 1: 59–74; *S.E.* 3: 41–61.
—— (1895b [1894]) "On the Grounds for Detaching a Particular Syndrome from Neurasthenia under the Description 'Anxiety Neurosis' ", *G.W.* 1: 315–342; *S.E.* 3: 85–115.
—— (1895c [1894]) "Obsessions and Phobias: Their Psychical Mechanism and their Aetiology", *G.W.* 1: 345–353 (in French); *S.E.* 3: 69–82.
—— (1895h) *Mechanismus der Zwangsvorstellungen und Phobien*, *G.W. Nachtr.*: 352–359.
—— (1896b) "Further Remarks on the Neuro-Psychoses of Defence", *G.W.* 1: 379–403; *S.E.* 3: 157–185.
—— (1897b) "Abstracts of the Scientific Writings of Dr. Sigm. Freud 1877–1897", *G.W.* 1: 463–488; *S.E.* 3: 223–257.
—— (1898a) "Sexuality in the Aetiology of the Neuroses", *G.W.* 1: 491–516; *S.E.* 3: 259–285.
—— (1898b) "The Psychical Mechanism of Forgetfulness", *G.W.* 1: 519–529; *S.E.* 3: 287–297.
—— (1899a) "Screen Memories", *G.W.* 1: 531–554; *S.E.* 3: 299–322.
—— (1900a) *The Interpretation of Dreams*, *G.W.* 2–3; *S.E.* 4–5.
—— (1901a) *On Dreams*, *G.W.* 2–3: 643–700; *S.E.* 5: 633–686.
—— (1901b) *The Psychopathology of Everyday Life*, *G.W.* 4; *S.E.* 6.
—— (1904a) "Freud's Psycho-Analytic Procedure", *G.W.* 5: 3–10; *S.E.* 7: 247–254.
—— (1905a) "On Psychotherapy", *G.W.* 5: 13–26; *S.E.* 7: 255–268.
—— (1905c) *Jokes and their Relation to the Unconscious*, *G.W.* 6; *S.E.* 8.
—— (1905d) *Three Essays on the Theory of Sexuality*, *G.W.* 5: 29–145; *S.E.* 7: 123–243.
—— (1905e [1901]) "Fragment of an Analysis of a Case of Hysteria" (Dora), *G.W.* 5: 163–286; *S.E.* 7: 1–122.
—— (1907a) *Delusions and Dreams in Jensen's* "Gradiva", *G.W.* 7: 31–125; *S.E.* 9: 1–95.
—— (1907b) "Obsessive Actions and Religious Practices", *G.W.* 7: 129–139; *S.E.* 9: 115–127.
—— (1907c) "The Sexual Enlightenment of Children", *G.W.* 7: 19–27; *S.E.* 9: 129–139.
—— (1908b) "Character and Anal Erotism", *G.W.* 7: 203–209; *S.E.* 9: 167–175.
—— (1908c) "On the Sexual Theories of Children", *G.W.* 7: 171–188; *S.E.* 9: 205–226.
—— (1908d) " 'Civilized' Sexual Morality and Modern Nervous Illness", *G.W.* 7: 143–167; *S.E.* 9: 177–204.
—— (1909b) "Analysis of a Phobia in a Five-Year-Old Boy ('Little Hans')", *G.W.* 7: 243–377; *S.E.* 10: 1–147.
—— (1909d) "Notes upon a Case of Obsessional Neurosis", *G.W.* 7: 381–463; *S.E.* 10: 151–249.
—— (1910c) *Leonardo da Vinci and a Memory of his Childhood*, *G.W.* 8: 128–211; *S.E.* 11: 57–137.
—— (1910d) "The Future Prospects of Psycho-Analytic Therapy", *G.W.* 8: 104–115; *S.E.* 11: 139–151.
—— (1910h) "A Special Type of Choice of Object Made by Men (Contributions to the Psychology of Love I)", *G.W.* 8: 66–77; *S.E.* 11: 163–175.
—— (1910k) " 'Wild' Psycho-Analysis", *G.W.* 8: 118–125; *S.E.* 11: 219–227.
—— (1911b) "Formulations on the Two Principles of Mental Functioning", *G.W.* 8: 230–238; *S.E.* 12: 213–226.
—— (1911c) "Psycho-Analytic Notes on an Autobiographical Account of a Case of Paranoia (Dementia Paranoides)", *G.W.* 8: 240–316; *S.E.* 12: 1–79.
—— (1911d) "The Significance of Sequences of Vowels", *G.W.* 8: 348; *S.E.* 12: 341.
—— (1911e) "The Handling of Dream-Interpretation in Psycho-Analysis", *G.W.* 8: 350–357; *S.E.* 12: 89–96.
—— (1912b) "The Dynamics of Transference", *G.W.* 8: 364–374; *S.E.* 12: 97–108.
—— (1912d) "On the Universal Tendency to Debasement in the Sphere of Love (Contributions to the Psychology of Love II), *G.W.* 8: 78–91; *S.E.* 11: 177–190.
—— (1912e) "Recommendations to Physicians Practising Psycho-Analysis", *G.W.* 8: 376–387; *S.E.* 12: 109–120.
—— (1912–1913) *Totem and Taboo: Some Points of Agreement between the Mental Lives of Savages and Neurotics*, *G.W.* 9; *S.E.* 13: 1–161.

—— (1913b) "Introduction to: Pfister's *The Psycho-Analytic Method*", *G.W.* 10: 448–450; *S.E.* 12: 327–331.
—— (1913c) "On Beginning the Treatment", *G.W.* 8: 454–478; *S.E.* 12: 121–144.
—— (1913i) "The Disposition to Obsessional Neurosis", *G.W.* 8: 442–452; *S.E.* 12: 311–326.
—— (1914b) "The Moses of Michelangelo", *G.W.* 10: 171–201; *S.E.* 13: 209–236.
—— (1914c) "On Narcissism: An Introduction", *G.W.* 10: 138–170; *S.E.* 14: 67–102.
—— (1914d) "On the History of the Psycho-Analytic Movement", *G.W.* 10: 44–113; *S.E.* 14: 1–66.
—— (1914g) "Remembering, Repeating and Working-Through", *G.W.* 10: 126–136; *S.E.* 12: 145–156.
—— (1915–1917) "Papers on Metapsychology", *G.W.* 10; *S.E.* 14: 105–259.
—— (1915a [1914]) "Observations on Transference-Love", *G.W.* 10: 306–321; *S.E.* 12: 159–171.
—— (1915b) "Thoughts for the Times on War and Death", *G.W.* 10: 324–355; *S.E.* 14: 273–300.
—— (1915c) "Instincts and their Vicissitudes", *G.W.* 10: 210–232; *S.E.* 14: 109–140.
—— (1915d) "Repression", *G.W.* 10: 248–261; *S.E.* 14: 141–158.
—— (1915e) "The Unconscious", *G.W.* 10: 264–303; *S.E.* 14: 159–215.
—— (1916–1917 [1915–1917]) *Introductory Lectures on Psycho-Analysis*, *G.W.* 11; *S.E.* 15–16.
—— (1917c) "On Transformations of Instinct as Exemplified in Anal Erotism", *G.W.* 10: 402–410; *S.E.* 17: 125–133.
—— (1917d) "A Metapsychological Supplement to the Theory of Dreams", *G.W.* 10: 421–426; *S.E.* 14: 217–235.
—— (1917e [1915]) "Mourning and Melancholia", *G.W.* 10: 428–446; *S.E.* 14: 237–258.
—— (1918b [1914]) "From the History of an Infantile Neurosis" (The "Wolf-Man"), *G.W.* 12: 29–157; *S.E.* 17: 1–122.
—— (1919a) "Lines of Advance in Psycho-Analytic Therapy", *G.W.* 12: 183–194; *S.E.* 17: 157–168.
—— (1919e) "A Child is Being Beaten (A Contribution to the Study of the Origin of Sexual Perversions)", *G.W.* 12: 197–226; *S.E.* 17: 175–204.
—— (1919h) "The 'Uncanny' ", *G.W.* 12: 229–268; *S.E.* 17: 217–252.
—— (1920a) "The Psychogenesis of a Case of Female Homosexuality", *G.W.* 12: 271–302; *S.E.* 18: 145–172.
—— (1920g) *Beyond the Pleasure Principle*, *G.W.* 13: 3–69; *S.E.* 18: 1–64.
—— (1921c) *Group Psychology and the Analysis of the Ego*, *G.W.* 13: 73–161; *S.E.* 18: 65–143.
—— (1921e) Extract from a letter to Claparède, *S.E.* 11: 214–215.
—— (1923a) "Two Encyclopaedia Articles", *G.W.* 13: 211–233; *S.E.* 18: 235–259.
—— (1923b) *The Ego and the Id*, *G.W.* 13: 237–289; *S.E.* 19: 1–59.
—— (1923e) "The Infantile Genital Organization: An Interpolation into the Theory of Sexuality", *G.W.* 13: 293–298; *S.E.* 19: 139–145.
—— (1924b) "Neurosis and Psychosis", *G.W.* 13: 387–391; *S.E.* 19: 147–153.
—— (1924c) "The Economic Problem of Masochism", *G.W.* 13: 371–383; *S.E.* 19: 155–170.
—— (1924d) "The Dissolution of the Oedipus Complex", *G.W.* 13: 395–402; *S.E.* 19: 171–179.
—— (1924e) "The Loss of Reality in Neurosis and Psychosis", *G.W.* 13: 363–368; *S.E.* 19: 181–187.
—— (1925d [1924]) "An Autobiographical Study", *G.W.* 14: 33–96; *S.E.* 20: 1–70.
—— (1925h) "Negation", *G.W.* 14: 11–15; *S.E.* 19: 233–239.
—— (1925j) "Some Psychical Consequences of the Anatomical Distinction between the Sexes", *G.W.* 14: 19–30; *S.E.* 19: 241–258.
—— (1926b) "Karl Abraham", *G.W.* 14: 564; *S.E.* 20: 277–278.
—— (1926d [1925]) *Inhibitions, Symptoms and Anxiety*, *G.W.* 14: 113–205; *S.E.* 20: 75–174.
—— (1926e) *The Question of Lay Analysis: Conversations with an Impartial Person*, *G.W.* 14: 209–286; *S.E.* 20: 177–250.
—— (1927c) *The Future of an Illusion*, *G.W.* 14: 325–380; *S.E.* 21: 1–56.
—— (1927d) "Humour", *G.W.* 14: 383–389; *S.E.* 21: 159–166.
—— (1927e) "Fetishism", *G.W.* 14: 311–317; *S.E.* 21: 147–157.
—— (1928a [1927]) "A Religious Experience", *G.W.* 14: 393–396; *S.E.* 21: 167–172.
—— (1930a [1929]) *Civilization and its Discontents*, *G.W.* 14: 421–506; *S.E.* 21: 57–145.
—— (1931b) "Female Sexuality", *G.W.* 14: 517–537; *S.E.* 21: 221–243.
—— (1933a [1932]) *New Introductory Lectures on Psycho-Analysis*, *G.W.* 15: 6–197; *S.E.* 22: 1–182.
—— (1933b [1932]) "Why War?", *G.W.* 16: 13–27; *S.E.* 22: 203–215.
—— (1933c) "Sándor Ferenczi", *G.W.* 16: 267–269; *S.E.* 22: 225–229.
—— (1936a) "A Disturbance of Memory on the Acropolis", *G.W.* 16: 250–257; *S.E.* 22: 237–248.
—— (1937a) "Lou Andreas-Salomé", *G.W.* 16: 270; *S.E.* 23: 297–298.
—— (1937c) "Analysis Terminable and Interminable", *G.W.* 16: 59–99; *S.E.* 23: 211–253.
—— (1937d) "Constructions in Analysis", *G.W.* 16: 43–56; *S.E.* 23: 256–269.
—— (1939a [1934–1938]) *Moses and Monotheism*, *G.W.* 16: 101–246; *S.E.* 23: 3–140.
—— (1940a [1938]) *An Outline of Psycho-Analysis*, *G.W.* 17: 67–138; *S.E.* 23: 139–207.
—— (1940e [1938]) "Splitting of the Ego in the Process of Defence", *G.W.* 17: 59–62; *S.E.* 23: 271–278.
—— (1941f [1938]) "Findings, Ideas, Problems", *G.W.* 17: 151–152; *S.E.* 23: 299–300.
—— (1942a [1905–1906]) "Psychopathic Characters on the Stage", *S.E.* 7: 303–310.
—— (1950a [1887–1902]) *The Origins of Psycho-Analysis*, London: Imago and New York: Basic Books (1954) (partly, including "Project for a Scientific Psychology", in *S.E.* 1: 175).

—— (1985a [1915]) "A Phylogenetic Fantasy: An Overview of the Transference Neuroses", edited and with an essay by I. Grubrich-Simitis; trans. A. Hoffer & P. T Hoffer; Cambridge, MA: Harvard University Press.
—— (1985c [1887–1904]) *The Complete Letters of Sigmund Freud to Wilhelm Fliess 1887–1904*, trans. and ed. J. Masson, London & Cambridge, MA: Harvard University Press.
—— (1987c [1908–1938]) *Correspondance Sigmund Freud-Stefan Zweig*, trans. G. Hauer and D. Plassard, ed. H. U. Lindken, Paris: Rivages (1991).
—— (1992 [1908–1938]) *The Freud–Binswanger Correspondence 1908–1938*, ed. G. Fichtner, trans. A. J. Pomerans and T. Roberts, New York: Other Press & London: Karnac (2003).
—— and Abraham, K. (2003) *The Complete Correspondence of Sigmund Freud and Karl Abraham, 1907–1925*, ed. E. Falzeder, trans. C. Schwarzacher, C. Trollope and K. Majthényi King, London: Karnac.
—— and Andreas-Salomé, L. (1985) *Letters*, ed. E. Pfeiffer, trans. W. Robson-Scott & E. Robson-Scott, London and New York: Norton.
—— and Breuer, J. (1893a [1892]) "On the Psychical Mechanism of Hysterical Phenomena: Preliminary Communication", *G.W.* 1: 83–98; *S.E.* 2: 1–17.
—— and Breuer, J. (1895d) *Studies on Hysteria*, *G.W.* 1: 77–312; *S.E.* 2: 1–309.
—— and Ferenczi, S. (1992) *The Correspondence of Sigmund Freud and Sándor Ferenczi, Volume 1: 1908–1914*, ed. E. Brabant, E. Falzeder and P. Giampieri-Deutsch, trans. P. Hoffer, London & Cambridge, MA: Harvard University Press.
—— and Jones, E. (1993) *The Complete Correspondence of Sigmund Freud and Ernest Jones, 1908–1939*, ed. R. A. Paskauskas, London & Cambridge, MA: Harvard University Press.
—— and Pfister, O. (1963a) *Psychoanalysis and Faith: The Letters of Sigmund Freud and Oskar Pfister*, ed. H. Meng & E. L. Freud, trans. E. Mosbacher, New York: Basic Books.
—— and Zweig, A. (1970) *The Letters of Sigmund Freud and Arnold Zweig*, ed. E. Freud, trans. E. Robson-Scott & W. Robson-Scott, New York: Harcourt Brace Jovanovich.
Gabbard, G. O. and Lester, E. (1995) *Boundaries and Boundary Violations in Psychoanalysis*, New York: Basic Books.
Gardiner, M. (ed.) (1971) *The Wolf-Man and Sigmund Freud*, New York: Basic Books and London: Hogarth Press (reprinted London: Karnac, 1989).
—— (1983) "The Wolf Man's Last Years", *Journal of the American Psychoanalytic Association*, 31: 867–897.
Gay, P. (1988) *Freud: A Life for our Time*, London: Dent.
Geissmann, C. and Geissmann, P. (1992) *Histoire de la psychanalyse de l'enfant*, Paris: Bayard; *A History of Child Psychoanalysis*, London: Routledge (1967).
Gibeault, A. (2000) "In Response to Otto F. Kernberg's *Psychoanalysis, Psychoanalytic Psychotherapy and Supportive Psychotherapy: Contemporary Controversies*", *International Journal of Psycho-Analysis*, 81: 379–383.
Glover, E. (1955) *The Technique of Psycho-Analysis*, New York: International Universities Press and London: Baillière, Tindall & Cox.
Graf, H. (1972) "Memoirs of an Invisible Man: A Dialogue with Francis Rizzo", *Opera News*, 5 February: 25–28; 12 February: 26–29; 19 February: 26–29; 26 February: 26–29.
Green, A. (1972) "De l' 'Esquisse' à 'L'interprétation des rêves': coupure et clôture", *Nouvelle Revue de Psychanalyse*, 5: 155–180.
—— (1973) *Le Discours vivant*, Paris : Presses Universitaires de France; trans. A. Sheridan (1999) *The Fabric of Affect in the Psychoanalytic Discourse*, London: Brunner-Routledge.
—— (1983) *Narcissisme de vie et narcissisme de mort*, Paris : Minuit; trans. A. Welle (2001) *Life Narcissism, Death Narcissism*, London: Free Association Books.
—— (1986) "Pulsion de mort, narcissisme négatif et fonction désobjectalisante", in *La pulsion de mort*, Premier Symposium de la Fédération Européenne de Psychanalyse, Paris: Presses Universitaires de France.
—— (1992) "La Psychanalyse et la science", *Médecine et Hygiène*, 50: 2350–2377.
Greenson, R. R. (1967) *The Technique and Practice of Psychoanalysis*, London: Hogarth Press.
Grinberg, L. (1962) "On a Specific Aspect of Countertransference due to the Patient's Projective Identification", *International Journal of Psycho-Analysis*, 43: 436–440.
—— and Grinberg, R. (1986) *Psychoanalytic Perspectives on Migration and Exile*, trans. N. Festinger, New Haven, CT: Yale University Press.
——, Sor, D. and Bianchedi, E. de (1973) *New Introduction to the Work of W. R. Bion*, New York: Jason Aronson.
Groddeck, G. W. (1921) *Le Chercheur d'âme* (*The Soul Seeker*), Paris: Gallimard (1982).
—— (1923) *Das Buch vom Es*, Vienna: Psychoanalytischer Verlag; trans. V. M. E. Collins (1946) *The Book of the It*, New York: International Universities Press; (1976) London: Vision Press.
Grosskurth, P. (1986) *Melanie Klein: Her World and her Work*, London: Hodder & Stoughton (reprinted Maresfield Library, London: Karnac, 1987); New York: Alfred A. Knopf.
Grubrich-Simitis, I. (1985) *Zurück zu Freud's Texten*; trans. P. Slotkin (1996) *Back to Freud's Texts*, New Haven, CT: Yale University Press.
Grunberger, B. (1971) *Le Narcissisme*, Paris: Payot; trans. J. S. Diamanti (1979) *Narcissism: Psychoanalytic Essays*, New York: International Universities Press.

Hanly, C. (1986) "Book Review of *The Assault on Truth : Freud's Suppression of the Seduction Theory*, by Jeffrey M. Masson, 1984", *International Journal of Psycho-Analysis*, 67: 517–519.
Hartmann, H. (1939) *Ego Psychology and the Problem of Adaptation*, trans. D. Rapaport (1958) New York: International Universities Press.
——, Kris, E. and Loewenstein, R. M. (1969) "Some Psychoanalytic Comments on 'Culture and Personality' ", in Münsterberger, W. (ed.) (1969) *Man and his Culture: Psychoanalytic Anthropology after "Totem and Taboo"*, London: Rapp & Whiting and New York: Taplinger.
Hawelka, E. R. (1974) "Introduction" and "commentaire", in *L'Homme aux rats : Journal d'une analyse*, Paris: Presses Universitaires de France.
Haynal, A. (1986) *La Technique en question: Controverses en psychanalyse*, Paris : Payot; trans. E. Holder (1988) *The Technique at Issue: Controversies in Psychoanalysis from Freud and Ferenczi to Michael Balint*, London: Karnac.
—— (2001) *Un Psychanalyste pas comme un autre: La renaissance de Sándor Ferenczi*, Neuchâtel and Paris: Delachaux et Niestlé.
—— and Falzeder, E. (2002) Introduction, in *The Complete Correspondence of Sigmund Freud and Karl Abraham, 1907–1925*, London and New York: Karnac.
Heimann, P. (1950) "On Counter-Transference", *International Journal of Psycho-Analysis*, 3: 8–17.
Hinshelwood, R. D. (1989) *A Dictionary of Kleinian Thought*, London: Free Association Books.
—— (2002) Introduction to the French edition of *A Dictionary of Kleinian Thought* (*Dictionnaire de la pensée kleinienne*, Paris: Presses Universitaires de France).
Hirschmüller, A. (1978) *The Life and Work of Josef Breuer*, New York: New York University Press.
Horney, K. (1922) *Feminine Psychology*, London: Routledge and New York: Norton.
Hug-Hellmuth, H. (1912a) "Analyse eines Traumes eines Fünfeinhalbjährigen", *Zentralbl. Psychoanal. und Psychother.*, 2/3: 122–127, trans. G. MacLean, in *Psychiat. J. Univ. Ottawa*, 11/1 (1986): 1–5.
—— (1921) "On the Technique of Child Analysis", *International Journal of Psycho-Analysis*, 2: 287–305.
Isaacs, S. (1948) "The Nature and Function of Phantasy", *International Journal of Psycho-Analysis*, 29: 73–97; also in Klein, M., Heimann, P., Isaacs, S. and Riviere, J. (eds) (1952) *Developments in Psycho-Analysis*, London: Hogarth Press and The Institute of Psycho-Analysis.
Israëls, H. (1981) *Schreber: Father and Son*, trans. H. S. Lake, New York: International Universities Press.
Jackson, M. and Williams, P. (1994) *Unimaginable Storms: A Search for Meaning in Psychosis*, London: Karnac.
Jeanneau, A. (1990) *Les Délires non psychotiques*, Paris: Presses Universitaires de France.
Jones, E. (1916) "The Theory of Symbolism", *British Journal of Psychology*, 9: 181–229; also in Jones, E. (1948) *Papers on Psycho-Analysis*, London: Baillière, Tindall and Cox (reprinted London: Karnac, 1977).
—— (1927) "The Early Development of Female Sexuality", *International Journal of Psycho-Analysis*, 8: 459–472.
—— (1935) "Early Female Sexuality", *International Journal of Psycho-Analysis*, 16: 263–273.
—— (1953–1957) *The Life and Work of Sigmund Freud*, 3 vols, London: Hogarth Press and New York: Basic Books.
—— (1959) *Free Associations: Memories of a Psychoanalyst*, New York: Basic Books.
Joseph, B. (1985) "Transference: A Total Situation", *International Journal of Psycho-Analysis*, 66: 447–454.
Jung, C. G. (1902) "On the Psychology and Pathology of So-Called Occult Phenomena", trans. M. D. Eder, in Long, C. (ed.) (1916) *Collected Papers on Analytical Psychology*, New York: Moffat, Yard and London: Baillière, Tindall & Cox.
—— (1906) *Über die Psychologie der Dementia praecox : Ein Versuch*, Halle : Marhold; trans. F. W. Peterson and A. A. Brill (1909) "The Psychology of Dementia Praecox", *Journal of Nervous and Mental Disease*, Monograph Series, no. 2; also in Read, H., Fordham, M., and Adler, G. (eds) trans. F. C. Hull and others (1953–1992) *The Collected Works of C. G. Jung*, vol. 3, Princeton, NJ: Princeton University Press.
—— (1911–1912) *Symbols of Transformation*, in Read, H., Fordham, M., and Adler, G. (eds) trans. F. C. Hull and others (1953–1992) *The Collected Works of C. G. Jung*, vol. 5, Princeton: Princeton University Press.
—— (1913) *Wandlungen und Symbole der Libido: Beiträge zur Entwicklungsgeschichte des Denkens*, Leipzig: Franz Deuticke; trans. B. M. Hinke, *Psychology of the Unconscious: A Study of the Transformations and Symbolisms of the Libido*, New York: Moffat, Yard (1916).
—— (1921) *Psychological Types, or, The Psychology of Individuation*, trans. H. Godwin Baynes, New York: Harcourt Brace (1923).
Kardiner, A. and Linton, R. (1939) *The Individual and his Society*, New York: Columbia University Press.
Kernberg, O. (1975) *Borderline Conditions and Pathological Narcissism*, New York: Jason Aronson.
King, P. and Steiner, R. (1991) *The Freud–Klein Controversial Discussions 1941–1945*, London: Brunner-Routledge (New Library of Psychoanalysis).
Klein, M. (1921) "The Development of a Child", in Klein, M. (1975) *The Writings of Melanie Klein*, vol. 1, London: Hogarth Press (reprinted London: Karnac, 1992).
—— (1928) "Early Stages of the Oedipus Conflict", in Klein, M. (1975) *The Writings of Melanie Klein*, vol. 1, London: Hogarth Press (reprinted London: Karnac, 1992).

—— (1930) "The Importance of Symbol-Formation in the Development of the Ego", in Klein, M. (1975) *The Writings of Melanie Klein*, vol. 1, London: Hogarth Press (reprinted London: Karnac, 1992).
—— (1932) *The Psycho-Analysis of Children*, in Klein, M. (1975) *The Writings of Melanie Klein*, vol. 2, London: Hogarth Press (1986).
—— (1935) "A Contribution to the Psychogenesis of Manic-Depressive States", in Klein, M. (1975) *The Writings of Melanie Klein*, vol. 1, London: Hogarth Press (reprinted London: Karnac, 1992).
—— (1940) "Mourning and its Relation to Manic-Depressive States", in Klein, M. (1975) *The Writings of Melanie Klein*, vol. 1, London: Hogarth Press (reprinted London: Karnac, 1992).
—— (1946) "Notes on Some Schizoid Mechanisms", in Klein, M. (1975) *The Writings of Melanie Klein*, vol. 3, London: Hogarth Press (reprinted London: Karnac, 1993).
—— (1957) *Envy and Gratitude and Other Works*, in Klein, M. (1975) *The Writings of Melanie Klein*, vol. 3, London: Hogarth Press (reprinted London: Karnac, 1993).
Kohut, H. (1971) *The Analysis of the Self*, New York: International Universities Press.
Kris, E. (1956) "The Recovery of Childhood Memories in Psycho-analysis", *Psychoanalytic Study of the Child*, 11: 54–88.
Kroeber, A. L. (1920) "Totem and Taboo: An Ethnologic Psychoanalysis", *American Anthropologist*, 22(1): 48–55.
Lacan, J. (1949) "Le stade du miroir comme formateur de la fonction de Je", in *Ecrits*, Paris: Seuil (1966), pp. 93–100; trans. A. Sheridan (1977) "The Mirror Stage as Formative of the Function of the I as Revealed in Psychoanalytic Theory", in *Écrits – A Selection*, London: Tavistock and New York: Norton. Also in *Écrits – A Selection*, new translation by B. Fink in collaboration with H. Fink and R. Grigg, New York and London: Norton (2004).
—— (1953) "Fonction et champ de la parole et du langage en psychanalyse", in *Ecrits*, Paris: Seuil (1966), pp. 237–322; "The Language of the Self, the Function of Language in Psychoanalysis", Baltimore, MD: Johns Hopkins University Press (1968).
—— (1955) "La Chose freudienne, ou Sens du retour à Freud en psychanalyse", in *Ecrits*, Paris: Seuil (1966), pp. 406–436; trans. A. Sheridan (1977) "The Freudian Thing or the Meaning of the Return to Freud in Psychoanalysis", in *Écrits – A Selection*, London: Tavistock and New York: Norton. Also in *Écrits – A Selection*, new translation by B. Fink in collaboration with H. Fink and R. Grigg, New York and London: Norton (2004).
—— (1957) "L'Instance de la lettre dans l'inconscient ou la raison depuis Freud", in *Ecrits*, Paris: Seuil (1966), pp. 493–528; trans. A. Sheridan (1977) "The Instance of the Letter in the Unconscious", in *Écrits – A Selection*, London: Tavistock and New York: Norton. Also in *Écrits – A Selection*, new translation by B. Fink in collaboration with H. Fink and R. Grigg, New York and London: Norton (2004).
—— (1981) *Le Séminaire, livre III, Les psychoses (1955–1956)* Paris: Seuil; ed. J-A. Miller, trans. R. Grigg (1993) *The Seminar Book III: The Psychoses (1955–1956)*, New York and London: Norton.
Ladame, F. (1991) "L'Adolescence, entre rêve et action", *Revue Française de Psychanalyse*, 55: 1493–1542.
Lansky, M. R. (1992) *Essential Papers on Dreams*, New York and London: New York University Press.
Laplanche, J. (1980) *Problématique I. L'angoisse*, Paris: Presses Universitaires de France.
—— (1987) "La Séduction généralisée aux fondements de la théorie et à l'horizon de la pratique psychanalytique", Conference in Geneva, 9 May 1987 (report written by J-M. Quinodoz, *Bulletin de la Société Suisse de Psychanayse*, 24 : 98–99).
—— and Pontalis, J. B. (1967) *Vocabulaire de la psychanalyse*, Paris : Presses Universitaires de France; trans. D. Nicholson-Smith (1973) *The Language of Psychoanalysis* (with an editorial preface by M. Masud Khan and an introduction by D. Lagache), London: Hogarth Press (reprinted London: Karnac, 1988).
Lax, R. (1992) "A Variation on Freud's Theme in 'A Child is Being Beaten' – Mother's Role: Some Implication for Superego Development in Women", *Journal of the American Psychoanalytic Association*, 40: 455–473.
Le Bon, G. (1895) *Psychologie des foules*, 28th edn, Paris: Alcan; *The Crowd: A Study of the Popular Mind*, New York: Macmillan (1896); Viking Press (1960) (2nd edn, Dunwoody, GA: Norman S. Berg).
Lipps, T. (1898) *Komik und Humor: Eine psychologish-ästetische Untersuchung*, Hamburg: L. Voss.
Lipton, S. D. (1977) "The Advantage of Freud's Technique as Shown in his Analysis of the Rat Man", *International Journal of Psycho-Analysis*, 58 : 255–273.
Little, M. (1951) "Counter-transference and the Patient's Response to it", *International Journal of Psycho-Analysis*, 32: 32–40; also in Little, M. (1986) *Transference Neurosis and Transference Psychosis: Toward Basic Unity*, London: Free Association Books and Maresfield Library.
Lothane, Z. (1992) *In Defense of Schreber: Soul Murder and Psychiatry*, Hillsdale, NJ and London: Analytic Press.
Luquet, P. (1985) Introduction to the series "Le fait psychanalytique", Paris: Presses Universitaires de France.
Macalpine, I. and Hunter, R. A. (1955) (translated, edited, with introduction, notes and discussion) *Daniel Paul Schreber: Memoirs of my Nervous Illness*, London: Dawson & Sons.
McDougall, W. (1921) *The Group Mind: A Sketch of the Principles of Collective Psychology with Some Attempt to Apply Them to the Interpretation of National Life and Character*, New York and London: Cambridge University Press.

Mack Brunswick, R. (1928a) "The Analysis of a Case of Paranoia. Delusion and Jealousy", *Journal of Nervous and Mental Disease*, 70: 1–22, 155–178.
—— (1928b) "A Supplement to Freud's 'History of an Infantile Neurosis' ", in Gardiner, M. (ed.) (1971) *The Wolf-Man and Sigmund Freud*, New York: Basic Books and London: Hogarth Press (1972) (reprinted London: Karnac, 1989).
Mahler, M., Pine, F. and Bergman, A. (1975) *The Psychological Birth of the Human Infant*, New York: Cambridge University Press.
Mahony, P. (1986) *Freud and the Rat Man*, New Haven, CT and London: Yale University Press.
—— (1993) "The Dictator and his Cure", *International Journal of Psycho-Analysis*, 74: 1245–1251.
—— (2002) "Remarques sur un cas de névrose obsessionnelle", in Mijolla, A. de (ed.) *Dictionnaire International de la Psychanalyse*, Paris: Calmann-Lévy.
Manzano, J. (1989) "La Séparation et la perte d'objet chez l'enfant", *Revue Française de Psychanalyse*, 53: 241–272.
Masson, J. M. (1984) *The Assault on Truth: Freud's Suppression of the Seduction Theory*, New York: Farrar, Strauss, and Giroux.
Masters, W. and Johnson, V. (1966) *Human Sexual Response*, Boston, MA: Little, Brown.
Meissner, S. J. and Meissner, W. W. (1984) *Psychoanalysis and Religious Experience*, New Haven, CT: Yale University Press.
—— (2002) "Religion and Psychoanalysis", in Edward, E. (ed.) *The Freud Encyclopaedia: Theory, Therapy, and Culture*, London and New York : Routledge.
Messier, D. (1988) "Notice terminologique du traducteur" [Translator's note on terminology], in Freud, S., *Le Mot d'esprit et ses rapports avec l'inconscient*, Paris: Gallimard, pp. 413–424.
Meyer-Palmedo, I. and Fichtner, G. (1989) *Freud–Bibliographie mit Werkkonkordanz*, Frankfurt: S. Fischer Verlag.
Mijolla, A. de (ed.) (2002) *Dictionnaire de la psychanalyse*, Paris: Calmann-Lévy.
Miller, J-A. (2003) "L'Avenir de la psychanalyse: Débat entre Daniel Widlöcher et Jacques-Alain Miller", *Psychiatrie, Sciences humaines, Neuro-sciences*, 1(1): 10–18.
Mitchell, J. (1972) *Psychoanalysis and Feminism*, Hardsmondsworth: Penguin.
Münsterberger, W. (ed.) (1969) *Man and his Culture: Psychoanalytic Anthropology after "Totem and Taboo"*, London: Rapp & Whiting and New York: Taplinger.
Neyraut, M. (1974) *Le Transfert*, Paris: Presses Universitaires de France.
Niederland, W. G. (1963) "Further Data and Memorabilia Pertaining to the Schreber Case", *International Journal of Psycho-Analysis*, 44: 208–212.
Obholzer, K. and Pankejeff, S. (1982) *The Wolf-Man: Conversations with Freud's Patient – Sixty Years Later*, New York: Continuum and London: Routledge.
Ophuijsen, J. H. W. van (1917) "Beiträge zum Männlichkeitskomplex der Frau", *Internationale Zeitschrift für ärztliche Psychoanalyse*, 4: 241; translated as "Contributions to the Masculinity Complex in Women", *International Journal of Psycho-Analysis*, 5 (1924): 39.
Oraison, M. (1950) *Vie chrétienne et problème de la sexualité*, Paris: Fayard (1970).
Palacio Espasa, F. (2003) *Dépression de vie, dépression de mort*, Toulouse: Erès.
Parin, P. and Morgenthaler, F. (1969) "Character Analysis Based on the Behaviour Patterns of 'Primitive' Africans", in Münsterberger, W. (ed.) (1969) *Man and his Culture: Psychoanalytic Anthropology after "Totem and Taboo"*, London: Rapp & Whiting and New York: Taplinger.
Perelberg, R. J. (ed.) (2000) *Dreaming and Thinking*, London: Karnac Books and The Institute of Psycho-Analysis.
—— (2002) "Féminisme et psychanalyse", in Mijolla, A. de (ed.) *Dictionnaire de la psychanalyse*, Paris: Calmann-Lévy.
Pfister, O. (1928) "Die Illusion einer Zukunft: eine freundschaftliche Auseinandersetzung mit Prof. Freud", *Imago: Zeitschrift für Anwendung der Psychoanalyse auf die Geiseswissenschaften*, vol. XIV (2/3), Vienna: Internationaler Psychoanalytischer Verlag.
Plath, Sylvia. (1982) *The Journals of Sylvia Plath*, ed. Ted Hughes and Frances McCullough, New York: Ballantine.
Pragier, G. and Faure-Pragier, S. (1990) "Un siècle après *l'Esquisse:* nouvelles métaphores? Métaphores du nouveau?", *Revue Française de Psychanalyse*, 54: 1395–1529.
Quinodoz, D. (1994) *Le Vertige: entre angoisse et plaisir*, Paris: Presses Universitaires de France; trans. A. Pomerans (1997) *Emotional Vertigo: Between Anxiety and Pleasure*, London: Brunner-Routledge.
—— (1999) "Deux grands méconnus: les parents adoptifs d'Œdipe. Du dédoublement des imagos parentales au dédoublement des affects", *Revue Française de Psychanalyse*, 63: 103–122; "The Oedipus complex revisited: Oedipus abandoned, Oedipus adopted." *International Journal of Psycho-Analysis*, 80: 15–30.
—— (2001) "The Psychoanalyst of the Future: Wise Enough to Dare to Be Mad at Times", *International Journal of Psycho-Analysis*, 82: 235–248.
—— (2002) *Des mots qui touchent: Une psychanalyste apprend à parler*, Paris : Presses Universitaires de France; trans. P. Slotkin (2003) *Words that Touch: A Psychoanalyst Learns to Speak*, London: Karnac.
Quinodoz, J-M. (1989) "Female Homosexual Patients in Psychoanalysis", *International Journal of Psycho-Analysis*, 70: 57–63.

—— (1991) *La Solitude apprivoisée: L'angoisse de séparation en psychanalyse*, Paris: Presses Universitaires de France; trans. P. Slotkin (1993) *The Taming of Solitude: Separation Anxiety in Psychoanalysis*, London and New York: Routledge.
—— (1997a) "Transitions in Psychic Structures in the Light of Deterministic Chaos Theory", *International Journal of Psycho-Analysis*, 78: 699–718.
—— (1997b) " 'A Child is Being Beaten': A Seminar with Candidates from the Perspective of Contemporary Psychoanalysis", in *On Freud's "A Child is Being Beaten"*, International Psychoanalytical Association Monograph no. 5, ed. E. Spector Person, New Haven, CT and London: Yale University Press, pp. 112–132.
—— (2000) "Mélancolie maniaque: quelle issue?" *Revue Française de Psychanalyse*, 64: 1825–1835.
—— (2001) *Les Rêves qui tournent une page*, Paris: Presses Universitaires de France; trans. P. Slotkin (2002) *Dreams that Turn Over a Page: Paradoxical Dreams in Psychoanalysis*, London: Brunner-Routledge.
—— (2002) "L'Identification projective: qu'en pensent les psychanalystes de langue française?" *Bulletin de la Fédération Européenne de Psychanayse*, 56: 148–156; "Projective Identification: What do French-Speaking Psychoanalysts Think?", EPF *Bulletin*, 56.
Racamier, P. C. and Chasseguet-Smirgel, J. (1966) "La Révision du cas Schreber", *Revue Française de Psychanalyse*, 30: 3–26.
Racker, H. (1953) "A Contribution to the Problem of Counter-transference", *International Journal of Psycho-Analysis*, 34: 313–324.
Rank, O. (1909) *The Myth of the Birth of the Hero: A Psychological Exploration of Myth*, 2nd edn (1922) trans. G. C. Richter and E. J. Lieberman, Baltimore, MD: Johns Hopkins University Press (2004).
—— (1924) *The Trauma of Birth*, London: K. Paul, Trench & Trubner (1929), New York: Brunner (1952).
Rice, E. (1990) *Freud and Moses: The Long Journey Home*, Albany, NY: State University of New York Press.
—— (2002) "Religion and Psychoanalysis", in Edward, E. (ed.) *The Freud Encyclopedia: Theory, Therapy, and Culture*, London and New York: Routledge.
Ricoeur, P. (1965) *De l'interprétation: Essai sur Freud*, Paris: Seuil; trans. D. Savage (1970) *Freud and Philosophy: An Essay on Interpretation*, New Haven, CT: Yale University Press.
Riesenberg Malcolm, R. (1988) "The Mirror: A Perverse Sexual Phantasy in a Woman Seen as a Defence against a Psychotic Breakdown", in E. B. Spillius (ed.) *Melanie Klein Today*, London and New York: Routledge.
Robert, M. (1964) *La Révolution psychanalytique*, 2 vols, Paris: Payot; trans. K. Morgan (1966) *The Psychoanalytic Revolution: Sigmund Freud's Life and Achievement*, New York: Harcourt and London: George Allen & Unwin.
Robbins, T., Cotran, R. S., and Kumar, V. (1974) *Pathologic Basis of Disease*, 6th edn, Philadelphia, PA: Saunders (1999).
Rodrigué, E. (1996) *Sigmund Freud: o século da psicanálise 1895–1995*, São Paulo: Escuta.
Roheim, G. (1950) *Psychoanalysis and Anthropology: Culture, Personality and the Unconscious*, New York: International Universities Press.
Roiphe, J. (1995) "The Conceptualisation and Communication of Clinical Facts", *International Journal of Psycho-Analysis*, 76: 1179–1190.
Rosenfeld, H. (1965) *Psychotic States: A Psychoanalytical Approach*, London: Hogarth Press and New York: International Universities Press (reprinted London: Karnac, 1982).
—— (1971) "A Clinical Approach to the Psychoanalytic Theory of Life and Death Instincts: An Investigation into the Aggressive Aspects of Narcissism", *International Journal of Psycho-Analysis*, 52: 169–178; reprinted in E. B. Spillius (ed.) (1988) *Melanie Klein Today*, vol. 1, London: Routledge.
Roudinesco, E. and Plon, M. (1997) *Dictionnaire de la psychanalyse*, Paris: Fayard.
Sandler, A. M. (1996) "The Psychoanalytic Legacy of Anna Freud", *The Psychoanalytic Study of the Child*, 51: 11–22.
Sandler, J. (ed.) (1991) *On Freud's "Analysis Terminable and Interminable"*, Newhaven, CT and London: Yale University Press (International Psychoanalysis Library).
Schaeffer, J. (1986) "Le Rubis a horreur du rouge: Relation et contre-investissement hystérique", *Revue Française de Psychanalyse*, 50: 923–944.
Schäppi, R. (2002) *La Femme est le propre de l'homme*, Paris: Odile Jacob.
Schapiro, M. (1956) "Leonardo and Freud", in Schapiro, M., *Theory and Philosophy of Art: Style, Artist and Society*, New York: George Braziller (1994).
Schmidt, W. (1929) "Der Oedipus-K der freudschen Psychoanalyse und die Ehegestaltung des Bolschevismus: Eine kritische Prüfung ihre ethnologischen Grundlagen", *Nationalwirtschaft*, 2: 401–436.
Schreber, D. (1903) *Memoirs of my Nervous Illness*, trans. and ed. R. Macalpine and I. A. Hunter, London: Dawson & Sons (1955); Cambridge, MA: Harvard University Press (1988).
Schur, M. (1972) *Freud: Living and Dying*, New York: International Universities Press.
Segal, H. (1957) "Notes On Symbol Formation", *International Journal of Psycho-Analysis*, 38: 391–397; reprinted in Segal, H. (1981) *The Work of Hanna Segal* (with a postscript, 1980) New York: Jason Aronson.
—— (1964) *Introduction to the Work of Melanie Klein*, London: Hogarth Press (reprinted London: Karnac, 1988).
—— (1979) *Melanie Klein*, Glasgow: Fontana/Collins and New York: Viking Press.
—— (1986) "De l'utilité clinique du concept de pulsion de mort", in *La pulsion de mort*, Premier Symposium de la Fédération Européenne de Psychanalyse, Paris: Presses Universitaires de France.

—— (1987) "Silence is the Real Crime", *International Review of Psycho-Analysis*, 14: 3–12; reprinted in Segal, H. (1997) *Psychoanalysis, Literature and War*, London: Routledge.
—— (1991) *Dream, Phantasy and Art*, London: Routledge (New Library of Psychoanalysis).
—— (1995a) "Comments on Ruth Riesenberg Malcolm's paper", UCL Conference on Projective Identification, London, October 1995 (unpublished).
—— (1995b) "Hiroshima, the Gulf War and After", in Elliot, A. and Frosch, S. (eds) *Psychoanalysis in Contexts: Paths between Theory and Modern Culture*, London: Routledge.
—— (2002) "Not Learning from Experience: Hiroshima, the Gulf War and 11 September", *International Psychoanalysis*, 11(1): 33–35; http://eseries.ipa.org.uk/prev/newsletter/newsletters.htm (consulted 2 October 2004).
Sellin, E. (1922) *Mose und seine Bedeutung für die israelitisch-jüdische Religionsgeschichte*, Leipzig.
Sharpe, E. F. (1937) *Dream Analysis*, London: Hogarth (1978).
Sherfey, M. J. (1966) "The Evolution and Nature of Female Sexuality in Relation to Psychoanalytic Theory", *Journal of the American Psychoanalytic Association*, 14: 28–128.
Silverman, M. (1980) "A Fresh Look at the Case of Little Hans", in Kanzer, M. and Glenn, J. (eds) *Freud and his Patients*, New York: Jason Aronson.
Solms, M. and Kaplan-Solms, K. (2000) *Clinical Studies in Neuro-Psychoanalysis: An Introduction to Depth Neuropsychology*, New York: Other Press and London: Karnac.
Spitz, R. A. (1957) *No and Yes: On the Genesis of Human Communication*, New York: International Universities Press.
—— (1965) *The First Year of Life: A Psychoanalytic Study of Normal and Deviant Development of Object Relations*, New York: International Universities Press.
Steiner, R. (2002) "Ernest Jones (1879–1958)", in Mijolla, A. de (ed.) *Dictionnaire international de la psychanalyse*, Paris: Calmann-Lévy.
Stoller, R. J. (1968) *Sex and Gender*, New York: Science House (2nd edn, New York: Jason Aronson, 1974).
Strachey, J. (1957) Editor's introduction to "Mourning and Melancholia", *Standard Edition*, 14: 239–242.
—— (1959) Editor's introduction to "Inhibitions, Symptoms and Anxiety", *Standard Edition*, 20: 77–86.
Sullivan, H. S. (1944–1945) *The Psychiatric Interview*, New York: Norton (1954).
Taylor, E. (2002) "Jung, Carl Gustav (1875–1961)", in Edward, E. (ed.) *The Freud Encyclopedia: Theory, Therapy, and Culture*, London and New York: Routledge.
This, B. (2002) "Dolto-Marette, Françoise", in Mijolla, A. de (ed.) *Dictionnaire international de la psychanalyse*, Paris: Calmann-Lévy.
Tous, J. M. (1996) "Hysteria one hundred years on", Panel report, *International Journal of Psycho-Analysis*, 77: 75–78.
Vallet, O. (2002) "Religion et psychanalyse", in Mijolla, A. de (ed.) *Dictionnaire international de la psychanalyse*, Paris: Calmann-Lévy.
Vassalli, G. (2001) "The Birth of Psychoanalysis from the Spirit of Technique", *International Journal of Psycho-Analysis*, 82: 3–25.
—— (2002) "*Erraten* ou *verraten*: deviner ou trahir", trans. M. Gribinski, *Penser/rêver*, 2002: 211–256.
Vermorel, H. and Vermorel, M. (1993) *Sigmund Freud et Romain Rolland, correspondance 1923–1936*, Paris: Presses Universitaires de France.
Weber, K. (2002) "Suisse alémanique", in Mijolla, A. de (ed.) *Dictionnaire international de la psychanalyse*, Paris: Calmann-Lévy.
Widlöcher, D. (2003) "L'Avenir de la psychanalyse: débat entre Daniel Widlöcher et Jacques-Alain Miller", *Psychiatrie, Sciences Humaines, Neuro-sciences*, 1(1): 10–18.
Winnicott, D. W. (1947) "Hate in the Counter-transference", *International Journal of Psycho-Analysis* (1949), 30: 69–74; also in Winnicott, D. W. (1958) *Collected Papers: Through Paediatrics to Psycho-Analysis*, London: Tavistock and New York: Basic Books (reprinted as *Through Paediatrics to Psycho-Analysis*, London: Hogarth Press and The Institute of Psycho-Analysis (1975); reprinted London: Karnac, 1992).
—— (1955–1956) "Clinical Varieties of Transference", *International Journal of Psycho-Analysis* (1956), 37: 386–388; also, *sub nomine* "On Transference", in Winnicott, D. W. (1958) *Collected Papers: Through Paediatrics to Psycho-Analysis*, London: Tavistock and New York: Basic Books (reprinted as *Through Paediatrics to Psycho-Analysis*, London: Hogarth Press and The Institute of Psycho-Analysis (1975); reprinted London: Karnac, 1992).
—— (1958 [1957]) "The Capacity to be Alone", *International Journal of Psycho-Analysis* (1958), 39: 416–420; *Psyche*, 1958, 12; also in Winnicott, D. W. (1965) *The Maturational Process and the Facilitating Environment: Studies in the Theory of Emotional Development*, London: Hogarth Press and The Institute of Psycho-Analysis and New York: International Universities Press (reprinted London: Karnac, 1990).
Wollheim, R. (1971) *Freud*, London: Fontana Press (2nd edn with a supplementary preface (1990), London: Fontana, Harper Collins, 1991).
Yerushalmi, Y. H. (1991) *Freud's Moses: Judaism Terminable and Interminable*, New Haven, CT: Yale University Press.
Young-Bruehl, E. (1988) *Anna Freud: A Biography*, New York: Summit Books (revised edition New York: Norton 1994).
Zilboorg, G. (1942) "The Catholic Doctor", *Psychoanalytic Quarterly*, 11: 419–421.

INDEX OF PROPER NAMES

Abraham, Karl, 74, 83, 101, 130, 136, 147–148, 218, 252
Abraham, R., 93
Adler, Alfred, 66, 93, 95, 122, 157, 222–223
Andreas-Salomé, Lou, 136, 172–173, 255
Andreassen, Nancy C., 30
Anna O., 13–14, 68
Anzieu, Didier, 38, 44, 114, 146
American Psychoanalytical Association, 235
Arlow, Jacob A., 262

Balint, Michael, 117, 132, 154
Bauer, Ida (see "Dora" case study), 65–66
Bellemin-Noël, Jean, 77
Bernays, Martha, 10, 37
Bernays, Minna, 58
Bernheim, Hippolyte, 11
Binswanger, Ludwig, 14, 71
Bion, Wilfred R., 56, 71, 93, 107, 114, 127, 133–134, 153, 201–202, 241
Blacker, Kay Hill, 93
Bleger, José, 114
Bleuler, Eugen, 69, 74, 104, 147, 228
Bonaparte, Princess Marie, 21, 149, 169, 181, 255, 264
Bourguignon, André, 51, 246
Bowlby, John, 225
Braunschweig, Denise, 127
Breen, Dana, 182
Brenman, Eric, 19
Breuer, Josef, 9–13, 68, 218
Breuer, Robert, 25
Brill, Abraham, 235
British PsychoAnalytical Society, 87, 168
Britton, Ronald, 14
Brücke, Ernst, 10–11
Bullitt, William, 285
Burghölzli (hospital), 74
Burlingham, Dorothy, 86, 172, 225

Canestri, Jorge, 252
Carlson, Rachel, 30
Charcot, Jean-Martin, 11, 17
Chasseguet-Smirgel, Janine, 19, 106, 146, 182, 255
Choisy, Maryse, 233
Claparède, Édouard, 58
Clark University, 74, 122

Cooper, Arnold M., 263
Cooper, S. H., 72

da Vinci, Leonardo, 94–97, 198
Darwin, Charles, 125
Deutsch, Hélène, 181
Deutsch, Félix, 66, 204
Devereux, Georges, 127
Diatkine, Gilbert, 106
Diatkine, René, 233
Dolto, Françoise, 233
Dor, Joël, 55
Dora (case-study), 57, 63, 65–72, 198, 180
Duparc, François, 55

Eissler, Kurt R., 97, 164
Eitingon, Max, 74, 186
Ellis, Havelock, 57, 58, 97
Emmy von N. (case-study), 14, 17
Erikson, Eric, 210
Eskelinen de Folch, Terttu, 263
Etchegoyen, R. Horacio, 109
European Psychoanalytical Federation, 193

Fairbairn, W. R. D., 106
Falzeder, Ernst, 172
Faure-Pragier, Sylvie, 29–30, 115
Federn, Paul, 132
Fenichel, Otto, 109
Ferenczi, Sàndor, 69, 74, 83, 94–95, 114, 116–117, 136, 139, 152, 154, 156, 165, 199–200, 218, 254–257, 259–260
Flanders, Sara, 44
Flechsig, Paul Emil, 102–103, 105
Fliess, Wilhelm, 21–25, 26, 34, 37–38, 46, 50, 58–59, 63, 65, 74, 92, 94–95, 105, 282
Foulkes, Siegmund Heinrich, 201
Frankiel, Rita V., 82
Frazer, Sir James G., 122, 125
Freeman, Derek, 126
Freud, Alexander (Freud's brother), 58, 73
Freud, Anna (Freud's daughter), 84, 85–87, 149, 169, 172–173, 204, 210, 225, 265
Freud, Ernst (Freud's son), 136, 265
Freud, Jakob (Freud's father), 37
Freud, Martha Bernays (Freud's wife), 10, 37, 84, 265

Freud, Martin (Freud's son), 136, 168
Freud, Oliver (Freud's son), 136
Freud, Sigmund : see Subject Index
— Biography, 10–11, 21–22, 37–38, 45–46, 50–51, 57–58, 65–66, 73–74, 78–79, 88–89, 94–95, 101–102, 121–122, 136, 157, 165–166, 172, 186, 195, 204–205, 212–213, 217–218, 227, 135–136, 250, 251, 254–255, 264–265
— Chronological Table, 10–11
Freud, Sophie (Freud's daughter), 166, 186
Freund, Anton von, 165, 186

Gabbard, Glen O., 118
Gardiner, Muriel M., 164
Gay, Peter, 186
Geissman, Pierre and Claudine, 83
Gibeault, Alain, 49,
Glover, Edward, 84, 109, 148
Glover, James, 148
Goethe, Johann Wolfgang von, 126
Graf, Herbert (cf. Little Hans), 78–79
Graf, Max, 78–79, 82
Graf, Olga, 78
Green, André, 19, 29, 44, 133–134, 146–147, 193, 263
Greenson, Ralph R., 109
Grinberg, Léon, 71–72, 201
Groddeck, Georg, 117, 204
Grosskurth, Phyllis, 84
Grubrich-Simitis, Ilse, 136, 154, 251
Grunberger, Béla, 133

Hajek, Marcus, 204
Halberstadt, Sophie Freud (Freud's daughter), 166
Hajek, Markus, 204
Hanly, Charles, 24–25
Hartmann, Heinz, 86, 127, 210
Hawelka, E. R., 89
Haynal, André, 117, 148
Heimann, Paula, 71
Hinshelwood, Robert D., 84, 253
Hirschmüller, Albrecht, 11, 14
Hitler, Adolf, 236, 254–255, 264
Hoffmann, E. T. A., 167
Horney, Karen, 148, 181
Hug-Hellmuth, Hermine, 83, 84
Hunter, R. A., 106

International Journal of Psycho-Analysis (The), 168–169, 195, 235
International Psychoanalytical Association, 55, 72, 74, 87, 95, 108, 113, 116, 119–120, 122, 148, 156, 168–169, 210, 233, 234, 262
Irma, 37, 41, 43
Israels, H., 126

Jackson, Murray, 49
Janet, Pierre, 14
Jeanneau, Augustin, 77
Jensen, Wilhelm, 73–77
Jolk, Katherin, 169
Jones, Ernest, 10, 14, 36, 56, 57, 83, 89, 117, 136, 165–166, 168–169, 181, 192, 195, 207, 212–213, 228, 235, 241, 255, 264

Joseph, Betty, 101
Jung, Carl Gustav, 63, 69, 73–75, 95, 101, 115, 121–122, 130, 147, 157

Kann, Loe, 169
Kaplan-Solms, Karen, 29
Kardiner, Abram, 127
Katharina (case-study), 15
Kernberg, Otto, 133–134
Khan, Masud R., 117
King, Pearl, 84
Klein, Arthur, 83
Klein, Melanie, 56, 83–85, 86, 93, 97, 106–107, 132–134, 148, 151–153, 168–169, 181, 192, 202, 207, 210, 225, 240, 252
Klein, Melitta (Schmideberg-), 83
Kohut, Heinz, 117, 133, 211
Kraepelin, Emil, 104, 157
Krafft-Ebing, Richard von, 34, 57, 58
Kris, Ernst, 21, 127, 149, 210, 224
Kroeber, Alfred L., 126

Lacan, Jacques, 49, 51, 54–55, 72, 106, 109, 129, 146–147, 211, 224, 255
Lacassagne, Antoine, 204
Ladame, François, 77
Laforgue, René, 233, 255
Lansky, Melvin R., 44
Lanzer, Ernst (the 'Rat Man'), 88–93
Laplanche, Jean, 19, 22, 45, 47, 115, 129, 216, 224
Lax, Ruth F., 176
Le Bon, Gustave, 196
Lester, Eva, 118
Leupold-Löwenthal, Harald, 289
Lipps, Theodor, 50
Lipton, Samuel D., 93
Little Hans, 78–87, 220
Little, Margaret, 71
Loewenstein, Rudolf M., 127, 210
Lothane, Zvi, 106
Lucy R. (case-study), 15
Luquet, Pierre, 146

Macalpine Ida, 106
Mack Brunswick, Ruth, 132, 156–157, 163–164
Mahler, Gustav, 79
Mahler, Margaret, 132–133, 225
Mahony, Patrick, 82, 93
Malinowski, Bronislaw, 127
Manzano, Juan, 224
Masson, Jeffrey Moussaieff, 24
McDougall, Joyce, 146, 255
Mead, Margaret, 127
Meissner, William W. and S. J., 272
Merezhkovsky, Dimitri, 94
Messier, Denis, 51
Meynert, Theodor, 147
Mijolla, Alain de, 210
Miller, Jacques-Alain, 72
Mitchell, Juliet, 172
Modell, Arnold, 117
Morgenthaler, F., 127
Moser, Baronness Fanny (cf. Emmy von N.), 14
Moses, 127, 228, 264–272

INDEX OF PROPER NAMES

Mostardeiro, A. L. Bento, 263
Münsterberger, Werner, 127

Nacht, Sacha, 255
Nersessian, Edward, 19
Neyraut, Michel, 71
Niederland, W. G., 106
Nietzsche, Friedrich, 172, 204

Obholzer, Karin, 164
Offenbach, Jacques, 167
Ophuijsen, J. H. W. van, 174
Oraison, Marc, 233

Palacio-Espasa, Francisco, 132
Pankejeff, Serguei̇ (the 'Wolf Man'), 156–157
Pappenheim, Bertha (cf. Anna O.), 13–14
Parin, Paul, 127
Perelberg, Rosine J., 44, 182
Pfister, Oskar, 97, 227–228, 230, 232, 241
Pichler, Hans, 204
Pine, Fred, 133, 225
Plath, Sylvia, 59
Plé, Father., O. P., 233
Plon, Michel, 54, 233
Poe, Edgar Allan, 255
Pontalis, Jean-Bertrand, 22, 45, 47, 129, 216
Pragier, Georges, 29–30, 115

Quinodoz, Danielle, 33, 37, 132, 168, 209, 273
Quinodoz, Jean-Michel, 30, 44, 48, 115, 178, 193, 225

Racamier, Paul-Claude, 106, 146
Racker, Heinrich, 71
Rado, Sandor, 148
Rank, Otto, 116, 195, 213, 217–218, 219, 223, 256, 266
Rée, Paul, 172
Reick, Theodor, 148
Rice, Emanuel, 272
Ricoeur, Paul, 272
Riesenberg, Malcolm R., 176
Rilke, Rainer Maria, 172
Robbins, Stanley L., 193
Robert, Marthe, 273
Rodrigué, Emilio, 204
Roheim, Géza, 117, 127
Roiphe, Jean, 29
Rolland, Romain, 195, 228, 235–236, 255
Rosenfeld, Herbert, 56, 107, 133, 153
Rosenfeld, David, 289
Roudinesco, Elisabeth, 54, 233

Sadger, Isidor, 83
Sandler, Joseph, 262
Sandler, Anne-Marie, 86
Saussure, Ferdinand de, 54

Saussure Raymond de, Centre Psychanalytique, 1
Schaeffer, Jacqueline, 19
Schäppi, Rolf, 127
Schapiro, Meyer, 97
Schmideberg, Melitta (Klein's daughter), 83
Schopenhauer, Arthur, 190
Schreber, Daniel Paul, 101–107
Schur, Max, 186, 265
Segal, Hanna, 44, 56, 76, 83, 84, 107, 133–134, 153, 192–193, 241
Sellin, E., 266
Shakespeare, William, 76
Sharpe, Ella Freeman, 44
Sherfey, M. J., 182
Silverman, Martin Arnold, 82
Société Psychanalytique de Paris (Paris Psychoanalytical Society), 255
Solms, Hugo, 79
Solms, Mark, 29–30
Sophocles, 76, 168
Spitz, René A., 225
Steckel, Wilhelm, 122
Steiner, Riccardo, 84, 169
Stoller, Robert Jesse, 182
Strachey, James, 136, 149, 217
Sullivan, Harry Stack, 132

Tausk, Viktor, 145, 186
Taylor, Eugen, 74
This, Bernard, 233–234
Tous, Joana M., 19
Trotter, Wilfred, 199

Vallet, Odon, 228
Vassalli, Giovanni, 115
Vermorel, Henri, 195
Vienna Psychoanalytical Society, 122
Vinci Leonardo da, 94–97, 198

Weber, Kaspar, 229
Wells, H. G., 255
Widlöcher, Daniel, 55, 72, 193
Williams, Paul, 49
Winnicott, Donald W., 71, 114, 117, 133
Wollheim, Richard, 18

Yerushalmi, Yosef Hayim, 272
Young-Bruehl, Elizabeth, 172

Zellenka, Hans (Mr K . . .) and Pepina (Mrs K . . .), 66
Ziehen, Theodor, 157
Zilboorg, Gregory, 233
Zimmermann, David, 289
Zweig, Arnold, 236
Zweig, Stefan, 14, 68, 255

SUBJECT INDEX

abreaction, 10, 16, 20
abstinence, 70, 118, 120
acquired (traces), 163
acting in, acting out, 48
active (technique), 117
activity, 187, 223
active tendency/passive tendency, 138, 160, 180
adaptation (theory of), 210–211
adolescence, 95, 179
affects, 32, 35, 62, 67, 135, 140–144, 146, 148, 152, 155, 196, 221
aggressiveness (see ambivalence, hate, aggressive drives), 81, 101, 134, 135, 138–139, 142, 148–150, 155, 161, 194, 197, 208–209, 221, 242; turning aggressiveness back against the self, 178, 220
aim (of a drive), 136–137
alarm signal (anxiety as), 217, 225
alpha-elements, 153
alpha-function, 154, 158
altruistic surrender (defence), 210
ambivalence, ambivalence between love and hate, 69, 80, 81, 93, 116, 123, 127, 138–140, 150, 155, 164, 221, 240–241
amnesia, 60, 174
anaclisis, 30, 64, 103, 193
anality, 61, 64, 93; anal character, 98; anal eroticism, 88–93, 161, 164
analysis; interminable analysis, 158, 254–260; of children, 78–87; of the analyst, 118–120, 259, 263; training analysis, 55, 119–120; wild analysis, 118
anatomical distinction between the sexes, 243, 246–248
anxiety, 24–25, 31, 142, 165–169, 217–226, 145; annihilation anxiety, 137, 217; anxiety as signal, 217, 225; anxiety at birth, 219; anxiety concerning separation from and loss of the object, 217–226; anxiety neurosis, 33, 35; automatic anxiety, 21, 226; castration anxiety, 64, 81, 87, 161–162, 220, 226, 247; separation anxiety, 217–226; separation anxiety in children, 225; stranger anxiety, 225;
animism, 124, 127
anthropologists, 126, 271–272; psychoanalytic anthropology, 127
anti-Semitism, 74, 255
aphanisis, 169, 181
apoptosis, 193

applied psychoanalysis, 73, 77
archaeology, 73, 260
archaic heritage, 272
army, 197, 200, 202
artificial groups, 197
atheist, 24, 270–271
attachment, 81, 225; homosexual attachment, 68, 161–162, 177–179
autism, autistic, 56
auto-eroticism, 62, 64, 103–104, 128–129
autonomous ego, 210, 258
awareness, 43–44, 142–145, 155, 203, 205

beating fantasies, 85, 171–173, 176; in boys, 175; in girls, 174
being in love, 118, 199, 202
beta-elements, 153–154
binding/unbinding (of the drives), 210
birth, 217
bisexuality, 21, 25, 59, 64, 82, 96, 177, 180; psychic bisexuality, 24–25, 64, 66, 162, 171, 179, 203, 206–207
borderline (patients, states), 49, 56, 132
bungled actions (parapraxes), 45–49, 50, 261

cancer (Freud's), 204, 250
cathartic method, 9, 13–17, 20, 110
cathexis, object cathexis, 129–130, 145, 149–150, 197–198, 206
clinical cases (Freud's); Anna O., 13–14; Elizabeth von R., 15–16; Emmy von N., 14; Katerina, 15; Leonardo da Vinci, 94–97; Little Hans, 78–87; Lucy R., 15; of female homosexuality, 177–178; Rat Man, 88–93; Senatspräsident Schreber, 101–107; Wolf-Man, 156–164;
clinical cases (other than Freud's), 176;
castration (anxiety), 82, 103, 159, 161, 164, 166–167;
castration complex (woman), 180
censorship, 20, 41–42, 43–44, 54, 142, 144; in dreams, 41–42, 132
ceremonial (ritual), 92, 123
change of object, 64, 181
child being beaten, 171–176, 182, 247
child analysis, 78–87
children's drawings, 86, 187

children's play, 187; repetitive play in children (wooden reel), 193
Christianity, 121, 125, 227, 268–269, 271–272
Church, 97, 197, 200, 202, 232–233, 265, 267
civilization, 60, 126, 235–241, 264–272
cloacal theory, 162
comic, 50–51, 53–54, 56
communication from unconscious to unconscious, 145
complex (see Oedipus complex), 63–64; castration complex, 80, 180, 246; masculinity complex, 179
complex systems (theory of), 30, 115
component instincts, 59, 62
compromise, 33–35, 41–42, 43–44, 82
compulsion to repeat, 70, 120, 165, 167, 169, 185–193, 208–209
compulsive actions, 90, 93
"conception" (Bion), 36, 154
condensation, 43–44, 47, 49, 50, 52, 54, 56
confidentiality, 66
conflict between life and death drives, 151, 185–193, 208, 239
consciousness, conscious (see also moral conscience), 43–44, 124, 131–132, 142–145, 150, 155, 167, 203, 205
constructions, reconstructions, 62, 160, 163, 178, 254, 260–263
content; latent, 39, 44; manifest, 39, 44
Controversial Discussions, 84
counter-cathexis, 144, 223
counter-projective identification, 71–72
counter-transference, 48, 55, 70–72, 93, 112–113, 118, 120; in Freud, 70–71; post Freudians, 70–71
conversion, 16–17, 20, 32
couch, 111–113
creation; artistic, 76, 94–97; literary, 76
criticism (of the ego), 150–151, 155
criticizing agency, 198
culture, 227–229, 231, 236, 238, 242
current; affectionate, 62, 199; sensual, 62, 199

damning-up of the libido, 130
day's residue, 41, 44
death drive (see drive, conflict), 185–193
deferred action, 22, 28–29, 31, 33–35, 141, 160, 164
defences, defence mechanisms, 40, 140, 210, 220–221, 243–253, 258; advanced, 106; primitive, 106, 146
defusion (unbinding) of the instinctual drives, 208–210
delusion, 73–77, 91–92, 101–107, 132, 164, 245, 261–263; as a defence against homosexuality, 107; as an attempt at recovery, 105, 261; delusions of grandeur, 130; hallucinatory delusions, 77, 102; paranoid delusions, 101–102, 106, 124; persecutory delusions, 102
delusional ideas (see delusion)
dementia praecox, 104–105
denial (disavowal), 153, 243–253; of castration, 248–249; of reality, 73, 91–92, 105, 243–253, 256
de-objectalizing function, 193
depression, 22, 151, 155, 178, 198; melancholic depression, 24, 148–151, 200
depressive position, 56, 85, 152–153, 192, 225
deterministic chaos theory, 30, 115

devour, 139
development of the libido, 152
discourse, 55
displacement, 40, 43–44, 47, 49, 50, 56, 272
dissociation, 104
double, 113, 169; narcissistic double, 169
doubling, dichotomization, 167–168, 170
dramatization, 41, 61
dreams, 36–44, 50, 67, 73, 75–77; of the "table d'hôte", 39; of wolves, 156; recurrent dreams, 187, 193; theory of dreams, 36–44, 135–136, 147;
dream-formation, 40–41
drive, drives, 59, 64, 122, 135–140, 146; aggressive (or destructive), 133, 134, 235, 238; auto-erotic, 139; component, 59, 62; conflict between life and death drives, 151–152, 189, 190–192, 212–216, 239–240; death drive, 85, 92, 134, 185–193, 203, 207, 211, 212, 225, 235, 239, 246; direct sexual drives and drives inhibited as to their aim, 201; ego drives, 155; incestuous, 82; libidinal, 133; life drive, 92, 134, 185–193, 203, 207, 211, 212, 235, 239, 246; primal instincts, 155; self-preservative, 122, 135, 137; sexual, 76, 135, 235, 238

economic factor, 244, 255
education, 60, 86; psychoanalytic education, 86
ego, 17, 27, 32, 192, 194, 229, 203–211, 219–220, 242, 258; autonomous ego, 210, 258; critical, 150–151, 155; ego and non-ego, 258; ego ideal (see superego), 131, 199–200, 203–211; ideal ego, 131, 211; pleasure ego, 139, 237, 246; purified pleasure ego, 152, 155; reality-ego, 139; skin-ego, 114, 146; whole ego, 139, 200;
Ego Psychology, 133, 210–211
Egypt, 96, 266–271
empathy, 211
enactment (see acting in and acting out)
end of an analysis, 158, 164, 256–260, 262–263
envy (see also penis envy), 85, 134
Eros (see life drive), 185–191, 208
erotogenic zones, 59–61, 64, 130
ethics, 113, 116, 118
Ethics Committee, 118
ethnology, 122, 126
ethno-psychoanalysis, 127
evenly-suspended attention, 110
experience of pain, 28
experience of satisfaction, 27, 31

faith (religious), 227–228, 230–233, 272
family, 238
fantasy; early fantasies, 83; fantasies of seduction, 22, 25; masturbatory fantasy, 245; passive homosexual fantasy, 96, 103; perverse fantasy, 182; sado-masochistic fantasies, 182; unconscious fantasy, 18, 20, 22, 23, 34, 61, 67, 76, 94, 97, 106, 167, 173, 245
father (see identification, killing, Oedipus complex, psychosexual development), 62, 63–64, 80–81, 97, 106, 160, 198, 207; of the primal horde, 125–126, 190–191, 240
fee (payment), 112, 118
feelings, unconscious feelings, 138, 143, 155, 205; feelings of guilt (unconscious) 92, 121, 125–127, 135, 142, 152, 155, 206–210, 211, 214, 221, 235,

239–240, 258, 268; feelings of guilt in the girl (towards her mother), 176; feelings of persecution, 101–105, 123; oceanic feeling, 235–236, 242
fellatio, 94, 96
feminine, femininity, 161, 169, 171–172, 177, 179–182; in Freud's writings, 179–182, 238, 248, 259–261
feminine attitude in men, 102–103, 161, 175
fetishism, 59, 77, 243, 249–202
first theory of anxiety, 24, 33, 35, 217
first theory of the instinctual drives, 135, 146
first topographical theory, 43, 135, 146, 186, 203
fixation, 173; fixation point, 103, 107, 148, 152, 173; the girl's infantile fixation on her mother, 179, 180, 182
foreclosure of the Name-of-the-Father, 106
forgetting (lapses of memory), 43, 45–46, 48–49; forgetting names, 49
free associations, 9, 13–16, 17, 36–37, 39, 42, 45, 89, 113
frequency of analytic sessions, 108
function of judgement, 246
fundamental rule, 89, 110, 113
fusion-defusion of the instinctual drives, 210

genital stage (phase), 61–62, 139, 148
Gradiva, 73–77, 92
groups (psychoanalytic), 201–202
groups (psychology), 194–202
guilt (see feeling of)

hate (see aggressiveness, ambivalence), 81, 101, 134, 135, 138–139, 142, 148–150, 152, 155, 181, 194, 197, 208, 239
hallucination, 76, 77, 245, 261–263
Hebrew, Hebrews, 264, 266, 271–272
helplessness (Hilflosigkeit), 223, 226, 230, 235
hero (myth of the), 200–201
heterogeneous (patients), 77
heterosexuality, 179, 182
holding, 114, 225
homosexuality, 58, 95–97, 106, 164; female homosexuality, 65, 171, 177–179; male homosexuality, 81, 96, 103, 161–162, 175
hostility (see aggressiveness, ambivalence), 124, 148, 229
humour, 54
hypnoid state, 13
hypnosis, 9, 11, 14–15, 17, 119, 194, 199, 202
hypnotist, 202
hypochondriasis, 130
hysteria 9–20, 66, 88, 262–263; anxiety hysteria, 142, 154; conversion hysteria, 141, 154

id, 151, 203–211, 242; hereditary id, 210
ideal, 192, 198, 202; ego ideal 131, 134, 194–195, 198–200, 202, 206–207, 211
idealization, 92, 133–134, 202; idealization of the object, 199
identification, 135, 138, 149, 182, 194, 198–200, 202, 203, 206–207; feminine identification, 161–162, 182, 255; hysterical identification, 198; introjective identification, 133–134; masculine identification in boys, 82, 177–178; masculine identification in girls, 179–182; melancholic identification, 148–151, 178; narcissistic identification, 96, 150, 155, 210–211; projective identification, 71–72, 85, 107, 133–134, 153; with the aggressor (defence), 210; with the lost object, 148–151, 179; with the parental couple, 82, 221, 215
identity (see identification, Oedipus complex, psychosexual development)
illusion, 227–233
incest (prohibition), 62, 113, 121–126
incorporation, 139–155
individuation, 225
infantile amnesia, 60, 64, 174
infantile neurosis (see neurosis), 60–64, 78–82, 88–93, 156–164
infantile psychosexual development, 59, 61, 63–64, 103, 173, 180; in boys, 63–64, 81, 246–248; in girls, 64, 81, 246–248
infantile sexual curiosity, 61, 94, 87, 176
infantile sexual theories, 78–82, 81, 84, 156–164
inherited (traces), 163
instincts (see drives), 135, 136
integration of love and hate, 152
interpretation, 49, 67, 90–91, 143
interpretation of dreams, 36–39, 41–44, 108, 160–163
interruption (of the treatment), 117
introjection, 149, 199, 250; of the lost object, 115, 148–151, 153, 155
introversion, 130
inversion, 43
"Irma's injection", 37, 41, 43
isolation, 221, 226

Jarbuch der Psychoanalyse, 74
jealousy, 63, 247
jokes, 50–56; innocent jokes, 53; tendentious jokes, 53
joke-formation, 51–53, 56
Judaism, 10, 227, 264, 268, 271–272

killing of the father, 63, 125–127, 155, 195, 200, 207, 268–270, 272

language (speech), 55, 145; organ-speech, 145, 155
latency period, 60, 63, 247, 267–268, 272
lay analysis (practised by non-doctors), 87, 227, 229, 233–234, 235
length of analytical treatment, 111
letters to Wilhelm Fliess, 21–25
libidinal organization, 122, 130, 136–141, 148
libido (see drives), 122, 130
literature (psychoanalysis and literature), 73, 76
loss of the object, 148–151, 245–254
love, 62–63, 67, 101, 116, 124, 128, 131, 135, 138–140, 142, 148, 150, 155, 194, 196–197, 202, 208, 232; affectionate, 199; genital love, 199; homosexual love, 180; object love, 103–104, 128–129, 131; primary object love (Balint), 132–133; sensual, 199; transference love, 70, 108, 118, 120; whole-object love, 148

magic, 124, 127, 130
mania, 148, 155, 200
manic-depressive (states), 132, 148

masochism, 138, 155, 180–181, 185, 190, 212–216, 221; feminine masochism, 216; feminine masochism in men, 212, 180, 182, 214, 216; moral masochism, 212, 214–216; original masochism (erotogenic), 191; primary erotogenic masochism, 190, 193, 212, 214–216; secondary masochism, 191, 216
masturbation, 60, 83, 92, 103, 128, 173, 176, 214
maturity, 62–63; genital sexual maturity, 238; growth of the ego, 86
megalomania, 130
melancholia (depression), 22, 24–25, 135, 148, 155, 198, 203, 208
memory, memories, 97, 117, 144, 160, 174, 269; childhood memories, 94, 96, 260–261; screen memories, 31, 34, 47; traumatic memories, 9, 17, 115, 187
memory traces, 144
metapsychology, 43, 135–155
mental apparatus (theory of), 36
models of the workings of the mind, 135
money, 91, 92, 161-2
monotheism (Moses), 264–272
moral conscience, 16, 124, 127, 131–132, 150–151, 207
morality, morals, 229
mother (see identification, Oedipus complex, psychosexual development), 62, 63–64, 97, 106, 131, 160–163, 175, 198, 207; genital mother figure, 181; mother's womb, 162–163; pregenital mother figure, 180–181
mourning (affect), 135, 142, 148, 224, 249; normal mourning, 148–149, 155; pathological mourning, 148–151, 155, 224, 249
mutual understanding, 28
myth, mythology, 63, 96, 122, 127, 128, 168, 201

Narcissus (myth of), 96, 128
narcissism (see narcissistic transference), 94, 97, 107, 124, 128–134, 139, 146, 149, 150, 167, 194; infantile narcissism, 131; narcissism as a phase of development, 131; narcissism of small differences, 239; narcissistic neurosis, 70, 129, 132, 145, 150, 252; object-less narcissism, 132; primary infantile narcissism, 132–133; primary narcissism, 85, 128–134, 139; secondary narcissism, 128–134, 208; symbiotic infantile narcissism, 133
narcissistic disorders, 132
narcissistic personality, 128
narcissistic states of mind, 133, 211
Nazism, 235
negation, 45, 243, 245–246, 252
negative therapeutic reaction, 203, 208, 211, 215, 258, 261–262
neurosciences, 29–30, 108, 115
neurosis 31, 34, 35, 49, 77, 91–93, 222, 237, 243–245, 251–252, 269; anxiety neurosis, 33, 35; infantile neurosis, 60–64, 78–82, 88–93, 156–164, 171; narcissistic neurosis, 70, 129, 132, 141, 145, 150, 244, 252; obsessional neurosis, 88–93, 123, 124, 141, 154, 158–159, 161, 220, 227; transference neurosis, 69–70, 129, 135, 137, 145, 154; traumatic neurosis, 187, 189, 193, 221; universal obsessional neurosis (religion), 231, 232; war neuroses, 107

neurotica, 22, 34, 101
neuro-psychoses (see neuroses); of defence, 31–33, 35, 140
Nirvana principle, 190–191, 193, 212–213, 216
normal, normality, 63, 77, 107, 222, 251–252
normal symbiotic phase, 133

object-cathexis (see cathexis)
object choice, 62, 64, 131, 228; anaclitic, 128, 131, 134; final object choice, 59; homosexual, 94, 97; in women, 131; narcissistic, 128, 131, 134; of love object, 63
objects, object relations, 59, 61–63, 64, 85, 135, 137, 138–139, 145, 148, 152–153, 198, 200, 229, 237; loss, 148–151, 217–226; object of the drives, 137; part-object, 62, 85, 152, 162; separate and distinct object, 132–134; whole-object, 62, 85
object relations (see objects); primitive object relations (archaic), 85
obsessions, 32, 88–91, 93; obsessive actions, 90–91; obsessive thoughts, 93; religious obsessions, 164; with rats, 90
oceanic feeling, 237
Oedipal myth, 167
Oedipus complex, 22–23, 63–64, 68, 85, 121, 126, 163, 168, 171, 175, 177, 198, 203–211, 218, 221, 247–248, 269; complete form, 64, 206–207, 210; direct (or positive), 23–24, 63, 82, 156, 162, 175–176; early stages, 85, 152; eroticization of incestuous objects in the Oedipus complex, 182; in boys, 206–207, 247; in girls, 206–207, 247–248; inverted (or negative), 23–24, 82, 156, 175, 198; pre-Oedipal, 164, 242
omnipotence, omnipotence of thoughts, 124, 130, 133, 153
onanism (see masturbation), 60
oral, oral stage, 64
organ-speech, 145
origin of anxiety, 217
over-determination, 44

pain, 224
pan-sexualism, 58
paranoia, paranoid, 22, 101–107, 163–164
paranoid-schizoid position, 56, 85, 114, 152–153192, 225
parapraxes (see bungled actions), 45–49, 50, 261
rents (see identification, Oedipus complex), 62, 168, 215
passive, passivity, 180, 187, 223
passive attitude in women, 159–161, 164
patients (see clinical cases), 77
penis (primacy of), 61, 64, 79, 96, 156, 162–163, 182
penis-envy, 64, 181–182, 247, 254, 259, 263
perception, 205, 209
perception of castration in women, 249
perception-consciousness (Pcpt-Cs) system, 205
persecutor, persecution, 101–107, 192
perverse, perversion, 58, 61, 64, 73, 146, 171, 173, 175–177, 182, 214, 243–245; masochistic, 171, 212–216; sado-masochistic, 61, 171
phallic, phallic stage, 64, 247
phallic monism, 64, 181–182, 247
phallocentric (theory), 61, 64, 81

phallus, 249, 252
phobia, phobias, 32, 78–82, 142, 158–158, 160, 164; infantile phobias, 81, 87, 125
phylogenesis, phylogenetic, 63, 116, 126–127, 154, 155, 163, 207, 223, 269, 271–272
play upon words, 52
pleasure, 50, 53–54
pleasure-unpleasure (principle), 50, 54, 137–138, 146, 185, 188, 212–213, 216, 237
point of view, 142, 144; dynamic point of view, 142, 144; economic point of view, 144; topographical point of view, 142, 144
polymorphous, 60
polymorphously perverse disposition, 60, 64
"preconception" (Bion), 127, 154
preconscious 43, 142–145,
presentation (see representation), 17, 32, 35, 141, 143, 146, 155, 205; thing-presentation, 145, 155; word-presentation, 145, 155
primal scene, 156, 159, 161–162, 164, 254
primitive emotional development, 133, 225
principle of constancy, 27, 31, 187, 190; Nirvana principle, 190–191, 193; pleasure-unpleasure principle, 137, 146, 185, 186, 212–213, 216, 237; principle of inertia, 27, 31; reality principle, 137, 187, 212–213, 216
process; of representation, 17, 32, 35, 141, 143, 146, 155, 205; of separation-individuation, 225; primary process, 27, 31, 43, 144, 145; secondary process, 27, 31, 43, 108, 110, 144, 145
projection, 24, 69, 101–107, 124, 153, 189
projective identification, 71–72, 85, 107, 133–134, 153
projective counter-identification, 71–72
protective shield, 188
proton-pseudos, 28, 31
psychical integration, 62, 192, 258
psychoanalytic educational methods 114-, 119–120
psychoanalytic groups, 132, 194–202, 268
psychoanalytic method, 108
psychoanalytic process, 110, 111, 114
psychoanalytic setting, 108, 110–111, 113–115
psychoanalytic training, 114, 119–120
psychoanalysis, 110; age limit for undertaking psychoanalysis, 110; child psychoanalysis, 88–99; fundamental rule, 89, 110, 113; psychoanalytic process, 111, 114; wild psychoanalysis, 108, 112
psychology; analytical psychology (Jung), 74; group psychology, 132, 194–202, 268; individual psychology, 202; scientific psychology, 31–35
psychopharmacology, 108
psychosexual development (girls and boys), 247–248
psychosis, 32, 73, 77, 91–92, 101–107, 129, 146, 163–164, 237, 243–245, 247, 248–251, 263; hallucinatory psychosis, 32, 244; symbiotic psychosis, 133
psychotherapy, 108–109; psychotherapy of hysteria, 9, 17

quantitative factor, 141
quota of affect, 141

rationalization, 91, 103, 107
reaction formation, 210, 220

reality, reality principle, 22, 25, 106, 160, 167, 187, 212, 213; difference between reality and fantasy, 160
reality-testing, 27, 31, 147, 209
realization (Bion), 127, 154
reconstructions, constructions, 67, 90, 162, 254
regression, 116, 130, 133, 209, 210; structural regression, 147, 155; temporal regression, 147, 155
regression point, 103, 107
religion, 121, 126, 207, 227–233, 235, 237, 242, 267–268, 272; monotheistic, 267, 272; Moses, 264–272; of Aton, 264, 266; totemic, 108, 117, 121–126
religious ideas, 159, 235, 272
remembering, 108, 117
reminiscences, 12
reparation, 76, 152
repetition, 69–70, 108, 117, 120, 169, 193
representability, 40, 44, 50
representative-representation, 141, 155
representation, 17, 32, 35, 141, 143, 146, 155, 205; symbolic representation
repressed, 14–15, 32, 41–42, 167, 188, 246
repression, 17, 20, 28, 32, 35, 41–42, 45, 76, 94, 105, 135, 136, 138, 140–145, 148, 153–154, 162, 210, 217, 219–221, 223, 226, 245, 260–261; deferred repression, 141; primal repression, 140, 144; repression *stricto sensu*, 140
re-sexualization of the Oedipus complex, 216
resistance, 9, 17, 20, 49, 112, 117, 205, 254, 258–259
return to Freud, 54, 146
return of the repressed, 141, 245, 270
return of split-off aspects, 252
reversal into the opposite, 138
rituals, 159
rivalry, 39

sadism, 138, 148, 150, 155, 171, 185, 190; reversal of sadism into masochism, 138
scenes of seduction, 15, 22, 66–67, 154, 156, 164
schizophrenia, 56, 104, 130, 145, 153
science, 26–31, 109, 227, 232, 235, 238; deterministic science, 115
scientific models, 26–29, 30–31
screen memories, 31, 34, 47
sessions (analytical), 111, 113; frequency, 108
second theory of anxiety, 217–226
second theory of instinctual drives, 135, 146
second structural (topographical) theory, 135, 146, 185, 203
secondary gain (from illness), 220
secondary revision, 41, 43, 44
secret committee, 116
seduction, actual seduction, 15, 22, 25, 60, 66–67
self, 134
self-analysis, 21, 23–24, 37, 44, 71, 259
self-destruction, 150, 151, 178, 239–240
self-disclosure, 72
Self-Psychology, 211
self-punishment, 178, 219
self-reproaches, 92, 124, 149–150, 155
seminar on a chronological reading of Freud's writings, 4–6, 275

sense of guilt (unconscious), 92, 121, 125–127, 135, 142, 152, 155, 206–210, 211, 214, 221, 135, 239–240, 258, 268
separation anxiety (see anxiety), 217–226
setting (see psychoanalytic setting), 110–111
sexual abuse, 15, 18, 22, 24–25, 66
sexuality (see psychosexual development, Oedipus complex), 17, 19, 31, 34, 57, 238; female sexuality, 81, 169, 172, 181–182, 246–248, 255; genital sexuality, 59, 61–62; infantile sexuality, 23, 34–35, 57–58, 60–63, 78–79, 82, 85, 92, 96, 156–163, 175, 214, 247
signifier, 54, 106, 146
signified, 54
situation; analytical situation, 114; Oedipal situation, 80–81; situations of danger, 22–223; traumatic situation, 187, 223–224, 226
sleep, 130, 147, 200
slips of the tongue, 45–49
source of an instinct, 137
splitting, 124, 153, 166, 169, 192
splitting of the ego, 73, 150–151, 174, 243–244, 249–251, 252–253, 256; in Freud and in Klein, 252
stage (or phase), 152; anal-sadistic, 61, 88–93, 148, 159, 174; developmental, 61–62, 64, 148; genital, 61–62, 139, 148; mirror stage, 129; narcissistic, 103, 107; oral, 61, 148; phallic, 61, 64, 246–248, 249; pregenital, 61
subject, 66, 210–211
sublimation, 60, 94, 96–97, 163, 174
substitution, 47, 49
suggestion, 9, 113, 194; hypnotic suggestion, 11
suicide, 47, 151, 178, 191, 208–209
superstition, 47, 91, 121–123
supervision (training), 119–120
superego (see ego ideal, censorship, conscience), 43–44, 92, 151, 175, 194, 200, 203–211, 215, 235, 239–241, 248; and civilization, 240–241; harshness of the superego in children, 240; in the melancholic patient, 208, 210; primitive, 85; protective, 209–210
suppress, suppression (see repress, repression)
symbiotic (phase), 114, 133
symbolic equation, 153, 248, 252
symbolism, symbols, 18, 42, 49, 54, 75, 90, 106, 145, 153, 155, 219, 145, 261; primitive symbolism, 56; symbolism in dreams, 44
symptom, symptoms, 22, 32, 67, 217–221, 223–225, 245, 261; hysterical symptoms, 9–13, 15, 17–18, 65, 67; obsessional symptoms, 88–89, 92

taboo, 121–127; incest taboo, 127
technique (psychoanalytic), 55, 93, 108–120, 192, 254; active technique, 115, 116; of mutual analysis, 116; play technique with children, 84
technique of jokes; based on thought, 53; based on words, 52
telepathy, 167

termination (analysis) (see end of), 254, 256–260, 262–263
terrorism, 241
therapeutic alliance, 90
therapeutic failure, 189
theories (infantile sexual), 57, 59, 61, 63, 64, 80–81, 156, 161, 179, 181
theory; of anxiety, 24, 33, 35, 209, 217–226; of object relations, 224; of seduction, 22, 24–25, 34; of symbolism, 269; of the libido, 74
totem, totemism, 121–123, 125
totem meal, 121, 125
tradition, 269, 272
transference, 18, 48, 55, 65–72, 82, 85, 101, 103, 108, 112–113, 117, 150, 162–164, 188–189, 284, 257, 259–260; heterosexual transference; homosexual transference, 68, 72; hostile transference, 134, 171, 178, 182; maternal transference, 65, 72, 180; narcissistic transference, 128, 129, 132, 133–134; negative transference, 69, 112, 116–117, 120, 129, 132, 179, 257; paternal transference, 65, 72, 90, 163; positive transference, 69, 112, 117, 120, 129, 132, 179, 257; transference love, 70, 108, 117, 120; transference neurosis, 154
transformation, 101
transformation into the opposite, 220
transgression, 116, 118, 123
transmission; phylogenetic, 126; telepathic, 115; trans-generational, 127
traumatic neuroses, 187–188
traumatism, 15, 18, 20, 155, 193, 217–218; early trauma, 116; sexual trauma, 18, 20, 33

uncanny (feeling of uncanniness), 165–169
unconscious, 20, 43–44, 45, 46, 50, 76, 85, 135–136, 140–147, 149, 152–153, 155, 203, 205
underlying bedrock, 254, 259–260, 263
undoing what has been done, 90–91, 93, 220–221, 226
unsuccessful treatment, 189
urethral, 60

vagina, 85, 161, 181–182
verbalization, 55
vertigo, 33
voyeurism-exhibitionism, 138, 176
vulture, 97

wild analysis, 113
wish (see also wish-fulfilment); death-wishes, 30; incestuous wishes, 63; passive feminine wishes, 64; repressed homosexual wishes, 101, 103; wish for a penis (see penis envy); wish for revenge, 67
wish-fulfilment, 40, 54, 55, 147
womb (mother's), 162–163
work; dream-work, 40, 143–144; of mourning, 219; of the analysis, 40, 44; working-through, 117
workings of the mind (a model of)
working-through, 108, 117; secondary revision, 41, 43, 44